Why Don't Women Rule the World?

This book is dedicated to the women who have cleared the rocky path of leadership by making the choice to run as well as all of those who will choose to run in the future. We thank you for your tenacity and service.

Sara Miller McCune founded SAGE Publishing in 1965 to support the dissemination of usable knowledge and educate a global community. SAGE publishes more than 1000 journals and over 800 new books each year, spanning a wide range of subject areas. Our growing selection of library products includes archives, data, case studies and video. SAGE remains majority owned by our founder and after her lifetime will become owned by a charitable trust that secures the company's continued independence.

Los Angeles | London | New Delhi | Singapore | Washington DC | Melbourne

Why Don't Women Rule the World?

Understanding Women's Civic and Political Choices

J. Cherie Strachan

Central Michigan University

Lori M. Poloni-Staudinger

Northern Arizona University

Shannon Jenkins

University of Massachusetts, Dartmouth

Candice D. Ortbals

Pepperdine University

FOR INFORMATION:

CQ Press
An imprint of SAGE Publications, Inc.
2455 Teller Road
Thousand Oaks, California 91320
E-mail: order@sagepub.com

SAGE Publications Ltd.
1 Oliver's Yard
55 City Road
London, EC1Y 1SP
United Kingdom

SAGE Publications India Pvt. Ltd.
B 1/I 1 Mohan Cooperative Industrial Area
Mathura Road, New Delhi 110 044
India

SAGE Publications Asia-Pacific Pte. Ltd.
18 Cross Street #10-10/11/12
China Square Central
Singapore 048423

Printed in the United States of America

Library of Congress Cataloging-in-Publication Data

ISBN 978-1-5443-1724-3

This book is printed on acid-free paper.

MIX
Paper from responsible sources
FSC
www.fsc.org
FSC® C008955

Acquisitions Editor: Scott Greenan
Editorial Assistant: Sam Rosenberg
Production Editor: Rebecca Lee
Copy Editor: Michelle Ponce
Typesetter: Hurix Digital
Proofreader: Rae-Ann Goodwin
Indexer: Jean Casalegno
Cover Designer: Alexa Turner
Marketing Manager: Erica DeLuca

19 20 21 22 23 10 9 8 7 6 5 4 3 2 1

CONTENTS

LIST OF TABLES, FIGURES, PHOTOGRAPHS, AND BOXES

TABLES

BOXES

PREFACE

As political scientists who teach and live women and politics, we each have had a keen interest in a women and politics book that would be comprehensive, unique, and address shortfalls that we found in other books on the market. Thus, over cocktail hour at a meeting of the American Political Science Association, this book was hatched, bringing together four authors who had previous collaborative experiences in dyads but never had worked all together. We were interested in ameliorating what we saw as holes in current women and politics books, including a thorough and theoretical introduction, broadening a U.S.-centric approach to allow for attention to comparative examples, and activities purposefully designed to bolster students' political interest and ambition. We also wanted to make sure that the concepts discussed in the book were tied to direct policy examples. Thus, the idea for *Why Don't Women Rule the World?* was born. The idea was further incubated and expanded at a café at the first Women's March in Washington, DC, in 2017. Over the following two years, the four of us have worked closely to draft a cohesive book that drew on our unique strengths as scholars and authors.

The title of this book, *Why Don't Women Rule the World?*, is a tongue-in-cheek response to a serious question. We know girls achieve as well as boys (often better) in school. We know that some of the traits considered "feminine" such as collaboration and listening work well in leaders. We also know that women are underrepresented in positions of power throughout the world. We also each have our own experiences as women in the male domain of academia and in leadership positions—questioning our reproductive choices, calling into question our right to be in the room of decision-makers, having ideas ignored only to be repeated by a male colleague, and yes, "mansplaining." So why don't women rule, and why don't they have more influence over the way the world is structured?

This book begins to explore this question by looking at how underrepresentation of women manifests comparatively and also by exploring how it plays out in policy. As four feminists who care deeply about dismantling patriarchal structures, we also had a normative reason for writing this book. We know that young men's political ambition begins to outpace young women's ambition in late high school/early college. The ambition activities at the end of each chapter specifically relate to the chapter material and prompt readers to think about their gendered assumptions of power and privilege, their role in reifying patriarchal structures, their own political ambition, and the ways they can address gender inequalities in their personal lives and in the broader world.

The book's cover is further intended to illicit thought. The globe represents our attempt to bring a more comparative focus to a U.S.-based women and politics textbook. The woman is supposed to represent an archetype of women's strength modeled after Rosie the Riveter—but based on a race neutral rendition, as we know women of color were working outside of the home long before Rosie appeared in World War II. The colors on the cover are meant to conform to gendered stereotypes around femininity while reclaiming them for a book that aims to bolster women's political ambition and calls into question patriarchal structures.

This book is meant to be a stand-alone textbook in a women and politics course. We also hope that those interested in the topic and women interested in pursuing a political career will be drawn to the content.

We had fun (yes, fun writing a book!) working with each other on this book. Over conference calls in hotel hallways, group chats through online platforms, dinners in sweltering restaurants, cocktails in a variety of locations, and an almost trolley ride, we learned, laughed, and sometimes cried with each other when grappling with the material. We hope that you, the reader, take away as much from reading this book as we did writing it.

ACKNOWLEDGMENTS

The authors would like to thank first and foremost our families for putting up with long work hours and travel schedules, as well as supporting us in our writing. We also wish to thank the entire editorial team at SAGE/CQ Press. Monica Eckman signed this project, and she has been amazing to work with. Sam Rosenberg has been a pleasure to work with and helpful in securing images when we needed them. We would like to thank Michelle Ponce for her excellent copyediting, Rebecca Lee and the rest of the production team, as well as Erica DeLuca for marketing. Thanks, as well, to those who provided helpful reviews on this project:

Erin Cassese, West Virginia University

Rebecca Deen, University of Texas at Arlington

Kathleen Dolan, University of Wisconsin – Milwaukee

Amanda Friesen, Indiana University – Purdue University Indianapolis

Revathi Hines, Southern University and A&M College

Mirya R. Holman, Tulane University

Karen Kedrowski, Winthrop University

Gabriel Kikas, University of Detroit Mercy – McNichols Campus

Susan S. Lederman, Kean University

Lanethea Mathews, Muhlenberg College

Heather Ondercin, University of Mississippi

Kathryn Pearson, University of Minnesota

Ronnee Schrieber, San Diego State University

We also want to offer a very special thanks to Will Kasso Condry, community muralist and educator at Middlebury College in Vermont. His amazing portrait, a mural featured at the Anderson Freeman Resource Center, is highlighted in Chapter 1. We are extremely grateful that he allowed us to use the photo and hope that people will take time to check out his work: https://willkasso.com/?page_id=47.

Cherie would like to thank Central Michigan University first for valuing and rewarding the development of instructional materials and second for providing institutional support to work on this project. In particular, she appreciated the opportunity to work with and mentor graduate assistants, including Grace Van-DeMark, Kwyn Trevino, and Shambika Raut. These three young women helped to implement various civic engagement initiatives for the College of Liberal Arts and Social Sciences. Their assistance with these projects, especially coordinating deliberative discussion sessions embedded in Introduction to American Government courses, freed time for writing in her schedule.

Lori is indebted to several people for their help on this book. First, she wishes to thank Dr. Karen Pugliesi, dean of Social and Behavioral Sciences, for allowing her time to maintain research after she moved into the associate dean role. Without this time, this book would not have been written. Thanks also goes to Nicole Olonovich, who provided background research for cases on Iceland and Pakistan and the women's equality index and who spent many hours proofreading and offering comments. Finally, Myann Bradley was instrumental in helping Lori conduct research on several cases. Myann's work can be seen in the cases on abortion worldwide, Black Lives Matter, and the Women's March. She also helped with formatting, citations, and many of the charts and graphs. Her research skills are well beyond her years, and her contributions to this book are valued.

Shannon would like to thank the University of Massachusetts Dartmouth for the time and institutional support provided to work on this project and travel to meet with her coauthors.

Candice would like to thank Pepperdine University for granting her sabbatical time to complete her portions of the book and for supporting her student research assistants. She greatly enjoyed working with the following assistants: Megan Johnston, Ryanne Gordon, Kevin Gordon, and Esther Chung. Megan was responsible for reading all the ambition activities and providing the student perspective on them. She helped us understand how her generation thinks about matters of equality and feminism. Megan compiled tables about women presidential candidates, women's policy agencies in the United States, and media frames used to present presidential candidates. Megan also investigated current equality politics in France. Ryanne, for instance, researched women's tribunals, peace huts, and native women in politics. Kevin, among other things, proofread all the chapters of the book, researched substantive representation offered by executives, and compiled a list of sexist statements made by Donald Trump. Esther worked closely with Candice summarizing the actions of peace movements and the global #MeToo movement. Moreover, Candice is thankful for the valuable input from Isabella Ordaz, Marisa Thompson, and Emilie Rohrbach regarding ambition activities. Finally, she would like to thank Marilyn and Dennis Ortbals for countless hours of babysitting.

ABOUT THE AUTHORS

J. Cherie Strachan (PhD, State University of New York at Albany, 2000) is professor of Political Science at Central Michigan University. Her research addresses the effects of partisan polarization on elections, the role of civility in a democratic society, and the effect of college-level civic education interventions, deliberative forums, and campus organizations on students' civic skills and identities. Her applied pedagogy research has resulted in on-going work with foundations such as the Kettering Foundation, the National Institute for Civil Discourse, and the American Democracy Project. Strachan currently serves as the Review Editor for the *Journal of Political Science Education*. She is also cofounder and codirector of the Consortium for Inter-Campus SoTL Research (CISR), which facilitates multicampus data collection for civic engagement and political science pedagogy research.

Lori M. Poloni-Staudinger (PhD, Indiana University, 2005) is associate dean for research, personnel, and graduate programs in the College of Social and Behavioral Sciences and a professor in the department of Politics and International Affairs at Northern Arizona University. Her research and publications focus on social movements, political contention and extrainstitutional participation, and political institutions, mainly in Western Europe. Her recent work examines questions around women and political violence. She was a Distinguished Fulbright Fellow at the Diplomatic Academy in Vienna, Austria, and has served as a consultant for the Organization for Security and Co-operation in Europe. She also taught at University of the Basque Country in San Sebastian, Spain. She served as treasurer, vice president, and president of the Women's Caucus for the Midwest Political Science Association. Lori is a Kettering Foundation Fellow and also serves as vice president of a school board and president of a nonprofit board in Flagstaff, Arizona.

Shannon Jenkins (PhD, Loyola University Chicago, 2003) is a professor in the Department of Political Science and the academic director of online learning at the University of Massachusetts Dartmouth. Her research and publications focus on decision making in U.S. state legislatures, with a specific interest in the role of political organizations and gender in shaping outputs in these institutions, and the impact of specific pedagogical practices on student learning outcomes in political science courses. She has been a Fulbright Lecturer at East China University of Political Science and Law in Shanghai in 2012 and at Yokohama National University and Tokai University in Japan in 2019. Previously, she taught at Central Michigan University. She was also elected to and currently serves on the School Committee in Dartmouth, Massachusetts.

Candice D. Ortbals (PhD, Indiana University, 2004) is professor of Political Science at Pepperdine University. Her publications relate to state feminism in Spain and gender and terrorism. She has been the newsletter editor, president-elect, and president of the Women's Caucus of the Midwest Political Science Association. She also served as president for the National Women's Caucus of Political Science. She has taught at the University of Seville, and she was winner of the Carrie Chapman Catt Prize for Research on Women and Politics. She has also received numerous grants from the government of Spain to study women in regional and local government.

CHAPTER ONE

WHY DON'T WOMEN RULE THE WORLD?

Why don't women rule the world? In most cultures across the globe, the rise of civilization meant that women were confined to domestic roles and denied positions of authority in the public sphere—including leadership positions in religion, civil society, and the marketplace. Of particular interest and concern to political scientists is the way that women's association with the household, children, and domestic responsibility has been used—not just in one culture, but in many—to exclude them not only from holding official positions of political authority but to deny them public voice and citizenship. Hence, this book explores the political status of women across the globe, with particular attention paid to women in the American context. It examines the tactics and strategies women use to insert themselves into the men-dominated arena of government and politics and also describes the way women currently participate in a wide array of political endeavors, ranging from protest politics and voting to running for elected office and serving as public officials. We also explore and address the **gender gap**, or the idea that women report less interest in participating in politics than men[1]—discussed more later in the section, Plan of the Book. Finally, we examine the ways in which particular policies either influence women or are *influenced by* women in both the United States and comparative context.

Before launching into in-depth details of these activities, it is important to understand the deep roots of women's subordination, which emerged along with the embrace of agriculture in the Neolithic age and spread across the globe as early agricultural-based civilizations flourished. Understanding this deep history is important for several reasons, not least is that it is difficult to dismantle a system of oppression without understanding why it was established in the first place. Moreover, understanding provides a response to those who use women's shared fate across much of the globe to claim that a gendered division of labor, with women excluded from the public sphere so that they can focus on children and the household, as simply "natural"—either divinely inspired or biologically determined. Those who only know the recent written history of women's subordinate status will be tempted to argue that **cisgender women's** (or women whose assigned sex at birth and intrinsic gender identity are both female) reproductive capacity means that they are somehow naturally ill-suited for participation in politics and public life. In fact, an overview of the origins of civilization suggests that public spaces and political institutions were purposefully designed to exclude women rather than vice versa. Learning about the purposeful creation of **patriarchies**—or social systems where men's dominance over women and children in the family is extended to men's dominance over women in society in general[2]—makes it possible to consider explanations other than the natural order for women's exclusion from public life.

Understanding the patriarchal roots of modern civilization also serves a broader social justice agenda. Early civilizations' successful subordination of women inspired ongoing and more egregious versions of oppression. For example, successful efforts to control cisgender women's bodies to benefit from their sexual and reproductive functions led to efforts to control others' bodies as well, resulting in the adoption of caste systems, slavery, feudalism, and colonialism. Organizing society around a gendered division of labor—with clearly defined roles for men and women—also required patriarchal societies to enforce **binary gender categories**, or those of man/masculine and woman/feminine. Those who did not or could not comply by conforming to the masculine and feminine gender roles prescribed for their assigned sex at birth represented a threat to the society and were sanctioned, suppressed, and threatened. In short, understanding and uprooting social structures that exploit cisgender women should also help to understand and disrupt class inequality and oppression against racial and ethnic minorities, as well as discrimination against queer and transgender people who do not conform to patriarchy's insistence on binary categories that conflate sex, gender identity, and sexual orientation.

BOX 1.1: POLICY FEATURE

Feminist Activism and Same-Sex Marriage

The legalization of same-sex marriage in the United States provides an example of the way overcoming one form of oppression can have an unintended domino-effect that helps others. Unlike other major civil rights achievements—including women's suffrage or interracial marriage—public support for and legalization of same-sex marriage seemed to occur swiftly, taking mere decades instead of centuries.

Same-sex couples often found ways to cohabitate throughout American history.[3] Yet, it seems no partner in a homosexual relationship fought to legally establish same-sex marriage prior to the 1970s. In 1972, the U.S. Supreme Court declined to hear an appeal challenging the Minnesota high court's decision that prohibiting same sex marriage was not a violation of the U.S. Constitution.[4] In response, several states enacted bans on same-sex marriage in the late 1970s. In 1993, the Hawaii Supreme Court, in *Baehr v. Lewin*,[5] suggested such prohibitions could be unconstitutional, while another decade later, in 2004, Massachusetts became the first U.S. state to legalize same-sex marriage in response to its own high court's decision in *Goodridge v. Department of Public Health*.[6] Both decisions resulted in spates of state laws and ballot initiatives—some legalizing same-sex marriage and some explicitly rejecting it—along with the 1996 federal Defense of Marriage Act (DOMA), which prohibited the federal government from recognizing, and allowed states the option of refusing to recognize, such unions. Laws opposing same-sex marriage were soon targeted in the courts by pro-gay-rights organizations such as the American Civil Liberties Union, Lamda Legal, and the National Center for Lesbian Rights, while gay rights advocates continued to press for changes through state policies. By 2012—when Maine, Maryland, and Washington became the first states to legalize same-sex marriage via legislation—same-sex marriage had become legal in 37 states and the District of Columbia, through a combination of court challenges, ballot initiatives, and state law. In 2013, the U.S. Supreme Court deemed DOMA unconstitutional.[7] In a 2015 decision rejecting marriage bans in Kentucky, Michigan, Ohio, and Tennessee, the Court essentially legalized same-sex marriage in all 50 states and required states to recognize other states' same-sex marriage licenses.[8]

As these legal battles were playing out, public opinion on same-sex marriage shifted dramatically. In 2001, 57% of the American electorate opposed same-sex marriage, while only 35% supported it. By 2017, 62% of Americans (along with 73% of self-identified Democrats and 85% of self-identified liberals) supported such unions, while only 32% opposed them (along with 40% of self-identified Republicans and 41% of self-identified conservatives).[9]

Unlike previous advances in civil rights, this stunning shift in public opinion preceded the Supreme Court's decision to protect minority rights. According to historian Stephanie Coontz, author of *Marriage, a History: How Love Conquered Marriage*,[10] same-sex marriage was able to gain acceptance so quickly not only because of the dedicated efforts of gay rights activists but also because it is the logical conclusion of egalitarian marriages that emerged from hundreds of years of feminist activism.

In Western culture, the institution of marriage mimicked the hierarchical structure of feudalism, featuring men as heads of the household with almost absolute authority over their wives and children. Marriages were arranged for economic advantage until the late 1700s, when people began to marry for love and to choose their partners. Notably, such matches dismayed traditionalists, who feared that men's ability to exercise authority over their wives would be diminished, and that an inevitable increase in divorced and unmarried

(Continued)

(Continued)

single women would result in chaos. By the 1920s, more Americans considered sexual fulfilment an important part of marriage, and by the 1960s, married heterosexual couples gained the right to use contraception to avoid having children.[11] Even so, many second wave feminists and queer theorists alike saw the institution as a hopelessly patriarchal institution mired in binary gender roles and best avoided. Yet, reformers continued to advocate for women's rights within the institution of marriage—changing norms and laws about property ownership, child custody, bodily autonomy, and sexual consent until most Americans viewed marriage as an egalitarian partnership based on affection, rather than as an economic necessity. "As marriage has become less gendered—with women becoming breadwinners and men doing more housework and child care—it became more difficult to explain why two men, or two women, couldn't participate in the institution as well as a man and a woman could."[12] Hence, the chain of events that early feminists set in motion when they tackled the task of reforming marriage, with the goal of improving the lives of cisgender women who had few options other than marriage, helped to make marriage a possibility for LGBTQIA+ (Lesbian, Gay, Bisexual, Transgender, Queer [or Questioning], Intersex, Asexual, etc.) individuals hundreds of years later.[13]

THE CREATION OF PATRIARCHY

Modern humans evolved about 200,000 years ago. For most of this time, up until around 7,000 years ago, humans lived in small bands of hunter-gatherers. Contrary to popular caricatures of men cavemen dragging women around by the hair and dominating other men with their size and strength, hunter-gatherers' societies were far more egalitarian than modern civilizations. Their social structures were not characterized by hierarchies where an elite ruling class makes all the decisions and demands loyalty and homage from lesser subjects. Even though men and women had different roles that grew out of their sex differences, these differences were not used to justify inequality. These prehistoric bands of hunter-gatherers—described by some scholars as **matristic societies** or as **matricentries**—often revolved around women's ability to care for their children. While we think about this historically, this way of organizing societies can also be seen in contemporary societies (see Box 1.2). While both sexes helped care for children, men often contributed to food needs by participating in big game hunting, while women focused on small game hunting and gathering. Both means of procuring food were valued, but women's activities were more reliable, and the majority of calories consumed often came from their efforts. One modern-day hunter-gathering tribe, the Hazda, provides an example of how people lived and survived prior to civilization. Among the Hazda, who have been hunter-gatherers in the same region of Tanzania for thousands of years, men's big game hunting efforts are successful only 3.4% of the time. Food needed to sustain the community overwhelmingly comes from women's collective efforts to gather tubers. While the growth of a woman's first child is correlated with her ability to gather food, the survival of additional children after the first is correlated to their grandmother's success in digging tubers. Among the Hazda, and likely among the many hunter-gather societies that at one time characterized human society, grandmothers have been more important to children's survival than their fathers. These insights help to explain why human women live so long beyond their ability to reproduce, as well as why advanced social traits—like pointing, smiling, and laughing—emerge at such an early age among human babies and toddlers.[14] Given women's role in sustaining their communities, it is not surprising that despite gendered activities and despite distinct biological functions, these small, simple societies placed few restrictions on men and women based on sex differences.[15] Indeed, some evolutionary biologists believe that early human men's low levels of testosterone, in comparison to other male primates, provided humans with a distinct advantage. Human men, in comparison, for example, to chimpanzees, were less aggressive and more willing to cooperate with weaker men and with women. This dynamic allowed intelligence and innovation to drive group decision-making rather than brute force by an alpha male—and this cooperative feature was essential for much of our species' success.[16]

BOX 1.2: COMPARATIVE FEATURE

Complementarian and Matriarchal Practices in Other Countries

Some ethnic groups do not perceive of sex in a way that matches the patriarchal experiences of much of the rest of the world. Men do not control all social, political, religious, and economic institutions among these groups even though they may be dominant in given contexts. The Mosuo minority in China, along with Igbo and Aka of Africa, are examples of groups that consider women fit to have agency and to be leaders in some domains. The Mosuo, an ethnic minority of about 40,000, have lived in relative stability for hundreds of years in a region of southwest China near Lugu Lake. The Mosuo are matriarchal, with no marriage system, as well as no indigenous terms for husband or father. When a girl turns fourteen, she is considered an adult and is given an adult ceremony and her own room where she can host visits from a boyfriend. These relationships, which may be short term or long term, are called *zuo hun*, or walking marriages, because boyfriends are invited to spend the night with women, but then must walk back to their mothers' houses in the morning. He belongs to his mother's family, and she

(Continued)

(Continued)

Christopher Pillitz/Getty Images

▶ **Photo 1.1** Two Mosuo women.

belongs to her mother's family—and multigenerational family members all related by blood rather than marriage live under one roof. In the Mosuo culture, the family carries through the mother's line, and children, cared for by their maternal aunts and uncles, stay with the mother their entire lives. A mother "passes" her power over family decision-making to her eldest daughter, although most decisions are made collectively with input from all family members.[17] As one photographer who spent a month documenting local practices noted, "Men and women are very much equals, but the women are just a little more in charge."[18]

Meanwhile, the Igbo, one of the largest ethnic groups in Nigeria with a population of over 30 million, have a **complementarian** society. Women in the Igbo group can achieve success normally attributed to men, such as acquiring wealth. Women who act in ways traditionally associated with men gain the full respect of their husbands and men peers. The politics of the Igbo people are collective and decentralized, but Igbo women tend to lack influence in politics as they play a consultative rather than active role. However, the Igbo have adopted a dual-sex political system, which allows women through women's groups to check men's power.

Santiago Urquijo Zamora / Contributor

▶ **Photo 1.2** Igbo women resting together.

Similarly, the Aka people in central Africa are very egalitarian. Women and men share economic responsibilities with the exception of shooting arrows to kill elephants (typically performed by men). Women and men are often together when hunting and collecting plants. As with the Igbo, men are more dominant in politics, but they do not hold absolute power. Men influence politics through hospitality, persuasiveness, humor, and knowledge. Aka women challenge men's authority regularly. Mothers are influential in the clan, and women participate in decisions about camp movements, extramarital affairs, and hunting. Violence against women is uncommon, which encourages women's autonomy and also supports the ability for men and women to work together. When disagreements occur, members of the Aka do not resort to physical or verbal abuse, but instead participate in a meditation or leave the camp until they have thought about reconciliation.

Anthropologists' insights into **prehistory**, or the long era preceding civilizations that recorded their own histories, are supported by egalitarianism characterizing the small handful of hunter-gatherer tribes that remain today. In these societies, both men and women influence decisions about where their group lives and who lives with them. Modern hunter-gatherer groups in the Congo and in the Philippines, for example, tend to live in groups of about 20 people, moving about every 10 days to hunt, fish, and gather in new locations. The result of equality in deciding who constitutes each core group is an array of loosely related individuals living together, with close kin scattered across a wider geographic area. If only men or only women influenced decisions about living conditions, however, anthropologists conclude the result would be more closely-related groups populated by one sex or the other's close relatives and siblings.[19] This clustering is precisely what happened with the dawn of agriculture in the **Neolithic Age** when men began to exercise more authority over collective decisions than women. The villages that emerged when humans began to focus on settled farming were organized around men's relatives—fathers, sons, uncles, nephews, and cousins. These living arrangements disadvantaged women, who sacrificed status in their own kinship groups to become laborers and producers—but not decision-makers or property-owners—for an entirely different kinship group. Women must have initially supported incremental decisions that made this transition possible, likely because these choices offered short-term benefits to their kinship groups, and they could not be expected to anticipate the long-term consequences for their sex that evolved over the centuries. Indeed, feminist historians and anthropologists prefer the word **subordination**, rather than the term *oppression*, to describe the gradual domination of men over women across time. Women, it seems, often voluntarily participated in creating a world that would undermine their own equality. Although they could not know it at the time, abandoning the egalitarian living arrangements that characterized past and current hunter-gathering societies had devastating effects on women's status in society; they became a resource acquired by men, similar to the way that land and domesticated animals became property acquired by men.[20]

Of course, this shift in living patterns happened gradually over thousands of years. In the beginning of the Neolithic Age, humans launched an agricultural revolution, learning how to domesticate plants and animals as a source of food. Domesticating animals made people aware that men played a role in paternity and that women's sexual and reproductive functions could be controlled to provide a valuable resource for their communities. Both of these realizations had dramatic consequences for the way civilizations would evolve. As labor-intensive forms of agriculture increased the value of children, women's bodies—so essential for reproduction and group survival—became a sought-after commodity, one that could be exchanged for the benefit of their kin-group. By the end of the Neolithic Era, as agricultural societies became settled and hierarchical, men leaders emerged and expanded their strategic advantages with a set of common practices anthropologists have labeled the **Exchange of Women**. These common practices included offering women in negotiated marriages to establish alliances with other groups, providing sex with women as a gesture of hospitality to men visitors, and expecting women to participate in fertility festivals that incorporated ritual rapes designed to ensure abundance.[21] WTF

While Marxist scholars such as Friedrich Engels have argued that the notion of private property was a prerequisite for the establishment of patriarchy, Gerda Lerner (1987), in her classic work, *The Creation of Patriarchy*, argues that men's appropriation of women's sexual and reproductive capacity as a commodity that could be exchanged for their own advantage actually serves as the foundation for notions of private property and ownership.[22] Lerner, a historian who relies on archeological evidence to explore how women's subordination took root in ancient Mesopotamia, concludes that "the first appropriation of private property consists of the appropriation of the labor of women as reproducers," and thus, "in the course of the agricultural revolution the exploitation of human labor and the sexual exploitation of women become inextricably linked".[23]

Gradually, over time, men's control over women's reproductive functions established the notion of ownership and private property. This process was exacerbated by men's awareness of their own paternity. After recognizing their role in procreation, men began insisting that brides be virgins and that their wives refrain from adultery after marriage. The desire to pass on fields and herds to their own male children helped extend the notion of men's control and ownership over *their* patriarchal family units, over *their* fields, and over *their* herds. As men organized their patriarchal households into settled communities, warfare increased which men used as an opportunity to expand the size, and hence the productivity, of their households by enslaving conquered women and children. Initially, slaves were integrated into domestic households, often as concubines and domestic servants. Yet, the practice of dominating women established the precedent that demographic traits could be used to determine people's status in society. Lerner's argument is straightforward and simple: "The stigma of belonging to a group which is enslavable is based on the precedent of seeing women as an inferior group."[24] Not long after this "crucial invention,"[25] men leaders began capturing and enslaving conquered men rather than killing them, institutionalizing more oppressive versions of slavery and forced labor. In short, men learned how to dominate other people by first subordinating, commodifying, and exchanging women in their own close kinship groups—practices which Engels described as the historical defeat of the female sex.

Lerner additionally provides an in-depth account of the way the Exchange of Women first led to patriarchal family units and then to the establishment of patriarchal civilization in the fertile crescent surrounding Mesopotamia. Similar processes, with regional variations, took place across the globe. Notably, however, scholars from various social science disciplines ranging from anthropology to economics have found a connection between agriculture and patriarchy. Societies with the earliest Neolithic revolutions, where agriculture has been embraced for a longer period of time, still have stronger patriarchal values, more restrictions on women's role in public life, lower labor force participation, and less sex-based equality.[26] The type of agriculture pursued also was related to equality (or inequality). Regions that required intense physical labor, often characterized by dry irrigation and reliance on the plow, still have more distinct and restrictive gender roles, as do regions of the world where people have a higher percentage of ancestors who were plow users.[27] Meanwhile, regions requiring less intense physical labor—where women were not entirely excluded from the means of production—still see higher levels of women's participation in the economy.[28–31] (See Box 1.3 for a discussion of women's participation in the workforce today.) In addition, the type of crop mattered. Domesticated grain was essential for the rise of patriarchal archaic states. Unlike other crops, grain produces a surplus—most notably a surplus that is easily observed and measured. It grows above ground, can be planted in rows, and has to be harvested all at once, making it easier to tax and regulate. Grain, in particular, provided early patriarchs with the agricultural surplus they needed to transform themselves into the rulers of city-states. Notably, the adoption of the plow and reliance on grain was widespread across the entire continent of Europe, which had implications for the status of women in hierarchical civilizations that laid the foundation for Western cultures.[32]

BOX 1.3: POLICY FEATURE

Women in the Workforce

Over the last 20 years, we have witnessed progress in the world of work for women. This change has come through sex-based equality, education, and participation in the labor market, as well as efforts to reduce poverty and boost economic development by allowing women into the workforce with "equal pay for equal work."[33]

(Continued)

(Continued)

According to the International Labor Organization in the United States, the percentage of eligible workers participating in the workforce is 65.3% men to 53.3% women; that is 12.9 million more men in the workforce, although the majority of eligible women outweighs men by 4.6 million.[34] Similar findings are seen in other democratic societies, such as Spain and Switzerland, where the eligible number of women outnumbers men, yet the rates of employment show similar disparities. In Spain, 53.8% of the men's population participates in the workforce as opposed to 42.2% of women. In Switzerland, 70.8% of men verses 59.7% of women are actively employed in the workforce.

Yemen fairs among the worst in the world in terms of percentage of women in the workforce. In Yemen, where the population of eligible working men to working women is comparable, only 4.3% of the women are employed in the workforce.[35] Similarly, in the Syrian Arab Republic, only 7.3% of eligible women are employed.[36] There are three underlying reasons for this low rate of employment. Challenges to women's economic participation include the following: "i) the patriarchal structure of states in the region, ii) dominant public-sector employment and weak private sector employment, and iii) an inhospitable business environment for women because of the conservative nature of gender roles and the lack of support for reproductive and family costs."[37] These regions lose an estimated 27% of income due to the employment gap in women's labor force participation.[38]

In stark contrast, countries like Cambodia where the available labor force between men and women only differs by 17,000, in favor of men, women are employed at 80.8% compared to their male counterparts at 88.5%. Cambodia has the highest level of women's participation in the workforce.[39] Nevertheless, in Cambodia, women report "earning $1 to $3 less per day than men for the same value of work. Furthermore, they often work jobs that are low-skilled, sign contracts with terms that they do not understand, and lack equal protections under the law."[40]

Overall, in the last 20 years, we have seen remarkable changes in closing the gap between men and women as it pertains to women's participation in the workforce—especially among developed and developing countries as well as democratic countries (see Table 1.1).[41] On the other hand, we have a long way to go in bridging those gaps. The worldview that women do not deserve equal and equitable employment even if they are eligible is a barrier. Women as the primary custodians of the household is another barrier. Religious and political views that place women in a lower status also are contributing factors. How women combat these blockades individually, politically, and collectively will be the determining mechanisms for access to equal and equitable reception into the labor market.

Table 1.1 Levels and Trends in Rates of Labor Force Participation and Unemployment by Sex, 2009–21

Country/region	Labor force participation rate (percentages) and sex-based gap (percentage points)					Unemployment rate (percentages) and women's-to-men's unemployment rate ratio				
	Men	Women	Gap (Men–Women)			Men	Women	Ratio (Women's rate/Men's rate)		
	2018	2018	2009–18	2018	2018–21 (Projection)	2018	2018	2009–18	2018	2018–21
World	**75.0**	**48.5**	**D**	**26.5**	**I**	**5.2**	**6.0**	**I**	**1.2**	**I**
Developing Countries	81.1	69.3	D	11.8	S	4.6	6.1	D	1.3	I
Emerging countries	76.1	45.6	I	30.5	I	5.2	6.1	I	1.2	I
Developed countries	68.0	52.4	D	15.6	D	5.3	5.6	S	1.1	S
Northern Africa	71.9	21.9	D	50.0	D	9.1	19.5	D	2.2	I
Sub-Saharan Africa	74.0	64.7	D	9.3	D	6.4	8.2	D	1.3	I
Latin America and the Caribbean	77.1	51.5	D	25.6	D	6.8	9.5	D	1.4	
Northern America	67.9	55.8	S	12.1	D	4.6	4.4	I	1.0	D
Arab States	77.2	18.9	I	58.3	D	6.8	16.3	I	2.4	D

(Continued)

(Continued)

Country/region	Labor force participation rate (percentages) and sex-based gap (percentage points)					Unemployment rate (percentages) and women's-to-men's unemployment rate ratio				
	Men	Women	Gap (Men–Women)			Men	Women	Ratio (Women's rate/Men's rate)		
	2018	2018	2009–18	2018	2018–21 (Projection)	2018	2018	2009–18	2018	2018–21
Eastern Asia	74.7	59.1	I	15.6	I	4.8	4.2	I	0.9	I
South-Eastern Asia and Pacific	79.4	56.5	D	22.8	D	3.5	3.3	D	0.9	S
Southern Asia	79.0	27.6	D	51.4	I	3.7	5.2	I	1.4	D
Northern, Southern and Western Europe	63.4	51.6	D	11.9	D	7.9	8.2	I	1.0	S
Eastern Europe	67.0	51.8	I	15.2	D	5.6	4.9	S	0.9	S
Central and Western Asia	73.5	45.1	D	28.4	D	8.0	9.4	I	1.2	D

Source: Adapted from International Labor Organization (2018). World employment social outlook. Retrieved from https://www .ilo.org/wcmsp5/groups/public/---dgreports/---dcomm/---publ/documents/publication/wcms_619577.pdf

Developments for the periods 2009 to 2018 and 2018 2021 are marked with an "I" if the gap in labor force participation (unemployment rate ratio) is projected to increase by more than 0.1 (0.01) percentage points, a D if it is projected to decrease by more than 0.1 (0.01) percentage points, and a "S" if it is expected to hold steady

Numbers in the "Gap" column refer to the percentage point difference between the men's and women's labor force participation rates but may not correspond precisely due to rounding.

Contrary to the assumptions of later political theorists like Thomas Hobbes and John Locke, who argued that people entered into a voluntary social contract with government to achieve a better life, most people did not flock to these fledgling city-states to benefit from civilization. Rather, archaic states emerged to institutionalize the elite position of the handful of men leaders (and their close relations) who benefited from the agricultural surplus they generated through the coerced reproductive labor of women and the forced labor of slaves. The patriarchal family unit, with a man in charge of wives, female relatives, children, and slaves provided the foundation on which civilizations were built, embedding hierarchy, subordination, and oppression into archaic states from their very inception.

As civilization evolved, the status of various groups within this formative patriarchal unit was embedded into formal law, and formal rule-based systems of slavery and oppression were established. This process fundamentally altered women's relationships to one another, as enslaved women and their children no longer shared a common fate, embedded within the family unit. Formalizing slavery led to distinct classes in society—and therefore distinct classes of women in society. All women were subordinate to men within their own class but were also separated from one another by their class status. In ancient Mesopotamia, for example, women attached to men rulers through marriage and kinship were at the top of this hierarchy, with slave women at the bottom, and slave-concubines holding a mid-level status.[42] While their own freedom and reproductive functions were controlled, wives still benefited from controlling the physical and reproductive labor of women beneath them in this social hierarchy. In patriarchal systems, men's class status results from their relationship to the means of production in society. For women, class status is mediated through their relationship to men.

Hence from their earliest versions, patriarchal systems were insulated from challenges by one half of the population by affording some women privileges at the expense of others. Wives who enjoyed status and privilege in ancient Mesopotamia, for example, were not likely to align themselves with slaves and concubines. Rather than a single demographic group with common experiences and a shared fate, civilization provided women with cross-cutting (or intersectional) identities that prevented them from developing a sense of group consciousness, a theme we'll see emerge in modern-day systems as well. Yet, if women lack **group consciousness**—or the recognition that their subordinate status results from a shared group trait—they are unlikely to engage in collective action to demand change. Even now, women's levels of group consciousness are typically much lower than other groups of people who are subject to discrimination based on shared traits.[43] Recent feminist scholarship and activism have relied on the concept of **intersectionality**—which was coined by legal scholar Kimberlé Crenshaw (1989) in the 1980s to describe the way different demographic traits combine, overlap, and intersect to create different versions of privilege and oppression—in an attempt to build a more inclusive feminist movement (see Box 1.4).[44]

It is important to note that the class and racial inequalities that divide women were built into patriarchy at the very beginning and are part of the reason why patriarchy has been so difficult to overcome. Sociologist Allan G. Johnson (2014), in *The Gender Knot*, also describes how patriarchy is built on overlapping systems of oppression. He argues patriarchy is not problematic simply because it features men's dominance over women but because it promotes dominance and control over others as the legitimate means to achieve a stable society. In that sense, all forms of privilege draw support from common roots, and undermining any single form of oppression can help to undermine them all.[45] Yet, if reformers fail to link patriarchy to other versions of oppressions, such as those based on race, class, and/or sexuality, they will simply enable some women to succeed at the expense of women who are disadvantaged by other demographic characteristics. This feature of patriarchy has made it difficult for women to advocate for reforms that benefit all women. Intersectionality has also prevented most men from actively attempting to dismantle patriarchy's oppression of women, ironically, even if they have recognized and fought against hierarchies based on class, race, ethnicity, or sexual orientation. Johnson argues men's reluctance stems from the fact that "men have no experience of being oppressed as men, and because all men, regardless of race or class, have access to some degree of men's privilege."[46] In short, patriarchy encourages everyone, men and women alike, to focus on preserving some of the privileges their identity provides. For women, this means preserving status based on aspects of their identity other than sex, while for men it means preserving status based on sex. But if men are not included in the quest to stymie patriarchy, the harm that hierarchy and oppression, along with strictly policed binary gender roles, do to everyone is more easily overlooked. According to Johnson, we are "stuck deep inside an oppressive gender legacy" that also castigates men who do not live up to strict standards of masculinity. The result is that many people experience "a great deal of suffering, injustice, and trouble" because of the so-called "gender knot" that constrains us all.[47]

BOX 1.4: KIMBERLÉ CRENSHAW'S TED TALK ON INTERSECTIONALITY

In 2016, Kimberlé Crenshaw presented at TEDWomen, part of the official TED Conferences—also known as TED talks. During this conference, she highlighted a national and global problem that women of color face when it comes to police violence and protections under the law. Crenshaw argued that, due to a lack of an available framework under the law, women of color were facing a double discrimination, which she beautifully described as "injustice squared."

Paul Zimmerman/WireImage for V-Day

BLACK WOMEN AR[...] HE POLICE TOO.
SAY THEIR NAM[...] [...]ER THEIR FACES.
THE MOVEM[...] [...]T THEM TOO.

▶ **Photo 1.3** Kimberlé Crenshaw speaking about police violence against Black women.

Crenshaw explores two main issues. Primarily, she offers an alternative framework that can help us better recognize the unique challenges faced by women of color, in order to broaden our current frame of understanding to evoke political change and equal justice under the law. Secondly, she explores the way in which communities, media, policy makers, politicians, and the law view matters of injustice that are central to change.

Crenshaw shares the case of Emma DeGraffenreid. DeGraffenreid is an African American woman who was seeking employment at a car manufacturing plant. She applied for employment and was denied. DeGraffenreid took this case to court where she argued she was not hired because she was a Black woman. Her case was dismissed because the judge believed that she would have had "preferential treatment" or "two swings at the bat" because she was both African American and a woman. The car manufacturer in question argued that they hired African Americans, though they were men working industrial and maintenance jobs. The manufacturer also argued that they hired women, who tended to work the secretarial or front office jobs and were white. Seeing this combination as unfair and with no framework to see the double discrimination at play, the judge dismissed DeGraffenreid's case.

The case of DeGraffenreid lends itself to the broader issue of combined race and sex discrimination. Crenshaw would offer an answer to this framing problem through the lens of intersectionality. That is, the understanding that two marginalized categories can overlap at the same time within a single entity, often causing multiple levels of social injustice. People can have the dilemma of facing intersections of racism, sexism, heterosexism, transphobia, xenophobia, and ableism. Furthermore, the realities lived by one person or group are not the same as the realities faced by others. Everyone has a uniquely lived experience and therefore faces injustice at tragically different levels, just as in the case of DeGraffenreid.

(Continued)

(Continued)

However, by recognizing these compounded injustices through broadening their understanding of the lived experience, lawmakers may be able to reevaluate these particular cases. The current framework of the law is partial and distorting. There is no name for this problem, and, as Crenshaw states, "where there is no name for this problem, you can't see the problem, and when you can't see the problem, you pretty much can't solve it." By labeling this problem one of intersectionality, individuals gain perspective on the matter at hand.

Stories such as DeGraffenreid's are not the only reason we should accept this idea of intersectionality and its place in our society. In a time where African American men are being shot to death by police, the public often does not hear about the vast number of African American women equally subjected to the same use of deadly force by the police. From grandmothers to 7-year-old girls, African American women are dying at just as alarming rates as Black men. The difference is that the public, media, and the law are not talking about these cases. These women are at the crossroad of intersectionality, and they are falling through the cracks.

Another reason why patriarchy is so difficult to overcome, somewhat ironically, is that the advantages that accrued to leaders in settled communities were difficult to sustain. Recorded history has tended to celebrate the dawn of civilization as a great leap forward for humanity, providing the security of a stable food source and settled communities. While elites in early archaic states enjoyed a dramatic—although precarious—improvement in their standard of living, average people most certainly did not. Hunting and gathering provided a more varied and nutritious diet, with far less effort than farming. The small size of hunter-gatherer bands, with no settled fields to cultivate and defend, meant that members could easily relocate if one source of food failed. It also prevented the spread of disease and protected members from new epidemics that swept through settled communities and domestic stock. Hunter-gatherers, who did not spend hours laboring to produce agricultural surplus to support the ruling class or to build infrastructure for the state, enjoyed more leisure time than village and city dwellers—and they had more freedom to use this time as they pleased, with fewer class-based and sex-based restrictions on their behavior. The claim that our ancestors were reluctant to become the ruling class's labor force in settled communities is supported by the 4,000-year gap between domestication of grain and the rise of the earliest states. Rather than embracing farming with enthusiasm, prehistoric people preferred to adopt subsistence strategies that combined hunting and gathering with easily domesticated crops. This tactic allowed them to maintain a hunter-gatherer lifestyle, supplemented with a more reliable source of food. Indeed, some scholars argue that our ancestors only settled down in response to a series of droughts that made foraging unsustainable.[48] Moreover, even after peasants and slaves were incorporated into the earliest states, they often had to be compelled to stay. The walls built around the earliest city states served a dual purpose; they kept "barbarians" and marauders out, but they also prevented the workforce from fleeing. Elites had a vested interest in compelling laborers to stay, as the most populous states were also the most successful states. In successful states, elites had access to skilled workers and technical expertise that could provide a competitive edge in trade, adequate warriors to defend the state and to plunder nearby regions, and enough peasants and slaves to feed the ever-expanding classes removed from agricultural labor, such as rulers, priests, administrators, and crafts people.

Yet, as a past littered with fallen and conquered societies makes clear, elites' ability to maintain this balance was precarious. This precariousness exacerbated the underpinning logic of patriarchal civilization—the **fear-control cycle**, or men's fear of being dominated by other men. Agriculture taught people how to control the natural environment to build food surpluses, and they quickly learned to extend this control to women and conquered men. But the men patriarchs who stepped into positions of authority in early agricultural settlements quickly realized the biggest threat to their security and status—even worse than environmental disasters from overuse of natural resources and high mortality rates from epidemics—was other men.

Living in settled communities increased the mortality rates for both infants and adults. Settled communities replaced some of this lost labor with increased fertility rates. Women living in settled communities gave birth far more often than women in hunter-gatherer societies, who would typically only have one child every four years. Despite outpacing the mortality rate, live births alone could not meet the labor needs of the rising archaic states—which have been described as "population machines" designed to control new sources of labor, domesticating other people in the same way that animals had been domesticated into herds.[49]

Early states were heavily reliant on agricultural labor, and low numbers were supplemented with what Max Weber described as "**booty capitalism**"—or raiding and conquering nearby settlements.[50] Hence, the root cause of patriarchy's expansion was men's fear of being conquered and dominated by other men. Men learned that control of the natural environment, women, and slaves, provided surplus resources that they needed to compete with each other. Eventually, control became the priority around which entire societies were organized. Yet as men, and by extension patriarchal systems, pursued control as a way to protect themselves, the same response is triggered from others. According to sociologist Allan G. Johnson, "Once this dynamic is set in motion, it forms the basis for an escalating spiral of control and fear. The result is an extended patriarchal history marked not only by the accomplishments that control makes possible, but also by domination, warfare, and oppression, all of which are male-dominated, male identified, male-centered pursuits that revolve around affirming, protecting, and enhancing men's standing and security in relation to other men."[51] In a more succinct statement, he concludes "this dynamic has provided patriarchy with its driving force for thousands of years."[52]

Patriarchal societies were also organized around assigning specific roles and functions to people based on sex, class, race, religion, and/or caste. For example, men and masculinity became associated with all aspects of control, including rationality, logic, strength, combat, leadership, and decision-making. Meanwhile, women and femininity became associated with the exact opposite traits, including emotion, submissiveness, weakness, and nurturing. Each sex's willingness to embrace roles associated with these traits became seen as essential for sustaining society and avoiding chaos.

Binary gender roles were so embedded as a foundational organizing structure in Western civilizations that they were still embraced during the earliest stages of democratization. During the **Enlightenment**, for example, Western societies perpetuated strict sex-based roles for men and women, even while rejecting other hierarchical structures that oppressed many men, such as monarchies, landed aristocracies, and feudalism. Scholars date the Enlightenment to the seventeenth and eighteenth centuries, following the so-called Dark Ages of Medieval Europe. Whereas Medieval Europe championed tradition and the top-down authority of the Church and monarchies, the Enlightenment embraced individualism and reason, or, in other words, the ability of every man to seek knowledge, experience liberation, and participate in government. The classical liberalism of the Enlightenment projected an archetype of an honorable man and citizen who relied on reason and avoided emotionalism, had courage to act on his own reason, and was seriously committed to his community.[53] Women during this era were not considered fit to be citizens, as the philosopher Jean Jacques Rousseau explained, because they were emotional and too tied to the home and family to be dedicated to their community and state. Perhaps, Rousseau's greatest pronouncement of gender stereotypes was in his book about the education of boys and girls, titled *Emile* or *On Education* (1762). In this book, the young man, Emile, is educated in the social and natural sciences to be a citizen and a leader, while his female counterpart, Sophie, is educated to be his helpmate.[54] She is expected to be emotional, to take care of her home and family, and to present herself in a becoming way. Rousseau also insisted women must be excluded from politics and leadership because their cunning and flirtatious ways could distract men from their noble duties. The Enlightenment, therefore, was exclusionary even as it hastened democratic forms of government. Women, like enslaved men at the time, were considered less than fully human and incapable of reason and thus undeserving of equality and unfit for leadership.

In the midst of the Enlightenment, as the notion of men's popular sovereignty and men's unalienable rights took root, political revolutions with the goal of establishing the first modern democratic states took place in the United States and France. (Box 1.5 explains how political thought failed to extend these unalienable rights to women.) Establishing democracy through war further cemented binary gender roles. Even though many women played a role in civil unrest and revolution (see Chapter 2), citizenship became associated with formal military service and with men who were willing to fight and die, not only for freedom, but to defend their property—which included their wives and their families—from tyrants. Political leadership was equated with military leadership and masculine traits, and war heroes like George Washington were expected to continue their service to the country by stepping into public office. Burgeoning nationalism, meanwhile, highlighted women's role in childbirth and childrearing, as women were expected to produce and socialize the next generation of patriotic citizens.

BOX 1.5 CAROLE PATEMAN AND THE SEXUAL CONTRACT

American political thought emphasizes that citizens have unalienable rights to life, liberty, and the pursuit of happiness, as famously celebrated by Thomas Jefferson in the Declaration of Independence; however, when Jefferson and his contemporaries referenced "all men" having rights, they generally meant only men. Social contract theorists imagined a society built on an agreement of the governed, namely citizens. John Locke (1632–1704), whose ideas influenced Jefferson, argued government only gains the legitimate right to exercise authority, depriving men of their natural sovereignty, when men voluntarily consent to enter a social contract and agree to be governed in exchange for the ability to better enjoy their life, liberty, and property. While Locke "was willing to elevate women's status,"[55] he remained silent on the question of their participation in the founding of political society. Hence, social contract theorists who worried about men's unalienable rights did not worry about women's much more than the political theorists who preceded them. Without the participation of women, the contract is indeed an agreement among men. This outcome is problematic for democracy because it means patriarchy is built into political theories that inspire Western democracies.

Sir Robert Filmer (1588–1683) wrote *Patriarcha: or the Natural Power of Kings* in 1680. Whereas social contract theorists thought citizens must agree to be governed, which then leads them to build democratic institutions, Filmer believed that kings had the divine right to rule over subjects, a right handed down from the first father and king, Adam, in the Bible. The king was also the patriarch in the sense that he was a father

(Continued)

(Continued)

and would rule his family, that is, the state and his subjects. Initially, patriarchy not only justified men's rule over women but also the most powerful man's rule over other men and all women. Carole Pateman, feminist theorist and author of *The Sexual Contract* (1988), points out that when social contract theorists critiqued kings' rule over subjects, they failed to critique men's rule over women. Put another way, contract theorists wanted to eliminate the most powerful man's rule over other men and give them rights but did not foresee an end to women's oppression or their attainment of rights. Pateman argues the social contract theorists left in place a so-called sexual contract that allows men to rule over women's bodies. Women do not consent to this rule; patriarchy allows for it, as it has since Adam, the first man, had access to Eve's body. Pateman further argues that the social contract would not be possible without the sexual contract, for there would be no men to challenge the king's rule and form a social contract without men's sexual access to women and women's reproductive role in bearing children. Even though women give birth to the men who become citizens and form social contracts, early democratic movements left them under men's authority without the right to participate.[56]

The *Sexual Contract* is at once a critique of social contract theory and the early history of democracies (see Chapter 2 for more discussion about women's lack of rights in early American history), and also a critique of politics today. Consent to sex is a current topic in American society, and it is particularly relevant on college campuses. Best consent practices now emphasize that both partners in a sexual encounter should affirm their desires. It is not good enough to say "no means no"; rather, sexual partners should verbally or physically indicate that, yes, they agree to sex. Unfortunately, many women are robbed of the ability to make this choice. Statistics from the World Health Organization show that one in three women will experience physical or sexual violence by a partner or sexual violence by a nonpartner.[57] The continued existence of sexual assault proves the longevity of the sexual contract. The sexual contract did not end with the formation of democracy, and as explained in Chapter 4, democracies today do not do enough to stop sexual violence or ameliorate its effects. The United States did not pass the Violence Against Women Act (VAWA) until 1994, and even in the year 2018, lawmakers were slow to commit to its reauthorization. The VAWA (see Chapter 4) largely funds social services to support victims of sexual assault and domestic violence.[58] All democracies that purport that women are citizens and have rights must respond to the question, how can women be considered equal citizens under the social contract if the state cannot ensure them a basic unalienable right to "life" that should, by definition, include bodily integrity?

Despite repeated waves of the women's movement, as women have sought the same status and legal rights as men in society, remnants of these prescribed gender roles remain today, and we will see them recur throughout this book. Thus, in the past, and today, a great deal of effort was and is expended to convince people that these sex-based roles are natural, so that men will fulfill the masculine functions society thinks it needs to sustain itself, and women will fulfill feminine ones.

REIFICATION AND THE SOCIAL CONSTRUCTION OF REALITY

Social scientists refer to this process—where people perceive their own society and their own role within it as the only possible way to structure society—as the **social construction of reality**. They claim that the **reification** that occurs as a result of this process helps to explain how so many people throughout recorded history have been willing to accept worldviews that result in their own oppression and also to perpetuate these worldviews by acting out their assigned roles within them. Specifically, reification describes perceiving the roles and institutions that human beings have created (which are actually social constructs) as unchanging features of the natural world (or reality). When people experience the world in reified terms, they lose historical consciousness. They forget the role people played in structuring human activities, which undermines demands for change. Indeed, people who experience the world in reified terms do not believe that it is possible, or sometimes even desirable, to change their own and others' roles in society, any more than they would want to change the color of the sky or believe they could stop the ocean from forming waves. Thus, the two sociologists who first fully explained these ideas, Thomas Luckmann and Peter Berger (1967), conclude that, "even while apprehending the world in reified terms, [people] continue to produce it. That is [people are] capable of paradoxically producing a reality that denies [them]."[59]

When a society's entire institutional order is encompassed within a single, symbolic worldview, the entire society makes sense to most people, like a puzzle with no missing pieces. This outcome is most apt to occur when all means of socialization—including **primary socialization** by parents as well as **secondary socialization** by political, civic, religious, and educational institutions—all reinforce the same messages about appropriate roles and behavior. Under these circumstances, most people experience the world in reified terms, and few people challenge the status quo. The handful of people who do challenge the status quo, either with arguments or by simply refusing to conform to expectations, are either perceived as eccentric and mentally unstable or as wicked and evil. They may be largely tolerated but subject to soft versions of suppression, such as ridicule, social sanction, or ostracism.[60] An example of social sanction against women who argue against patriarchy is exemplified in John Adams's befuddled reaction when his wife, Abigail Adams, wrote a letter to him during the American Revolution, titled *Remember the Ladies,* asking him to consider extending the rights of citizenship to women. He found the request amusing and provided a patronizing reply but clearly did not feel threatened by the request. Alternatively, noncompliance is more likely to be framed as evil or heresy when people are perceived as a genuine threat to social stability. These protestors are more likely to be forcibly corrected by being beaten, institutionalized, arrested, or even assassinated. For example, when women recently took to the streets of Tehran, Iran, with chants of "We are women, we are human, but we don't have any rights," they were met with state forces who beat them with batons.[61]

All social realities are, at the end of the day, human inventions, constructed to serve a particular purpose. As such, all social realities are inherently fragile. Change can occur when people are exposed to alternative ideas that challenge their worldview's underpinning assumptions—and when they are willing to risk the inevitable cognitive dissonance that occurs when they take disruptive ideas seriously. Human beings are social creatures who crave stability and the assurance of knowing their place in the world in relation to other people and how to behave accordingly. Hence, the sharpest justification of cultural norms occurs after people come into contact with other societies, as they reject alternative worldviews that may cause them to question their own. Yet, when these ideas take hold, people can form deviant groups that adopt an alternative worldview, that embrace different roles to guide members' choices and behavior. This inevitably leads them to behave in ways that challenge the status quo. It is important not to overlook the importance of these new legitimizing worldviews, as humans need a common understanding of the world in order to coordinate and construct social lives. Large numbers of people are not apt to reject stable society for chaos, but they may be willing to embrace an alternative way of understanding the world. If **deviant groups** can sustain their alternative worldview, despite soft and violent versions of sanction, their ideas can spread throughout the population like a virus, changing beliefs and transforming the dominant culture. Here, the term *deviant* is not intended to imply that the group is evil or wrong but to convey its status within society. Members of the group *deviate* from widely accepted cultural norms and expected practice.[62]

Unfortunately, there is no guarantee that the worldview embraced by a small group that rejects mainstream culture will be any less grounded in hierarchy and oppression than patriarchy. It is entirely possible—and perhaps even quite likely after 7,000 years of civilization built on hierarchy and oppression—that the alternative worldview imagined by a deviant group will simply replace one dominant demographic group with another without upending hierarchy and oppression as the building blocks of society. How can we evaluate the new world that these groups envision? How can we make choices among the myriad possibilities for structuring a new and improved society?

Allan G. Johnson (2014), in *The Gender Knot,* suggests addressing all forms of oppression with simple actions. People often think activism requires heroic endeavors to achieve immediate change, and, while social movements and protest politics have played a role in advancing women's rights, everyday choices can also help to dismantle patriarchy, bit by bit, over time. Some of these simple choices include acknowledging that patriarchy exists, paying attention to its effects on others, and learning to listen attentively when women and other marginalized people describe its effects on their lives. Other choices might include speaking up after noticing that these outcomes are unfair and engaging in collective action to challenge unfair decisions and policies whenever possible. Johnson also recommends openly supporting others who step off the path of least resistance and by refusing to police binary gender roles. Similarly, whenever possible, avoid unthinkingly performing traditional gender roles in personal or professional relationships out of habit or fear of social sanction. Simply choosing not to participate in oppressive practices sets an example and normalizes egalitarian alternatives, making it easier for others to follow a similar path. Johnson notes that it is likely impossible to change the hearts and minds of outright misogynists who insist that women fulfill subordinate gender roles in society, but personal choices subverting these roles now will result in well-trod alternative pathways that provide different options for these same misogynists' children and grandchildren years later.[63]

In addition, scholars argue that familiarity with critical theory, which focuses on achieving the normative ideals of justice and equality, plays an important role in guiding efforts to restructure society.

Critical Theory, Feminist Theory, and Feminist Activism

The term *theory* is typically linked to natural sciences like biology, chemistry, and physics. When a series of related hypotheses are supported by careful empirical observations—or data—they are used to develop a broader explanation—or **theory**—about how the world works. When social scientists began using the same careful research methods to describe and explain human activity and to develop theories of their own, some scholars became concerned that their empirical, descriptive findings would further disguise the social construction of reality, reinforcing perceptions that the status quo is natural and inevitable. These critics feared that empirical social science was "in danger of reifying social phenomenon," and that it "all too frequently ends by confusing its own conceptualization for the laws of the universe."[64] Their solution was to argue for an interdisciplinary approach, integrating philosophy's normative concern with empirical social science research methods.

This interdisciplinary approach is referred to as **critical theory**. When the term Critical Theory is capitalized, it refers to the Frankfurt School—a group of like-minded scholars in 1930s Germany who developed and promoted this approach, along with their students. Specifically, the neo-Marxist scholars associated with the Frankfurt School believed that their work should identify and help to overcome all of the circumstances that limit human freedom. These circumstances, they argued, were the result of **ideologies** (another word for world views) that justified economic and social oppression. They believed social scientists were responsible not only for identifying these oppressive social constructions (i.e., institutions, practices, beliefs, and norms) but also responsible for recommending strategies to change them. When critical theory is not capitalized, it refers to the numerous philosophical traditions that do not have specific links to a scholar affiliated with the Frankfurt School but that adopt a similar approach—and that developed a way to address a wide array of underpinning reasons why people are oppressed. These include **neo-Marxism**, which emphasizes the consequences of organizing societies around class status; **critical race theory** and **postcolonial criticism,** which address the effects of being non-white and non-Western on individual freedom; **queer theory and transgender theory,** which address the effects of not conforming to heteronormative assumptions about sexual orientation and gender identity on individual freedom; and of most relevance to this particular book, **feminist theory,** which focuses on the effects of biological sex and gender identity on individual freedom.

Types of Feminist Theory

Of course, given the way that cross-cutting identities create a wide variety of women's experiences, there are also many distinct categories of critical feminist theory—so many that students can take semester-long college courses dedicated to learning about these varied approaches. Hence, the summary provided below is only intended to give a broad overview of these often overlapping—but sometimes contradictory—recommendations for how to best eliminate women's subordination across the globe.

Perhaps the most familiar feminist theory is **liberal feminism**, sometimes called mainstream feminism. Liberal feminism, most associated with women's suffrage and women's rights movements in Western democracies like the United States and England, emphasizes equal standing and rights within an existing political and social structure. Liberal feminism's focus is on gaining access to, and fair treatment within, these institutions rather than seeing the institutional structures themselves as a source of oppression. This leads those who embrace this approach to focus on specific legal and social reform. Examples of classic feminist contributions written from the liberal feminist perspective include Mary Wollstonecraft's *A Vindication of the Rights of Women*, published in 1792, which argued that women should receive an education commensurate with their class status in society. Another is *The Declaration of Sentiments*, written primarily by Elizabeth Cady Stanton in 1848 to proclaim that women had the same inalienable rights that Thomas Jefferson attributed to men in America's *Declaration of Independence*. A more modern example is the text of the proposed U.S. Equal Rights Amendment, which was almost ratified in the late 1970s and would have overturned laws that treat men and women differently. While this approach yielded important gains for women—such as the right to vote and legislation eliminating sex-based discrimination and sexual harassment in the workplace—it has also been criticized for overlooking the root cause of oppression for all women and for prioritizing the agenda of white upper-class women whose racial and class privilege is linked to sustaining at least some aspects of the status quo.

This criticism must be taken seriously and must inform future waves of feminist activism. Yet, it is also important to realize how difficult it can be for women to make change in patriarchal systems at all if they are deprived of an education, financial independence, and legal rights. The women first able to advocate for these essential resources were often those who could leverage the privilege of their class and race, and, unfortunately, their intersectional experiences made it less likely that they would advocate for more fundamental changes. In addition, imagining a completely different reality than the one that has been constructed over thousands of years is difficult—even for the most visionary feminist. Envisioning a different world is even more unlikely in closed, homogeneous societies, where deviant groups are easily suppressed, contact with different cultures is limited, and socializing agents, such as parents, teachers, civic and political leaders, religious teachings, and so on, reinforce messages about the way the world should work. From this perspective, liberal or mainstream feminism, and the type of reforms it inspires, can provide a foundation upon which future activists can build. It took hundreds of years, with gradually shifting behaviors and beliefs, for the subordination of women to take root and for patriarchy to spread across the globe. Overturning it has required, and will continue to require, similar incremental changes that gradually shift the trajectory of civilization along a more egalitarian path.

In addition to liberal feminism, several versions of feminist theory address experiences of women based on different aspects of their intersectional identities. Traditional Marxist theorists believed that eliminating capitalism and exploitation of lower-class labor would end much of women's oppression. **Neo-Marxist and socialist feminists** often build on the connection between class status and sex to emphasize women's subordinate role within the domestic sphere and not simply the workplace. For example, they point out that patriarchal family units—where women's unpaid domestic labor enables men to be ideal workers focused exclusively on the workplace—is essential for sustaining capitalism. This concern over the effect of capitalism is mirrored by contemporary **transnational or global feminists**, who are concerned about the way globalization and global capitalism negatively affect women from different national, racial, and ethnic identities. Similarly, **ecofeminism** highlights the way societies motivated by a fear-control cycle are willing to exploit both natural resources (thereby damaging the environment) and women's reproductive labor (thus oppressing women) to build surpluses and bolster control. **Religious feminism** seeks to combine feminist discourses with the beliefs of a religious paradigm (see Box 1.6).

BOX 1.6: COMPARATIVE FEATURE

Islam, Sharia, and Feminist Thought

Many Americans and Europeans who fear the influence of Islam in Western societies view *sharia* law very negatively. In the media as well, **sharia**, translated literally as "a path," comes across as uniform and immutable, thereby making *sharia* understood as a tradition that forces inequalities such as head coverings and underage marriage upon women. This textbox draws on Muslim feminist thought and casts *sharia* differently, as a path leading to a destination, which is restrictive to women in many instances but also diverse, complex, and dynamic. Because of the important role of law in the interpretation of *sharia*, in the following text, we clarify the practice of Muslim jurisprudence and its legal outcomes as they relate to family law (marriage, divorce, child custody, etc.), often also referred to as personal status law (marriage, divorce, and child custody but also including inheritance laws), which also ties into themes discussed in Chapter 7. In doing so, we become acquainted with the interpretation tools that Muslim feminist scholars want to use in order to push *sharia* law in a more empowering direction for women. Many Muslims worldwide support *sharia* law as the official law of the land (Afghanistan (99%), Iraq (91%), Pakistan (84%), Turkey (12%), Kazakhstan (10%), and Azerbaijan (8%). As a result, Muslim feminists believe that reform from within *sharia* law is more likely to empower and liberate women than a liberal tradition forced on Muslims from without.

What factors determine personal status laws in individual Muslim countries? The answer to this question rests on multiple variables: *sharia* law, legal interpretation, local political actors, and colonial influence, among others. Delineating what makes up *sharia* is our first task. *Sharia* is inspired by the Quran as well as the traditions associated with how the prophet Mohammed lived (*sunnah*). The *hadith* captures *sunnah*, as they are the evidence of Muhammad's actions as recorded by his associates. *Sharia* gives instructions on how to live, including hygiene, how to pray, and how to fast. *Sharia* law also covers more complex issues, like crime, economics, and politics, as well as ethical behavior, that is, how to treat others justly and do good.

How complex issues and ethics are understood requires interpretation. Whereas the Quran as a text originally put forth the main tenets of the law, Islam gradually developed more concrete rules over time. The major Sunni schools of jurisprudence were established in the ninth and tenth centuries, but they continue to evolve over time. They are the Hanafi, Mālikī, Shafi'i, and Hanbali schools; the former two are considered more progressive than the latter two. Saudi Arabia, considered to be a very conservative country, uses the Hanbali tradition; whereas Tunisia and Morocco, more progressive countries, follow the Mālikīte school. Several caveats are in order. First, the relative progressive or conservative nature of these schools in terms of women's rights is debatable. For example, Egypt is under Hanafite interpretation, considered to be more progressive, but, as of 2017, Egypt permitted *talaq*, a practice allowing a man to divorce his wife without a court proceeding by simply "saying 'you are divorced' three times."[65] Egyptian women, on the other hand, must seek divorces in court and are only granted them "under certain conditions such as domestic violence or illness."[66] Second, these legal traditions produce various outcomes depending on the interpretations of national and local actors. In this way, the law is diverse and dynamic even within schools.

The dynamic nature of *sharia* is best understood through the Muslim principle of *ijtihad*, namely the idea that a judge can use his own intellect and reasoning to come to new interpretations of issues to fit Quranic principles. This process can occur in Sunni and Shia contexts. According to Ali, *ijtihad* is an "exercise" that can "liberate Muslim thought from outmoded tribal shackles."[67] This exercise is both ancient and contemporary.

In more recent times, Muslim feminists have suggested that women's rights can be pursued as a matter of justice in Islam and new legal interpretations. Practices can change, they argue, as legal experts change *sharia* to meet modern social contexts. Particularly, feminists emphasize that the Quran imparts justice and equality, thus the lack of justice and equality in Muslim countries results from old patriarchal practices that, in their opinion, no longer belong in the faith. Practicing *ijtihad* requires a judge to have extensive legal training and a comprehensive understanding of ethics and justice. As such, the training for and practice of *ijtihad* has not been afforded to many women historically, which, in turn, means that feminist interpretations do not predominate. Moreover, *ijtihad* is not without backlash from fundamentalists who reject reinterpretations of the holy book of Quran. Though proponents of *ijtihad* see it as a way to reestablish a lost history of *sharia* dynamism, opponents see it as surrender to secular ideals, and particularly to the secularism and liberalism of the West.

Yet another interpretive tool in the Muslim tradition is *takhayyur*, which translates as "selection." This tool is used when a judge uses the "principles of one school alone or a range from different schools" to promote a new practice.[68] For example, Indian Muslims follow Hanafite interpretations, but they chose to follow rules from the Mālikī and Hanbali traditions when the Muslim Marriage Act 1939 was enacted and permitted women to seek divorces. According to Ali, "takhayyur has been of enormous significance in developing a number of women friendly codes of family laws in Muslim jurisdictions."[69]

(Continued)

(Continued)

Morocco

Morocco's reforms of its personal status law over the last 30 years provide examples of how *sharia* law can be dynamic and improve women's lives depending on interpretation. The Morocco case also shows that a country's codified personal status law is a result of multiple variables, including the influence of political actors, protesters, and religious leaders. Morocco's personal status law became codified in 1958 and is referred to as the Moudawana. Previously, under French colonialism, Morocco followed Berber customary law, and it was considered a nationalist feat to develop laws based on *sharia* that embodied the new country's Islamic identity.[70] Ten religious scholars, all men, worked on the law, and it was based on traditional Mālikī jurisprudence. The law was disadvantageous to women in many ways, for example, permitting men to have multiple wives, giving fathers the ability to marry off daughters, and obliging women to obey their husbands. The law was criticized from the start, and women stepped up activism in the early 1990s to seek reform. A women's group collected over a million signatures to petition the king, and he sanctioned a commission to practice *ijtihad* on the Moudawana—which included "twenty male and one female religious scholars and one representative of the Royal Court."[71] The reform to the Moudawana in 1993 was not extensive and represented Mālikī standards, but it did, for example, require a woman to verbally give her consent to marriage.[72] Greater reforms to the Moudawana came in 2004 after a socialist minister, in 1999, proposed changes in line with the United Nations' women's rights standards. Some religious scholars repudiated the reforms, and citizens also protested at this point, some in favor of reform and others against it.[73] Also in 1999, King Mohammed VI followed his father to the throne and sought social and political change, and, to reform the Moudawana, he appointed a commission that included three women. This new commission, once again, practiced *ijtihad*. The Moudawana preamble now insists that reform comes from the heart of Islam itself as it "adheres to Islam's tolerant ends and objectives, namely justice, equality, solidarity, ijtihād and receptiveness to the spirit of our modern era and the requirements of progress and development."[74] Some of the changes made in 2004 include women no longer owe obedience to their husbands, women are allowed to sign contracts at marriage to establish community property, the marriage age of women was raised from 15 to 18 to be the same as that of men, and processes for seeking a divorce were standardized for women and men.[75]

Other feminist theories underscore the connection between sex and racial/ethnic identities. **Postcolonial and multiracial feminism** highlight the overlapping oppression experienced by non-Western and non-white women. They argue that women's experiences with oppression are not universal and that overlooking their lived experiences with racism is not only ethnocentric but ignores discrimination against women through racial bias. **Black feminism**, which emerged in the 1970s to address the distinct version of oppression experienced by African American women, offers a similar intersectional approach that expanded to include not simply race and sex but all forms of oppression that affect women. Writer Barbara Smith, a prominent activist associated with the National Black Feminist Organization (NBFO), defined feminism as "the political theory and practice that struggles to free all women: women of color, working class-women, poor women, disabled women, Jewish women, lesbians, old women—as well as white, economically-privileged, heterosexual women. Anything less than this vision of total freedom is not feminism, but merely female self-aggrandizement."[76] This definition's focus on eliminating all justifications for subordination and oppression in society corresponds to feminist scholar bell hooks's (see Box 1.7) argument that feminism must attempt to eradicate all social systems that lead to domination, including not simply patriarchy but also racism, imperialism, and capitalism.[77]

BOX 1.7: BELL HOOKS EXPLAINS HOW FEMINISM HELPS EVERYONE

Middlebury College/Todd Balfour

▶ **Photo 1.4** Mural of feminist scholar bell hooks, by Will Kasso Condry, community muralist and educator at Middlebury College in Vermont.

Contrary to some popular arguments, feminists and feminist theorists are not trying to reverse the position of men and women in patriarchal civilizations. They are not trying to displace men so that women can take over, to maintain a hierarchical society where women are privileged rather than subordinate. The fear that feminists want power and authority for themselves, rather than freedom for everyone, underscores how difficult it is to imagine and construct an alternative world. After 7,000 years of hierarchy, it is difficult to imagine a new world characterized by egalitarianism. Yet, many feminist scholars point out that

(Continued)

(Continued)

men would also be better off in a world characterized by egalitarianism. Without a doubt, men are rewarded with privilege and status for performing masculine roles in patriarchal societies. But performing these roles comes at a cost.

According to feminist scholar bell hooks,[78] "The first act of violence that patriarchy demands of men is not violence toward women. Instead patriarchy demands of all men that they engage in psychic-mutilation, that they kill off the emotional parts of themselves. If an individual is not successful in emotionally crippling himself, he can count on patriarchal men to enact rituals of power that will assault his self-esteem."

To achieve "manhood" in a patriarchal society, sociologist Allan G. Johnson (2014) argues that boys must first sacrifice a portion of their humanity. They are praised (typically by other men) for devaluing and suppressing any emotion or reaction associated with women, and they are ridiculed when they do not. The result "precludes them from knowing true intimacy with other people, estranges them from their own feelings and the bodies through which feelings are felt, and denies them powerful inner resources for coping with stress, fear, and loss."[79] Expecting men to be in control at all times not only undermines their ability to feel empathy for those they are controlling, it encourages them to use violence, both to establish control and to avoid being controlled by others. Yet, the fear-control cycle established by using violence, or the threat of violence, to achieve control inevitably leads back to fear. Hence, "men's frequent complaints about their lives often reflect the patriarchal paradox that organizing yourself around control, power, and privilege usually makes you feel worse rather than better."[80]

Additional feminist approaches tend to emphasize what women have in common, rather than intersectional identities that result in different experiences. One of these approaches, **cultural feminism**, is more apt than liberal feminism to acknowledge essential differences between men and women but argues that female attributes have been undervalued and suppressed under patriarchy—and that the subordination of empathy, nurturing, and caring are at the core of oppression. Rather than working to change the status quo by seeking access to men-dominated institutions of government and power, however, cultural feminists often encourage the formation of separate, women-only spaces where women's culture—one that promotes an alternative world view— is more apt to flourish. Keep in mind that this approach, which emphasizes changing society through lifestyle choices over political reforms, was only possible after women first gained legal rights and economic independence through political activism.

Radical feminism is similarly focused on the root cause of all women's oppression, which it also identifies as patriarchal gendered relationships and the institutions that grew up around them. Indeed, the term *radical* is related to the Latin adjective *radicalis*, which simply meant "of or relating to a root," as well as the noun *radix*, which meant "root." Unlike cultural feminism, radical feminism argues that the patriarchal institutional structures that evolved to subordinate women and remove them from the public sphere must be eliminated—along with all other hierarchical institutional structures that oppress people based on their race, ethnicity, class, and ability—before feminists can achieve significant reform. They argue that all hierarchical institutional structures must be uprooted and replaced to dramatically improve all women's status in a more egalitarian society (see Box 1.8).

BOX 1.8: RADICAL FEMINISTS AND GENDER CONSTRUCTIVISM

The term *radical feminist* has recently been used in a different way by both feminist scholars and activists who developed the term **TERF**—which stands for trans-exclusionary radical feminist (see Chapter 2). Some now use the term *radical* in a more conventional way, to imply that feminists who embrace the social construction of gender but reject the social construction of sex—leading them to also reject transgender women's status as women—embrace an extreme and unacceptable version of feminism. Some **gender constructionists**, or feminists who question the social construction of sex, aggressively reject trans women and seek to exclude them from participation in the all-women spaces advocated by cultural feminists. This practice is discussed in more detail in Chapter 2.

Conflict between **gender critical scholars**, who focus on the social construction of gender rather than the social construction of sex, and those who fully embrace the social construction of both sex and gender continues to play out in both academic and nonacademic settings. A British philosopher at the University of Sussex, Kathleen Stock, for example, recently published a statement expressing concern that potential differences of interest between cisgender (or "cis") and transgender (or "trans") women are not being addressed in the discipline's work, because those who embrace a gender critical approach are worried that they will be labeled TERFS and ostracized. On the other hand, her concerns have been

(Continued)

criticized for not delving deeply enough into existing work in trans theory, as well as for being willing to consider an approach that invalidates people's identity and lived experience. Prominent trans-scholar Rachel Williams, for example, noted that scholarship questioning trans women's status as women should be considered as problematic as if a queer theorist questioned whether homosexuality is immoral.[81]

This concern flared up recently when a group of scholars complained that the author of an article in the journal *Philosophy and Phenomenological Research* used the term *TERF* as an ad hominem attack against all gender constructionists and gender critical scholars rather than in general discussion. The author refused to apologize for her use of the term, noting that those who reject trans women's status as women to deny them access to women-only spaces, services, and protection deserve to be labeled as bigots.[82] The problem some now have with the term *TERF* is that it has now been used in more aggressive ways outside of academia—to malign those who question whether sex is entirely socially constructed, including lesbians who maintain that same-sex attraction is not equivalent to transphobia, as well as women who believe that much of the oppression of women is sex-based and who do not want to erase discussions of cis women's bodies and biological functions from feminist activism.[83] These tensions played out in the aftermath of the Women's March, an issue we discuss in depth in Chapters 2 and 9. One feminist scholar responded to these concerns, arguing that the next stage of the women's movement should focus on an issue that unites all women, such as the assumption that people who present feminine gender identities are often assumed to be incompetent.[84]

Gender critical feminists, on the other hand, express concern that this focus will displace activism grounded in anatomy and biological functions, which has been at the core of many women's activism in the past. Throughout most of recorded history, women often had no bodily autonomy or right to refuse sex and no access to reliable contraception, which meant they had no control over how many times they became pregnant and gave birth. Limited access to consent and contraception are still issues for many women, even more so in developing countries than in the United States. Similarly, while women in the United States are mobilizing around the high cost of feminine hygiene products—sometimes called the tampon tax—menstruation has far more damaging consequences in developing countries. In places where women lack access to feminine hygiene products, girls often drop out of school after their periods start.[85] In other places, menstruating women are still considered unclean and are not allowed to sleep inside their families' homes. This practice is still common in rural Nepal, for example, where a young, menstruating woman recently died of smoke inhalation after warming her outdoor hut with a fire.[86] According to the United Nations, approximately 303,000 women die in childbirth each year, many from complications that could be avoided with access to adequate medical care.[87]

Some gender critical feminists, even those who want to be inclusive allies to trans women, worry that avoiding conversations about the connection between sex and biological functions will mean these types of issues will no longer receive adequate attention. Others acknowledge the traumatic effects of living with **gender dysphoria,** or the distress individuals experience when there is a mismatch between the sex assigned at their birth and their gender identity, but emphasize that trans women and cis women have different lived experiences that both deserve empathy and attention. Cis women have not struggled with gender dysphoria and have not risked being ostracized or violently attacked for presenting themselves as women. But they have experienced a lifetime of day-in-and-day-out gender socialization that reinforces intrinsic gender identity and penalizes them for failing to behave in appropriately feminine ways. Gender critical feminists worry that the language around the social construction of sex undermines this aspect of the social construction of gender. They are dismayed by prominent trans women's claims—such as Caitlyn Jenner's and Chelsea Manning's—that they have women's brains trapped in men's bodies. Yet, for centuries, feminists grounded their claim to equal treatment in the argument that behavioral differences result largely from socialization and institutionalized sexism and that there is no such thing as a "man's" brain or a "woman's" brain. Gender critical scholars embrace the social construction of gender. Unlike cultural feminists, they reject **gender essentialism,** or the belief that men and women have inherently different (i.e., "natural") interests, traits, and abilities. They worry that descriptions of men's and women's brains reinforces the binary gender roles and stereotyped assumptions about men and women that should be dismantled. Unlike the most hostile gender constructionists, many of these feminists believe in fighting violence and discrimination against trans people, even if they question whether all aspects of biological sex are mutable.

The concept of intersectionality serves as a tool for bridging these differences. Transgender and cisgender women have different lived experiences, which may lead them to prioritize fighting different types of discrimination and marginalization. **Intersectional feminism,** which focuses on building understanding, empathy, and allies across such differences, allows scholars and activists to focus on eliminating all forms of oppression rather than elevating one over the other.

Radical feminism more directly addresses the dilemma of critical theories grounded in acceptance of the claim that reality is, to a large extent, socially constructed and reified through institutional structures. The dilemma is that challenging gender norms in everyday lives does not necessarily immediately alter the social structure. Yet, gaining access to the social structure, in order to promote reforms that promote equality, typically requires some level of conformity with prescribed gender roles to achieve influence. Individual actions and institutional structures reinforce each other in ways that make achieving radical change in one fell swoop quite difficult. Indeed, a common criticism of ground-breaking women who do manage to achieve influential positions within prominent institutions—whether these are business, government, educational, or religious organizations—is that they are reluctant to sacrifice their hard-fought status by advocating for substantial feminist reforms, especially when the response to their efforts is likely to be social sanction and loss of their own status instead of change. Reform is more apt to take place when women hold a threshold of positions in a given institution, rather than a single, prominent position. Hence, aside from more dramatic shifts accomplished through social movements, advances for women often come slowly. That said, we recognize that the worldviews underpinning the social construction of reality can change. They may not only change in ways that advance equality but also in ways that erode equality between men and women—as recent backlashes that attempt to reinvigorate binary gender roles and strict division of labor make clear. This knowledge motivates feminist scholars and activists to remain vigilant.

The point of this overview is not to encourage readers to pick which versions of feminist theory are "right" and which are "wrong." What is important is to realize that while different traditions within feminist theory disagree about how to promote equality and how to eliminate oppression, they do agree on the common goal of creating a more egalitarian world. At the close of this chapter, we hope that you now recognize the intentional play on words embedded in the title of this book, which poses the question *Why Don't Women Rule the World?* The history of patriarchy provides in-depth understanding of why women have been denied positions of authority as "rulers" in most civilizations around the world. Yet, it is important to keep in mind that feminists do not simply want women to displace men as rulers in the hierarchical governing structures that spread across the globe 7,000 years ago. Rather, feminists aspire to replace hierarchy with egalitarianism and reject the notion that anyone—man or woman, binary or nonbinary—should have the authority to rule over others.

CONCLUSION

The remaining chapters in the book relay many empirical findings describing women's political attitudes and political behavior—often revealing the way they differ from each other across racial, ethnic, class, and religious lines but also the way they differ from men. When reviewing this data—especially when stark patterns between the sexes emerge—it is tempting to resort to gender essentialism as an explanation. The subordination of women takes place in regions and nations across the globe that otherwise may seem quite different from one another. A knee-jerk reaction could be to simply infer that women really are different and the opposite of men, that they just simply prefer to direct their attention to the domestic sphere, and that they are either uninterested in politics or unprepared to wield political power. Yet, reaching this simplistic conclusion means the reader has failed to heed the social constructionists' warning—that empirical data should not be unquestioningly used to endorse world views that evolved to justify inequality and oppression. Familiarity with the intertwined origins of patriarchy and agriculture in the Neolithic era, combined with an overview of feminist theory, is intended to encourage readers to seek alternative explanations for women's status in society than the ones offered by the dominant culture. Rather than using social science data to infer that the status quo is somehow natural and inevitable, poke and prod at the data from various feminist perspectives to see what it reveals about women's status in civilizations across the globe. Follow the lead of historian Judith Bennett (2006), who argues that evidence of women's ongoing subordination—or what she describes as the **patriarchal equilibrium** that emerges when the means of oppressions shift to sustain women's second-class status in societies over long periods of time—speaks more to patriarchy's resilience and ability to adapt to changing circumstances than it does to the natural order of society.[88] The authors of this book agree with critical theorists, firmly believing that social science research should be used to promote freedom from oppression rather than to bolster ideologies that justify enslaving people, and we hope this introductory chapter has encouraged our readers to embrace this agenda along with us.

PLAN OF THE BOOK

Each chapter explores concepts not only from a U.S. perspective but also from a comparative perspective. This comparative feature should increase readers' awareness of their own intersectional identities (across nationalities, ethnicities, class, and cultures) as well as the common and varying effects of patriarchy on women worldwide. Each chapter also has a policy feature, focusing on one or two policy areas. These policy areas are highlighted throughout the chapter, including in the comparative element. Attention to public policy matters a great deal, as even subtle changes in the law can gradually shift patterns of behavior enough to yield major social and cultural transformations years later. Legal scholar Catharine A. MacKinnon (2017) describes this effect as **butterfly politics**, arguing that just as the flutter of a butterfly wing can trigger change in chaos theory, even minor shifts in law and public policy can trigger a chain of events that lead to a completely different world over time.[89] Finally, each chapter concludes with review questions, designed to highlight key concepts and information relayed throughout the chapter, along with ambition activities, with prompts purposefully intended to bolster political interest, efficacy, and ambition. The inclusion of these activities is a direct response to recent research by Jennifer L. Lawless and Richard L. Fox (2014) revealing that the gap between men and women in political ambition in the United States first emerges among college students and calling on higher education to be far more proactive in bolstering young women's political interest and ambition.[90]

Chapter 2 continues to explore the historical status of women as antecedents to today's understandings of feminisms and women's place in politics. This chapter addresses patriarchy, along with prominent feminist critiques of its effects. We discuss First, Second, and Third Wave feminism in this chapter.

Chapter 3 shifts our focus to contemporary public opinion. We explore theories of opinion formation as well as how our understanding of gender and sex influences policy opinion and gaps between men and women in opinion and political interest. Comparatively, we explore reproductive rights around the world, and for the policy features, we examine reproductive rights as well as sex differences in opinions about terrorism/counterterrorism policy.

Chapter 4 examines political ambition and candidate emergence, asking if there is a gap in men's and women's willingness to run for political office. The chapter unpacks why a gap in political ambition first emerges among college-aged women and men in the United States, as well as why women are still reluctant to become candidates despite gaining access to educational and professional opportunities that were only available to men prior to the activism of the second wave. The chapter's comparative feature details women's levels of political ambition around the globe, while the policy feature explores efforts to reduce violence against women in general and against women politicians in particular. The chapter further explores how ongoing socialization into traditional gender roles along with institutional features and public policy interact in ways that affect women's levels of political ambition.

Chapter 5 explores women's experiences as candidates. It notes that when women run, they are just as likely to win as men in similar electoral contexts, and partisan polarization means that voters are more reliant on party cues than sex and gender cues when casting their ballots. Yet, the chapter also explores how women experience campaigning differently and must still overcome obstacles, ranging from difficulty fund-raising and gaining their respective parties' support to sexism and misogyny on the campaign trail. Implications of the sheer number of women who ran in 2018, as well as their willingness to break away from campaign styles that encouraged women to downplay sex differences and imitate men, are also addressed.

Chapter 6 looks at the representation of women in legislatures. We examine theories for why women should be represented, and we define the different types of representation that legislators can offer women citizens. We also present data about the number of women in legislatures in the United States and around the world. In making a comparison to countries other than the United States, we develop a conversation about why certain electoral systems and rules more successfully advance women's representation. The policy features in this chapter address the role of legislatures in debates about abortion and human trafficking. One comparative feature expands our discussion of electoral rules, and the other presents data about the representation of women in local governments.

Chapter 7 is an examination of executive institutions and the women represented in them. This chapter first discusses the masculine expectations of executive leadership and how the public and media judge women negatively for lacking masculine attributes and for acting in ways that display emotions associated with femininity. An analysis of representation looks at women as presidents, prime ministers, cabinet secretaries, governors, mayors, and as bureaucrats in women's policy agencies. This analysis focuses on the United States and also draws on examples from the rest of the world. The policy issues in this chapter are poverty and foreign policy, and the comparative features discuss Latin American women presidents and women's policy agencies in Spain and France.

Chapter 8 analyzes the judiciary as it relates to women's representation and influence. We document the presence of women in the legal profession and in judicial institutions, and we discuss the perspective of feminist jurisprudence. We ask how women judges influence rulings, and our policy features look at employment discrimination and policies influenced by intersectional oppression. The comparative features in this chapter present information on different kinds of legal systems found worldwide and specifically the common law and civil law systems. We also debate the influence and importance of women on international courts in a comparative feature.

Chapter 9 examines interest groups (social movements), with a focus on women's movements. We focus on definitional aspects of women's movements and feminist movements and examine how groups act and why they act differently under different institutional settings. Comparatively, we explore the difference between groups in the United States and in Germany and also action under authoritarian societies like Saudi Arabia. We also examine the use of the maternal discourse in the politics of women's movements to understand why groups would choose to engage a maternal framing and explore such framing among Black Lives Matter and peace groups.

Chapter 10 reflects on findings across the array of subjects covered in these preceding chapters, allowing readers to assess for themselves the balance between patriarchy's ongoing legacy and women's progress toward equality, both in the United States and across the globe. In addition, it outlines specific steps that readers can take to promote a more equal world, which include acknowledging that various versions of patriarchy still exist, listening to women's concerns even when they sound angry, using post-2016 activism as an opportunity to practice listening, monitoring backlash and progress to update priorities, and taking action to advance this agenda.

REVIEW QUESTIONS

1. Consider the link between patriarchy and the spread of labor-intensive agriculture across the globe. Was the spread of patriarchy, described by Friedrich Engels as "the historic defeat of the female sex," inevitable? How do the handful of matristic societies that still exist manage to survive? Does their success provide any insights into how to dismantle contemporary patriarchies?

2. Explain the fear-control cycle that Allan G. Johnson and others argue is the root cause of patriarchy. Do you think that the fear-control cycle still affects the everyday lives of men in the United States and in other countries? Do you think it affects decisions of nation-states and international relations? How much does the fear-control cycle still affect the world we live in today?

3. Some people argue that women in the United States and other well-established democracies now have more behavioral latitude than men. After several waves of the women's movement, they have more freedom to make choices about the way that they dress, the type of careers they pursue, and the way they express themselves than do most men. Should men engage in similar activism, to break down assumptions about acceptable male behavior and masculinity? Given that masculinity has historically needed femininity as a foil, would this type of activism also benefit women? Sociologist Allan G. Johnson argues that men have not been more proactive in dismantling restrictive gender roles and stereotypes because even though patriarchy exacts a painful cost from them, it also rewards them with status and privilege. Do you agree that this is why men have not been more active in dismantling patriarchy? Why, or why not?

4. Now that you have learned about the social construction of reality, can you identify aspects of your own life that you have experienced as "reified" or believed were "real" and "inevitable," when they are truly socially constructed? Does this recognition give you insights about the ability to make changes in the way we collectively construct our world?

5. How are feminist transformations of *sharia* law taking place in Muslim countries similar to women's efforts to overcome patriarchal legacies in Western culture? How are they different?

6. This chapter reviews a wide array of feminist theories and approaches, ranging from liberal feminism to radical feminism. Which theory or theories do you think currently provide the most insight into the obstacles that must be overcome to achieve a more egalitarian world? Explain your choices.

AMBITION ACTIVITIES

Dismantling Systems of Oppression by Building Alliances and Taking Action: Overcoming patriarchy requires active intervention in our social and political systems. Yet, feminist activism is hard to cultivate, in part because intersectionality discourages women from identifying with one another and in part because all men—even if they are discriminated against because they are also gay, disabled, poor, or belong to a minority racial/ethnic group—benefit from men's privilege under the status quo. How can people build alliances and work together to address many systems of oppression? Recall Allan G. Johnson (2014), the author of *The Gender Knot*, encourages students to take action in small, humble, and do-able ways ranging from acknowledging that patriarchy exists and taking the complaints of marginalized people seriously, to actively supporting people who violate prescribed gender roles in their private and professional lives, up through engaging in collective action or running for public office in order to challenge oppressive practices or policies.

Given these ideas for action,

1. *Think to yourself*: Who are you in terms of gender identity (female, nonbinary, gender fluid, or male?), and how do your identities and experiences relate to gender and sex-based discrimination and feminism? Do you have a cross-cutting trait, such as being transgender, of color, from the working class, or disabled? What systems of oppression affect you most acutely, and which ones are you most likely to work actively against? Which type of activism, to overcome a specific type of oppression, is not as close to your heart, and why? How do the oppressions you experience overlap with or overlook the oppressions of others?

2. *By yourself or with a group, list actions:* Make a list of all the things you actually could imagine doing to reduce the influence of a given system of oppression. Consider how these actions help to overcome patriarchy, the subordination of women, and other kinds of oppression. Rank these actions from the most risky to the least. Start with the least risky and set reasonable goals for the next few months. As long as you are doing something, it counts!

3. *Discuss how your list of actions addresses intersectionality and multiple systems of oppression*: Which types of privilege/oppression did you decide to tackle first, and why? To what extent does your list of actions appeal to many people, making them willing to participate in feminist activism? In what ways does your list of actions cultivate allies across intersections of oppression that typically divide people into separate groups?

4. *Keep track of your list*: Throughout the semester, add or subtract activities from the list as your ideas about feminist activism evolve.

Recognizing and "Preventing" Sexual Assault: In 2018 a table went viral on social media that depicted the disparity between how women and men think about sexual assault and its prevention. Crediting earlier feminist work for giving him the inspiration, Dr. Jackson Katz, co-founder of Mentors in Violence Prevention, asks attendees at his lectures to report what they do daily to prevent sexual assault. He presents women's and men's daily strategies to prevent assault in a table, which is widely available online by searching for the following terms: Jackson Katz viral sexual assault prevention table. One column of the table presents answers from men and the other answers from women. The column listing men's responses includes just one simple answer: "Nothing. I don't think about it."[91] The column with women's responses lists, among many others: "Don't go jogging at night;" "Park in well-lit areas;" "Lock my car doors as soon as I get in the car;" "Watch what I wear;" and "Make sure I see my drink being poured."[92] The disparity between the two columns reveals the fear of assault that women live with daily, and the many more things they do to "prevent" assault.

In posts on Facebook and Twitter, Katz's exercise is often accompanied by the following quotation that captures the sentiment of women who always face the possibility of assault: "That, my friends, is what it's like to be thought of as prey."[93] Katz's viral table, therefore, illustrates how the sexual contract described by Carole Pateman continues to influence people's lives. That is, Pateman too draws attention to the fact that women are subjected to unwanted sexual attention and abuse, and that they face this threat on a regular basis. According to the US Center for Disease Control's National Intimate Partner and Sexual Violence Survey, as well as the 2015 US Transgender Survey, those who identify within the LGBTQIA+ spectrum experience higher levels of sexual assault than cisgender heterosexuals. Elevated rates of assault occur because LGBTQIA+ people are more apt to experience poverty and marginalization, and to be stereotyped as hypersexual, all of which place them at risk. They are also more apt to be targets of hate crimes, which often include an element of sexual assault.[94,95]

Go online and find Katz's viral table and then discuss its contents. Are the "prevention" strategies he lists shocking to you or are they familiar, and in what ways? If you are LGBTQIA+, do you use tactics similar to those used by cisgender and heterosexual women? Choose two strategies women tend to use and discuss the last time you used them. When and from whom did you learn to practice these strategies? What will it take, in your opinion, for all people to be able to live safely without using these strategies? Who is responsible for making necessary changes and why? Use this discussion to think about the types of activities you would be willing to add to the list you began developing in the previous activity.

Recognizing and Dismantling Unfair Practices in the Workplace: In workshops about sex discrimination in the workplace, Allan G. Johnson (2014) asks participants to brainstorm four lists, first identifying the advantages and then identifying the disadvantages that men and women experience at work. Either alone or in groups, replicate this exercise. In addition to Johnson's initial four lists, consider the way intersectional identities and being LGBTQIA+ might affect these advantages and disadvantages. Discuss the items on your lists, looking for similarities and differences. What, if anything, should be done to ensure that all people have similar experiences at work? Whose responsibility is it to advocate for those changes? Use this exercise as an opportunity to practice the simple acts that Johnson recommends. Listen attentively and take the concerns of women and marginalized people seriously. Consider ways to support people who violate traditional gender role expectations in the workplace, as well as whether such activities create an alternative pathway that others will be able to follow. Consider whether collective action would help achieve changes in policies and practices that affect people at work. Use this exercise to think about adding items to the list of activities you began keeping in the first Ambition Activity.

KEY WORDS

Binary gender categories 2

Black feminism 29

Booty capitalism 17

Butterfly politics 35

Cisgender women 1

Complementarian 6

Critical race theory 24

Critical theory 23

Cultural feminism 30

Deviant groups 22

Ecofeminism 25

Enlightenment 18

Exchange of Women 8

Fear-control cycle 17

Feminist theory 24

Gender constructionists 31

Gender critical scholars 31

Gender dysphoria 33

Gender essentialism 33

Gender gap 1

Group consciousness 13

Ideologies 23

Intersectional feminism 33

Intersectionality 13

Liberal feminism 24

Matricentries 4

Matristic societies 4

Neolithic Age 7

Neo-Marxism 24

Neo-Marxist and socialist feminists 25

Patriarchal equilibrium 35

Patriarchies 2

Postcolonial and multiracial
    feminism 28

Postcolonial criticism 24

Prehistory 7

Primary socialization 21

Queer theory and transgender
    theory 24

Radical feminism 31

Reification 21

Religious feminism 25

Secondary socialization 21

Sharia 26

Social construction of reality 21

Subordination 7

Talaq 27

TERF 31

Theory 23

Transnational or global feminists 25

REFERENCES

1. Lawless, J. L., & Fox., R. L. (2014, November). "Not a 'Year of the Woman'. . . and 2036 doesn't look so good either." *Brookings Institute: Issues in Governance Studies*. Retrieved from https://www.brookings.edu/wp-content/uploads/2016/06/apsr.pdf.

2. Lerner, G. (1987). *The creation of patriarchy*. New York, NY: Oxford University Press.

3. Kaplan, S. (2015). The improbably, 200-year-old story of one of America's first same sex "marriage." *The Washington Post*. Retrieved from https://www.washingtonpost.com/news/morning-mix/wp/2015/03/20/the-improbable-story-of-one-of-americas-first-same-sex-marriages-from-over-200-years-ago/?utm_term=.e8f7d33f3cdb; Cleves, R. H. (2014). *Charity and Sylvia: A same-sex marriage in early America*. New York, NY: Oxford University Press.

4. *Baker v. Nelson*, 291 Minn. 310 (Minn. 1971).

5. *Baehr v. Lewin*, 852 P.2d 44 (Hawai'I 1993).

6. *Goodridge v. Department of Health*, 798 N.E.2d 941 (Mass. 2003).

7. *United States v. Windsor*, 570 U.S. 744 (2013).

8. *Obergefell v. Hodges*, 576 U.S. (2015); Lopez, G. (2016). The Supreme Court legalizes same-sex marriage after years of legal battles. *Vox*. Retrieved from https://www.vox.com/2015/6/26/17937530/supreme-court-same-sex-gay-marriage-obergefell-v-hodges.

9. Pew Research Center. (2017). Changing attitudes on gay marriage. Retrieved from http://www.pewforum.org/fact-sheet/changing-attitudes-on-gay-marriage.

10. Coontz, S. (2006). *Marriage, a history: How love conquered marriage*. New York, NY: Penguin Group.

11. *Griswold v. Connecticut*, 381 U.S. 479 (1965).

12. Lee, T. B. (2015). The most radical changes to marriage happened decades ago. *Vox*. Retrieved from https://www.vox.com/2015/6/26/8853495/same-sex-marriage-history.

13. Coontz, S. (2006). *Marriage, a history: How love conquered marriage*.

14. Hawkes, K. (2012). Grandmothers and their consequences. Contribution to Calcano & Fuentes. What makes us human? Answers from evolutionary anthropology. *Evolutionary Anthropology* 21(5):189.

15. Foster, J., & Derlet, M. (2013). *Invisible women in prehistory: Three million years of peace, six thousand years of war.* North Melbourne, Australia: Spinifex Press.

16. Cieri, R. L., Churchill, S. E., Franciscus, R. G., Tan, J., & Hare, B. (2014). Craniofacial feminization, social tolerance, and the origins of behavioral modernity." *Current Anthropology* 55(4), 419–443.

17. China Buddhist Temple. Accessed online at https://www.gettyimages.com/detail/news-photo/mu-ze-latso-with-a-friend-also-from-the-mo-suo-minority-news-photo/600641296?fbclid=IwAR1iDeyKZ_IuUIsapMqqCKzfvbXzj2GQulXOYawckZ7whP3uE9juKl3W7mY. December 7, 2018.

18. Shaitly, S. (December 18, 2010). Is China's Mosua Tribe the world's last patriarchy?" *The Guardian.* Retrieved from https://www.theguardian.com/lifeandstyle/2010/dec/19/china-mosuo-tribe-matriarchy.

19. Dyble, M., Salali, G. D., Chaudhary, N., Page, A., Smith, D., Thompson, J., Vinicius, L., Mace, R., & Migliano, A. B. (2015). Sex equality can explain the unique structure of hunter-gatherer bands. *Science 348*(6236), 796–798.

20. Coontz, S., & Henderson, P. (1986). *Women's work, men's property: The origins of gender and class.* Thetford, Norfolk: Thetford Press.

21. Levi-Strauss, C. (1969). *The elementary structures of kinship.* Boston, MA: Beacon Press.

22. Lerner, G. (1987). *The creation of patriarchy.* New York, NY: Oxford University Press.

23. Ibid.

24. Ibid., 99.

25. Ibid., 77.

26. Hansen, C. W., Jensen, P. S., & Skovsgaard, C. V. (2015). Modern gender roles and agricultural history: The Neolithic inheritance. *Journal of Economic Growth 20*(4), 365–404.

27. Alesina, A. F., Giuliano, P., & Nunn, N. (2013, May). On the origin of gender roles: Women and the plough. *Quarterly Journal of Economics, 128*(2), 469–530.

28. Burton, M. L., & White, D. R. (1984). Sexual division of labor in agriculture. *American Anthropologist, 86*(3), 558–583.

29. Alesina, A. F., Giuliano, P., & Nunn, N. (2013). On the origin of gender roles: Women and the plough. *Quarterly Journal of Economics, 128*(2), 469–530.

30. Boserup, E. (1970). *Woman's role in economic development.* London, UK: George Allen and Unwin Ltd.

31. Blumberg, R. L. (2015). "Dry" versus "wet" development and women in three world regions." *Sociology of Development 1*(1), 91–122.

32. Scott, J. C. (2017). *Against the grain, a deep history of the earliest states*. New Haven, CT: Yale University Press.

33. International Labor Organization. (2018). *World employment social outlook*. Retrieved from https://www.ilo.org/wcmsp5/groups/public/---dgreports/---dcomm/---publ/documents/publication/wcms_619577.pdf.

34. International Labor Organization. (2017). Retrieved from https://www.ilo.org/ilostat/faces/oracle/webcenter/portalapp/pagehierarchy/Page3.jspx?MBI_ID=7&_adf.ctrlstate=19kzwvr02q_4&_afrLoop=1325244429792146&_afrWindowMode=0&_afrWindowId=19kzwvr02q_1#!@@?_afrWindowId=19kzwvr02q_1&_afrLoop=1325244429792146&MBI_ID=7&_afrWindowMode=0&_adf.ctrl-state=11yrxthqa9_4.

35. Ibid.

36. Ibid.

37. El-Swais, M. (2016, March 9). *Despite high education levels, Arab women still don't have jobs*. Retrieved from http://blogs.worldbank.org/arabvoices/despite-high-education-levels-arab-women-still-don-t-have-jobs.

38. Ibid.

39. International Labor Organization. (2017). *Key indicators of the labor market*. Retrieved from https://www.ilo.org/ilostat/faces/oracle/webcenter/portalapp/pagehierarchy/Page3.jspx?MBI_ID=7&_adf.ctrlstate=19kzwvr02q_4&_afrLoop=1325244429792146&_afrWindowMode=0&_afrWindowId=19kzwvr02q_1#!@@?_afrWindowId=19kzwvr02q_1&_afrLoop=1325244429792146&MBI_ID=7&_afrWindowMode=0&_adf.ctrl-state=11yrxthqa9_4.

40. Sokunthea, H., & Hawkins, H. (2016, September 09). *Women's work*. Retrieved from https://www.cambodiadaily.com/features/womens-work-117817.

41. International Labor Organization. (2018). Retrieved from https://www.ilo.org/wcmsp5/groups/public/---dgreports/---dcomm/---publ/documents/publication/wcms_619577.pdf.

42. Lerner, G. (1987). *The creation of patriarchy*. New York, NY: Oxford University Press.

43. Gurin, P. (1985, January). Women's gender consciousness. *Public Opinion Quarterly, 49*(2), 143–163.

44. Crenshaw, K. (1989). Demarginalizing the intersection of race and sex: A Black feminist critique of antidiscrimination doctrine, feminist theory and antiracist politics. *University of Chicago Legal Forum* (1), 138–167.

45. Johnson, A. G. (2014). *The gender knot, unraveling our patriarchal legacy*, 3rd ed. Philadelphia, PA: Temple University Press.

46. Ibid., 206.

47. Ibid.

48. Scott, J. C. (2017). *Against the grain, a deep history of the earliest states*. New Haven, CT: Yale University Press.

49. Ibid.

50. Ibid.

51. Johnson, A. G. (2014). *The gender knot, unraveling our patriarchal legacy*, 3rd ed. Philadelphia, PA: Temple University Press.

52. Ibid., 51.

53. Honeywell, R. (2016). *The man problem, destructive masculinity in Western culture*. New York, NY: Palgrave Macmillan.

54. Trouille, M. S. (1997). *Sexual politics in the Enlightenment: Women writers read Rousseau*. New York, NY: SUNY Press.

55. Butler, M. A. (1978). Early roots of feminism: John Locke and the attack on patriarchy. *The American Political Science Review*, 72(1), 135–150, 144.

56. Pateman, C. (1988). *The sexual contract*. Stanford, CA: Stanford University Press.

57. The World Health Organization. (2018). Violence against women. Retrieved from https://www.who.int/news-room/fact-sheets/detail/violence-against-women.

58. Thayer, K. (October 1, 2018). The Violence Against Women Act could expire soon. Here's what's at stake. *The Chicago Tribune*. Retrieved from https://www.chicagotribune.com/lifestyles/ct-life-violence-against-women-act-explainer-20180927-story.html.

59. Berger, P., & Luckmann, T. (1967). *The social construction of reality, a treatise on the sociology of knowledge*. New York, NY: Anchor Books.

60. Ibid.

61. Karimi, N. (2006). Women's rights activists beaten in Tehran. *The Washington Post*. Retrieved from http://www.washingtonpost.com/wp-dyn/content/article/2006/06/12/AR2006061201034.html.

62. Berger, P., & Luckmann, T. (1967). *The social construction of reality, a treatise on the sociology of knowledge*. New York, NY: Anchor Books.

63. Johnson, A. G. (2014). *The gender knot, unraveling our patriarchal legacy*, 3rd ed., 244.

64. Berger and Luckman. (1967). *The social construction of reality*.

65. Human Rights Watch. 2004. *Divorced from justice: Women's unequal access to divorce in Egypt*. Retrieved from https://www.hrw.org/reports/2004/egypt1204/egypt1204.pdf.

66. United Nations. (2017). *Spring forward women programme: Egypt*. Retrieved from https://spring-forward.unwomen.org/en/countries/egypt.

67. Ali, Z. S. (2014). The dynamic nature of Islam's legal system with reference to Muslim women. *The Federal Lawyer*. Retrieved from http://www.fedbar.org/Resources_1/Federal-Lawyer-Magazine/2014/July/Features/The-Dynamic-Nature-of-Islams-Legal-System-with-Reference-to-Muslim-Women.aspx?FT=.pdf.

68. Ibid.

69. Ali, S. S. (2011). Teaching and learning Islamic law in a globalized world: Some reflections and perspectives. *Journal of Legal Education, 61*, 206–230.

70. Harrack, F. (2009, March). The history and significance of the New Moroccan Family Code. *Institute for the Study of Islamic Thought in Africa (ISITA)Working Paper Series*, Working Paper No. 09-002. Retrieved from https://buffett.northwestern.edu/documents/working-papers/ISITA_09-002_Harrak.pdf.

71. Ibid., 3.

72. Yavuz, M. (2016). Allah (God), al-Watan (the Nation), al-Malik (the King), and the role of ijtihād in the family law reforms of Morocco. *Journal of the Middle East and Africa*, 7(2), 207–227.

73. Harrack, F. (2009, March). The history and significance of the New Moroccan Family Code." *Institute for the Study of Islamic Thought in Africa (ISITA)Working Paper Series, Working Paper No. 09-002*. Retrieved from https://buffett.northwestern.edu/documents/working-papers/ISITA_09-002_Harrak.pdf.

74. Yavuz, M. (2016). Allah (God), al-Watan (the Nation), al-Malik (the King), and the role of ijtihād in the family law reforms of Morocco. *Journal of the Middle East and Africa*, 7(2), 207–227.

75. Prettitore, P. S. (2015, September). Family law reform, gender equality, and underage marriage: A view from Morocco and Jordan. *Review of Faith & International Affairs, 13*(3), 32–40.

76. Smith, B. (1998). *The truth that never hurts: Writings on race, gender, and freedom*. New Brunswick, NJ: Rutgers University Press.

77. hooks, bell. (1984). *Feminist theory: From margin to center*. Cambridge, MA: South End Press.

78. hooks, bell. (2004). *The will to change masculinity and love*. New York, NY: Simon and Schuster.

79. Johnson, A. G. (2014). *The gender knot, unraveling our patriarchal legacy*, 3rd ed. Philadelphia, PA: Temple University Press.

80. Ibid.

81. Flaherty, C. (2018). By any other name. *Inside Higher Ed*. Retrieved from https://www.insidehighered.com/news/2018/06/06/philosophy-really-ignoring-important-questions-about-transgender-identity.

82. Flaherty, C. (2018). "TERF war." *Inside Higher Ed*. Retrieved from https://www.insidehighered.com/news/2018/08/29/philosophers-object-journals-publication-terf-reference-some-feminists-it-really.

83. Ibid.

84. Bovy, P. M. (2017). It's time to drop the vagina as a protest symbol. *The Washington Post*. Retrieved from https://www.washingtonpost.com/posteverything/wp/2017/03/31/its-time-to-drop-the-vagina-as-a-protest-symbol/?utm_term=.ca7183e52229.

85. Higgins, A. 2(017). Having a period is unaffordable in Kenya, yet no one wants to talk about it. *The Guardian*. Retrieved from https://www.theguardian.com/global-development-professionals-network/2017/jan/05/having-a-period-is-unaffordable-in-kenya-yet-no-one-wants-to-talk-about-it.

86. Bowman, V. (2018). Woman in Nepal dies after being exiled to outdoor hut during her period. *The Guardian*. Retrieved from https://www.theguardian.com/global-development/2018/jan/12/woman-nepal-dies-exiled-outdoor-hut-period-menstruation.

87. Ford, L. (2018). Why do women still die giving birth?" *The Guardian*. Retrieved from https://www.theguardian.com/global-development/2018/sep/24/why-do-women-still-die-giving-birth.

88. Bennett, J. M. (2006). *History matters: Patriarchy and the challenge of feminism*. Philadelphia: University of Pennsylvania Press.

89. MacKinnon, C. (2017). *Butterfly politics*. Cambridge, MA: Harvard University Press.

90. Lawless, J. L., & Fox, R. L. (2014, November). Not a 'Year of the Woman' . . . and 2036 doesn't look so good either. *Brookings Institute: Issues in Governance Studies*.

91. *Katz, J. (2006). The macho paradox: Why some men hurt women and how all men can help*. Naperville, IL: Sourcebooks, 2.

92. Ibid., 2.

93. Riben, M. (2017, October 18). "#MeToo: In the Wake of the Harvey Weinstein Scandal." Huffington Post. Retrieved from https://www.huffpost.com/entry/metoo-in-the-wake-of-the-harvey-weinstein-scandal_b_59e6ca0ae4b0432b8c11eb36.

94. Smith, S.G., Zhang, X., Basile, K.C., Merrick, M.T., Wang, J., Kresnow, M., Chen, J. 2018. "The National Intimate Partner and Sexual Violence Survey (NISVS): 2015 Data Brief – Updated Release." Atlanta, GA: National Center for Injury Prevention and Control, Centers for Disease Control and Prevention. Retrieved from https://www.cdc.gov/violenceprevention/pdf/2015data-brief508.pdf.

95. James, S. E., Herman, J. L., Rankin, S., Keisling, M., Mottet, L., & Anafi, M. 2016. "Executive Summary of the Report of the 2015 U.S. Transgender Survey." Washington, DC: National Center for Transgender Equality. Retrieved from https://transequality.org/sites/default/files/docs/usts/USTS-Executive-Summary-Dec17.pdf.

HISTORY OF WOMEN IN POLITICS

O n January 21, 2017, millions of people across the globe gathered to protest in the Women's Marches; marches were held in over 400 locations in the United States and in more than 150 locations in 81 countries around the world. Wearing pink "pussy" hats and waving creative signs and banners, people gathered to voice their concern about a variety of issues—women's rights, immigration reform, LGBTQIA+ rights, the environment, and more. Most of all, the protests were a rebuttal to Hillary Clinton's defeat and Donald Trump's victory in the 2016 United States presidential election, particularly in the aftermath of Trump's sexist comments about women.

The marches in 2017 and the protest movements that are still active today are a continuation of a long history of marches, protests, and political activism against the exclusion of women from the public realm and the subjugation of women in the private realm as well. While the patriarchal roots of modern culture and civilization are deep, as detailed in Chapter 1, concerted efforts to elevate the status of women really began to emerge in the seventeenth and eighteenth centuries, coinciding with the Industrial Revolution. The Industrial Revolution was a period of dramatic political, economic, and social upheaval as new technological developments, like the steam engine and the factory system, transformed society. While there is debate about whether this change was good for the status of women, questions about the role of women in society came to the fore. This chapter traces the history of activism for the advancement of women's rights and efforts to transform the patriarchal roots of modern society, describing both the successes and failures of these efforts. After identifying key themes in this chapter, we start by examining women's activism in the United States around the time of the Industrial Revolution and the emigration of the colonists from Europe to the colonies.

Several themes emerge in this examination, building on themes from the previous chapter. First, as described in Chapter 1, while women have historically been excluded from the public realm, the exclusion to and subjugation in the private realm are critical to their oppression. Historically though, efforts to give women fuller voice and extend to them the rights of citizenship in the public realm have generally been more successful than efforts to eliminate the roots of the patriarchy in the private realm. Such transformation challenges the social construction of reality for so many, which has made the achievement of true equality for women an unfulfilled goal. Second, the success of efforts to advance the status of women have been hampered by the fact that those active in these movements were and are often divided by cross-cutting identities that prevented them from developing a sense of group consciousness. In particular, early waves of feminist organizing were marred by classism and racism. A deeper understanding of the intersectionality of oppression has only recently emerged, but divisions among those fighting for women's equality can impede progress. This is a theme we will revisit in Chapter 9. Finally, bringing these two themes together, feminist organizing has been more successful when there is a single overarching goal focused on eliminating barriers to women's equality in the public realm around which to organize. But as more voices have emerged and been given equal status and preliminary gains have been secured, a unifying focus has become more elusive. This is a vexing conundrum that faces the women's movement to this day—how to advance the cause of women's rights when there are so many flourishing and legitimate issues that motivate political activism.

COLONIAL HISTORY

While early settlers in the United States migrated predominantly from England in and around the time of the Industrial Revolution, bringing with them English common law tradition, the common law patriarchal view of the status of women in society was not the only one that existed in the colonial era. As seen in Chapter 1, alternative arrangements that elevated the status of women coexisted with the dominant patriarchal arrangements. Quaker tradition, for example, allowed women to act as public ministers, and because of this role in the church, they were also granted a role in secular society.[1] Many Native American tribes maintained matrilineal kinship and residence systems, as described in Box 2.1.[2] Women also played a central role in early colonial economies; in Boston and Philadelphia, women were nearly half of all licensed retailers in the mid to late 1700s.[3] Given the centrality of women to colonial society and the economy, some colonies recognized the legal status of women, too, allowing them to enter into contracts, testify against their spouses, and seek a divorce.[4]

BOX 2.1: COMPARATIVE FEATURE

Sex and Gender Roles in Native American Culture

As noted in Chapter 1, regions that were remote and harder to reach sustained hunter-gatherer lifestyles for longer, and, thus, alternatives to patriarchal systems emerged. This is true around the globe, but it was also true of the United

States when the colonists first immigrated. After first coming to North America sometime around 4,000 BCE, the transition from a hunter-gatherer lifestyle was slow for Native Americans; furthermore, different tribes settled around different advantageous locations (some fished, and some cultivated crops, for example), such that there was a good deal of variation in the social arrangements of Native American communities. Contrary to discussions of the connections between agriculture and

▶ **Photo 2.1** Iroquois women doing agricultural work.

the patriarchy from Chapter 1, in Native American societies, "the more central hunting was to survival, the more extensive were men's prerogatives; the greater the dependence upon cultivation, the greater the realms of authority and autonomy for women."[5] This pattern emerged because, unlike the type of labor intensive agriculture focused on producing a surplus that emerged in much of the rest of the world, the type of cultivation practiced in North America left women in charge, much in the way women of the Hazda in Tanzania are largely responsible for calories provided by gathering. Because women were responsible for cultivation and were more place bound, they became responsible for group maintenance in societies where this version of agriculture was important, so matrilocal and matrilineal systems emerged in some Native American societies.

Carol Berkin (1996) provides a detailed account of relations between men and women in precolonial Native American societies in her book *First Generations: Women in Colonial America.*[6] She argues that what we know about Native American societies must be taken with a grain of salt, as much of the recorded history was written by white men colonists who were baffled by the cultural arrangements of many Native societies. Because systems of private property did not exist in many Native American tribes, the driving force behind the development of patriarchal systems was missing, and different patterns of work and sex-based relations emerged, which the colonists could not understand. For instance, colonists traditionally visited Native communities to do

(Continued)

(Continued)

business during the summer because this was the only time the men were present; during other times, the men were off hunting. But because summer was farming and not hunting season, it appeared to the colonists that only Native women were industrious whereas the men were indulgent and lazy.

Importantly, because women were responsible for crop production, they also controlled the means of production for this work and the fruits of this labor. Berkin (1996) notes that women's control over this surplus gave them immense power; for example, Iroquois warriors could only go to war if the Iroquois women released surplus cornmeal to sustain this effort.[7] In some cases, women wielded power directly as was the case of Wetamoo, queen of the Wampanoag tribe. In other cases, women wielded power behind the scenes, as was the case with the Iroquois women who nominated men tribal chiefs and could have them removed.

Despite the wide variety of sex-based relations in Native American tribes and the existence of systems that gave women much greater power than they enjoyed in the colonies, these arrangements had little impact on relations between men and women among the colonial settlers—in large part because the social reification of gender roles in the colonies made them blind to what they could have seen before them.

By the time of the Revolutionary War, these alternative visions of the status of women gave way to a common understanding of the subordinate role of women in American society. As Langley and Fox (1994) argue,

> Everything seems to have been arranged to effect the oppression of women: religious doctrines as interpreted and practiced, the legal tradition as revered and taught, the institutions of family and property as promoted and nurtured, the republican ideology as understood and preached, and even popular sentiments as fostered and used for governing.[8]

Critical to this crystallization of the status of women was Sir William Blackstone's *Commentaries on the Laws of England*. In these *Commentaries*, Blackstone clearly lays out the idea of coverture as the way to understand women's legal status in the United States. He writes,

> By marriage, the husband and wife are one person in law: that is, the very being or legal existence of the woman is suspended during the marriage or at least is incorporated and consolidated into that husband; under whose wings, protection, and *cover*, she performs every thing. . . . For this reason, a man cannot grant any thing to his wife, or enter into any covenant with her: for the grant would be to suppose her separate existence.

It is difficult to underestimate the effect of this interpretation of the status of women under common law on the actual status of women in the United States. For nearly a century, *Commentaries* was a standard textbook for legal training in the United States and was commonly cited by those opposed to the efforts to improve the status of women.[9]

Unmarried women, "femmes soles," enjoyed some degree of legal autonomy, as they could enter into contracts and accumulate personal property. Given the diminished social status that accompanied "spinsterhood," most women chose to marry during this period, despite the loss of legal autonomy.[10] The reality of many women, then, was that they never legally existed; they passed from complete legal control by their fathers to complete legal control by their husbands. According to the legal concept of coverture, women had no legal existence outside the authority of their husbands. They could not enter into contracts or own property; their husbands had rights to all their wages and any personal property that they brought into the marriage. Women could not appear in court as independent actors because under coverture, women did not have legal personhood. The diminishment of women's autonomy was not just legal; coverture also denied women bodily autonomy. Men had the right to absolute control over their wives' bodies. This, combined with women's lack of legal autonomy, meant that the concepts of domestic violence or marital rape did not exist. Of course, for a large portion of American women, these distinctions were meaningless as the legality of slavery meant much of federal and state law disregarded their rights to autonomy, freedom, and personhood, regardless of their marital status. The net result was that few women had any autonomy—political, legal, financial, economic, or bodily—during this period.

This legal interpretation coincided with the Industrial Revolution, which meant that more men began to work outside the home for wages, leaving women behind in the home. A "cult of true womanhood" developed, which viewed the proper role of women as pure, pious, and domestic.[11] Women's economic role in colonial economies diminished as did the scope of their responsibilities and, indeed, existence.

Given this decline after contributing so much to the Revolutionary War effort in traditional roles such as nurses and cooks but also as soldiers (secretly) and spies, women in the 1700s agitated to improve the status of women. For instance, as mentioned in Chapter 1, Abigail Adams implored her husband to "remember the ladies" in the writing of the Constitution, or else the women would be determined to "foment a Rebellion" should they have no voice or representation.

Despite the fact that colonial women were not successful in improving the status of women, they laid the ground work for women activists who continued their quest to elevate the status of women through obtaining the right to vote. Murphy (2013) argues, "in the end, historical interpretations that defended domestic citizenship would triumph, but not before alternative historical views were registered that supported the possibility of broader citizenship for women."[12]

THE FIRST WAVE

The question of the status of women in society in the United States simmered on low burn during the late 1700s and the early 1800s with bursts of activism and victories here and there. Mary Wollstonecraft published *A Vindication of the Rights of Women* in 1792; in this work, one of the earliest examples of feminist philosophy, Wollstonecraft lays out the argument that women's character and status were not the result of their nature, but the environment in which they were raised. She argued for equal education for men and women, so they could equally succeed academically and professionally. Because the Constitution allows states to determine who votes in elections, women were able to secure the right to vote in some places. In New Jersey, single women with property could vote for approximately two decades until a law passed in 1807 limited the franchise to free white men.

But it was as women took up activism around other issues that the question of their own political status came back to the fore in the late nineteenth and early twentieth centuries—what was known as the **First Wave** of the feminist movement. For instance, Catharine Beecher led the first national women's campaign in an effort to prevent President Jackson's Cherokee Indian Removal Act. Women mill workers in Lawrence and Lowell, Massachusetts, engaged in industrial labor activism. Women also became involved in the temperance movement (a movement to outlaw alcohol in the United States) in organizations such as the Women's Christian Temperance Union, although such temperance activism can be seen as largely conforming to society's views of the primarily domestic role of women.[13,14]

Women's activism in the movement to abolish slavery was particularly important in launching the first wave of feminist activism in the United States. Women's involvement in the abolitionist movement allowed women to acquire "important skills in speaking, organizing and agitating for social change at the very same time that they encountered resistance to their participation."[15] Women active in these abolitionist organizations forged connections that they drew on in leading the suffrage movement. For instance, Lucretia Mott formed the Philadelphia Female Anti-Slavery Society with Black and white women colleagues, which became a focal point for the advancement of women's rights. Susan B. Anthony and Elizabeth Cady Stanton gathered nearly 400,000 signatures and delivered them to Congress in support of the Thirteenth Amendment, which abolished slavery, later turning these organizing skills toward efforts to promote women's suffrage.

Denial of leadership roles in these organizations pushed women to fight for their own political place. Angelina and Sarah Grimké were widely criticized for speaking to "promiscuous" (men and women) audiences in support of the abolition movement. Sarah Grimké defended their actions in her *Letters on the Equality of the Sexes and the Condition of Women* in which she asserted that "whatever is right for man to do, is right for woman."

Importantly, Mott, Stanton, and other women traveled to London in 1840 to attend the World Anti-Slavery Convention. However, after considerable debate, the men delegates voted to deny seating to the women delegates, forcing them to sit behind a curtain in an observer's gallery and remain silent. The experience moved Stanton to draft the *Declaration of Sentiments*, which was presented at the Seneca Falls Convention, organized by many of the same women who were denied their place in London.

The Seneca Falls Convention in July of 1848 was a critical moment in the first wave of the feminist movement. The issues raised in the *Declaration* seem to be a matter of fact these days—the right of women to vote, to acquire a good education, and to pursue meaningful work—but at the time these were revolutionary demands. From the *Declaration*, attendees to the convention laid out 11 resolutions to demand equal rights for women. The most controversial of these was the ninth, which demanded the right to vote for women; this was the only resolution that did not pass unanimously and would have foundered were it not for the impassioned speeches in favor by Stanton and famed abolitionist leader Frederick Douglass.

When the issue of voting rights came after the abolition of slavery, many men abolitionists told the women that it was the "Negro's hour" in order to avoid tainting the question of suffrage for Black men with the question of suffrage of women. The passage of the Fourteenth Amendment, which prohibited the denial of the right to vote on the basis of race, in 1868 marked an important victory for the abolitionist movement. But it was a disappointment to Stanton, Anthony, Sojourner Truth, and many women activists who worked in the abolitionist movement as section two of this amendment introduced the word "male" into the U.S. Constitution for the first time, prohibiting states from denying any "male inhabitant" the right to vote. Due to their frustrations with the setting aside of women's rights, Anthony and Stanton organized the American Equal Rights Association, which sought to advance the cause of voting rights for Black people and white women simultaneously.

Nonetheless, as time went on, there were certainly tensions between the abolitionist and women's suffrage movements. On the one hand, many women's rights advocates were not happy when it became clear that the push for suffrage after the Civil War might not include women. They felt the push to secure voting rights ought to encompass both women and Black men. On the other hand, many activists were displeased with the "racism, ethnocentrism, and class privilege" in the women's suffrage movement.[16] For instance, Frances Gage, who presided over the Women's Convention in Akron, Ohio, recounts how many in the audience warned her to prevent Sojourner Truth (Box 2.2) from delivering her famous "Ain't I a Woman" speech, lest the cause of suffrage be mixed with the abolition movement.[17] As we will see in Chapter 9, these tensions continue.

BOX 2.2: SOJOURNER TRUTH

Truth, a former slave from New York who was active in the abolition movement, gave her speech extemporaneously. While there are varying accounts of the text of the speech, the most famous includes multiple repetitions of the phrase "Ain't I a Woman," thus giving the speech its name. Her speech was a rebuke to the reasoning of men as to why women should be denied their rights—they were weak and intellectually inferior to men. As a former slave, Truth was well aware of the strength and intellectual fortitude of women and drew on her experiences working in the fields and bearing the indignities of slavery as forceful arguments for the granting of rights to women.

This racism is evident in a close reading of the *Declaration of Sentiments*, which elevated white women above immigrants and Black people, and cited issues that were relevant primarily to middle- and upper-class white women—reflective of the liberal feminism discussed in Chapter 1. This debate continues in feminist circles today and will be one we revisit in future chapters. Ultimately, Terborg-Penn (1978) argues that while prominent leaders of the suffrage movement emerged from the abolitionist movement, their commitments to racial equality were the exception rather than the rule, such that discrimination against Black women in the suffrage movement was routine.[18] Elizabeth Cady Stanton, a preeminent suffragette, has been called a classic liberal racist who talked about fairness in the abstract while enunciating racist and bigoted views of African American men. She referred to them as "Sambos" and rapists in the time just after the Civil War.[19]

Despite these differences, these activists managed to coalesce around the issue of women's suffrage, even though this resolution was the most controversial at Seneca Falls. Some women felt that the expansion of suffrage was a matter of human equality. Others believed that allowing women the right to vote would have a civilizing effect on society. What "civilizing" meant differed amongst these women, though. Those in the temperance movement saw women's suffrage as a means to restrict access to alcohol, for example, while others saw a white woman's vote as a way to maintain racial hegemony. In addition to differences about rationale, these women were deeply divided on how to achieve this goal and what means they were willing to use to achieve it.

Even though the word "male" was inserted into the Constitution, Virginia and Francis Minor, leaders of the suffrage movement in Missouri, believed provisions that already existed in the Constitution provided for women's suffrage—they just needed the courts to recognize women were citizens because of the Fourteenth amendment and therefore should be able to vote. So, Virginia attempted to register to vote in Missouri; when she was denied by the state, she sued.

In 1875, the United States Supreme Court effectively ruled out judicial means as a way to secure the right to vote for women in their *Minor v. Happersett* decision. In its ruling, the Supreme Court agreed that Minor was a citizen but that the Fourteenth Amendment did not give her the right to vote. The amendment had used the word "male," and the Court articulated that voting was a state-level issue. By stating that "the United States has no voters in the States of its own creation," the Court ensured that suffrage activists would then have to persuade state legislatures to vote on whether to give suffrage to women or seek an amendment to the U.S. Constitution.

The passage of the Fourteenth Amendment convinced the leaders of the suffrage movement of the need for an organization focused solely on the issue of women's suffrage, so Stanton and Anthony launched the National Women's Suffrage Association (NWSA) in early 1869. A few months later, Lucy Stone and others who opposed what they perceived as Stanton's elitism, classism, and racism formed an alternative suffrage organization known as the American Women Suffrage Association (AWSA). As Buechler (1990) argues, the rivalry between these two organizations "was the logical, organizational expression of prior ideological, strategy, and personal differences within the women's movement."[20] The NWSA, led solely by women, was more radical and highlighted the connections between women's oppression and the patriarchal structure of the family and work in society; as such, the NWSA focused on a variety of issues, in addition to suffrage. The AWSA, on the other hand, focused only on the issue of suffrage and included men among its leaders.

In addition to ideological and personal differences, the two main organizations differed with regard to strategy as well. The NWSA adopted a national strategy, focusing on securing an amendment to the national Constitution, while the AWSA pursued a strategy of amending state constitutions, believing that they could win smaller victories in favorable venues, which would make it easier to eventually secure voting rights for women nationally. There was a good foundation to this logic as western states were more amenable to the idea of women's suffrage than the eastern states. Wyoming adopted women's suffrage while still a territory, and when it looked like Congress might not approve statehood if women could vote, the legislature said, "we will remain out of the Union a hundred years rather than come in without the women."[21] According to Banaszak, "in every year between 1870 and 1890, 4.4 states considered legislation giving women the vote" through state constitutions."[22] For example, Oregon introduced state legislation for woman suffrage in 1884, 1900, 1906, 1908, 1910 and 1912—at which point the state legislature voted for it.

Despite the fact that these two groups had different strategies, they both relied on similar tactics, focusing on educating the public about their cause through the press.[23] These educational campaigns did not lead to many concrete victories, so in 1890, the two rival organizations merged to become the National American Women's Suffrage Association (NAWSA). New leaders, such as Carrie Chapman Catt and Alice Paul, recognized the need to expand beyond educational strategies and build organizational and activist strategies. After leading the effort to secure the right to vote in Colorado, Catt stepped up to helm the NAWSA, which now focused on passing an amendment in Congress and then getting state legislatures to ratify the amendment.

Paul, along with Lucy Burns, was the leader of the more militant wing of the suffrage movement, the "Iron-Jawed Angels" of the National Woman's Party (NWP).[24] While much smaller than the NAWSA (just 50,000 members to the NAWSA's two million members), the radical tactics of the NWP pushed the envelope and prodded the NAWSA into greater activity. They staged protests and pickets and marched in a suffrage parade before President Wilson's inauguration. In 1917, some of these activists were arrested after picketing outside the White House; in jail, they went on a hunger strike and were brutally force fed. The pressure put on Wilson by these militant feminists was critical in eventually securing his support for women's right to vote. These activists challenged conventional assumptions of appropriate behavior for women and, in doing so, challenged the status quo.

When President Wilson finally spoke before Congress in 1918, endorsing the right of women to vote, it was a pivotal moment for the First Wave. Nineteen states already had granted women suffrage, and Congress ultimately voted in favor of the Nineteenth Amendment, sending it to the states to be ratified as a part of the U.S. Constitution. Because ratification required the approval of the states, leaders of the NAWSA recognized it was critical to expand their support beyond western and eastern states, as such, racist and nativist sentiments came to the fore. The "Southern" strategy pursued by the NAWSA rested on the argument that allowing women to vote would provide for the continuation of white supremacy in the South. Suffrage organizations in the South routinely excluded Black people—both men and women—from their membership, and leaders actively excluded them from participating in events like conventions and marches.[25,26]

Despite this overt hostility, many Black women actively campaigned for suffrage during this period, including but not limited to Sojourner Truth, Ida B. Wells, and Adella Hunt Logan, who made the intersectional argument that Black women, as victims of both racism and sexism, needed the right to vote even more.[27] The movement still relied on support from Black people, particularly Black men who had recently been enfranchised (and not yet thoroughly disenfranchised by Jim Crow laws codifying segregation in the South). For instance, in order to put pressure on Tennessee to ratify the Nineteenth Amendment, Alice Paul appealed to the NAACP to have Black men contact their state legislators; the NAACP complied but not before pointing out Paul's racist exclusion of Black women.

In the states, the movement faced stiff opposition from a variety of well-financed and well-funded groups. Business interests and the liquor industry, fearful that women would vote to restrict their economic interests through reforms like the prohibition of alcohol or child labor laws, campaigned against ratification in the states. But decades of work meant that there were existing women's organizations in every state who worked tirelessly to secure approval. The Nineteenth Amendment to the Constitution was ratified in Tennessee by a one-vote margin in 1920, the 36th and final state necessary to the ratification campaign.

The First Wave of the feminist movement ultimately achieved success in reaching the goal that united the disparate factions who supported suffrage for a variety of reasons; primarily though, they did so by studiously avoiding most other issues, to ensure that divisions did not distract them from their key goal. Thus, the success of the First Wave of the feminist movement rested precisely on the fact that it avoided tackling other issues that contributed to the subordinate status of women in the domestic and work worlds. By focusing on the civic and public sphere, suffragists were able to unite people around the idea of public citizenship. So while suffrage was an important first step in securing greater equality for women, the First Wave of the feminist movement left much business unfinished.

THE SECOND WAVE

Pushing for the right to vote united women around a common cause and allowed them, for a time, to overlook important differences on other issues. The passage of the Nineteenth Amendment represented a victory for the women's movement, but it also meant this centralizing focus disappeared. As such, the women's movement splintered as leaders began to take up different causes. For example, Carrie Chapman Catt founded the League of Women Voters in 1920, which focused on nonpartisan efforts to educate women voters. Alice Paul and other leaders of the militant suffrage movement took up the cause of an Equal Rights Amendment (ERA). Their efforts were opposed by social justice feminists such as Jane Addams who were fearful of an ERA overturning laws that afforded women special protection, such as working conditions and wages, in the work realm.

But while this period did see the decline of women's organizations focused primarily on women's rights, many women were still active on behalf of issues that affected women. There was a robust group of working class and minority women fighting in mixed gender political, labor, and civil rights movements and organizations such as the United Auto Workers, the NAACP, the Communist Party, and the Hotel Employees and Restaurant and Employees Union to advance the social and economic status of women.[28] For instance, in 1937, a group of young women workers locked themselves into the downtown Detroit Woolworth store for six nights, demanding better wages and a voice in decisions at work, which they ultimately earned.

During World War II, women mobilized into the work force in support of the war effort, taking on a variety of roles once reserved exclusively for men, who were off fighting the war (Box 2.3). Rosie the Riveter and her "We Can Do It" slogan symbolized the mindset of women during this period. Women felt they were making progress toward true equality, not just political equality.

BOX 2.3: WOMEN IN THE WORKFORCE IN WORLD WAR II

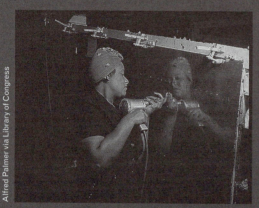

▶ **Photo 2.2** A "Rosie the Riveter" working on a Vengeance dive bomber in World War II.

Alfred Palmer via Library of Congress

With the enlistment of so many men into the armed services during WWII, there was a great need to replace them in the workforce. Importantly, women were desperately needed to fill industrial jobs to support the war effort, despite the fact that these jobs had been historically reserved for men. During the period from 1940 to 1944, the percentage of women in the workforce had increased by almost half, and 37% of all women over the age of 14 held paying jobs.[29] While the employment of women increased in fields across the board, their employment gains in industrial work were substantial; for instance, there was a 112% increase in the number of women working in factories. Rosie the Riveter, a fictionalized version of a real factory worker, was part of a campaign to recruit women to work in the defense industries. Interestingly, the original poster wasn't meant for public display and was forgotten for decades; in the 1980s, a copy in the National Archives was discovered, and it became a feminist icon.[30] While there is some debate about the inspiration for Rosie the Riveter, the most credible claim was that of Naomi Parker Fraley, who worked in a machine shop in Alameda, California. She passed away in January of 2018, although her legacy, in the image of Rosie, endures.

Many women were vastly disappointed when American service men returned home from the war. Rather than keeping their place in the work world, women were asked to step back into a primarily domestic role once again. As Dicker (2008) argues, "domesticity was celebrated in the postwar years as it had been in the Victorian era."[31] To be sure, this transition was primarily the plight of the middle- and upper-class white women. For poor, working class, and minority women, work was a constant, and the option to return to the home, whether forced or by choice, was not available to them.

This transition, though, forged some degree of common cause between middle- and upper-class and poor, working, and minority women. While the latter had been focused on issues such as women's wages, access to education, and access to good work throughout this time period, the abrupt withdrawal of meaningful work for the former formed the basis for the **Second Wave** of the feminist movement.

Perhaps nothing crystalized the feelings of this group of middle- and upper-class women more than the publication of Betty Friedan's *The Feminine Mystique* in 1963. Friedan herself was educated at Smith College and worked as a journalist before marrying and staying home to raise her children, like most educated women of the period did. Friedan did some freelance writing during this period, however, and while researching a story about her fellow Smith alumnae, she found that many of them were as discontented with their lives and roles as she was. She called this the "problem that has no name." Friedan argued that women, namely housewives, could no longer ignore their discontent and the voice inside that told them they wanted more than a house, a husband, and children—they wanted a place in society.[32]

While Friedan's book was narrow in scope, drawing on interviews with affluent and educated women and focusing on issues such as isolation in their home and lack of meaningful work, the book also resonated with working-class and minority women who felt similarly unhappy with their lot in life. To be sure, their discontent stemmed from different causes. While Friedan and others like her were unhappy about their ability to work outside the home, working women were unhappy about their second-class citizenship in the work world. Thus, *The Feminine Mystique* helped crystalize this sense of discontent and was an important catalyzing force for the Second Wave of the feminist movement. Buechler (1990) argues that a strong sense of collective identity is a prerequisite for a social movement to emerge; during this period, it was this sense of marginality as a result of secondary status in employment, education, and other institutions that provided that organizing focus.[33] In Chapters 3 and 9, we explore further this idea of linked fate among women.

For instance, in 1963 when *The Feminine Mystique* was published, many women worked outside the home, but it was common for them to be fired if and when they got pregnant. A married woman could not open a credit card without her husband's permission, even if she had a job of her own. There were little to no protections against sexual harassment or domestic violence. Job segregation was the norm; women had access to low-skilled, low-paying jobs, but ads for jobs that promised more money and better potential for advancement announced that women need not apply.

Clearly, Friedan had tapped into a growing source of discontent that was bubbling forward across the nation. For instance, in 1961, President Kennedy established the Presidential Commission on the Status of Women. The commission was chaired by Eleanor Roosevelt, wife of former president Franklin Delano Roosevelt and a known champion of women's causes. The makeup of the commission reflected tensions amongst those who were working on behalf of women. On one side, liberal feminists argued for the revision of laws to eliminate sex discrimination and to recognize the full legal equality of women. On the other side, labor activists were worried that such changes would nullify protective legislation. They saw these laws as protecting women and children from harsh working conditions with long, unregulated hours with low pay, although others believed they had the practice of limiting women's economic mobility. Nonetheless, the Commission had some immediate impact. President Kennedy barred sex discrimination in federal employment in 1962 per the Commission's request, and the Equal Pay Act was passed in 1963 after the Commission endorsed the idea in 1962.

Additionally, in 1964, the issue of discrimination against women was drawn into the debate about passage of the Civil Rights Act. While the initial wording of the act focused on employment discrimination based on race, a last-minute amendment was passed in the House of Representatives that would prohibit sex discrimination. Many felt that this addition was a poison pill; while some members of the House voted in favor of this amendment earnestly, others voted for it because they believed that the addition of the word "sex" would sway others against the measure, thus dooming passage of the Civil Rights Act in the Senate. But a group of feminist activists working to advance women's rights saw this as an opportunity, so Pauli Murray, one of the leaders of this movement and a member of the Commission, drafted a memo to be sent to lawmakers and the White House. In this memo, Murray argued that the distinction between sex and race discrimination was a false dichotomy; instead, she drew parallels between the two and insisted they could not be separated.

Murray's argument in the memo and in her other academic works was instrumental in recognizing the intersectionality of racism and sexism; she used the term "Jane Crow" to highlight the ways that sex and race discrimination overlap and reinforce the subordinate status of Black women.[34] Murray saw herself as a man trapped in a woman's body. Despite the mores of her time, Murray traveled the country dressed as a man, with her woman partner; as Orleck (2015) argues, "it is difficult to imagine the courage and bravado she had to summon to wander through the American Southwest in the mid-1930s, a cross-dressed, mixed-race woman traveling with her white female lover."[35] Importantly, Murray's experiences as a queer, Black woman are perhaps what made her uniquely qualified to identify the intersectionality of varying forms of discrimination; while the term *intersectionality* did not emerge until later, Murray's work was foundational to this concept. The Civil Rights Act ultimately passed both chambers of Congress and was signed in to law, with protections against sex discrimination in employment included.

The Commission ultimately reported on its findings in October of 1963, although the assassination of President Kennedy a month later overshadowed its release. Nonetheless, it sold over 64,000 copies and spurred the creation of state commissions on the status of women across the nation. The report contained a variety of specific recommendations for change, such as increasing access to education, a basic income, and child care. However, the report largely conformed to conventional expectations about the role of women; while it advocated for reforms to make women more equal, it also largely endorsed traditional gender roles and a liberal feminist approach to equality.[36] Importantly, the report did not endorse the passage of an Equal Rights Amendment, largely on the guidance of Pauli Murray who believed it was not necessary because women's equality could be advanced under the Fourteenth Amendment.[37]

Even though the Civil Rights Act protected women, many felt that the Equal Employment Opportunities Commission (EEOC) was not doing enough to enforce these protections and did not take sex discrimination seriously. For instance, in 1966, the EEOC upheld the legality of sex-segregated help wanted ads, so these ads continued to separate postings for men's jobs, like lawyers, engineers, and managers, from women's jobs, like secretaries, teachers, and nurses. As described in Box 2.4, the **pay gap**, or the difference in earnings between men and women, had not budged since the passage of the Civil Rights Act; women still earned approximately $0.59 to every one dollar men earned in 1966.[38] Buechler (1990) argues that this gap created a sense of rising expectations for equality with declining satisfaction, which is essential for protest movements, as it creates an intolerable gap between what people want and what they get, or **relative deprivation**.[39] The EEOC's lack of attention to sex discrimination certainly fostered this gap.

BOX 2.4: POLICY FEATURE

The Pay Gap

Equal pay for equal work has been one of the main motivating forces behind women's political activism for generations, both in the United States and around the world. In 2017, in the United States, women still earn approximately $0.80 on the dollar as compared to white men, with larger disparities for Black ($0.68 on the dollar) and Hispanic ($0.62 cents on the dollar) women.[40] Globally, women earn approximately $0.63 on the dollar as compared to men. According to research from the Institute for Women's Policy Research, if the pay gap continues to decrease at the same pace as it has in recent years, pay parity in the United States should be expected in 2059 for white women, 2124 for Black women, and 2233 for Hispanic women; the intersectional nature of the pay gap is discussed in greater detail in Chapter 3.

The causes of the wage gap are diverse, but a few are important to highlight. A large part of the gap is caused by occupational segregation; even though women have access to more kinds of work than they did in the past, they still tend to be concentrated in lower paying fields. Low pay in these fields is due at least in part to the fact that society values women's work less;

(Continued)

(Continued)

one study demonstrated that as women enter fields in greater number, the pay in that field declines.[41] Fields that require similar education, experience, and duties can have vastly different median pay based on whether the field is dominated by women or not; for instance, janitors, who tend to be men, are paid 22% more than maids and housekeepers, who tend to be women.[42]

Differences in pay can also be traced to differences in experience, as women are more likely to take time off work to assume caregiving responsibilities. As we discuss in Chapters 4 and 5, cultural norms place the expectation of child rearing and elder care largely on women, and the lack of domestic supports, such as paid family leave and affordable child care, makes it more likely that women in the United States take time out of work to shoulder these responsibilities. Internationally, the size of the wage gap varies from country to country, and research suggests this is due to differences in the strength of wage-setting mechanisms such as the minimum wage and collective bargaining by unions.[43] That said, every advanced industrial democracy has a wage gap between men and women. Research suggests this is a penalty for having children. After the first child, women's wages drop with no concomitant drop for men who have children. Thus, some argue that what we often refer to as a gender penalty is more aptly referred to as a childbearing pay gap or a motherhood penalty.[44]

Governments have pursued a variety of policy solutions to reduce the pay gap. For instance, Massachusetts passed a pay equity law in effect in 2018 that bars employers from asking job applicants about their previous salary until a job offer is made and from preventing employees from discussing their wages; it also prohibits retaliating against employees who exercise their rights under this act. The intent of the law was to prevent past wage disparities from carrying forward into new work and to give employees new tools for determining if wage discrimination exists. Other countries provide generous leave and child care for working parents; Denmark provides 52 weeks of paid leave to a family after the birth of a child, and child care is highly subsidized. While the United States only provides limited unpaid leave for some workers under the Family Medical Leave Act, states are beginning to provide paid leave to more workers. California, Washington, New Jersey, and Rhode Island have all recently passed laws to require paid family leave, and other states are considering adopting such provisions.

Yet, even in countries like Denmark, which provides extensive support for working parents, the pay gap persists. The pay of men and women in that country when they begin their careers is roughly equal, yet women's pay collapses by 30% on average when they have children; women's pay is still one fifth lower 10 years after the birth of a child as compared to before they had children. This continued gap is partially the result of cultural expectations about child rearing and work, passed down from parents to daughters, but not sons.[45] Until cultural norms about child rearing are challenged, progress on eliminating the pay gap will likely remain slow.

Thus, in 1966, when a group of women convened in Washington, DC, for a meeting of the state commissions on the status of women, frustrations were high. Some of these women met outside of the official meeting in Betty Friedan's hotel room to devise a plan to launch a new organization, focused exclusively on promoting women's rights. They realized, just as the leaders of the First Wave of the feminist movement did, that they needed an organization to serve as the focal point of this movement. Working together, Murray and Friedan drafted a statement of purpose that was adopted in October 1966, founding the National Organization for Women (NOW). Friedan was named the first president of the nascent organization.

However, the issues that divided Paul and Addams in the immediate aftermath of the passage of suffrage continued to plague NOW and the women's movement. On one side, liberal or equal rights feminists believed that the movement ought to focus on the elimination of legal barriers to the differential treatment of women; equality could be achieved by equal treatment under the law, with no special recognition or treatment for either sex. On the other side were **social justice feminists** who believed that women as a sex were disadvantaged, so women needed more than legal equality; the advancement of women's rights depended also on racial and economic justice.[46] In some cases, such as maternity leave, differential treatment was not only justified but needed. These divisions were evident at the second conference of NOW, where members adopted a Bill of Rights but were divided over whether to support planks supporting an ERA and reproductive rights. The majority of women in NOW came down on the side of liberal feminism; indeed, NOW's 1966 manifesto explicitly stated a belief in the power of American law to ensure equality of opportunity for women.

But almost concurrently with the formation of NOW, whose leadership was dominated by upper- and middle-class elite women who believed in liberal feminism, younger and more radical women were also engaged in the struggle for women's equality. For instance, young Black women were raising issues of sexist treatment in the civil rights movement. In December of 1965, the Students for a Democratic Society, a left-wing student group organized to protest the Vietnam War, racial discrimination, and capitalism, held their annual conference, and women there organized a women's workshop, an exercise in feminist consciousness raising.[47] Demands for women's equality in other leftist movements emerged, too, such as at the National Conference for New Politics, where women drafted resolutions calling for things like equal pay, child care, and half the convention votes. They were ridiculed for their request, and one organizer told Jo Freeman and Shulamith Firestone, organizers of these women, that they "had more important things to do here than talk about women's problems."[48]

Importantly, these more radical women focused not just on transforming institutional structures in the public realm but in the private realm as well. For them, "changes in consciousness mattered as least as much as changes in the law."[49] For instance, Carol Hanisch (1970) argued that what had previously been seen as personal problems, such as appearance, sex, child care, and the division of household labor, are actually political problems.[50] This gave rise to the saying—*the personal is political*. For radical feminists, class, sex, race, age, and sexuality were interrelated; they raised questions about family, lesbianism, abortion, colonialism, and other issues.[51]

These radical feminists drew on political theater to emphasize their points; for example, they protested the sexism of the Miss America contests by burning bras, girdles, and fake eyelashes in a freedom trash can, giving rise to the image of feminists as bra burners. Important works like Firestone's *The Dialectic of Sex* highlighted how women's role in the home, and particularly child bearing, was fundamental to women's oppression. Kate Millettt's *Sexual Politics* demonstrated how patriarchal family units were a political institution. Thus, like the First Wave, the Second Wave of feminism focused on advocating the advancement of women in the public realm. But unlike the First Wave, the Second Wave of feminism began to draw attention to how the private realm and patriarchal systems, systems that encompassed both the domestic and public spheres, were instrumental in women's oppression.

In 1968, representatives from a variety of these groups met at the first Women's Liberation Convention. While these women debated whether the primary focus of their activism should be around women's rights, racial and economic justice, or antiwar protests, they agreed that they should focus on drawing more women into the movement through a process of consciousness-raising.[52] Radical feminism saw women's oppression as the first and oldest form of oppression to which other forms of oppression are related, and the way to get women to see their shared status was through these consciousness-raising groups.[53] The Redstockings, a women's liberation group, articulated the need for and the process by which consciousness raising would work in their 1969 manifesto. They argued,

> Because we have lived so intimately with our oppressors, in isolation from each other, we have been kept from seeing our personal suffering as political. This creates the illusion that a woman's relationship with her man is a matter of interplay between two unique personalities, and can be worked out individually. In reality, every such relationship is a *class* relationship, and the conflicts between individual men and women are *political* conflicts that can only be solved collectively. . . . Our chief task at present is to develop female class consciousness through sharing experiences and publicly exposing the sexist foundation of all our institutions.

Thus, consciousness-raising groups sprung up around the country; in these meetings, women would share personal experiences about a given topic, such as marriage, work, or child care. The process of sharing personal experience was designed to demonstrate to women that the problems they felt were uniquely their own were, in fact, common. Hanisch (1970) saw these groups as an important part of the political action necessary to achieve women's equality.[54] But for others, the issues that radical women's movement raised were ahead of the time and thus a distraction from the goal of obtaining legal equality for women.

Despite differences in approaches and focus, the movement for women's equality marched forward, making advances on several fronts. Both liberal and radical feminist groups organized protests and demonstrations. NOW organized pickets at EEOC offices in 1967, demanding an end to sex segregated help wanted ads. In 1970, radical feminists staged a sit-in in the offices of *Ladies Home Journal*, protesting how the magazine depicted women and their interests.

Importantly, these women secured significant victories through their work. In 1973, the Supreme Court struck down sex segregated job ads in *Pittsburgh Press vs. Pittsburgh Commission on Human Relations*. In 1972, Congress passed Title IX of the Elementary and Secondary Education Acts. It stated, "[n]o person in the United States shall, on the basis of sex, be excluded from participation in, be denied the benefits of, or be subjected to discrimination under any education program or activity receiving Federal financial assistance." This act has been instrumental in opening educational and athletic opportunities to women. The Equal Employment Opportunity Act was also passed in 1972; it gave the EEOC the ability to sue when it finds evidence of employment discrimination.

Perhaps the most important step taken in 1972 to advance women's rights was the passage of the ERA by Congress. The ERA was taken up by Alice Paul and the National Women's Party after the passage of the Nineteenth Amendment; it was first introduced in Congress in 1923. Because Paul and the NWP took "equal rights" to mean ending special benefits for women, this was met with immediate opposition from other women's and labor organizations; opposition from these groups, as well as conservatives, meant that the ERA, which was introduced in Congress for 20 years after this, was roundly defeated.[55] However, with the passage of the Civil Rights Act, both the courts and the EEOC held that protective legislation was no longer permissible, removing left-leaning opposition to the passage of the ERA.

As such, much of the energy and focus of the mainstream Second Wave feminist movement began to coalesce around the passage of the ERA. Mansbridge (1990) argues that in this regard, the movement to pass the ERA was like the suffrage movement; "feminists of widely differing intellectual priorities, personal styles, and collective needs pooled their energies for a short, intense period in order to produce the near national consensus required to pass a constitutional amendment."[56] Entities such as the United Auto Workers and the Department of Labor, which had long opposed the ERA, voiced support. Seizing on the moment, feminists convinced Senator Birch Bayh to hold hearings on the ERA, and Representative Martha Griffiths (D-MI) collected signatures on a discharge petition to remove the ERA from the House Judiciary Committee where it had been stuck. There were still issues to be worked on with respect to the wording of the amendment; in particular, these debates focused on whether women could be drafted and whether an ERA would impact laws regarding family and marital support. While amendments to the ERA to deal with these issues were rejected, they were important harbingers of the debate over ratification that was to come. Finally, nearly 50 years after it was first introduced, Congress voted in favor of the Equal Rights Amendment to the Constitution in 1972.

After ratification, the next step in the amendment process is for three fourths of the states to ratify the amendment. Immediately following adoption by Congress, it looked like the ERA would attain this mark easily. Hawaii became the first state to ratify on the same day the ERA was passed by Congress; five more states (Delaware, Idaho, Iowa, Nebraska, and New Hampshire) followed in the next two days. By early 1973, 30 states had ratified the amendment, often with little to no debate, which seemed to imply that the amendment would easily meet the 38-state benchmark by the 7-year ratification deadline imposed by Congress. But then, ratification efforts stalled as opposition to the amendment emerged. Ultimately, the 7-year window expired, with only 35 states having ratified the amendment. Congress extended the ratification deadline to 1982, but no other states ratified the amendment during this time period. While there have been attempts to revive the ratification process and fresh Equal Rights Amendments have been introduced annually in Congress, the odds for actually adding the ERA to the U.S. Constitution are long (Box 2.5).

Why did the ERA fail? A variety of explanations have been offered, but it is important to highlight a few here. Jane Mansbridge (1986), in her book *Why We Lost the ERA*, argues that because the ERA applied only to government action and not private entities, it would not have had the impact that both proponents and opponents claimed it would.[57] This is what the American public wanted; while committed to equality in the abstract, they were not committed to real changes in gender roles. For instance, in 1977, 62% of Americans supported the notion that married women should not hold jobs if jobs were scarce and their husbands could

BOX 2.5: POLICY FEATURE

The Equal Rights Amendment

While Congress has not extended the deadline for ratification of the ERA, efforts to ratify the amendment and to pass state versions of this amendment still persist. For instance, on March 22nd, 2017, Nevada became the 36th state to ratify the ERA, 45 years to the day after Congress passed it; Illinois became the 37th state to ratify the ERA in May of 2018. In some of the remaining states that have not yet ratified the amendment, state legislators have introduced bills to ratify; for instance, there have been several attempts to ratify the amendment in Arizona. If 38 states ratify the amendment, it would require Congressional action to extend the deadline for ratification. These bills have been introduced regularly in the U.S. Congress but have not yet been approved. The Equal Rights Amendment organization keeps a list of which states have ratified the amendment; check their website to see if yours has.

support them.[58] Had the argument been framed as a symbolic advancement for women, Mansbridge argues, proponents might have been successful. But because the ERA would have few immediate effects, those who worked for ratification were the most committed. And the most committed indeed supported changes that the American public did not want. For instance, many proponents contended that the ERA would require that women be drafted and serve in combat, just like men—a change that the broader public did not support. We discuss this difference between equity policies and role policies (like the draft) and how this influences public opinion in Chapter 3.

This tension played into the hands of the emerging opposition, led by Phyllis Schlafly. Schlafly founded Stop ERA, which was devoted to preventing ratification of the ERA. While there were certainly other opponents of the amendment, such as conservative business interests that financed the opposition, the fact that some women opposed the amendment gave them ammunition. Conservatives opposed to the ERA put forward a variety of arguments against it: it would lead to the drafting of women to serve in the military, it would require unisex bathrooms, and it would lead to abortion on demand. This women-led opposition had two key effects. First, pitting women on the right against women on the left meant that the ERA lost its aura of benefiting all women, and second, the result of this was that the ERA became controversial, and controversial amendments rarely pass.[59] Importantly, this opposition resonated with the emerging new right. While the new right and the women involved in this movement are not monolithic in their beliefs, Schlafly's arguments—which focused on patriarchal family values and morals and which framed the ERA as an attack on homemakers and mothers— appealed to social conservatives who believe women are naturally subordinate to men.[60,61] The Supreme Court's landmark *Roe v. Wade* decision in 1973 galvanized the opposition as some of their worst fears appeared to be coming true. Schlafly was at the forefront of this new movement, which was successful in rolling back some of the gains secured by the Second Wave and creating a hostile political environment for future feminist action.

Despite the failure of the ERA, the Second Wave of the feminist movement was extraordinarily successful in advancing the status of women, mainly in the political and economic realm. Starting in the late 1960s and into the early 1970s, landmark legislation and Supreme Court decisions advanced women's access to reproductive freedom, work, and education. The effect of these victories is profound. For instance, in 1970, just prior to the passage of Title IX, women earned 10.6% of all doctoral degrees; by 2012 (the 40th anniversary of Title IX), that number had increased to 50.6%.[62] Women, for the first time, could receive a prescription for birth control and had access to abortion. In addition, no longer could employers limit applications to jobs on the basis of sex. But while there were important legal victories in the public realm during this period, there was still much work to be done, both in the public and private realms, to advance women's equality; furthermore, as we discuss in Chapter 8, some of these victories are currently under attack.

THE THIRD WAVE

It is fairly easy to mark the emergence of the First and Second Waves of the feminist movement. Organized around an important goal, the right to vote in the First Wave and the ERA in the Second Wave, activists were able to temporarily put aside their ideological and political differences. But these temporary alliances masked real differences in opinion about the sources of women's oppression and the necessary solutions. Furthermore, while the First and Second Wave of the feminist movement did much to advance the status of women, both movements were marred by racism and classism. For instance, during the debate over the ERA, Representative Martha Griffiths (D-MI) argued that without protection against sex discrimination "white women will be last at the hiring gate," and Representative Catherine Dean May (R-WA) argued these protections were necessary to prevent discrimination against white native-born American Christian women.[63] As another example, women of color in the 1970s waged a campaign against forced sterilization campaigns run by various states as part of antipoverty programs; these forced sterilizations disproportionately affected women of color, yet NOW refused to endorse any legislation they felt might be used to restrict access to sterilization on demand.[64]

But the issues raised by the Second Wave, and the radical women's movement in particular, simmered for many years. The sexual revolution of the 1960s and 1970s, along with women's newfound access to reproductive choice, moved discussion about sexuality out into the open. In some ways then, the consciousness raising of the Second Wave was successful, if incomplete. Issues that had seemed primarily private, such as domestic violence, rape, and sexual harassment, burst out into the open as more and more women began to see these as public issues demanding public solutions. While prominent national women's organizations declined in membership, women remained active in many other organizations that affected the lives of women. For instance, women played prominent roles in the 1970s movements representing the interests of Native Americans, farm workers, and the poor and working class.[65]

Thus, finding a beginning moment for the Third Wave of the women's movement is difficult. During the 1970s and 1980s, women were active on behalf of a variety of issues and organizations—there was no centralizing focus. And women were often on both sides of the debate on many issues. For example, many feminists were deeply divided about the issue of pornography. On one side, antipornography feminists like Catharine MacKinnon (1991) and Andrea Dworkin argued that pornography violated women's rights.[66] MacKinnon and Dworkin helped write local municipal ordinances banning pornography based on their theories. On the other side, liberal feminists, as exemplified by Nadine Strossen's work *Defending Pornography* (1995), argued that banning pornography was a violation of the First Amendment right to freedom of expression and that suppressing pornography would be used as a tool to also suppress women's sexuality.[67]

But as more and more women gained access to higher education and as the issues raised during the Second Wave began to take root, many more perspectives of feminism came to the fore: Black and Latina feminism, postcolonial and multiracial feminism, queer theory, lesbian feminism and more, many of which were described in Chapter 1. Given the centrality of this blossoming of feminist thought to the Third Wave, it is worth reviewing and highlighting several of these different approaches that developed during this period.

While women of color have always been involved in and at the forefront of the advancement of the rights of women, the 1980s saw the emergence of many powerful feminist voices taking up the mantle of intersectionality from Pauli Murray. For instance, bell hooks (1984) argued that "much feminist theory emerges from privileged women who live at the center, whose perspectives on reality rarely include knowledge and awareness of the lives of women and men who live in the margin."[68] Because these women accepted capitalist values, hooks argues, they would never be able to achieve women's economic liberation, an important goal for those who lead less comfortable lives. Novelist Alice Walker (1983) coined the term **womanist** to describe feminists of color, but also to put forth a more encompassing vision of feminism; many Black women activists did not identify with the term feminist, given the racism of earlier feminist movements.[69] This new term was designed to be more universal, including and representing more voices, particularly those of Black feminists.

Transnational feminism critiqued the largely white, North American perspective in the modern feminist movement; Mohanty (1984) in *Under Western Eyes* argues that feminist thought has tended to portray non-Western women as monolithic victims, thus creating two groups: liberated and educated Western women and victimized Third World women.[70] This leads Western feminists to engage in projects to save women in these regions, denying these women the agency to liberate themselves.[71] But there are strong feminist movements in many non-Western countries; see Box 2.6 for an example of the feminist movement in India.

BOX 2.6: COMPARATIVE FEATURE

The Indian Feminist Movement

There is a good deal of overlap between the issues that feminists in non-Western countries like India and feminists in Western countries confront. At the most basic level, the feminist movement in India is focused on issues like access to the public sphere and the basic safety of women. For instance, in 2012, thousands of people took to the streets across India to protest the brutal gang rape

(Continued)

(Continued)

▶ **Photo 2.3** Police facing women in a protest march in Kolkata, India.

of a young woman on a public bus. Violence against women is not uncommon in India, but it is uncommon for perpetrators to be punished. Something about the Delhi bus rape sparked outrage, and it became "a landmark in the fight for women's rights and feminism in India, leading to legislative changes and moving sex and gender to the center stage of political debates."[72] Despite fairly severe restrictions on women's access to public space, Indian women have been active on a whole host of issues, starting in the nineteenth century. Women in India have long paved the way not only on women's issues but also on significant socioeconomic movements, such as the Chipko movement focusing on ecological balance, the anti-liquor movement in Andhra Pradesh, and the movement against *khap panchayats* or honor killings.[73] Making choices about one's body and dress is just as important in India as it is in Western countries. Millennial women in India have challenged moral policing of women regarding "sexist curfew rules in student halls," and conservative men who disapprove of Valentine's Day and women's presence in places like pubs. In terms of the latter, feminists waged the Pink Chaddi campaign against right-wing men who want to limit women in public places.[74] "Chaddi is a childish word for underwear and slang for right-wing hardliner;" feminists sent pink underwear to a conservative right-wing leader as a joke but also as a way to emphasize that women have freedom in public to embrace a man, have consensual sex, or simply enjoy a run in the park.[75] However, as in the United States, the feminist movement in India is challenged by the vast diversity of women in India, with divisions along class, caste, religion, sexuality, and disability lines, which we describe in more depth in Chapter 9. And just as in the West, one of the difficult tasks that Indian feminists face is changing underlying attitudes toward women, which activists see as necessary for an end to the violence, persecution, and abuse women in India experience.[76]

The sexual liberation of the 1960s and 1970s also coincided with and led to the rise of sex-positive, lesbian, and queer feminism. **Sex-positive feminists** celebrated women's sexuality and placed consent and empowerment at the center of the sexual experience. Thus, these feminists focused on constructing a personalized and individualized approach to women's issues such as sex, pornography, and prostitution. While social conservatives saw feminists as man haters,

lesbian feminism emerged as a result of what they saw as the Second Wave's hostility toward lesbians; for instance, Betty Friedan, as president of NOW, used the phrase "lavender menace" to describe what she saw as the threat of lesbianism to the organization. Lesbian radical feminists claimed this phrase for their own and argued for the inclusion of lesbians and lesbian issues in the feminist movement. **Queer theorists** argued against the creation and use of binaries (such as male/female or straight/gay) and saw these as artificial constructs used to maintain the power of dominant groups.[77] Contrary to many feminists who argued that sex was biological and gender socially constructed, queer theorists argue that both are socially constructed.[78] Importantly, these feminists demonstrated that our notions of what is considered masculine and feminine are socially constructed and constantly changing. For instance, in the late 1800s and early 1900s, pink was a boys' color, while blue was a girls' color, and young boys, including future president Franklin Roosevelt, routinely wore dresses.

It is important to note that these diverse voices emerged in a culture that was growing increasingly hostile to contemporary feminism. Conservative women, who began to organize during the ERA campaign, were energized by three political developments that they believe threatened traditional values.[79] In addition to the passage of ERA and the *Roe v. Wade* decision, these activists were alarmed by the growing LGBTQIA+ movement. Along with Schlafly, other women activists like Connie Marshner at the Heritage Foundation and Beverly LaHaye at Concerned Women for America, organized in defense of traditional values and families. The three women worked together to elect over 15% of the delegates to President Carter's White House Conference on Families and staged protests at the event over what they saw as the antifamily agenda of the conference. Like the women's movement on the left, the women's movement on the right is not monolithic in its views. Laissez-faire conservative women, such as the Independent Women's Forum, tend to be opposed to government intervention in the private realm and so are less driven to defend traditional families and values as compared to their socially conservative counterparts.[80] Such women tend to be less prominent and visible in the New Right political movement, though, which is motivated by concerns about what the rise of feminism and women's rights means for the traditional family structure characterized by marriage between a cisgender man and a cisgender woman, with the man serving as the head of the household.

Additionally, even those who were not directly opposed to the women's rights movement were, at best, ambivalent about it and at worst, hostile to it. For instance, *Elle* magazine, in 1986, stated that "young women no longer need to examine the whys and hows of sexism. . . . All those ideals that were once held as absolute truths—sexual liberation, the women's movement, true equality—have been debunked or debased."[81] The writings of Camille Paglia (1990) and Katie Roiphe (1994) encapsulate these "post-feminist" sentiments.[82,83] Susan Faludi (1991) argues this rejection of feminism was a media-driven "backlash" against the threat that gains made by women represented to the status quo.[84]

To be sure, the success of the Second Wave of the feminist movement led to education and economic advancement for women. Women had access to higher education and jobs that had previously been denied to them. Yet, despite the gains of the Second Wave, women were far from achieving equal status in society. The pay gap remained stubbornly intact, and the **glass ceiling**, a metaphorical barrier that prevents women from advancing into high-ranking positions, was immune to attempts to break it, leaving women outside of executive management and board-rooms. Furthermore, many women born in the 1970s were mothered by women active in the Second Wave; Rebecca Walker, Jennifer Baumgardner, and Amy Richards, prominent authors during this period writing about feminism, all had mothers who were active in the Second Wave. These women came of age during rising expectations for women; women believed they could "have it all." But there was a wide gap between expectations and reality. Nonetheless, as these women were raised with different expectations, their approach to feminism was different. Rampton argues,

> the Third Wave of feminism . . . was informed by post-colonial and post-modern thinking. In this phase, many constructs were destabilized, including the notions of "universal womanhood," body, gender, sexuality, and heteronormativity. . . . Its transversal politics means that differences such as those of ethnicity, class, sexual orientation, etc. are celebrated and recognized as dynamic, situational, and provisional.[85]

These women reclaimed many of the trappings of womanhood that their mothers had railed against: lipstick, high-heels, and push-up bras; they also reclaimed words such as *girl*, *slut*, and *bitch*. Riot grrrl activism that emerged during this time was a good example of this aesthetic. Emerging out of the Pacific Northwest, these activists expressed themselves through music in bands such as Bikini Kill, Sleater Kinney, and 7 Year Bitch and in zines like *Jigsaw*, *Girl Germs*, and *Riot grrrl*.

> ▶ **Photo 2.4** Riot grrrl 1992 convention poster.

Yet, while the Third Wave of feminism was more successful in engaging with the issues of racism, classism, and heteronormativity than the earlier waves of the feminist movement, it was less successful in advancing a political agenda. Because there was no central organizing goal of this movement (indeed, Rampton argues that rejection of communal objectives is an important characteristic of the Third Wave), it is difficult to say whether the Third Wave was successful; nor is it easy to say if and when the Third Wave ended. Thompson (2016) argues the Third Wave focused little on a political agenda but instead focused on breaking boundaries and conceptions of gender, which has sometimes caused disagreements among those involved as Box 2.7 explains.[86]

BOX 2.7: TRANS-EXCLUSIONARY RADICAL FEMINISM?

Even as feminism has become more inclusive, there are still debates about who belongs as well as claims of exclusionary behavior within the movement. **Trans-Exclusionary Radical Feminism**, or **TERF**, is a collective idea rooted in exclusion of transgender people and particularly trans women from the feminist movement. Note, the way the term *radical* is used in this context is different from the definition of radical feminist theory provided in Chapter 1. In academic theory, the term *radical* refers to women who want to dismantle hierarchical institutional structures rather than gain access to them. Here, radical is used in a more conventional way, to imply that feminists who reject trans women embrace an extreme and unacceptable version of feminism. Kelsie Brynn Jones, a trans woman, writes on the effects of TERF in one of her articles. She cites the definitive emergence of TERF to be when Janice F. Raymond (1979) published *The Transsexual Empire: The Making of the She-Male.*[87] Rather than grapple with **gender dystopia**—which is the clinical term for the distress a trans person feels when forced to present as the wrong gender—and the social construction of both sex and gender, Raymond argued that transsexual women reduced the female form to an artifact so that they could appropriate it for themselves. By minimizing transitioning to merely aesthetic choice, she denied trans women the status of women, suggesting that transsexuals' participation in women's spaces and culture amounted to a "she-male" invasion, metaphorically comparable to rape.

Aggressive disputes between some feminist activists and the trans community are not new. Goldberg (2017) dates the beginning of the dispute to the Second Wave feminist movement and the refusal of some Second Wave feminists to acknowledge transgender women as women.[88] For example, the Michigan Womyn's Music Festival, or MichFest, originally began in 1976 and promotes itself as "womyn-born womyn" only. Musical acts such as the Indigo Girls and Hunter Valentine boycotted the festival to advocate for trans inclusivity. Trans activists have seen the exclusion of women who were assigned male at birth to be trans-exclusionary, and some refer to women who argue for cis-women spaces as TERFS.

(Continued)

(Continued)

Some gender-critical feminists (those who the trans community labels radical) argue that "gender is less an identity than a caste position. Anyone born a man retains male privilege in society; even if he chooses to live as a woman—and accept a correspondingly subordinate social position—the fact that he has a choice means that he can never understand what being a woman is really like."[89] They argue that sex and gender should not be seen as interchangeable. These gender critical feminists argue that "sex-based gender roles are oppressive social constructs—not natural states of being in need of protection and celebration—and that the well-documented threats of violence against women who defend women-only space are an abusive and unacceptable response to political disagreement."[90] A long-time MichFest attendee described how while at the camp, women were free to be themselves, clothed or unclothed, walk alone at night and have no fear for their safety. She explained that there was always controversy at the camp. One year, a group of women involved in S&M (sadism and masochism) attended, which made other women uncomfortable because they argued it promoted violence against women (many there had histories of abuse). The camp organizers created a solution whereby the S&M women had their own "neighborhood" within the camp, just like there were neighborhoods for the over 60 group, the loud and rowdy group, or the alcoholics anonymous group. When women started to arrive with boys (not allowed in the camp), a neighborhood was developed at the camp's entrance where women could stay with their children and have childcare services while they attended different events. According to a personal interview, the only issue that wasn't solved through a dialogue with organizers was that of the inclusion of trans women. Although it is documented that there were trans women at MichFest, no one was ever asked about their sexual or gender identity upon entry. The removal of a trans woman from the camp and subsequent protests became a rallying cry for those who accused the feminists at MichFest of being TERFs. In alternative accounts, attendees state that the woman was removed for being disruptive, not because of her trans status.

While the women's movement has at times been bigoted and exclusionary (as discussed earlier in this chapter and revisited in Chapter 9), the term "TERF" is not without its own baggage. It is viewed by those it describes as a slur and has been perceived as a way for some in the trans community to threaten cis women (lesbian or straight). According to Hungerford (2013) "TERF is not meant to be explanatory, but insulting. These characterizations are hyperbolic, misleading, and ultimately defamatory. They do nothing but escalate vitriol and fail to advance the conversation in any way."[91]

In the twenty-first century, some continue to use the concepts of waves to study feminist activism; they argue a new wave of feminism began in the United States and elsewhere in the 2010s. This "Fourth Wave" is centered on technological mobilization, social action and justice, bodies, and identity. The Fourth Wave uses the Internet to call out misogyny found in politics and culture, and its actions center around a young generation of women who are tech savvy.[92] The #MeToo campaign is a prime example of tech mobilization in support of feminist issues, like sexual harassment and violence perpetrated by men in entertainment, business, and politics. The actions of feminists in the Fourth Wave are "defined by technology," but they also manifest in real life through protests, whether that be an organized march, gathering, or even personal protests such as refusing to shave body hair.[93]

Body and sexual positivity in the Fourth Wave also relates to gender identity. According to the feminist magazine *Bustle*, the Fourth Wave is queer and trans inclusive. The Fourth Wave does not just talk about queer theory or sex positivity, it was founded upon and celebrates the queering of gender. Building on the Riot grrrl movement in the Third Wave, it continues to reclaim language used to denigrate women. For instance, the slutwalk movement began in January 2011 as a response to the idea that a woman's dress makes her vulnerable to rape.

However, others now argue that the idea of "waves" in the feminist movement has less meaning.[94,95] The success of the Second Wave of the women's movement in opening educational opportunities to women means that there are more and more women in academia, and nowadays it is common to see women's centers and women's and gender studies departments on college campuses. Feminist theorizing continues regardless of whether there is a wave or not. Collectively then, while women still have a ways to go to achieve true equality, feminist activists have ensured that great strides have been made. Furthermore, while there is often push back against gender studies or research into women's interests, the academic and theoretical arms of the feminist movement are well established.[96] The feminist movement, while far from unified in its vision or goals, has become more open to diverse perspectives and ways of seeing and thinking. As Kang, Lessard, Heston, and Nordmarken (2017) argue, "feminists have increasingly realized that a coalitional politics that organizes with other groups based on their shared (but differing) experiences of oppression, rather than their specific identify, is absolutely necessary."[97]

Thus, in the early twenty-first century, it is unclear where the feminist movement is headed. On the one hand there are definitely signs of renewed political activity on feminist causes in the aftermath of Hillary Clinton's loss to Donald Trump in the 2016 general election (see Chapter 9). Rampton (2008) argues activism is "emerging because (mostly) young women and men realize that the Third Wave is either overly optimistic or hampered by blinders.[98] Feminism is moving from the academy and back into the realm of public discourse. Issues that were central to the earliest phases of the women's movement are receiving national and international attention . . . sexual abuse, rape, violence against women, unequal pay, slut-shaming, the pressure on women to conform to a single and unrealistic body type."

This emerging movement combines a First and Second Wave focus on concrete political issues and Third Wave consciousness about diverse perspectives. The Black Lives Matter movement (discussed in Chapter 9) is a prime example of contemporary activism around intersectional issues of oppression. The movement is a broad based coalition of activists focused on the issue of police brutality against people of color. Cofounded by three Black women community organizers, Alicia Garza, Patrisse Cullors, and Opal Tometi, the women created a "chapter-based, member-led organization whose mission it is to build local power and to intervene in violence inflicted on Black communities by the state and vigilantes."[99] The organization's website explicitly recognizes the unique needs of Black women, queer, trans, and disabled individuals.

Another example is the #MeToo movement, referenced above, that emerged in 2017, which we discuss in more detail in Chapter 9. The hashtag, originated by Tarana Burke—an activist who works with marginalized teens—has been used by women and, to a lesser extent, men and nonbinary individuals around the world to share stories of sexual harassment and assault. The hashtag gained prominence in reporting about the sexual assault and battery by movie producer Harvey Weinstein and has brought down dozens of prominent men such as NBC TV host Matt Lauer, U.S. Senator Al Franken (D-MN), and actor Kevin Spacey. As a result of this movement, millions of dollars have been raised for a legal fund, the Time's Up fund, at the National Women's Law Center to provide legal support to victims of sexual harassment and assault.

But as Susan Faludi (2017) argues,

> Women's activism has historically taken two forms. One is an expression of direct anger at the ways individual men use and abuse us. It's righteous outrage against an unambiguous enemy with a visible face, the male predator who feeds on our vulnerability and relishes our humiliation. Mr. Weinstein's face is the devil's face du jour, and the #MeToo campaign fits squarely in this camp. The other form is less spectacular but as essential: It's fighting the ways the world is structurally engineered against women. Tied to that fight is the difficult and ambiguous labor of building an equitable system within which women have the wherewithal and power to lead full lives.[100]

Where the feminist movement goes and whether it takes on the labor of building a more equitable system remains to be seen.

CONCLUSION

Over the past several centuries, there has been significant progress in advancing the status of women in society. Prior to the First Wave of the feminist movement, women were routinely denied access to the public realm and full citizenship; indeed, most women did not enjoy any legal protections or bodily autonomy whatsoever. Women have now secured the legal right to vote, access to education, and the workplace. These efforts have largely been successful when these movements have been able to focus on legal changes to improve the status of women. When these movements have a concrete goal upon which to focus, such as the right to vote or the passage of the ERA, they have been able to temporarily set aside differences in pursuit of the cause, which has allowed for significant progress.

But the move to achieve true equality for women and dismantle patriarchal systems is incomplete. As we have noted above and in Chapter 1, women identify with demographic traits other than shared sex, such as class, race, or religion, which makes it difficult for them to recognize their shared status as a cohesive marginalized group. Because of these cross-cutting identities and the social reification of sex roles, movements to advance women's rights have always met with opposition from others, both men and women, making dismantling these roles a difficult challenge. It is far easier to unify movements around legal changes; changes to the private realm are more divisive. The association of women with the domestic realm, fundamental to patriarchal systems of oppression, is seen to many as natural; and to this day, women still assume a greater burden of the work in this realm, what many call the "second shift," a concept we investigate further in Chapter 4. In order to better understand these cross-cutting identities and often divergent viewpoints among women, we turn now to an examination of public opinion to see how women differ from both men and each other in terms of the political opinions they hold.

REVIEW QUESTIONS

1. Discus the difference between the private and public realms as it relates to women's rights. Where have women made the most gains? Give some examples.

2. What rights did women have during the revolutionary war period? How did this differ if they were married or single? How was society structured to impact the rights of women?

3. Describe the activities and advances of the First Wave. Who were the key players? What were the key issues? What were the key events and key advancements? In what way was women's activism during the First Wave tied to the abolition of slavery? Where were the tensions?

4. Describe the activities and advances of the Second Wave. Who were the key players? What were the key issues? What were the key events and key advancements? Where were the tensions within the women's movement during this time?

5. What is the pay gap? How did this motivate the Second Wave? In what way does the pay gap persist?

6. In what ways are the Third and Fourth Waves different from the first two? Can we still talk about a "wave?" How did the women's movement broaden and change after the Second Wave? What type of "feminisms" did we see emerge during the Third and Fourth Wave eras?

AMBITION ACTIVITIES

Analyzing Changes in Women's Lives: As this chapter discusses, tremendous changes in the status of women have occurred over the past generations, particularly from the late 1960s and on. We have moved away from a society in which only two genders (male or female) were recognized and each sex was proscribed certain gender roles: previously the public realm was the domain of men and the private realm was the domain of women. Get a sense of how society has changed by interviewing a woman who was an adult during the period of change, that is, someone who was born before 1960. Talk to your mother, grandmother, or someone who is living in a nursing home. Ask her how things have changed, both generally and for women specifically, during her life. Did women go to college when she was growing up? Did women she knew work outside the home? What kind of jobs did most women have? What did her family expect of her? What life accomplishments were expected out of men? How did race factor into these expectations? For tips on how to conduct interviews, see Appendix 1.

Build Civic Skills in Student Organizations and Citizens' Academy: Political scientists and sociologists are concerned about declining social capital in American society. Social capital refers to networks of people in community clubs, groups, and organizations that can be mobilized to address and resolve civic and political issues. These types of groups, where people learn valuable civic skills about organizing for collective action, have provided an important staging ground for every new wave of the women's movement. Since the number of formally organized clubs and organizations in the United States has declined over the past two decades, it is useful to seek out opportunities to replace experiences—in registered student organizations on your college campus or in a Citizen Academy in your local community.

Discuss your participation in current clubs and organizations: Are you or your classmates members of any organizations, either on campus or in your communities? These might range from churches and unions in the community to honors clubs, professional societies, and sororities/fraternities on campus. Those who are members should describe any civic and political skills they have learned by being a member, as well as how these abilities could be used to coordinate collective action about a civic or political issue on campus, in your community.

Find new opportunities to participate on campus: Most college websites include a page dedicated to student life, with access to a complete list of registered student organizations. Explore the list and identify a list of campus clubs that you might like to join. Do you think you would gain access to social capital, as well as civic and political skills, by participating? Discuss why or why not.

Find new opportunities to participate in your community: Research whether or not there is a Citizens' Academy in your community. Citizens' Academies, defined as programs conducted by local officials to "help educate, inform and engage citizens," encourage the growth of social capital, local democratic practices, and political change. Citizens' Academies "are a relatively new phenomenon in U.S. local government . . . [as they] began to appear in the late 1990s," and not all local governments have them even today. Local governments with academies invite citizens to attend classes about multiple topics, including city finances, crime, transportation, land use, and public works projects such as parks. During class time, citizens meet local leaders and government officials. Citizens attend classes for approximately 6 to 12 weeks and spend, on average, 20 hours in class time. What do local communities and citizens get out of this experience? The local communities get educated and engaged citizens, some of whom will go on to be involved in local government and politics. Citizens likely will better trust government leaders after learning more about them. If your community has a Citizens' Academy, consider joining. If not, contact the National League of Cities about setting up a Citizens' Academy in your region.

Brainstorm 1: Consider which women in your life, including yourself, might be interested in attending an academy and becoming active in public life. What issues/initiatives might these women pursue once they are public leaders, and how might participation in a Citizens' Academy help them to pursue these issues? Try to identify at least three women whom you know personally and whom you believe would attend a Citizens' Academy and why they might do so.

Brainstorm 2: A lot of the content presented in Citizens' Academies pertain to policing, transportation, and public spaces. What about these local issues should be of particular concern to women? For instance, local policing includes responses to sex trafficking as well as hate crimes based on race and trans/queer identities. What might be taught in a Citizens' Academy that pertains to women and a variety of women from diverse backgrounds? Design a teaching unit for one meeting of a Citizens' academy that you believe pertains to a local issue of interest to women. What local guest speakers could teach in the unit, what issues would citizens learn about, and what policy changes could citizens discuss during the course of that unit?

Practice Using Parliamentary Procedure: One of the most important skills people learn in civic groups and local government is how to use parliamentary procedure to discuss an issue. Becoming comfortable with "parli-pro" can make participating in civic and political life less intimidating. Pick an issue related to class, such as the preferred format for an exam or whether to take attendance. Take turns being chair and use the guide below to practice the basic steps required to pass a motion.

The basic five steps for passing a motion include the following:

Be recognized—It's important that a member of an organization first have the floor before presenting a motion or new order of business. This is typically done simply by the raise of a hand and recognition by the president or chair.

Motion is presented—The proper language you should use is, "I move that we . . . " An example of the correct language is simply, "I move that we [*insert specific details here*]."

Motion is seconded—The proper language is, "I second," or "I second the motion." Seconding a motion simply means that you are to move the item to discussion, seconding a motion does not necessarily indicate support.

Motion is discussed—Only motions that have been properly moved and seconded can be discussed. A common mistake in many meetings is that many ideas are discussed before any are presented in the form of a motion.

Vote is taken on motion—after an appropriate period of discussion, the chair should call for a vote for the motion on the floor. Voting can be conducted in several ways, a voice vote ("aye" or "nay"), by raising of hands, by roll call, or by secret ballot. Practice using all of these means of voting as each of you takes a turn at being chair.

KEY WORDS

First Wave 54

Glass ceiling 74

Lesbian feminism 73

Pay gap 63

Queer theorists 73

Relative deprivation 63

Second Wave 61

Sex-positive feminists 72

Social justice feminists 65

Trans-Exclusionary Radical
   Feminism 75

Transnational feminism 71

Womanist 71

REFERENCES

1. Langley, W. E., & Fox, V. C. (1994). *Women's rights in the United States: A documentary history*. Westport, CT: Greenwood Press.

2. Berkin, C. (1996). *First generations: Women in colonial America*. New York, NY: Hill and Wang.

3. Murphy, T. A. (2013). *Citizenship and the origins of women's history in the United States*. Philadelphia: University of Pennsylvania Press.

4. Williams, S. R. (1976). *Demeter's daughters: The women who founded America, 1587–1787*. New York, NY: Atheneum Books.

5. Berkin, C. (1996). *First generations: Women in colonial America*.

6. Ibid.

7. Ibid.

8. Langley, W. E., & Fox, V. C. (1994). *Women's rights in the United States: A documentary history.*

9. Beard, M. R. (1976). *Women as force in history: A study in traditions and realities.* New York, NY: Octagon Books.

10. Salmon, M. (2012). "The legal status of women 1790–1830." *The Gilder Lehrman Institute of American History.* Retrieved from https://www.gilderlehrman .org/history-by-era/womens-history/essays/legal-status-women-1776%E2%80%931830.

11. Buechler, S. M. (1990). *Women's movements in the United States: Woman suffrage, equal rights, and beyond.* New Brunswick, NJ: Rutgers University Press.

12. Murphy, T. A. (2013). *Citizenship and the origins of women's history in the United States,* p. 39.

13. Buechler, S. M. (1990). *Women's movements in the United States*

14. DuBois, E. Carol. 1998. *Woman suffrage and women's rights.* New York: New York University Press.

15. Buechler, S. M. (1990). *Women's movements in the United States.*

16. Orleck, A. (2015). *Rethinking American women's activism.* New York, NY: Routledge.

17. Stanton, E. C., Anthony, S. B., & Gage, M. J. (1889). *History of woman suffrage,* (Vol. 1. 2nd ed.). Charles Mann (Ed.). Rochester, NY: Authors.

18. Terborg-Penn, R. (1978). Discrimination against Afro-American women in the woman's movement, 1830–1920. In S. Harley & R. Terborg-Penn (Eds.), *The Afro-American women: Struggles and images.* Baltimore, MD: Black Classic Press.

19. Staples, B. (2018). How the suffrage movement betrayed black women. *New York Times.* Retrieved from https://www.nytimes.com/2018/07/28/opinion/ sunday/suffrage-movement-racism-black-women.html?fbclid=IwAR1ok_ WdEE78Sy78T2wglplco1RjaNHrP5Dscym4z0B110a98JNpmtF1aJM.

20. Buechler, S. M. (1990). *Women's movements in the United States: Woman suffrage, equal rights, and beyond.*

21. Wheeler, M. S. (1995). *One woman, one vote: Rediscovering women's suffrage.* Troutdale, OR: New Sage Press.

22. Banaszk, L. A. (1996). *Why movements succeed or fail: Opportunity, culture, and the struggle for woman suffrage.* Princeton, NJ: Princeton University Press.

23. Hoffert, S. D. (1995). *When hens crow: The woman's rights movement in antebellum America*. Bloomington, IN: Indiana University Press.

24. Ford, L. G. (1991). *Iron-jawed angels: The suffrage militancy of the national woman's party, 1912–1920*. Lanham, MD: University Press of America.

25. Terborg-Penn, R. (1995). African American women and the woman suffrage movement. In M. S. Wheeler (Ed.), *One woman, one vote: Rediscovering women's suffrage*. Troutdale, OR: New SAGE Press.

26. Wheeler, M. S. (1995). *One woman, one vote: Rediscovering women's suffrage*.

27. Ibid.

28. Orleck, A. (2015). *Rethinking American women's activism*.

29. Schweitzer, M. M. (1980, March). World War II and female labor force participation. *The Journal of Economic History, 40*(1), 89–95.

30. Fox, M. (2018). Naomi Parker Fraley, the real Rosie the Riveter, unrecognized for 7 decades, dies at 96. *New York Times*. Retrieved from https://www.nytimes.com/2018/01/22/obituaries/naomi-parker-fraley-the-real-rosie-the-riveter-dies-at-96.html.

31. Dicker, R. (2008). *A history of U.S. feminism*. Berkeley, CA: Seal Press.

32. Frieden, B. (1963). *The feminine mystique*. New York, NY: W.W. Norton and Company.

33. Buechler, S. M. (1990). *Women's movements in the United States: Woman suffrage, equal rights, and beyond*.

34. Murray, P., & Eastwood, M. O. (1965, December). Jane Crow and the law: Sex discrimination and Title VII. *George Washington Law Review, 34*(2), 232–256.

35. Orleck, A. (2015). *Rethinking American women's activism*.

36. President's Commission on the Status of Women. (1963). *American women: Report of the President's Commission on the Status of Women*. Washington, DC: U.S. Department of Labor.

37. Murray, P., & Eastwood, M. O. (1965). Jane Crow and the law: Sex discrimination and Title VII.

38. National Committee on Pay Equity. (2016). *The wage gap over time: In real dollars, women see a continuing gap*. Washington, DC: Author.

39. Buechler, S. M. (1990). *Women's movements in the United States: Woman suffrage, equal rights, and beyond*.

40. Hegewisch, A., & Williams-Baron, E. (2018). *The gender wage gap: 2017 earnings differences by race and ethnicity*. Retrieved from https://iwpr.org/wp-content/uploads/2018/03/C464_Gender-Wage-Gap-2.pdf.

41. Levanon, A., England, P., & Allison, P. (2009, December). Occupational feminization and pay: Assessing causal dynamics using 1950–2000 U.S. Census data. *Social Forces, 88*(2), 865–891.

42. Miller, C. C. (2016). As women take over a male-dominated field, the pay drops. *New York Times*. Retrieved from https://www.nytimes.com/2016/03/20/upshot/as-women-take-over-a-male-dominated-field-the-pay-drops.html.

43. Blau, F., & Kahn, L. M. (2001). Understanding international differences in the gender pay gap. *National Bureau of Economic Research*. Retrieved from http://www.nber.org/papers/w8200.

44. Kliff, S. (2018). A stunning chart shows the true cause of the gender pay gap. *Vox*. Retrieved from https://www.vox.com/2018/2/19/17018380/gender-wage-gap-childcare-penalty?fbclid=IwAR3PiPgSUyeFO-Tm1ko9dz0g-BjxQePmHhPzW961ot1klXnQUKLl5i8PF8w.

45. Klevin, H., Landais, C., & Sogaard, J. E. (1992). Children and gender inequality: Evidence from Denmark National Bureau of Economic Research. *National Bureau of Economic Research*. Retrieved from http://www.nber.org/papers/w24219.pdf.

46. Cobble, D. S., Gordon, L., & Henry, A. (2014). *Feminism unfinished: A short, surprising history of American women's movements*. New York, NY: W.W. Norton and Company.

47. Buechler, S. M. (1990). *Women's movements in the United States: woman suffrage, equal rights, and beyond*. New Brunswick, NJ: Rutgers University Press.

48. Orleck, A. (2015). *Rethinking American women's activism*.

49. Ibid., 106.

50. Hanisch, C. (1970). The personal is political. In S. Firestone & A Koedt, *Notes from the second year: Women's liberation*. New York, NY: New York Radical Women.

51. Crow, B. A. (2000). *Radical feminism: A documentary reader*. New York: New York University Press.

52. Orleck, A. (2015). *Rethinking American women's activism*.

53. Crow, B. A. (2000). *Radical feminism: A documentary reader*. New York, NY: New York University Press.

54. Hanisch, C. (1970). The personal is political.

55. Mansbridge, J. L. (1986). *Why we lost the ERA*. Chicago, IL: University of Chicago Press.

56. Mansbridge, J. L. (1990). Organizing for the ERA: Cracks in the façade of unity. In L. A. Tilly & P. Gurin (Eds.), *Women, politics, and change*. New York, NY: Russell Sage Foundation.

57. Mansbridge, J. L. (1986). *Why we lost the ERA*.

58. Ibid., 20.

59. Ibid.

60. Klatch, R. E. (1987). *Women of the new right*. Philadelphia, PA: Temple University Press.

61. Matthews, D. G., & De Hart, J. S. (1992). *Sex, gender, and the politics of the ERA: A state and the nation*. New York, NY: Oxford University Press.

62. National Center for Education Statistics. (2013). Table 318.10. Degrees conferred by degree-granting postsecondary institutions, by level of degree and sex of student: Selected years, 1869–70 through 2023–24. Retrieved from https://nces.ed.gov/programs/digest/d13/tables/dt13_318.10.asp.

63. Cobble, D. S., Gordon, L., & Henry, A. (2014). *Feminism unfinished: A short, surprising history of American women's movements*.

64. Orleck, A. (2015). *Rethinking American women's activism*.

65. Ibid.

66. MacKinnon, C. (1991). *Toward a feminist theory of the state*. Cambridge, MA: Harvard University Press.

67. Strossen, N. (1995). *Defending pornography*. New York, NY: Scribner.

68. hooks, b. (1984). *Feminist theory: From margin to center*. Boston, MA: South End Press.

69. Walker, A. (1983). *In search of our mothers' gardens: Womanist prose*. New York, NY: Harcourt.

70. Mohanty, C. T. (1984, Spring). Under Western eyes: Feminist scholarship and colonial discourses. *Boundary 2, 12/13*(3/1), 333–358.

71. Kang, M., Lessard, D., Heston, L., & Nordmarken, S. (2017). *Introduction to women, gender, and sexuality studies*. Amherst: University of Massachusetts Amherst Libraries.

72. Bagri, N. T. (2013). Where is India's feminist movement headed? *The New York Times*. Retrieved from https://india.blogs.nytimes.com/2013/03/08/where-is-indias-feminist-movement-headed.

73. Roychowdhury, A. (2018). International Women's Day 2018: Five mass movements spearheaded by women in India. *The Indian Express*. Retrieved from https://indianexpress.com/article/research/international-womens-day-2017-five-mass-movements-spearheaded-by-women-in-india-4559761.

74. Kurian, A. (2018). Millennial Indian women have been leading a new kind of feminism since the early 2000s, long before the present day feminist resurgence in the U.S. *The Wire*. Retrieved from https://thewire.in/gender/metoo-campaign-brings-the-rise-of-fourth-wave-feminism-in-india.

75. Susan, N. (2009). Why we said pants to India's bigots. *The Guardian*. Retrieved from https://www.theguardian.com/commentisfree/2009/feb/15/india-gender.

76. Bagri, N. T. (2013). Where is India's feminist movement headed.

77. Fisher, J. A. (2013). Today's feminism: A brief look at Third Wave feminism. Retrieved from https://beingfeministblog.wordpress.com/2013/05/16/todays-feminism-a-brief-look-at-third-wave-feminism.

78. Butler, J. (1990). *Gender trouble: Feminism and the subversion of identity*. New York, NY: Routledge Classics.

79. Orleck, A. (2015). *Rethinking American women's activism*.

80. Klatch, R. E. 1987. *Women of the new right*.

81. Dicker, R. (2008). *A history of U.S. feminism*.

82. Paglia, C. (1990). *Sexual personae: Art and decadence from Nerfetiti to Emily Dickinson*. New Haven: Yale University Press.

83. Roiphe, K. (1993). *The morning after: Fear, sex and feminism*. New York, NY: Little, Brown and Company.

84. Faludi, S. (1991). *Backlash: The undeclared war against American women*. New York, NY: Crown.

85. Rampton, M. (2008). Four waves of feminism. *Pacific Magazine*. Retrieved from https://www.pacificu.edu/about/media/four-waves-feminism.

86. Thompson, D. L. (2016). Third-wave feminism: A valid distinction. *Odyssey*. Retrieved from https://www.theodysseyonline.com/third-wave-feminism.

87. Raymond, J. (1979). *The Transsexual Empire: The Making of the She-Male*. Boston: Beacon Press.

88. Goldberg, M. (2014). What is a woman? *The New Yorker*. Retrieved from https://www.newyorker.com/magazine/2014/08/04/woman-2.

89. Ibid.

90. Hungerford, E. *Sex is not gender*. Retrieved from https://www.counterpunch.org/2013/08/02/sex-is-not-gender.

91. Ibid.

92. Munroe, E. (2018). Feminism: A fourth wave? *Political Insight*. Retrieved from https://www.psa.ac.uk/insight-plus/feminism-fourth-wave.

93. Cochrane, K. (2013). The fourth wave of feminism: Meet the rebel women. *The Guardian*. Retrieved from https://www.theguardian.com/world/2013/dec/10/fourth-wave-feminism-rebel-women.

94. Kang, M., Lessard, D., Heston, L., & Nordmarken, S. 2017. *Introduction to women, gender, and sexuality studies*.

95. Thompson, D. L. (2016). Third-wave feminism: A valid distinction.

96. Rampton, M. (2008). Four waves of feminism.

97. Kang, M., Lessard, D., Heston, L., & Nordmarken, S. (2017). *Introduction to women, gender, and sexuality studies*.

98. Rampton, M. (2008). Four waves of feminism.

99. Black Lives Matter. (n.d.). *Black Lives Matter*. Retrieved from https://blacklivesmatter.com/about.

100. Faludi, S. (2017). The patriarchs are falling. The patriarchy is stronger than ever. *The New York Times*. Retrieved from https://www.nytimes.com/2017/12/28/opinion/sunday/patriarchy-feminism-metoo.html

CHAPTER THREE

PUBLIC OPINION

"Why can't a woman vote more like a man?" opined Alexis Toufexis in a 1982 *Time Magazine* piece titled "Waking Up to the Gender Gap."[1] It seemed that the Republican Party had what they termed a GG (or a gender gap) problem that was receiving a great deal of attention. The **gender gap** (which actually describes a sex-based gap) refers to the difference in political opinion and behavior between men and women. Previously, many women had followed the voting patterns of their fathers and husbands, but times and voting patterns were changing, and pollsters were noticing a break between men's and women's public opinions and voting patterns. The Second Wave (discussed in Chapters 1 and 2) had taken place, and it seemed that for some women, previous opinions were not holding. This chapter deals with issues of public opinion and voting behavior in three areas. First, we examine how individuals form opinions about sex and gender issues and how ideas about gender influence public opinion. Second, we look at how sex influences public opinion. Finally, we explore how these opinions impact voting behavior.

Before we delve much further, certain terms need to be explored. **Sex** refers to the categories of male (men) and female (women) and the biological characteristics and properties of bodies placed in these categories.[2,3] While for many years we thought of sex as binary, that is, men and women, new research suggests that sex is not binary but rather fluid like gender.[4] Additionally, experts agree that anatomy does not determine one's gender.[5] That is, anatomy does not determine assignment as a female, male, or binary mixed-gendered individual. **Gender** is "the assignment of masculine and feminine characteristics to bodies in cultural contexts."[6] "Gender uncovers how women, men, and nonbinary people act according to expectations of what is feminine, masculine, and fluid, and it references what is expected of men and women,"[7] and "meanings of masculinity and femininity vary across cultures, over historical time."[8] Gender is **socially constructed**, as we discuss in Chapter 1. To say something is socially constructed means that it is an artifice of a given society. For example, in the United States, society associates the color pink with girls and the color blue with boys, although as Chapter 2 notes, this has not always been the case. This preference is socially constructed, that is, it is an artifact of American society and not based in any sort of objective reality.

Additionally, one's gender identity interacts with other personal identities, all the while interacting with gender structures. Thus, throughout the book, we attempt to elucidate intersectionality as it influences gender in political contexts. **Intersectionality**, as discussed in earlier chapters, references one's interacting identities, such as race, sex, gender, class, age, disability, and religion. Each identity "intersects" and produces specific life experiences, many of which are experiences of discrimination.[9] Thus, women of various ages, ethnicities, racial backgrounds, social backgrounds and religions may experience politics differently. As laid out in Chapters 1 and 2, this book follows Michael Kimmel's suggestion to "account [for] these different definitions of masculinity and femininity constructed and expressed by different groups of men and women."[10] That said, given the topic of the book, we prioritize the experiences and actions of women—and a variety of women—in given cultural and political contexts.

Public opinion refers to the aggregated opinions and beliefs held by a population, or the general population's thoughts on an issue. **Voting behavior** refers to voting patterns. Analysis of these patterns focuses on determining why people vote as they do and how they arrive at the decisions they make. Voting behavior is most definitely influenced by public opinion. Social scientists measure public opinion in a variety of ways, but the most common way is through **public opinion polls**, surveys conducted by individuals or groups to determine people's thoughts on particular issues. For example, if a politician from Arizona wanted to see what her constituents thought about banning abortions after 6 weeks gestation, she would ask a polling organization to conduct a poll asking people what their thoughts were. This poll might be conducted over the phone, by mail, by e-mail, or in person. A **polling organization** is a business that measures public opinion. Typically, polling organizations do this strategically through surveys using best practices. The best-known polling organization in the United States is the **Gallup Organization**. Other prominent polling organizations include Pew as well as news outlets like CNN, *New York Times*, CBS, and others.

BOX 3.1: THE GALLUP ORGANIZATION

The Gallup Organization was founded by George Gallup in 1935 as the American Institute of Public Opinion. He wanted to objectively determine public opinion and, from the beginning, refused money from organizations with entrenched interests in electoral outcomes, like the Democratic and Republican parties.[11] Gallup's interest in polling was sparked in 1932 when he conducted a poll for his mother-in-law, Ola Babcock Miller, who was running for Secretary of State in Iowa. Pundits' commentary held that Miller was a long shot for winning the race, but the polls told differently. She won in the 1932 Democratic wave that swept that election, making her Iowa's first woman Secretary of State.[12] In 1936, most newspapers were claiming that Alfred Landon would win the presidency, based on **straw polling** results. A straw poll is an unofficial, nonscientific ballot to test public opinion. In particular, the editors of the *Literary Digest* asked their readers to send in whom they planned to vote for in the 1936 presidential election. The 2 million responses they received pointed to a Landon win. You may be scratching your head saying, "Who is Alfred Landon?" Gallup, on the other hand, conducted a scientific poll of only 50,000 respondents and predicted Franklin D. Roosevelt (FDR) as the winner.[13] FDR is probably a name you have heard of, as Roosevelt went on to serve as President of the United States throughout World War II. Why did Gallup's poll succeed where *Literary Digest* failed? Gallup used scientific sampling methods. When races are close, it is easy to misinterpret polling data. For example, while national polling in 2016 accurately predicted Hillary Clinton's popular vote within the margin of error, many reporters used this data to predict that she would win without taking state-by-state polling and the impact of the Electoral College into account. While polling is not always correct, Gallup's 1936 poll cemented scientific public opinion polling into the American political landscape.

How does polling work? Legitimate polling organizations try to gather accurate statistics. That is, they want to make sure that they are truly measuring the opinions of a population. In order to do this, **pollsters** (people who run the polls) must make sure that questions are properly and objectively worded, that is, that the questions do not reflect the answer the pollster or person commissioning the poll wants to hear. For example, the politician from Arizona would not ask, "Don't you think it's wrong to kill a baby after 6 weeks in the womb?" Instead, it would be more appropriate to ask, "The government is considering banning abortions after six weeks gestation. Do you support this proposal? Why, or why not?" Polling organizations must also select a **polling sample**, which is a selection of people chosen to accurately reflect the overall population of a polling area. In the above example, the polling sample needs to accurately reflect the population of Arizona. In order to collect a poll, pollsters do not need to ask all people in a polling area their opinion. A much smaller random sample, where every member of the population being studied has an equal chance of being included as a respondent, will work just fine. If participants are truly selected at random, they will constitute a **representative sample**. This means that it has the same basic characteristics of the population. If it does not, then the pollster has introduced **sampling error**. For example, if Arizona is 30% Latinx, then the sample would need to also be 30% Latinx. In order to produce a sample that is representative of the entire population of the United States, a typical poll will sample approximately 1,000 to 1,500 people.

HOW INDIVIDUALS FORM OPINIONS ABOUT GENDER ISSUES

Theories of Public Opinion Formation

Having described how we measure public opinion, we now turn to what we know and have learned about sex, gender, and public opinion from these measures. Several theories exist that explain how individuals form opinions. In this section, we will provide a quick review of public opinion formation and then explore how this process specifically interacts with gender. We also examine how individuals, Americans in particular, form preferences about **gender issues**, that is, the appropriate roles and spaces for men and women, responses to systematic gender injustices, and the belief that men and women share a common fate. Much of the research around this topic draws upon psychological research or political psychology. In addition, political socialization and mass media, described later in the chapter, are thought to contribute to opinion formation in different ways. Political socialization is more likely to contribute to long-term **predispositions**, or "enduring, consistent ideas" about issues like "gender and gender relations that individuals possess."[14] Mass media plays upon predispositions to influence **policy views**, or short-term reactions to issues of the day.[15] While predispositions tend to be more stable, policy views can be more variable.

One of the first questions that emerges in this sort of discussion is "what constitutes a gender issue?"[16] Carroll (1985) suggested it is one that disproportionately and intentionally affects women.[17,18] These types of classifications, however, conflate sex and gender, making the two synonymous. Others worked to broaden the definition[19] of a gender issue, suggesting that it is any issue dealing with relationships between men and women (also conflating gender with sex), or with the representation of feminine traits.[20] Burns and Gallagher (2010) offer the most inclusive definition, explaining that issues are "about gender" when people use gendered tools or cultural ideas about gender to think about them.[21] Gender issues typically emerge from two categories of public policies: equity policies and role policies.[22,23] **Equity policies** are those that are put in place to encourage equal treatment of the sexes or genders.[24-26] In contrast, **role policies** argue for a full-scale restructuring of society and gender roles. For example, allowing cis women and trans people to serve in combat is a role change issue, while equal pay (discussed in Chapters 2, 8, and later in this chapter) is an equity issue. By and large, research suggests that there is higher support, that is, public opinion is more favorable, for equity policies than for role policies; and there is less of a sex gap in attitudes about changing roles than there is about promoting equity.

Political Socialization

Political socialization is the process whereby people develop attitudes, opinions, and beliefs about politics and learn how to be citizens within their political system.[27,28] We think of political socialization happening during childhood when young people develop an understanding of the political world through their interactions with adults. Through political socialization, people learn about politics, power, and the world around them and develop a sense of how they should act in the world. Political socialization also influences how individuals develop values and opinion.[29] While primary sources of socialization include direct interactions with parents, family, and teachers, media also play a role in political socialization. In fact, research shows that, as young as ages 5 to 6, children have come to believe gender is fixed, and gender differences between men and women are natural. Gender at this age becomes central to children's personal identity, as well as how they think of others.[30] We'll see in Chapter 4 how girls and boys are socialized differently, leading to possible differences in political ambition.

Mass Media

Mass media influence public opinion primarily through **agenda setting**, or the ability of media to influence the amount of attention given to particular topics. In other words, news outlets (aka **mass media**) like the Internet, television, newspapers, magazines, and so on, decide which stories to tell and which to ignore. These decisions influence the public agenda and help to shape public opinion, particularly the identification of which topics publics deem important. In the age of social media, opinion formation and agenda setting can become skewed as individuals tend to receive messaging only from people who think like they do. This tendency is why your Uncle Fred may have completely different "facts" about a particular social issue than you do; the information he is consuming is different because he is watching, reading, and accessing different media sources. Mass media and social media also frame stories. Frames present little tacit theories about what exists, what happens, and what matters, and they articulate how reality is defined and interpreted by various actors and institutions. In short, **framing** is the central organizing principle or storyline that prevails about a given topic.[31] Framing can have a large influence on shaping opinion. For example, if a politician votes for banning abortions past 6 weeks gestation, media can frame that act as "politician X votes against women" or as "politician X votes for babies." This is an extreme example but shows how important framing can be in influencing public opinion.

The media also play a role in influencing the social desirability of a policy. **Social desirability** is the idea that people form opinions based on what they believe is the prevalent opinion of groups with whom they identify and agree.[32] Social media, in particular, can repeat stories as "truth," thus influencing opinion. **Motivated cognition** describes the phenomenon of individuals (re)interpreting evidence from their own perspectives.[33] When the motivation is protecting in-group identity, such interpretations are referred to as **identity-protective cognition**[34] and are consistent with social identity theory. The desire to be internally consistent, to agree with the preferences of those who share important social and demographic identities, has a powerful influence on individual policy opinions. This need to conform is the reason why simply providing more facts to individuals will not change their minds, shift their opinions, or change their behavior. For example, motivated reasoning can help explain why no matter how valiantly you provide an in-depth, fact-based argument for equal pay at Thanksgiving dinner, your Uncle Fred may never be swayed. Framing can influence support as well by influencing the degree to which individuals see policies as threatening or inclusive to their worldviews and in-groups.[35] Importantly, other identities aside from sex and gender tend to dominate the identity-protective cognition of women; this affects their gender predispositions, an issue we turn to next.

Gender Predispositions

Predispositions are relevant for thinking about public opinion formation about gender issues. Particularly when we consider gender predispositions, we are talking about

1. views on motherhood and gender roles;

2. a sense of group **interdependence**—the extent to which individuals believe their life chances and outcomes are intertwined with others in their group—also called **linked fate**; and

3. an embrace of a **structural critique**—the idea and acknowledgement that inequality is socially constructed and sustained through systematic discrimination.

Motherhood Predispositions and Opinions About Gender

Views on motherhood shape opinions about roles and equity and are some of the most enduring predispositions to influence public opinion about gender. In fact, when women won the right to vote with the ratification of the Nineteenth Amendment to the U.S. Constitution, First Wave feminists hoped that women would support candidates who promoted "maternalist" policies, such as labor laws and housing and health subsidies, as we saw in Chapters 1 and 2. However, a "women's vote" never materialized, as parties did little to try to mobilize the "women's vote."

Political discourse often focuses on Soccer Moms and Hockey Moms (suburban married women with children), Walmart Moms (working class, often single mothers), and Security Moms (women with children who vote for strong defense or security policies), that is, those women whose identities don't extend beyond their children. The essentialist idea that women are suited for the home or that children must be "mothered" by cisgender women, can lead to acceptance of inequality among men, women, and the LGBTQIA+ community. Views on family roles have been evolving over time among the American public. For example, between 1977 and 1998 the percentage of people who disagreed or strongly disagreed that it was more important for a man to achieve outside the home while a woman took care of the home and family rose by 30 percentage points for both men and women, from close to 30% to 60% disagreement. Since the mid-1990s, however, we have seen a steady march back toward traditionalism, so that in 2014, just over 40% of respondents agreed with this statement.[36] It is likely that people socialized during the feminist activism that characterized the Second Wave of the women's movement are more committed to equality, while those who were socialized during the backlash against feminist activism that characterized the 1980s and 1990s are less supportive. In addition, failure to make changes in the workplace—where policies and expectations still assume employees are ideal workers with no responsibility for domestic work and child care—make it difficult to live up to egalitarian ideals in everyday life. For example, after experiencing how difficult it is to juggle paid and domestic work responsibilities without experiencing career setbacks, many Millennial-aged men, although initially egalitarian, revert back to a preference for traditional gender roles.[37] This is applicable to women as well. In an editorial, Valenti (2018) argues that efforts to make the term "feminism" less scary to younger women and mainstream had unintended consequences: Women in powerful positions who do not hold feminist values are held up by those with traditional or conservative values as manifesting feminism.[38]

Intersectionality plays a role here as well. For example, younger, more educated working women married to well-educated working men shifted toward egalitarian views on sex-roles in the 1970s. Conversely, women with large families with fundamentalist Christian identities never made this shift and continue to hold on to traditional views of the family.[39] That said, since the mid-1990s, the gap between these groups has remained rather steady, while *both* groups have moved toward traditionalism. Age is a major influence in opinion formation about gender roles among both men and women. Americans who came of age in 1996 to 2004 base partisanship and opinions about roles more on issues such as race and gender than older generations and are more likely to question traditional gender roles. In short, ideas about motherhood and gender roles can help to explain opinions on a variety of gender policies.

Interdependence, Structural Critique, and Opinion

Interdependence or a sense of linked fate can lead to a sense of anger about group mistreatment and pride in group accomplishments.[40–42] Linked fate is based on the idea that what happens to members of my group also influences me. Thus, "what happens to other women, also influences what happens to me." Together with

▶ **Photo 3.1** Anti-Trump protests.

a structural critique, a sense of interdependence leads to consciousness of a group. The idea of structural critique finds its roots in Karl Marx.[43] Marx argued that class struggle requires both the existence of objective classes in society and the development of consciousness. This consciousness-raising then means that groups can agitate toward a common goal. We saw this consciousness-raising take form during First, Second, and to a lesser extent, Third Wave feminism, as covered in Chapter 2. We have also seen it recently in the Women's Marches and their outgrowths since the election of Donald Trump in 2016. The #MeToo movement of 2017 to 2018 can also be considered a form of consciousness raising about harassment universally experienced by women, girls, and femme-identified individuals (more on #MeToo in Chapter 9).

There are complications that come with conceptualizing women as a group.[44] Thus, linked fate translates for women and gender issues less powerfully than it does for a racial group. In short, women as a whole are less likely to report a sense of linked fate than those in racial/ethnic groups, concepts we discussed in Chapters 1 and 2. This does not mean that interdependence is not important in shaping public opinion. For example, Sears and Huddy (1986) found that interdependence among women was the most influential variable in views on women's issues such as childcare, affirmative action, and social services.[45] Belief in linked fate was also found to be a predictor of support for Geraldine Ferraro's vice-presidential candidacy in 1984, and over 20 years later, was an important predictor in determining support for Hillary Clinton over Bernie Sanders.[46] At least among Democratic women, at every age group, women agreed that what happens to women in general impacts them personally.[47] While interdependence rarely matters for men, it does influence women's opinions.

Opinions About Differences Between Men and Women

Pew, a major U.S. polling agency, conducted a poll in the United States in 2017 asking Americans about differences between men and women. Most Americans say that men and women are different in terms of expression of feelings (87%), physical abilities (76%), hobbies and personal interests (68%), and approach to parenting (64%).[48] Of respondents, 63% say that men and women are similar in terms of what workplace skills they have. Pew also asked whether or not people thought these differences were rooted in biology or were socially constructed.[49] The only clear area where we see opinion that sex differences are biological is in physical abilities. In contrast, while majorities of respondents think men and women express feelings differently, a majority (58%) point to the reason as societal expectations rather than biological;[50] however, women were more likely than men to point to social constructions as the reason for differences. For example, while majorities of respondents thought men and women were good at the same things in the workplace, among those who do see a difference, 65% of women say they are mostly based on differences in societal expectations. Conversely, 61% of men who think men and women are good at different workplace tasks say that the reason is biological. Interestingly, Republicans are more likely to see differences between men and women than Democrats, across all the categories.[51] Additionally, "about half of Americans (49%) say society isn't accepting enough of women taking on roles that are typically associated with men, while 36% say society is about right, and 14% say it is too accepting of women doing this. Similarly, 46% say society is not accepting enough of men taking on roles that are typically associated with women; 39% say it is about right, and 14% say it is too accepting."[52] These views vary by sex and party identification, with 58% of women saying society isn't accepting enough of women taking on roles associated with men and 53% of women saying the same thing about men taking on traditionally female roles. Only 39% and 38% of men say that society should be more accepting of women and men, respectively, taking on roles traditionally assigned to the opposite sex.[53]

Hostile sexism pits men and women against each other, seeing men and women locked in a "battle of the sexes" or a zero-sum game. Defined as a "set of attitudes that are antagonistic toward women and stem from a belief that women want to control men," hostile sexists are contrasted with **benevolent sexists** who have a set of beliefs that come from ideas that women should be protected by men.[54] The consequences of hostile sexism along with benevolent sexism—the belief that women are communal, other-oriented, and need protection—and **ambivalent sexism**—the combination of these attitudes—are further described in Chapter 4. Cassese, Barnes, and Holman (2018) attempted to measure hostile sexism in society.[55] About 13% of respondents held hostile sexist views; 17% did not, and the remaining 70% fell somewhere in the middle. Interestingly, among those with very high levels of hostile sexism, men (51%) and women (49%) score similarly. Republican men and women are more likely than Democratic men and women to hold these views. Among women, white women are most likely to hold hostile sexist views, even when controlling for party.[56] This also predicts women's support for Donald Trump. Hostile sexism is dangerous because it can be manipulated and activated through political discourse. Cassese et al. (2018) found that hostile sexists became stronger supporters of Donald Trump when reading stories that said Hillary Clinton played "the woman card."[57] Additionally, in experimental work, they found that "those who scored high in hostile sexism were more likely to want to punish a female candidate for alleged sexual misconduct than people who scored low on hostile sexism—but that scandal had no effect on their opinions toward a male candidate."[58] This can also explain why some Republicans were energized by the Brett Kavanaugh Supreme Court hearings. For hostile sexists, the allegations of sexual assault were viewed as a he said–she said debate where women were trying to elevate themselves over men, thus energizing their support for Kavanaugh and Donald Trump by extension as the one who nominated him. In fact, Kavanaugh's angry response mirrored hostile sexists' own response to such events, thus garnering him greater favor among this subset of the population. The rise of misogynistic "incel" (involuntarily celibate) communities on the Internet is an example of hostile sexism at its most extreme. Members of such hate groups believe that they are entitled to sex with women of their choice and that they would have had access to desirable sexual partners if not for women's empowerment. In some instances, their online discussions of how to punish the women who reject them have led to acts of domestic terrorism targeting women. Examples include college student Elliot Rodger, who killed six people in May 2014, including two members of a campus sorority that he targeted for rejecting him, and Scott Paul Beierle, who killed two people in a November 2018 attack on a Tallahassee yoga studio.[59]

We also see predispositions toward gender influence opinions about LGBTQIA+ communities. In the early 2000s, Herek (2002) found that attitudes toward lesbians differed from attitudes toward gay men in several areas, and significant differences were observed between men and women heterosexual respondents.[60] Heterosexual men and women were more likely to believe gay men were mentally ill and less likely to support adoption rights for gay men than for lesbian women. Herek (2002) did find difference in opinion based on sex.[61] Heterosexual women were more supportive than heterosexual men of employment protection and adoption rights for gay people, more willing to extend employee benefits to same-sex couples, and less likely to hold stereotypical beliefs about gay people. This difference was primarily driven by heterosexual men's negative reactions to gay men. This reaction suggests cisgender straight men are often influenced by **hegemonic masculinity**, which is defined as a hyper masculinity that embraces all the stereotypical and expected ways of "being a man" (rational, powerful, controlling) and uses this identity to privilege men's position in society in relation to women.

BOX 3.2: COMPARATIVE FEATURE

Attitudes and Outcomes of Gender Equality

On November 2, 2017, the World Economic Forum released the Global Gender Gap Report, ranking countries across the globe on equity and equality for women (see Table 3.1 for top 20 and bottom 20 countries).[62] Western Europe fairs the best at equality of outcome, while the Middle East and North Africa fair poorly. The United States ranks 48th out of 144 countries.[63] The report focuses on *economic participation and opportunity* (i.e., women's to men's income, wage equality, and top level employment), *educational attainment* (i.e., women's literacy and women's to men's educational achievement at each level of education), *health and survival* (i.e., life expectancy, "missing women," and birth/death rates), and *political empowerment* (i.e., participation in decision making and office holders).

Progress on achieving equality of outcomes for men and women worldwide is slow and is intimately related to opinions on equality. While we see outcomes related to equality vary, more than half of the citizens in all countries believe in the principle of equality, with the exception of Burkina Faso.[64] Not surprisingly, women more than men were most likely to hold this sentiment. In Europe, 86% say equality between men and women is important. This is similar to opinions held in Latin America. The Middle East and Africa at 48% and 50%, respectively, have much lower percentages of their populations saying sex-based equality is important. Worldwide, women, individuals on the political left, and the more educated are more likely to say that equality between the sexes is important.[65]

In the United States, 91% say that such equality is important.[66] Interestingly, there is not much of a difference between men's and women's opinions: 93% of American women and 90% of American men say equality between the sexes is important. This does not mean pluralities of Americans think equality has been achieved. Satisfaction with progress on equality varies by party identification. Of Democrats, 69% say the country hasn't gone far enough when it comes to giving women equal rights. Among Republicans, 54% say things are about right when it comes to equality, and only 26% say there is more work to be done.[67] In the United States, women are also more likely than men to say that the country does not have equality between the sexes. In addition, opinion polls show that Democratic men are more likely to support such equality than Republican women. In fact, Democratic men are 31 percentage points more likely to say the country has not gone far enough to promote sex-based equality than Republican women.[68]

(Continued)

(Continued)

At the top of the equality scale, attitudes in Iceland are similar to the United States. Over 96% of Icelandic women and 91% of Icelandic men believe equality between the sexes is important.[69] Iceland leads the world in having the most equality of outcomes for women. In Pakistan, 52% of men and 76% of women say that the principle of equality is very important.[70] When we look at equality of outcomes, however, Pakistan is at the bottom of the world, only beating out war-torn Yemen. Next, we discuss the cases of Iceland and Pakistan in a bit more depth.

Iceland

Why is Iceland the most equal country in the world? First, we can look to historical answers. Iceland has always been a seafaring country, and when the men were away, the women took over traditional male roles such as hunter, builder, farmer, and at some points in history, defender of the land.[71] Thus, from an early point in history, the "strong woman" was part of the national discourse and influenced attitudes toward sex-based equality. As early as 1850, the women of Iceland fought and won equal rights of inheritance; in 1881, women were allowed to vote in local and parish elections, although it wasn't until 1917 that women won equal rights to vote.[72] The "Women's Day Off" strike that took place on October 24, 1975 had a major impact on advancing women's equality in Iceland. On this day, over 90% of women in the population disengaged from all activities so their men counterparts could recognize them as "indispensable" and address wage and unfair pay practices.[73]

Wiki Commons, national archive public domain
https://commons.wikimedia.org/wiki/Category:Vigd%C3%ADs_Finnbogad%C3%B3ttir#/media/File:Vigdis_Finnbogadóttir_(1985).jpg

▸ **Photo 3.2** Vigdís Finnbogadóttir.

The Women's Day Off was the antecedent to Icelandic women voting their first woman president into office, Vigdís Finnbogadóttir, who happened to be a divorced single mother; she served in office for over 16 years.[74]

By 2009, Iceland had elected its first woman prime minister, who also happened to be the first openly gay head-of-government.[75] Having women in power allowed sweeping legislative changes to take place, increasing demand for equal pay for equal work. Additionally, Iceland made profiting off nudity and prostitution illegal; was at the forefront of same-sex and nonbinary gender issues making changing names on documents legal; and began to close the gaps in terms of management positions and broadcast television spearheaded by women.[76] Both women and men in Iceland have access to socialized healthcare and the opportunity to use up to 90 days each of maternity and paternity leave with an option for an additional 30 days that can be split in any way they see fit.[77] Since the beginning of the Global Gender Gap Report in 2006, Iceland has closed the economic gender gap by approximately 10% (as of 2018), making it one of the fastest improving countries in the world.[78]

Pakistan

Taking the 143rd position on the Global Gender Gap Report is Pakistan. While Pakistan has made some progress in women's basic literacy and labor force participation, they often reverse policy on issues such as equal wages and access to higher education for women.[79] Women won the right to vote in Pakistan in 1956; nevertheless, barriers such as religion and proper identification stand in the way of exercising it.[80] Though allowed to work, women and men are segregated by occupation, and employees in industries where women predominate are paid less than their men counterparts.[81]

Women have very little control over finances in Pakistan unless they are retail shop owners, beauty parlor owners, or seamstresses, which grants them access to banking and mobile phones for banking purposes.[82] Opening a bank account, engaging with institutions, and conducting transactions are typically tasks done by men.[83] Thus, while opinions related to equality between men and women are not as low in Pakistan as we see in some other countries, policies to improve equality for women are lacking, and opportunities for women in education and the workforce are not equal to those of men.[84] Women only represent 3% of the legislators and senior officials in power, and even in these governmental roles, their positions are often viewed more as tokenism than as positions of actual authority.[85]

The difference between Icelandic and Pakistani women can be summed up in their agency. Women in Iceland have, and have historically had, access to media on a global scale and therefore are able to "shame" their country for inequality or coordinate strikes on a global stage that grants them equal treatment.[86] Voice combined with media have been a powerful tool for the women of Iceland—not only by enacting change but placing themselves on the international radar and putting themselves in positions of power to ensure gaps between men and women are closed. The opposite is true for the women of Pakistan, where many of the avenues to equality—such as calling out men politicians or refusing to do domestic work—can result in "dishonor" to the family.[87]

(Continued)

Table 3.1 Global Equality Rankings, 2017

Country	Global Index		Economic Participation and Opportunity		Educational Attainment		Health and Survival		Political Empowerment	
	Rank	Score	Rank	Score	Rank	Score	Rank	Score	Rank	Score
Iceland	1	0.878	14	0.798	57	0.995	114	0.969	1	0.750
Norway	2	0.830	8	0.816	38	0.999	80	0.973	4	0.530
Finland	3	0.823	16	0.793	1	1.000	46	0.978	5	0.519
Rwanda	4	0.822	7	0.820	113	0.951	1	0.980	3	0.539
Sweden	5	0.816	12	0.809	37	0.999	112	0.969	8	0.486
Nicaragua	6	0.814	54	0.702	34	1.000	1	0.980	2	0.576
Slovenia	7	0.805	13	0.801	1	1.000	1	0.980	11	0.440
Ireland	8	0.794	50	0.710	1	1.000	96	0.971	6	0.493
New Zealand	9	0.791	23	0.768	43	0.998	115	0.969	12	0.430
Philippines	10	0.790	25	0.764	1	1.000	36	0.979	13	0.416

11	France	0.778	64	0.683	1	1.000	54	0.9777	9	0.453
12	Germany	0.778	43	0.720	98	0.970	70	0.975	10	0.447
13	Namibia	0.777	9	0.813	41	0.999	1	0.980	26	0.318
14	Denmark	0.776	36	0.728	1	1.000	95	0.971	16	0.406
15	United Kingdom	0.770	53	0.705	36	0.999	100	0.971	17	0.404
16	Canada	0.769	29	0.744	1	1.000	105	0.970	20	0.361
17	Bolivia	0.758	60	0.692	108	0.956	69	0.976	14	0.408
18	Bulgaria	0.756	51	0.710	80	0.990	36	0.979	23	0.346
19	South Africa	0.756	89	0.652	64	0.993	1	0.980	18	0.399
20	Latvia	0.756	15	0.798	1	1.000	1	0.980	41	0.246
21	Switzerland	0.755	31	0.743	63	0.993	90	0.972	28	0.314
(United States Comparative)										
48	Peru	0.719	98	0.632	82	0.988	49	0.978	33	0.277
49	United States	0.718	19	0.776	1	1.000	82	0.973	96	0.124
50	Zimbabwe	0.717	49	0.710	89	0.986	68	0.976	62	0.197

(Continued)

(Continued)

Country	Global Index		Economic Participation and Opportunity		Educational Attainment		Health and Survival		Political Empowerment	
	Rank	Score	Rank	Score	Rank	Score	Rank	Score	Rank	Score
Bottom 20:										
Fiji	125	0.638	127	0.479	71	0.991	36	0.979	105	0.104
Bahrain	126	0.632	120	0.537	75	0.991	136	0.961	137	0.037
Algeria	127	0.629	132	0.442	107	0.957	106	0.970	86	0.145
Timor-Leste	128	0.628	136	0.393	117	0.934	43	0.979	60	0.205
Kuwait	129	0.628	125	0.518	52	0.996	117	0.969	141	0.027
Qatar	130	0.626	122	0.523	33	1.000	127	0.965	143	0.016
Turkey	131	0.625	128	0.471	101	0.965	59	0.977	118	0.088
Mauritania	132	0.614	134	0.417	131	0.853	107	0.970	57	0.214
Cote d'Ivoire	133	0.611	115	0.575	137	0.800	121	0.968	108	0.102
Egypt	134	0.608	135	0.413	104	0.960	99	0.971	119	0.087

Jordan	135	0.604	138	0.377	51	0.996	113	0.969	126	0.075
Morocco	136	0.598	137	0.391	122	0.920	128	0.965	100	0.117
Lebanon	137	0.596	133	0.440	109	0.956	109	0.970	142	0.019
Saudi Arabia	138	0.584	142	0.320	96	0.975	130	0.965	124	0.077
Mali	139	0.583	126	0.518	140	0.741	139	0.956	99	0.118
Iran, Islamic Rep.	140	0.583	140	0.357	100	0.965	135	0.963	136	0.046
Chad	141	0.575	77	0.667	144	0.572	73	0.974	120	0.087
Syria	142	0.568	144	0.274	110	0.956	1	0.980	130	0.063
Pakistan	143	0.546	143	0.309	136	0.802	140	0.948	95	0.127
Yemen	144	0.516	141	0.345	141	0.737	119	0.968	144	0.014

Source: The Global Gender Gap Report 2017, World Economic Forum.

HOW SEX INFLUENCES PUBLIC OPINION

Gender Gap: Policy Opinions

The gap between men and women, that is, the persistent differences in the political opinions of men and women, have been found in extant survey data dating to the 1960s and even earlier.[88-91] Differences in attitudes about war, foreign policy, the use of force, capital punishment, gun control, and some social welfare policies have been stable over time.[92-98] On the whole, when examining social survey data going back to the 1970s, research shows that women's views about politics remain more stable, while men's views are more likely to fluctuate.[99] That is, if women move just a little bit in opinion to the right or the left on an issue, men will move more percentage points.[100] This **asymmetry** (not moving at the same rate) in movement causes the gap to increase and decrease based on the variability in men's opinions and the stability in women's. Surprisingly, it does not appear that "women's issues," like abortion rights or the Equal Rights Amendment (ERA), drive the gap. Women and men have similar opinions about abortion and the ERA.[101] This seems counterintuitive, but Barkan (2014) argues that women are more religious than men.[102] Thus, religiosity serves to suppress the difference that we would expect to show up between men and women over abortion. When religiosity is controlled (i.e., taken into account), the expected difference between men and women appears. On the whole, research suggests that men tend to be ideologically more conservative than women. But as noted elsewhere and explained later in the chapter, this pattern could be due to intersecting identities of race and sex for women of color, as people of color tend to be more liberal and Democratic.[103]

BOX 3.3: POLICY FEATURE

Gender Differences About Attitudes on Terrorism

When we consider the relationship between public opinion and terrorism, we can consider many aspects including investigating how publics respond to terrorism and how responses influence support for certain counterterrorism policies.[104] Studies show that terrorism influences the emotions and mental health of those witnessing it, and public opinion data show that emotions influence policy preferences.[105-108] Anxiety promotes preferences for isolationism and less aggressive foreign policy.[109-111] Anger causes citizens to prefer policies associated with force.[112] Media, as discussed earlier, influences emotional responses and opinions particularly when it comes to fear through framing. This is because media emphasize the dangerous nature of terrorism and provide terrorists with a large audience for their extremist messages.[113-117]

In experimental settings, inducing fear by way of media leads respondents to be more supportive of hawkish (promilitary force) foreign policy.[118-120] Public opinion data also suggest that women display more fear and depression related to terrorism than do men.[121,122] Women also report more stress and experience anxiety and anger following attacks as well as more mental illness and depression.[123-127] This is because social norms (i.e., socialization discussed earlier) may make it more acceptable for women than men to express fear.[128,129] Additionally, women are more worried about personal victimization in many aspects of life, thus they also may feel more victimized by terrorism.[130,131] Previous research has shown that women generally express less hawkish opinions than men in terms of foreign policy, and they prefer less use of force or antimilitarism.[132-139] For example, Eichenberg (2016) found sex differences in support of major wars among Americans between 1982 and 2013, with men generally being more supportive of war than women.[140] Women tend to be more sensitive to casualties than men, thus depressing their support for war when they hear people have been killed.[141,142] This pattern is not static; however, in the wars in Iraq and Afghanistan, men's sensitivity to casualties increased over time, and thus the gap between sexes decreased.[143] The gap between men's and women's military support shows up in other countries as well (such as Germany, the U.K., and Canada).[144] While research suggests that there is a sex-based gap in terms of opinions related to military involvement in conflicts, including combating of terrorism, new research is nuancing our understanding of this relationship. Newer research by Mendez, Poloni-Staudinger, Ortbals, and Osborn (2016) found that fear associated with terrorism is so great that traditional gender differences in public opinion related to militarism and force break down,[145] with both men and women likely to support military action at similar levels of fear.[146] Additionally, women tend to be more fearful of terrorism, and this fear can be so great that they are often even *more likely* than men to support military action.[147] Thus, intense fear mimics anger in support of hawkish policies. The Mendez et al. study examines whether or not the sex of the terrorist also influences public opinion, showing that Americans react similarly to men and women terrorists as well as to mothers and fathers who are terrorists.[148]

Studies out of Western Europe, Canada, and Australia consistently find (at least since the 1980s) that women are more leftist in their issue preferences than men.[149] Women are also more supportive of feminist values, welfare state policies, and social spending, and less supportive of market-based solutions than men.[150-153] Women tend to be more likely to support humanitarian aid and less likely to support military interventions as discussed in the earlier policy feature on terrorism.[154] Given these differences, elections that highlight social welfare issues or security/military issues may yield larger gaps between men and women in vote outcomes.[155]

In 2012 and 2016, Pew conducted polls to assess sex differences in policy priorities in the 2012 and 2016 U.S. presidential elections. The results can be found in Table 3.2. In 2016, while nearly equal numbers of men and women said the economy was "very important" to their vote (83% and 85%, respectively), on other issues men and women diverged. The largest difference was with those saying "treatment of racial and ethnic minorities" was "very important" to their vote with 69% of women and 56% of men agreeing with this; abortion with 52% of women and 38% of men saying this was "very important to their vote" (note, this does not mean that men and women have different opinions on abortion as noted, simply that they prioritize its importance differently); and "treatment of gay, lesbian, and transgendered people" with 49% of women and 32% of men saying this was "very important" to their vote. This also illustrates how the gap between the sexes can fluctuate over time.

Race also intersects with sex to influence public opinion in part because lived experiences are different for racial minorities than for white people, no matter their sex.

Table 3.2 Priorities of Women and Men in the 2012, 2016 U.S. Elections

Issue	2012		2012 Gender Gap	2016		2016 Gender Gap
	Women	Men		Women	Men	
	88	85	3	83	85	2
Terrorism	60	57	3	78	82	4
Health Care	80	69	11	71	77	6
Gun Policy	50	44	6	69	74	5
Foreign Policy	52	51	1	74	76	2
Immigration	42	42	0	71	69	2
Treatment of Racial/ Ethnic Minorities	not asked	not asked	not asked	69	56	13
Education	79	65	14	69	63	6
Social Security	not asked	not asked	not asked	68	65	3
Supreme Court	not asked	not asked	not asked	64	66	2
Environment	55	46	9	57	47	10
Abortion	34	44	10	52	38	14
Trade Policy	not asked	not asked	not asked	52	62	10
Treatment of LGBTQ	not asked	not asked	not asked	59	32	27

Source: Data derived from Pew Research Center Staff (2012; July 7 2016; July 28 2016).
Data entered as percentages.

Black men are far more likely than white men to say their sex has made it harder for them to get ahead in life (20% vs. 5%, respectively). Similar shares of Black women (28%) and white women (27%) say their sex has set them back.[156] Thus, we tend to see gaps between Black men and women that are smaller than between white men and women.

Interestingly, Jensen (2014) found that many of the sex-based gaps that exist in the broader population disappear or reverse direction among sexual minorities.[157] "LGB men and women are more likely than straight men and women to hold liberal political views, to identify as Democrats, and to support policies that favor sexual minorities, such as legal recognition of same-sex relationships, allowing LGB men and women to serve openly in the military, and protection against employment discrimination on the basis of sexuality."[158–164] There are fewer studies about sexual minorities than those that look at the gap between men and women in part because the General Social Survey (GSS) began to measure sexual identity only in 2008; thus, data is relatively new. That said, it is important to understand that sexual orientation can intersect with sex to influence opinion.

BOX 3.4: COMPARATIVE FEATURE

Abortion Rights Around the World

Abortion policies around the world can range from complete bans to unfettered access. Most countries fall somewhere in between. Tables 3.3, 3.4, 3.5, 3.6, and 3.7 categorize countries according to their abortion policies. Two countries, Canada and Poland, provide interesting cases for further analysis, as well as an interesting comparison to U.S. policies. Canada is a country that has gradually loosened abortion restriction over time to have one of the least restrictive policies in the world. Poland, on the other hand, has increasingly restricted abortion access, making its policy one of the most restrictive in Europe.

Table 3.3   Abortion Prohibited Altogether
Andorra
Angola
Congo (Brazzaville)
Democratic Republic of the Congo
Dominican Republic
Egypt

(Continued)

(Continued)

El Salvador
Gabon
Guinea-Bissau
Haiti
Honduras
Iraq
Madagascar
Marshall Islands
Mauritania
Nicaragua
Palau
Philippines
Senegal
Suriname

Table 3.4 Abortion Allowed to Save a Woman's Life

Afghanistan
Antigua and Barbuda
Bangladesh
Bhutan
Brazil
Cote D'Ivoire
Central African Republic
Chile
Dominica
Guatemala
Indonesia
Iran
Kiribati
Lao People's Democratic Republic
Lebanon
Libya

Mali
Myanmar
Mexico
Nigeria
Oman
Panama
Papua New Guinea
Somalia
Solomon Islands
South Sudan
Sri Lanka
Sudan
Syria
Tanzania
Timor-Leste
Uganda
United Arab Emirates
Venezuela
West Bank and Gaza Strip
Yemen

Table 3.5 Abortion Allowed to Preserve Health (Not Just in Case of Certain Fatality)
Algeria
Argentina
Barbados
Benin
Bolivia
Botswana
Burkina Faso
Burundi
Cameroon

(Continued)

(Continued)

Chad
Colombia
Costa Rica
Djibouti
Ecuador
Equatorial Guinea
Eritrea
Ethiopia
Gambia
Ghana
Guinea
Jamaica
Kenya
Lesotho
Liberia
Liechtenstein
Mauritius
Monaco
Morocco
Namibia
Niger
North Ireland
Peru
Poland
Republic of Korea
Rwanda
Saudi Arabia
Seychelles
Sierra Leone
St. Kitts and Nevis

| St. Lucia |
| St. Vincent and Grenadines |
| Swaziland |
| Togo |
| Trinidad and Tobago |
| Zimbabwe |

Table 3.6 Abortion Allowed on Socioeconomic Grounds

| Belize |
| Cyprus |
| Fiji |
| Finland |
| Great Britain |
| Iceland |
| India |
| Japan |
| Taiwan |
| Zambia |

Table 3.7 No Restriction on Abortions

Country	Caveat
Albania	Parental authorization
Austria	Gestational limit of 14 weeks
Belgium	Gestational limit of 14 weeks
Bosnia-Herzegovina	Parental authorization
Canada	Law does not indicate gestational limit; regulatory mechanisms vary
Croatia	Parental authorization
Cuba	Parental authorization Required

(Continued)

(Continued)

Czech Republic	Parental authorization
Denmark	Parental authorization
France	Gestational limit of 14 weeks
French Guiana	None
Germany	Gestational limit of 14 weeks
Greece	Parental authorization
Greenland	Parental authorization
Guyana	Gestational limit of 8 weeks
Hungary	None
Ireland	Gestational limit of 12 weeks (as of May 2018)
Italy	Gestational period of 90 Days
Kosovo	Parental authorization, sex selective, gestational limit of 10 weeks
Montenegro	Parental authorization
Netherlands	Law does not limit previability abortion
Norway	Parental authorization
Portugal	Parental authorization, gestational limit of 10 weeks
Puerto Rico	Law does not limit previability abortion
Serbia	Parental authorization
Slovak Republic	Parental authorization
Slovenia	Parental authorization
Spain	Parental authorization, gestational limit of 14 weeks
Sweden	Gestational limit of 18 weeks
Switzerland	None
United States of America	Federal system, parental authorization required in some states
Uruguay	Parental authorization

Canada. Abortion in Canada is legal at all stages of pregnancy, and Canada is one of the only countries with no legal restrictions on abortion, although there is some variability by provinces.[165] The procedure is also publicly funded under the Canadian Health Act.[166] Canada's abortion policy was not always so open. Prior to 1969, all abortion was illegal until Pierre Trudeau's Liberal government legalized abortion, provided a committee of doctors signed off on the procedure. The Canadian Supreme Court ruled in R. v Morgentaler in 1988 that the existing laws were unconstitutional, striking down the 1969 law. The government at that time, led by the Progressive Conservatives, tried to pass a new abortion law but failed. Ever since, Canada has had no criminal laws governing the subject, and abortion is a decision made by a woman with her doctor. Most abortions in Canada are done in early stages and have been decreasing over time.[167] In a recent poll, 77% of Canadians believe that abortion should be legal;[168] 53% of Canadians said the procedure should be permitted whenever a woman decides she wants it; and 24% favor some limits.[169] Interestingly, while Canada has some of the least restrictive abortion policies in the world, other countries show higher rates of support for legal abortion. France, Sweden, and Belgium all have support rates around 87%. Only 5% of Canadians believe that abortion should never be allowed. Just as in the United States, there is little difference between men and women on the abortion issue.[170]

Poland. While Canada provides a case where abortion policy has become increasingly less restrictive over time (a common pattern among democracies), Poland presents the opposite case. Abortion in Poland has become more restrictive over time to the point where Poland has among the most restrictive abortion policy in the European Union. (Interestingly, a similar chipping away of abortion rights has happened in the United States.) Under communism, abortion in Poland was completely legal for over 4 decades. Once the country transitioned to a post-communist state (1990), policies gradually became more restrictive. The current policy was adopted in 1993 and states that abortion is banned except when the woman's life or health is endangered by the continuation of pregnancy, the pregnancy is the result of a criminal act, or when the fetus is seriously malformed. Abortions in these instances may only be performed within the first 12 weeks of pregnancy.[171] Consent of a doctor is required for determining fetal malformation or health endangerment, and prosecutors must certify if the pregnancy was the result of a crime (rape). Persuading a woman to have an abortion is also an illegal act.[172] The 1993 law was considered a "compromise" position between the communist era policy and those who wanted a complete abortion ban.[173] Even though Poland has the most restrictive abortion policies in Europe (excepting Malta and the Vatican), the policy continues to be debated. In 2011, 2015, and 2016, various proposals were introduced into the Polish parliament to ban abortion all together and to institute tough sentences for anyone who performed or received an abortion.[174]

(Continued)

(Continued)

Far-right political parties have even run on introducing an amendment to the Polish constitution that would ban abortions in all instances. Why is abortion so restrictive in Poland? Even though Poland was communist from the end of World War II until 1990, religion was not wiped out in the country. In fact, today 95% of people in Poland identify as Catholic. This high level of religiosity coupled with far-right political leadership, to the extent that some now characterize Poland as having an authoritarian as opposed to a democratic government, helps to explain the policy. The move to make a restrictive abortion policy even more restrictive led to many women taking to the streets in Poland in 2016 in what is known as the Black Protest.[175] On April 4, 2016, women and men across Poland walked out of mass when priests read the Catholic Church's position on the ban. The protest was "against open and direct church involvement in politics, and especially the perception that the Church is exploiting social tensions and political conflict to attain its goals,"[176] and in fact forced the government to withdraw its plans for a complete ban. This does not mean that the Polish population favors less restrictive abortion policies. In fact, public opinion in Poland is against abortion. A 2014 poll found 65% of respondents thought abortion was "morally inappropriate."[177] Opinion may be shifting, however, as a 2017 poll found 51% of Poles thought abortion should be illegal in most or all cases, with 41% wanting it legalized for most or all situations.[178] As of 2017, the 1993 law still stands, and the topic continues to be debated in the parliament. The restrictive nature of Polish abortion policy means that most women in Poland who can afford to will travel in order to seek abortions.

The United States. By 1880, abortion—once openly practiced in the United States up through the pregnancy stage called "quickening"—was banned in most U.S. states except to save the mother's life. Even when it was illegal, women still sought out abortions, often sharing information through personal networks about where to obtain one (sometimes from well-trained doctors and sometimes from unqualified hacks).[179] In response, early Second Wave feminist groups like the Abortion Counseling Service of the Chicago Women's Liberation Union or the Citizen Committee for Humane Abortion Laws in San Francisco undertook illegal activities including referring women to safe alternatives; training lay-women to provide safe, affordable abortions; offering classes on how to perform a safe DIY abortion; and raising money to send women to locations where legal abortion was available.[180,181] They also lobbied state legislatures, achieving reforms in 14 states and outright repeal of restrictive abortion laws in four states and Washington, DC, by 1973.

This strategy of state-by-state reform was cut short by the Supreme Court's 1973 decision in *Roe v. Wade*, which found that a woman's decision to terminate a pregnancy in the first trimester was protected by an individual right to privacy grounded in the Fourteenth Amendment. The decision allowed states to impose second trimester restrictions to protect a woman's health and third trimester restrictions to protect a viable fetus, while rejecting restrictions at any time if a woman's life or health were at risk.[182] The Court modified this standard in the 1992 case *Planned Parenthood of Southeastern Pennsylvania v. Casey*—allowing restrictions during the first trimester (including mandatory waiting periods and parental consent but not spousal consent) as long as they did not place an "undue burden" on access.[183]

Since this time, social conservatives have focused their political energy not only on supporting the nomination and appointment of justices who will overturn *Roe v. Wade* but also on passing state laws to test and expand the Court's definition of a reasonable burden on access. Efforts to impose new restrictions spiked after 2010, when conservative Republicans swept control of state legislatures across the country and enacted bans on late term abortion, restrictions on medication abortion, enforcement of waiting periods, informed consent requirements (even when information provided is not medically accurate), and targeted regulation of abortion providers (TRAP) regulations.[184] TRAP regulations are state laws that single out facilities that provide abortions, imposing strict requirements that do not apply to other types of clinics that provide medical procedures of similar risk. Examples include requiring unusually wide hallways or demanding that physicians have admitting privileges at a nearby hospital when no nearby hospital is willing to grant them. According to the Guttmacher Institute, 24 states had TRAP laws in place by 2017.[185]

Further restrictions on access to abortion may occur under the Trump administration. In the third 2016 presidential debate, moderator Chris Wallace asked then-candidate Trump if he wanted to see the Supreme Court overturn *Roe v. Wade*. Trump replied "yes," explaining, "If we put another two or perhaps three justices on. . . . that will happen automatically, in my opinion, because I'm putting pro-life justices on the Court."[186] Not only has Trump appointed federal judges approved by antiabortion groups, he has appointed two conservative Supreme Court justices, Neil Gorsuch and Brett Kavanaugh, who many suspect will be willing to substantially expand the type of restrictions that meet the "reasonable burden" on women's access to abortion (in the tradition of *Casey*), even if they do not directly overturn *Roe*.

However, a test case with the potential to overturn *Roe* altogether will likely make it to the Supreme Court soon, as the 2019 state legislative session saw four states (Ohio, Kentucky, Mississippi, and Georgia) restrict all access to abortion after four weeks (joining Iowa and North Dakota with such laws already in place). Missouri passed a similar ban on access after eight weeks, while Alabama passed a ban on abortions altogether. The Alabama and Ohio state laws are particularly stringent, providing no exemptions for pregnancies that result from rape or incest, and allowing both doctors who provide abortions and women who seek them out to be charged with a felony (possibly even for women who travel to other states to obtain one). The overarching goal, according to state legislators who sponsored and supported these bills, is to trigger a challenge that overturns *Roe* entirely.

Gender Gap: Interest and Participation

Another area where sex influences public opinion is in expressions of opinion. Expression of opinions is important in a democracy. One of the main predictors of expressiveness is sex, with women speaking less than men in deliberative settings.[187] Lower levels of political interest among women have been documented,[188] and recent research shows that this gap persists and is not isolated to the United States.[189] For example, "in Hungary just three percent of women said they were 'very interested' in politics, making them 63 percent less interested in politics than Hungarian men. This is the largest gap between men and women registered in the countries surveyed. Hungary also has the lowest level of women's representation in parliament of the countries surveyed at 10 percent."[190] In contrast, in Norway the gap in interest was 21%, and women's participation in the national parliament is the highest in the world. Data such as these lead some to suggest that the interest gap is in part caused by young women not having role models in the national parliament; however, while the data show some support for this idea, the evidence for this is mixed at best, as discussed in Chapter 7. In countries like Germany where there is (relatively) high representation of women in parliament, we also see low levels of political interest among women and girls. We examine the connection between interest and ambition in greater detail in Chapter 4.

Women and men also perceive women to have lower levels of political knowledge than men.[191] That said, this is an attitude that appears to be changing as it disappears in younger voters.[192] Education is an important mediator as it serves to increase women's interest and perceptions of women's knowledge more in other women than in men.[193]

Research also shows a persistent gap in women and men citizens' political participation, with women less politically engaged than men, particularly in the United States.[194-199] This is important because inequality in political involvement undermines the quality of deliberation, representation, and legitimacy in the democratic process.[200] These differences are not unique to the United States but are found throughout advanced industrial democracies. A 2010 study of 18 advanced industrial democracies showed that while women were more likely to have voted and engaged in "private" activism, men were more likely to have engaged in direct contact with elected officials and in participation requiring collective action. They are also more active members of political parties.[201] In the United States alone, one study shows the stark impact differential participation can have: When survey findings are translated into actual activity, even seemingly modest gaps between the sexes accumulate to sizable differences in total political inputs—"2,000,000 fewer phone calls or letters to public officials from women than men . . . 7,000,000 fewer campaign contributions from women than from men . . . 9,000,000 fewer women than men affiliated with a political organization." In the United States, throughout the 1950s and 1960s, women's participation in voting was about 10 percentage points below men, almost entirely the result of women's lower participation in the South.[202] Since 1980, women vote slightly more than men in U.S. presidential elections.

It is possible the participation gap is narrowing, as we will discuss when describing the resistance movements that have built up around the Trump administration in Chapter 9—primarily led by women. Or as Coffé and Bozendahl (2010) argue, women may not participate less; they just may participate differently.[203-207] That is, past studies have measured political interest and participation in terms of political parties and formal politics. Research is beginning to show, however, that women participate as much as men in informal politics and private politics—that is, things that can be done from the home like shopping, boycotts, or engagement with social movements. When we measure interest in these areas as well as social movements, we see the gap disappear or reverse.[208,209] For Latina women, this preference for informal activism may even be more of the case. According to Hardy-Fanta (1995), Latinas are triple burdened with sex, ethnicity, and cultural expectations about the role of women. Thus, their engagement is even more "behind the scenes" and not counted in typical surveys.[210] When we expand our definition of participation, Latina women are actually political leaders, engaging in more activities than other groups.[211]

Explanations for Opinion and Behavior Differences

Why do we see these differences in opinion and behavior? Explanations can be generally grouped into three broad categories: concern for the disadvantaged, political mobilization, or gender socialization (others have referred to this as socialization, attitudes, and opportunities).[212] The first explanation argues that since women are economically disadvantaged relative to men, they are more likely to support social welfare and redistributive policies. Their relative deprivation also causes them to hold opinions that express more concern for the disadvantaged.[213-215] Gay and Tate (1998) found that such concern is particularly pronounced for Black women who experience intersecting disadvantage due to their race and sex.[216] Mobilization, meanwhile, refers to the divergent targeting of men and women by political campaigns. The discussion of the gap that emerged in the 1980 campaign in the introduction to this chapter is an example of this practice. Additionally, as the messages and information about issues from political elites have become more partisan, men and women have been increasingly drawn to different partisan identities.[217-220] Finally, socialization arguments suggest that women are socialized to vote based upon an identity of motherhood[221,222] or are socialized more into an "ethics of caring" than are men.[223] Additionally, gender socialization may predispose men and women to hold different values and the development of feminist values, or consciousness.[224] Kittilson (2016) suggests a confluence of several interrelated factors (resources, economy, socialization, political context, mobilization) work together to cause this gap.[225] This conclusion is reinforced in a comparative study by Nir and McClurg (2015), who find that those institutions that set up opportunities for equality between the sexes have greater opportunities for women to participate.[226] This is an idea we will explore more deeply in the following chapters.

BOX 3.5: POLICY FEATURE

Attitude Toward Fair Wage

Intersectionality is not only important for understanding individual opinion, but it is also important for understanding support for certain policies, particularly when policies are viewed in racialized or gendered ways. As discussed earlier, different subgroups of women experience distinctive forms of discrimination. This is reflected in the concept of **"double jeopardy."**[227] "Double jeopardy suggests that Black and Hispanic women experience discrimination differently from white women or men of color because they simultaneously belong to a low-status gender group and a low-status racial/ethnic group."[228,229] Thus, double jeopardy refers to a type of cumulative discrimination faced by women of color. This can impact public opinion on policies, particularly those policies that are seen to benefit women of color in a disproportionate way. In a 2015 study, Cassese et al. explored the intersection of race and sex on policies related toward **fair wages**, or the idea that men and women should be paid the same for the same type of work. Wage discrimination based on sex is often reported as a single figure, that is, women make 77 cents for every dollar a man makes, but this is misleading. As of 2015, white women made about 80 cents for every dollar a man made, but for Latina women, the wage gap was 54 cents for every dollar.[230] African American women made 63 cents for every dollar a man made.[231] Cassese et al. (2015) find that support for fair-pay policy increases among those who think women face systemic discrimination. That said, opinions of racial discrimination also influence support for fair pay.[232] For example, white liberals who have high levels of racial resentment reported lower support for fair wages when Black and Hispanic workers were mentioned.[233] White conservatives on the other hand universally have low opinions of fair wage policies, no matter the racial makeup of the beneficiaries. "The significant role played by both modern sexism and racial resentment in shaping policy attitudes lends support to the concept of double jeopardy. But, the moderating effect of ideology suggests the intersectional biases held by white Americans are relatively complex and inherently politicized."[234]

PARTISAN PREFERENCES AND VOTING BEHAVIOR

Opinions are not only seen through opinion polls but also have real consequences at the ballot box as they influence voting behavior. When political scientists explain voting behavior, they draw upon one (or a combination) of several different approaches. **Structural approaches to voting behavior,** also sometimes called **sociological approaches** or the **Columbia model**, *focus on the relationship between individual and social structure by placing the decision to vote in a social context and relating it to individuals' social status.*[235,236] Thus, structuralists look to variables such as social class, language, religion, and sex as explanatory variables for voting behavior. A structuralist may argue women are more likely to vote based upon security concerns because they are more fearful; the idea that the gap in voting will be larger when social welfare is an electoral emphasis is a structural argument. **Ecological approaches**, sometimes referred to as **aggregate statistical approaches**, *relate voting behavior to characteristic features of a geographical area.* Those relying on this approach would be likely to argue that European women are more likely to be interested in politics because they have more women in parliaments due to quotas (we discuss quotas in Chapter 4). **Social psychological approaches**, also called the **Michigan model**, *suggest that voters make voting decisions based on psychological predispositions or attitudes and focus on attitudes and party identification as explanatory variables.*[237] The exact mechanism through which partisanship shapes public opinion is debated by scholars,[238,239] but partisanship has been important in determining opinion on gender issues, particularly candidate evaluations. In fact, Winter (2009) has argued that partisanship itself is gendered.[240] Several studies find that partisanship influences men's opinions more than women's, with examples documented in Conover (1988) and Conover and Sapiro (1993).[241,242] Finally, **rational choice approaches**, also called **economic approaches**, *explain voting behavior as the outcome of a series of cost and benefit analyses on the part of the voter where the voter is trying to maximize a particular "payoff."*[243] If, for example, the voter values maintaining *Roe v. Wade* as the most important calculus in voting, the voter will evaluate the costs and benefits to *protecting Roe v. Wade* by voting for particular candidates and choosing the candidate who maximizes the payoff—in this case keeping abortion legal—for the voter.[244]

How do sex and gender influence voting? For one, today, the majority of voters are women. After **enfranchisement**, or the right to vote, women were more politically conservative than men in their ideology, party attachment, and vote choice across most democracies.[245] "Scholars typically reasoned that women's higher levels of religiosity encouraged stronger ties to religious and conservative parties. Further, fewer women participated in the paid workforce, and thus they were less likely to join trade unions, the very organizations that historically connected workers to leftist parties."[246] More recently, women across Western European countries have increasingly supported leftist parties, while in postcommunist countries they tend to favor the right. Part of the explanation for the move of women toward the left in advanced democracies has to do with declining religiosity among women.[247] Additionally, due to differences in opinion about immigration, women in Western Europe are significantly less likely to cast their vote for radical right parties than men.[248,249]

For decades in the United States, women have been more closely aligned with the Democratic Party (see Table 3.8) and men more likely to identify as Republicans. The gender gap—the difference between how men and women

Table 3.8 Long-Standing Gap Between Men and Women in Presidential Voting: Percentage Who Voted for Democratic Candidate

Election Year	Men	Women
1972	36	38
1976	50	50
1980	36	45
1984	37	44
1988	41	49
1992	41	45
1996	43	54
2000	42	54
2004	44	51
2008	49	56
2012	45	55

Sources: Based on exit polls from CBS, CBS/New York Times, Voter News Service, and National Election Pool. All information courtesy of Pew Research Center (2016).

vote—represents on average an 8 to 10 percentage point gulf between the sexes during presidential elections.[250] Though there was evidence of some voting differences between the sexes as far back as the 1960s, many political scientists date the emergence of the modern gap to the 1980 election introduced at the beginning of this chapter, which served as the culmination of years of change in women's lives. By then, more women were working and more were single and living on their own. The women's movement reinforced the growing sense that women's political interests could and should be different than those of their husbands and fathers. Why was 1980 such an important year in delineating the gap between men and women in voting? For one, Reagan ran on a hawkish (i.e., military strength and aggressiveness) platform, and women tend to report lower levels of support for defense spending and the use of military force. Additionally, Reagan attempted to cut back the welfare state. Women are more likely to be the recipients of government aid. They are also more likely to be older and more likely to be single parents. Thus, Reagan's attack on the welfare state had had far more negative effects on women than it did on men. Additionally, from the 1950s through the 1980s, both white men and women became more Republican. Men—in particularly white men—however, disproportionately moved toward the Republican Party, which accounts for the sex-based gap.[251] In other words, women did not necessarily move toward the Democratic Party, but decline in support for the Democrats happened less dramatically among women than men.[252] Kaufmann, Petrocik, and Shaw (2008), of the University of Maryland, have looked at American National Election Study data from 1952 to 2004 and observed that white men's support for the Democratic Party declined from the mid-1970s through 1988 (the eight years of Reagan's presidency).[253] It has remained at this lower level ever since the Reagan years. This pattern is similar to how church goers aligned themselves with the Republican Party in 1972 and have stayed there ever since. In contrast, at least until 2016, women's voting and party identification looked similarly to how it looked in the 1970s.

There is some evidence that women are moving now to the Democratic Party. Some Republican women have chosen to leave the party. Susan Bevan and Susan Cullman were leaders of the Republican Majority for Choice. They used to support Republicans who supported freedom of choice (abortion rights) and decided to leave the party because this position was no longer feasible within the Republican Party. In recent years, lifelong Republicans were booed out of state committee meetings for raising abortion rights and family planning ideas. Hence Bevan's and Cullman's editorial explained: "We don't have the space to outline President Trump's transgressions, but it is important to understand that his rise is an inevitable result of the hostility to women within the Republican culture." After the 2018 midterms, there is not a single prochoice Republican member of the House and only Susan Collins (R-ME) and Lisa Murkowsi (R-AK) in the Senate.[254]

Post-2016 party identification among young women voters has shifted dramatically. Millennial women, aged 18 to 34, have been trending toward the left for the past several years, a pattern exacerbated by the 2016 presidential election. Prior to 2016, about 55% of young women identified with the Democratic Party; as of 2018, 70% do. Similarly, their identification with the Republican Party dropped from the mid 30s to 23%. Meanwhile, millennial men's party identification has remained fairly static with 49% identifying with Democrats and 41% with Republicans. Unlike past gaps, this 20-point gap between millennial men and women was created because women moved while men stayed relatively static. It remains to be seen whether this shift is merely a "Trump effect" or whether it will become a permanent part of the political landscape. If so, it will be historically significant as women are also less likely to identify as political independents than men, opting more for weak partisanship than independent identification in opinion polls.[255] Research suggests this is because women prefer connections to others while men prefer separateness.[256]

There is variation in this trend across racial and ethnic groups. Among Latinx Americans, women are more likely to hold liberal ideology and to support the Democratic Party than men, and this gap is especially pronounced among younger Latinx populations. Among African Americans, support for the Democratic Party

Table 3.9 2016 Presidential Exit Poll Data by Sex, Race

	Clinton	Trump	Other/No Answer
White men	31%	62%	7%
White women	43%	52%	5%
Black men	82%	13%	5%
Black women	94%	4%	2%
Latino men	63%	32%	5%
Latina women	69%	25%	6%
Others	61%	31%	8%
24,558 total respondents			

Source: All information courtesy of CNN Exit Poll data (2016).

is strong among men and women alike, and sex-based differences in voting behavior are minimal. It is also important to compare among groups of women. Smooth (2006) finds that Democratic support among Latinas and Black women accounts for much of the total gap between men and women in the United States.[257] That is, such large percentages of Latinas and Black women break for the Democratic Party that their support accounts for most of the difference between sex support for the Democratic and Republican parties. "Despite the importance of Latina and Black support, the news media most often relies on stories about white suburban 'soccer moms' to account for the gap between men and women."[258] This is misguided and not supported by the data. For example, in the 2016 U.S. presidential election, white women voted 52% for Trump, compared to 25% of Latinas and only 4% of Black women (see Table 3.9).

CONCLUSION

This chapter explored the gap between men and women in public opinion, or the difference between the sexes on a host of public opinion issues. The first place we see this manifest is in how individuals form opinions about gender issues and how ideas about sex and gender influence public opinion. Gender is socially constructed, and we find that because women have intersectional identities, linked fate arguments can be harder to make for women than for other groups, like racial/ethnic groups. We also explored the degree to which opinions about sex and gender roles and conceptions of motherhood influences politics. This is a theme we'll see reemerge throughout the book. This chapter also explored how sex influences public opinion, finding that a gap between men and women exists about certain policy issues as well as in terms of party identification. Women tend to be more supportive of social welfare and humanitarian policies and men of military policies. Women also tend to be more supportive of the Democratic Party than men. Intersectionality is important to take into account, though, as we discussed most of the difference between the sexes is due to women of color leaning strongly Democrat and also having a cohesiveness of public opinion. Interestingly, the gap disappears or reverses when we take into account LGBTQIA+ individuals. We also noted a gap in terms of political interest and participation, with women in many different political settings indicating less political interest than men. We suggested this may be changing with the resistance movements against Donald Trump, which are strongly women-led. The intersection between interest and ambition will be something we pick up in Chapter 4. Finally, we explored voting behavior, showing that voting behavior mirrored party identification, with women more likely to vote for Democrats than men. Again, this pattern is driven primarily by the voting patterns of women of color. So, why can't women vote more like men? In some instances they do, primarily when we look at white women. However, women's lived experiences are changing and varied; this means their opinions and voting behavior will be as well.

REVIEW QUESTIONS

1. What changed electorally in the United States with the 1980 election? Why do you think we saw this change?

2. Explain how polling works. What was unique about the Gallup organization?

3. How do individuals form opinions about sex and gender issues?

4. Explain the difference between equity policies and role policies. Give an example of each.

5. How does intersectionality impact gender predispositions? Think about your own socialization, media influence, and intersectional identity. How do you think this influences your gender predispositions?

6. What is hostile sexism? Where do you see hostile sexism manifest in the United States and elsewhere today?

7. What is the relationship between sex and political ideology? In the United States? In other democracies?

8. Pick a policy issue. How does the United States stack up on that policy relative to other countries? Are there differences in the policy? Differences by sex or gender?

9. In what way do sex and gender influence political interest, participation, and voting behavior?

AMBITION ACTIVITIES

Tweaking Political Interest: This activity is designed to cultivate individual and group consciousness. Choose a policy area (education, reproductive health, security, foreign aid, welfare, use of military force, transgender service in military, family leave, or another policy area approved by your instructor). For the chosen policy area, discuss the following questions:

1. How does this policy affect me, and do my life experiences influence how I see this policy? How does it affect others including people like me and people different from me?

2. To what extent do women participate in political discussions and political activism related to this issue? Considering the degree of women's engagement on this issue, do you believe it will make it onto the public's and elected officials' agendas? Why, or why not?

3. How might policy related to this issue be different if women's voices and preferences are not heard as policymakers consider solutions?

Brainstorming Political Action About Public Policy: Make a short list of two or three equity-based public policies (those that encourage equal treatment of the sexes) that you think women should care about. Choose one, and discuss how to build group consciousness and coalitions regarding this policy.

1. What actions would your group be willing to take together?

2. How could you cultivate group consciousness that cuts across intersectional identities?

3. Discuss how the policy could be addressed with informal activism as well as the ways it could be addressed through formal political participation. Which approach do you think would be more effective, and why?

Repeat the same assignment for role-based public policies (those that require full-scale restructuring of society to change gender roles).

Practice Using Parliamentary Procedure: Revisit the guidelines from the Ambition Activity in Chapter 2 to practice using parliamentary procedure. Using one of the issues you discussed above, use parliamentary procedure to pass a resolution identifying a preferred policy solution. Switch chairs. Use parliamentary procedure to pass a resolution to identify a preferred activism strategy for encouraging elected officials to implement your preferred policy solution.

Practice Using Turn-Taking and Reaching Consensus: During the activism of the Second Wave, many feminist groups avoided using parliamentary procedure, as they associated the structured rules with the types of organizations and governments they were trying to reform. Instead, members took turns speaking about important decisions, as they attempted to reach consensus rather than a simple majority vote. To facilitate this practice, and to prevent those who feel comfortable in the public sphere (who are more apt to be men) from dominating discussion, they handed out a specified number of tokens or poker chips before the meeting. After taking the floor and speaking, members were required to discard a token. When their tokens were gone, they were no longer allowed to contribute to the discussion. Pass out three slips of paper to each classmate to use as tokens, and revisit the two decisions you made about a policy position and a preferred strategy that you made in the previous activity. Did your group reach the same decision? Discuss whether people feel more comfortable participating and make different types of contributions. With your classmates, try to decide when groups should rely on parliamentary procedure and voting to make decisions and when they should rely on turn-taking and consensus.

KEY WORDS

Agenda setting 93

Aggregate statistical approaches 121

Ambivalent sexism 97

Asymmetry 106

Benevolent sexists 97

Columbia model 121

Double jeopardy 120

Ecological approaches 121

Economic approaches 121

Enfranchisement 121

Equity policies 92

Fair wages 120

Framing 93

Gallup organization 90

Gender 89

Gender gap 89

Gender issues 92

Hegemonic masculinity 98

Hostile sexism 97

Identity-protective cognition 94

Interdependence 94

Intersectionality 90

Linked fate 94

Mass media 93

Michigan model 121

Motivated cognition 93

Policy views 92

Political socialization 93

Polling organization 90

Polling sample 91

Pollsters 91

Predispositions 92

Public opinion 90

Public opinion polls 90

Rational choice approaches 121

Representative sample 91

Role policies 92

Sampling error 91

Sex 89

Social desirability 93

Social psychological approaches 121

Socially constructed 89

Sociological approaches 121

Straw polling 91

Structural approaches to voting
        behavior 120

Structural critique 94

Voting behavior 90

REFERENCES

1. Toufexis, A. (1982). Waking up to the gender gap. *Time Magazine*. Retrieved from http://content.time.com/time/magazine/article/0,9171,949585,00.html.

2. Poloni-Staudinger, L., & Ortbals, C. D. (2012). *Terrorism and violent conflict: Women's agency, leadership and responses*. New York, NY: Springer Press.

3. Poloni-Staudinger, L., & Ortbals, C. (2017). *Memory and counter-memory following violence and terrorism: A feminist perspective*. Paper presented at the Midwest Political Science Association, Chicago, IL.

4. National Geographic Staff. (2017). How science is helping us understand gender. *National Geographic Magazine*. Retrieved from http://www.nationalgeographic .com/magazine/2017/01.

5. Grady, D. (2018). Anatomy does not determine gender, experts say. *New York Times*. Retrieved from https://www.nytimes.com/2018/10/22/ health/transgender-trump-biology.html?action=click&module=Well &pgtype=Homepage&section=Health&fbclid=IwAR2V6BoE4bzDt-QSdVt6DC8wkksUOKiUKUX3q09lXcO_jnQGvaMtOHvCeEI.

6. Oudshooen, N. (2006). Sex and the body. In I. Grewal & C. Kaplan (Eds.), *An introduction to women's studies: Gender in a transnational world*. New York, NY: McGraw-Hill.

7. Poloni-Staudinger, L., & Ortbals, C. *Memory and counter-memory following violence and terrorism: A feminist perspective*.

8. Kimmel, M. (2010). *The gendered society*. London, UK: Oxford University Press.

9. Crenshaw, K. W. (1991). Mapping the margins: Intersectionality, identity politics, and violence against women of color. *Stanford Law Review, 43*(6), 1241–1299.

10. Kimmel, M. (2010). *The gendered society*.

11. Gallup Staff. (n.d.). George H. Gallup, Founder: 1901–1984. *Gallup*. Retrieved from http://www.gallup.com/corporate/178136/george-gallup.aspx.

12. Ibid.

13. Ibid.

14. Burns, N., & Gallagher, K. (2010). Public opinion on gender issues: The politics of equity and roles. *Annual Review of Political Science, 13*, 425–443.

15. Ibid.

16. Ibid.

17. Carroll, S. (1985). *Women as candidates in American politics*. Bloomington: Indiana University Press.

18. Wolbrecht, C. (2000). *The politics of women's rights: Parties, positions, and change*. Princeton, NJ: Princeton University Press.

19. Sanbonmatsu, K. (2002). *Democrats, Republicans, and the politics of women's place*. Ann Arbor: University Michigan Press.

20. McDonagh, E. (2009). *Motherless state*. Chicago, IL: University Chicago Press.

21. Burns, N., & Gallagher, K. (2010). Public opinion on gender issues: The politics of equity and roles.

22. Sanbonmatsu K. 2002. *Democrats, Republicans, and the politics of women's place*.

23. Burns, N., & Gallagher, K. (2010). Public opinion on gender issues: The politics of equity and roles.

24. Ibid.

25. Carden, M. (1977). *Feminism in the mid-1970s: The non-establishment, the establishment, and the future*. New York, NY: Ford Foundation.

26. Gelb, J., & Palley, M. (1982). *Women and public policy*. Princeton, NJ: Princeton University Press.

27. Greenstein, F. (1968). The need for systematic inquiry into personality and politics: Introduction and overview. *Social Issues, 24*(3), 1–14.

28. Glasberg, D. S., & Shannon, D. (2011). *Political sociology: Oppression, resistance, and the state*. Thousand Oaks, CA: Pine Forge Press.

29. Powell, L., & Cowart, J. (2013). *Political campaign communication: Inside and out*. Boston, MA: Allyn & Bacon.

30. Burns, N., & Kinder, D. (2012). Categorical politics: Gender, race and public opinion. In A. J. Berinsky (Ed.), *New directions in public opinion* (pp. 139–168). New York, NY: Routledge Press.

31. Gamson, W. A., & Modigliani, A. (1989). Media discourse and public opinion on nuclear power: A constructionist approach. *American Journal of Sociology, 95*(1), 1–37.

32. Walker, J. D., Wassenberg, D., Franta, G., & Cotner, S. (2017). What determines student acceptance of politically controversial scientific conclusions? *Journal of Scientific College Teaching, 47*(2), 46–56.

33. Chen, S., Duckworth, K., & Chaiken, S. (1999). Motivated heuristic and systematic processing. *Psychological Inquiry, 10*(1), 44–49.

34. Kahan, D. M. (2007). Culture and identity-protective cognition: Explaining the white male effect in risk perception. *Faculty Scholarship Series 101*. Retrieved from https://digitalcommons.law.yale.edu/fss_papers/101.

35. Walker, J. D., Wassenberg, D., Franta, G., & Cotner, S. (2017). What determines student acceptance of politically controversial scientific conclusions?

36. Pepin, J., & Cotter, D. (2017). Trending towards traditionalism? Changes in youths' gender ideology. *Council on Contemporary Families*. Retrieved from https://contemporaryfamilies.org/2-pepin-cotter-traditionalism.

37. Coontz, S. (2017). Why do men want stay at home wives? *New York Times*. Retrieved from https://www.nytimes.com/2017/03/31/opinion/sunday/do-millennial-men-want-stay-at-home-wives.html.

38. Valenti, J. (2018). The myth of conservative feminism. *The New York Times*. Retrieved from https://www.nytimes.com/2018/05/19/opinion/sunday/conservative-feminism.html?mabReward=CBMG1&recid=14sCf3V48dS6Eu0S VYP2Tq3CJXS&recp=4&action=click&pgtype=Homepage&region=CColumn &module=Recommendation&src=rechp&WT.nav=RecEngine&fbclid=IwAR3v KvkRDlx5qK5rFDnvCsOBT7knuVBl2S9QVUQnzyskYLOdai2uc_5s-58.

39. Thornton, A., & Freedman, D. (1979). Changes in the sex role attitudes of women, 1962–1977: Evidence from a panel study. *American Sociology Review, 44*(5), 831–842.

40. Lewin, K. (1948). *Resolving social conflicts*. New York, NY: Harper & Row.

41. Campbell, D. (1958). Common fate, similarity, and other indices of the status of aggregates of persons as social entities. *Behavioral Sciences, 3*(1),14–25.

42. Dawson, M. (1994). *Behind the mule: Race and class in African-American politics*. Princeton, NJ: Princeton University Press.

43. Marx, K., & Fowkes, B. (1976). *Capital: A critique of political economy*. Harmondsworth, NY: Penguin Books.

44. Young, I. (1994). Gender as seriality: Thinking about women as a social collective. *Signs, 19*(3), 713–38.

45. Sears, D., & Huddy, L. (1986). *Social identities and political disunity among women*. ANES Pilot Stud. Rep. No. nes002258.

46. Poloni-Staudinger, L., Strachan, J. C., & Shaffner, B. (2016). In six graphs here is why young women don't support Hilary Clinton as much as older women do. *The Washington Post, Monkey Cage*. Retrieved from https://www.washingtonpost.com/news/monkey-cage/wp/2016/04/11/in-6-graphs-heres-why-young-women-dont-support-hillary-clinton-as-much-as-older-women-do.

47. Ibid.

48. Parker, K., Cilluffo, A., & Stepler, R. (2017). 6 facts about the U.S. military and its changing demographics. *Pew Research Center*. Retrieved from http://www.pewresearch.org/fact-tank/2017/04/13/6-facts-about-the-u-s-military-and-its-changing-demographics.

49. Ibid.

50. Ibid.

51. Ibid.

52. Ibid.

53. Ibid.

54. Cassese, E., Barnes, T., & Holman, M. (2018). Who supports Kavanaugh after last week's angry hearings? Our research helps explain. *Washington Post*. Retrieved from https://www.washingtonpost.com/news/monkey-cage/wp/2018/10/02/who-supports-kavanaugh-after-last-weeks-angry-hearings-our-research-helps-explain/?noredirect=on&utm_term=.848a226f0a0c.

55. Ibid.

56. Ibid.

57. Ibid.

58. Ibid.

59. See, for example, https://www.theguardian.com/world/2018/apr/25/raw-hatred-why-incel-movement-targets-terrorises-women; and https://www.washingtonpost.com/nation/2018/11/03/man-with-groping-history-opens-fire-tallahassee-yoga-class-killing-two-policesay/?utm_term=.ebafbe4f23db.

60. Herek, G. M. (2002). Gender gaps in public opinion about lesbians and gay men. *Public Opinion Quarterly, 66*, 40–66.

61. Ibid.

62. The World Economic Forum. Retrieved from www.weforum.org.

63. The World Economic Forum. (2017). *The global gender gap report 2017*. Retrieved from www.weforum.org/reports/the-global-gender-gap-report-2017.

64. Fetterolf, J. (2017). Many around the world say women's equality is very important. Pew Research Center. Retrieved from http://www.pewresearch.org/fact-tank/2017/01/19/many-around-the-world-say-womens-equality-is-very-important.

65. Ibid.

66. Ibid.

67. Menasce Horowitz, J., Parker, K., & Stepler, R. (2017). Wide partisan gaps in U.S. over how far the country has come on gender equality. *Pew Research Center*. Retrieved from http://www.pewsocialtrends.org/2017/10/18/wide-partisan-gaps-in-u-s-over-how-far-the-country-has-come-on-gender-equality.

68. Beinart, P. (2017). The partisanship of feminism. Retrieved from https://www.theatlantic.com/politics/archive/2017/12/the-partisanship-of-feminism/548423/?utm_source=atlfb&fbclid=IwAR2maE_3iIz6FP9HBe4FUZt3aiORbB5WbtNEl7c3Bu7N48yX49IaseJviro.

69. Center for Gender Equality Iceland. (2012). Gender equality in Iceland. Retrieved from https://www.stjornarradid.is/media/velferdarraduneyti-media/media/rit-og-skyrslur2012/Gender-Equality-in-Iceland.pdf.

70. Fetterolf, J. (2017). Many around the world say women's equality is very important.

71. Chapman, M. (2013). Gender equality in Iceland. *Guide to Iceland*. Retrieved from https://www.guidetoiceland.is/history-culture/gender-equality-in-iceland.

72. Ibid.

73. Ibid.

74. Ibid.

75. Ibid.

76. Ibid.

77. Weller, C. (2016). These 10 countries have the best parental leave policies in the world. *Business Insider*. Retrieved from www.businessinsider.com/countries-with-best-parental-leave-2016-8?r=UK&IR=T.

78. The World Economic Forum. (2017). *The global gender gap report 2017*.

79. Ibid.

80. Stone, M. (2018). Where are the women in Pakistan's elections this week? Retrieved from https://www.cfr.org/blog/where-are-women-pakistans-elections-week.

81. Ibid.

82. Khan, I. (2016). Pakistan's gender gap in financial inclusion. *CPAG*. Retrieved from http://www.cgap.org/blog/pakistan's-gender-gap-financial-inclusion.

83. Ibid.

84. Moin, A., Fatima, H., & Qadir, T. F. (2018). Pakistan's slow progress toward gender partially. *The Lancet*. Retrieved from https://www.thelancet.com/journals/langlo/article/PIIS2214-109X(17)30498-9/fulltext.

85. Ibid.

86. Noack, R. (2018). Iceland is trying to close the gender pay gap by publicly shaming companies. *Washington Post.* Retrieved from https://www.washingtonpost.com/news/worldviews/wp/2018/01/04/icelands-trying-to-close-the-gender-pay-gap-by-publicly-shaming-companies/?noredirect=on&utm_term=.68d68f8ce4ae.

87. Khan, I. (2016). Pakistan's gender gap in financial inclusion.

88. Erskine, H. (1971). The polls: Women's role. *Public Opinion Quarterly, 35*(2), 275–290.

89. Smith, T. W. (1984). The polls: Gender and attitudes towards violence. *Public Opinion Quarterly, 48*(1), 384–396.

90. Schneider, W. (1984). Opinion outlook: The Democrats are counting on the gender gap, but it may not be much help. *National Journal,* 1242–1245.

91. Shapiro, R., & Mahajan, H. (1986). Gender differences in policy preferences: A summary of trends from the 1960s to the 1980s. *Public Opinion Quarterly, 50*(1), 42–61.

92. Jensen, M. K. (2014). *Public opinion gender gaps among sexual minorities.* Paper presented at the American Political Science Association annual meeting. Retrieved from https://ssrn.com/abstract=2451404.

93. Rapoport, R. B. (1982). Sex differences in attitude expression: A generational explanation. *Public Opinion Quarterly, 46,* 86–96.

94. Fite, D., Genest, M., & Wilcox, C. (1990). Gender differences in foreign policy attitudes: A longitudinal analysis. *American Politics Quarterly, 18,* 492–512.

95. Conover, P. J., & Sapiro, V. (1993). Gender, feminist consciousness, and war. *American Journal of Political Science, 37*(4), 1079–1099.

96. Kaufmann, K. M., & Petrocik, J. R. (1999). The changing politics of American men: Understanding the sources of the gender gap. *American Journal of Political Science, 43*(3), 864–887.

97. Sapiro, V. (2001). It's the context, situation, and question, stupid: The gender basis of public opinion. In B. Norrander & C. Wilcox, *Understanding public opinion.* Washington, DC: CQ Press.

98. Sapiro, V. (2003). Theorizing gender in political psychology research. In D. O. Sears, L. Huddy, & R. Jervis, *Oxford handbook of political psychology.* New York, NY: Oxford University Press.

99. Kellstedt, P. M., Peterson, D. A., & Ramirez, M. D. (2010). The macro politics of a gender gap. *Public Opinion Quarterly, 74*(3), 477–498.

100. Ibid.

101. Kaufmann, K. M., Petrocik, J. R., & Shaw, D. R. (2008). *Unconventional wisdom: Facts and myths about American voters*. Oxford, UK: Oxford University Press.

102. Barkan, S. E. (2014). Gender and abortion attitudes: Religiosity as a suppressor variable. *Public Opinion Quarterly, 78*(4), 940–950.

103. Fisher, P. (2014). *Demographic gaps in American political behavior*. Boulder, CO: Westview Press.

104. Ortbals, C., & Poloni-Staudinger, L. (2018). *Gender and political violence: Women changing the politics of terrorism*. Cham, Switzerland: Springer International.

105. Fischer, P., & Ai, A. L. (2008). International terrorism and mental health: Recent research and future directions. *Journal of Interpersonal Violence, 23*(3), 339–361.

106. Huddy, L., Feldman, S., Lahav, G., & Taber, C. (2003). Fear and terrorism: Psychological reactions to 9/11. In P. Norris, M. Kern, & M. Just (Eds.), *Framing terrorism: The news media, the government, and the public* (pp. 255–278). New York, NY: Routledge.

107. Huddy, L., Feldman, S., Taber, C., & Lahav, G. (2005). Threat, anxiety, and support of antiterrorism policies. *American Journal of Political Science, 49*(3), 593–608.

108. Huddy, L., Feldman, S., & Cassese, E. (2007). On the distinct political effects of anxiety and anger. In W. Russell, G. E. Marcus, A. N. Crigler, & M. Mackuen (Eds.), *The affect effect: Dynamics of emotion in political thinking and behavior* (pp. 202–230). Chicago, IL: University of Chicago Press.

109. Ortbals, C., & Poloni-Staudinger, L. (2018). *Gender and political violence: Women changing the politics of terrorism*.

110. Brader, T., Marcus, G. E., & Miller, K. I. (2011). Emotion and public opinion. In R. Y. Shapiro & L. R. Jacobs (Eds.), *Oxford handbook of American public opinion and the media* (pp. 384–401). Oxford, UK: Oxford University Press.

111. Huddy, L., Feldman, S., Lahav, G., & Taber, C. (2003). Fear and terrorism: Psychological reactions to 9/11.

112. Ortbals, C., & Poloni-Staudinger, L. (2018). *Gender and political violence: Women changing the politics of terrorism*.

113. Ibid.

114. Tuman, J. S. (2010). *Communicating terror: The rhetorical dimensions of terrorism*. Thousand Oaks, CA: SAGE.

115. Nacos, B. L. (2007). *Mass-mediated terrorism: The central role of the media in terrorism and counterterrorism*, 2nd ed. Lanham, MD: Rowman & Littlefield.

116. Nacos, B. L. (2016). *Terrorism and counterterrorism*. New York, NY: Routledge, Taylor & Francis Group.

117. Nacos, B. L., Bloch-Elkon, Y., & Shapiro, R. Y. (2011). *Selling fear: Counterterrorism, the media, and public opinion*. Chicago, IL: University of Chicago Press.

118. Ortbals, C., & Poloni-Staudinger, L. (2018). *Gender and political violence: Women changing the politics of terrorism*.

119. Gadarian, S. K. (2010). The politics of threat: How terrorism news shapes foreign policy attitudes. *Journal of Politics*, *72*(2), 469–483.

120. Mendez, J., Poloni-Staudinger, L., Ortbals, C., & Osborn, T. (2016). *Emotionally evocative women: The influence of women suicide bombers on the American public*. Article manuscript.

121. Ortbals, C., & Poloni-Staudinger, L. (2018). *Gender and political violence: Women changing the politics of terrorism*.

122. Huddy, L., Feldman, S., & Cassese, E. (2009). Terrorism, anxiety, and war. In W. G. Stritzke, S. Lewandowsky, D. Denemark, J. Clare, & F. Morgan (Eds.), *Terrorism and torture: An interdisciplinary perspective* (pp. 290–312). Cambridge, MA: Cambridge University Press.

123. Ortbals, C., & Poloni-Staudinger, L. (2018). *Gender and political violence: Women changing the politics of terrorism*.

124. Fischer, P., & Ai, A. L. (2008). *International terrorism and mental health: Recent research and future directions*.

125. Huddy, L., Feldman, S., & Cassese, E. (2009). Terrorism, anxiety, and war.

126. Heskin, K. (1980). *Northern Ireland: A psychological analysis*. New York, NY: Columbia University Press.

127. Huddy, L., Feldman, S., Lahav, G., & Taber, C. (2003). Fear and terrorism: Psychological reactions to 9/11.

128. Ortbals, C., & Poloni-Staudinger, L. (2018). *Gender and political violence: Women changing the politics of terrorism*.

129. Brody, L. R., & Hall, J. A. (2008). Gender and emotion in context. In M. Lewis & J. M. Haviland-Jones (Eds.), *Handbook of emotions* (pp. 395–408). New York, NY: Guilford Press.

130. Huddy, L., Feldman, S., & Cassese, E. (2009). Terrorism, anxiety, and war.

131. Mendez, J., Poloni-Staudinger, L., Ortbals, C., & Osborn, T. (2016). *Emotionally evocative women: The influence of women suicide bombers on the American public.*

132. Ortbals, C., & Poloni-Staudinger, L. (2018). *Gender and political violence: Women changing the politics of terrorism.*

133. Clements, B. (2012). *Men and women's support for war: Accounting for the gender gap in public opinion.* Retrieved from http://www.e-ir.info/2012/01/19/men-and-womens-support-for-war-accounting-for-the-gender-gap-in-public-opinion.

134. Fite, D., Genest, M., & Wilcox, C. (1990). *Gender differences in foreign policy attitudes: A longitudinal analysis.*

135. Gentry, C. E. (2009). Twisted maternalism: From peace to violence. *International Feminist Journal of Politics, 11*(2), 235–252.

136. Huddy, L., & Feldman. S. (2011). Americans respond politically to 9/11: Understanding the impact of the terrorist attacks and their aftermath. *American Psychologist, 66*(6), 455–467.

137. Huddy, L., Feldman, S., Lahav, G., & Taber, C. (2003). Fear and terrorism: Psychological reactions to 9/11.

138. Sapiro, V. (2003). Theorizing gender in political psychology research. In D. O. Sears, L. Huddy, & R. Jervis, *Oxford handbook of political psychology.*

139. Shapiro, R., & Mahajan, H. (1986). Gender differences in policy preferences: A summary of trends from the 1960s to the 1980s.

140. Eichenberg, R. C. (2016). Gender difference in American public opinion on the use of military force, 1982–2013. *International Studies Quarterly, 60*(1), 138–148.

141. Ibid.

142. Burris, V. (2008). From Vietnam to Iraq: Continuity and change in between-group differences in support for military action. *Social Problems, 55*(4), 443–479.

143. Ortbals, C., & Poloni-Staudinger, L. (2018). *Gender and political violence: Women changing the politics of terrorism.*

144. Clements, B. (2012). *Men and women's support for war: Accounting for the gender gap in public opinion.*

145. Mendez, J., Poloni-Staudinger, L., Ortbals, C., & Osborn, T. (2016). *Emotionally evocative women: The influence of women suicide bombers on the American public.*

146. Ortbals, C., & Poloni-Staudinger, L. (2018). *Gender and political violence: Women changing the politics of terrorism.*

147. Mendez, J., Poloni-Staudinger, L., Ortbals, C., & Osborn, T. (2016). *Emotionally evocative women: The influence of women suicide bombers on the American public.*

148. Ibid.

149. Kittilson, M. C. (2016). Gender and political behavior. *Oxford Research Encyclopedias*. Retrieved from http://politics.oxfordre.com/view/10.1093/acrefore/9780190228637.001.0001/acrefore-9780190228637-e-71.

150. Gidengil, E., Blais, A., Nadeau, R., & Nevitte, N. (2001). Women to the left? Gender differences in political beliefs and policy preferences." In M. Tremblay & L. Trimble (Eds.), *Gender and elections in Canada* (pp. 140–159). Don Mills: Oxford University Press.

151. Jelen, T. G., Thomas, S., & Wilcox, C. (1994). The gender gap in comparative perspective. *European Journal of Political Research, 25*(2), 171–186.

152. Studlar, D. T., McAllister, I., & Hayes, B. C. (1998). Explaining the gender gap in voting. *Social Science Quarterly, 79*(4), 779–798.

153. Kittilson, M. C. (2016). Gender and political behavior.

154. Ortbals, C., & Poloni-Staudinger, L. (2018). *Gender and political violence: Women changing the politics of terrorism.*

155. Kittilson, M. C. (2016). Gender and political behavior.

156. Pew Research Center Staff. (2016). Long-standing gender gap in presidential voting. Pew Research Center. Retrieved from http://www.pewresearch.org/fact-tank/2016/07/28/a-closer-look-at-the-gender-gap-in-presidential-voting/ft_16-7-29-gender1.

157. Jensen, M. K. (2014). *Public opinion gender gaps among sexual minorities.*

158. Ibid.

159. Hertzog, M. (1996). *The lavender vote: Lesbians, gay men, and bisexuals in American electoral politics.* New York: New York University Press.

160. Sherrill, K. (1996). The political power of lesbians, gays, and bisexuals. *PS: Political Science and Politics, 29,* 469–473.

161. Egan, P. J., & Sherrill, K. (2005). Marriage and the shifting priorities of a new generation of lesbians and gays. *PS: Political Science and Politics, 38,* 229–232.

162. Schaffner, B., & Senic, N. (2006). Rights or benefits? Explaining the sexual identity gap in American political behavior. *Political Research Quarterly, 59,* 123–132.

163. Lewis, G. B., Rogers, M. A., & Sherrill, K. (2011). Lesbian, gay, and bisexual voters in the 2000 election. *Politics and Policy, 39*(5), 655–677.

164. Egan, P. J. (2012). Group cohesion without group mobilization: The case of lesbians, gays and bisexuals. *British Journal of Political Science, 42,* 597–616.

165. Ammer, C. (2009). *The encyclopedia of women's health*. New York, NY: Infobase.

166. Long, L., & Foot, R. (2016). Abortion in Canada. *The Canadian Encyclopedia*. Retrieved from https://www.thecanadianencyclopedia.ca/en/article/abortion.

167. Statistics Canada Staff. (n.d.). Data quality in the therapeutic abortion survey. *Statistics Canada*. Retrieved February 15, 2018 from http://www23 .statcan.gc.ca/imdb-bmdi/pub/document/3209_D4_T2_V6-eng.pdf.

168. Scotti, M. (2017). Support for abortion rights strong in Canada, but Ipsos poll shows we are "middle of the pack" globally. *Global News Canada*. Retrieved from https://globalnews.ca/news/3290006/support-for-abortion-rights-strong-in-canada-but-poll-shows-we-are-middle-of-the-pack-globally.

169. Ibid.

170. Ibid.

171. Gryzmala-Busse, A. (2016). Why would Poland make its already strict abortion law Draconian? *The Washington Post*. Retrieved from https://www.washingtonpost.com/news/monkey-cage/wp/2016/04/18/why-would-poland-make-its-already-strict-abortion-law-draconian/?utm_term=.228c474ade17.

172. United Nations Staff, Office on Drugs and Crime. (n.d.). Rape at the national level, number of police-recorded offences. *UNODC*. Retrieved from http://www.unodc.org/documents/data-and-analysis/Crime-statistics/Sexual_violence_sv_against_children_and_rape.xls.

173. Gryzmala-Busse, A. (2016). Why would Poland make its already strict abortion law Draconian?

174. Ibid.

175. Ibid.

176. Ibid.

177. Harris, C. (2017). Poland and abortion: A year on from Mass Street protests. *Euronews*. Retrieved from http://www.euronews.com/2017/10/17/how-women-s-rights-have-still-been-hit-despite-abortion-ban-climbdown-in-poland.

178. Gryzmala-Busse, A. (2016). Why would Poland make its already strict abortion law Draconian?

179. Reagan, L. (1996). *When abortion was a crime: Women, medicine, and law in the United States, 1867–1973*. Berkeley: University of California Press.

180. Kaplan, L. (1995). *The story of Jane: The legendary underground feminist abortion service*. Chicago, IL: University of Chicago Press.

181. Loofbourow, L. (2018). They called her "the Che Guevara of abortion reformers". *Slate*. Retrieved from https://slate.com/human-interest/2018/12/pat-maginnis-abortion-rights-pro-choice-activist.html.

182. *Roe v. Wade*, 410 U.S. 113 (1973).

183. *Planned Parenthood of Southern Pennsylvania v. Casey*, 505 U.S. 833 (1992).

184. Guttmacher Institute. (2016). Last five years account for more than one-quarter of all abortion restrictions enacted since Roe. Retrieved from https://www.guttmacher.org/article/2016/01/last-five-years-account-more-one-quarter-all-abortion-restrictions-enacted-roe.

185. Guttmacher Institute. (2018). Targeted regulation of abortion providers. Retrieved from https://www.guttmacher.org/state-policy/explore/targeted-regulation-abortion-providers.

186. "Full Transcript: Third 2016 presidential debate." (2016). *Politico*. Retrieved from https://www.politico.com/story/2016/10/full-transcript-third-2016-presidential-debate-230063.

187. Nir, L., & McClurg, S. D. (2015). How institutions affect gender gaps in public opinion expression. *Public Opinion Quarterly, 79*(2), 544–567.

188. Inglehart, M. (1981). Political interest in West European women: A historical and empirical comparative analysis. *Comparative Political Studies, 14*(3), 299–326.

189. Kiel, A. (2016). The gender gap in political interest. *Millennial Dialogue*. Retrieved from https://www.millennialdialogue.com/blog/the-gender-gap-in-political-interest.

190. Ibid.

191. Fisher, P. (2014). *Demographic gaps in American political behavior*. New York, NY: Routledge.

192. Ibid.

193. Ibid.

194. Burns, N., Lehman Schlozman, K., & Verba, S. (1997). The public consequences of private inequality: Family life and citizen participation. *American Political Science Review, 91*(2), 373–389.

195. Dalton, R., & Russell, J. (2008). Citizenship norms and the expansion of political participation. *Political Studies, 56*(1), 76–98.

196. Gallego, A. (2007). *Inequality in political participation: Contemporary patterns in European countries*. Irvine: Center for the Study of Democracy: University of California.

197. Norris, P. (2002). *Democratic phoenix: Reinventing political activism*. New York, NY: Cambridge University Press.

198. Paxton, P., Kunovich, S., & Hughes, M. H. (2007). Gender in politics. *Annual Review of Sociology*, *33*, 263–284.

199. Schlozman, K. L., Burns, N., & Verba, S. (1999). What happened at work today?: A multistage model of gender, employment, and political participation. *The Journal of Politics*, *61*(1), 29–53

200. Kittilson, M. C. (2016). Gender and political behavior.

201. Coffé, H., & Bolzendah, C. (2010). Same game, different rules? Differences in political participation. *Sex Roles*, *62*(5–6), 318–333.

202. Fisher, P. (2014). Demographic gaps in American political behavior.

203. Coffé, H., & Bolzendah, C. (2010). Same game, different rules? Differences in political participation.

204. Bourque, S., & Grossholtz, J. (1998). Politics an unnatural practice: Political science looks at female participation. In A. Phillips (Ed.), *Feminism and politics* (pp. 23–43). Oxford, UK: Oxford University Press.

205. Harrison, L., & Munn, J. (2007). Gendered (non)participants? What constructions of citizenship tell us about democratic governance in the twenty-first century. *Parliamentary Affairs*, *60*, 426–436.

206. Lister, R. (1997). Citizenship and difference: Towards a differentiated universalism. *European Journal of Social Theory*, *1*, 71–90.

207. Parry, G., Moyser, G., & Day, N. (1992). *Political participation and democracy in Britain*. Cambridge, MA: Cambridge University Press.

208. Kiel, A. (2016). The gender gap in political interest.

209. Fisher, P. (2014). *Demographic gaps in American political behavior*.

210. Hardy-Fanta, C. (1995). Latina women and political leadership: Implications for Latino community development. *New England Journal of Public Policy*, *11*(1),221–235.

211. Ibid.

212. Coffé, H., & Bolzendah, C. (2010). Same game, different rules? Differences in political participation.

213. Jensen, M. K. (2014). *Public opinion gender gaps among sexual minorities*.

214. Miller, A. H., Gurin, P., Gurin, G., & Malanchuk, O. (1981). Group consciousness and political participation. *American Journal of Political Science*, *25*(3), 494–511.

215. Ransford, H. E., & Miller, J. (1983). Race, sex and feminist outlooks. *American Sociological Review, 48*(1), 46–59.

216. Gay, C., & Tate, K. (1998). Doubly-bound: The impact of gender and race on the politics of black women. *Political Psychology, 19*, 169–184.

217. Zaller, J. (1992). *The nature and origins of mass opinion*. New York, NY: Cambridge University Press.

218. Hetherington, M. J. (2001). Resurgent mass partisanship: The role of elite polarization. *American Political Science Review, 95*(3), 619–631.

219. Jensen, M. K. (2014). *Public opinion gender gaps among sexual minorities.*

220. Abramowitz, A. I., & Saunders, K. L. (1998). Ideological realignment in the U.S. electorate. *Journal of Politics, 60*(3), 634–652.

221. Gilligan, C. (1977). In a different voice: Women's conceptions of self and of morality. *Harvard Educational Review, 47*(4), 481–517.

222. Tronto, J. C. 1987. Beyond gender difference to a theory of care. *Signs, 12*(4), 644–663.

223. Ibid.

224. Conover, P. J. (1988). Feminists and the gender gap. *Journal of Politics, 50*(4), 985–1010.

225. Kittilson, M. C. (2016). Gender and political behavior.

226. Nir, L., & McClurg, S. D. (2015). How institutions affect gender gaps in public opinion expression.

227. Cassese, E., Barnes, T., & Holman, M. (2018). How "hostile sexism" came to shape our politics. *The Washington Post.* Retrieved from https://www.washingtonpost.com/news/monkey-cage/wp/2018/10/02/who-supports-kavanaugh-after-last-weeks-angry-hearings-our-research-helps-explain/?fbclid=IwAR3jRunbrS-QCyVhjAvLR1BzCv_3ZYR4F3tTl4pxJhg4AnlnpyDehrB9Qro&noredirect=on&utm_term=.45df287823b6.

228. Ibid.

229. Sidanius, J., & Veniegas, R. (2000). Gender and race discrimination: The interactive nature of disadvantage." In S. Oskamp (Ed.), *Reducing prejudice and discrimination, The Claremont Symposium on Applied Social Psychology* (pp. 47–69). Mahwah, NJ: Lawrence Erlbaum Associates.

230. Vasel, K. (2017). 5 things to know about the gender pay gap." *CNN Money.* Retrieved from http://money.cnn.com/2017/04/04/pf/equal-pay-day-gender-pay-gap/index.html?iid=EL.

231. Ibid.

232. Cassese, E., Barnes, T., & Holman, M. (2018). How "hostile sexism" came to shape our politics.

233. Ibid.

234. Ibid.

235. Bartels, L. M. 2008. *Unequal democracy: The political economy of the New Gilded Age*. Princeton, NJ: Princeton University Press.

236. Poloni-Staudinger, L., & Ortbals, C. D. (2012). *Terrorism and violent conflict: Women's agency, leadership and responses*.

237. Bartels, L. M. 2008. *Unequal democracy: The political economy of the New Gilded Age*.

238. Bartels, L. (2002). Beyond the running tally: Partisan bias in political perceptions. *Political Behavior, 24*(2), 117–50.

239. Gerber, A., & Green, D. (1998). Rational learning and partisan attitudes. *American Journal of Political Science, 42*(3), 794–818.

240. Winter, N. (2010). Masculine Republicans and feminine Democrats: Gender and Americans' explicit and implicit images of the political parties. *Springer Science*. DOI: 10.1007/s11109-010-9131-z.

241. Conover, P. J. (1988). Feminists and the gender gap.

242. Conover, P. J., & Sapiro, V. (1993). Gender, feminist consciousness, and war.

243. Bartels, L. M. 2008. *Unequal democracy: The political economy of the New Gilded Age*.

244. Poloni-Staudinger, L., & Ortbals, C. D. (2012). *Terrorism and violent conflict: Women's agency, leadership and responses*.

245. Lipset, S. M. (1960). *Political man*. New York, NY: Doubleday.

246. Kittilson, M. C. (2016). Gender and political behavior.

247. Ibid.

248. Givens, T. (2004). The radical right gender gap. *Comparative Political Studies*.

249. Kittilson, M. C. (2016). Gender and political behavior.

250. Fisher, P. (2014). *Demographic gaps in American political behavior*.

251. Ibid.

252. Ibid.

253. Kaufmann, K. M., Petrocik, J. R., & Shaw, D. R. (2008). *Unconventional wisdom: Facts and myths about American voters*.

254. Bevan, S., & Cullman, S. (2018). Why we are leaving the G.O.P. *The New York Times*. Retrieved from https://www.nytimes.com/2018/06/24/opinion/abortion-rights-republican-party-women.html?action=click&pgtype=Homepage&clickSource=story-heading&module=opinion-c-col-left-region&region=opinion-c-col-left-region&WT.nav=opinion-c-col-left-region&fbclid=IwAR1ArnGMo1BSYQ9Zt8iS5Z9k2cWKp7zd2_7do9pXTGOE44-OZcGx0e4dhzQ.

255. Fisher, P. (2014). *Demographic gaps in American political behavior*.

256. Ibid.

257. Smooth, W. (2006). Intersectionality in electoral politics: A mess worth making. *Politics & Gender, 2*(3), 400–414.

258. Kittilson, M. C. (2016). Gender and political behavior.

CHAPTER FOUR

POLITICAL AMBITION

Chapter 3 opened with a story about the gap between American men and women and their affiliation with the Republican and Democratic parties, respectively. Another striking gap that occurs in U.S. politics, as well as in other countries with patriarchal roots, is that women engage in many traditional political acts at lower rates than men. U.S. women, for example, not only have lower levels of political knowledge and self-report lower levels of political interest but are also less apt to engage in political discussions, attempt to persuade others' vote choice, donate money to a political candidate or cause, or volunteer to work for a candidate or political party.[1-7] Of particular consequence is that this reluctance to engage in traditional political activity extends to women's **political ambition**, or their willingness to run for public office.[8] This chapter first unpacks reasons why women have low levels of political ambition compared to men, in particular exploring why motivating women to run for office has been so much more difficult than most Second-Wave scholars anticipated. It also explores what happens when women do put themselves forward as candidates, as well as whether the sheer number of women inspired to run in the 2018 midterm elections finally will help transform the electoral arena in ways that bolster women's political ambition in the future.

Women's tendency to avoid most forms of traditional political participation does not mean that they are uninterested in political outcomes. Women were initially precluded from formal means of participation linked to elections and office holding—like working on a campaign, making a campaign contribution, or contacting a government official. Their participation in these tactics still falls short of men's. But women always have embraced informal activities—including boycotting products and services, signing petitions, joining voluntary associations, volunteering in the community, and organizing social movements.[9] Channeling political interest through these gender-conforming tactics emerges with adolescence.[10] For example, Alozie, Simon, and Merril (2003) found that school-aged girls were more likely to see voting as important—and were more interested in media coverage of political issues and of electoral campaigns—than similarly-aged boys. Yet young women often claim to be disinterested in "politics" even when they have strong opinions about inherently political issues, like reproductive rights, use of military force, and public policies.[1112] Similarly, while women are reluctant to engage in political discussion in **masculine-coded public settings** (i.e., those typically considered the domain of men, like radio call-in shows, letters to the editor, or town hall meetings), they are willing to engage in public talk about the issues they care about in feminized public settings. These include carefully organized deliberative forums, where preferred modes of talk and action emphasize feminine values over masculine ones (for example, favoring civility over conflict or helping over winning).[13] By the time they reach college, young women are much more apt to claim that the best way to make their community and country a better place is to volunteer for a charity (at 40%, compared to only 27% of young men), while young men are more likely to embrace running for office (at 28%, compared to only 15% of young women).[14] At some point in their political socialization, women learn to express political opinions and to seek political influence in gender-conforming settings and in gender-conforming ways that differ markedly from men's.

Yet, a knee-jerk reaction, grounded both in patriarchy's embrace of gender essentialism and in Americans' embrace of radical individualism, is to use these differences to bolster the claim that men and women really are different and suited for different functions in society. Some women began running for public office, including the office of the presidency, in the 1800s, even before they earned the right to vote. Since women have been enfranchised fully for nearly 100 years, one simplistic explanation of persistent patterns is to assume that if women really wanted to debate political issues, volunteer for a political party, or stand for public office, they would. For some, women's failure to opt in to these activities in larger numbers serves as evidence that women, unlike men, are "naturally" apolitical and disinterested in wielding political influence. Before drawing this simplistic conclusion, this chapter asks you to consider other explanations, including the long reach of our patriarchal history. Further, as Box 4.1 indicates, comparing other countries to the United States reveals that institutional and cultural factors—and not innate gender differences—play an important role in whether women consider running for office.

BOX 4.1: COMPARATIVE FEATURE

Studies of Women's Political Ambition in Comparative Perspective

Americanists are political scientists who focus on the United States, but **comparativists** focus on countries other than America. When studying women's political participation, comparativists tend to explore how institutional (often called **demand variables**) and cultural factors that vary across countries influence women's political behavior. They are less likely to investigate how individual traits (often called **supply variables**) such as political ambition propel or impede women's candidacies. Although no comprehensive worldwide study of women's political ambition exists, scholars have studied women's political ambition in an array of countries, listed in Table 4.1.[15-19] Findings suggest that women worldwide often do not *significantly* differ from men in their political ambition, and sometimes women have more ambition than men, as ambition (supply) interacts with institutional structure (demands).

Table 4.1 Studies of Women's Political Ambition in Comparative Perspective

Country (Electoral system and quotas)	Authors (Publication date)	Study's Respondents (Year of data)	Findings on Political Ambition of Women and Men	Women Less Ambitious than Men? (Yes or no; statistically significant?)
Argentina	Schwindt-Bayer (2011)	68 national legislators, women and men (2001–2002)	43.8% of women legislators and 50% of men legislators aspire to stay in the current office they hold.	*Yes*, but statistically significant *only* for legislators aspiring to higher political office.
			31.3% of women legislators and 77.3% of men legislators aspire to higher political offices.	
Colombia	Schwindt-Bayer (2011)	176 national legislators, women and men (2001–2002)	66.7% of women legislators and 77.5% of men legislators aspire to stay in the current office they hold.*	*Yes*, but *not* statistically significant.
			64.3% of women legislators and 77.3% of men legislators aspire to higher political offices.*	

(Continued)

(Continued)

Costa Rica	Schwindt-Bayer (2011)	50 national legislators, women and men (2001–2002)	20.0% of women legislators and 43.6% of men legislators aspire to stay in the current office they hold.	*Yes*, but *not* statistically significant.
			44.4% of women legislators and 68.4% of men legislators aspire to higher political offices.	
Germany	Davidson-Schmich (2016)	465 high ranking members of political parties (date needed)	50% of women and 59% of men in parties with voluntary quotas had considered running for a political position.	*Yes*, but *only* statistically significant for willingness to accept a hypothetical nomination for local elective office.
			65% of women and 73% of men in parties with voluntary quotas would be willing to accept a hypothetical nomination for local elected office.	
			30% of women and 38% of men in parties with voluntary quotas would agree to appear on the ballot for high-level elective office.**	
Japan	Dalton (2015)	17 national legislators, women only (2007–2008)	Women avoid claiming overt ambition and instead frame their political participation as a matter of caring and working for others and as a result of their connections with men in politics.***	*NA— interviews with no statistical test

Pakistan	Rincker, Aslam, and Isani (2017)	62 supporters of the Pakistani Lawyers' Movement, women and men who tended to be urban, elite, and highly educated. (2007–2009)	72% of women and 68% of men who are supporters of the movement had considered running for office.	*No* for considering running for office, but *not* statistically significant.
			48% of women and 50% of men had talked to a political party leader about running for office.	*Yes* for talking to political party leader, but *not* statistically significant.
			5% of women and 34% of men had discussed running for office with a community leader.	*Yes* for talking to political party leader, *and* statistically significant.
Spain	Galais, Öhberg and Coller (2016)	133 national legislators, women and men (2009–2011)	55% of women legislators and 44% of men legislators wanted to stay in politics.	*Yes*, but *not* statistically significant.
Sweden	Galais, Öhberg and Coller (2016)	181 national legislators, women and men (2011)	50% of women legislators and 50% of men legislators wanted to stay in politics.	*No*

Sources: Dalton, E. (2015). *Women and politics in contemporary Japan.* New York, NY: Routledge; Davidson-Schmich, L. K. (2016). *Gender quotas and democratic participation: Recruiting candidates for elective offices in Germany.* Ann Arbor: University of Michigan Press; Galais, C., Öhberg, P., & Coller, X. (2016). Endurance at the top: Gender and political ambition of Spanish and Swedish MPs. *Politics and Gender* 1(2); Rincker, M., Aslam, G., & Isani, M. (2017). Crossed my mind, but ruled it out: Political ambition and gender in the Pakistani lawyers' movement 2007–2009. *International Political Science Review,* 38(4), 246–63; Schwindt-Bayer, (L). 2011. Women who win: Social backgrounds, paths to power, and political ambition in Latin American Legislatures. *Politics and Gender,* 7(1),1–33.

*These numbers represent percentages for respondents from the lower house of the legislature in Colombia. Swindt-Bayer (2011) also reports numbers from the Senate that are not included here.

** the Landtag, Bundestag, or European Parliament.

***Due to Japanese culture, men would also avoid overt ambition.

What might explain why women in countries other than the United States are more ambitious? Ambition is stifled when women, who tend to be more risk-adverse than men, believe they will not succeed in politics.[20] Institutional factors such as the proportional representation electoral system (PR), sex-based electoral quotas, and reserved parliamentary seats for women can improve the "recruitment environment" for women, pulling them into politics (see Chapter 6 for greater discussion).[21,22] These factors also increase women's chances to win and arguably lower their fear of losing. In the United States, the majoritarian electoral system still favors incumbents who tend to be white men (see Chapters 5 and 6). Thus, many other countries have institutional settings with greater political opportunities that cultivate ambition.[23] This seems to be the case in Pakistan. In Pakistan, Rincker, Aslam, and Isani (2017) find that *more* women than men have thought of running for office because the "presence of reserved seats in Parliament for women [i.e., 17 percent of Parliament seats are is legally required to be fill by women] . . . and the presence of a recent executive role model [i.e., Benazir Bhutto as Prime Minister]."[24] Similarly, voluntary political party quotas in Germany bring more women into politics because some parties have promised to increase the number of women within their organizations; however, fewer German women than men who are eligible candidates actually want to run for election, suggesting that quotas may not be enough of an incentive to overcome other factors influencing German women's political ambition.[25]

The gap in participation in the United States, meanwhile, at least partially reflects a "hang-over" effect from women's historic exclusion from public life. Even after winning the right to vote in 1920, it took women time to become habitual voters—in the same way that it takes other newly enfranchised groups of citizens, such as first generation immigrants, time to become regular voters. Not only did American women who came of age just before the Nineteenth Amendment was passed continue to vote at lower rates than women born after them, they passed on their ambivalence toward the ballot to their daughters.[26,27] Hence in the 1920 election, only one third of eligible women voted,[28] and women's voter turnout did not exceed 50% until the 1948 presidential election. Women continued to underperform at the ballot box, in comparison to men, until 1968. Yet since 1984, women overall (as well as when compared

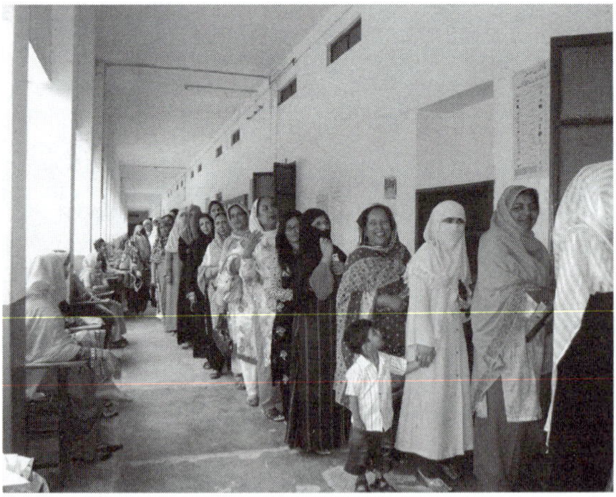

▶ **Photo 4.1** Women standing in line to vote in Pakistan.

to men who share their racial and ethnic identity) have slightly out-voted men in national elections. Intersectional identities, however, affected patterns of voter turnout from the time of women's suffrage, as native-born, middle-to-upper-class, and white women initially had higher levels of turnout than immigrant, rural, and poor women.[29,30] Up until 2004, white women voted at higher rates than other women—a distinction they ceded to African American women in 2008 and 2012. African American women's strong participation in these elections was likely a response to Barack Obama's historic presidential campaigns. Their participation rates dropped in 2016 but rebounded in 2018.

PROMOTING WOMEN'S ACCESS AND AMBITION

Both academics and activists initially anticipated that women's participation in governance would gradually increase over time, like voting, until women were fully integrated into the political process. Because similar educational and occupational opportunities transpired for men and women after the First and Second Waves of feminism, many anticipated that women's lived experiences would converge with men's, at which point women would overcome barriers to full participation and would assimilate into the existing political structure. This expectation overlaps with the liberal feminist tactics described in Chapter 1; it suggests that if women have opportunities and resources they will gain access to political processes and institutions rather than having to fundamentally transform them so that they better accommodate women's lives and how they are different from men's.

Women's full participation in public life—especially serving in political office—is an important indicator of a robust democracy. The United States has a federal system of government designed to disperse power away from the central, national government. Diffusing government authority throughout the federal system means that about 500,000 citizens at any given time must be willing to serve in local, state, and national elected positions, so that the electorate has a choice in representation. Holding contested elections requires that at least twice this number must be interested in running for office. As political scientist Joseph Schlesinger noted, "A political system unable to kindle ambitions for office is in danger of breaking down as one unable to restrain ambitions."[31] The failure to generate political ambition among more than half the population has implications for our ability to recruit an adequate number of public servants, especially in recent decades when Americans, men and women alike, have turned toward private life and away from public service and civic duty.[32] Moreover, as the ensuing chapters on the effect of women legislators, executives, and judges indicate, women have different lived experiences than men—which affects the types of issues they prioritize, as well as their approach to deliberation and problem-solving. When women do not seek public office, the types of issues government addresses, as well as the way elected officials discuss and resolve issues are affected.

Early studies of **candidate emergence**—when someone throws his or her hat into the ring and runs for office—treated political ambition as a given. Scholars assumed that some subset of U.S. men citizens would always have political ambition. So instead of studying how people developed political ambition in the first place, they studied how those with ambition decided whether or not to run. This research started with the assumption that politicians are rational actors, and it attempted to understand which factors—including the likelihood of winning—the potential politicians were likely to include in an internal cost-benefit analysis before seeking office.[33]

Thus, early studies noting that women were often reluctant to run for office assumed that after the Second Wave in the 1960s and 1970s, women would gain access to higher education and professional careers, and their lives and experiences would start to more closely resemble men's. Political scientist Susan Welch first developed this argument in a 1977 article, noting that women's full participation in public life was constrained by situational, socialization, and structural factors.[34] **Situational factors** described women's ongoing domestic responsibilities. Given the way families and households were structured in the 1970s, women still often found themselves primarily responsible for not only managing their households but also for the care and feeding of husbands and children. **Socialization factors**, meanwhile, emphasized the way influential actors in society (parents, teachers, and authority figures) overwhelmingly encouraged women to embrace traditional feminine traits such as passivity and traditional feminine roles, such as caregiver. Finally, **structural factors** focused on the fact that few women fell into the demographic categories typically associated with successful political careers, including holding bachelors and professional degrees, earning a high income, or working as business executives and lawyers. Nearly 20 years later, another major study of political participation reached similar conclusions. Sidney Verba, Kay Lehman Schlozman, and Henry Brady[35] found three key experiences affected everyone's ability to participation in politics. These include experiences that cultivate necessary resources (which includes money but more importantly civic and political skills), provide engagement (such as processing political information, developing political preferences, and cultivating political interest), and extend invitations (whereby people are regularly asked to participate in civic and political affairs). They found that women's historical confinement to the domestic sphere meant that far fewer women were capable of cultivating key political resources (money and civic skills), which in turn resulted in less engagement and fewer invitations to participate. Similar to Welch,[36] Verba and Schlozman (along with Nancy Burns) later concluded that once women gained equal access to the type of education and careers that cultivate civic and political skills and yield higher incomes, "then it would follow as the day the night: gender differences in political participation would disappear."[37] Focusing on women's access to education and occupations as the primary barrier to their political ambition led others to build statistical models predicting that, excluding incumbents, half of the challengers running for state legislature in 2006 would be women.[38] They concluded that "a substantial part of the underrepresentation of women in public office in the United States is because of their underrepresentation in this eligible pool" and that, "changing the occupational distribution of women would influence their recruitment to public office."[39]

As predicted, young women were eager to take advantage of the broad access to education provided to them for the first time, when Congress passed Title IX of the Education Amendments in 1972. **Title IX** bars sex discrimination in education programs and activities offered by any school that receives federal funding. Before Title IX, women had difficulty going on to college or university.

▶ **Photo 4.2** The ratio of men to women on college campuses prior to Title IX.

Los Angeles Times photographic archive, UCLA Library

Elite private universities and colleges (like Harvard and Yale or Bates and Dartmouth) had quotas to restrict the number of women admitted—if they admitted them at all. Requiring women applicants to have higher GPAs and test scores than men was common practice on many public and private campuses. Yet despite being more qualified, women were either officially prevented or informally discouraged from pursuing traditionally men-dominated programs in medicine, law, and business. For example, Ruth Bader Ginsburg, and decades later Hillary Clinton, were discouraged by administrators and faculty members from attending Harvard Law School. In her memoir, Clinton (2017) describes her decision to attend Yale Law School after a Harvard professor told her, "We don't need any more women at Harvard,"[40] during a campus visit.

Not surprisingly, then, only 8% of women age 19 and older were college graduates in 1970, compared with 14% of men. Yet by 2009, approximately 28% of U.S. women had a college degree.[41] Women students quickly achieved parity with men on college campuses by the late 1970s, and their numbers have advanced steadily ever since. By 2010, they constituted approximately 58% of college students nationwide, while simultaneously earning higher grades and being more likely to complete college than their men peers. Now, not only are women more likely than men to earn bachelor's degrees among most racial and ethnic groups and across all socioeconomic distributions,[42,43] since 2011, they have also been more likely to earn a graduate degree.[44]

BOX 4.2: COMPARATIVE FEATURE

Access to Medical School Scandal in Japan

While many take women's access to higher education and professional schools for granted in established democracies, a recent scandal in Japan makes it clear that women's battle for access to education is ongoing. In 2018, an investigation into the admission process at Tokyo Medical University revealed university officials regularly altered women applicants' test scores in order to reduce the number of women admitted. The practice, while likely in use by at least 2006, was ramped up in 2010, when successful women applicants spiked up to 38% of incoming students—which admissions officials deemed too many. As a result, hundreds of women across nearly a decade were systematically discriminated against and were denied admission in favor of less-qualified men. In Japan, women are expected to be almost entirely responsible for the household and family caregiving, while men are expected to be ideal workers who work long hours without complaint. (These same expectations also mean that Japanese voters historically have been leery of electing mothers to serve in public office, as Box 4.1 notes). A former admissions official anonymously explained that women were denied entry to medical school because officials believed that they were likely to quit after marrying and starting families and that they would not want to pursue the most time-consuming and rigorous assignments, such as pursuing surgical specialties or working in remote areas. Clearly, binary gender roles and expectations still affect women's opportunities—even in countries where laws officially prohibit discrimination based on sex.[45-47]

© The Asahi Shimbun/Getty Images

▶ **Photo 4.3** Japanese women protest medical school admission scandal.

Despite their dramatic success in undergraduate, graduate, and professional programs, however, women are still underrepresented in the fields long associated with men's political careers. In 2017, for example, women were 50.3% of law school graduates but constituted just over 34% of lawyers at law firms. Further, their share of equity partnerships, a position associated with decision-making authority and higher income, remained stuck at just 20%.[48]

Women faired even less well in business, where women made up 48% of entry-level positions in 2017 but just 21% of those in the **C-suite**, which refers to women in the highest levels of senior management that normally have titles starting with C (i.e., CEO). Only 3% of these top executive positions were held by women of color.[49] The **glass ceiling** (the metaphor used to describe how women can see the top of a company/government but not reach it) is even thicker in Fortune 500 Companies, where the number of women executives dropped in 2017—which meant that women comprised only 4.8% of the chief executives at America's most profitable companies.[50] Among women of color, rates are even lower, occupying only 1 in 30 of senior level positions.

Given these statistics, perhaps it is no surprise to learn that lack of anticipated progress also characterizes women in politics, which we cover in greater depth in Chapters 6, 7, and 8. The puzzle of too few women American elected officials persists even when the most likely explanations, including access to education and voter bias and incumbency, covered in Chapter 5, are eliminated as explanations.

GENDER SOCIALIZATION AND POLITICAL AMBITION

The interrelated problems of a half-empty pipeline and a persistent plateau led scholars to reexamine sex, gender, and candidate emergence, in order to understand why—despite access to higher education, professional employment, supportive voters, and political opportunities—women still have comparatively lower levels of political ambition than men. Rather than taking political ambition as a given, scholars began to ask how ambition emerges in the first place. Jennifer L. Lawless and Richard L. Fox undertook two studies—titled *It Takes a Candidate* and *It Still Takes a Candidate*—to explore the emergence of **nascent political ambition**, which they define as the inclination to consider becoming a candidate.[51,52] They argued that nascent political ambition must precede **expressive political ambition**, where individuals engage in a cost-benefit analysis and consider whether to run for a specific seat.[53] Lawless and Fox conducted two waves of the Citizen Political Ambition Panel Study in 2001 and 2008, each time surveying men and women working in law, business, education, and politics—the four professions previous scholars had identified as most associated with a political career. Unlike average citizens, both the women and men included in this study regularly interacted with elected officials, engaged in traditional political activity, and—not surprisingly—were more interested in political issues and events than most people. Despite these similarities, men had much higher levels of nascent and expressive political ambition.

Lawless and Fox identified a consistent 16-point difference when men and women answered the question: "Have you ever considered running for office?"[54,55] In their 2001 survey, 59% of likely men candidates responded affirmatively, compared to only 43% of their women counterparts. The follow-up study revealed that of those who responded affirmatively, 20% of the men actually ran for a public office, compared to only 15% of the women. The result is that across the eight years from 2001 to 2008, 12% of the men included in the study actively sought public office, compared to only 7% of women.[56] Keep in mind that intersectionality likely affects the reasons why women with different cross-cutting identities are less interested in pursuing political careers, as women are not a monolithic group. Scholars are now beginning to explore nuanced differences in the way women develop political ambition. Moreover, the type of positions that women and men were interested in pursuing differed. While both were interested in running for local positions, such as school board or town council seats, women were far less interested in running for more prominent local and state positions, like mayor, governor, or state legislator or for positions at the national level, like U.S. representative, U.S. senator, or president. Men, for example, were 40% more likely to consider running for state legislature and about 50% more likely to consider pursuing federal office.[57]

Therefore, simply waiting for the second round of educational and professional gains that women made in the 1970s and 1980s to take root and flourish is not likely to yield more progress in numbers of women in government for two reasons. First, the gap in nascent political ambition among members of the overall general public actually grew between 2001 and 2011—a result of men's interest in public office remaining constant (at about 22%), with women's dropping 4% (from 18% to 14%).[58] Research measuring political ambition in which subjects were asked to watch Hillary Clinton's 2016 campaign ads confirms that while her candidacy inspired her women supporters to run for office, it suppressed other women's, along with men's, political ambition.[59] Lawless and Fox further speculate that contrary to the anticipated impact of visible women politicians, women's enthusiasm for public service likely diminished after observing what other women endured throughout their bids for national office.[60] While Hillary Clinton and Sarah Palin served as role models for many in 2008, they also provided a prominent reminder that women candidates have barriers to overcome that men do not, barriers such as sexist media coverage, questions about their family and life choices, overt sexual harassment, and misogynist online abuse (all covered in more detail in Chapters 5 and 7). This should give us pause as the 116th Congress, elected in the 2018 election, is more female and more diverse than ever before. While having women of color represented in Congress may serve to be important in raising the ambition of some, if they are attacked, we may see a decrease in the political ambition of girls and women of color down the road. Second, generational replacement does not appear likely to fix the problem, as young women have been no more ambitious than older women by the time they begin their professional careers. While adolescents report similar levels of political ambition, with about two-thirds in each group rejecting a political career, a gap emerges between the sexes by the time they are college-aged and persists into adulthood.

By this point in their lives, 14% of men indicate that they definitely plan to run for office, compared to only 7% of women in their age cohort. Meanwhile, 36% of college-aged young women claim to have "absolutely no interest" in running for office, compared to only 23% of their men peers.[61,62]

BOX 4.3: THE "CHILLY" CAMPUS CLIMATE AND YOUNG WOMEN'S POLITICAL AMBITION

Lawless and Fox (2013) attribute the decline in college-women's political ambition to newfound freedom to control activities and coursework.[63] While high school curricula has structured requirements for all students, women can self-select into college electives, majors, and co-curricular activities that conform to traditional gender roles—and that exposes young women to fewer experiences that bolster political interest (like taking a political science course or talking about political issues with friends). Yet, research by scholars who study higher education has long suggested that women experience a "chilly" climate on most campuses that systematically undermines their self-esteem.[64-67] Women enter college with higher levels of academic achievement, for example, but lower levels of perceived academic ability and intellectual self-confidence, as well as lower expectations for their own performance in college. The decline of girls' self-esteem and self-confidence begins in adolescence.[68-70] Yet, rather than ameliorating this disparity between achievement and perception, the college experience exacerbates it—even for the highest-performing women students.[71,72] Once arrived on campus, women and men continue to enact sex-differentiated patterns established in elementary and high school, as women spend more time engaged in academic endeavors (studying), while men typically choose to pursue leisure activities (playing video games) instead.[73] Women are rewarded for this investment with higher levels of academic achievement.[74] Indeed, women earn higher grades than men even when men match them in the amount of time devoted to coursework.[75] Yet, gaps in the two sexes' perceptions of their academic ability continue to widen.[76] Just as troubling, women enter college rating themselves lower than men on a number of measures of psychological well-being such as emotional health and stress levels. Women are also more likely than men to report feeling overwhelmed and being depressed. Again, rather than helping to close the distance

(Continued)

(Continued)

between men and women, spending four years in college makes it worse.[77] Even after successful women college students become accomplished professionals, many continue to suffer from **imposter syndrome**—or the feeling that they are unqualified and undeserving of recognition. Imposter syndrome can be exacerbated for young women of color or for those with low socioeconomic status. Far more women than men attribute their success to luck than to their own talent and hard work.[78]

Sax and colleagues (2008) summarize recent findings on women and college experiences, noting that while women dominate enrollments and earn high grades, they are still underrepresented in traditionally male majors and careers, while reporting higher levels of stress and lower levels of academic self-confidence.[79] While the behaviors and orientations that produce these differences are established before students enter college, educational programs appear to "preserve and strengthen stereotyped differences in behavior, personality, aspirations and achievements."[80]

Even when women and men have similar college experiences, the outcomes are often different. For example, the more time men students spend interacting with professors outside of the classroom, the more apt they are to embrace egalitarianism. Frustratingly, the exact opposite is true for women students—as those same interactions push them toward traditional gender roles. Challenging a professor in the classroom heightens women's (but not men's) self-reported anxiety. Similarly, when women students perceive that faculty members do not take their comments seriously, they are more likely than their men peers to experience an erosion of academic self-confidence and professional aspirations.[81] Yet, in campus climate studies, few women complain of overt sexism or describe the behavior of their professors or their fellow students as offensive. Many women claim that they are satisfied with their college experience and sometimes even claim that they have received preferential treatment from professors—which makes it difficult to attribute the outcomes described above to patterns of behavior that can be readily identified through survey research.

Yet, a student may claim to be satisfied with her educational experiences on a questionnaire but still report troubling incidents of "everyday sexism" when interviewed in person.[82] Research suggests that women regularly experience an array of **microaggressions**, indirect or subtle discriminations, grounded in objectification[83] and patronizing assumptions.[84] These include brief, commonplace comments or actions—a sexist joke here, a wolf-whistle there—that convey slights about women's inherent abilities or convey criticisms when women fail to conform to traditional gender roles.[85,86] Swim et al. (2004) conclude that college women are subjected to one or two such acts each week.[87] This constant presence of microaggressions helps to explain the erosion of academic self-confidence and psychological well-being throughout women's college careers, as microaggressions are linked to negative consequences such as stress, depression, anger, rage, and hopelessness.[88]

Moreover, it also helps to explain why women themselves fail to recognize and report a hostile campus climate, as microaggressions are intended to serve as subtle social sanctions. As such, they can be effective in encouraging women to question their own abilities and to accept their role as a helpmate to men relatives and professional colleagues in a patriarchal status quo. For example, when women are asked to recall a specific incident of objectification—even when they can accurately label and describe the incident as such—their acceptance of traditional gender norms increases and their willingness to engage in feminist social activism decreases.[89] It is likely that immersion in a chilly campus climate is not only the root cause of women's declining confidence and elevated stress levels during college but also erodes their political ambition.

Rather than identifying Welch's structural factors (access to education and professions) as the reason women avoid politics, Lawless and Fox (2010) point to traditional gender socialization as the culprit,[90,91] noting "[t]he pervasive influence of traditional gender socialization clearly might affect the cost-benefit calculus eligible candidates employ, but it has been largely disregarded."[92] Their research identifies three aspects of gender socialization that still suppress women's nascent political ambition, including traditional family role orientations, a masculinized ethos, and a gendered psyche among eligible candidates.

BOX 4.4: POLICY FEATURE

Violence Against Women in Politics Worldwide

Americanists have tended to focus on traditional gender socialization's effect on women, overlooking its effect on men. Yet, when explaining why patriarchy is inherently violent—and in particular why men overwhelmingly commit acts of violence—sociologist Allan G. Johnson (2014) notes "because violence is the most extreme instrument of control, then the capacity for

(Continued)

violence—whether or not individual men actually make use of it—is central to the cultural definition of manhood."[93] Traditional patriarchy positions men as heads of households, responsible (using violence if necessary) for ensuring that the women and children under their authority conform to prescribed roles.[94] As a result, patriarchy encourages men "to dismiss or not even to be aware of the needs and experiences of others, and to base moral decisions, including whether to use violence, solely on abstract notions of principle and dignity, honor and authority and 'being in the right' without also taking into account the consequences of what they do."[95] Until this aspect of gender identity is dismantled, some men who embrace traditional definitions of masculinity will commit acts of violence against nonconforming women—and especially against women who step into public leadership roles. The tactic often works, as even just the perception that their neighborhoods are unsafe is enough to suppress women's (but not men's) civic engagement.[96]

U.S. policy focuses on helping women victims rather than changing men. Consider the **Violence Against Women Act** enacted in 1994. The legislation created an Office of Violence Against Women in the Department of Justice (DOJ). Along with the Department of Health and Human Services (HHS), the DOJ awards tribal, state, and local grants, funding programs that help to provide a coordinated response (from courts, law enforcement, prosecutors, lawyers, and community organizations) to address domestic violence, child abuse, sexual assault, rape, and stalking. A provision of the bill, identifying sex-based crimes as hate crimes—thus enabling victims to seek civil rights remedies in federal court—was overturned by the Supreme Court in *U.S. v. Morrison*.[97] While successful in preventing violence and helping victims, reauthorization of the law became controversial in 2013 and 2018 over new provisions intended to help at-risk individuals, including Native American women (by permitting nontribal perpetrators to be prosecuted in tribal court), undocumented immigrant women (by increasing the number of visas available), and victims of sex trafficking (by mandating provision of reproductive health services), as well as to LGBTQIA+ individuals (by prohibiting denial of remedial services or access to shelters). Another addition to the version of the 2018 reauthorization passed in the House of Representatives expanded law enforcement's ability to restrict gun purchases by those convicted of domestic violence.

In the meantime, the U.S. #MeToo movement is revealing the extent of sexual harassment/assault and violent threats experienced by women candidates and public officials in the United States, as well as ways women are grappling with these incidents, either personally or via policy changes (see Chapters 5, 6, 7, and 8). Such violence is called **violence against women politicians (VAWP)**, and it occurs in many countries around the world. Violent acts against women candidates and politicians are frequent, as the Inter-Parliamentary Union's 2016 survey of 55 women parliamentarians from 39 countries revealed that 82% of respondents reported being subjected to psychological violence; 44% to threats of death, rape, kidnapping, or beatings targeting themselves or their children; 26% to direct physical violence; and 22% to sexual violence.[98] Recent events in Kenya are illustrative, as when four men forced Ann Kanyi, a primary candidate for the legislature, from her car at gunpoint[99] or when Elizabeth Manyala, an official from Nairobi County, was "smashed" into a wall by a man colleague when she refused to reallocate funds from the "county women's caucus to one of his pet projects."[100]

Scholars define VAWP as "1) aggressive acts aimed largely or solely at women in politics; 2) because they are women, often using gendered means of attack; and 3) with the goal of deterring their participation in order to preserve traditional gender roles and undermine democratic institutions."[101] Acts that meet this definition, categorized in Table 4.2, include murder, kidnapping, or sexual assault (real or threatened), as well as pressuring women to resign their government posts and propagating rumors maligning their commitment to being wives and mothers or questioning their sexual morality. Physical and/or verbal intimidation is key, as the goal is to scare women into to abandoning politics.

Table 4.2 Categories of Violence Against Women in Politics

Category of Violence	Definition	Example
Physical Violence	Bodily injuries inflicted upon women political actors or their families, including domestic abuse, beating, abduction, and assassination.	After being sworn in as her town's first woman mayor, a Mexican politician was gunned down in her home in 2016.
Sexual Violence	Sexual acts and attempts at sexual acts by coercion, along with unwelcome sexual comments and advances. This includes sexual harassment, rape, and sexual exploitation.	In Sudan, women human-rights defenders have been sexually assaulted and told that they will be raped again if they continue their activities.
Psychological Violence	Hostile behavior and abuse intended to cause emotional damage to a person, including death and rape threats, stalking, character assassination, and social boycotts.	In Uganda, police stripped a woman opposition activist naked at a party rally in 2015, leaving her shocked and humiliated in front of men colleagues.

(Continued)

(Continued)

| Economic Violence | Degradation and coercion through control over access to economic resources | Local officials in Bolivia denied women— but not men—officeholders their salaries and expense reimbursements. |
| Symbolic Violence | Abuse and aggression in terms of false portrayals that seek to deny women's competence as political actors. | Highly sexualized images of women politicians are found easily via Google. |

Source: Krook, Mona Lena. "Violence Against Women in Politics." Journal of Democracy 28:1 (2017), 79–81. © 2017 National Endowment for Democracy and Johns Hopkins University Press. Reprinted with permission of Johns Hopkins University Press.

Sometimes violence against women occurs as backlash against an increasing number of women in politics. Reforms to increase the number of women in politics, such as quotas (see Chapter 6), make women a "key voting demographic," as well as more visible, powerful politicians.[102] Some men believe that women's newfound public positions detract from their own power, while others (men and women alike) think women should not be in public life at all. Such beliefs contribute to violent attacks—as in a 2015 bombing in Afghanistan that killed Angiza Shinwari, a provincial council member and defender of women's rights, who exacerbated fundamentalists' ire by refusing full body covering in favor of a face covering (*niqab*).[103] Contextual variables also contribute to violence against women politicians. In countries already rife with political and social violence, for example, violent crimes targeting women are also apt to go unprosecuted. Advanced democracies are not immune. In 2018, Jess Phillips, a feminist member of the U.K. parliament, received at least 600 rape threats (via Twitter) in one night; in 2017, French candidate Nathalie Kosciusko-Morizet was attacked while campaigning in Paris.[104]

Solutions to VAWP range from media campaigns to new laws. The #NotTheCost campaign, emphasizing "violence is NOT the cost of politics," was started in 2016 by the National Democratic Institute (NDI)—a nonprofit, nonpartisan nongovernmental organization that supports democracy worldwide. The #NotTheCost hashtag is used almost every day to publicly denounce violence against women in politics. For example, @Farida_N tweeted, "When someone tells me women shouldn't get involved in politics because it is too violent for them, I tell them men should stay away from politics because they are too violent for it. #africansrising #notthecost." Meanwhile, political parties can establish zero-tolerance policies and refuse to support perpetrators, while states can establish commissions to track violence or pass laws penalizing those who commit violent acts.[105]

The difficulty of suppressing VAWP is illustrated by Bolivia—which has a *machismo* culture, rife with violence against women, along with quotas that have yielded parity among men and women in its national legislature and city councils. Bolivia became the first country to pass a law prohibiting such violence in 2012. Efforts to enact this legislation took over a decade, as women legislators first gathered to discuss the problem in 2000, with a policymaking initiative launched by the Bolivian Association of Councilwomen (*La Asociación de Concejalas de Bolivia*) shortly thereafter.[106] Similar legislation has been considered in in Costa Rica, Ecuador, Mexico, and Peru. Even so, as of 2018, no Bolivian perpetrators have been convicted. According to the Association of Bolivian Councilwomen, 70 complaints were filed in just the first six months of 2018—more than the 64 filed in 2017 or 65 in 2017.[107] Some Bolivian women were locked in or out of their offices for days, while others were beaten. In a particularly egregious incident, one pregnant councilwoman was kicked so hard that she miscarried.[108] Despite legislation, failure to change Bolivians' definition of masculinity makes it difficult to check these ongoing violent attacks against women politicians.

TRADITIONAL FAMILY ROLE ORIENTATIONS

As described in Chapters 2 and 3, associating women with domestic responsibilities has deep roots in the United States. Women were excluded from the public sphere first because they were deemed inherently unqualified for such participation and second because most people thought such participation would undermine society's stability. These conclusions were based on assumptions about women's natural ability and character. Women's supposed inability to engage in reason and their overly passionate natures justified somber male guidance, while their physical weakness necessitated men's provision and protection.[109] Beyond their inability to meet the criteria for full citizenship, women were also associated with an uncontrollable craving for all forms of self-gratification, so much so that their participation in the public sphere would result in chaos and corruption. Hence women who attempted to be active in public life were perceived not only as inappropriate individuals, reaching beyond their limited abilities, but as a threat that could inspire other women to misbehave, thus undermining society's fragile stability with their craven demands in the public sphere. Such unfortunate outcomes could be avoided if women were guided into their natural role as submissive helpmates within the domestic sphere, where they could be encouraged to direct their passionate nature into fiercely protecting their children and fulfilling the needs of their families rather than their own grasping ambitions. Indeed, patriarchy defines masculinity, in large part, as the ability to successfully control wives and daughters, ensuring that they conform to these gender appropriate roles.[110]

It is important to recognize the weight of this history. None of our civic, political, and economic institutions evolved to accommodate women, along with their unique lived experiences or even with cisgender women's distinct biological functions. These institutions also evolved with the expectation that men would be "ideal workers"—able to dedicate all of their time to civic, political, and economic endeavors—because they were expected to off-load all of their domestic responsibilities onto their mothers, wives, and daughters (along with servants, serfs, and slaves if available). Even now, our civic, political, and economic institutions make little-to-no accommodation for those who cannot be "ideal workers" (fully able, young, healthy, straight men with no domestic responsibilities).

When women first entered the workforce, they were expected to manage their households, a phenomenon that resulted in women—especially married, heterosexual women with children—putting in a **"second shift"** at home, after the workday ended.[111] Many assumed, however, that women's participation in the workforce would eventually result in a more equitable distribution of household chores and child care. Yet, revisiting time diaries of working women in traditional marriages over time reveals how little has changed.[112] Women as of 2018 do less household labor than their mothers and grandmothers (down from 32 hours per week in the 1960s to 18 hours per week by 2013), whereas men are doing more than their fathers and grandfathers (up from 4 hours to 10 across the same time span). Yet, women are more apt to undertake boring, rote chores (such as laundry, food prep, and clean up) that need to be performed day in and day out. On an average day in 2017, 19% of men did this type of housework, compared with 49% of women. Meanwhile, 46% of men did food preparation or cleanup, compared with 69% of women. The percentage of men on "kitchen duty" has increased 11 points from 2003 to 2017.[113,114] Yet, the slow pace of change means that women still do far more household labor than men, even when they are working full time.

This pattern becomes even more dramatic when heterosexual couples have children. When both partners work, women still perform 65% of the family's child-care responsibilities and are 2.5 times more likely than their husbands to care for their children in the middle of the night. Women are also overwhelmingly responsible for the myriad tasks associated with managing a busy household—coordinating calendars, filling out forms, managing doctors' appointments, hiring babysitters, remembering to restock household items, and so on—termed **invisible labor** by social scientists.[115] The gendered expectations of parenting are so entrenched that working women still spend more time on child care, even when their husbands do not work.[116–118]

The small number of women who already have nascent political ambition are willing to juggle family and child care responsibilities to pursue a political career, just as they do to pursue any other profession.[119] But a 2011 study found that likely women candidates were more apt than men to be single, separated, or divorced, less apt to have children, and less apt to have children still living at home. In addition, they are willing to multitask their way through hectic days, as 43% of these women claimed that they were responsible for the majority of household tasks, compared to only 7% of men. Similarly, 60% of women reported being responsible for the majority of childcare responsibilities, compared to only 6% of men. And, while some women are willing to campaign under such circumstances, prioritizing family responsibilities likely keeps many other women from developing an interest in electoral politics in the first place. Indeed, more women run for state legislative seats when living nearby the state capital, which makes juggling family and professional demands easier, and undergraduate women in an experimental design weighed proximity to home twice as much as men students when asked to decide whether to run for a hypothetical elected position.[120]

Young women and men have claimed to support egalitarian relationships—where no partner does more than 60% or less than 40% of domestic work—for decades.[121] But when specifically asked, young men anticipated doing less housework and parenting than their young women partners. Although young men generally agreed that either partner could work full time after having children, they personally expected to be employed full time for their entire careers. Meanwhile, even though they preferred egalitarian relationships, young women anticipate doing significantly more housework than their husbands and to be the ones to interrupt their careers for children.[122-126]

Moreover, as discussed in Chapter 3, even abstract support for egalitarian marriages among 18- to 25-year-olds has declined over the past 20 years, as embracing equal partnerships grew steadily from the 1970s up through the mid-1990s but then fell. In 1994, only 16% of young adults agreed with the statement that a woman's place is in the home, compared to 25% in 2014. Across this same time period, those agreeing that husbands should make all the important decisions for a family grew 10%, from 30% to 40%.[127] This decline in support for egalitarian gender roles is occurring in part because the percentage of Latinx young people in the population is increasing. Latinx young people—especially young men—are more inclined than other demographic groups to prefer traditional family arrangements. Similarly, young African Americans are less apt to embrace egalitarian gender roles than white millennials.[128]

Attitudes toward egalitarian family structures also shift after couples have children. Only 35% of employed millennial men (those born between 1981 and 1996) without children thought that men should be traditional breadwinners, compared to 53% of those with children. Similarly, 24% of college-educated young men in 2015 anticipated taking on substantial child care duties, but only 8% of those with children actually followed through.[129] Sociologists believe millennials are reverting to traditional parenting roles and to gender essentialism to explain those choices as a way to avoid feeling bad when lack of family friendly policies (paid sick, parental, and vacation leave, along with subsidized child care) make it hard to live up to their ideals. Hence, they focus on the notion that women have choices but prefer to take time off or to pursue more flexible careers because they are "naturally" more nurturing.[130,131] Notably, however, broad public support for egalitarian partnerships has continued to rise in some European countries, where family leave policies are more generous and child care more affordable.[132]

Patterns among same-sex partners in the United States provide further evidence that public policy affects family structures. Prior to having children, same-sex couples divide chores more equally. After having children, however, one partner often transitions to the breadwinner role, while the other often takes on more responsibility for household chores and child care—in large part because the workplace still rewards ideal workers unconstrained by domestic responsibility.[133] Claims of gender essentialism, that heterosexual women voluntarily choose to take on domestic roles because it comes naturally, are undermined by the fact that heterosexual women are far less satisfied with this arrangement than gay and lesbian partners—likely because heterosexual husbands assume that if anyone stays home or makes career sacrifices, it will be their wives. Meanwhile this "deal" must be more explicitly negotiated among other types of couples.[134-136]

It is important to recognize that as of 2018 both men and women claim to want partners and families. Men high school students are only slightly less likely to aspire to marriage (at 79%) than women high school students (at 84%). But both sexes are equally likely to want children (at about 70%), to earn a lot of money (at about 85%), and to be successful at their jobs (at 96%).[137] Yet, young heterosexual women who envision men partners in this future scenario are not naïve about the work achieving their goals will entail. While young women prefer egalitarian relationships, they know from observing men and women all around them in everyday life that they will likely work far harder to care for their households and children than their husbands.

Young women consciously factor these responsibilities into their life choices. They intuitively act on the insight explicitly offered by Supreme Court Justice Ruth Bader Ginsberg when she advised, "You can't have it all at once."[138] Hence, the one shift in mass behavior that women overwhelmingly have embraced since the 1960s is to purposefully delay marriage and childbirth. By 2009, the proportion of American women who were married dropped below 50%, while the average age at the time of first marriages rose dramatically to 27, up from only 20 in the 1950s. Fertility rates among millennial women dropped to a record low of 60.2 births per 1,000 women of childbearing age in 2017. On average, women had 1.8 children, which is shy of the 2.1 children per woman required to replace the current U.S. population. When asked, women explain that they are having fewer children in part because affordable high-quality childcare is not available and in part because they are purposefully delaying the responsibilities that come with marriage and family until they have established careers.[139] Interestingly, Susan B. Anthony, in a speech titled *The Homes of Single Women*, predicted a stage when women would use their newfound freedom and economic power to avoid marriage before equality among the sexes would be achieved. She argued that "long existing customs and laws" would affect the behavior of even well-intentioned men, and that these domestic patterns would not change until women purposefully chose to remain single.

Her prediction that this reluctance to marry would result in change may be coming true. The same pattern of delayed marriage and fewer children is happening in other countries, especially in those where women have the greatest difficulty achieving work-life balance. These patterns have even started playing out in the socially conservative countries of West Africa, where women with access to education and employment are not only delaying marriage and family but also shifting cultural norms resulting in women seeking divorces when their marriages are not based on affection between partners.[140]

Until more change occurs, however, women's ongoing obligations in the private sphere force them to undergo a careful juggling act and to consider whether and when to have children. This balancing act not only helps to explain the drop in fertility rates, but it is almost certainly responsible for women's failure to break through glass ceilings in the workplace, as well as for their low levels of nascent political ambition.[141,142]

THE MASCULINIZED ETHOS OF POLITICS

Part of the reason it has been so difficult to shift responsibility for household chores and childcare is that stereotypes about masculinity and femininity have been difficult to displace. Despite repeated waves of social movement activism, many Americans still embrace binary sex categories connected to distinct, gendered traits. The ideal "**agentic male**" makes decisions and takes action, while the ideal "**communal female**" is supportive, other-oriented, and nurturing. Most importantly, she is not ambitious but willingly serves as a resource for others' aspirations. Such stereotyped thinking is persistent. In 2017, for example, Pew Research Center conducted a national survey where Americans across the nation were asked to describe the traits they think society associates with men and women, as well as whether these associations were positive or negative. Researchers found that Americans are much more likely to use the adjective "powerful" to describe men in a positive way (67% positive), while this description had negative connotations for women (92% negative). Similarly, the words "compassionate" and "caring" were positively associated with women but viewed negatively when linked to men. Americans thought that "leadership" and "ambition" are traits that society values more in men, while women were positively associated with "kindness" and "responsibility."[143]

The enforced division of labor over the past 7,000 years means that the domestic sphere still has a traditionally **feminine ethos**, where women are expected to excel precisely because they are "naturally" communal and other-oriented. Similarly, the public sphere—and in particular the hyper-masculine sphere of politics—has a traditionally **masculine ethos**, where men are expected to excel because they are "naturally" ambitious and agentic leaders. People expect politics to be a competitive, rough and tumble man's world—and these expectations tend to become a self-fulfilling prophecy. Many aspects of public office involve listening to others, finding consensus, and solving problems to help other people. But few people emphasize these aspects of the job—choosing instead to highlight competition and conflict. Politicians adopt the language of warfare (using phrases such as waging campaigns, developing strategies and tactics, or mobilizing their foot soldiers) to describe running for office. These metaphors are often repeated by journalists and media pundits—who typically only set aside battle imagery when they use the metaphor of a competitive horse race (who's ahead and who's fallen behind) in their campaign reporting. Similarly, legislative debates are described as battles with winners and losers, when they could be described as deliberation to identify the best solutions for society's shared concerns. Even coverage of politics within party caucuses emphasize conflict, power, and authority—as majority and minority leaders "whip" the votes to build support for their legislative agendas when their efforts could be described as persuading colleagues. Given this masculine ethos, political leadership is still strongly associated with men, and women are often inherently viewed as ill-equipped intruders when they become involved in politics.[144-148]

One major consequence of politics' masculine ethos is that women—from the time they are young girls throughout their adult lives—are rarely encouraged to participate in traditional political activities or to run for office. Parents and families are the primary agents of political socialization, giving them great influence over young people's political identities, attitudes, and behaviors. Indeed, the biographies of successful women politicians and political activists often relay anecdotes of atypical fathers who encouraged their daughters' political interests. It comes as no surprise that people of both sexes are much more likely to think about running for political office if their parents have encouraged them. Yet, even as late as 2013, men college students were more likely (at 40%) to report being encouraged to run for office by their parents than women college students (at only 29%). This pattern holds true for other significant adults in their lives, including other family members, teachers, coaches, religious leaders, and friends.[149]

Similarly, adult women are less likely than men to be encouraged to run for office by their family, friends, and colleagues or to be recruited to run by party officials, elected officials, or activists—even when they have experiences, professions, and civic activism typically associated with political careers.[150] Notably, these patterns held in all of Lawless's and Fox's repeated surveys from 2005 to 2012 about the emergence of nascent political ambition among likely political candidates.[151-153] Fewer women than men were asked to run for office, despite the fact that more women's organizations dedicated to recruiting women (albeit primarily Democratic women) to run for office emerged while they were conducting their research.[154]

Women are less likely than men to be "self-starters" and more likely to run only after being encouraged.[155] Yet, women respond just as positively as men when they are asked, suggesting that nascent political ambition can be cultivated through such requests.[156-158] Currently, however, when people think of politicians, they think of men engaged in hypermasculine endeavors. Unfortunately, more work must be done to dispel the masculine ethos surrounding politics before it will occur to people—from parents and family members to friends, colleagues, and political actors—to ask more women to run.

WOMEN'S GENDERED PSYCHE

The combined effect of traditional gender roles and gendered spheres of activity not only affects broader society but also the internal identities, attitudes, and choices of girls and women. In short, the masculinized ethos of traditional political endeavors leads people to believe that politicians are focused on wielding power over others and are mired in conflict. Hence, women and girls see politics as a masculine endeavor and learn to think that they should avoid traditional political participation.[159]

Even now, many people, including both men and women, still expect women to exemplify the idealized traits of the communal female. Many women still internalize expectations that they be communal, nurturing, and other-oriented. The benevolent nature of many of the prescriptive stereotypes used to confine women to the domestic sphere and to nurturing roles have made this tendency a particularly troublesome gender trap for women to overcome. Unlike the stereotypes used to justify oppressing other minority groups, the attributes that constrain women sound quite positive—leading some to describe this form of sexism as **sugar-coated oppression**. Girls and women who demonstrate nurturing, self-sacrificing characteristics are praised and upheld as exemplary. Members of other marginalized groups often try to overcome negative beliefs by becoming "model minorities" and working hard to contradict assumptions about their inherent abilities and traits. While stressful and unfair to the individuals involved, this strategy can be effective when minorities positively exceed negative stereotypes. When women adopt this strategy by acting agentic, self-promoting, ambitious, and forceful, it can backfire because women are believed to be violating "positive" stereotypes—and thus undermining the reasons why society has placed women on a pedestal. Hence, agentic women often are intensely disliked. A more intense, misogynist reaction is to dehumanize such women as unnatural and deserving of punishment, up to and including threats and violence.

Those who strongly embrace traditional gender roles are apt to have the most intense, negative reactions to women who violate their expectations. This dynamic is labeled **ambivalent sexism** because it combines **benevolent sexism** and **hostile sexism**, and it explains the paradox of how those who cling to traditional gender norms can simultaneously claim that they love and admire (appropriately behaved) women while harshly sanctioning those who dare violate the natural order by rejecting traditional gender roles.[160]

As discussed elsewhere in the book, those with hostile sexist attitudes often mistrust women's motives and see men and women in a zero-sum game for power.

On social science surveys, they are apt to agree with the claims like, "many women get a kick out of teasing by seeming sexually available and then refusing advances," or "most women interpret innocent remarks or acts as being sexist." Those with benevolent sexist attitudes, on the other hand, will agree with statements such as "Women should be cherished and protected by men," or "Women, compared to men, tend to have a superior moral sensibility." According to psychologist Peter Glick, these attitudes create a reinforcing cycle, where society assumes that the only women who are mistreated are those who violate expectations of appropriate feminine behavior—and deserve it. He notes that the basic agreement of ambivalent sexism is that women will cater to men's needs, so that men will cherish and protect them in return. In the most patriarchal cultures, where women have less access to education and economic independence, women are more inclined to go along. Indeed, under such circumstances, women are more likely to embrace benevolent sexism than men.[161]

For girls and women, the risk of social sanction and being disliked is amplified not only by lack of resources but by the fact that they typically have close, intimate relationships (as parents, daughters, friends, spouses, and lovers) with boys and men who benefit from their subordinate status. In the 2014 book *The Gender Knot*, sociologist Allan G. Johnson notes that patterns of oppression seem the most normal when dominate and subordinate groups interact in close, interdependent ways.[162] He concludes,

> As a result, the path of least resistance is to experience patriarchy as normal, consensual, and serving everyone's needs and values. It should not surprise us, then, to find no shortage of women who seem to accept their lot, and not a few who do their part to keep it going in the "natural order" of things.[163]

Similarly, social psychologist Laurie A. Rudman (2005), who studies benevolent sexism, describes why there are not more out-right misogynists, as well as why it is so difficult for women to reject the role of the communal female.[164] She notes, "It is simply not feasible for men to be overtly hostile to women, on whom they depend for a variety of services, including sexual gratification, emotional intimacy, child raising and domestic labor. Similarly, women depend on men for romantic love, economic stability, and social prestige. Thus, one could hardly invent a stronger context in which dominant and subordinate groups are equally invested in preserving the status quo."[165] However, note, just as Susan B. Anthony predicted, women's advances over the past several decades emerged as they became less dependent on men for romantic love, economic stability, and social prestige.

Cultural myths surrounding romance are one of the ways society perpetuates women's subordinate status. When women idealize traditional romance and being protected by chivalrous men, they become less interested in seeking prestigious careers for themselves and more willing to invest in their male partner's economic success. In a nod to Cinderella and Prince Charming, social psychologists refer to this phenomenon as the **glass slipper effect**.[166]

To the extent that women themselves co-opt their own empowerment by internalizing such identities, it can be difficult for them to identify and advocate for their own best interests in the public sphere.[167] Political theorists initially raised these very same concerns not with regard to women but the lower classes. In 1859, John Stewart Mill argued that the habit of deferring to the aristocracy should play no role in a modern democracy, as the practice would encourage those from the lower classes to moderate their demands and to "desire nothing strongly."[168] Echoing John Stuart Mill's concerns that British commoners who knew their place would be incapable of fully recognizing their own self-interests, some feminist scholars fear the same pattern can make it difficult for women to identify and voice their legitimate political concerns. They note, for example, that women have been and still are socialized to be more polite than men.[169–172] According to the seminal work on sex and politeness by Robin T. Lakoff (1972), "Little girls were indeed taught to talk like little ladies, in that their speech is in many ways more polite than that of boys or men, and the reason for this is that politeness involves an absence of strong statement, and women's speech is devised to prevent the expression of strong statements."[173] The absence of strong preferences is essential if women are expected to be a resource for others' agendas rather than their own. Of course, not all women modify their preferences, speech, or activities accordingly, but those who do not risk being disliked and subjected to social sanction as a result.

Not only are girls and women socialized to avoid advocating for their own interests, they are more prone than others to prioritize social harmony over political participation, often choosing to avoid face-to-face conflict and political disagreement within their interpersonal networks altogether.[174,175] Given that people discussing public affairs will almost inevitably disagree with one another at some point over some issues, perhaps it should not be surprising that women are also far less likely than men to participate in political activities that require them to persuade others,[176–178] and they avoid conflict-laden activities, like debates, protests, and partisan disagreements.[179] Women are more likely than men to have conflict-avoidant personality traits, which reduces political participation.[180–182] Hence, women often see themselves as the type of people who should not participate fully in the public sphere, especially when that participation requires them to fight about contested political issues or to debate wicked, divisive issues in their communities.[183]

As noted in Box 4.2, women are generally inclined to underestimate their intelligence, experiences, and abilities—especially in traditionally male-dominated endeavors. This tendency follows them into the electoral arena. When Lawless and Fox questioned people with professional experiences linked to political careers, for example, women were more than twice as likely (at 28%) to claim that they were not at all qualified to run for office compared to men (at 12%).[184]

Men (at 26%), on the other hand, were nearly twice as likely as women (at 14%) to claim that they were very qualified.[185] These same women were less likely than their men counterparts to believe that they knew about public policy issues and had relevant professional experience—or that they were good public speakers, fundraisers, or self-promoters.[186] Women's self-effacing claims about their abilities had already taken root by the time women entered college. When Lawless and Fox asked college students whether they would know enough to run for political office after finishing school and working a while, just over half of young women said no, while only one third of young men doubted themselves.[187] Meanwhile, nearly a quarter of young men confidently anticipated future competence, compared to only about one tenth of young women.[188]

Even when women believe they are just as professionally accomplished and qualified as their men colleagues, many have serious doubts about whether they have the character traits required to withstand the conflict, rudeness, and negative attacks of professional politics.[189] Women are less apt than men to describe themselves as competitive, risk-taking, entrepreneurial, and, perhaps most important of all for a political career, as thick-skinned. They recognize the importance of these traits for candidates willing to enter the fray of electoral campaigns, which convinces many that even if they would be good public servants, they just are not cut out to run for office.[190,191] An even more discouraging finding is that women often believe that they will face sexism and misogyny on the campaign trail and after winning elections—which convinces them that they will need to be more experienced, more qualified, and will need to work twice as hard as their men peers in order to win elections and to have a successful political career.[192] Until the masculine ethos of the political sphere changes, or political socialization and lived experiences transform women's gendered psyche, women will be less likely to want to run for office than men, even when they are highly qualified to do so.

Solving Women's Political Ambition Dilemma— Liberal Versus Radical Feminist Solutions

Scholars have embraced both liberal and radical feminist, including intersectional, solutions to this dilemma. Some have continued to focus on reforms grounded in liberal feminism, which emphasize more women gaining access to the political sphere rather than changing it to accommodate women. Since girls' and women's political socialization cultivates a gendered psyche, they believe efforts should be made to eliminate differences in men's and women's political socialization. The goal is to bolster experiences that better prepare women to participate in explicitly political environments.

Those adopting this approach, for example, have emphasized that the gap in political ambition could be closed if more parents encouraged their daughters, as well as their sons, to consider a career in politics. They also point out that fewer girls than boys play competitive sports. Yet, playing competitive sports encourages girls to prioritize winning, respond to aggression, and take risk—which are all traits associated with successful politicians.

Other recommendations for bolstering young women's political interest and efficacy are to make sure that they continue to have experiences associated with political ambition in young men, including taking political science courses, discussing politics with friends and family members, and seeking out political information in the media.[193]

Making women's experiences more similar to men's assumes that they will evoke similar reactions from women; yet as Box 4.2 indicates, men's and women's

▸ **Photo 4.4** Women who play competitive sports cultivate traits that help them run for office.

distinct reactions in college make it clear that convergence does not always occur even when both sexes have similar experiences. If political science courses and media sources are male-coded public spaces and emphasize the masculine ethos of politics, increasing women's exposure to them may also increase exposure to microaggression and social sanctions, reinforcing women's sense that they do not belong. Such experiences may suppress women's political ambition instead of cultivating it. Hence, other scholars and reformers adopt a radical feminist approach and recommend changing the public sphere instead of changing women.

These scholars point out that given women's historic exclusion from the public sphere, researchers' descriptions of men's political behavior became the "standard" or the "norm" by which others are evaluated. When women make different choices, they are deemed deficient or abnormal in comparison.[194,195] In response, some political scientists have argued that "rather than focus on the individual as the thing that needs fixing—more motivation, higher resources, stronger democratic values—a higher level of scrutiny should be directed at the institutions and practice of the democratic system itself."[196]

The differences that more women would bring to political office may be good for democratic government. As Susan J. Carroll and Kira Sanbonmatsu (2013) demonstrate in their book *More Women Can Run*, women typically develop political ambition differently than most men.[197] Women are more apt than men to consider the effects of their decisions on other people and especially on those close to them. This trait—which has also been found to differentiate women's moral reasoning and leadership decisions from men's—is grounded in women's socialization to be other-oriented, as well as in many women's lived experiences as primary caregivers for children, spouses, and elderly relatives. This **Relationally-Embedded Model** of decision-making extends to the decisions they make about political participation. Hence, women's political ambition is often cultivated when people in their lives encourage them to run.[198] When Carroll and Sanbonmatsu (2013) conducted a survey of state legislators, for example, they found that 42.7% of men legislators said it was entirely their own idea to run, compared to only 26.4% of women legislators.[199] Beyond being asked, these women also overwhelmingly attribute their decision to run not to a longstanding desire to be involved in politics but to concern over public policy issues that affect people's lives.[200]

Research shows that women's low tolerance for interpersonal conflict reduces their willingness to pursue careers—including political careers—associated with power-related goals such as self-promotion and competition. To the contrary, women are attracted to careers that fulfill communal goals such as solving problems and helping others. Yet, the masculine ethos of politics was socially constructed and has become a self-fulfilling prophecy. Elected officials do not spend all of their time fighting with people. They spend considerable time on communal tasks—like helping constituents, meeting with community members, and collaborating with others to draft effective policies that solve problems and improve people's lives. If stories about these aspects of public service replaced war metaphors and conflict narratives, politics could have a feminine ethos that attracts rather than repels women. An experimental design with college students as subjects demonstrated that emphasizing the communal aspects of public life does substantially narrow the sex-based gap in political ambition.[201] Further, if more women were elected to office, narratives that bolster politics' feminine ethos could also become self-fulfilling, as women politicians do actually spend more time than men on communal tasks.[202,203]

Women's avoidance of conflict can be seen as a deficiency that needs to be "fixed" before women will run for office; however, it may be the case that conflict should be seen as less central to the political process. Given voter complaints about partisan polarization and legislative gridlock, willingness to listen, negotiate, and compromise instead could also be considered positive attributes that more men politicians should emulate. Studies of interpersonal communication show that women avoid interpersonal conflict by being more polite than men—and that their politeness can facilitate **exploratory talk**—where people construct shared meanings as they develop ideas. Polite interactions are characterized by soliciting others' opinions, qualifying one's claims, providing supportive feedback, acknowledging others' contributions, and avoiding confrontation. All of these conversational patterns encourage collaboration and are especially useful in deliberation.[204] On the contrary, interactions characterized by challenges, disagreements, and interruptions lead to entrenched positions, especially when these tactics are used in a public.[205,206] "Those attacked often respond defensively, and little progress is made in exploring the issues and ideas proposed."[207]

It should come as no surprise that women's involvement in decision-making processes can increase a group's capacity for decision-making by improving cooperation and increasing understanding of complex issues. Such efforts are more apt to lead to innovative solutions to public problems—often labeled win-win or third way solutions—that are unlikely to be developed during a heated debate between entrenched opponents.[208] Research on the composition of deliberative groups suggests that more inclusive processes and more empathetic policy recommendations result when women deliberate exclusively with other women and even when group composition substantially favors women.[209]

Transforming electoral politics is important because, "mitigating the effects of gendered institutions is not only better for the women who otherwise get shut out of the democratic process, but is better for the health of democracy as a whole."[210] Yet, the dilemma remains: How will a male-coded public space be transformed into to a gender-neutral or female-coded public space unless enough women's political socialization better prepares more of them to participate in contemporary politics, despite its masculine ethos? As Box 4.5 on the phenomenon of backlash notes, relying on a gradual erosion of traditional gender roles over time has not been a reliable strategy to improve the status of women.

BOX 4.5: BACKLASH AND THE RESURGENCE OF TRADITIONAL GENDER ROLES

Progress in overcoming the public sphere's masculine ethos and women's gendered psyche is not inevitable. Binary sex categories and associated gender roles are constructed, and when perceived as useful, they can be resurrected in different eras. Indeed, a backlash against egalitarian roles often takes place immediately after women have made significant strides in achieving equality. U.S. women's experiences during and after World War II serve as a poignant example. The United States had done little to prepare for participation in another war. When working-age men were drafted, too few men laborers were left behind—not only to sustain the economy but to build the planes, tanks, and munitions that the military needed. During the war, 6.5 million women joined the labor force to take

(Continued)

their place. As a result, society embraced a tomboyish version of womanhood, celebrating confident, independent women who wore overalls, tucked their hair in bandannas, rolled up their sleeves, and went to work. This ideal woman was epitomized by Rosie the Riveter, part of a media campaign to entice more women into the paid workforce, described in Chapter 2 and highlighted in the Preface and cover of this book. These women often had young children, and the government responded to the problem of unsupervised children in the home by supporting federally subsidized daycare centers across the nation. After the war ended, the Child Welfare League of America, along with prominent child welfare advocates like Eleanor Roosevelt, tried to keep the centers open. But public sentiment about the value of women in the workplace shifted. Some of this concern focused on making space for returning soldiers in the workplace. Yet, as historian Elaine Tyler May (1988) notes, postwar anxieties about the rise of communism were linked to unconventional lifestyles and to sex outside of marriage.[211] White women in the burgeoning middle class were once again encouraged to embrace early marriage, child care, and domesticity, and subsidized child care centers were shuttered. Fashion became more restrictive, with a return of skirts and heels that confined women's gait. And, despite increasing access to time-saving household appliances like washing machines and vacuum cleaners, domestic routines became more complex as a way to consume more of women's time.[212] Ironically, women's diminished opportunities and status set the stage for activism in coming decades. "The stuffing of middle class American women back into the box of early marital expectation and domestic confinement—a box that chafed all the more thanks to the revolutionary opportunities that had too recently been made available to their mothers and grandmothers—by the 1960s had created a world so airless that it was nearly destined to combust more forcefully than ever before."[213] Journalist Susan Faludi (1991) argued that a similar, although less effective, backlash occurred in the 1980s, with a spate of prominent media stories inaccurately describing educated, working women as unlikely to marry, unhappy, and unfulfilled.[214]

The phenomenon is not restricted to the United States, nor to the dustbin of history, as backlash against women's progress is currently playing out in both China and Saudi Arabia. In China, the Communist Party has responded to a sluggish economy, a shrinking population—and concern that educated women would exacerbate the lull in fertility by rejecting marriage and children in favor of careers—by purposefully socializing women to embrace restrictive gender roles celebrated in traditional Chinese culture. At Shenjiang College, under the guise of preparing women for upcoming job interviews, the All-China Women's

Federation instructs women students on comportment, including how to pour tea, sit demurely, dress appropriately, and adopt a "sunny" demeanor.

"According to traditional culture, women should be modest and tender, and men's role is working outside and providing for the family," one 21-year-old student told a reporter from *The Washington Post*. While waiting for a class on tea ceremonies to begin, she also said, "I want to be a model for my children." Similarly, a company in Northern China operates a "traditional culture school" where women are told to focus on wifely virtues, to defer to their husbands, and no matter what, not to get divorced! Notably, there are no comparable courses targeting young men.[215]

Meanwhile, the backlash in Saudi Arabia is more coercive. The current crown prince, Mohammed bin Salman, has recently acceded to women's rights activists' decades long push for equality by granting women the right to drive. At the same time, however, these same activists—many of whom staged illegal driving protests decades ago—have been arrested under charges that they are traitors who threaten national security and deserve the death penalty (see Chapters 8 and 9). In both countries, it remains to be seen whether repression of women after recent gains will inspire future activism or whether women's progress will be curtailed.[216][217]

CONCLUSION

Over the past several decades, cultivating political ambition has become the Holy Grail of scholars and activists who believe patriarchal legacies cannot be completely addressed until women are more fully represented in government. Research consistently shows that when American women run, they are just as likely to win as men. This is a topic we turn to in Chapter 5. The problem is that even after gaining access to higher education and professional careers typically associated with political aspirations, many women are still reluctant to run for office. Liberal feminists' emphasis on converging men's and women's experiences did not take the tenacity of traditional gender socialization, and its ability to produce gendered psyches among both men and women, into account, nor did they anticipate that women would continue to find the masculine ethos of politics alienating.

It remains to be seen whether the sharp uptick in the number of women who ran in the 2018 midterm elections will provide the "jolt" to the system that Lawless and Fox (2014) recently claimed was needed to upend the long-term factors that have suppressed American women's political ambition—and their representation among elected public servants—for so long.[218] This possibility is addressed more fully in Chapter 5, which explores women's experiences as candidates.

REVIEW QUESTIONS

1. Political scientists have identified three main influences on the number of women who run for office—institutional, cultural, and individual factors. Which of these three factors do you think has the greatest influence on the number of women willing to serve in public office? Why?

2. What is the difference between nascent and expressed political ambition? Why did Americanist scholars who study candidate emergence need to develop a difference between these two aspects of political ambition?

3. Why did Second Wave scholars believe the convergence of men's and women's educational and professional experiences would close the gap between men's and women's participation and ambition? Why did their predicted outcomes fail to occur?

4. How are "chilly" campus climates for women related to the erosion of women's self confidence in their academic and intellectual ability, as well as in the emergence of the imposter syndrome?

5. How do benevolent and hostile sexism work in tandem to constrain women's ability to step into political leadership roles? How are the concepts of sugar-coated oppression and the glass-slipper effect related to benevolent sexism?

6. Can the Relationally-Embedded Model of Decision Making, which describes the way many women make political decisions, help to develop better strategies for recruiting women candidates?

7. Why do some feminist writers believe that delayed marriage and declining U.S. birthrate are the fulfillment of Susan B. Anthony's prediction that women would need to avoid responsibilities that accompany marriage and parenthood before achieving equality?

8. Explain how traditional, patriarchal definitions of masculinity expect men to control women's behavior and lead to elevated levels of violence against women.

9. Why does politics still have a "masculine" ethos in so many countries around the globe, including the United States? How could politics be reframed to have a "feminine" or gender neutral ethos?

AMBITION ACTIVITIES

Measuring Implicit Gender Bias: Social psychologists at Harvard have developed an online test designed to measure implicit biases, or those unconscious, knee-jerk reactions based on common stereotypes in mainstream American culture that affect our reactions to members of marginalized groups. Project Implicit is a nonprofit organization that studies individuals' thoughts and feelings about social attitudes and mental health. The test labeled Gender-Career on the organization's website measures a person's association of women with home and men with career, and, particularly, the individual's association outside of conscious awareness.

Search for Project Implicit's webpage, and log in to take the test labeled Gender-Career, to determine whether you instinctively associate women with family-related topics and men with career-related topics. Your score may surprise you, as very few people can completely avoid effects from the day-in and day-out exposure to traditional gender socialization over years. Discuss with classmates your result, how the result was generated, and your degree of surprise about the result. Then discuss how to eliminate ingrained biases. To what extent is it possible to reshape your own ingrained biases about men and women? What actions could change the biases you have discussed.

Discussing the Balance of Caregiving and Household Responsibilities With a Partner: One partner is often saddled with unequal responsibility for household chores and childcare. Frequently this is a woman in a heterosexual relationship, and her double workload creates stress and difficult decisions about work-life balance. Unequal responsibilities for household chores and childcare also are thought to suppress nascent political ambition in American women. Greater balance of responsibilities requires conversations between partners, regardless of their sexual or gender orientation, but what would partners discuss, and at what point in their relationship? Brainstorm answers to the following questions, and consider when you would discuss them with a partner. Consider how the type of relationship you have might affect your ability to be involved in civic and political affairs.

Questions about the home or caregiving:

- Who will be responsible for grocery shopping and preparing meals? Who will be responsible for cleaning the house? Doing the dishes? Keeping up with the laundry? What would be an equal division of labor?

- Who is responsible for "invisible household scheduling," that is, keeping track of who in the family goes where and when?

- Do you want children, and, if you do, who will be the primary caregiver? Or will you share caregiving equally? What would equal caregiving mean in practical, everyday terms?

- Who will do the household finances? Who will do home repair and yard work?

Questions about careers and public service:

- How would you decide whether to prioritize your career or your partner's career as it relates to moving to live near one of your places of employment?

- How will each partner help the other in terms of balancing career and family life? For instance, who takes off work when a child is sick? Who leaves work early to pick a child up from school?

- How do you think your future work-life balance will influence your ability to be involved in civic and political affairs?

Questions about how to have this conversation with a partner:

- At what point in a relationship would you be willing and prepared to discuss these ideas with a partner? When and how would you reassess these ideas as the relationship progresses?

- Do your ideas offer fair expectations of your partner? Are they fair questions to yourself? To what extent, are your ideas influenced by stereotypes about men's and women's innate abilities or prescribed roles?

Asking a Woman to Run for Political Office: Research indicates that women need to be asked before they seriously consider running for political office, and they are more motivated by the prospect of passing policies that solve problems and help others than they are by wielding power or holding a prominent position. Write a letter to classmates to ask them to run for office, and, in doing so, reframe public service in terms of solving problems and helping people. Do this by conducting the interview described below.

Interview classmates about their hobbies, voluntarism, political interests, work experience, and people skills. Additionally, ask them questions about the types of social problems they would like to solve and the type of people they would like to help. Use this information to write them letters, explaining the reasons why they are qualified for public service and why they should run for elected office. In order to reframe politics as more than a chance to hold power and be aggressive, include in the letter references to empathy for others, the ability to facilitate deliberation, and the ability to implement change, when applicable. Finally, reflect on your letter. How do the letters present why people are motivated to run for office and the skills it takes to be a good public servant? Do your letters tend to frame public service as "feminine," "masculine," or gender-neutral work?

Addressing Microaggressions: According to social psychologist Derald Wing Sue, examples of gender-based microaggressions include the following:

- An assertive woman manager is labeled as a "bitch," while her male counterpart is described as "a forceful leader." (Hidden message: Women should be passive and allow men to be the decision makers.)

- A woman physician wearing a stethoscope is mistaken as a nurse. (Hidden message: Women should occupy nurturing and not decision-making roles. Women are less capable than men.)

- Whistles or catcalls are heard from men as a woman walks down the street. (Hidden message: Your body/appearance is for the enjoyment of men. You are a sex object.)[219]

When women challenge microaggressions, they often are told that they are overreacting, being too emotional, or misunderstanding the speaker's true intent—which is simply another form of microaggression sometimes called "gaslighting." Make a list of sex-based microaggressions you have experienced personally or have observed directed at other students. With classmates, analyze your lists, and plan to take action. Use this exercise to practice developing the "thick skin" that so many women believe is a prerequisite for a political career.

Analyze Lists:

- Compare and contrast your listed experiences. What experiences are similar, and why?

- How do intersectional identities affect the microaggressions experienced by different kinds of women?

- Consider the effect of regular, ongoing exposure to aggressions. How do microaggressions make you (and others) feel or make you (and others) adjust your everyday actions?

Action:

- A wide array of sources on the Internet provide suggestions for how to respond to microaggressions—ranging from giving a quick verbal comeback, attempting to educate others, or simply walking away. Which actions are you most inclined to choose? What are the pros and cons of this choice?

- Microaggressions make women feel like unqualified interlopers in male-coded spaces like politics, or like imposters. Ellen Hendriksen, PhD, a clinical psychologist, suggests the following actions for overcoming imposter syndrome: remind yourself of all that you've accomplished, ask someone who is "fan" of you to affirm you, find a mentor (with a similar intersectional identity), and teach something to someone younger, and, in doing so, recall all you know and have to offer.[220] What actions will you and your classmates take to prevent internalizing the negative messages of microaggressions and developing imposter syndrome?

KEY WORDS

Agentic male 167

Ambivalent sexism 169

Americanists 146

Benevolent sexism 169

REFERENCES

1. Atkeson, L. R., & Rapoport, R. (2003. The more things change, the more they stay the same: Examining gender differences in political attitude expression, 1952–2000. *Public Opinion Quarterly, 67,* 495–521.

2. Jacobs, L., Cook, F., & Delli-Carpini, M. (2009). *Talking together: Public deliberation and political participation in America.* Chicago, IL: University of Chicago Press.

3. Burns, N., Lehman Schlozman, K., & Verba, S. (2001). *The private roots of public action: Gender, equality, and political participation.* Cambridge, MA: Harvard University Press.

4. O'Connor, K., & Yanus, A. B. (2009). The chilly climate continues: Defrosting the gender divide in political science and politics. *Journal of Political Science Education, 5*(2),108–118.

5. Wolak, J., & McDevitt, M. (2011). The roots of the gender gap in political knowledge in adolescence. *Political Behavior, 33,* 505–533.

6. Karpowitz, C., & Menderlberg, T. (2014). *The silent sex: Gender, deliberation, and institutions.* Princeton, NJ: Princeton University Press.

7. O'Connor, K., & Yanus, A. B. (2009). The chilly climate continues: Defrosting the gender divide in political science and politics.

8. Lawless, J. L., & Fox, R. L. (2010). *It still takes a candidate: Why women don't run for office.* New York, NY: Cambridge University Press.

9. Matthews, G. (1992). *The rise of public woman: Woman's power and woman's place, 1630–1970.* Oxford, UK: Oxford University Press.

10. Alozie, S., Simon, J., & Merrill, B. (2003). Gender and political orientation in childhood. *Social Science Journal, 40*(1), 1–18.

11. Briggs, J. E. (2008). Young women and politics, an oxymoron? *Journal of Youth Studies, 11,* 579–592.

12. Taft, J. K. (2014). The political lives of girls. *Sociology Compass, 3,* 259–267.

13. Polletta, F., & Chen, P. C. B. (2014). Gender and public talk: Accounting for women's variable participation. *Public Sphere, 31*(4), 291–317.

14. Lawless, J. L., & Fox, R. L. (2013). *Girls just wanna not run: The gender gap in young Americans' political ambition.* Washington, DC: Women and Politics Institute. Retrieved from https://www.american.edu/spa/wpi/upload/girls-just-wanna-not-run_policy-report.pdf.

15. Davidson-Schmich, L. K. (2016). *Gender quotas and democratic participation: Recruiting candidates for elective offices in Germany.* Ann Arbor: University of Michigan Press.

16. Galais, C., Öhberg, P., & Coller, X. (2016). Endurance at the top: Gender and political ambition of Spanish and Swedish MPs. *Politics and Gender, 1*(2).

17. Rincker, M., Aslam, G., & Isani, M. (2017). Crossed my mind, but ruled it out: Political ambition and gender in the Pakistani Lawyers' Movement 2007–2009. *International Political Science Review, 38*(4), 246–63.

18. Dalton, E. (2015). *Women and politics in contemporary Japan.* New York, NY: Routledge.

19. Schwindt-Bayer, L. (2011). Women who win: Social backgrounds, paths to power, and political ambition in Latin American legislatures. *Politics and Gender, 7*(1), 1–33.

20. Kanthak, K., & Woon, J. (2014). Women don't run? Election aversion and candidate entry. *American Journal of Political Science, 59*(3), 595–612.

21. Davidson-Schmich, L. K. (2016). *Gender quotas and democratic participation: Recruiting candidates for elective offices in Germany.*

22. Matland, R. E., & Montgomery, K. A. (Eds). (2003). *Women's access to political power in post-communist Europe.* Oxford, UK: Oxford University Press. 19–42.

23. Davidson-Schmich, L. K. (2016). *Gender quotas and democratic participation: Recruiting candidates for elective offices in Germany.*

24. Rincker, M., Aslam, G., & Isani, M. (2017). Crossed my mind, but ruled it out: Political ambition and gender in the Pakistani Lawyers' Movement 2007–2009.

25. Davidson-Schmich, L. K. (2016). *Gender quotas and democratic participation: Recruiting candidates for elective offices in Germany*.

26. Firebaugh, G., & Chen, K. (1995). Voter turnout of Nineteenth Amendment women: The enduring effect of disenfranchisement. *American Journal of Sociology, 100,* 972–996.

27. Dinas, E. (2014). The long shadow of parental political socialization on the development of political orientations. *The Forum, 12*(3), 397–416.

28. Corder, J. K., & Wolbrecht, C. (2016). *Counting women's ballots: Female voters from suffrage through the New Deal*. New York, NY: Cambridge University Press.

29. Klein, E. (1984). *Gender politics*. Cambridge, MA: Harvard University Press.

30. Anderson, K. (1996). *After suffrage: Women in partisan and electoral politics before the New Deal*. Chicago, IL: University of Chicago Press.

31. Schlesinger, J. A. (1966). *Ambition and politics: Political careers in the United States*. Chicago, IL: Rand McNally and Co.

32. Putnam, R. (2000). *Bowling alone, the collapse and revival of American community*. New York, NY: Simon & Schuster.

33. Schlesinger, J. A. (1966). *Ambition and politics: Political careers in the United States*.

34. Welch, S. (1977). Women as political animals? A test of some explanations for male-female political participation differences. *American Journal of Political Science, 21*(4), 711–730.

35. Verba, S., Schlozman, K. L., & Brady, H. E. (1995). *Voice and equality: Civic voluntarism in American politics*. Cambridge, MA: Harvard University Press.

36. Welch, S. (1977). Women as political animals? A test of some explanations for male-female political participation differences.

37. Burns, N., Lehman Schlozman, K., & Verba, S. (2001). *The private roots of public action: Gender, equality, and political participation*.

38. Darcy, R., Welch, S., & Clark, J. (1994). *Women, elections, and representation*, 2nd ed. Lincoln: University of Nebraska Press.

39. Ibid.

40. Clinton, H. (2017). *What happened?* New York, NY: Simon and Schuster.

41. White House Council on Women and Girls. (2011). Women in America: Indicators of social and economic well-being. Retrieved from https://digitalcommons.ilr.cornell.edu/cgi/viewcontent.cgi?referer=https://www.google.com/&httpsredir=1&article=1804&context=key_workplace.

42. Buchmann, C., & DiPrete, T. (2006). The growing female advantage in college completion: The role of family background and academic achievement. *American Sociological Review, 71*(4), 515–541.

43. Goldin, C., Katz, L., & Kuziemko, I. (2006). The homecoming of American college women: The reversal of the college gender gap. *Journal of Economic Perspectives, 20,* 133–156.

44. Yen, H. (2011). Women lead men in graduate degrees. *Star Tribune.* Retrieved from http://www.startribune.com/nation/120750509.html?refer=y.

45. Yamaguchi, M. (2018). Reported med school discrimination sparks protests in Japan. *U.S. News.* Retrieved from https://www.usnews.com/news/world/articles/2018-08-03/japan-urges-quick-probe-of-female-med-school-discrimination.

46. Ramzy, A., & Ueno, H. (2018). Japanese medical school accused of rigging admissions to keep women out. *New York Times.* Retrieved from https://www.nytimes.com/2018/08/03/world/asia/japan-medical-school-test-scores-women.html.

47. Nagano, Y. (2018). In Japan, voters are wary of mothers in public office. *New York Times.* Retrieved from https://www.nytimes.com/2018/03/07/world/asia/japan-mothers-politics.html?action=click&module=RelatedCoverage&pgtype=Article&region=Footer.

48. Olsen, E. (2017). "A bleak picture" for women trying to rise at law firms. *New York Times.* Retrieved from https://www.nytimes.com/2017/07/24/business/dealbook/women-law-firm-partners.html.

49. Krivkovich, A., Robinson, K., Starikova, I., Valentino, R., & Yee, L. (2017). *Women in the workplace 2017.* McKinsey & Company. Retrieved from https://www.mckinsey.com/featured-insights/gender-equality/women-in-the-workplace-2017.

50. Fortune Editors. (2017). These are the women CEOs leading Fortune 500 companies. *Fortune.* Retrieved from http://fortune.com/2017/06/07/fortune-500-women-ceos.

51. Lawless, J. L., & Fox, R. L. (2010). *It still takes a candidate: Why women don't run for office.*

52. Ibid.

53. Ibid.

54. Ibid.

55. Ibid.

56. Ibid.

57. Ibid.

58. Lawless, J. L., & Fox, R. L. (2012). *Men rule, the continued under representation of women in politics*. Washington, DC: Women and Politics Institute. Retrieved from https://www.american.edu/spa/wpi/upload/2012-Men-Rule-Report-web.pdf.

59. Bonneau, C. W., & Kanthak, K. (2018). Stronger together: Political ambition and the presentation of women running for office. *Politics, Groups, and Identity*.

60. Ibid.

61. Lawless, J. L., & Fox, R. L. (2014). *Not a "Year of the Woman" . . . and 2036 doesn't look so good either*. Fox Brookings Institute Issues in Governance Studies. Retrieved from https://www.brookings.edu/wp-content/uploads/2016/06/apsr.pdf.

62. Lawless, J., & Fox, R. (2013). *Girls just wanna not run: The gender gap in young Americans' political ambition*.

63. Ibid.

64. Hall, R., M., & Sandler, B. R. (1982). *The campus climate: A chilly one for women? (Report of the Project on the Status and Education of Women)*. Washington, DC: Association of American Colleges.

65. Hall, R. M., & Sandler, B. R. (1984). *Out of the classroom: A chilly campus climate for women? (Report of the Project on the Status and Education of Women)*. Washington, DC: Association of American Colleges.

66. Astin, H. S. (1990). Educating women: A promise and a vision for the future. *American Journal of Education, 98*(4), 479–493.

67. Martin, J. R. (1997). Bound for the promised land: The gendered character of higher education. *Journal of Gender Law and Policy, 4*(1), 3–26.

68. American Association of University Women. (1992). How schools short-change girls: A study of the major findings on girls in education. Washington, DC: AAUW Foundation.

69. Mann, J. (1994). *The difference: Growing up female in America*. New York, NY: Warner Books.

70. Pipher, M. (1994). *Reviving Ophelia: Saving the selves of adolescent girls*. New York, NY: Putnam.

71. Arnold, K. (1996). *Lives of promise: What becomes of high school valedictorians*. San Francisco, CA: Jossey-Bass.

72. Sax, L., Astin, A., & Astin, H. (2008). *The gender gap in college: Maximizing the developmental potential of women and men*. San Francisco, CA: Jossey-Bass.

73. Ibid.

74. Conger, D., & Long, M. C. (2010). Why are men falling behind? Gender gaps in college performance and persistence. *The Annals of the American Academy of Political and Social Sciences, 627*, 184–214.

75. Sax, L., Astin, A., & Astin, H. (2008). *The gender gap in college: Maximizing the developmental potential of women and men*.

76. Ibid.

77. Ibid.

78. Pinker, S. (2009). *The sexual paradox: Men, women and the real gender gap*. New York, NY: Simon and Schuster.

79. Sax, L., Astin, A., & Astin, H. (2008). *The gender gap in college: Maximizing the developmental potential of women and men*.

80. Astin, A. W. (1993). *What matters in college? Four critical years revisited*. San Francisco, CA: Jossey-Bass.

81. Sax, L., Astin, A., & Astin, H. (2008). *The gender gap in college: Maximizing the developmental potential of women and men*.

82. Swim, J., Mallett, R., & Stangor, C. (2004). Understanding subtle sexism: Detection and use of sexist language. *Sex Roles, 51*(3–4), 117–128.

83. Fredrickson, B., & Roberts, T-A. (1997). Objectification theory. *Psychology of Women Quarterly, 21*, 173–206.

84. Glick, P., & Fiske, S. T. (2001). An ambivalent alliance: Hostile and benevolent sexism as complementary justifications of gender inequality. *American Psychologist, 56*, 109–118.

85. Capodilupo, C. M., Nadal, K. L., Corman, L., Hamit, S., Lyons, O., & Weinberg, A. (2010). The manifestations of gender microaggressions. In D. W. Sue (Ed.), *Microaggressions and marginality: Manifestations, dynamics and impact* (pp. 193–216). Hoboken, NJ: Wiley and Sons.

86. Nadal, K. L. (2010). Gender microaggressions: Implications for mental health. In M. A. Paludi (Ed.), *Feminism and women's rights worldwide, Volume 2: Mental health and physical health* (155–175). Santa Barbara, CA: Praeger.

87. Swim, J., Mallett, R., & Stangor, C. (2004). Understanding subtle sexism: Detection and use of sexist language.

88. Sue, D. W. (Ed). (2010). *Microaggressions and marginality: Manifestations, dynamics and impact*. Hoboken: Wiley & Sons.

89. Calogero, R. M. (2013). Objects don't object: Evidence that self-objectification disrupts women's social activism. *Psychological Science, 24*(3), 312–318.

90. Lawless, J. L., & Fox, R. L. (2010). *It still takes a candidate: Why women don't run for office.*

91. Ibid.

92. Ibid.

93. Johnson, A. G. (2014). *The gender knot: Unraveling our patriarchal legacy*, 3rd ed. Philadelphia, PA: Temple University Press.

94. Kann, M. E. (1999). *The gendering of American politics: Founding mothers, founding fathers, and political patriarchy.* Westport, CT: Greenwood Press.

95. Johnson, A. G. (2014). The gender knot: Unraveling our patriarchal legacy, 3rd ed.

96. Caiazza, A. (2005). Don't bowl at night: Gender, safety, and civic participation. *Journal of Women in Culture and Society, 30*(2), 1607–31.

97. *United States v. Morrison.* 529 U.S. 598 (2000).

98. Berry, M., Bouka, Y., & Muthoni Kamuru, M. (2017). Kenyan women just fought one of the most violent campaigns in history. *Foreign Policy*, Retrieved from https://foreignpolicy.com/2017/08/07/kenyas-female-politicians-just-fought-the-one-of-the-most-violent-campaign-in-history-election.

99. Krook, M. L. (2017). Violence against women in politics. *Journal of Democracy, 28*(1), 79–81.

100. Berry, M., Bouka, Y., & Muthoni Kamuru, M. (2017). Kenyan women just fought one of the most violent campaigns in history.

101. Krook, M. L. (2017). Violence against women in politics.

102. Ibid.

103. Donati, J., & Harooni, M. (2015). Bomb attack in Eastern Afghanistan kills female politician. *Reuters.* Retrieved from https://www.reuters.com/article/us-afghanistan-women-idUSKBN0LK1EI20150216.

104. France 24. (2017). Leading French conservative politician Nathalie Kosciusko-Morizet briefly lost consciousness after being attacked while handing out leaflets for Sunday's legislative poll at a Paris market Thursday, her team has reported. *France 24.* Retrieved from http://www.france24 .com/en/20170615-france-legislative-elections-top-conservative-politician-unconscious-campaign-clash.

105. Krook, M. L. (2017). Violence against women in politics.

106. Krook, M. L., & Restrepo Sanin, J. (2016). Gender and political violence in Latin America: Concepts, debates, and solutions. *Politica y Gobierno, XXIII(1).*

107. Elton, C. (2018). In Bolivia, shattering the glass ceiling can cause bodily harm. *Ozy*. Retrieved from https://www.ozy.com/fast-forward/in-bolivia-shattering-the-glass-ceiling-can-cause-bodily-harm/87970?utm_source=dd&utm_medium=email&utm_campaign=07182018&variable=88a4990cbb3505a38c5ad1d347bd272d.

108. Ibid.

109. Kann, M. E. (1999). *The gendering of American politics: Founding mothers, founding fathers, and political patriarchy.*

110. Ibid.

111. Hochschild, A. R. (1989). *The second shift: Working families and the revolution at home*. New York, NY: Penguin Books.

112. Ibid.

113. Bureau of Labor Statistics. (2018). *Economic news release*. United States Department of Labor. https://www.bls.gov/news.release/atus.nr0.htm.

114. National Bureau of Economic Research. (2004). *Hours spent in homemaking have changed little this century*. Retrieved from https://www.nber.org/digest/oct08/w13985.html.

115. Walzer, S. (1998). *Thinking about the baby: Gender and transitions into parenthood*. Philadelphia, PA: Temple University Press.

116. Raley, S., Bianchi, S., & Wang, W. (2012). When do fathers care? Mothers' economic contribution and fathers' involvement in child care. *American Journal of Sociology, 117*(5), 1422–1459.

117. Pedulla, D. S., & Thébaud, S. (2015). Can we finish the revolution? Gender, work family ideals, and institutional constraint. *American Sociological Review, 80*(1), 116–139.

118. Yavorsky, J., Kamp-Dush, C., & Schoppe-Sullivan, S. (2015). The production of inequality: The gender division of labor across the transition to parenthood. *The Journal of Marriage and Family, 77*(3), 662–679.

119. Fox, R. L., & Lawless, J. L. (2014). Reconciling family roles with political ambition: The new normal for twenty-first century U.S. politics. *The Journal of Politics, 76*(2), 398–414.

120. Silbermann, R. (2015). Gender roles, work-life balance, and running for office. *Quarterly Journal of Political Science 10*(2), 123–153.

121. Ferber, M., & Young, L. (1997). Student attitudes toward roles of women and men: Is the egalitarian household imminent? *Feminist Economics, 3*(1), 65–83.

122. Ibid.

123. Askari, S. F., Liss, M., Erchull, M. J., Staebell, S.E., & Axelson, S. J. (2010). Men want equality, but women don't expect it: Young adults' expectations for participation in household and child care chores. *Psychology of Women Quarterly*, *34*(2), 243–252.

124. Ganong, L., Coleman, M., Thompson, A., & Goodwin-Watkins, C. (1996). African American and European American college students' expectations for self and for future partners. *Journal of Family*, *17*(6), 758–75.

125. Orrange, R. M. (2002). Aspiring law and business professionals' orientations to work and family life. *Journal of Family*, *23*, 287–317.

126. Stone, L., & McKee, N. P. (2000). Gendered futures: Student visions of career and family on a college campus. *Anthropology & Education Quarterly*, *31*(1), 67–892000.

127. Pepin, J., & Cotter, D. (2018). *Trending towards traditionalism? Changes in youths' gender ideology.* A briefing paper prepared for the Council on Contemporary Families. Retrieved from https://contemporaryfamilies.org/2-pepin-cotter-traditionalism.

128. Bradford Wilcox, W. B., & Sturgeon, S. (2017). Why would millennial men prefer stay-at-home wives? Race and Feminism. *The Washington Post*. Retrieved from https://www.washingtonpost.com/posteverything/wp/2017/04/05/why-would-millennial-men-prefer-stay-at-home-wives-race-and-feminism/?utm_term=.7040e7ae4de5.

129. Cain Miller, C. (2015). Millennial men aren't the dads they thought they'd be. *The New York Times*. Retrieved from http://www.nytimes.com/2015/07/31/upshot/millennial-men-find-work-and-family-hard-to-balance.html.

130. Pepin, J., & Cotter, D. (2018). *Trending towards traditionalism? Changes in youths' gender ideology.*

131. Coontz, S. (2017). Do millennial men want stay-at-home wives? *The New York Times*. Retrieved from https://www.nytimes.com/2017/03/31/opinion/sunday/do-millennial-men-want-stay-at-home-wives.html.

132. Van Bavel. (2017, January). *The reversal of the gender gap in education and the continued push towards gender equality.* A briefing paper prepared for the Council on Contemporary. Retrieved from http://www.contemporaryfamilies.org/6-van-bavel-reversal-of-gender-gap.

133. Gotta, G., Green, R-J., Rothblum, E., Solomon, S., Balsam, K., & Schwartz, P. (2011). Heterosexual, lesbian, and gay male relationships: A comparison of couples in 1975 and 2000. *Family Process*, *50*(3), 353–376.

134. Goldberg, A., Smith, J., & Perry-Jenkins, M. (2012). The division of labor in lesbian, gay, and heterosexual new adoptive parents. *Journal of Marriage and Family*, *74*(4), 812–828.

135. Gotta, G., Green, R-J., Rothblum, E., Solomon, S., Balsam, K., & Schwartz, P. (2011). Heterosexual, lesbian, and gay male relationships: A comparison of couples in 1975 and 2000.

136. Goldberg, A. (2013). "Doing" and "undoing" gender: The meaning and division of housework in same-sex couples. *Journal of Family Theory and Review*, 5(2), 85–104.

137. Lawless, J. L., & Fox, R. L. (2013). *Girls just wanna not run: The gender gap in young Americans' political ambition*.

138. Izadi, E. (2014). Ruth Bader Ginsburg's advice on love and leaning. *The Washington Post*. Retrieved from https://www.washingtonpost.com/news/post-nation/wp/2014/07/31/ruth-bader-ginsburgs-advice-on-love-and-leaning-in/?utm_term=.21b2f947c3f4.

139. Cain Miller, C. (2018). Americans are having fewer babies. They told us why. Women have more options, for one. But a new poll also shows that financial insecurity is altering a generation's choices. *The New York Times*. Retrieved from https://www.nytimes.com/2018/07/05/upshot/americans-are-having-fewer-babies-they-told-us-why.html.

140. Searcey, D. (January 6, 2019). A quiet revolution: More women seek divorces in conservative West Africa. *The New York Times*. Retrieved from https://www.nytimes.com/2019/01/06/world/africa/niger-divorce-women.html.

141. Anthony, S. B. (1877). *Susan B. Anthony papers: Speeches and writings, -1895; 1877, homes of single women*. [Manuscript/Mixed Material]. Retrieved from the Library of Congress, at https://www.loc.gov/item/mss11049049/.

142. Traister, R. (2016). *All the single ladies: Unmarried women and the rise of an independent nation*. New York, NY: Simone and Schuster.

143. Walker, K., Bailik, K., & van Kessel, P. (2018). Strong men, caring women: How Americans describe what society values (and doesn't) in each gender. *Pew*. Retrieved from http://www.pewsocialtrends.org/interactives/strong-men-caring-women.

144. Campbell, D., & Wolbrecht, C. (2006). See Jane run: Women politicians as role models for adolescents. *The Journal of Politics*, 68(2), 233–247.

145. Huddy, L., & Terkildsen, N. The consequences of gender stereotypes for women candidates at different levels and types of office. *Political Research Quarterly*, 46(3), 503–525.

146. Niven, D. (1998). Party elites and women candidates. *Women & Politics*, 19(2), 57–80.

147. Norris, P., & Lovenduski, J. (1995). *Political recruitment: Gender, race and class in the British Parliament*. Cambridge, MA: Cambridge University Press.

148. Miller Rosenwasser, S., &. Dean, N. G. (1989). Gender role and political office: Effects of perceived masculinity/femininity of candidate and political office. *Psychology of Women Quarterly, 13*(1), 77–85.

149. Lawless, J. L., & Fox, R. L. (2013). *Girls just wanna not run: The gender gap in young Americans' political ambition.*

150. Lawless, J. L., & Fox, R. L. (2012). *Men rule, the continued under representation of women in politics.*

151. Lawless, J. L., & Fox, R. L. (2010). *It still takes a candidate: Why women don't run for office.*

152. Ibid.

153. Lawless, J. L., & Fox, R. L. (2012). *Men rule, the continued under representation of women in politics.*

154. Ibid.

155. Moncrief, G., Squire, P., & Jewell, M. (2001). *Who runs for the legislature?* Upper Saddle River, NJ: Prentice Hall.

156. Lawless, J., & Fox, R. L. (2012). *Men rule, the continued under representation of women in politics.*

157. Fox, R. L., & Lawless, J. L. (2010). If only they'd ask: Gender, recruitment, and political ambition. *The Journal of Politics, 72*(2), 310–326.

158. Carroll, S., & Sanbonmatsu, K. (2013). *More women can run: Gender and pathways to the state legislatures.* New York, NY: Oxford University Press.

159. Burns, N., Lehman Schlozman, K., & Verba, S. (2001). *The private roots of public action: Gender, equality, and political participation.*

160. Glick, P., & Fiske, S. T. (2001). An ambivalent alliance: Hostile and benevolent sexism as complementary justifications of gender inequality.

161. Crockett, E. (2016). Why misogyny won. *Vox.* Retrieved from https://www.vox .com/identities/2016/11/15/13571478/trump-president-sexual-assault-sexism-misogyny-won.

162. Johnson, A. G. (2014). *The gender knot: Unraveling our patriarchal legacy*, 3rd ed.

163. Ibid.

164. Rudman, L. A. (2005). Rejection of women? Beyond prejudice as antipathy. In J. Dovidio, P. Glick, & L. Rudman (Ed.), *On the nature of prejudice: Fifty years after Allport* (pp. 106–120). Malden, MA: Blackwell.

165. Ibid.

166. Ibid.

167. Becker, J. C., & Wright, S. (2011). Yet another dark side of chivalry: Benevolent sexism undermines and hostile sexism motivates collective action for social change. *Journal of Personality and Social Psychology, 101*(1), 62–77.

168. Mill, J. S. (1859). *On liberty*. London, UK: John W. Parker and Son.

169. Sapiro, V. (1983). *The political integration of women: Role, socialization, and politics*. Chicago, IL: University of Illinois Press.

170. Holmes, J. (1995). *Women, men and politeness*. New York, NY: Longman.

171. Lakoff, R. T. (1990). *Talking power*. New York, NY: Basic Books.

172. Lakoff, R. T. (1975). *Language and women's place*. New York, NY: Harper & Row.

173. Ibid.

174. Mutz, D. C. (2006). *Hearing the other side: Deliberative versus participatory democracy*. New York, NY: Cambridge University Press.

175. Miller, P. M., Danaher, D. L., & Forbes, D. (1986). Sex-related strategies for coping with interpersonal conflict in children aged five and seven. *Developmental Psychology, 22*(4), 543–548.

176. Mansbridge, J. (1983). *Beyond adversary democracy*. Chicago, IL: University of Chicago Press.

177. Mutz, D. C. (2006). *Hearing the other side: Deliberative versus participatory democracy*.

178. Jacobs, L., Cook, F., & Delli-Carpini, M. (2009). *Talking together: Public deliberation and political participation in America*.

179. Ulbig, S. G., & Funk, C. L. (1999). Conflict avoidance and political participation. *Political Behavior, 21*(3), 265–282.

180. Fox, R. L., & Lawless, J. L. (2010). If only they'd ask: Gender, recruitment, and political ambition.

181. Gerber, A., Huber, G. A., Doherty, D., &. Dowling, C. M. (2011). The big five personality traits in the political arena. *Annual Review of Political Science, 14*, 265–287.

182. Kam, C. D. (2012). Risk attitudes and political participation. *American Journal of Political Science, 56*(4), 817–836.

183. Polletta, F., & Chen, P. C. B. (2014). Gender and public talk: Accounting for women's variable participation.

184. Fox, R. L., & Lawless, J. L. (2010). If only they'd ask: Gender, recruitment, and political ambition.

185. Ibid.

186. Ibid.

187. Lawless, J., & Fox, R. (2013). *Girls just wanna not run: The gender gap in young Americans' political ambition.*

188. Ibid.

189. Lawless, J., & Fox, R. (2010). *It still takes a candidate: Why women don't run for office.*

190. Ibid.

191. Lawless, J., & Fox, R. L. (2012). *Men rule, the continued under representation of women in politics.*

192. Lawless, J., & Fox, R. (2010). *It still takes a candidate: Why women don't run for office.*

193. Lawless, J., & Fox, R. (2013). *Girls just wanna not run: The gender gap in young Americans' political ambition.*

194. Bourque, S. C., & Grossholtz, J. (1974). Politics an unnatural practice: Political science looks at female participation. *Politics & Society, 4*(2), 225–66.

195. Burt-way, B., & Kelly, R. M. (1992). Gender and sustaining political ambition: A study of Arizona elected officials. Political Research Quarterly Volume, *45*(1), 11–25.

196. Junn, J. (2007). Square pegs and round holes: Challenges of fitting individual level analysis to a theory of politicized context of gender. *Politics & Gender, 3*, 124–134.

197. Carroll, S., & Sanbonmatsu, K. (2013). *More women can run: Gender and pathways to the state legislatures.*

198. Ibid.

199. Ibid.

200. Ibid.

201. Schneider, M., Holman, M., Diekman, A., & McAndrew, T. (2016). Power, conflict and community: How gendered views of political power influence women's political ambition. *Political Psychology, 37*(4), 515–531.

202. Duerst-Lahti, G., & Johnson, C. M. (1990). Gender and style in bureaucracy. *Women and Politics, 10*(1), 67–120.

203. Kathlene, L. (1989). Uncovering the political impacts of gender: An exploratory study. *Politics Research Quarterly, 42*(2), 397–421.

204. Strachan, J. C., & Wolf, M. R. (2012). Political civility: Introduction to political civility. *PS–Political Science & Politics*, *45*(3), 401–404.

205. Tannen, D. (1990). Gender differences in topical coherence: Creating involvement in best friends' talk. *Discourse Processes*, *13*, 73–90.

206. Tannen, D. (1990). *You just don't understand: Women and men in conversation*. New York, NY: William Morrow.

207. Holmes, J. (1995). *Women, men and politeness*.

208. Hannagan, R. J., & Larimer, C. W. (2010). Does gender composition affect group decision outcomes? Evidence from a laboratory experiment. *Political Behavior*, 32, 51–67.

209. Karpowitz, C., & Menderlberg, T. (2014). *The silent sex: Gender, deliberation, and institutions*.

210. Kanthak, K. (2017). Gender differences in political ambition," In A. Bos & M. Schneider (Eds.), *The political psychology of women in U.S. politics* (pp. 133–147). New York, NY: Routledge.

211. Tyler, E. M. (1988). *Homeward bound: American families in the Cold War era*. New York, NY: Basic Books.

212. Kurtz, D. (2018). We have a child-care crisis in this country. We had the solution 78 years ago. *The New York Times*. Retrieved from https://www .washingtonpost.com/news/posteverything/wp/2018/07/23/we-have-a-childcare-crisis-in-this-country-we-had-the-solution-78-years-ago/?utm_ term=.fc6f2215be98.

213. Traister, R. (2016). *All the single ladies: Unmarried women and the rise of an independent nation*.

214. Faludi, S. (1991). *Backlash: The undeclared war against American women*. New York, NY: Broadway Books.

215. Rauhala, E. (2018). Hold in your belly . . . legs together: Chinese college teaches female students to be perfect. *The Washington Post*. Retrieved from https://www.washingtonpost.com/world/asia_pacific/hold-in-your-belly--legs-together-chinese-college-teaches-female-students-to-be-perfect/2018/06/25/c0e1205e-6a21-11e8-bbc5-dc9f3634fa0a_story .html?utm_term=.e8ad4a18dca7.

216. Fahim, K., and & Morris, L. (May 19, 2018). In harsh Saudi crackdown, famous feminists are branded as traitors. *The Washington Post*. Retrieved from https:// www.washingtonpost.com/world/middle_east/in-harsh-saudi-crackdown-famous-feminists-are-branded-as-traitors/2018/05/19/b3bc3502-5b63-11e8-9889-07bcc1327f4b_story.html?utm_term=.66f0b47d4982.

217. Harrison-Graham, E. (2018). Saudi Arabia seeks death penalty against female human rights activist. *The Guardian*. Retrieved from https://www.theguardian .com/world/2018/aug/22/saudi-arabia-seeks-its-first-death-penalty-against-a-female-human-rights-activist.

218. Lawless, J. L., & Fox, R. L. (2014). *Not a "Year of the Woman" . . . and 2036 doesn't look so good either*.

219. Sue, D.W. (November 17, 2010). Microaggressions: More than just race. *Psychology Today*. Retrieved from https://www.psychologytoday.com/us/blog/ microaggressions-in-everyday-life/201011/microaggressions-more-just-race.

220. Hendrikson, E. (August 8, 2017). Nine ways to fight imposter syndrome. *Psychology Today*. Retrieved from https://www.psychologytoday.com/us/blog/ how-be-yourself/201708/nine-ways-fight-impostor-syndrome.

CHAPTER FIVE

WHEN WOMEN RUN

Despite the fact that women tend to have lower political ambition than men, many women do, in fact, make the decision to run. That decision is not always supported by others. For instance, Maura Healey, Massachusetts's current attorney general, was a first-time candidate when she decided to run for office in 2014. "Democratic insiders told her she wasn't ready. They told her she couldn't raise the money. They told her it wasn't her turn yet. They actively worked to derail her candidacy."[1] Yet, she won. Other Democratic women politicians in Massachusetts, supposedly one of the bluest of the blue states, have faced similar opposition. Elizabeth Warren, the senior U.S. senator for the state, says she was told the state was not ready to send a woman to the Senate when she ran in 2012.[2] In 2018, Boston City Councilor Ayanna Pressley challenged 18-year incumbent Michael Capuano in the Democratic primary for the 7th Congressional district. Because Capuano generally had a liberal voting record in the House, many Democratic party insiders threw their weight behind his candidacy, including Boston Mayor Marty Walsh, the state's first African American, Governor Deval Patrick, who served from 2006 to 2010, civil rights icon Representative John Lewis, and the Congressional Black Caucus.[3] But Pressley was not deterred. At a campaign kick-off event, she said,

> I am running for Congress against the wishes of many good Democrats. I've been told to wait my turn. I've been accused of naked ambition. I've been called a traitor for challenging an incumbent, told simply this isn't the way things are done here in Massachusetts. . . . When the challenges we are confronted with are this big, this deep, and growing, I can't and I won't wait my turn.[4]

Pressley went on to defeat Capuano in the primary and was elected to serve in the U.S. House of Representatives, becoming the first woman of color for the Massachusetts Congressional delegation. She joins a wave of women who won historic victories in the 2018 election, including Deb Haaland (D-NM) and Sharice

Davids (D-KS) who are the first Native American women elected to Congress; Rashida Tlaib (D-MI) and Ilhan Omar (D-MN) who are the first Muslim women elected to Congress; Kyrsten Sinema (D-AZ), the first openly bisexual U.S. Senator; and Alexandria Ocasio-Cortez (D-NY) and Abby Finkenauer (D-IA) who are the youngest women to serve in Congress.

In all, the 2018 elections saw a wave of historic women candidates along with a wave of women victories, confirming the conventional wisdom that when women run for office, women win. However, that doesn't mean that the experience of women who run for office is the same as the experience of men who run for office. Observers note that the experience of women candidates, as compared to men candidates, is like doing everything "backward and in high heels," a reference to what famous dancer Ginger Rogers had to do with her partner Fred Astaire while dancing. Barack Obama gave credit to Hillary Clinton using this phrase at the 2008 Democratic National Convention; former Texas governor Ann Richards used the same phrase to describe her political work at the 1988 Democratic Convention.[5] This is recognition of the fact that women face numerous obstacles on the campaign trail, from voter perceptions to media coverage to fund-raising, that they must overcome in order to secure victory.

In this chapter, we examine the experiences of women candidates who decide to run for office. We start by examining when and where women candidates are more likely to emerge, as some political environments are more hospitable to women candidates. We then examine some of the obstacles women candidates face, including how voters react to women candidates, how the media covers them, and the efforts they have to undertake to even the playing field. Given the wave of women candidacies and victories in 2018, we describe how this historic election cycle may change our understanding of how to run as a woman. Importantly, while theories of political ambition often focus on the lack of ambition amongst women, research examining the experience of women candidates in office focuses more on the patriarchal barriers to women's candidacies. Overall, the political environment is less hospitable for women candidates. In light of this, women's reluctance to run may be a rational response. When considering whether to run, women may see that they will have to work long and hard (and longer and harder than men) to run, so they may choose not to run (Jenkins 2007, 237).[6] As such, we conclude with observations on how to dismantle the masculine ethos of politics, as getting more women to run for office will require not just fostering political ambition but also creating a political environment that is more welcoming of their candidacies.

WHEN AND WHERE WOMEN CANDIDATES EMERGE

Initially, scholars anticipated that the biggest obstacles for ambitious women politicians to overcome would be a lack of political opportunity in the form of winnable electoral contests. Generally speaking, when incumbent candidates run for office they win. For instance, in 2016, 97% of House incumbents seeking reelection won, and 93% of Senate incumbents seeking reelection won.[7] This is in line with historic averages; at the congressional level, for example, incumbents win reelection approximately 90% of the time. Because incumbents are more likely to be men, and because they rarely step down after serving a single term, barring a prominent scandal or mishap, women are at a disadvantage. Incumbents have such high success rates because they already have attracted broad support from the public, and their status as a current public official makes it easier to raise money and to garner favorable media coverage.

Historically, ambitious politicians often have waited for incumbents to step down, because challengers in an open race have a better chance of winning. Indeed, recent research suggests this pattern holds true for both Democrat and Republican women candidates. Both respond to the opportunity structure, discussed in more detail in Chapter 9, in a given election cycle, and just like men, when they decide to run, they are more apt to run for **open seats** (seats that no candidate currently occupies) than they are to challenge an incumbent.[8] Hence, scholars initially feared that a bottleneck of men incumbents would impede women's access to elected office.[9–12]

In the 1990s, there was a push to enact term limits in the United States; proponents often argued that restrictions on the number of terms state legislative candidates could serve would smooth women's pathways to elected office. While 21 states initially enacted term limits in the 1990s, they were challenged and overturned in all but 15 states. And while forced retirements in these 15 states did create more opportunities for women to run in open seats, too few ran to make a substantial difference in the overall composition of these states' legislatures. One major study, for example, found that term limits had no effect on the demographic characteristics—including the sex—of those elected to state legislative seats.[13] In 1998, the number of women state senators in these 15 states increased, and this bump in numbers was sustained in 2000, but only because women incumbents termed out of the state house ran for senate seats instead of retiring. Hence, the number of women holding state house seats declined, because few new women candidates stepped forward to run for these recently vacated seats.[14] While researchers initially noticed a promising increase in the number of Latina challengers (that unfortunately did not extend to African American women) winning seats in these term-limited states' majority white districts, the overall composition of state legislatures did not shift.[15]

Initial assessment about the impact term limits would have on women candidates failed to take partisan polarization around feminist issues into account. As discussed in Chapter 3, Republicans were concerned about the emerging gap in voting in the 1980s, with women tending to slightly favor the Democratic Party and its candidates. So they made a concerted effort to recruit and assist women candidates—including the chair of the **Republican Senatorial Campaign Committee's** (RSCC) unprecedented offer to support women candidates during primary elections.[16] Both parties wanted to appeal to women in the electorate by supporting women for high-visibility leadership positions. As a result, in 1988, both major political parties' platforms endorsed recruiting and supporting women for public office. At the time, some prominent feminist leaders even thought that the Republican Party was doing a better job of supporting women candidates, as Republican women credited men politicians with recruiting them to run for office.[17,18] Thus, scholars initially anticipated that both Republican and Democratic women alike would benefit from the open seats created by term limits.

Over the past several decades, however, the parties have developed distinct gendered cultures—as those who organized to advance Second Wave feminist issues increasingly have identified with the Democratic Party, while the backlash against Second Wave successes was increasingly concentrated in the Republican Party. As a result, women's caucuses and support groups are more influential within the Democratic coalition, and the party has sustained efforts to recruit and support women candidates for office. Republicans, meanwhile, have eschewed identity politics. While the National Federation of Republican Women still offers campaign trainings and other support to women Republican candidates, enthusiasm for purposeful efforts to diversify the party have waned. As noted later in this chapter, Democratic and Republican women experience different reactions from voters when they run for office, but they also experience different opportunity structures within their respective parties.[19–22] As a result, term limits have affected candidates from the two parties differently, helping more Democratic women seeking elected office but fewer Republican women. In short, Democratic women's success since term limits were adopted has compensated for the success of fewer Republican women. Prior to the 2018 midterm elections, 33% of women serving in Congress were Democrats compared to the 9.7% who were Republicans. Of women state legislators, 61% were Democrats, compared to only 37.6% who were Republican.[23]

Despite these nuances in the types of women who have been able to leverage open seats to their advantage, the biggest take-away from research on term limits is that, contrary to expectations, creating more open seats—and more opportunities for women challengers to run for office—did not yield parity among men and women U.S. elected officials. Even with open seats available, too few women decided to run. The issue was not voter bias or limited opportunity but rather too few women in the pipeline, discussed in Chapter 4. While term limits do not yield more women candidates, other electoral arrangements and rules, like proportional representation and quotas described in Chapter 6, can increase the representation of women. In addition, the electoral environment can shape candidate entry decisions.

Aside from these electoral arrangements, though, certain types of districts are more likely to elect a woman. These "woman-friendly" districts tend to have higher average incomes, more people who work in professional occupations, and are more urban; because of these characteristics, these districts have more resources and are more amenable to electing women.[27–28] In other words, women candidates are more likely to emerge when they face fewer barriers. Like most candidates, women are strategic politicians, assessing their chances of winning before running and emerging in conditions that are most hospitable. Because women are more risk averse, on average, than men, this means they tend to be more election averse than men. For instance, Kanthak and Woon (2014) ran an experiment where they randomly assigned people to groups and selected leaders from those groups; women were just as likely to volunteer for leadership as men when leaders were randomly selected but were less likely to volunteer when leaders would be elected.[29] Thus, women are most likely to emerge when the environment is receptive and when there are fewer obstacles.

BOX 5.2: THE 2018 ELECTORAL ENVIRONMENT

Just as districts can be more or less welcoming to women candidates, so can electoral environments. Box 5.1 demonstrates how this can affect candidate entry decisions in other countries, but even within a given country, the electoral environment can change. At some points in time, as when issues related to war and terrorism dominate, this can disadvantage women candidates as these issues are seen as more masculine, as described in Chapter 3, while at other times, the electoral environment may be more welcoming. In 2018, there was a sharp divide among voters as to what were the most important issues (see Table 5.1).

Table 5.1 Most Important Electoral Issues, 2018 Midterm Election in the United States			
Most Important Issue Overall	Democrat	Republican	No Answer
Health care (41%)	75%	23%	2%
Immigration (23%)	23%	75%	2%
Economy (22%)	34%	63%	3%
Gun Policy (10%)	70%	29%	1%

Source: 2018 CNN Exit Polls.

While Republican campaign messages focused heavily on immigration and the economy, Democratic political messages focused on issues like health care and the environment. As Table 5.1 indicates, this advantaged Democrats, as there were more voters who identified health care as the most important issues, and these voters broke primarily for the Democrats. For example, political newcomer Debbie Mucarsel-Powell (D-FL), who immigrated to the United States from Ecuador as a young girl, focused her campaign on access to health care and her opponent Carlos Curbelo's (R-FL) vote to repeal the Affordable Care Act (ACA), winning a narrow victory in 2018.[30] Additionally, the environment featured prominently in at least five hotly contested House races, and in those races, the Democratic candidates prevailed, including three women candidates who knocked off Republican incumbents.[31] For instance, Democrat Lizzie Pannill Fletcher (D-TX) defeated Republican incumbent John Culberson (R-TX) in a district that includes part of suburban Houston, which was hit by Hurricane Harvey in 2017. Like many other women candidates in 2018, Fletcher decided to run in reaction to President Trump's 2016 victory but focused heavily on climate change, particularly flood control in the Houston area, during her campaign.[32] Mucarsel-Powell also focused on the environment heavily in her campaign, highlighting her opponent's poor record on environmental issues. Thus, while there were sharp partisan divides among voters about the most important issues, more voters, and particularly voters in competitive districts, favored issues that were beneficial to Democratic and women candidates. As described in Chapter 4, issues like the environment and health care are seen as more feminine, so when these issues dominate the electoral environment, women candidates can benefit.

The prominence of these issues in the 2018 midterm election cycle helped the Democrats take back control of the House, but the Senate and the presidency are still controlled by Republicans. As such, the actual policy gains that come in these areas for Democrats may be small. On the health care side, the ACA, which was passed during the Obama administration, remains in place, so control over the House is important for the Democrats, as it gives them the ability to block any attempts to repeal the ACA during the 2019–2020 term. Given that three states with predominantly Republican representation in Congress (Idaho, Nebraska, and Utah) voted to expand health care coverage for the poor and working class under the ACA's expansion of Medicaid in 2018, further efforts to repeal the ACA seem unlikely.

On the environment, control of the House by Democrats means Republicans need Democratic support to pass any environmental legislation; proposals to roll back parts of the Endangered Species Act and revisions of the Farm Bill to limit controls on pesticides that were part of the Republican Congressional agenda will likely die. However, Republicans gained seats in the Senate, which is the body that confirms key judicial and political appointments, which means they will have the power to confirm someone to head the Environmental Protection Agency and judges throughout the federal court system. Environmental activists continue to push Congress to act on environmental issues though; days after the midterm elections, climate activists protested outside of House Speaker Nancy Pelosi's (D-CA) office and were joined by newly elected Representative Alexandria Ocasio-Cortez (D-NY). Members of the Sunrise Movement (2018), which organized the protests, have called for Democrats to create a select committee for a Green New Deal to fully transition the United States away from a fossil-fuel economy.[33] Overall then, 2018 was a positive electoral environment for many women candidates, and while the policy impacts may be small, more women will have a seat at the table in crafting policy, which can have important impacts on legislatures and legislation, as Chapter 6 describes.

Thus, despite lower levels of political ambition overall, many individual women do make the decision to run for office. As with men, they tend to be strategic about these decisions, thinking about district and political environment in making the decision to run for office. And overall, when women run, women win. Despite this, women candidates' experiences during the campaign are not the same as men's experiences; they still face numerous obstacles in the political environment—obstacles that their men opponents do not necessarily face, which means they often have to work longer and harder to secure similar outcomes.

Voter Perceptions of Women Candidates

Even after women were enfranchised and gained the right to run for office, stereotyped thinking about women's natural abilities and proper place biased some voters against women candidates. In 1937, for example, a Gallup poll found that 64% of Americans would not support a woman for president, "even if she were qualified in every other respect,"[34] a percentage that increased to 73% in 1940. Perhaps a looming war triggered a preference for a man commander in chief. But by 1948, the public was evenly split on a revised version of this question. In 1958, Gallup settled on the final version of this question which reads, "If your party nominated a woman for president, would you vote for her if she were qualified for the job?"—which it began consistently including in national surveys after the 1970s. Majority opinion shifted, with 66% professing support for a hypothetical woman presidential candidate in 1971, 76% in 1978, 82% in 1987, and 92% in 1999. Aside from another slight dip in the early 2000s, perhaps once again driven by prominent overseas military engagements, the percentage of Americans who claimed they would support a woman president continued to rise until it hit 95% in 2011. This is a topic we reconsider in Chapter 7.

It is important to note that the overwhelmingly high number of respondents who say yes to this question likely underestimates voter bias against women candidates. Even when providing anonymous answers in a telephone interview, **social desirability**—or an effort to avoid being judged for giving a politically incorrect or inappropriate response—affects the way people answer. Some people inevitably adjust their response in order to avoid appearing sexist. Researchers at Gallup have addressed this likelihood by also asking a question that allows respondents to attribute sexist bias to other voters rather than themselves. In 2015, for example, 20% of Americans indicated that they did not think "the voters of this country are ready to elect a woman president." In another creative attempt to identify how many Americans would be upset by a prominent woman candidate, respondents were asked to identify the number of public issues that upset them from a given list. Half of the respondents were randomly assigned to review a list of likely public concerns, while half were assigned an identical list with the addition of having a woman serve as president of the United States. An increase in the number of concerning issues identified by those who received the second list allows researchers to avoid social desirability while estimating sexist voter bias. This list experiment indicated that about 26% of the electorate was still biased against women candidates in 2008,[35] but that such opposition had been cut in half, down to 13% by 2017.[36] Perhaps resulting from Hillary Clinton's prominent campaigns in 2008 and 2016, the Democratic Party's embrace of feminist issues, and the Republican Party's pushback against identity politics and political correctness, opposition to women candidates was clustered among Independents and Republicans and was almost nonexistent among Democrats in the electorate by 2017.

The most important take-away from this overview is that by every measure, voter bias against women candidates has steadily declined over time and no longer prevents women from winning elections. Given the rise of partisan polarization and increased strength of party identification over the same time period, voters are more apt to rely on a candidate's partisanship than her sex when making choices in a general election. But voter bias has not been completely eliminated, and running for office as a woman still comes with difficult challenges, described in more detail later in the chapter. Further, sex-based bias is exacerbated when voters prioritize issues associated with stereotypical male strengths (i.e., war and budgets) over those associated with women and nurturing others (i.e., health care or education)—as well as when women run for prominent executive offices, such as governor or president, that are still linked to stereotypically male leadership traits, as described in more detail in Chapters 6 and 7. Thus, women must undertake a careful balancing act—often referred to as the **double bind**—conforming to traditional feminine norms to establish likability, while also proving their competency, prior to achieving influence over others.[37] Even in 2018, voters were more confident that men would do a better job overseeing military intervention, interacting with foreign leaders, and handling a terrorist attack or war, while women were trusted to handle domestic issues.[38] Yet when women run—after controlling for factors like incumbency status that would affect any candidate's success—they are just as likely to attract voter support and to win elections as men candidates.[39–41] Thus, there are still some voters who are biased against women candidates, but because these voters are more likely to identify as Independents and Republicans, these biases present a greater barrier for Republican women candidates, which we discuss later in the chapter.

Media Coverage of Women Candidates

As described in Chapter 3, the media plays a large role in shaping the way individuals and society think about politics. As a result, politicians are highly reliant on the media to communicate with voters. Information about the candidates comes to voters both directly, through running campaign ads that politicians themselves shape, and indirectly, through coverage of candidates and their campaigns. Candidates are less reliant on the media when running for local offices, such as school board member or city councilor, especially in smaller cities where candidates may be able to personally contact a large number of voters. But as the scope of the district and the number of voters represented grows, candidates increasingly rely on the media to communicate with voters, which means the media can play a large role in shaping voter perceptions of candidates.

Campaign advertising allows candidates to communicate directly with voters without media interpreting and framing these messages, thus they are very important to candidates' campaigns. Candidates use advertising to persuade voters to support them and to mobilize supporters; the effects of these ads is typically short term, but they can influence the behavior of voters.[42] While men and women candidates prefer to focus on policy issues in their ads, men candidates historically focus more on economic issues, and women candidates focus more on social issues like education and health care.[43,44] Women candidates also are more likely to present a "soft" image in their ads, both in the United States and in Finland.[45] Additionally, women candidates are more likely to run ads that are generally positive, as these sorts of ads are perceived by voters as more socially desirable for women candidates.[46] As such, campaign strategists often recommend women candidates avoid running negative ads. Negative ads are effective though, particularly with respect to mobilizing voters,[47] so the backlash associated with these ads can be an obstacle for women candidates. There are ways for women candidates to overcome this. For instance, the Barbara Lee Foundation (ND), which provides training to help women candidates prepare and run for office, acknowledges that it is important to run ads that provide contrast with opponents, so they provide detailed strategies, such as using real people to deliver negative information and citing sources, to help women candidates avoid backlash from voters for these contrasting ads.[48]

Despite the fact that early research showed differences between men and women candidates in terms of their messaging and advertising strategies and voter reactions, other research suggests that these differences are diminishing, such that men and women candidates' communication strategies are converging.[49] Importantly, newer research has demonstrated that voters do not punish candidates, men or women, of their own party for running negative ads, but they do punish candidates of the opposing party for going negative, with the harshest evaluations reserved for women candidates from the opposing party who run negative ads.[50] Thus, as with voters' evaluations of candidates, evaluations of candidates' campaign messages are increasingly driven by partisan polarization. As such, some research suggests that negative advertising can, in some contexts, be a positive weapon for women candidates.[51] In 2018, it appears that differences in the campaign ads of candidates started to diverge again, with women increasingly running "as women." That is, rather than avoiding gender and ads that activate gender stereotypes about women, women candidates seemed to turn the conventional wisdom about how to run as a woman on its head, running ads featuring stories of sexual abuse and images of breastfeeding. Many of these ads were featured on the Internet, where the cost of running ads is lower than on TV, creating a low risk, high reward situation if the ads go viral.[52] We discuss the 2018 campaign in greater detail later in the chapter, but it is important to note that this confirms existing research that women are more likely adopt innovative campaign communication strategies, such as using Twitter earlier and more often than men candidates.[53]

Because candidates cannot reach all voters through personal connections or advertising, they also rely on the media to indirectly communicate with voters. When examining how the media indirectly conveys information about candidates through their coverage of them and their campaigns, research demonstrates that the media has historically treated women candidates differently than their men counterparts. To start, early research suggested that women candidates received less campaign coverage as compared to their men counterparts, and the coverage they did receive was more negative, focusing on their unlikely chances of winning.[54] A study of the news media in Europe, published in 2005, found that women were just 21% of all news subjects—those who are interviewed or who the news is about—and were just 10% of the politicians in the news media.[55] More recent research in the U.K. suggests that as more women run, this imbalance in the quantity of coverage is diminishing or even flipping to benefit women. For instance, in the 2015 U.K. General Election, women candidates received more coverage than their men counterparts, after controlling for factors like incumbency and party.[56] With unprecedented numbers of women running in the Democratic primary for the 2020 presidential election, it will be important to watch the amount of media coverage women receive relative to the men in the race. Early observations seem to indicate that women are losing out in coverage to the white men in the race. That said, this increased coverage can be a double-edged sword for women candidates of color, as coverage may be narrowly focused on the novelty of their candidacies and fixated on their ethnicity and sex as was the case for women candidates of color in the 2010 U.K. General Election.[57]

In addition to the volume and tone of the coverage, the content of media messages about women candidates is different. First, women receive less issue coverage than their men counterparts.[58] Instead, coverage tends to focus on their traits, as opposed to issues.[59] Beaudoux (2017) identifies five ways the media hurts women politicians by focusing on traits and relationships; they 1) focus on women's domestic life, 2) attach them to powerful men, 3) highlight any display of emotions, 4) discuss their looks, and 5) comment on their voice.[60] Examples for each of these strategies illuminate how they can undermine women candidates. For example, Sarah Palin was asked how she would balance being a mother and vice president during the 2008 election cycle. But House Speaker Paul Ryan, who was the Republican vice presidential nominee in the next election cycle, was not asked similar questions, despite the fact the he also had young children. As an example of the second issue, Beaudoux describes how 32-year-old Bibiana Aído was named Minister of Equality and Innovation in Spain in 2008, and one of the prominent papers ran the story with the headline, "Dad, they're going to make me minister!" In 2014, *Perfil*, an Argentinian political magazine, ran a story called "Cristina's Emotional Default," which described Argentinian President Cristina Fernández's errors and argued she suffered from a mood disorder. As an example of the media's focus on appearance, the German media ran a story called "Merkel's Weapons of Mass Destruction;" this story described a dress German Chancellor Angela Merkel wore to the opera, which the media apparently felt was too low cut and revealing. Finally, Hillary Clinton's voice has been the subject of much media attention, having been described as shrill, monotone, bitter, angry, and screaming by various outlets.

The media often uses frames, or central organizing principles (as defined in Chapter 3), when covering a given topic, and analysis of women candidates demonstrates that certain frames are commonly deployed when describing them. Kanter (1977) identified four common stereotypes used to describe professional women: seductress or sex object, mother, pet, and iron maiden;[61] Carlin and Winfrey (2009) demonstrate how these stereotypes extend into media coverage of political women.[62] The first, the **seductress frame**, refers to both sexuality and sex roles and includes everything from coverage of a woman candidates' clothing and speculation about her sexuality and marital status. The media are more likely to comment on the appearance of women, and all types of this coverage, neutral, negative, and positive, have negative impacts on women's campaigns, reducing voters' perceptions of likeability and their likelihood of voting for women candidates.[63] The **mother frame** can cut both ways for women candidates, Carlin and Winfrey argue. Women who are seen as mothering and caring, can be advantaged as these are generally seen as positive traits. Conversely, women candidates are often questioned about their competency to run given maternal responsibilities and about their ability to control their emotions when needed. The **pet frame** occurs when women are taken along as symbolic tokens, diminishing expectations about their capacity for leadership. Finally, Carlin and Winfrey describe the **iron maiden frame**; women in this frame are seen as cold and uncaring. By displaying masculine tendencies, women cast in this frame lose any of the few advantages that come from being a woman, mainly because they are seen as failing to conform to expected gender roles. Carlin and Winfrey found evidence of all four frames in use in the 2008 election campaign; Palin was frequently framed using the first three frames, while coverage of Clinton more commonly used iron maiden and mother frames.

Black women candidates are framed in even more narrow terms, drawing on racist, historical images of Black women.[67] West (1995) identifies numerous ways that Black women are portrayed in the media, although the use of these frames in covering women candidates has not yet been studied.[68] The **mammy**

BOX 5.3: COMPARATIVE FEATURE

Iron Maidens Around the World

The Iron Maiden frame is used commonly throughout the world in media coverage of women leaders who display stereotypically masculine traits in office. Margaret Thatcher is perhaps the most frequently associated with this frame and most likely the contemporary origin of this frame. The first woman to lead a major political party in the United Kingdom, Thatcher served as prime minister from 1979 until 1990. In 1976, Thatcher gave a speech, widely known as the Britain Awake speech, where she warned world leaders of the rising threat of the Soviet Union. The Soviet Media dubbed her the "Iron Lady" in the wake of this speech, a nickname that she fully embraced. In 1976, she said in a speech to fellow conservatives,

> I stand before you tonight in my Red Star chiffon evening gown, my face softly made up and my fair hair gently waved. The Iron Lady of the Western world. A cold war warrior, an amazon philistine, even a Peking plotter. Well, am I any of these things? Yes, I am an iron lady, after all it wasn't a bad thing to be an iron duke, yes if that's how they wish to interpret my defense of values and freedoms fundamental to our way of life.[64]

However, while the use of the term "Iron Lady" is contemporary, the frame itself is not. Historically, as now, this frame is employed to describe a strong-willed woman leader who does not conform to societal gender expectations of female passivity and caring. For instance, Queen Wilhelmina, who ruled the Netherlands from 1890 to 1948, was called "the only man in the Dutch cabinet" by Winston Churchill.[65]

Since then, the iron lady/maiden frame has been applied to many women politicians around the world. Angela Merkel, the German chancellor, has been called the Iron Chancellor. Ellen Johnson Sirleaf, Africa's first democratically elected leader and president of Liberia from 2006 to 2018, has also been called the Iron Lady. A behind-the-scenes documentary about her first year in office was called *The Iron Ladies of Liberia* (2007). Wikipedia maintains a page to guide people who search for the term "Iron Lady," the page lists dozens of additional women politicians who have been dubbed Iron Ladies, including Benazir Bhutto, former prime minister of Pakistan; Indira Gandhi, former prime minister of India; Dalia Grybauskaité, president of Lithuania; Golda Meir, former prime minister of Israel; and Wu Yi, former vice premier of China. This frame does not only apply to leaders of the national government; Jane Byrne, the

(Continued)

(Continued)

first woman mayor of Chicago, was called "Atilla the Hen" by her critics.[66] Frequently, this frame is applied to women firsts: first prime minister, first secretary of state (in the United States, Madeleine Albright was called the "Titanium Lady"), and first mayor.

While these frames commonly have been used as an attempt to denigrate these women for their nonconformity, many of these women, just like Thatcher, are embracing the label. In addition to the documentary about Johnson Sirleaf, she appointed a predominantly woman cabinet who collectively have embraced the "Iron Ladies" nickname.

frame emphasizes Black women's role in domestic service, whereby she is portrayed as a large, caring woman who sacrificed self for those under her care. The **sapphire frame** portrays Black women as loud and angry, who seek to emasculate Black men. For example, during the 2008 campaign, Michelle Obama was frequently covered using the sapphire frame, such as when *The New Yorker* ran a cover featuring her with an afro and a gun slung over her back. The final frame described by West is the **jezebel frame**, which is akin to the seductress frame.

However, as with voter bias against women candidates and campaign communication strategies, more recent research suggests media bias in covering women candidates may be diminishing. Smith (1997) finds that bias was more prevalent prior to 1990 than it was at end of the 1990s.[69] Despite the fact that the gap in how men and women candidates are covered is shrinking, the examples above demonstrate that unequal coverage still persists. Hillary Clinton's 2008 and 2016 presidential campaigns, described in more detail later in this chapter and in Chapter 7, demonstrate this effectively. Some have argued there has been a shift in the coverage of women candidates post-2016, with the media more likely to focus on women's partisanship and ideology given the levels of party polarization in contemporary politics.[70]

The bias in media coverage of women candidates also extends to coverage of women politicians once they are in office, and increasingly, this bias in coverage is driven by party polarization. Nowhere is this more evident than in coverage of Nancy Pelosi (D-CA). Pelosi is the only woman to have served as Speaker of the U.S. House, from 2007 to 2011, before being reelected to the position in 2019. Many regard her as one of the most effective people to ever have served in this role; for instance, *New York Times* columnist Paul Krugman (2018) calls her "the greatest Speaker of modern times and . . . among the most impressive people to ever hold that position."[71] Perhaps her signature accomplishment may have been keeping the Democratic Party caucus in the House together to secure the passage of President Obama's Affordable Care Act in a difficult political climate. Republicans focused a great deal of direct, negative coverage on Pelosi in the

2018 election cycle; in September and October of 2018, nearly 100 ads funded by Republicans featured Nancy Pelosi, Hillary Clinton, or both, framing the 2018 election as a choice between Pelosi and Trump. This framing was largely ineffective as an electoral strategy, as Democrats picked up over 30 House seats in the election. This uptick resulted in Democrats gaining control of the House, allowing them to once again choose Pelosi as Speaker of the House. However, the Republican advertising strategy was effective in undermining support for Pelosi; polls at the time of the election found that 52% of respondents had an unfavorable view of Pelosi, while just 28.5% had a favorable view.[72] Since Democratic ads have not featured Pelosi, voters' information about her has come either from ads aired directly by the Republican party or indirect media coverage. Research suggests that the coverage of Pelosi relies heavily on the iron maiden and mother frames, framing her as having a "spine of steel and a heart of gold."[73] As such, the nomination of Pelosi to become Speaker was contentious. Given her success in the role, many have argued that this should not have been a contentious decision, so obviously the negative direct and indirect coverage of Pelosi has been damaging to her.

CAMPAIGN FINANCE

Importantly, mounting a campaign for office requires a good deal of resources. Money is critical to any effort to run for elected office. Money can be used to hire campaign workers, contact potential voters, or buy media time. All other things being equal, candidates who raise more money are more likely to win.[74,75] Thus, in order for women to successfully seek elected office, they must raise money. Generally speaking, research suggests that women candidates raise as much money as men candidates, but there are obstacles that women must overcome to reach this parity.

One of the primary determinants of how much money candidates raise is their incumbency status; people who already hold a given office raise more money than those who do not hold that office.[76] Because there are more men elected office holders, as noted earlier, it appears on the face that men raise more money when running for office than women. When we compare men and women who have the same credentials though, those differences tend to disappear.[77] Women incumbents raise as much as men incumbents;[78] women challengers raise as much money as men challengers.[79–82] This is true across different levels of office seeking from city council and mayoral elections to state legislative races all the way up to races for the U.S. Congress.[83–85] However, these similar outcomes mask obstacles that women candidates may have to overcome.

First, in order to achieve financial parity, women have to work harder at fundraising. Women candidates rely on a broader variety of fund-raising techniques for their campaign money and devote more time to this task as compared to men candidates.[86] Given that nearly all candidates dislike fund-raising, this disliked task may partially explain why fewer women seek elected offices. Indeed, in interviews of women officials, Witt, Paget, and Matthews (1994) find that currently elected women commonly cite the need to raise money as a reason why they were not interested in seeking higher office.[87] Senfronia Thompson, a Democratic state representative from Texas representing Houston and the nation's longest serving woman representative, says she has a harder time raising money than her white men colleagues because she is a woman and she is Black.[88]

Second, potential donors are less likely to contribute to women's campaigns,[89] which also explains why women have to work longer and harder at this task. In particular, men donors are less likely to give to women candidates.[90] Additionally, women are less likely to have developed financial networks and are less connected to affluent donors.[91] Given wealth disparities between men and women, men are a large portion of the donor pool, and they tend to dominate in these financial networks, which disadvantages women candidates. In 2018, as described later in the chapter, women have increased their political donations substantially, to the benefit of women candidates, and diminish this participatory gap between the sexes.

Women candidates are also more likely to rely on a broader variety of sources for their campaign funding,[92] and donations that come early in the campaign cycle are particularly important to women candidates. Women's **Political Action Committees (PACs)** that focus on raising money early in a woman's bid for office, like EMILY'S List, give a boost to women candidates, as these group donations lead to more small donations from individual donors.[93] This dynamic provides an advantage for women Democrats as compared to women Republicans as these women's PACs tend to be liberal in their focus and because Democratic donors value the election of women, while Republican donors focus more on ideology than sex or gender.[94,95]

BOX 5.4: POLICY FEATURE

Women Supporting Women—
Donations To Women Candidates

Few things have done more to support the candidacies of women candidates than the emergence of PACs that focus exclusively on providing support to women candidates. PACs are political committees organized for the purpose of raising and spending money to elect and defeat candidates.[96] PACs can give up to $5,000 to a candidate per election (primary or general); they can also solicit donations from individuals and often help guide individual decision-making about which candidates should receive individual contributions.

One of the earliest and now largest organizations to focus exclusively on women candidates is EMILY's List. Founded in 1985, the name is an acronym for

Early Money Is Like Yeast; the founders chose this name because they felt that early money—that is, money donated at the beginning of an election cycle—was like yeast, in that it made the dough rise.[97] In other words, they saw their

Table 5.2   Top 10 Women's Issues Contributors in 2018

Group	Total	To Democrats	To Republicans
EMILY's List	$603,239	$603,239	$0
Value in Electing Women PAC	$375,000	$0	$375,000
Women's Political Committee	$238,375	$238,375	$0
Tri-state Maxed Out Women	$186,699	$186,699	$0
Winning for Women PAC	$127,753	$0	$127,753
RightNow Women	$73,500	$0	$73,500
Maggie's List	$50,300	$0	$50,300
Los Angeles Women's Giving Collective	$47,800	$42,400	$5,400
National Organization for Women	$47,200	$47,200	$0
Electing Women San Francisco	$30,420	$30,420	$0
Overall Totals for all Women's Issue PACs	$1,884,413	$1,238,260 (66%)	$646,153 (34%)

Source: Center for Responsive Politics.

role as providing early donations to promising women candidates, in the hopes that these early donations would signal to individual donors that these candidates were worth investing in. This strategy had early success as Senator Barbara Mikulski (D-MD), who was one of EMILY's List's first candidates, won election to the U.S. Senate in 1986.[98]

Since then, the number of PACS and groups specifically focused on funding and supporting women candidates has exploded. For instance, in 2018, PACs focused on women's issues donated over $1.84 million dollars to midterm candidates as Table 5.2 shows; the majority of this money (66%) went to Democratic candidates. EMILY's List led the way with over $600,000 in contributions. As with

(Continued)

other aspects of our current political system, partisan considerations dominate giving patterns for these groups. Of the top 10 groups giving to women, only one gave to candidates of both parties; instead, these groups tend to focus on either Democratic women or Republican women.

These figures represent only the amounts donated directly to women candidates. In addition to PACs, there are **Super PAC**s. These groups cannot donate directly to campaigns under current campaign finance regulations, but they can raise unlimited sums of money from corporations, unions, and individuals and then spend unlimited sums to advocate for or against political campaigns, so long as these expenditures are made independently from candidates' campaigns. The amounts raised and spent by these groups dwarfs the direct contributions to candidates by PACs. For instance, Women Vote! is the Super PAC associated with EMILY's List; in 2018, it raised over $33 million and spent over $28 million overwhelmingly in support of Democratic women candidates and in opposition to Republican women candidates, making it one of the largest Super PACs overall. Given that there were fewer Republican women candidates in 2018, Republican Super PACs were less active. That said, Susan B. Anthony List, a prolife Super PAC supporting predominantly Republican women, raised and spent over $2.6 million on the 2018 election.

This money and these groups have been instrumental to supporting women candidates. For example, EMILY's List, last updated in 2017, claims to have helped elect over 100 Democratic women to Congress and statewide office.

Overall, then, while women candidates are just as likely to win when they run as similarly situated men, this does not mean their experience on the campaign trail is the same. They must overcome voter and media bias and work harder to secure the necessary resources for their campaign; these obstacles may be diminishing, but they still persist. This leads to what Anzia and Berry (2011) term the "Jackie (and Jill) Robinson effect;" women candidates have to be harder working and more talented to reach the same levels of achievement as men politicians.[99] As a result, they argue only the most qualified and most ambitious women emerge as candidates. As Lazarus and Steigerwalt (2018) describe in their book *Gendered Vulnerability*, women candidates are more electorally vulnerable than their men counterparts because they get lower quality media coverage, face higher quality opponents, and receive less support from political parties, making it more difficult for them to succeed.[100] This dynamic has important implications for women's performance in office, which we examine over the next few chapters.

While some find that women candidates use campaign strategies and tactics that are similar to their men peers and use these similarities to infer that women candidates face few challenges in the electoral arena,[101,102] the abundance of evidence suggests that women achieve this parity by simply working harder. So, it is certainly true that polarization makes partisanship the overwhelming criteria that voters used to evaluate candidates—and that when women run, they are just as likely to win as men. Yet, it is difficult to assess the nuanced effects of the double bind on women's lived experiences. Survey data, for example, failed to capture the sexual harassment and threats of violence that women in the public sphere experienced. The stories relayed in the wake of the #MeToo movement make it clear that far more women candidates and public officials have these experiences than do men. Moreover, in their 2018 campaigns, many Democratic women ran campaigns that looked distinctly different than their men counterparts, allowing them to act more naturally and to be more authentic. The number of women in the public eye and in public office after 2018 may well help to shift politics from a male coded to a female coded or gender-neutral space—which will encourage more women to run for office in the long run. Furthermore, the 2018 "Year of the Woman" upended conventional wisdom about what women candidates need to do in order to win office, so we turn next to examining the campaign cycle in greater detail.

WOMEN AS CANDIDATES IN 2018

In 2014, Lawless and Fox predicted that barring a "jolt" to the political system, they could not foresee another Year of the Woman in the next several decades. (The first **Year of the Woman** was in 1992 when record numbers of women were elected into Congress.) Yet, Donald J. Trump's successful presidential bid provided just such a jolt, motivating women across the country to become more involved in politics.

Democrats across the country had a strong reaction to Donald Trump's campaign rhetoric, which included sexist statements about women and negative stereotypes about racial and ethnic minorities. While Democratic men were upset, the demographic group most outraged by Donald Trump's election has been Democratic women. This intensity led to hundreds of thousands of people—many of them women participating in a protest for the very first time—to travel to Washington, DC, the day after the inauguration to join the Women's March on Washington (see Chapter 9 for a more thorough discussion). On the same day, approximately three million participated in similar protests of Trump's presidency in marches and rallies in 550 towns throughout the United States.[103]

Some questioned whether the Women's March protest was a one-time event or whether participants would engage in sustained political activism. Organizers encouraged protesters to follow through by posting "10 Actions for the first 100 Days." Participants not only followed through by writing post cards and contacting their elected officials, they went on to found grassroots organizations—sometimes collectively referred to as "the resistance" despite their lack of coordination—where they honed organizing skills as they began canvassing and raising money to support politicians and learning the nit-picky rules that govern local politics and voter registration drives, as well as coordinating letter-writing campaigns, phone banks, and protests. Their efforts have spawned an overlapping array of civic organizations that range from bare-bones local organizations to well-funded national networks such as Indivisible, Action Together, and Together We Will. College-educated mid-career women—many in their 40s, 50s, and 60s—have taken the lead in these organizing efforts, which have focused not only on recruiting candidates to run for office in the 2018 midterm elections but also on rebuilding the Democratic Party from the grassroots up by stepping up to serve on party committees and volunteering to serve on local governing boards.[104,105]

It is important to note that this commitment to organizing and activism extends beyond white middle-aged women. The Trump era has also inspired African American women, angry over his disparaging comments about prominent Black women like Congresswomen Maxine Waters (D-CA) and Frederica Wilson (D-FL), to get involved. African American women, for example, leveraged their connections to community organizations and voluntary associations to help Alabama Democrat Doug Jones narrowly defeat Republican Roy Moore, who was accused of sexual misconduct with underage girls, in a special election for U.S. Senate. Quentin James, founder of Collective PAC, summarized the sentiment of women who reach out to his political action committee for donations. "You have a president who attacks Black women. . . . They're fed up, we're fed up, and . . . It's crucial we have more voices on the public stage to fight back."[106]

It stands to reason that some of these activists would not only recruit other women to run for office but would also decide to run themselves. In 2017, nonprofit organizations opposed to Trump's agenda reported a surge in donations, while organizations that recruit and train women to run began to report record numbers of women at their events.

Emily's List reported a significant increase in the number of women reaching out for assistance after the 2016 presidential election. Stephanie Schriock, the organization's president, described their motivation with the following claim: "It's not just Trump's victory motivating women to run. . . . It's also about Clinton's loss. I met so many women before the election with tears in their eyes about how important this victory was going to be."[107] Some of these women transformed their motivation into political ambition. The organization, which supported a record-setting 1,200 women running for state legislative seats in 2018, had been contacted by 16,000 potential women candidates by August of 2017. This number had nearly doubled to 30,000 contacts by March of 2018. In comparison, only 900 women reached out to seek support during the entire 2016 election cycle. Other campaign-oriented nonprofits report a similar spike in interest. For example, Emerge America, which provides a 6-month, 70-hour training program, saw a 90% increase in requests for its services after the 2016 presidential election. Other partisan counterparts (like Rise to Run and She

Should Run) and nonpartisan counterparts (like VoteRunLead) also report recent exponential growth in demand for their services. VoteRunLead, for example, trained 9,700 women online and in person in 2017 and anticipates training 30,000 by 2020.[108–112]

Similar to Anita Hill's testimony at Justice Clarence Thomas's nomination hearings, which motivated women to run for office in 1992 (see Chapter 8), President Trump's success gave rise to a sharp increase in the number of women candidates in the 2018 midterm elections. For example, 53 women filed to compete in U.S. Senate races, breaking the last record of 40 women set in 2016. Then 23 (15 Democrats and 8 Republicans) went on to compete in the general election. In House races, 476 women filed in 2018, far exceeding the previous record of 298 set in 2012, and 239 (187 Democrats and 52 Republicans) moved on to the general election. This pattern was consistent with gubernatorial races, as 61 women competed in primaries, almost doubling a previous high of 35 women candidates running for governor in 1994. Of those, 16 (12 Democrats and 4 Republicans) competed in the general election. Similarly, 3,381 women (2,381 Democrats, 980 Republicans, and 48 nonpartisan/others) won the right to compete in the 2018 general elections for state legislature, compared to only 2,649 in 2016.[113]

BOX 5.5: WHAT ABOUT REPUBLICAN WOMEN?

As these numbers make clear, the 2018 midterms exacerbated the existing gender gap between the two parties discussed in Chapter 3, as politically ambitious women were more apt to identify with and run as Democrats than as Republicans. The number of Republican women who ran in primaries and general elections increased in 2016 to over 100, in large part because of the efforts of Rep. Elise Stefanik (R-NY), who directed the GOP's recruitment efforts. Despite such efforts, along with support from nonprofit organizations—such as Maggie's List, the Values in Electing Women PAC, and the RightNOW Women PAC—that bolster conservative women's electoral bids, Republicans could not match the record-breaking number of Democratic women in the 2018 midterms.[114]

One reason may be that President Trump's campaign rhetoric has made it more difficult for Republican women to campaign effectively. Voters in the Republican Party are less inclined to embrace the type of identity politics that has allowed Democratic candidates to push back against the double bind by transforming their intersectional identities into candidate strengths. Republican women can-

(Continued)

(Continued)

didates have been more likely to maintain traditional candidate images and campaign themes, downplaying their sex and gender identity rather than embracing it. Now, in addition to having less ability to push back against the double bind, Republican women are forced to develop a strategy for responding to the president's sexist rhetoric in a way that addresses concerns of moderate and independent women, without alienating base voters who are fiercely loyal to Trump. Rep. Martha Roby (R-AL) faced this dilemma. She publicly rejected Trump's candidacy in 2016, claiming "I cannot look my children in the eye . . . and justify a vote for a man who promotes and boasts about sexually assaulting women."[115] The following year, however, she found herself in need of Trump's support to mobilize the base and defeat a conservative challenger in her own primary election.

Other Republican incumbents have found creative ways to publicize their work on issues important to women without taking on the president directly. Former Rep. Mimi Walters (R-CA), who lost to a Democratic challenger in 2018, highlighted her efforts to help battered and raped women, while Rep. Cathy McMorris Rodgers (R-WA), who defeated her Democratic challenger in 2018, has made sure to prominently feature women supporters in her campaign literature. Yet, many women GOP lawmakers privately admit that they face a "difficult situation" under the current administration. Retiring Rep. Ileana Ros-Lehtinen (R-FL), the first Cuban American and the first Latina elected to Congress, has been blunt, worrying that Republican women will become an "endangered species" and noting that while the absolute number of Republican women has increased since she first came to Congress, the proportion of women in the Republican Party has fallen substantially.[116] She explicitly blames Donald Trump for their poor showing in the 2018 midterms, imploring him to "Just stop with the name calling. It turns women off. It turns a lot of people off, but especially young women. They just say this is ugly."[117] It remains to be seen whether 2018 is an anomaly or whether more Republican women can be encouraged to run in the future.[118,119]

Again, it is important to note that many of the candidates most motivated to run in response to Trump's 2016 win are women whose intersectional identities will further diversify the racial, ethnic, religious, immigrant, and sex of American public officials, as described in the introduction to this chapter. For instance, Paulette Jordan was the first Native American woman gubernatorial candidate in U.S. history. Jordan, who created a two-woman ticket by selecting Kristin Collum as her running mate, explained, "For someone to say, 'Step aside,' that's something women have heard before. . . . This is our time."[120]

Current evidence suggests, however, that the spike in political ambition that drove more women to run for office in the 2018 midterms is likely a short-term reaction to Trump's campaign and presidency. To assess how much women changed their political behavior and attitudes in response to Trump, Lawless and Fox (2017) conducted a survey of likely political candidates in 2017.[121] Democratic women were much more likely, at 28% to claim that they had first thought about running within the past 6 months. Only 11% of Democratic men gave a similar answer. Rather, most Democratic men, much like both men and women Republican candidates, indicated that they first thought about running for office nearly a decade ago. Despite this stark uptick, the aftermath of 2016 will likely be similar to 1992, which led to an increase in the number of women who ran and won elections but did not transform women's low levels of nascent and expressed political ambition in the long term. Simply put, the deeply rooted factors that affect women's political ambition—such as socialization into traditional gender roles—are not likely to be overcome in one fell swoop. Indeed, Lawless and Fox's 2017 survey of potential candidates revealed that despite Democratic women's visceral reactions to Donald Trump and enthusiastic embrace of political activism, few anticipated running for office themselves. In fact, Lawless and Fox (2017) found that in 2017, men's and women's levels of political ambition looked essentially unchanged, with the same gap between men and women that has characterized responses for the past 15 years.[122]

Of course, this "Trump Effect" may boost the number of women who run over time. When women are politically active, they are more likely to be recruited to run for office. Being asked to run several times typically precedes women's political ambition. Hence, recruitment has the potential to substantially increase the number of women who think of themselves as potential candidates in the future. Just as important, however, the sheer number of women running for office in 2018 may finally be helping to shift the hypermasculine ethos that portrays politics as men's work and the gendered psyches that convince women they are not qualified for such work.

The Trump Effect already appears to be having this effect on women's confidence in their ability to run for office. Trump's ability to win the presidency as a first-time candidate with no prior experience made many realize that they did not need to burnish their political credentials, serving for years on city councils and school boards, before running for state legislature or even Congress.[123] Cecile Richards, the daughter of former Texas Governor Anne Richards and former president of Planned Parenthood, expressed her approval of this turn of events, saying, "My mom would be thrilled to see that women aren't waiting their turn—they're just jumping in. Back in the day, a woman had to have an entire resume of accomplishments, three times as long as a man running. A lot of things that women already do—running the PTA, raising children, balancing a job and family—those are all attributes that make them highly qualified to be in public office."[124] For instance, Rep. Abigail Spanberger (D-VA) defeated Tea Party star David Brat in 2018, despite having never run for or held elected office in the past.

The number of women candidates running is not only shifting candidates' perceptions about who is qualified to run for office, it may be shifting voters' perceptions as well. Gubernatorial candidate Kelda Roys (D-WI) claimed to notice a difference, stating, "I don't have to credential myself as much anymore. In previous elections, I thought it was a disadvantage—you had to prove yourself capable and worthy of winning voter support in a way that was assumed for men. This year, I think women and men are excited about voting for a woman."[125]

DISMANTLING THE MASCULINE ETHOS OF POLITICS IN 2018 AND BEYOND

In the past, women have dealt with the assumption that political leaders should have stereotypically masculine traits by imitating men. Yet, until quite recently, women were associated with lower status domestic positions in society, and they are still expected to be more communal and other-oriented than men as a result. These expectations place women candidates in a precarious situation. Their behavior is scrutinized when they step into traditionally masculine roles, as they must prove that they are competent. Yet, women who engage in displays of competence, self-promotion, and assertiveness are less well-liked and wield less influence than other women. People—including other women—have often disliked and sanctioned women who display such traits, as demonstrated by opinions about Nancy Pelosi. This consequence occurs because such behaviors are linked to efforts to gain status or to promote narrow agendas, which violate expectations grounded in the traditional ideal of the communal female. In the past, women in leadership positions have avoided being disliked—and subject to social sanction—when they managed to combine high levels of perceived competence with a warm, communal style of communication that focuses on helping others. In short, women's femininity is linked to their likeability—and both are a prerequisite to their ability to influence others—and is often more important to others than their expertise and competence.[126] Men face far fewer hurdles in their attempts to influence others, as the success of their efforts is not predicated on displays of competence or communality. They are already assumed to be competent, and they are not expected to be communal, another example of the double bind. Yet, when women try to fulfill both sets of expectations, they almost always fail, because anything they do to fulfill one set of expectations violates the other. As prominent linguist Deborah Tannen explains, "The requirements of a good leader and a good woman are mutually exclusive. A good leader must be tough, but a good woman must not be. A good woman must be self-deprecating, but a good leader must not be."[127]

Hillary Clinton's long political career provides examples of how difficult it can be—even for experienced women—to overcome the double bind. In her 2000 bid for U.S. Senate, for example, Hillary Clinton presented herself at her most authentic when she framed her campaign as a listening tour and traveled around the state to hear voters' stories as a way to inform her legislative agenda and policy positions. Listening corresponds to a more feminine leadership style, as the goal is to establish relationships, win allies, and build coalitions. While Clinton won, the press disliked covering her campaign because Clinton's approach violated expectations of campaign events, where candidates typically adopt a masculine leadership style by giving speeches to establish the value of their own ideas and enhance their status. While Clinton's campaign style could have been described as a strength, the press framed it as a weakness instead.[128] Clinton changed her approach in the 2008 presidential primaries, instead emphasizing her political experience and ability to make tough decisions. She adopted a more masculine demeanor, reinforced by television ads describing her as the only candidate in the race who was ready to answer "a 3 a.m. phone call" requiring the next president to handle an international crisis. After losing, in part because her likability suffered, Clinton tried to adopt a warmer, more feminine style in her 2016 presidential bid, where she more openly expressed concern for her constituents and played up her role as a new grandmother. According to consultant, Mark Penn, this approach simply opened her up to the accusation that she was inauthentic.[129] Indeed, pundits scolded Clinton's performance on the campaign trail so often—variously complaining that she appeared too serious and demanding that she smile more often, that she was too flippant and not serious enough, or simply that she appeared uncomfortable—that it became the basis for a skit on the late night show, Jimmy Kimmel Live! In the skit, Kimmel proceeds to offer helpful advice about how to dress stylishly without appearing to try, giving Clinton contradictory advice about lowering and raising her voice and telling her to smile but then telling her the effort appears forced.[130]

Clinton never managed to master the trick of portraying herself as likeable during her campaigns for public office (although, somewhat ironically, she was well-liked while serving in the appointed position of Secretary of State when she wielded power but did not have to seek it in a campaign). The fact that she won the popular vote in 2016—by more than 3 million ballots cast—is impressive, given that she was the least liked major party presidential nominee ever, except for Donald Trump—even dropping below the favorability of losing presidential candidates like John McCain, John Kerry, Al Gore, and Bob Dole. Pollsters described candidate Clinton's unfavorability rating as "freakishly bad" when it spiked into the mid-50s. As a point of comparison, the number of people who disliked her was 20 points higher than Barack Obama in 2012.[131]

Frustrated with carefully calculated—and often contradictory advice—about how to behave, many Democratic women in 2018 threw out the rules and simply tried to be authentic on the campaign trail. As one political journalist noted, "After years of being told to put on a suit and recite their resume—and smile!—women candidates are revealing themselves in more complex ways. They aren't running as men, but they aren't exactly running as women in a stereotypical way. They're running as individuals—something like the voters they are trying to reach."[132] This approach meshes well with recent research on voters' expectations. After Clinton lost in 2016, the Barbara Lee Foundation, which was established to support women in politics, conducted focus groups to determine how average voters respond to women candidates.

▸ **Photo 5.1** Alexandria Ocasio-Cortez, House of Representatives.

Researchers found that voters still expect to know more about women candidates' personal lives than they do men's—a likely side-effect of associating women first and foremost with the domestic sphere. Further, when women candidates failed to provide information about their private lives, voters were prone to speculate and make assumptions. Hence, the foundation recommends that women run as "360 degree candidates" who explain how both their personal and professional experiences qualify them for public service.[133] For some, this has meant sharing personal stories about private issues that candidates have been reluctant to address in the past. Gubernatorial nominee Stacey Abrams D-GA, for example, reached out to voters by discussing her brother's struggles with mental illness and her own credit card debt. Others explicitly have incorporated aspects of their lives that highlight, rather than diminish, their status as women and mothers. Normalizing women's daily routines, Alexandria Ocasio-Cortez (D-NY) won her primary election after airing an ad where she talked to Brooklyn voters while applying mascara and changing into pumps on a subway platform.[134]

Meanwhile, Liuba Grechen Shirley (D-NY), a Congressional candidate from Long Island, New York, made headlines when the Federal Election Commission approved her request to spend campaign funds on child care. In a *Washington Post* editorial explaining her request, she argued, "It's time to take down the institutional barriers blocking mothers from running for office. And if I'm going to win, then I need a babysitter."[135] Not surprisingly, her preschool age children feature prominently on her campaign's social media page and literature.

▸ **Photo 5.2** Liuba Grechen Shirley taking time from campaign to spend with her son.

Other candidates have highlighted their infants in campaign commercials. Gubernatorial candidate Kelda Roys (D-WI) breastfed on camera while discussing the importance of banning the suspected carcinogen BPA from baby bottles, while counterpart Krish Vignarajah (D-MD) aired a similar ad to underscore that Maryland has failed to elect women to statewide or federal office.[136]

A 2016 survey by the Barbara Lee Foundation found that voters are still reluctant to support mothers with young children but not fathers.[137] The scrutiny Sarah Palin received about who would care for her children, when she was tapped as John McCain's vice presidential running mate, has not dissipated over the years. By purposefully demonstrating that they can juggle domestic responsibilities with public service, these 2018 candidates may help normalize mothers in the public sphere, as they contradict stereotypes that women should set aside political ambition until they have met their family responsibilities.

The flexibility in approach has extended to how women present themselves in their public appearances and campaign advertisements. Fewer women candidates in the 2018 cycle felt the need

Getty Images

▸ **Photo 5.3** MJ Hegar shows her tattoo.

to mask their femininity behind dark pant suits and perfectly coifed hair. Instead, they wore their hair up, down, in braids, and styled naturally. Rather than the expected campaign "uniform," women candidates chose clothing that women typically wear in their everyday lives, ranging from blue jeans to skirts and, sometimes, suits—but in a fuller array of colors and styles. Women military veterans chose to highlight their service in unique ways. Unsuccessful U.S. Senate candidate Martha McSally (R-AZ), who served as a colonel in the Air Force, aired a more traditional television ad that featured her in a flight suit.[138] Congressional candidate MJ Hegar (D-TX), a helicopter pilot with three tours in Afghanistan, instead chose to show voters the cherry blossom and dragon tattoo that covers scars and battle injuries on her arm.[139]

Women are using these personal narratives not only for television advertisements but for online videos that help them overcome limited experience, low name recognition, and less access to wealthy donors. When used effectively, the videos can go viral and make or break candidate's chances, as they gain traction with voters and raise money from donors across the country interested in helping women candidates. Congressional candidate Amy McGrath's (D-KY) experiences are illustrative. Her video, introducing herself to Kentucky voters, was viewed nearly 2 million times, helping her to overcome a 47 percentage point disadvantage in early polling and lack of support from national and state party

Getty Images

▸ **Photo 5.4** Martha McSally in the Air Force.

organizations.[140] Such approaches—in an online environment where candidates can raise money from small donations without a face-to-face ask—can help women compensate for difficulty raising money. Women historically have struggled to raise money, in part because juggling domestic and professional responsibilities, combined with gendered career paths, results in fewer acquaintances who can give large donations. Further, asking for campaign contributions requires self-promotion, which tends to violate gendered norms of appropriate behavior. Men candidates not only tend to have more contacts on their lists of likely donors, they also have an easier time asking them for money. Further, just as men have historically been more apt to run for office, they are also more likely to contribute, constituting almost two thirds of all donors even in 2018. In 2016, for example, the top 10 men political donors gave $155.4 million, more than the amount given by the top 100 women donors combined, according to OpenSecrets.org. Yet, political activism on the left is beginning to shift this narrative, as contributions from Democratic women to support women on the left are increasing. In 2018, 61% of donations from women to candidates or parties went to Democrats. In 2014, in comparison, 51% went to Republicans. By March of 2018, 44% of the contributions to Democratic women congressional candidates came from women. According to the Center for Responsive Politics, this represents a five-point increase over women's support for such candidates in 2014. By July of 2018, 329,000 women had donated at least $200 to a federal campaign or PAC in the 2018 cycle, according to the Center for Responsive Politics—far outpacing the 198,000 women who donated similar amounts over the entire 2014 midterms. This field of women candidates' willingness to adopt innovative approaches to fund-raising is at least partially responsible for this trend.[141–143]

The influx of women into campaigns is overturning traditional advice on strategic choices. Women are reconsidering choices as mundane as the appropriate color for yard signs, to how to handle sexual harassment and misogyny on the campaign trail. The 2018 midterms became the year that the traditional, patriotic yard sign palette of red, white, and blue designs was rejected. A congressional candidate from El Paso, for example, purposefully used hot pink to highlight her sex, while Alexandria Ocasio-Cortez (D-NY), in a nod to colors used by the United Farm Workers, chose purple and yellow. Meanwhile, Deb Haaland (D-NM), who is Native American, a member of the Pueblo of Laguna, and regularly wears turquoise jewelry, featured turquoise signs with a Zia sun symbol to reinforce her identity with voters.[144]

On a more serious note, women candidates, along with consultants and campaign schools, have adopted a different approach to sexism on the campaign trail. As noted in Chapter 4's discussion of ambivalent sexism, the most hostile versions of sexism occur when women violate traditional gender norms. Given that they have entered the political realm, one of the last bastions of men's dominance, women politicians often evoke sexist reactions. In patriarchies, unchaperoned women in the public sphere are typically assumed to be either prostitutes or promiscuous.[145] Thus, women politicians are often subject to jokes where their bodies or assumptions about their sexual habits become the punch line. Anti-Hillary souvenirs at the 2016 Republican National

Convention, for example, included not only a blow-up sex doll featuring Clinton's face but also an array of buttons and t-shirts featuring the following slogans: *Hillary Sucks, But Not Like Monica*; *Trump vs. Tramp*; *KFC Special, 2 Fat Thighs, 2 Small Breasts, Left Wing*; and *Feminists are Sluts!*[146]

▸ **Photo 5.5** Buttons from the Republican National Convention, 2016.

The seriousness of Sarah Palin's (R-AK) vice presidential candidacy was similarly undermined, when delegates at the 2012 RNC wore buttons describing her as *The Hottest Governor from the Coolest State*.

Another common trope is to argue that women politicians are unnatural—frigid, unattractive, and power-hungry—for not being communal and other-oriented enough. Those framed as too attractive to take seriously, such as Palin or Michele Bachmann (R-TN), are still often framed as dangerously unstable, unreasonable, and insatiable. Powerful older women like Hillary Clinton or House Speaker Nancy Pelosi (D-CA), meanwhile, are more typically parodied as cackling witches and tagged with adjectives like "shrill" or "abrasive."[147]

Finally, a more intense, misogynist reaction is to dehumanize women in the public sphere. Women politicians are often subject to both threats and acts of harassment, punishment, and violence, which were deemed acceptable, or even necessary, ways to restrict women to the domestic sphere in our patriarchal past.[148] There is no way to determine how many likely women candidates have been alienated by such threats, as many likely simply walked away. Patti Russo, executive director of Yale University's bipartisan Campaign School points out, "There have always been women who have just decided that the risk to their personal safety or their families' personal safety is just too high a price to pay, and so they decide not to run, and they don't tell anyone why they are pulling out."[149] Some, like the first woman mayor of Greenville Mississippi, upon receiving a letter describing her decapitation and rape, decide to request a police detail and stick it out. Even when social media, along with intersecting marginalized identities, multiply the number and intensity of such threats, some women persist—as did gubernatorial candidate and transgender woman Christine Hallquist (D-VT). Despite a steady torrent of vicious online attacks, and being advised to seek help from the FBI, Hallquist continued her campaign for governor, ultimately losing to incumbent Governor Phil Scott (R-VT).[150] Others, like congressional candidate Kim Weaver (D-IA) feel so threatened that they drop out. Weaver continued her first 2016 congressional campaign after receiving tweets calling her a traitor and threatening her with lynching on "the day of the rope," but dropped out of her second bid for office after receiving angry e-mails calling her a cunt, being subject to acts of intimidation, and fielding death threats.[151,152] See Chapter 4 for a deeper conversation about violence against women candidates.

The number of women now willing to publicly share these experiences in the era of the #MeToo movement makes it clear that women public figures are subject to far more sexual harassment and violent threats than previously assumed. As a result, campaign schools and consultants are making a concerted effort to train women how to respond to such incidents.

BOX 5.6: COMPARATIVE FEATURE

Candidate Training in Pakistan

In Pakistan, like in the United States, various entities—the Pakistani government, non-governmental organizations (or NGOs), the United Nations, and other countries—seek to bolster women's ambition through political training. The United States government itself, through the United States Agency for International Development (USAID), has worked with the Pakistani government to increase women's participation. The two programs summarized here, which encourage girls' political ambition and train elected officials on how to succeed in office, are supported by NGOs. **Aware Girls**, aimed at young women, was established in 2002 by seven girls, and in particular by Gulalai Ismail. Ismail was inspired to found Aware Girls at 16 years old, after witnessing Taliban violence on the border between Afghanistan and Pakistan, near Peshawar. She wanted to inspire and train girls because, as she explains, "All around me I saw girls being treated differently to boys. My girl cousin was 15 when her marriage was arranged to someone twice her age; she couldn't finish her education while my boy cousins were [doing so]. This was considered normal."[153] Rather than watching girls submit to men, she dreamed that girls could be "taught leadership skills and how to negotiate within their families and with their parents to get education and to have control over their own lives."[154] Focusing on the rural areas surrounding urban Peshawar, Aware Girls conducts political training to help young women become active in civic life. Aware Girls also seeks change by holding "meetings with men and women at the grassroots level to educate and inform them about the importance of women's participation in electoral processes."[155] Meanwhile, the NGO, Search for Common Ground (SFCG), headquartered in Washington DC, promotes peace and nonviolence in many countries. One of its programs, **The Women's Initiative for Learning and Leadership (WILL)**, seeks to increase women's political participation in Pakistan by improving the political and leadership skills of women elected as local councilors. The organization's handbook describes what councilors learn in training sessions, which includes the history of women in elected politics and in women's movements in Pakistan, existing Pakistani legislation related to women's status, procedural rules in Pakistani legislatures, how to run a women's caucus in a legislature, and how to engage the media.[156]

For negative attacks by opponents that are sexist but do not convey a threat, women are being encouraged to simply name and shame the incident, before pivoting back to highlight issues important to their own campaign. In her memoir of the 2016 campaign, *What Happened*, Hillary Clinton (2017) agonizes over her decision to ignore Donald Trump when he lurked uncomfortably close behind her during a town hall format debate at Washington University in St. Louis.[157] She writes that she decided to keep her cool, even though his behavior made her skin crawl, and her knee-jerk reaction was to interrupt the debate format to tell him, "Back up, you creep."[158] Clinton likely made her decision to ignore Trump based on years of advice from consultants, whose standard recommendation to women candidates until recently was to avoid such confrontations, because it would make them look angry or weak or both. In the future, women will be more likely to have a practiced a response to sexist behavior. Fewer will be caught off guard, forced to make Clinton's split-second decision about what to do.

Similarly, women are encouraged to resist wasting time or resources responding to sexist comments from average people who will never support them anyway. "Thank them, and hand them a flier," one consultant advised, because, "That guy is never going to vote for you."[159] For more serious threats, organizations like VoteRunLead recommend immediately contacting the police and providing an in-depth response to the incident in a newspaper editorial or speech. Finally, to ensure women find supportive peers who can help them determine how to respond, some campaign schools are facilitating small conversation networks for women who share similar intersectional identities.[160]

CONCLUSION

The results of the 2018 midterm elections suggest that perhaps, finally, a change is coming. While women still face challenges when they run for office, these challenges are diminishing. And it bears repeating: When women run, women win. In 2018, a historic number of women took the leap and ran for office; as a result, a historic number of women won. There will be over 100 (102 to be precise) in the U.S. House for the first time in history; the previous record was 85. There are more women of color in Congress (45) than ever before. There are 35 newly elected women; the past record was 24.[161] These women appear to be taking the Capitol by storm, serving in a more transparent and open way. Newly elected Congresswomen Ayanna Pressley (D-MA), Rashida Tlaib (D-MI), Ilhan Omar

(D-MN), and Alexandria Ocasio-Cortez (D-NY) have been tweeting and Instagramming pictures of their new "squad" on Capitol Hill. Ocasio-Cortez has been using Instagram Live while cooking dinner to answer questions posed by voters, in an effort to humanize government. She said, "I think it's really important when we actually show people that government is a real thing, that it is something you can be a part of, it's a process that we can transition into. It really kind of opens up the window to show that anyone can serve."[162] A longtime consultant to Democratic women responded to all of the changes, noting, "These different women who are running, and the way they're running, is going to change politics forever. They're rewriting the playbook. But we don't know exactly what the new playbook will look like."[163]

Indeed, it remains to be seen whether this new playbook will be radically transformed, or whether it will just provide women better advice about how to compete in a "man's world." Will the 2018 midterm wave of women candidates and politicians demonstrate new ways to overcome sexist and gendered obstacles when they run for office, providing examples of innovative ways to juggle the demands of motherhood with a political career, better tactics for balancing the double bind to avoid alienating supporters, or new strategies for responding to benevolent and hostile sexism? Or, will the sheer number of women running and serving hit a critical mass, allowing women to fundamentally transform institutional constraints and cultural norms that overwhelm women with domestic responsibilities, undermine their confidence, suppress their political ambition, and, ultimately, sustain the masculine ethos of politics? We don't yet know. But what we do know is that having more women serving in office, in the legislative, executive and judicial branches, does matter, which we examine in the next few chapters. It's worth keeping the historic gains of the 2018 election in mind when reading this chapter and those that follow to think about whether this Year of the Women will mark an important critical moment in the way politics is performed.

REVIEW QUESTIONS

1. What factors influence women's decisions to run? What factors don't seem to make much of a difference?

2. When women do run for office, how are they framed in the media? How is this different for Black women?

3. How much does cultural context influence whether or not women run for office?

4. Why do you think Republicans have "a woman problem"?

5. Was 2018 a second "Year of the Women?" Why, or why not? How were the women who ran in 2018 different than past generations of candidates? What will it take to sustain political activity and ambition by women?

6. If you were to open a campaign school and advise women running for office, what would you advise? How might your advice change based upon their intersectional identities (think of age, class, race/ethnicity, transgender status)?

AMBITION ACTIVITIES

Read the News About Women Candidates With an Eye Toward Sex and Gender: In this chapter we learned that the media frame women and men who are candidates in gendered ways. Even trustworthy media sources are sometimes sexist in their criticism of women candidates, thereby making one question how it is possible to find accurate and fair-minded coverage of women in politics. Below are some questions to ask yourself as you read media sources. Choose a news article and practice answering the questions. How would you critique or praise the author of your chosen article in terms of the gender frames they employ?

1. *Source*: Who owns this media source, and who wrote the article? Is the article an op-ed, meant to take a position and critique or praise the candidate? How do you think the media source and the article's author influence how sex is portrayed? What sources/quotations does the author use to substantiate the article's main points and arguments? Would you consider these sources to be reliable (including women's voices, such as women politicians themselves or gender experts in academia), or would you consider these sources to be sexist in any way, and why?

2. *Reader*: Who are you in terms of your political persuasion and biases? Are you more or less likely to agree or disagree with the article based on your own political preferences or personal identity? How does your identity as a reader possibly influence the extent to which you notice frames related to gender, race, or sexuality, and so on?

3. *Spin and frames*: Is the article written in a way to present a favorable or unfavorable representation of the politician? How does this positive or negative "spin" relate to the gender content of the article? Of the frames presented in this chapter, which ones are most present in the article you chose? What statements/quotations in the article are evidence of the frame?

Become a Candidate: Alexandria Ocasio-Cortez was 28 and turned 29 as she was campaigning for a seat in the House of Representatives. Pretend you are thinking about running for office. How do you do it, and, especially, what funds do you need to raise for it? Running for office requires extensive preparation even before publicly announcing one's campaign. Preparation tasks a candidate must complete include, among others, researching the office, setting up social media, identifying and communicating with key supporters and local party organizations, establishing a bank account, and developing fundraising and press strategies. Choose one of the tasks below, research it, and report back to your classmates about what it takes to be a candidate.

1. *Research the office:* Check the county clerk's or your state's Secretary of State's website to see available elected offices and note how a candidate can get on the ballot. Does the office require a candidate to gather signatures or pay a filing fee? What is the filing deadline, and what is the fee?

2. *Network with the party:* Find local party websites, and note the leaders in the party who you should come to know. What means of communication or special events are available for you to network with these individuals? What candidate resources do the websites list? Does the party offer resources or available training for people wanting to become a political candidate?

3. *Opening a bank account and campaign costs:* You'll need to open a bank account in the name of the candidate. Research a bank of your choosing and how to open an account there. Brainstorm your campaign expenses. How much funds will you need, for what, and at what cost? In your estimates, consider the following expenses: website, office space rental and utilities, salaries, office supplies, mail costs, and yard signs. (See the following website for more information: https://candidatebootcamp.com/candidate-training-resources.)

Write a Stump Speech: Political speech writers agree that a campaign speech must be to the point, convey the candidate's personality, include engaging elements, and be delivered effectively. (See https://medium.com/national-democratic-training-committee/writing-a-stump-speech-6f14a9c80aff; https://www.scholastic.com/teachers/articles/teaching-content/tips-insiders-how-write-political-speech.) Use the suggestions that follow to write a campaign speech about a policy issue. After doing so, consider the extent to which your speech might include gendered components and how those components might be received by your audience. (e.g., If you share your personal story, might you be framed by the press in a feminine or feminist way? Or, will fellow voters judge you as more or less compassionate given your sex, gender identity, and the policy issue at hand?)

1. *Be brief and clear.* The National Democratic Training Committee accurately captures this sentiment when it states, "Everyone knows politicians love to talk, but try keep your remarks to ten minutes or less (or even five!)" (https://medium.com/national-democratic-training-committee/writing-a-stump-speech-6f14a9c80aff). You should also get to your major point right away, and you should be able to express the point in no more than one sentence. What's your "sound bite," and how can you start the speech with it and reiterate it throughout the speech? Focus on this one point, and don't get distracted talking about other policy issues. Try not to be too complex in your discussion of the policy issue. According to Paul Begala, a Democratic speech writer, "Always remember you're writing a speech, not an essay. Your points have to be clearer and your sentences have to be shorter, because people can understand a lot more complex things when they're reading than when they're listening" (https://www.scholastic.com/teachers/articles/teaching-content/tips-insiders-how-write-political-speech).

2. ***Be personal.*** Voters want to know the "real person" (https://medium.com/national-democratic-training-committee/writing-a-stump-speech-6f14a9c80aff). Let the audience know who you are and why you care about the policy issue. Try telling a story from your life that links who you are to the policy issue under discussion.

3. ***Be compelling.*** Be passionate, and use anecdotes and humor (when appropriate). According to Mary Kate Cary, a speechwriter for President George H.W. Bush, one can establish rapport with an audience by telling a quick joke, and, preferably, by making the joke "specific to the location" (https://www.scholastic.com/teachers/articles/teaching-content/tips-insiders-how-write-political-speech). Beware of too much humor, which distracts from your serious political concerns, and avoid insensitive humor (for example, telling jokes at a memorial site or mocking others). Here are a couple examples of good speeches:

   https://projects.fivethirtyeight.com/democratic-stump-speech

   https://projects.fivethirtyeight.com/republican-stump-speech

4. ***State your plan.*** Offer solutions, but don't be too complex in your explanations (recall, keep it short). Conclude by telling audience what you need from them: donations, votes, and volunteers.

5. ***Practice and practice again!***: The speech's content is important, but so is delivery. Always practice and know the speech by heart.

Learn to Pivot: Campaign schools are encouraging women to use a technique called Name It, Shame It, Pivot when their opponents make sexist comments or air advertisements grounded in either benevolent or hostile sexism. Below is a list of sexist comments and accusations that women candidates have experienced while campaigning. Pair off with a partner in class. Develop a script for these women candidates' responses and practice delivering them. Remember, the goal is to quickly pivot back to an issue-based discussion that highlights candidate strengths.

– During a debate, a challenger prefaced a claim that an incumbent U.S. Senator was an ineffective legislator by describing her as a "nice lady."

– A man politician has a habit of giving his opponents nicknames. One woman candidate, whose first name is Jacky, has been labeled with the moniker "Wacky Jacky."

– A negative mailer portrayed a woman candidate for local government surrounded by silk scarves, make-up, and curling irons, framing her as too girly and frivolous to be taken seriously as a public official.

– A woman in her 30s with two small children served as a city councilor and mayor before running for state legislature. During a contested primary, her opponents' supporters repeatedly described her as "not yet ready" for the state capital, while others asked questions about how she would care for her children with such a demanding job.

– A negative ad against a woman gubernatorial candidate, featuring ominous music and dark overtones, displayed the words "radical" and "feminist" emblazoned over a full-screen picture of her face.

– A woman candidate's opponent repeatedly questioned whether she had enough "stamina" to "get the job done."

KEY WORDS

Aware Girls 226
Double bind 205
Iron maiden frame 208
Jezebel frame 210
Mammy frame 208
Mother frame 208
Open seats 199
Political Action Committees
(PACs) 212
Pet frame 208

Republican Senatorial Campaign
Committee 199
Sapphire frame 210
Seductress frame 208
Social desirability 204
Super PACs 214
Women's Initiative for
Learning and Leadership
(WILL) 226
Year of the Woman 215

REFERENCES

1. Leung, S. (2016). Could one of these women be our next mayor or governor?" *Boston Globe*. Retrieved from https://www.bostonglobe.com/magazine/2016/10/26/could-one-these-women-our-next-mayor-governor/ubgMzJgZXs01NDmkDBaqRJ/story.html.

2. Devitt, P. (2017). Sen. Elizabeth Warren celebrates health care win at UMass Dartmouth town hall. *South Coast Today*. Retrieved from http://www.southcoasttoday.com/special/20170829/sen-elizabeth-warren-celebrates-healthcare-win-at-umass-dartmouth-town-hall.

3. King, A. (2018). Rep. Michael Capuano receives surprising endorsement in Democratic primary. *New England Cable News*. Retrieved from https://www.necn.com/news/new-england/Rep-Michael-Capuano-Receives-Surprising-Endorsement-in-Democratic-Primary-483074971.html.

4. Jonas, M. (2018). Pressley: "I can't and won't wait my turn." *Common Wealth*. Retrieved from https://commonwealthmagazine.org/politics/pressley-cant-wont-wait-turn.

5. Novey, B. (2016). Can we finally stop doing things "backwards and in heels"? *National Public Radio*. Retrieved from https://www.npr.org/2016/08/04/488213995/can-we-finally-stop-doing-things-backwards-and-in-heels.

6. Jenkins, S. (2007). A woman's work is never done? Fund-raising perception and effort among female state legislative candidates. *Political Research Quarterly, 60*(2), 230–239.

7. Kondik, & Skelley. (2016). Incumbent reflection rates higher than average in 2016. University of Virginia Center for Politics. Retrieved from http://www.centerforpolitics.org/crystalball/articles/incumbent-reelection-rates-higher-than-average-in-2016.

8. Pettey, S. (2017). Female candidate emergence and term limits: A state-level analysis. *Political Research Quarterly, 71*(2), 318–29.

9. Burrell, B. (1994). *A woman's place is in the House: Campaigning for Congress in the feminist era*. Ann Arbor: University of Michigan Press.

10. Carroll, S. J. (1994). *Women as candidates in American politics*, 2nd ed. Bloomington: Indiana University Press.

11. Darcy, R., Welch, S., & Clark, J. (1995). *Women, elections, and representation*. Lincoln: University of Nebraska Press.

12. Fox, R. L. (2000). *Gender and congressional elections: Women, men, and the political process source*. New York, NY: Sharpe.

13. Carey, J. M., Niemi, R. G., Powell, L. W., & Moncrief, G. F. (2006). The effects of term limits on state legislatures: A new survey of the 50 states. *Legislative Studies Quarterly, 31*(1), 105–134.

14. Carroll, S. J., & Jenkins, K. (2001). Unrealized opportunity? Term limits and the representation of women in state legislatures. *Women & Politics, 23*(4), 1–30.

15. Carroll, S. J., & Jenkins, K. (2001). Do term limits help women get elected? *Social Science Quarterly, 82*(1), 197–201.

16. Luga, R. (1983, August 21). A plan to elect more women. *The Washington Post*.

17. Freeman, J. (1989). Feminist activities at the Republican convention. *PS–Political Science & Politics, 26*, 39–47.

18. Romney, R., & Harrison, B. (1988). *Momentum: Women in American politics now*. New York, NY: Crown.

19. Cooperman, R., & Oppenheimer, B. (2001). The gender gap in the House of Representatives. In L. C. Dodd & B. L. Oppenheimer (Eds.), *Congress reconsidered*, 7th ed. Washington DC: CQ Press.

20. Stambough, S., & O'Regan, V. (2007). Republican lambs and the Democratic pipeline: Partisan differences in the nomination of female gubernatorial candidates. *Politics & Gender 3*(3), 349–368.

21. O'Regan, V., & Stambough, S. J. (2017). Term limits and women's representation: A Democratic opportunity and a Republican dead-end. *Politics, Groups, and Identities 6*(4), 650–665.

22. Sanbonmatsu, K., & Dolan, K. (2009). Do gender stereotypes transcend party? *Political Research Quarterly, 62*(3), 485–494.

23. National Conference of State Legislatures. (2015). The term-limited states. Retrieved from http://www.ncsl.org/research/about-state-legislatures/chart-of-term-limits-states.aspx.

24. Galais, C., Öhberg, P., & Coller, X. (2016). Endurance at the top: Gender and political ambition of Spanish and Swedish MPs. *Politics & Gender, 12*(3), 596–621.

25. Allen, P. (2013). Gendered candidate emergence in Britain: Why are more women councilors not becoming MPs? *Politics 33*(3), 147–159.

26. Rinker, M., Aslam, G., & Isani, M. (2017). Crossed my mind, but ruled it out: Political ambition and gender in the Pakistani Lawyers' Movement 2007–2009. *International Political Science Review, 38*(3), 246–263.

27. Mitchell, N. K., & Monroe, B. (2014). Where do women run? A case for the study of "women friendly districts" in state legislative primaries. *Journal of Social Science for Policy Implications, 2,* 37–57.

28. Palmer, B., & Simon, D. (2006). *Breaking the political glass ceiling: Women and congressional elections.* New York, NY: Routledge.

29. Kanthak, K., & Woon, J. (2014). Women don't run? Election aversion and candidate entry. *American Journal of Political Science, 59,* 595–612.

30. Sesin, C. (2018). Two latinos, Carlos Curbelo and Debbie Mucarsel-Powell battle for Florida congressional seat. *NBC News.* Retrieved from https://www.nbcnews.com/news/latino/two-latinos-carlos-curbelo-debbie-mucarsel-powell-battle-florida-congressional-n913091.

31. Rosane, O. (2018). The best and worst midterm results for the environment. *EcoWatch.* Retrieved from https://www.ecowatch.com/midterm-results-environment-climate-change-2618493194.html?fbclid=IwAR1xdHGJCJdVd9OUFCrIozv_4Vpkw5W09flbYIwP7A9VFzSrNPreOL_twt0.

32. Scherer, J. (2018). Lizzie Fletcher looks to legislate the way she won: In moderation. *Houston Chronicle.* Retrieved from https://www.houstonchronicle.com/news/houston-texas/houston/article/Lizzie-Fletcher-looks-to-legislate-the-way-she-13380859.php.

33. Sunrise Movement. (2018). Retrieved from https://www.sunrisemovement.org.

34. Roper Center. (n.d.). Madame president: Changing attitudes about a woman president. Accessed December 1, 2018 from https://ropercenter.cornell.edu/changing-attitudes-about-a-woman-president.

35. Streb, M. J., Burrell, B., Frederick, B., & Genovese, M. A. (2008). Social desirability effects and support for a female American president. *The Public Opinion Quarterly, 72*(1), 76–89.

36. Burden, B. C., Ono, Y., & Yamada, M. (2017). Reassessing public support for a female president. *The Journal of Politics, 79*(3), 1073–1078.

37. Carli, L. L. (2004). Gender effects on social influence. In J. S. Seiter & R. H. Gass (Eds.), *Perspectives on persuasion, social influence, and compliance gaining* (p. 144). San Francisco, CA: Jossey-Bass.

38. Caygle, H. (2018). Poll: Partisan gap could limit women's gains in November. *Politico*. Retrieved from https://www.politico.com/story/2018/06/05/women-elections-midterms-partisan-gap-623658.

39. Darcy, R., & Schramm, S. S. (1977). When women run against men. *Public Opinion Quarterly, 41*(1), 1–12.

40. Burrell, B. (1994). *A woman's place is in the House: Campaigning for Congress in the feminist era.*

41. Seltzer, R. A., Newman, J., & Voorhees Leighton, M. (1997). *Sex as a political variable: Women as candidates and voters in U.S. elections.* Boulder, CO: Lynne Rienner.

42. Motta, M. P., & Franklin Fowler, E. (2016). The content and effect of political advertising in U.S. campaigns. *Oxford Research Encyclopedia.* DOI: 10.1093/acrefore/9780190228637.013.217

43. Kahn, K. F. (1993). Gender differences in campaign messages: The political advertisements of men and women candidates for the U.S. Senate. *Political Research Quarterly, 46*, 481–502.

44. Debelko, K. L. C., & Herrnson, P. (1997). Women's and men's campaigns for the U.S. House of Representatives. *Political Research Quarterly, 50*, 121–135.

45. Carlson, T. (2001). Gender and political advertising across cultures: A comparison of male and female political advertising in Finland and the U.S. *European Journal of Communication, 16*, 131–154.

46. Hitchon, J. C., Chang, C., & Harris, R. (1997). Should women emote? Perceptual bias and opinion change in response to political ads for candidates of different genders? *Political Communication, 14*, 49–69.

47. Motta, M. P., & Franklin Fowler, E. (2016). The content and effect of political advertising in U.S. campaigns.

48. Barbara Lee Family Foundation. (2017). Modern family: How women candidates can talk about politics, parenting, and their personal lives. Retrieved from https://www.barbaraleefoundation.org/wp-content/uploads/BL_Memo_Final-3.22.17.pdf.

49. Debelko, K. L. C., & Herrnson, P. (1997). Women's and men's campaigns for the U.S. House of Representatives.

50. Krupnikov, Y., & Bauer, N. M. (2014). The relationship between campaign negativity, gender, and campaign context. *Political Behavior, 36*, 167–188.

51. Gordon, A., Shafie, D. M., & Crigler, A. N. (2003). Is negative advertising effective for female candidates? *The International Journal of Press/Politics, 3*, 35–53.

52. Caygle, H. (2018). Female candidates take on taboos in new campaign ads. *Politico*. Retrieved from https://www.politico.com/story/2018/04/03/women-rule-campaign-ads-495799.

53. Evans, H. K., Cordova, V., & Sipole, S. (2014). Twitter style: An analysis of how House candidates used Twitter in their 2012 campaigns. *PS: Political Science & Politics, 47*, 454–462.

54. Kahn, K. F. (1994). The distorted mirror: Press coverage of women candidates for statewide office. *Journal of Politics, 56*, 154–73.

55. MedMedia. (2006). *Portraying politics: A toolkit on gender and television*. Retrieved from http://www.med-media.eu/wp-content/uploads/2016/10/Portraying-Politics.pdf.

56. Rek, B.,& Murphy, J. (2016). Candidate gender and the quantity of media coverage in the 2015 General Election. *The Political Studies Association*. Retrieved from https://www.psa.ac.uk/sites/default/files/conference/papers/2016/Rek_Murphy_Gender_0.pdf.

57. Ward, O. (2016). Intersectionality and the press coverage of political campaigns: Representations of Black, Asian, and minority ethnic female candidates at the U.K 2010 General Election. *The International Journal of Press/Politics, 22*, 43–66.

58. Kahn, K. F. (1994). The distorted mirror: Press coverage of women candidates for statewide office.

59. Dunaway, J., Lawrence, R. G., Rose, M., & Weber, C. R. (2013). Traits versus issues: How female candidates shape coverage of Senate and gubernatorial races. *Political Research Quarterly, 66*, 15–726.

60. Beaudoux, V. G. (2017). Five ways the media hurts female politicians—and how journalists everywhere can do better. *The Conversation*. Retrieved from http://theconversation.com/five-ways-the-media-hurts-female-politicians-and-how-journalists-everywhere-can-do-better-70771.

61. Kanter, R. M. (1977). *Men and women of the corporation*. New York, NY: Basic Books.

62. Carlin, D. B., & Winfrey, K. L. (2009). Have you come a long way baby? Hillary Clinton, Sarah Palin, and sexism in the 2008 campaign coverage. *Communication Studies, 60*, 326–343.

63. Women's Media Center. (2013). An examination of the impact of media coverage of women candidates' appearance. Retrieved from http://www.womensmediacenter.com/reports/name-it-change-it-an-examination-of-the-impact-of-media-coverage-of-women-candidates-appearance-executive-summary-2013.

64. Margaret Thatcher Foundation. (n.d.). Speech to Finchley conservatives (admits to being an "Iron Lady"). Accessed December 1, 2018 from https://www.margaretthatcher.org/document/102947.

65. International Museum of Women. (n.d.). Iron ladies uncovered. Accessed December 1, 2018, from http://exhibitions.globalfundforwomen.org/exhibitions/women-power-and-politics/appearance/iron-ladies.

66. Ibid.

67. Dolan, J., Deckman, M. M., & Swers, M. S. (2018). *Women and politics: Paths to power and political influence*. New York, NY: Rowman and Littlefield.

68. West, C. (1995). Mammy, sapphire, and jezebel: Historical images of Black women and their implications for psychotherapy. *Psychotherapy Theory Research & Practice, 32*, 458–466.

69. Smith, K. B. (1997). When all's fair: Signs of parity in media coverage of female candidates. *Political Communication, 14*, 71–82.

70. Waters, K. (2018). 2018 midterms seeing better media coverage of women candidates. *Media File*. Retrieved from http://www.mediafiledc.com/2018-midterms-seeing-better-media-coverage-of-women-candidates.

71. Krugman, P. (2018). Who's afraid of Nancy Pelosi? *New York Times*. Retrieved from https://www.nytimes.com/2018/08/13/opinion/nancy-pelosi-midterms-democrats-republicans.html?fbclid=IwAR1lj7EBkbiV07tZquG3ZJhnV78FJv4zQz3XEF8hLbIuuw5IEcY_TBM2Z0Q.

72. Real Clear Politics. (2018). Nancy Pelosi: Favorable/unfavorable. Retrieved from https://www.realclearpolitics.com/epolls/other/nancy_pelosi_favorableunfavorable-6673.html.

73. Dabbous, Y., & Ladley, A. (2010). A spine of steel and a heart of gold: Newspaper coverage of the first female Speaker of the House. *Journal of Gender Studies, 19*, 181–194.

74. Gierzynski, A., & Breaux, D. (1991). Money and votes in state legislative elections. *Legislative Studies Quarterly, 16*(2), 203–217.

75. Abramowitz, A. I. (1988). Explaining Senate election outcomes. *American Political Science Review, 82*(2), 395–403.

76. Krasno, J. S., Green, D. P., & Cowden, J. A. (1994). The dynamics of campaign fundraising in House elections. *Journal of Politics, 56*(2), 459–474.

77. Uhlaner, C. J., & Schlozman, K. L. (1986). Candidate gender and congressional campaign receipts. *Journal of Politics, 48*(1), 30–50.

78. Barber, M., Butler, D. M., & Preece, J. (2016). Gender inequalities in campaign finance. *Quarterly Journal of Political Science, 11*(2), 219–248.

79. Burrell, B. (1994). *A woman's place is in the House: Campaigning for Congress in the feminist era.*

80. Burrell, B. (1998). *Campaign finance: Women's experience in the modern era.* New York, NY: Oxford University Press.

81. Fox, R. (2000). *Gender and congressional elections: Women, men, and the political process source.*

82. Darcy, R., Welch, S., & Clark, J. (1995). *Women, elections, and representation.*

83. Adams, B. E., & Schreiber, R. (2011). Gender, campaign finance, and electoral success in municipal elections. *Journal of Urban Affairs, 33*(1), 83–97.

84. Burrell, B. (1985). Women's and men's campaigns for the U.S. House of Representatives, 1972–1982: A finance gap? *American Politics Research, 13*(3), 251–272.

85. Hogan, R. E. (2007). The effects of gender on campaign spending in State legislative elections. *Social Science Quarterly, 88,* 1092–1105.

86. Jenkins, S. (2007). A woman's work is never done? Fund-raising perception and effort among female state legislative candidates. *Political Research Quarterly,* 60 (2), 230–239.

87. Witt, L.,. Paget, K. M., & Matthews, G. (1994). *Running as a woman: Gender and power in American politics.* New York, NY: Free Press.

88. Fifield, J. (2018). Nation's longest-serving female legislator sees some progress. *Daily Hampshire Gazette.* Retrieved from http://www.gazettenet.com/Legislator-who-stood-up-to-sexism-in-73-sees-some-progress-13839389.

89. Witt, L.,. Paget, K. M., & Matthews, G. (1994). *Running as a woman: Gender and power in American politics.*

90. Barber, M., Butler, D. M., & Preece, J. (2016). Gender inequalities in campaign finance.

91. Carroll, S. J., & Sanbonmatsu, K. (2013). *More women can run: Gender and pathways to state legislatures.* New York, NY: Oxford University Press.

92. Jenkins, S. (2007). A woman's work is never done? Fund-raising perception and effort among female state legislative candidates.

93. Crespin, M. H., & Deitz, J. L. (2010). If you can't join 'em, beat 'em: The gender gap in individual donations to congressional candidates. *Political Research Quarterly, 63*(3), 581–593.

94. Francia, P. L. (2001). Early fundraising by nonincumbent female congressional candidates. *Women & Politics, 23*(1–2), 7–20

95. Thomsen, D. M., & Swers, M. L. (2017). Which women can run? Gender, partisanship, and candidate donor networks." *Political Research Quarterly, 70*(2), 449–463.

96. Open Secrets. (n.d.). What is a PAC?" Accessed November 21, 2018 from https://www.opensecrets.org/pacs/pacfaq.php.

97. EMILY's List. (n.d.). Our history." Retrieved from https://www.emilyslist.org/pages/entry/our-history.

98. EMILY's List. (n.d.). Retrieved from https://www.emilyslist.org/pages/entry/our-history.

99. Anzia, S. F., & Berry, C. R. (2011). The Jackie (and Jill) Robinson effect: Why do congresswomen outperform congressmen?" *American Journal of Political Science, 55*(3), 478–493.

100. Lazarus, J., & Steigerwalt, A. (2018). *Gendered vulnerability: How women work harder to stay in office.* Ann Arbor: University of Michigan Press.

101. Lawless, J. L., & Hayes, D. (2018). *Women on the run: Gender, media, and political campaigns in a polarized era.* New York, NY: Cambridge University Press.

102. Burrell, B. (2014). *Gender in campaigns for the U.S. House of Representatives.* Ann Arbor: University of Michigan Press.

103. Waddell, K. (2017). The exhausting work of tallying America's largest protest. *The Atlantic.* Retrieved from www.theatlantic.com/technology/archive/2017/01/womens-march-protest-count/514166.

104. Robertson, C. (2018). These women mostly ignored politics. Now activism is their job. *The New York Times.* Retrieved from https://www.nytimes.com/2018/05/10/us/democratic-women-campaigning.html.

105. Colvin, R. (2017). Resistance efforts are taking root in pro-Trump country—and women are leading the charge. *The Washington Post.* Retrieved from https://www.washingtonpost.com/national/resistance-efforts-are-taking-root-in-pro-trump-country--and-women-are-leading-the-charge/2017/08/14/91e69daa-7874-11e7-8f39-eeb7d3a2d304_story.html?utm_term=.5e3ee53e06be.

106. Gstalter, M. (2018). Record number of Black women running for office in Alabama after Roy Moore defeat. *The Hill.* Retrieved from https://thehill.com/homenews/state-watch/379900-record-number-of-black-women-running-for-office-in-alabama-after-roy?amp.

107. North, A. (2017). We've never seen anything like this: How Trump inspired women to run for office. *Vox*. Retrieved from https://www.vox.com/identities/2017/11/6/16571570/female-candidates-trump-clinton-2016-election.

108. Lah, K., & Moya, A. (2018). Republicans left behind in blue Democratic wave of new women candidates. *CNN Politics*. Retrieved from https://www-m.cnn.com/2018/04/20/politics/gop-women-candidates/index.html?r=https%3A%2F%2Fwww.google.com%2F.

109. Dohrmann, S. (2017). The radical way women running for office are being trained to fight sexism in Trump's America. *Bustle*. Retrieved from https://www.bustle.com/p/the-radical-way-women-running-for-office-are-being-trained-to-fight-sexism-in-trumps-america-75683.

110. Margolin, E. (2018). How a new wave of female candidates is training to fight the trolls. *Politico*. Retrieved from https://www.politico.com/magazine/story/2018/03/12/how-a-new-wave-of-female-candidates-is-training-to-fight-the-trolls-217350.

111. Cirillo, J (2018). EMILY's List celebrates surge in women candidates for state offices. *Roll Call*. Retrieved from https://www.rollcall.com/news/politics/emilys-list-celebrates-surge-women-candidates-state-offices.

112. North, A. (2017). We've never seen anything like this: How Trump inspired women to run for office.

113. Center for American Women and Politics. (2018). Election watch. Retrieved from http://www.cawp.rutgers.edu/potential-candidate-summary-2018.

114. Zanona, M. (2018). GOP doubles female recruits for congressional races. *The Hill*. Retrieved from https://thehill.com/homenews/house/390339-gop-doubles-female-recruits-for-congressional-races.

115. Bade, R. (2018). A difficult situation: Republican women run in the Trump era. *Politico*. Retrieved from https://www.politico.com/story/2018/07/19/republicans-women-trump-midterms-731615.

116. Ibid.

117. Lah, K., & Moya, A. (2018). Republicans left behind in blue Democratic wave of new women candidates.

118. Bade, R. (2018). A difficult situation: Republican women run in the Trump era.

119. Lah, K., & Moya, A. (2018). Republicans left behind in blue Democratic wave of new women candidates.

120. Lah, K. (2018). Idaho woman challenges establishment and history in hope of becoming nation's first Native American governor. *CNN*. Retrieved from https://www.cnn.com/2018/05/15/politics/idaho-governor-native-american-candidate-paulette-jordan/index.html.

121. Lawless, J. L., & Fox, R. L. (2017). The Trump effect. Washington, DC: Women & Politics Institute. Retrieved from https://www.american.edu/spa/wpi/upload/The-Trump-Effect.pdf.

122. Ibid.

123. Boshma, J. (2017). Why women don't run for office. *Politico*. Retrieved from https://www.politico.com/interactives/2017/women-rule-politics-graphic.

124. Chira, S. (2018). Mom is running for office. *The New York Times*. Retrieved from https://www.nytimes.com/2018/04/14/sunday-review/mom-is-running-for-office.html.

125. Lu, D., & Zernike, K. (2018). The women who could shatter ceilings in governor's' races this year. *New York Times*. Retrieved from https://www.nytimes.com/interactive/2018/08/06/us/politics/women-governors-primaries.html.

126. Carli, L. L. (2004). Gender effects on social influence.

127. Kaufman, E. (2016). Sexist insults have dogged Clinton for years. And now they're part of presidential elections. *Vox*. Retrieved from https://www.vox.com/2016/8/1/12325014/sexist-language-hillary-clinton-donald-trump.

128. Klein, E. (2016). Understanding Hillary: Why the Clinton America sees isn't the Clinton colleagues know. *Vox*. Retrieved from https://www.vox.com/a/hillary-clinton-interview/the-gap-listener-leadership-quality.

129. Yglesias, M. (2016). The race is tightening for a painfully simple reason. *Vox*. Retrieved from https://www.vox.com/2016/9/15/12919800/clinton-trump-polls-tighter.

130. Kimmel, J. (2016). *Jimmy Kimmel mansplains to Hillary Clinton*. Filmed at El Capitan Theater, Hollywood, CA. Video, 3:29. Retrieved from https://www.youtube.com/watch?v=j2wBpYT6Zlo.

131. Yglesias, M. (2016). The race is tightening for a painfully simple reason.

132. Zernike, K. (2018). Forget the suits. Show the tattoo. Female candidates are breaking all the rules. *New York Times*. Retrieved from https://www.nytimes.com/2018/07/14/us/politics/women-candidates-midterms.html.

133. Barbara Lee Family Foundation. (2017). Modern family: How women candidates can talk about politics, parenting, and their personal lives.

134. Zernike, K. (2018). Forget the suits. Show the tattoo. Female candidates are breaking all the rules.

135. Shirley, L. G. (2018). Want women to run for Congress? We need someone to watch our kids first. *The Washington Post*. Retrieved from https://www.washingtonpost.com/news/posteverything/wp/2018/04/09/want-women-to-run-for-congress-we-need-someone-to-watch-our-kids-first/?utm_term=.585d0ff5c0fd.

136. Chira, S. (2018). Mom is running for office.

137. Chira, S. (2017). Mothers seeking office face more voter doubts than fathers. *The New York Times*. Retrieved from https://www.nytimes.com/2017/03/14/us/women-politics-voters.html.

138. Isenstadt, A. (2018). McSally 'pink tutu' ad hammers Sinema. *Politico*. Retrieved from https://www.politico.com/story/2018/08/23/martha-mcsally-kyrsten-sinema-attack-ad-794337.

139. Kurtz, J. (2018). Texas House hopeful shows off her tattoos in new ad. *The Hill*. Retrieved from https://thehill.com/blogs/in-the-know/in-the-know/404965-texas-house-hopeful-shows-off-her-tattoos-in-new-ad.

140. Jordan, M. (2018). With blunt talk and compelling stories, viral videos are turning unknown women candidates into political sensations. *Washington Post*. Retrieved from https://www.washingtonpost.com/politics/with-blunt-talk-and-compelling-stories-viral-videos-are-turning-unknown-women-candidates-into-political-sensations/2018/06/30/de823cd6-7a31-11e8-80be-6d32e182a3bc_story.html?utm_term=.79cffcd55b9b.

141. Sarlin, B. (2018). "Giving circles': Female fundraisers are powering women candidates. *NBC News*. Retrieved from https://www.nbcnews.com/politics/elections/giving-circles-female-fundraisers-are-powering-women-candidates-n895276.

142. Jordan, M. (2018). With blunt talk and compelling stories, viral videos are turning unknown women candidates into political sensations.

143. Ebbert, S. (2018). You can't do that in politics. (She just did). *Boston Globe*. Retrieved from https://www.bostonglobe.com/metro/2018/04/02/you-can-that-politics-she-just-did/hGBnEXWgpJ2MKobuFINqUM/story.html.

144. Martinez, D. (2018).Surge of female candidates sparks an explosion of color. *Politico*. Retrieved from https://www.politico.com/story/2018/07/07/women-candidates-campaign-signs-posters-logo-design-701664.

145. Kahn, K. F. (1994). The distorted mirror: Press coverage of women candidates for statewide office.

146. Goldberg, M., & Hassler, C. (2016). A children's treasury of misogyny at the Republican National Convention. *Slate*. Retrieved from https://slate.com/news-and-politics/2016/07/misogyny-is-alive-and-well-at-the-republican-national-convention.html.

147. Chira, S. (2017). Nancy Pelosi, Washington's latest wicked witch. *The New York Times*. Retrieved from https://www.nytimes.com/2017/06/26/opinion/nancy-pelosi-washingtons-latest-wicked-witch.html.

148. Kahn, K. F. (1994). The distorted mirror: Press coverage of women candidates for statewide office.

149. Margolin, E. (2018). How a new wave of female candidates is training to fight the trolls.

150. Schreckinger, B. (2018). Democrats poised to pick transgender woman for Vermont governor. *Politico*. Retrieved from https://www.politico.com/story/2018/08/07/vermont-transgender-governor-hallquist-764951.

151. Margolin, E. (2018). How a new wave of female candidates is training to fight the trolls.

152. Dohrmann, S. (2017). The radical way women running for office are being trained to fight sexism in Trump's America.

153. Bunting, M. (2011). Young women fight the "Talibanisation" of rural Pakistan. *The Guardian*. Retrieved from https://www.theguardian.com/global-development/poverty-matters/2011/may/16/pakistan-young-women-fight-prejudice.

154. Ibid.

155. Aware Girls. (2013). *Strengthening Democracy through increasing political participation of women*. Retrieved from http://www.awaregirls.org/strengthening-democracy-through-increasing-political-participation-of-women.

156. Hasmit, S. S. (2014). Leading the way: A handbook for Pakistan's women parliamentarians and political leaders. *Common Ground*. Retrieved from https://www.sfcg.org/wp-content/uploads/2014/06/Finding-the-Way-WILL-A4-Half.pdf.

157. *The Guardian*. (2016). Trump "prowls" behind Clinton during presidential debate—video. Retrieved from https://www.theguardian.com/us-news/video/2016/oct/10/donald-trump-behind-hillary-clinton-debate-video.

158. Clinton, H. R. (2017). *What happened*. New York, NY: Simon and Schuster.

159. Margolin, E. (2018). How a new wave of female candidates is training to fight the trolls.

160. Ibid.

161. *Politico*. (2018). Women rule: Candidate tracker. Retrieved from https://www.politico.com/interactives/2018/women-rule-candidate-tracker.

162. Burke, M. (2018). Ocasio-Cortez says she's using Instagram to "humanize" government. *The Hill*. Retrieved from https://thehill.com/blogs/blog-briefing-room/news/417542-ocasio-cortez-says-shes-using-instagram-to-humanize-government.

163. Zernike, K. (2018). Forget the suits. Show the tattoo. Female candidates are breaking all the rules.

CHAPTER SIX

WOMEN IN LEGISLATURES

In the early 1980s, near the end of a session, the Vermont state legislature was scrambling to find a way to balance the budget; doing so would allow legislators to close the legislative session and go home. Leaders in the legislature put together a budget that imposed a variety of cuts, including the elimination of $30,000 that funded the Women's Caucus, a group that represented women state legislators. The typical process for the budget in the Vermont House was for all legislators to unanimously agree to move the budget forward, but the women legislators, across party lines, refused to agree. As former Vermont state legislator Ralph Wright (2005) recounts, leaders in the legislature tried a variety of maneuvers to bypass the women, but they held strong. Working across party lines and with just two men legislators (including Wright) supporting them, the women managed to hold up the entire business of the legislature and prevent the session from ending until their demands were met—full restoration of funding for the Women's Caucus. Ultimately, this and other events over the course of working in the Vermont legislature for decades and serving as the Speaker of the House in that state led Wright (2005) to conclude that "pound for political pound, women made the better candidates—and often the better lawmakers."[1]

Whether women are better legislators is a question that several researchers have examined; there are certainly many stories of women's impact on legislatures in the United States and around the world, even though they are the minority of legislators in most of these institutions. The presence of women legislators has an impact on policy outcomes at all levels of government, and their presence has been particularly important for broadening the types of issues that government considers and addresses, such as social services and health care. For instance, as the presence of women in Norwegian municipal governments increased, municipal child care policies became more generous.[2] In the United States, Black women legislators are a small minority of legislators in state legislatures, but in the 1990s, they made stronger and more consistent efforts to alleviate "get tough" provisions of welfare reform than their white women, Black men, or Latinx colleagues.[3] In 2017, while Republican Arizona Senator John McCain was widely credited for casting the deciding vote to prevent the repeal of the Affordable Care Act, a law that has helped women gain access to health care,[4] that moment was only made possible by the fact that two women Republican Senators, Lisa Murkowski of Alaska and Susan Collins of Maine, had already announced their opposition. And it wasn't the first time that women senators were showing up to get the work of the Senate done; in January of 2016, Senator Murkowski remarked on the fact that only she and Senator Collins had shown up for an administrative session to postpone Senate business after a snowstorm shut down the U.S. capitol; none of the men senators had made it.

As the above examples demonstrate, having women in legislative bodies surely matters at least in some circumstances. In recognition of this, there have been efforts around the globe to elect more women into office, which is significant as conscious acts to increase the representation of women by political actors are an important factor behind increases in the number of women serving in legislatures.[5] As a result, there are now more than 30 lower legislative chambers around the world where more than a third of all legislators are women in 2018, and three—Rwanda, Cuba, and Bolivia—where women are more than half of lower chamber legislators.[6]

As women have made inroads into previously all-men bodies like legislatures, important questions have emerged about women's representation. Traditionally, research has looked at the question of "do women represent women?" but as Celis, Childs, Kantola, and Krook (2008) argue, we ought to also look at "where, how, and why does the substantive representation of women occur?"[7] We start to address these questions here and continue to examine them in Chapters 7 and 8; we examine women's representation in legislative bodies by looking at the history of women serving as legislators, from the national to the local level. Next, we turn the question of whether women's representation matters. We address this question in two ways. First, we look at the different ways political science and feminist scholars have theorized why women's representation might matter, and then we look at research that examines the impact of women officeholders. Both lines of research demonstrate that women's representation does make a difference, so finally, we examine efforts to increase the representation of women and to achieve parity between men and women in legislatures around the globe.

WOMEN'S REPRESENTATION IN LEGISLATURES AROUND THE WORLD

Over time, women's representation in legislatures has increased significantly. But there is considerable variation across national, subnational, and local governments in the number of women who currently serve in these institutions. Generally speaking, women first began serving in legislatures in the early 1900s. In the United States, the first woman to serve in the U.S. Congress was Republican Jeannette Rankin, who was elected to represent Montana in the U.S. House in 1916, several years before women secured the right to vote nationally. In the year following, Louise McKinney was the first woman elected to a provincial legislature in Canada.

Initially, the most common path for women to gain elected office in legislatures was through **widow's succession,** whereby the widow of a deceased officeholder was appointed or elected to serve out the remainder of her deceased husband's term. While not unheard of in current times (for instance, U.S. Representative Mary Bono (R-CA) served in the U.S. House until 2013 after being elected to her seat in 1998, just months after the death of her husband, U.S. Representative Sonny Bono (R-CA)), such a path to elected office is now far less common for women.

Since Rankin served in the House, the number of women serving in the U.S. Congress has increased such that in 2018, women accounted for just under 20% (19.8%) of all members of Congress and increased to 23.4% in 2019.* But the number of women who have served in the U.S. Congress over the course of its history is very low—just over 2.5% of all people who have *ever* served in Congress. Furthermore, when compared to other countries, the United States does not compare well. For instance, as noted elsewhere, women comprise more than 50% of the members of the lower chamber in Rwanda and Bolivia (61.3% and 53.1% respectively in 2018) due in part to the fact that both have sex quotas in their legislature, an issue we discuss in further depth later in the chapter. Across the globe, 101 countries have more women in the legislature than the United States; the United States ranks 102 out of the over 200 countries tracked by the Inter-Parliamentary Union (IPU, 2018), similar to Saudi Arabia and Kyrgyzstan.[8]

Overall though, few countries in the world have achieved or come close to parity between men and women in the legislature. The percentage of women in national legislatures worldwide is fairly low—just 22%. This is due in part to the fact that women are less likely to run for office, as we discussed in Chapter 4, and because cultural barriers to women's representation, including beliefs about the appropriate role of women and the burden of the second shift, still remain. But as the National Democratic Institute notes, this is also because political bodies, like political parties and legislatures, remain unwelcoming to women; at the end of this chapter, we examine efforts to make these political bodies more receptive to women's representation.[9]

There is considerable variation in the number of women who serve in subnational institutions, although once again, there are few places where women are close to achieving political parity. In the United States, just over 28% of all state legislators are women (see Table 6.1). At the high end, 50.8% of the state legislators in Nevada and 47% of the state legislators in Colorado are women, while at the low end, two states (West Virginia, and Mississippi) have fewer than 15% women state legislators. The IPU (2018) reports data on regional parliaments elected by direct suffrage in Central America and Europe.[10] In Central America, 21.6% of regional parliamentarians are women, ranging from a high of 33.3% women in Nicaragua to a low of 10% women in Guatemala. In Europe, 35.2% of regional parliamentarians are women; Finland has the most women (61.5%), while Malta (0%) and the Czech Republic (18.2%) have the lowest.

---

* Data on the representation of women in U.S. state and national legislatures throughout this chapter come from the Center for American Women and Politics and are for 2018.

Table 6.1 Women's Representation in U.S. State Legislatures

Rank	State	Total	Rank	State	Total
1	Nevada	50.8%	41	Kentucky	22.5%
2	Colorado	47.0%	42	Oklahoma	21.5%
3	Oregon	41.1%	43	North Dakota	21.3%
4	Washington	40.1%	44	South Carolina	15.9%
5	Vermont	39.4%	45	Alabama	15.7%
6	Arizona	38.9%	46	Wyoming	15.6%
7 (T)	Alaska	38.3%	47	Louisiana	15.3%
7 (T)	Maryland	38.3%	48	Tennessee	15.2%
9	Maine	38.2%	49	West Virginia	14.2%
10	Rhode Island	37.2%	50	Mississippi	13.8%
	Overall Average	28.7%		U.S. Congress	23.4%

Source: National Conference of State Legislatures. (2019). *Women in state legislatures for 2019.* Retrieved from http://www.ncsl.org/legislators-staff/legislators/womens-legislative-network/women-in-state-legislatures-for-2019.aspx.

There are less data about women's representation at the local level. There is no systematic collection of data on the sex, racial, and ethnic composition of most local legislative institutions in the United States, in part because there are so many local governments (over 89,000), and their forms of government are so diverse. Women are most likely to serve at this level, though, for a variety of reasons. First, given women's higher levels of risk aversion, a topic discussed in Chapters 3 and 4, the lower stakes of local office can seem less overwhelming to women considering a run for office. Second, most of these positions are part-time and are by their nature close in location, which means the time demands are less imposing and are therefore less likely to impose a severe burden on women who are already juggling a second shift at home. Next, there are more opportunities to serve at the local level, given the large number and great variety of offices at the local level. Finally, women tend to be motivated by policy concerns and personal connections to these issues, making them more likely to run for the offices that address their personal concerns. Kathlene (1989) calls these **gendered political priorities** and describes how they emerge in response to personal experience with a problem or policy matter that leads to efforts to remedy these problems.[11] For instance, MacManus, Bullock, Padgett, and Penberthy (2006) find that a high percentage of women school board members in the United States first ran for office when they had school-aged children.[12] These personal connections are particularly motivating for minority women, who are more likely to have community-oriented motivations for their political engagement.[13, 14]

While we do not know the exact number of women serving in these local legislative bodies, we do know that women are underrepresented in local legislatures. In the

United States, studies examining women's representation in city councils in various localities find that women make up approximately 20% to 30% of these councilors;[15] nonwhite women make up about one third of all nonwhite representatives on these bodies.[16] Aside from city councils, we know even less about women's representation on other local elected boards, like county commissions and special districts. One recent study found that more than half of county boards have *no* women representatives.[17] There is one set of local governments where women tend to fare better: school boards. The National School Board Association (2017) found that 44% of these local office holders are women.[18] As Holman (2017) argues, this may be due to the fact that voters see education as a stereotypically women's issue, so they also see the school board as a feminine office, leading to greater representation on these local boards.[19] Given that women still bear a larger burden of child-rearing, their personal connection to this issue may make them more likely to run for this office.[20]

BOX 6.1: COMPARATIVE FEATURE

Women in Local Government

As in the United States, it is difficult to find systematic data on women in local government worldwide, but women's participation in local government has been shown to be vital for the participatory health of a democracy.[21] "Including women, especially in local governments is an essential step towards creating gender equal opportunities and gender sensitive policies."[22] According to the United Nations, "consistently measuring the participation of women in local governments across countries and regions remains a challenge, since internationally agreed-upon standards, definitions and indicators for monitoring this area are yet to be developed."[23] Additionally, local government structures vary from one country to the next, making comparisons difficult.[24] While women's representation in local government has grown throughout much of the world over the last decade, parity has not been achieved, with women underrepresented compared to men throughout all regions of the world.[25] When women are present, they tend to be mayors or councilors in smaller municipalities, as described in greater detail in Chapter 7.[26]

Not all countries fare as poorly as the United States. For example, in India the 73rd Amendment created a three-tier system of local government that has allowed women greater participation, especially at the village level.[27] This has resulted in 30% to 50% of local seats (depending on the locality) being held by women. Overall, India's local representation of women is just over 30%.[28] Across different regions, there is wide variability in the percentage of women involved in local government. Figures 6.1, 6.2, and 6.3 indicate the percentage of women in local government in Europe, Latin America and the Caribbean, and Asia.

(Continued)

(Continued)

Figure 6.1   Percent Women in Local Government, Latin America

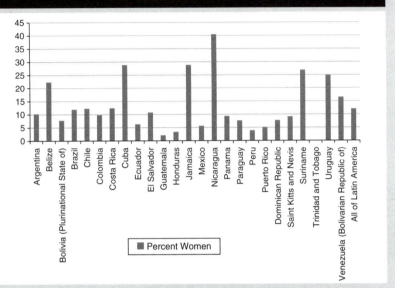

Source: https://unstats.un.org/unsd/gender/downloads/WorldsWomen2015_chapter5_t.pdf

Figure 6.2   Percent Women in Local Government, Europe

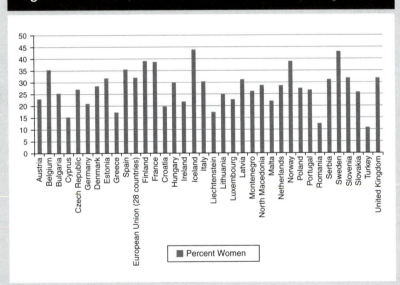

Source: https://unstats.un.org/unsd/gender/downloads/WorldsWomen2015_chapter5_t.pdf

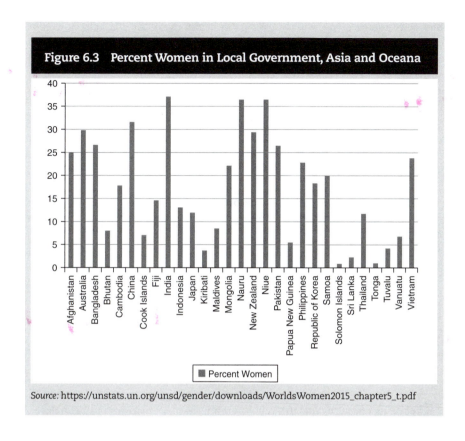

Figure 6.3   Percent Women in Local Government, Asia and Oceana

Source: https://unstats.un.org/unsd/gender/downloads/WorldsWomen2015_chapter5_t.pdf

In the United States, the majority of these women legislators are Democratic, at the national and state levels.* In Congress as of 2019, approximately 87% of all woman representatives are Democrats, while in state legislatures, nearly 68% are Democrats. Interestingly, these woman legislators are fairly diverse; 37% of the women members of Congress are women of color, although just 24.3% of women state legislators are women of color. Women of color make up a larger proportion of minority representatives, while white women are a smaller proportion of white representatives overall. In the 116th Congress (2019–2021), for example, over 39% of all legislators of color are women, while under 20% of white legislators are women. This pattern occurs because the Democratic party is more racially and ethnically diverse than the Republican party; men representatives are more likely to be Republican and white. According to one analysis, two thirds of Republican members of Congress are white men over the age of 50.[29] The women serving on local elected boards are starting to reflect the increasing diversity in

---

* In the United States, we have little data about the party affiliation of local office holders, in large part because many of these offices are nonpartisan seats. That is, candidates for these offices do not run under party labels.

their constituencies, too, with historic gains beginning in the 2017 elections. For instance, six women of color were elected to the Boston City Council, joining seven men councilors. In Palm Springs, California, 100% of the city council is LGBTQIA+; they represent the range of identities across this spectrum, as voters elected openly transgender and bisexual women candidates in 2017.[30] Andrea Jenkins became the first openly transgender woman of color elected to public office in the United States when she won a seat on the Minneapolis City Council, and in Iowa City, Iowa, Mazahir Salih became the first Muslim and the first immigrant to win a seat on the city council there.[31] In 2018, Democrat Christine Hallquist of Vermont became the first openly transgender major party nominee for governor in the United States.

However, while the representation of women has increased over time, progress has plateaued in recent years.[32,33] For instance, at the state level in the United States, the percentage of women serving has quintupled since 1971. But since breaking the 20% mark for overall representation in 1993, women's representation in U.S. state legislatures has increased by just over 8% since then. According to the Center for American Women in Politics, at the current rate of increase, there will be parity between men and women in the U.S. Congress by 2121. That is only slightly ahead of the estimate for global parity in politics; the National Democratic Institute (NDI) estimates global political parity will be achieved in 2080. A study by the National League of Cities (n.d.) found that U.S. city councils were no more diverse with respect to sex in 2001 than they were two decades earlier.[34] In the U.K., just 33% of representatives on local councils are women; in order to reach equal representation, an additional 3,000 woman councilors would be needed.[35]

While increases in women's representation have hit plateaus in many places, there have been periods in time where there have been dramatic gains in the representation of women. In the United States in 1992, law professor Anita Hill testified about being sexually harassed by Supreme Court nominee Clarence Thomas before an all-men committee of U.S. Senators. After her testimony was basically ignored and Thomas confirmed to the Supreme Court, many women were inspired to run for office. After that election, the number of women in the U.S. Senate nearly doubled (from 4 to 7), and the number of women in the U.S. House increased from 28 to 47; this election became widely known as the "Year of the Woman." Women's success in 2018 was foreshadowed by 2017. In 2017, as noted earlier, women made some historic gains. In Virginia, a record number of women ran for office in the state legislature, and 11 men were replaced by women, such that after the 2017 elections, there were more women in that legislature than ever before. Their members included the first Latina, the first transgender woman, the first lesbian, and the first Asian American; one of these newly elected women was the first legislator to nurse her baby on the floor of the House of Delegates.[36] In 2018, a record number of women filed to run for Congress. Nearly three quarters of congressional and gubernatorial candidates were woman; according to the Center for American Women and Politics, 529 women ran for Congress in 2018, compared to 338 in 2016.[37] And as Chapter 4 describes, women made historic gains in the 2018 elections, such that more than 100 women are serving in Congress for the first time in history, and the Nevada legislature and Colorado House will have woman majorities in 2019. With these increases in women's representation and in women seeking representation, an important question to ask is whether women's representation matters.

THEORIES OF REPRESENTATION

Under authoritarian and aristocratic systems of representation, the question of how politicians ought to act is not particularly prominent—leaders do as they wish. But with the advent of democratic forms of government, political philosophers began to wrestle with the question of how elected representatives ought to act in representing the interests of the people who elected them to office. Edmund Burke, an Irish Member of Parliament and political philosopher in the 1700s, was one of the first to tackle this question. In a speech given to his constituents, Burke argued against the notion that representatives should merely reflect the wishes of the people who elected them (**the delegate model of representation**); rather, he argued representatives ought to act in favor of the greater good, even if this may come at the short-term expense of their constituents (**the trustee model of representation**). As Dovi (2017) argues, "delegate conceptions of representation require representatives to follow their constituents' preferences, while trustee conceptions require representatives to follow their own judgment about the proper course of action."[38] Burke apparently failed to convince his constituents of this argument, as he was not returned to Parliament in the election following his speech. Importantly, research suggests that legislators adopt different approaches to legislating that mirror these theoretical models, and the approach they adopt has significant effects on how they act as legislators.[39]

Perhaps no one did more to advance theories of and questions about representation than Hanna Pitkin. A professor of political science at the University of California Berkley until 2014, her book *The Concept of Representation* (1967) is one of the most important works that addresses representation.[40] Pitkin argued that representation is the act of making citizens' voices, opinions, and perspectives present in policy making and identified four types of representation: formalistic, descriptive, symbolic, and substantive. For Pitkin, representation was important not just because it affects the sorts of policies governments produce but also because it affects how people feel about their government and lends it legitimacy. **Formalistic representation** simply describes how representatives attain their position (authorization) and how constituents can punish their representatives (accountability), as Burke's constituents did. Because formalistic representation simply describes how a representative attains a position of authority, it has no implicit standard for evaluating the actions of representatives.[41] However, the mechanisms for how officials are selected can serve to increase or decrease the representation of women, an issue we turn to later in this chapter.

▸ **Photo 6.1** MEP Licia Ronzulli voting in the European Parliament while holding her baby Vittoria.

Pitkin's three other forms of representation have important implications about women's presence in legislatures. Symbolic and descriptive representation focus on the ways that representatives stand for the represented, both through the meaning the represented attach to the representative (**symbolic representation**) and the extent to which representatives resemble those they represent (**descriptive representation**). For instance, a picture of Italian MP Licia Ronzulli breastfeeding her baby while voting in the Italian Parliament went viral in 2012, largely because of the newness of the image.

In 2018, U.S. Senator Tammy Duckworth (D-IL) became their first woman senator to give birth while in office. At the time, Senate rules prohibited bringing babies on the floor of the Senate; Senator Duckworth was told that she and her baby could go to the cloakroom, and the Senator could poke her head in to vote. This suggestion was quickly rebuffed by Senator Duckworth, as the cloakroom is not accessible to people with disabilities and Sena-

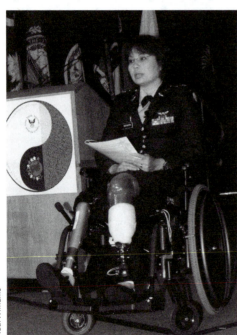

tor Duckworth largely relies on a wheelchair to move around because she lost both of her legs and severely injured one of her arms while serving as a helicopter pilot in Iraq. Through the efforts of Senator Duckworth and other colleagues, the Senate changed its rules in 2018, allowing all Senators to bring babies on to the floor, the first rule change expanding floor access in the Senate since 1977. Both of these examples were important symbolic moments for many women. Thus, women and other minorities may attach particular symbolic importance to representatives who look like them because they do not often see their own life experiences reflected in those who represent them.

▸ **Photo 6.2** U.S. Senator Tammy Duckworth (D-IL).

Symbolic representation ties in closely with descriptive representation and is particularly important to disadvantaged groups. In discussing descriptive representation, Mansbridge (1999) argues these groups desire representatives that resemble them for several reasons.[42] First, these representatives may increase disadvantaged groups' confidence in their ability to govern and their belief in the legitimacy of government. Additionally, descriptive representatives may foster improved communication between government and the represented in contexts of mistrust; these representatives may also think differently about important issues. These latter two reasons for descriptive representation are connected to the substantive representation of the interests of disadvantaged groups. Importantly, representatives from disadvantaged groups often feel compelled to represent not just members of their group who are part of their constituency but also members of the disadvantaged group from outside their constituency, a form of representation that Mansbridge terms **surrogate representation.**

The importance of symbolic and descriptive representation stands in direct contrast to the concept of liberal representation. Williams (1998) argues that the traditional concept of **liberal representation**, which is the idea that the social identity of representatives does not bear on their quality as representatives so long as the electoral process is fair, does not work for marginalized groups who have reasons to distrust representatives and government.[43] For Williams (1998), representation is an act of mediation, and representatives must mediate constituent-legislator relations to build trust among marginalized groups and to give voice to their interests.[44] As such, Williams argues that self-representation is important to marginalized groups as it both increases trust among members of these groups and gives them voice in developing policy outcomes. U.S. Supreme Court Justice Sonia Sotomayor's comment about how her experiences as a "wise Latina" shape her decision-making, which we describe in greater detail in Chapter 8, reflects this understanding of the importance of self-representation.

Young (1986) points out the challenges of descriptive representation as elected officials represent constituents with many intersecting identities, so it is impossible for one official to effectively represent all of these identities.[45] She uses the example of a Latinx representative who might represent the interests of straight Latinxs, which may conflict with the interests of LGBTQIA+ Latinx constituents (1986).[46] As Dovi (2009, 2017) argues, democratic citizens must be vigilant about the ways that representation for some groups may come at the expense of representation of other groups, such that democratic representation may require limiting the influence of overrepresented privileged groups.[47,48]

Pitkin's final type of representation is substantive representation. While the other types of representation are important in affecting perceptions of democratic governments, **substantive representation** focuses on whether the actions of the elected official reflect the policy preferences, priorities, and interests of those who are represented. To be sure, there are important links between descriptive and substantive representation; as Phillips (1995) argues in *The Politics of Presence*, differences between men and women in their everyday lives mean that women are more likely to substantively represent women's interests than are men.[49] But while descriptive representation requires that representatives look like those they represent, substantive representation carries with it no such requirement. Men representatives can substantively represent the interests of women, just as women representatives may act in ways that are counter to the substantive interests of women. Given the range of policy views that women hold, as described in Chapter 3, and the variety of women who are elected to office, Democrats and Republicans in the United States, and far-right to communist activists in Europe, the question of whether all women representatives substantively represent the interests of women is valid. But the research generally holds that increasing women's descriptive representation matters for substantive policy outcomes. As Mansbridge (2005) argues, "descriptive representation by gender improves substantive outcomes for women in every polity for which we have a measure."[50] Thus, we now look at the research that examines the impact of women's representation to understand where, how, and why women's representation matters.

THE EFFECT OF WOMEN'S REPRESENTATION IN LEGISLATIVE BODIES

Before examining whether women think and act differently as legislators, it is useful to think about why women might act differently in these roles. **Social role theory** argues that women are socialized to inhabit different roles in society; as a result, women may approach the job of legislating differently, focusing on relations to others, the need for help and empathy, and mutually beneficial problem solving.[51-53] Thus, differences in behavior between men and women legislators may emerge because women are socialized to act differently.

Women legislators may also act differently because they have different life experiences and a **shared social identity**.[54,55] As Swers (2002) argues, "women may bring unique experiences and viewpoints to the policy debate and different issues to the legislative agenda."[56] For instance, as discussed in Chapter 2, when Second Wave feminists began to argue that the "personal is political," a whole host of new issues like domestic violence and sexual harassment were moved out of the private realm and into the public realm because of women's experiences with these issues. Thus, women legislators behave differently because of differences in life experiences.

Finally, these differences may emerge because of **voters' expectations**. As discussed throughout this book voters perceive women to have different policy strengths, being better suited to "women's" issues like education and health. Because voters also expect women to be helpful and kind,[57] voters might expect women legislators to be more attentive to requests for constituency service and to pay more attention to what they see as feminine issues, like education and health care. The desire to remain in office is fairly universally held among politicians; so, if voters expect women to act differently, then women legislators may need to act this way in order to retain their positions.

THE BEHAVIOR OF INDIVIDUAL WOMEN LEGISLATORS

It's difficult to definitively say why differences in legislative behavior might emerge, as there is not a good deal of research examining this question. But there is a substantial body of research that establishes these differences do exist. First, research in the United States demonstrates that women legislators tend to be more liberal than their men counterparts.[58–63] This is also true in other legislatures, such as those in Latin America and Sweden.[64,65] As Wängnerud (2009) argues, there is agreement that women in parliaments are more leftist than their men counterparts, although the size of the gap in opinion varies from issue to issue, with women being more liberal on new issues, like environmental protection, and on women's interests.[66]

Additionally, women legislators think differently about their jobs. Women legislators are more likely to say representing women's interests is an important part of their job;[67,68] they are more likely to see themselves as delegates as opposed to trustees both in the United States[69] and in other places, such as the European Parliament.[70] These women also see themselves as working harder and being more attuned to constituency needs.[71,72] Part of this drive to work harder comes from the fact that many women legislators serve as surrogate representatives;[73] in addition to representing their own constituents, women legislators are more likely to see representing the interests of all women as part of their work.

These differences in beliefs about their work carry over into differences in actions at their work. For instance, women are more likely to spend more time interacting with their constituents in a variety of contexts, as the delegate theory of representation holds. At the U.S. state level, women legislators report spending more time on constituency service, as compared to their counterparts who are men,[74] and they are more likely to respond to requests for constituency service.[75] Women legislators also work harder for, and have more contact with, their constituents and grassroots organizations in the British Parliament,[76] in Spanish municipalities,[77] in the Rwandan Parliament,[78] and the Norwegian Parliament.[79] Indeed, in looking at a dozen types of potential interactions legislators may have with constituents, researchers have found that women in the U.S. Congress do more of *all* of these things. For instance, women legislators secure more federal spending for their districts and devote more time and energy to constituent service. Lazarus and Steigerwalt (2018) term this **"gendered vulnerability."**[80] They argue that women legislators are convinced they must work hard to win elections because they face more quality opponents and receive less support from political parties. As such, women feel more pressure to keep constituents happy in order to win reelection.

The most important task that legislators engage in, and the task they spend the most time on,[81] is legislating, and there is abundant evidence that women legislators legislate differently than their counterparts who are men. Across a variety of contexts, women legislators are more likely to prioritize women's issues in their bill sponsorship.[82–85] Issues such as health care, abortion, sexual harassment, and discrimination receive more attention in legislatures when there are more women because women are more likely to put forward bills that address these issues. It is not that men cannot and do not support these issues; they are simply less likely to sponsor bills to push for government action on these issues. For instance, U.S. House Speaker Nancy Pelosi (D-CA) argued that the passage of the Affordable Care Act in 2010 was achieved because it was a personal issue for women; she stated, "my sisters here in Congress, this was a big issue for us."[86]

Women are more likely to talk about these issues in legislatures as well. Pearson and Dancey (2011) analyzed the 1-minute speech that members of the U.S. House of Representatives give, and they found that women legislators are significantly more likely than men to discuss women and women's issues in these speeches.[87] Thus, the presence of women in these institutions brings more attention to the issues that affect women. Interestingly, one study examined the vocal pitch, which can be used to measure the emotional intensity of speech, used by Members of Congress giving these floor speeches.[88] Women legislators were not only more likely to speak about women and women's issues, but they were also more likely to talk with heightened vocal pitch, indicating greater emotional commitment to these issues. Their emotional intensity spread to men legislators who also spoke on the same issue and voted with the women.

BOX 6.2: POLICY FEATURE

Vaginas in the Legislature

In 2012, the Michigan State legislature, which was controlled by the Republican Party, was considering House Bill 5711 that would impose new regulations on abortion providers.[89] During debate over the bill, Representative Lisa Brown, a Democrat from West Bloomfield, delivered an impassioned speech, describing how her Jewish religious faith allowed women to seek an abortion regardless of the stage of the pregnancy if the mother's life was in danger. At the end of her speech, Rep. Brown said, "and finally, Mr. Speaker, I'm flattered that you're all so interested in my vagina, but 'no' means 'no.'"[90]

Some in the chamber were offended by her remarks. Republican Representative Mike Callton said, "What she said was offensive. It was so offensive I don't even want to say it in front of women. I would not say that in mixed company."[91] The "offensive" language that Representative Brown used was the word "vagina" on the House floor. Fellow Representative Barb Byrum, a Democrat from Onondaga, also found herself at odds with the House leadership after introducing an amendment to the abortion bill that would have banned men from having vasectomies unless their lives were in danger. She was ruled out of order by the leadership after protesting that she had not been allowed to speak about the issue.

After the debate over the abortion bill, which passed the House 70 votes for to 39 against, both women were not allowed to speak on the floor the next day because their comments and actions "failed to maintain the decorum of the House of Representatives."[92] The backlash to the punishment was swift. Shortly after the incident, a performance of the Vagina Monologues was staged on the steps of the Michigan statehouse, to an audience of thousands. Despite this protest and widespread outrage over the punishment of these two women legislators, House Bill 5711 passed both the House and the Senate, becoming law in March of 2013.

Despite the fact that women legislators pursue their interests in institutions in which they are a numerical minority, there is also a good deal of research that finds women legislators are more effective than their men counterparts.[93-95] Volden, Wiseman, and Wimmter (2013) argue this is due to three key factors: high effort, consensus building, and issue specialization.[96] Women work harder to secure the passage of the bills they sponsor. They also approach coalition building differently when working to secure passage of their bills; women legislators adopt a more collaborative and consensual approach to legislating as opposed to their men counterparts who adopt a more individualistic approach.[97] As U.S. Senator Susan Collins (R-ME) said in 2011, while surrounded by her women colleagues, "if we (women) were in charge of the Senate and of the administration we would have a budget deal by now. What I find is, with all due deference to our men colleagues, that women's styles tend to be more collaborative."[98]

Finally, because women tend to focus on particular issues that align with their beliefs, they developed specialized expertise that allows them to be more effective when working on these issues. These strategies are particularly effective for women who are in the minority party in legislative institutions as compared to men minority party legislators; building coalitions across party lines increases the legislative success of women minority party members.[99] As the U.S. Congress has become more divided along party lines, the advantage of these strategies is diminishing, though, and the situations under which these strategies work has waned. A recent study suggests that women are more likely to work across party divisions when they are Republicans working on bills that focus on health, education, or welfare.[100]

Anzia and Berry (2013) argue that these differences in effectiveness are due to sex-based selection; only the best or most qualified women run due to concerns about perceived or actual discrimination.[101] So in effect, the women who do run and win are likely to be above average performers; they are the cream of the crop. Alternatively, Pearson and Dancey (2011) argue that these differences are due to women legislators' desire to prove themselves in men-dominated institutions, in order to demonstrate their ability and expertise.[102] So, women have to work longer and harder to be effective legislators.

WOMEN AS INSTITUTIONAL LEADERS

As more women have gained entry into legislative institutions, they are also making inroads into positions of leadership in these institutions. There has been only one woman party leader in the U.S. Congress; Representative Nancy Pelosi (D-CA) who served as the Speaker of the House of Representatives from 2007 until 2011 and who was reelected to this position for the term starting in 2019. Her potential return to the Speaker position was the focus of a great many attacks in the 2018 election cycle; part of the reason why the attacks were successful is because voters are less likely to view powerful and ambitious women favorably.[103]

There have been more women legislative leaders in state legislatures in the United States; the first woman to serve in one of these roles was State Senator Vesta Roy (R-NH) in 1982. According to the Center for American Women and Politics, in 2019, women held 76 of 352 (21.6%) state legislative leadership positions. Thirty-seven women hold leadership in both state House and Senate chambers across the United States. Most of these women (75%) are Democrats, and approximately 18.4% of them are women of color.[104] The diversification of women legislative leadership happened fairly recently, as the first woman of color to lead a state legislative chamber, State Senator Colleen Hanabusa (D-HI), was elected to that position in 2007. As with membership in these institutions, there is considerable variation in the number of women in these leadership positions. At the low end are the twelve states with no women in legislative leadership; at the high end, 66.7% of the legislative leadership are women in Vermont, while in Oregon, half of the leaders are women. Outside the United States, few women preside over national parliaments; in 2016, just 19.1% of all parliamentary leadership positions were held by women, although this number

US House of Representatives

▶ **Photo 6.3** Nancy Pelosi (D-CA), the first woman Speaker of the House.

is the highest it has ever been. As the IPU (2018) notes, "while the number of women in parliaments grew at a remarkably slow pace throughout the 20th century, that of women presiding over parliament has grown at an even slower pace."[105] Prior to the turn of the century, only 42 countries had a woman preside, mostly in Europe, but since the 2000s, their presence has expanded. Women parliamentary leaders now span the globe, including in the Middle East, where Amal Al-Qubaisi was elected to serve as president of the Federal National Council in the United Arab Emirates in 2015.

▶ **Photo 6.4** Amal Al Qubaisi, President of the Federal National Council of the United Arab Emirates.

Aside from the formal party and institutional leadership positions in these institutions, legislative committees play a key role in these chambers in the United States, and women have also made inroads into these positions as well. Because women legislators were initially primarily assigned to "women's issues" committees like education and health, they first became chairs of these committees. As the positions women are appointed to in legislatures has diversified, women have assumed leadership roles across a variety of committees in these institutions. In the 115th Congress (2017–2019), Senator Lisa Murkowski (R-AK) chaired the Senate Energy and Natural Resources Committee, and Senator Susan Collins (R-ME) chaired the Special Committee on Aging; in the House, Representative Diane Black (R-TN) chaired

the House Budget Committee, and Representative Virginia Foxx (R-NC) chaired the Education and Workforce Committee. Committees are chaired by members of the majority party in these institutions, so there tend to be more women chairs during Democratic control of these chambers, as the Democratic party is more diverse than the Republican party. In the 113th Congress (2013–2015), the Senate was controlled by the Democrats, and seven women served as committee chairs.

▶ **Photo 6.5** U.S. Senator Lisa Murkowski (R-AK) talks with Lt. General Caldwell during a tour of Afghanistan.

There is ample evidence that having women serve in these roles makes a difference because they have different leadership styles; Whicker and Jewell (1998) label this the "feminization" of legislative leadership.[106] The differences in women leaders' style are similar to the differences in women legislators' approach to legislating. Women legislative leaders focus more on working with others, building consensus, and seeking input from a broader array of groups and voices.[107–109] As committee chairs, women speak less and make fewer interruptions than their men counterparts; men leaders focus on controlling hearings, while women leaders focus on facilitating discussion.[110] As Rosenthal (1998) argues, rather than pursuing power over others, women leaders focus more on getting things done through group effort.[111] Importantly, these different leadership styles can have transformative effects beyond the tenure of these woman leaders. Whicker and Jewell (1998) find that men leaders are increasingly gravitating toward women leadership styles, perhaps after seeing the effectiveness of this mode of operation.[112]

EFFECTS OUTSIDE THE INSTITUTION

Concepts of representation focus both on the represented and the representatives, so we can also look at the effect of women's representation in public office on the public. Generally speaking, research confirms theories about the effect of symbolic and descriptive representation—increases in women's representation in government are associated with increases in trust and confidence in government as well as women's engagement with and interest in government. Karp and Banducci's (2006) study of women candidates in 35 countries finds that women's representation in government is positively associated with political engagement for women and men.[113] A similar effect is found in Africa, where increases in women's representation in government lead to decreases in the gap in political engagement.[114] Wolbrecht and Campbell (2007) examined women's representation in parliaments in 23 countries (mostly in Europe) and found that women and girls are more likely to discuss politics with friends and to indicate they are interested in participating in politics when there are more women in parliament, with the strongest impact for adolescent girls.[115] In the United States, the same authors (2006, 2017) have found that when women politicians receive more news coverage and become more visible, adolescent girls are more likely to indicate an intention to be politically active, an effect they attribute to an increased propensity to discuss politics, particularly amongst family members.[116, 117] Burns, Schlozman, and Verba (2001) argue that if women were represented equally in government, the gap in men's and women's political engagement would be eliminated.[118]

Women's representation may also serve to increase women's ambition for seeking public office as women candidates serve as role models for other women and promote their political engagement—although, the evidence on this is mixed at best. On one hand, Brockman (2014) finds no evidence that having women on the ballot in state legislative elections leads to more women candidates in future elections.[119]

In India, though, the election of women has been shown to increase other women's presence in office.[120] It may be that state legislative races are not visible enough to the public to increase political ambition, and it may be that higher profile women candidates are necessary for the role model effect. The 2017 Women's Marches and the increase in women candidates for office in 2017 and 2018 in the aftermath of Hillary Clinton's high-profile candidacy are good examples of this role model effect.

Importantly, increases in symbolic and descriptive representation can have substantive effects beyond political engagement and policy outcomes as well. Beaman, Duflo, Pande, and Topalova (2012) surveyed over 8,000 girls and their parents in India where a 1993 law reserved some positions on local councils for women.[121] In comparing those areas where seats were and were not reserved for women, the authors found that parental aspirations for their sons remained unchanged, while parental aspirations for their daughters increased significantly in villages where council seats were reserved for women. By the second cycle of women's leadership, sex-based gaps in educational outcomes were erased, and girls spent less time on household chores.

Backlash/Critical Mass

While there is an abundance of evidence that the presence of women in legislative institutions matters for the policies these institutions produce, the way these institutions operate, and the people who are represented, that does not mean the advancement of women in these institutions has proceeded without any backlash. For instance, as the presence of women increases in legislative committees, men become more verbally aggressive, interrupt women more frequently, and control more of the committee hearings; in essence, men legislators are taking up and taking away the floor from women legislators.[122] To combat this backlash, Kathlene (1998) offers a number of recommendations, including having women committee members sit next to each other or in eye contact with other women.[123] In these legislatures, positions on committees are typically assigned by party leaders, and these predominantly men leaders frequently assign women legislators to less prestigious committees. For example, women legislators in Latin American legislatures are less likely to be assigned to power, economic, and foreign affairs committees.[124]

Furthermore, legislative institutions are not as receptive to proposals put forward by women on the whole. Volden, Wiseman, and Wittmer (2016) find that legislatures are more likely to pass bills related to education, health, and housing when they are sponsored by men, even though women sponsor more legislation on these issues.[125] And legislatures are more likely to take concrete action and commit resources to these issues when these issues are taken up by men and women, as opposed to when they are only championed by women. For instance, as described in Box 6.3, states are less likely to invest resources in combatting human trafficking when bill sponsors are primarily women; as Wittmer and Bouche (2013) argue, "framing what is actually a human issue as a women's issue triggers women to lead the charge but may suppress men's legislative support."[126]

BOX 6.3: POLICY FEATURE

Human Trafficking Legislation

While many think of human trafficking as a problem that happens elsewhere, it is unfortunately all too common in the United States. Polaris, a not-for-profit organization dedicated to fighting modern slavery, released a report about the state of human trafficking in the United States in 2017. The organization identified over 10,600 individual victims of human trafficking in 8,759 cases, a 13% increase from the past year.[127] The most common form of human trafficking in the United States is sex trafficking. As such, the vast majority of human trafficking victims in the United States are women (over 80%); the average age of sex trafficking victims is 19.

In the United States, both state and federal governments can pass legislation to combat this problem, which has been a persistent issue over the past few decades. The first federal legislation to combat this issue, the Victims of Trafficking and Violence Protection Act was passed in 2000, and shortly thereafter, the issue began appearing on the legislative agenda in state legislatures. Primarily, women have taken the lead on sponsoring legislation to combat this issue; because women are the primary victims of this crime, it has traditionally been seen as a "women's issue." Wittmer and Bouche (2013) studied this issue to determine whether women's leadership on the issue of human trafficking affects the extent to which the state takes this issue seriously.[128] While a good deal of research has demonstrated that women legislators are more likely to sponsor legislation related to women's issues, little research has examined the impact of this leadership on these issues. Given that some research shows women to be more effective legislators, it could be that such leadership produces policy that improves the lives of those affected by these issues. Alternatively, given the research showing the backlash against women leaders and legislators, it may be that leadership on these issues has unintended consequences.

States can take a variety of positions on this issue, from no action at all to bills that have little fiscal impact all the way to committing serious resources to combat this problem. Wittmer and Bouche wanted to find out the circumstances under which states were moved to act and to commit resources to fighting this problem; in essence, they wanted to know whether women's leadership on this issue led to greater investment in fighting the problem.

Significantly, the authors find that women played an important role in moving this issue on to the agenda and through the legislative process in state legislatures. When there are more women in the state legislature, bills that invest state resources, like money and personnel, in combatting trafficking are more likely to advance. However, they also find that as more of the sponsors of human trafficking legislation are women, states are less likely to pass bills investing in this problem. Having more women sponsors seems to indicate that the issue under consideration is just a women's issue and therefore not worthy of significant state investment. Wittmer and Bouche (2013) argue that if women legislators disproportionately speak out on issues like these, then the other state legislators and even the public pick up the signal that these are issues that women should care about more than men, with the unintended consequence being that men are exonerated from being responsible and accountable for these issues.[129] Thus, the presence of women in legislative bodies is important to get institutions to pay attention to "women's issues," but until legislative bodies are more receptive to the presence of these women and their leadership, their impact may be muted.

The backlash to the presence of women legislators and their concerns is both subtle, as outlined above, and overt. In the U.S. Congress, the pool in the U.S. Senate workout facility was men's only until 2008 because some of the men senators liked to swim naked. Women representatives in the U.S. House did not get their own bathroom until 2011. Women senators could not wear pants on the floor of the Senate until 1993, and women representatives held a "sleeveless Friday" in July 2017 in protest of U.S. House rules that prohibited women from wearing sleeveless dresses. The #MeToo movement has also brought to light the pervasive culture of sexual harassment in many legislative institutions. In California, the "We Said Enough" movement was organized in 2017 in response to the numerous claims of sexual harassment in the state legislature that emerged; more than 150 lobbyists, staffers, lawmakers, and consultants signed on to the movement. While the California legislature had just recently established a Subcommittee on Harassment, Discrimination, and Retaliation, the woman assigned to chair this subcommittee was a first-term legislator, signaling to some that the chamber was not taking this issue very seriously. An AP investigation into the issue found that the majority of state legislatures in the United States had no publicly available records of any sexual misconduct claims made in those institutions.[130] Beyond harassment, women legislators also face threats to their bodily integrity and lives. Two women who work in the Pennsylvania state legislature accused Republican State Representative Nick Miccarelli of sexual abuse, causing him to not seek reelection in 2018. In 2018, Marielle Franco, a city councilor in Rio de Janeiro and an outspoken advocate for the city's poor and fierce critic of the city police, was assassinated in retaliation for her advocacy. For women legislators of color, the intersectional nature of the harassment can be particularly intense; in 2018, Democrat Kiah Morris, a Black woman state legislator from Vermont, suspended her reelection campaign and resigned her seat after experiencing racially motivated harassment and threats.[131] Given the constraints and outright hostility that women face in these gendered institutions, the link between descriptive representation and substantive representation has not been always present.[132, 133] For instance, sex does not directly influence the roll call votes that women legislators cast—their votes are no different than those cast by men with similar party identification and personal beliefs.[134] Because these institutions are dominated by gender norms and expectations of behavior, the low rate of women's representation in these institutions can inhibit the ability of women to effectively advocate for women. "Increasing women's representation is a serious threat to scarce political resources . . . and men legislators will sideline women in an effort to preserve those resources."[135]

As Yoder (1991) argues, increasing women's presence in institutions to combat negative effects of tokenism ignores the pervasive sexism found in these bodies; highly masculinized occupations become more, not less, resistant to rapidly increasing numbers of women, what Yoder calls the "intrusiveness" effect.[136] Rather than accepting these women as equals, they are subject to ridicule, interruption, and harassment, which quite obviously interferes with their ability to succeed.

This has led some feminist theorists to ponder whether there is some magic number at which women have the ability to transform these institutions. For example, a study of Romanian women representatives found that women Romanian representatives to the EU parliament, where they make up 36% of the Romanian delegation, are more active on issues related to the substantive representation of women, but in the national parliament, where they make up 11.7% of members, these women are not particularly active on women's issues.[137]

Critical mass theory essentially argues that women in men-dominated institutions will remain tokens until they meet some threshold of representation. This theory was originally developed by Rosabeth Moss Kanter (1977), who argued that the relative numbers of members in a group are critical in shaping dynamics in that group; as these numbers begin to change, so do the social experiences in those groups.[138] Some groups are skewed, such that the minority in that group serve as tokens, are reduced to symbolic representation, and are forced to conform to the existing social norms of the group. For Kanter, there must be enough women to challenge these dynamics, although she does not clearly delineate the point at which these dynamics begin to change. Importantly, Kanter's work focused on women in the business world, so there has been debate over how and whether this theory applies in political institutions. Dahlerup's (1988) application of Kanter's theory to Scandinavia identified 30% as the specific threshold at which women will begin to transform these institutions, although this specific number has generated considerable debate.[139] Some research finds that women make a difference even when their presence is small numerically,[140] while others find that having more women reduces their likelihood of standing for women.[141] As Grey (2006) notes, "few have confirmed a straightforward causal link between female politicians reaching a critical mass and the substantive representation of women."[142]

Childs and Krook (2008) argue that this is because many have fundamentally misunderstood one of the important components of Kanter's work: It is not just the presence of women that matters but the presence of women who are supportive of women's interests.[143] As more women are elected to legislative bodies, their diversity increases such that not all women are interested in representing women's interests or in transforming these institutions. Thus, Childs and Krook (2006) argue, there is neither a single nor a universal relationship between the percentage of women elected to political office and the passage of legislation beneficial to women as a group.[144] In some cases, women work more effectively when numbers grow, but in other cases, women are more effective as a small minority, as they are able to avoid the backlash effect. In examining the New Zealand parliament, Grey (2006) finds that in addition to the number of women, transformative effects require women to have a group of women of sufficient size with feminist leanings and supportive colleagues in order to have some impact.[145]

As such, it is important to note that not all women necessarily represent women's interests, and in some situations, they may act counter to these interests. In the United States, women are more liberal than their men counterparts in both parties, but even though Republican women are more liberal than Republican men, they are not necessarily more liberal than Democratic men.[146] In Norway, women from right-wing parties favor private solutions to work-family balance issues, while women legislators from left-wing parties favor state solutions.[147]

HOW TO INCREASE THE NUMBER OF WOMEN IN LEGISLATIVE OFFICE

Despite the fact that not all women are supportive of women's issues and work to advance the cause of women, the consensus among researchers is that the presence of women in legislative bodies is positive for a variety of reasons; hence, a good deal of research has focused on ways to increase the representation of women in these chambers. The number of women in office is affected both by factors influencing both the supply of women candidates and the demand for women candidates.[148] In Chapter 4, we identified the lack of women running for office as one of the critical barriers to increasing the number of women in elected office; this is the supply of women candidates. However, that does not mean that other factors do not affect women's presence in office. For example, in the U.S. Congress, incumbents who seek reelection almost always earn it as described in Chapter 5; even in 2018, an election cycle with tremendous change, 91% of House candidates seeking reelection won, while 84% of Senate incumbents were reelected. Because most incumbents are men, most incumbents who win reelection are men, who are likely to box women out even if they decided to run. That said, it is worth noting that several Democratic women defeated prominent, well-ensconced incumbents in the 2018 midterm primaries, including Alexandria Ocasio-Cortez (D-NY) who sidelined Rep. Joe Crowley (D-NY), Dana Balter

(D-NY) who defeated Rep. Juanita Perez-Williams (D-NY), Liuba Grechen Shirley (D-NY) who beat Rep. DuWayne Gregory (D-NY), and Ayanna Pressley (D-MA) who knocked off Rep. Mike Capuano (D-MA). Furthermore, political parties and their leaders play a role in promoting the representation of women as parties generally serve as gatekeepers of access to the ballot. Generally speaking, left-leaning parties across the globe have been more supportive of women candidates, and left party prominence increases the presence of women in government.[149] Having women party leaders can help increase the number of women in government. Party leaders tend to rely on personal networks in promoting candidates for office, and when party leaders are men, their personal networks are dominated by men. As a result, they often literally don't see any women when looking to recruit someone for office.[150]

Indeed, some argue that systemic and institutional factors are greater barriers to women's presence in legislatures around the world than the dearth of women candidates. Importantly, the rules of the game, or our choices about how we select our political leaders, can have a profound impact on the level of women's representation. As Paxton, Kunovich, and Hughes (2007) argue, "features of political systems shape the rules of the game and strongly influence whether women can attain, and how they can attain, political power."[151]

Interestingly, when looking at the most fundamental feature of a political system, the form of government, democracy does not fare well. Democracy does not appear to be the most conducive form of government to women's representation; large cross-national studies do not find that democratic countries have more women in parliament than less democratic countries.[152] Of course, democratic governments have more to recommend them than the representation of women, so it is worth examining the features of democratic governments that can increase the representation of women. On the whole, parliamentary-styled governments with closed list proportional representation (PR) are more likely to produce higher levels of women in governments than other types of systems, particularly when this type of electoral system is coupled with legislated or voluntary party quotas (see below for an explanation of quotas). A **proportional representation** system awards parties seats in the national parliament based upon the proportion of the vote they get in elections. Voters simply choose the party they prefer, rather than the candidate herself or himself. For example, in a 100-member parliament, if the Pink Party gets 40% of the national vote, they put in 40 people to the parliament—the first 40 people of the possible 100 people on their list.

The United States does not have a PR system, and this is one explanation why fewer American women are in office than are women in other countries. Instead, the United States has a single member, simple **plurality** or **first-past-the-post system** (with exceptions in few states and local election systems). In this type of electoral system, voters chose one winner, who is the person who gets the most, not necessarily a majority, of the votes. Why is this system less preferable for women? The plurality system is candidate-centered, and one-on-one elections between candidates typically cost the candidates a lot. Women candidates historically have fewer resources than men and face sexism; thus, plurality systems present women with hurdles. On the other hand, the List PR system is based on the principle that parties or political groupings present a list of candidates, and the candidates, with party resources, run for office collectively.

List systems can be open or closed. The majority of List PR systems in the world are **closed,** which means that the order of candidates on the list is fixed by the party, and voters cannot choose a particular candidate but instead vote for a party. For example, in South Africa, the ballot contains party names and symbols and a photograph of the party leader but no names of individual candidates.[153] Closed lists do not make women compete as individuals, and this helps them avoid the hurdles of plurality systems discussed previously. The negative aspect of closed lists is that voters have no say in determining who the representatives of their party will be.[154] Lists can also be **open**, a system more common in Western Europe than in other regions. In an open list PR system, voters can indicate not just their preferred party but also their preferred candidate within that party. In these systems, voters often vote only for a party, so the candidate-choice aspect of the ballot has limited effect. That said, in Sweden, 25% of the voters regularly choose a candidate as well as a party, and a number of individuals are elected who would not be if the list were closed.[155] Brazil is a good example of how open lists can produce lower numbers of women in legislatures. Brazilian voters prefer to vote for a candidate more than a party; they can choose to do one or the other under their open list system. The result is that women find it hard to compete financially and have the same level of name recognition as men, and, as of 2018, men are 85% of the Brazilian legislature.[156]

Quotas are measures used to "recruit women into political positions and to ensure that women are not only a few tokens in political life."[157] In Table 6.2, we see that on the whole, countries (outside of Scandinavia) with large numbers of women in government have legislated quotas or voluntary party quotas. Whereas **legislated quotas** (also called legal candidate quotas) require political parties to present lists balanced with men and women candidates, some parties choose to do so voluntarily. Closed list systems function particularly well with quotas as party leaders are the ones responsible for choosing candidates and constructing lists, and, they can do so with gender in mind. However, when open lists are coupled with voluntary party quotas or norms of equality (as seen in Scandinavian countries), they, too, can result in higher numbers of women in legislatures.[158] **Reserved seats**, another form of quota system, designates certain political positions as positions only for women. Rwanda is a primary example of this, as 24 members of its 80-member legislature are reserved for women.

Proportional representation and quotas generally have been successful in increasing the number of women in legislatures, but Brazil presents an exception. In Brazil, 30% of party lists should be women, but the quota law does not mandate the order in which men and women are to be placed on the lists. Thus, the quota system lacks **placement mandates**, defined as rules for how parties must order candidates on the party list. It is possible, therefore, for political parties to put all women at the bottom of their lists, resulting in few women being elected. For this reason, academic experts on quotas suggest the use of a **"zipper" rule**, "where women's and men's names alternate on the party lists."[159]

As Table 6.2 shows, countries with high levels of women in government are more likely to be those with instituted quotas in closed list proportional representation systems. In fact, in the top 25 countries for women's legislative representation, only Cuba does not have some sort of quota system. Clearly, quotas increase the numbers of women in legislatures (particularly if women are placed in an equitable fashion on the list), and as noted earlier, increasing descriptive representation for women typically increases substantive representation for women.

Table 6.2 Women's Representation in Top 20 Countries, 2018

Rank	Countries	Percentage of Women in Lower/Single House	Percentage of Women in Upper House/ Senate	Electoral System	Open or Closed List
1	Rwanda	61.3	38.5	PR*	Closed party list
		Quotas: Legislated candidate and reserved Seats in both houses.			
2	Cuba	53.2	---	Plurality/ majority	N/A
		Quotas: Legislated quotas for the Lower and Upper House. Voluntary quotas adopted by political parties			
3	Bolivia	53.1	47.2	PR	Closed party list
		Quotas: No.			
4	Grenada	46.7	15.4 percent	Plurality	N/A
		Quotas: No.			
5	Namibia	46.2	24.4	PR*	Closed party list
		Quotas: Legislated Subnational quotas. Voluntary quotas adopted by political parties.			
6	Nicaragua	45.7	---	PR	Closed party list
		Quotas: Legislated quotas for the lower and upper house. Voluntary quotas adopted by political parties.			
7	Costa Rica	45.6	---	PR	Close party list

		Quotas: Legislated quotas for the lower and upper house. Legislated quotas at the subnational level. Voluntary quotas adopted by political parties.			
8	Sweden	43.6	---	PR	Open
		Quotas: Legislated quotas at subnational level. Voluntary quotas adopted by political parties.			
9	Mexico	42.6	36.7	Mixed* Lower house is part plurality part PR	Closed party list
		Quotas: Legislated quotas for the lower and upper house. Voluntary quotas adopted by political parties.			
10	South Africa	42.4	35.2	PR	Closed party list
		Quotas: Legislated subnational quotas. Voluntary quotas adopted by political parties.			
11	Finland	42	---	PR	Open
		Quotas: Voluntary quotas adopted by political parties.			
12	Senegal	41.8	---	Mixed Plurality and PR	Closed party list
		Quotas: Legislated candidate quotas.			
13	Norway	41.4	---	PR	Open
		Quotas: Legislated subnational quotas. Voluntary quotas adopted by political parties.			
14	Mozambique	39.6	---	PR	Closed party list
		Quotas: Legislated subnational quotas. Voluntary quotas adopted by political parties.			
15	Spain	39.1	38	PR*	Closed party list (lower house) Open for Senate (Upper House)
		Quotas: Legislated quotas for the lower and upper house. Legislated quotas at the subnational level. Voluntary quotas adopted by political parties.			

(Continued)

Rank	Countries	Percentage of Women in Lower/Single House	Percentage of Women in Upper House/ Senate	Electoral System	Open or Closed List
16	France	39	29.3	Plurality/2 round	Closed party list
		Quotas: Legislated quotas for the lower and upper house. Legislated quotas at the subnational level. Voluntary quotas adopted by political parties.			
17	Argentina	38.9	41.7	PR	Closed party list
		Quotas: Voluntary quotas adopted by political parties.			
18	Ethiopia	38.8	32	Plurality/ Majority*	N/A
		Quotas: Legislated subnational quotas. Voluntary quotas adopted by political parties.			
19	New Zealand	38.3	---	PR	Closed party list
		Quotas: No, "soft targets" and norm development of equality. Voluntary quotas adopted by political parties.			
20	Iceland	38.1	---	PR	Open
		Quotas: Legislated quotas for the lower and upper house. Legislated quotas at the subnational level. Voluntary quotas adopted by political parties.			
102	United States	19.5	22	Plurality	N/A
		Quotas: No.			

*The upper house is elected in a different election system than the lower house. Data compiled from Africans Elections (http://africanelections.tripod.com); IPU (2018, https://www.ipu.org); Election Guide (2016, http://www.electionguide.org); IDEA (https://www.idea.int/); and Wadley, N. (2015). The truth about gender equality in Cuba. Washington, DC: Berkley Center for Religion, Peace, & World Affairs. Retrieved from https://berkleycenter.georgetown.edu/posts/the-truth-about-gender-equality-in-cuba.

While quotas are much more common place outside the United States, there are some places in the United States where they exist. For instance, Iowa passed a law in 1987 requiring balance between men and women on city and county boards and commissions; and a few other states, including Connecticut, Illinois, and Montana, have laws mandating good faith efforts to make boards balanced between men and women.[160] Of course, these laws affect just appointed positions, not elected positions; there are no legislative or major party quotas for elected positions in the United States.

Akin to proportional representation in other countries, some states in the United States have multimember state legislative districts. Most commonly in the United States, each district, whether in a state Senate or House of Representatives, elects one person to represent the district. But in some state legislatures, voters elect two or more representatives. Research shows that electing more than one member per district increases the representation of women;[161] one study estimates there are 3.3% more women elected in two-member districts (as compared to the national average in state legislatures) and 4.6% more women in multimember districts.[162] Nearly 75% of all people living in multimember districts in the United States are represented by at least one woman in their state legislature.

Thus, the arrangements of political systems can do much to promote the representation of women. And, as described earlier, increased representation of women in legislatures generally leads to better political and policy outcomes for women. But this is not always the case; Rwanda and Cuba present two interesting examples of countries with high levels of women in government based on quotas (Rwanda) and no quotas (Cuba), where we have not seen a concomitant rise in women's equality nationwide.

BOX 6.4: COMPARATIVE FEATURE

The Effects of Descriptive Representation on Substantive Representation in Cuba and Rwanda

Cuba

Cuba is ranked third in terms of number of women in their national parliament. Due to the socialist system, sex-based equality is embraced in the abstract, and education is equally provided to boys and girls. Women make up 66% of the labor force, and more than 70% of professionals are women.[163] "The surge of women in the workforce over the past 50 years can be attributed to the women's movement, which began during the revolution under the rule of Fidel Castro. The movement dates back to 1960 when Castro formed the Federación de Mujeres Cubanas (FMC), the official, non-governmental organization (NGO) that advocates for women's rights."[164] The FMC is charged with advocating for women's equality, but some privately say that true gender equality is always in second place to the main ideal—maintaining the revolution.[165]

Nearly perfect equity in the legislature (49% women) has not necessarily translated into societal equity, particularly in the home. While Cuban law grants women and men equal rights and responsibilities in raising children, maintaining the home, and pursuing a career, traditional sexist

(Continued)

(Continued)

behavior and gender stereotypes persist, and laws that mandate equality in day-to-day life are not enforced.[166] On an American Academy of University Women research trip to Cuba in 2011, many Cuban women professionals spoke of a "double day," that is, their paid work day and then their duties as wife, mother, and homemaker after work.[167] If women in Cuba involve themselves in politics or community work, they would have a "triple burden" of work, home, and activism.[168] This mirrors what local French politicians indicated in personal interviews to the authors and also is a prominent theme among American working women (see Chapter 7 for discussion of French politicians).[169] One difference for Cuban women is that some of the conveniences of advanced developed countries—frozen meals, washing machines, dishwashers, and so on—are not prevalent in Cuba, creating more household burdens.

Journalists write of a pervasive **machismo,** a strong sense of masculine pride or power that places men as more important than women, that pervades Cuba. "Cuban machismo is strange in that it survives when women are working outside the home, receive the same paycheck as men for doing the same job, are the majority in universities and have a right to decide over their bodies, etc."[170] Machismo manifests in high levels of domestic violence and violence against women in general. Domestic violence is rarely prosecuted or results in only minimal fines, sometimes as low as the equivalent of 4 U.S. dollars.[171,172] Women are considered the property of their husbands, and sexual assault and domestic violence is viewed as "a family problem."[173]

Even in the halls of government, many women are put into positions to make it look as if there is equality between the sexes, and the ideals of the Revolution were realized, while in reality, they hold no real power.[174] In fact, women do not rise into power positions in the government at the same rate as men, even though they make up nearly half of governmental officials.[175] In the professional realm, women tend to hold positions more in the "helping" fields like nursing, education, administrative support, and so on, than in the hard sciences, technology, and business.[176] In sum, while Cuba is third in terms of women in government, descriptive representation has not translated into substantive changes in gender roles or equality, particularly in the private sphere.

Rwanda

Rwanda underwent a bloody genocide in 1994 that lasted 100 days; 800,000 to 1 million people were killed, the majority of them men. Additionally, many men in leadership positions were killed. In the immediate aftermath of the genocide, 60% to 70% of the population were women. Thus, when forming a government, society had to look toward women. This practice continues today, with Rwanda having more women in its legislature than any other country at 61% as of 2018. With this many women in parliament, one would think that Rwanda has an egalitarian culture. This is not the case. As illustration, according to Warner (2016) "feminism is a bad word" in Rwanda.[177] Perhaps this shouldn't be surprising. Before the genocide, it was rare for girls to be educated as well as boys and rarer still for women to work outside the home (Warner 2016).[178]

How then did women rise to predominance in Rwanda? Men were still 30% to 40% of the population postgenocide. Unlike in other countries where quotas and the rise of women in politics coincided with strong women's movements, Rwanda's path to sex-based equity was pushed by one man, Paul Kagame, who has led Rwanda since the country's return to peace.[179] Kagame believed that Rwandan society was so broken by the genocide that it needed radical change. He instituted a quota law in 2003 that said 30% of parliamentary seats must be held by women (reserved seats quotas). The country embraced the idea, and in 2003 elected 48% women. Subsequent elections have seen women elected between 60% to 70%.[180]

What did this top down push for equality mean for Rwandan sex-based equality across sectors of society? Do we see both descriptive and substantive equality in Rwanda, and have more women in positions of government led to a societal change? The short answer is no. A research study found in countless interviews with Rwandan political leaders that no matter the women's power in their public lives, this power did not extend to their private lives.[181] Woman after woman related that she was expected to carry out ceremonial household duties herself (even if she had the means to hire help), and that some even feared violence from husbands if they did not fulfill these roles.[182] For these women, their public roles felt more like a burden—a duty to their country—that had to be born rather than the achievement of equality.[183] "Because of the way that gender equality came so rapidly to Rwanda, from the outside in, with no psychological buildup or women's lib movement, it was harder for these politicians to talk about equality without appearing disloyal, not just to their spouses but to their country."[184] Thus, even in the country with the most women in the legislature, we see that descriptive representation is not enough to change predominant cultural attitudes related to gender roles in society, and while quotas do work to increase the number of women in government, it remains to be seen the degree to which this results in actual societal change.

Thus, while Heath, Schwindt-Bayer, and Taylor-Robinson (2005) state that, "institutional design may well be the most important influence on the marginalization of women," features like quotas and proportional representation systems are not sufficient to advance the status of women in society, as the case studies of Rwanda and Cuba show;[185] nor is the presence of women in government. Absent a supportive cultural environment, women are neither likely to make inroads into government nor to advance the cause of women. Paxton et al. (2007) argue, "cultural ideas about women can affect women's levels of representation throughout the political process, from an individual woman's decision to enter politics, to party selection of candidates, to decisions made by voters on election day."[186] For instance, the authors note that when asked whether men make better political leaders than women, the average response of a Norwegian is between strongly disagree and disagree, while the average response of a Nigerian is between agree and strongly agree. In order to advance the status of women, both the presence of women in positions of power and authority and a supportive cultural environment in which to exercise that power and authority are necessary.

CONCLUSION

In 1992, a record number of women were elected to the U.S. Congress. "Then they were promptly told how to vote by senior men colleagues, ignored in the elevators, and even turned away at the chamber doors because 'staff' weren't allowed on the floor."[187] Women are making strides into legislatures around the world, but even after the 2018-midterms, women have a long way to go. While U.S. Senator Tammy Duckworth (D-IL) can now bring her baby on to the floor of the Senate, she could not take maternity leave as the U.S. Congress has no maternity leave policy. Women's gains in representation have plateaued in recent years, and even when women are elected to office, they may face unsupportive colleagues and resistance to their efforts.

That having been said, the presence of women in legislatures matters. While women may not be a critical mass, little by little, they are changing these institutions. They interact more with their constituents and invite more people into the decision-making process. They work more collaboratively. They bring different issues to the table. Take Ilhan Omar (D-MN). As a child, she fled Somalia during a civil war and spent four years in a refugee camp in Kenya; she then came to the United States, learned English, and became engaged in local politics. As a Black, Muslim woman who wears a headscarf, she faced questions from the Somali community about the appropriateness of a woman serving in elected office. She faced false accusations during her campaign that she had married her brother to commit immigration fraud. Nevertheless, she persisted, and in 2016, she was elected to serve in the Minnesota State House of Representatives, and in 2018, she won a seat in the U.S. House of Representatives. As she says, "I think I bring the voice of young people. I think I bring the voice of women in the East African community. I bring the voice of Muslims. I bring the voice of young mothers looking for opportunity."[188] Our political systems are strengthened when more voices are heard and a variety of people have a seat at the table.

REVIEW QUESTIONS

1. How does the United States compare to the rest of the world in terms of the representation of women at the federal, state, and local level? Why do you think the United States generally fares poorly when compared to other nations?

2. Describe the different theories of representation. Some have argued that democratic representation may require limiting the influence of overrepresented privileged groups. Would you support a move to limit the representation of some groups? Why, or why not?

3. What are the effects of electing more women to legislatures? In other words, how do women legislators act differently than their men counterparts?

4. Once women are elected to office, they often face a backlash to their presence. Describe this backlash. Critical mass theory holds that having a certain threshold of women in these institutions is critical to avoiding this backlash. Explain what critical mass theory is. Do you believe there is some critical mass of women needed? If so, what level of representation is needed to overcome the backlash? If not, why not?

5. In looking around the world, there are a variety of ways that the representation of women can be increased. Describe the mechanisms that can be employed to increase women's representation. Would you support the implementation of any of these mechanisms in the United States? Why, or why not?

AMBITION ACTIVITIES

How Do Women Participate in Governance? Go to a student government or city government meeting, and observe parliamentary procedure. Do you notice any sex-based dynamics? How do the sex-based dynamics of leadership and participation play out in local settings, as in meetings of a city council, in volunteer organizations, or in religious institutions? What are the dynamics between men and women on your college campus—within the student government, for example?

As described earlier, Kanter (1977) found that women can be treated as tokens when there are few women; in these situations, they are considered anomalies and face stereotyping and discrimination.[189] As the presence of women increases, men start to interrupt more and take control of the proceedings.[190] Kanter also observed when women were a larger minority or a critical mass, they were able to form coalitions, influence the culture of their local context, and effect change. Alternatively, as women reach higher numbers, they may no longer act as a special interest minority with coherent goals.

Consider these lessons from scholars in the context of your campus's student government organization. Observe a meeting of the organization, interview a student who participates in student government, or, with the assistance of your professor, invite a panel of student government representatives to class for a Q&A session. Questions to consider during your observation of the meeting or to ask the panel participants include the following:

1. What percentage of the student government participants and primary leaders in student government are women? Are there leaders with other salient identities—race, ethnicity, LGBTQIA+, and so on?

2. Are women "tokens" in student government, or is representation between women, men, and/or gender-fluid individuals balanced? How or why might that matter?

3. Who does the most speaking in student government, men or women, and who interrupts whom the most? Women or men of different racial identities? Who appears to have the most voice, how can you tell, and why do you believe that is the case?

4. Are there any issues addressed by student government that you would say are particularly related to women (or men or nonbinary gender identity/LGBTQIA+) on campus? If so, who is acting on these issues: women acting as a group, women and men acting together, or one particular man or woman working as a "critical actor?"

5. If there are many women present and speaking in the council, do they appear to act together like a group, or do their interests seem to diverge from one another?

6. Do the men who are present seem to dismiss the women as a group or act in any way as a backlash against women when they united as a group? If yes, what were the women united about when they faced backlash?

How would you summarize your overall findings, and why are they significant for women at your school? Consider answering these same questions about other local contexts in your community—a city council meeting or a meeting of a community group.

Amplifying Women's Voices: In business meetings and in politics, it is not uncommon for men to speak over women or to talk down to them, telling them something they already know in an authoritative way. Jokingly, people have called these phenomena *manterrupting* and *mansplaining*. Men also sometimes take credit for women's ideas, which can be referred to as *bropropriating*.[191]

The fact that women are not heard or that men appropriate their ideas challenges the representation of women in politics. Some have argued that this has happened in the White House over history. Men have occupied the presidency for over 200 years, and women have only played important roles in the Oval Office, for example, as aides and as department heads, in recent decades. Only one third of Obama's closest aides were women at the beginning of his first term, thus necessitating the strategy of **amplification** used by his staffers who were women. Juliet Eilperin explains how this strategy was used in meetings. "When a woman made a key point, other women would repeat it, giving credit to its author. This forced men in the room to recognize the contribution—and denied them the chance to claim the idea on their own."[192] Women staffers used the strategy on an everyday basis, and President Obama "began calling more often on women and junior aides."

Think of a time in a college class when a person, perhaps a woman, has made a point, but no one has engaged her idea. Or, have you ever noticed when a man, a student or professor, has expressed an idea earlier stated by a woman as his own idea? Using the strategy of amplification could help in these situations to give weight to women's voices (or other voices that get overlooked in classrooms). Try using amplification in groups, specifically by (a) repeating and/or rephrasing the thoughts of the original speaker and (b) stating the speaker's name to tie her identity to her ideas (see sample scenario below). Practice restating and giving credit to a person in a conversation.

Sample: In a class discussion about political culture in the United States:

Classmate 1: American political culture puts a lot of emphasis on individualism. In what ways are Americans individualistic?

Classmate 2 (Mary): I think Americans tend to emphasize citizens' rights, like the right to assemble and free speech. People like to talk about this right and that right, and the focus is on what individuals should be able to do.

Classmate 3: *Mary's* idea makes sense to me. *She claims* that people frequently discuss rights to do things like assemble or have free speech. In this way, Americans are focusing on the rights of citizens, specifically the rights of individuals.

Interviewing a Woman Who Has Been Elected to Public Office: Find a woman who has been elected to a local, state, or national office; learn about her personal trajectory as well as her opinion about the influence of sex and gender on politics. After you complete the interview, summarize the candidate's understanding of how sex influences politics. To learn how to conduct an interview, see Appendix 1.

Interview Questions:

1. Who and/or what circumstances influenced you to run for office? Why were these people/circumstances so influential?

2. What factors, if any, do you believe deter young women from wanting to run for public office? How could these factors be mitigated?

3. To what extent do you believe that women's and men's experiences with politics and public policy are distinct? For example, are the policies and proposals you put forward any different from those of your men colleagues? Do you approach the way you work with others differently? Why do you think so, and what evidence from your personal experiences can you offer as examples?

Comparing Biographies of Members of Congress: Working with a partner, choose two members of Congress (MOC) to compare, one woman and one man or two women (with varying personal attributes). For each MOC, write a biography highlighting a particular aspect of her or his personal life and career; in addition, write a summary of how these MOCs are similar or different on the issue you chose to examine. The goal of the activity is to evaluate how women and men (or two women) serving in Congress have different (or similar) personal, career, and political trajectories. Recall, women are a heterogeneous group with various sex-based and gender experiences. This means the comparison of two women is just as theoretically interesting as a comparison between a woman and a man.

Political scientists typically compare cases (countries, political parties, politicians, etc.) that are somewhat similar rather than entirely different, because if cases are too different it is difficult to understand all the differences at once and which ones are most significant. If we examine relatively similar cases, we can come closer to isolating why particular variables (such as sex, gender, race, age, sexual orientation, or political party of a member of Congress) influence a MOC's personal or career trajectory. If we wanted to know how sex matters, you would need to compare a man and a woman with similar attributes—same party, about the same age, and same race. This way, you know sex accounts for differences more so than the variables of party, age, or race. Similarly, if we wanted to know how race influences women MOCs, you would need to compare two women of about the same age and same party but from different races. In comparing your two MOCs, you might examine a variety of different aspects of their background and political career. You could detail how these two MOCs vary in terms of early career and early life choices (marriage, kids, etc.) and how that influenced their road to political power. You could examine committee assignments, major advocacy issues, webpages, Twitter accounts, bill sponsorship, and more. For more information on comparison in political science, see Appendix 2.

KEY WORDS

Amplification 278

Closed party list 269

Critical mass theory 266

Delegate model of representation 253

Descriptive representation 254

First-past-the-post system 268

Formalistic representation 253

Gendered political priorities 248

Gendered vulnerability 257

Legislated quotas 269

Liberal representation 255

Machismo 274

Open party list 269

Placement mandates 269

Plurality 268

Proportional representation 268

Quotas 269

Reserved seats 269

Shared social identity 256

Social role theory 256

Substantive representation 255

Surrogate representation 255

Symbolic representation 254

Trustee model of
   representation 253

Voters' expectations 256

Widow's succession 247

"Zipper" rule 270

REFERENCES

1. Wright, R. (2005). *Inside the statehouse: Lessons from the speaker*. Washington, DC: CQ Press.

2. Bratton, K. A., & Ray, L. P. (2002). Descriptive representation, policy outcomes, and municipal day-care coverage in Norway. *American Journal of Political Science, 46* (2), 428–137.

3. Reingold, B., & Smith, A. R. (2012). Welfare policymaking and intersections of race, ethnicity, and gender in U.S. state legislatures. *American Journal of Political Science, 56*(1), 131–147.

4. Gunja, M. Z., Collins, S. R., Doty, M. M., & Beutel, S. (2017). How the Affordable Care Act has helped women gain insurance and improved their ability to get health care. *Common Wealth Fund*. Retrieved from http://www .commonwealthfund.org/publications/issue-briefs/2017/aug/aca-helped-women-gain-insurance-and-access.

5. Wängnerud, L. (2009). Women in Parliaments: Descriptive and substantive representation. *Annual Review of Political Science, 12*, 51–69.

6. Inter-Parliamentary Union (IPU). (2018). *Women in national Parliaments*. Retrieved from http://archive.ipu.org/wmn-e/classif.htm.

7. Celis, K., Childs, S., Kantola, J., & Krook, M. L. (2008). Rethinking women's substantive representation. *Journal of Representative Democracy, 44*(2), 99–110.

8. Inter-Parliamentary Union (IPU). (2018). *Women in national parliaments*. Retrieved from http://archive.ipu.org/wmn-e/classif.htm.

9. National Democratic Institute (NDI). (n.d.). *Gender, women and democracy*. Accessed on March 3, 2018 at https://www.ndi.org/what-we-do/gender-women-and-democracy.

10. Inter-Parliamentary Union (IPU). (2018). *Women in national parliaments*. Retrieved from http://archive.ipu.org/wmn-e/classif.htm.

11. Kathlene, L. (1989). Uncovering the political impacts of gender: An exploratory study. *The Western Political Quarterly, 42*(2), 397–421.

12. MacManus, S. A., Bullock III, C. S., Padgett, K. L., & Penberthy, B. (2006). Women winning at the local level: Are county and school board positions becoming more desirable and plugging the pipeline to higher office? In L. D. Whitaker (Ed.), *Women in politics: Outsiders or insiders?* (pp. 117–136). Upper Saddle River, NJ: Pearson.

13. Garcia, S. R., & Marquez, M. (2001). Motivational and attitudinal factors among Latinas in U.S. electoral politics. *NWSA Journal, 13*(2), 112–122.

14. Hardy-Fanta, C. (1995). Latina women and political leadership: Implications for Latino community empowerment. *New England Journal of Public Policy, 11*(1), 221–235.

15. Holman, M. R. (2017). Women in local government: What we know and where we go from here. *State and Local Government Review, 49*(4), 285–296.

16. Hardy-Fanta, C., Lien, P., Pinderhughes, D., & Sierra, C. M. (2016). *Contested transformation: Race, gender, and political leadership in 21st century America.* Cambridge, MA: Cambridge University Press.

17. Kellogg, L. D., Gourrier, A. G., Bernick, E. L., & Brekken, K. (2017). County governing boards: Where have all the women gone? *Politics, Groups, and Identities.* DOI: 10.1080/21565503.2017.1304223

18. National School Board Association. (n.d.). *Frequently asked questions.* Retrieved from http://www.nsba.org/about-us/frequently-asked-questions.

19. Holman, M. R. (2017). Women in local government: What we know and where we go from here.

20. MacManus et al. (2006). Women winning at the local level: Are county and school board positions becoming more desirable and plugging the pipeline to higher office?

21. Shanker, R. (2014). *Measurement of women's political participation at the local level: India experience.* United Nations Statistics Division. Retrieved from https://unstats.un.org/unsd/gender/mexico_nov2014/Session percent206 percent20India percent20paper.pdf.

22. Ibid., 1.

23. United Nations. *Power and decision-making.* United Nation Statistics Division. Retrieved from https://unstats.un.org/unsd/gender/downloads/WorldsWomen2015_chapter5_t.pdf.

24. Ibid.

25. Ibid.

26. Ibid.

27. Shanker, R. (2014). *Measurement of women's political participation at the local level: India experience.*

28. United Nations. *Power and decision-making.*

29. Kertscher, T. (2017). Diversity in Congress: Democrats have women and minorities, Republicans have white men over 55? *Politifact.* Retrieved from http://www.politifact.com/wisconsin/statements/2017/apr/28/mark-pocan/congress-democrats-have-women-and-minorities-repub.

30. Ring, T. (2017). With election of trans, bi women, Palm Springs City Council now entirely queer. *Advocate*. Retrieved from https://www.advocate.com/politics/2017/11/08/election-trans-bi-women-palm-springs-city-council-now-entirely-queer.

31. Farmer, L. (2017). Election 2017 was a historic night for women. *Governing*. Retrieved from http://www.governing.com/topics/politics/gov-election-2017-historic-night-women-candidates.html.

32. Holman, M. R. (2017). Women in local government: What we know and where we go from here.

33. Osborn, T. (2012). *How women represent women: Political parties, gender, and representation in state legislatures*. New York, NY: Oxford University Press.

34. National League of Cities. (n.d.). *City councils*. Accessed on March 9, 2018 at http://www.nlc.org/city-councils.

35. McNeil, C., Roberts, C., & Snelling, C. (2017). Power to the people? Tackling the gender imbalance in combined authorities and local government. *IPPR*. Retrieved from https://www.ippr.org/research/publications/power-to-the-people-tackling-gender-imbalance.

36. Nirappil, F. (2018). Women hit a record high in Virginia legislature. Can they break the boys' club? *Washington Post*. Retrieved from https://www.washingtonpost.com/local/virginia-politics/women-hit-a-record-high-in-virginia-legislature-can-they-break-the-boys-club/2018/01/11/e1d5f2f4-f4aa-11e7-beb6-c8d48830c54d_story.html?utm_term=.62cf2b39b1a3.

37. Center for American Women and Politics. (2018). *By the numbers: Women congressional candidates in 2018*. Retrieved from http://cawp.rutgers.edu/congressional-candidates-summary-2018.

38. Dovi, S. (2017, Winter). Political representation. *The Stanford Encyclopedia of Philosophy*.

39. Cooper, C. A., & Richardson, L. E. (2006). Institutions and representational roles in American state legislatures. *State Politics and Policy Quarterly, 6*(2), 174–194.

40. Pitkin, H. F. (1967). *The concept of representation*. Berkeley: University of California Press.

41. Dovi, S. (2017, Winter). Political representation.

42. Mansbridge, J. L. (1999). Should blacks represent blacks and women represent women? A contingent "yes." *Journal of Politics, 61*(3), 628–657.

43. Williams, M. (1998). *Voice, trust, and memory: Marginalized groups and the failure of liberal representation*. Princeton, NJ: Princeton University Press.

44. Ibid.

45. Young, I. M. (1986). *Deferring group representation*. New York: New York University Press.

46. Ibid., 351.

47. Dovi, S. (2009). In praise of exclusion. *Journal of Politics, 71*(3), 1172–1186.

48. Dovi, S. (2017, Winter). Political representation.

49. Phillips, A. (1995). *The politics of presence*. Oxford, UK: Oxford University Press.

50. Mansbridge, J. L. (2005). Quota problems: Combating the dangers of essentialism. *Politics & Gender, 1*(4), 622–638.

51. Jenkins, S. (2012). How gender influences roll call voting. *Social Science Quarterly, 93*, 415–432.

52. Karpowitz, C. F., & Mendelberg, T. (2015). *The silent sex: Gender, deliberation, and institutions*. Princeton, NJ: Princeton University Press.

53. Swers, M. L. 2002. *The difference women make: The policy impact of women in Congress*. Chicago, IL: University of Chicago Press.

54. Mansbridge, J. L. (1999). Should blacks represent blacks and women represent women? A contingent "yes."

55. Swers, M. L. 2002. *The difference women make: The policy impact of women in Congress*.

56. Ibid., 3.

57. Bauer, N. M. (2017). Gender stereotypes and voter evaluations of woman candidates. In A. L. Bos & M. C. Schneider (Eds.), *The political psychology of women in U.S. politics* (pp. 167–183). New York, NY: Routledge.

58. Burrell, B. (2014). *Gender in campaigns for the U.S. House of Representatives*. Ann Arbor: University of Michigan Press.

59. Carey, J. M., Niemi, R. G., & Powell, L. W. (1998). Are women state legislators different? In S. Thomas & C. Wilcox (Eds.), *Women and elective office: Past, present, and future* (pp. 87–108). New York, NY: Oxford University Press.

60. Dodson, D. L. (2006). *The impact of women in Congress*. New York, NY: Oxford University Press.

61. Dolan, J. (1997). Support for women's interests in the 103rd Congress: The distinct impact of Congressional women. *Women & Politics, 18*, 81–94.

62. Poggione, S. (2006). Women state legislators: Descriptive and substantive representation. In L. D. Whitaker (Ed.), *Women in politics* (pp. 182–198). Upper Saddle River, NJ: Pearson/Prentice Hall.

63. Swers, M. L. 2002. *The difference women make: The policy impact of women in Congress.*

64. Schwindt-Bayer, L. (2012). *Political power and women's representation in Latin America.* New York, NY: Oxford University Press.

65. Wängnerud, L. (2009). Women in Parliaments: Descriptive and substantive representation.

66. Ibid.

67. Reingold, B. (1992). Concepts of representation among men and women state legislators. *Legislative Studies Quarterly, 17,* 509–537.

68. Thomas, S. (1994). *How women legislate.* New York, NY: Oxford University Press.

69. Cooper, C. A., & Richardson, L. E. (2006). Institutions and representational roles in American state legislatures.

70. Katz, R. S. (1997). Representational roles. *European Journal of Political Science, 32*(2), 211–226.

71. Dolan, K., & Ford, L. E. (1998). Are all women state legislators alike?" In S. Thomas & C. Wilcox (Eds.), *Women and elective office: Past, present, and future* (pp. 73–82). New York, NY: Oxford University Press.

72. Richardson, L. E., &. Freeman, P. K. (1995). Gender differences in constituency services among state legislators. *Political Research Quarterly, 48*(1), 169–179.

73. Carroll, S. (2001). Representing women: State legislators as agents of policy-related change. In S. Carroll (Ed.), *The impact of women in public office* (pp. 3–21). Bloomington: University of Indiana Press.

74. Carey et al. (1998). Are women state legislators different?

75. Thomsen, D. M., & Sanders, B. D. (n.d.). Gender and representation: A tradeoff between constituency service and policy? *Gender Studies.* Retrieved from https://genderstudies.nd.edu/assets/253419/gender_and_representation_abstract.pdf.

76. Norris, P. (1996). Women politicians: Transforming Westminster?" *Parliamentary Affairs, 49*(1), 89–102.

77. Rodriguez-Garcia, M. J. (2015). Local women's coalitions: Critical actors and substantive representation in Spanish municipalities. *European Journal of Women's Studies, 22*(2), 223–240.

78. Devlin, C., & Elgie, R. (2008). The effect of increased representation in Parliament: The case of Rwanda. *Parliamentary Affairs, 61*(2), 237–254.

79. Esaiasson, P. (2000). Focus of representation." In P. Esaiasson & K. Heider (Eds.), *Beyond Westminster and Congress: The Nordic experience* (pp. 51–82). Columbus: Ohio State University Press.

80. Lazarus, J., and Steigerwalt, A. (2018). *Gendered vulnerability: How women work harder to stay in office*. Ann Arbor: University of Michigan Press.

81. Francis, W. L. 1989. *Legislative committee game: A comparative analysis of fifty states*. Columbus: Ohio State University Press.

82. Holman, M. R. (2014). *Women in politics in the American city*. Philadelphia, PA: Temple University Press.

83. Osborn, T. (2012). *How women represent women: Political parties, gender, and representation in state legislatures*.

84. Poggione, S. (2006). Women state legislators: Descriptive and substantive representation.

85. Thomas, S. (1994). *How women legislate*.

86. Bzdek, V. (2010). Why did health-care reform pass? Nancy Pelosi was in charge. *The Washington Post*. Retrieved from http://www.washingtonpost.com/wp-dyn/content/article/2010/03/26/AR2010032602225.html.

87. Pearson, K., & Dancey, L. (2011). Elevating women's voices in Congress: Speech participation in the House of Representatives. *Political Research Quarterly, 64*, 910–923.

88. Dietrich, B. J., Hayes, M., & O'Brien, D. Z. (2017). Pitch perfect: Vocal pitch and the emotional intensity of Congressional speech on women. Retrieved from http://www.brycejdietrich.com/files/working_papers/DietrichHayesOBrien.pdf.

89. Jones, S. (2012). Vaginagate: U.S. politician banned for saying "vagina" in abortion bill debate. *The Guardian*. Retrieved from https://www.theguardian.com/world/2012/jun/15/michigan-politician-banned-using-word-vagina.

90. Ibid.

91. Ibid.

92. Ibid.

93. Anzia, S. F., & Berry, C. R. (2011). The Jackie (and Jill) Robinson effect: Why do congresswomen outperform congressmen? *American Journal of Political Science, 55*(3), 478–493.

94. Bratton, K., & Haynie, K. L. (1999). Agenda setting and legislative success in state legislatures: The effects of gender and race. *The Journal of Politics, 61*, 658–679.

95. Jeydel, A., & Taylor, A. J. (2003). Are women less effective legislators? Evidence from the U.S. House in the 103rd-105th Congress. *Political Research Quarterly, 56*, 19–27.

96. Volden, C., Wiseman, A. E., and Wittmer, D. E. (2013). When are women more effective legislators than men? *American Journal of Political Science* 57, 326–341.

97. Jeydel, A., & Taylor, A. J. (2003). Are women less effective legislators? Evidence from the U.S. House in the 103rd-105th Congress.

98. McGill, A. (2016). Would electing more women fix Congress? *The Atlantic*. Retrieved from https://www.theatlantic.com/politics/archive/2016/08/would-electing-more-women-fix-congress/495989.

99. Volden, C., Wiseman, A. E., & Wittmer, D. E. (2016). Women's issues and their fate in Congress. *Political Science Research and Methods*, 1–18.

100. Gagliarducci, S., & Paserman, M. D. (2016). Gender differences in cooperative environments? Evidence from the U.S. Congress. Retrieved from http://www.nber.org/papers/w22488.

101. Anzia, S. F., & Berry, C. R. (2011). The Jackie (and Jill) Robinson effect: Why do Congresswomen outperform Congressmen?

102. Pearson, K., & Dancey, L. (2011). Elevating women's voices in Congress: Speech participation in the House of Representatives.

103. Chira, S. (2017). Nancy Pelosi, Washington's latest wicked witch. *The New York Times*. Retrieved from https://www.nytimes.com/2017/06/26/opinion/nancy-pelosi-washingtons-latest-wicked-witch.html.

104. *Center for American Women and Politics. (2019).* Women in state legislative leadership. Retrieved from http://cawp.rutgers.edu/sites/default/files/resources/stleg-leadership-2019.pdf.

105. Inter-Parliamentary Union. (2018). *Women Speakers of Parliament*. Retrieved from https://www.ipu.org/our-work/gender-equality/women-in-parliament/women-speakers-parliament.

106. Whicker, M. L., & Jewell, M. (1998). The feminization of leadership in state legislatures. In S. Thomas & C. Wilcox (Eds.), *Women and elective office: Past, present, and future* (pp. 163–174). New York, NY: Oxford University Press.

107. Frederick, B., & Jenkins, S. (2017). The impact of gender in the legislative process. In A. L. Bos & M. C. Schneider (Eds.), *The political psychology of women in U.S. politics* (pp. 205–220). New York, NY: Routledge.

108. Kathlene, L. (1989). Uncovering the political impacts of gender: An exploratory study.

109. Whicker, M. L., & Jewell, M. (1998). The feminization of leadership in state legislatures.

110. Kathlene, L. (1989). Uncovering the political impacts of gender: An exploratory study.

111. Rosenthal, C. S. (1998). Getting things done: Women committee chairpersons in state legislatures. In S. Thomas & C. Wilcox, *Women and elective office: Past, present, and future* (pp. 175–187). New York, NY: Oxford University Press.

112. Whicker, M. L., & Jewell, M. (1998). The feminization of leadership in state legislatures.

113. Karp, J. A., & Banducci, S. A. (2006). When politics is not just a man's game: Women's representation and political engagement. *Electoral Studies, 27*, 105–115.

114. Barnes, T. D., & Burchard, S. M. (2013). "Engendering" politics: The impact of descriptive representation on women's political engagement in Sub-Saharan Africa. *Comparative Political Studies, 46*(7), 767–790.

115. Wolbrecht, C., &. Campbell, D. E. (2007). Leading by example: Woman members of Parliament as political role models. *American Journal of Political Science, 51*, 921–939.

116. Campbell, D. E., & Wolbrecht, C. (2006). See Jane run: Women and political role models for adolescents. *Journal of Politics, 68*, 233–247.

117. Wolbrecht, C., & Campbell, D. E. (2017). Role models revisited: Youth, novelty, and the impact of woman candidates. *Politics, Groups, and Identities, 5*, 418–434.

118. Burns, N., Schlozman, K. L., & Verba, S. (2001). *The private roots of public action.* Cambridge, MA: Harvard University Press.

119. Brockman, D. (2014). Do woman politicians empower women to vote or run for office? A regression discontinuity approach. *Electoral Studies, 34*, 190–204.

120. Nagarajan, H. K., Deininger, K., & Jin, S. (2011). Can political reservations affect political equilibria in local elections in rural India? *Proceedings of the German Development Economics Conference, 59.*

121. Beaman, L., Duflo, E., Pande, R., & Topalova, P. (2012). Woman leadership raises aspirations and educational attainment for girls: A policy experiment in India. *Science, 335*(6068), 582–586.

122. Kathlene, L. (1994). Power and influence in state legislative policymaking: The interaction of gender and position in committee hearing debates. *American Political Science Review, 88*, 560–576.

123. Kathlene, L. (1998). In a different voice: Women and the policy process. In S. Thomas & C. Wilcox (Eds.), *Women and elective office: Past, present, and future* (pp. 188–202). New York, NY: Oxford University Press.

124. Heath, R. M., Schwindt-Bayer, L. A., & Taylor-Robinson, M. M. (2005). Women on the sidelines: Women's representation on committees in Latin America. *American Journal of Political Science, 49*, 420–436.

125. Volden, C., Wiseman, A. E., & Wittmer, D. E. (2016). Women's issues and their fate in Congress.

126. Wittmer, D. E., & Bouche, V. (2013). The limits of gendered leadership: Policy implications of woman leadership on "women's issues." *Politics & Gender 9*, 245–275.

127. Polaris Project. (2017). *Growing awareness, growing impact: 2017 statistics from the National Human Trafficking Hotline and Be Free Textline*. Retrieved from http://polarisproject.org/sites/default/files/2017NHTHStats percent20 percent281 percent29.pdf.

128. Wittmer, D. E., & Bouche, V. (2013). The limits of gendered leadership: Policy implications of woman leadership on "women's issues."

129. Ibid., 217.

130. Lieb, D. A. (2018). Most state legislatures have no public records on sex harassment. *Chicago Tribune*. Retrieved from http://www.chicagotribune.com/news/nationworld/ct-legislature-public-sex-harassment-records-20180411-story.html.

131. Stack, L. (2018). Black woman lawmaker in Vermont resigns after racial harassment. *New York Times*. Retrieved from https://www.nytimes.com/2018/09/26/us/politics/kiah-morris-vermont.html.

132. Jenkins, S. (2012). How gender influences roll call voting.

133. Wittmer, D. E., & Bouche, V. (2013). The limits of gendered leadership: Policy implications of woman leadership on "women's issues."

134. Jenkins, S. (2012). How gender influences roll call voting.

135. Heath, R. M., Schwindt-Bayer, L. A., & Taylor-Robinson, M. M. (2005). Women on the sidelines: Women's representation on committees in Latin America.

136. Yoder, J. D. (1991). Rethinking tokenism: Looking beyond numbers. *Gender and Society, 5*, 178–192.

137. Garboni, E. S. (2015). The impact of descriptive representation on substantive representation of women at European and national Parliamentary levels. Case study: Romania. *Procedia: Social and Behavioral Sciences, 183*, 85–92.

138. Kanter, R. M. (1977). *Men and women of the corporation*. New York, NY: Basic Books.

139. Dahlerup, D. (1988). From a small to a large minority: Women in Scandinavian politics. *Scandinavian Political Studies, 11*, 275–297.

140. Crowley, J. E. (2004). When tokens matter. *Legislative Studies Quarterly, 29,* 109–136.

141. Carroll, S. J. (2001). Representing women: State legislators as agents of policy-related change.

142. Grey, S. (2006). Numbers and beyond: The relevance of critical mass in gender research. *Politics & Gender, 2,* 492–502.

143. Childs, S., & Krook, M. L. (2008). Critical mass theory and women's political representation. *Political Studies, 56,* 725–736.

144. Childs, S., & Krook, M. L. (2006). Should feminists give up on critical mass? A contingent yes. *Politics & Gender, 4,* 522–530.

145. Grey, S. (2006). Numbers and beyond: The relevance of critical mass in gender research. *Politics & Gender, 2,* 492–502.

146. Carey et al. (1998). Are women state legislators different?

147. Skjeie, H. (1992). *The political importance of gender: A study of Norwegian top politics.* PhD. Institutt for samfunnsforskning.

148. Paxton, P., Kunovich, S., & Hughes, M. M. (2007). Gender in politics. *Annual Review of Sociology, 33,* 271–284.

149. Matland, R. 1993()0. Institutional variables affecting woman representation in national legislatures: The case of Norway. *The Journal of Politics, 55,* 737–755.

150. Sanbonmatsu, K. 2006. *Where women run: Gender and party in the American states.* Ann Arbor: University of Michigan Press.

151. Paxton, P., Kunovich, S., & Hughes, M. M. (2007). Gender in politics.

152. Ibid.

153. Ace Project. (n.d.). *About ACE.* Accessed March 9, 2018 at http://aceproject.org/about-en.

154. International Institute for Democracy and Electoral Assistance. (2009). *Gender quotas database.* Accessed March 9, 2018 at http://www.idea.int/data-tools/data/gender-quotas/quotas.

155. Ibid.

156. Sacchet, T. (2018). Why gender quotas don't work in Brazil? The role of the electoral system and political finance. *Colombia Internacional* (95), 25–54.

157. Dahlerup, D. (2009). What are quotas? Retrieved from https://www.idea.int/data-tools/data/gender-quotas/quotas#what.

158. International Institute for Democracy and Electoral Assistance. (2009). *Gender quotas database*.

159. Ballington, J., & Karam, A. (Eds.). (2005). *Women in Parliament: Beyond numbers, a revised edition (38)*. Stockholm: International IDEA.

160. Carrie Chapman Catt Center. (n.d.). *States with gender balance laws*. Accessed May 25, 2018 at https://iastate.app.box.com/v/GenderBalanceLaws.

161. Matland, R. R., & Brown, D. D. (1992). District magnitude's effect on woman representation in state legislatures. *Legislative Studies Quarterly 17*, 469–492.

162. Solomon, S. (2015). *The ripple effect of multi-member districts on women's representation*. Retrieved from http://www.representwomen.org/the_ripple_effect_of_multi_member_districts_on_women_s_representation.

163. American Association of University Women (AAUW). (2011). *Gender equality and the role of women in Cuban society*. Retrieved from http://www.aauw.org/files/2013/01/Cuba_whitepaper.pdf.

164. Pershall, K. (2017). Portraits of working women: Overcoming *"machismo"* in Cuba. *The Pioneer*. Retrieved from http://thepioneeronline.com/34450/study-abroad-cuba/essays/portraits-of-working-women-overcoming-machismo-in-cuba.

165. Ibid.

166. American Association of University Women (AAUW). (2011). *Gender equality and the role of women in Cuban society*.

167. Ibid.

168. Krull, C., & Davidson, M. (2011). Adapting to Cuba's shifting food landscapes: Women's strategies of resistance. In C. Krull, K. L. Stoner, G. M. Garcia, J. Stubbs (Eds.), *Rereading women and the Cuban Revolution, Cuban studies series* (pp. 59–77). Pittsburgh, PA: University of Pittsburgh Press.

169. Ibid.

170. Echarry, I. (2016). Cuba's strange *machismo*. *Havana Times*. Retrieved from https://www.havanatimes.org/?p=120694.

171. Vega, V. (2013). Cuba: The serious issue of *machismo*. *Havana Times*. Retrieved from http://www.havanatimes.org/?p=90110.

172. Echarry, I. (2016). Cuba's strange *machismo*.

173. Vega, V. (2013). Cuba: The serious issue of *machismo*.

174. Pershall, K. (2017). Portraits of working women: Overcoming *"machismo"* in Cuba.

175. American Association of University Women (AAUW). (2011). *Gender equality and the role of women in Cuban society.*

176. Ibid.

177. Warner, G. (2016). It's the No. 1 country for women in politics—But not in daily life. *NPR.* Retrieved from https://www.npr.org/sections/goatsandsoda/2016/07/29/487360094/invisibilia-no-one-thought-this-all-womans-debate-team-could-crush-it.

178. Ibid.

179. Ibid.

180. Ibid.

181. Ibid.

182. Ibid.

183. Ibid.

184. Ibid.

185. Heath, R. M., Schwindt-Bayer, L. A., & Taylor-Robinson, M. M. (2005). Women on the sidelines: Women's representation on committees in Latin America.

186. Paxton, P., Kunovich, S., & Hughes, M. M. (2007). Gender in politics.

187. Caygle, H. (2018). Women rule: Record-breaking number of women run for office. *Politico.* Retrieved from https://www.politico.com/story/2018/03/08/women-rule-midterms-443267.

188. Xaykaothao, D. (2016). Somali refugee makes history in U.S. election. *NPR.* Retrieved from https://www.npr.org/sections/goatsandsoda/2016/11/10/501468031/somali-refugee-makes-history-in-u-s-election.

189. Kanter, R. M. (1977). *Men and women of the corporation.*

190. Kathlene, L. (1994). Power and influence in state legislative policymaking: The interaction of gender and position in committee hearing debates.

191. Bennett, J. (2015). How not to be "manterrupted" in meetings. *Time.* Retrieved from http://time.com/3666135/sheryl-sandberg-talking-while-woman-manterruptions.

192. Eilperin, J. (2016). White House women want to be in the room where it happens. *Washington Post.* Retrieved from https://www.washingtonpost.com/news/powerpost/wp/2016/09/13/white-house-women-are-now-in-the-room-where-it-happens.

CHAPTER SEVEN

WOMEN IN THE EXECUTIVE

Former Australian Prime Minister Julia Gillard (2010–2013) gave her famous "Misogyny Speech" in 2012. The speech was a reaction to Tony Abbott, the opposition leader, who had suggested the unmarried and childless Gillard should "make an honest woman of herself." He also had appeared in photographs near protesters with signs identifying Gillard as a "bitch." Abbott, at other points in his career, had claimed women were "physiologically unsuited to leadership." For these reasons, Gillard, in her speech, stated that Abbott should look in a mirror if "he wants to know what misogyny looks like in modern Australia."[1] Prime Minister Gillard concluded her speech with the following refrain: "I think the best course for him [Abbott] is to reflect on the standards he's exhibited in public life … [he] should think seriously about the role of women in public life and in Australian society because we are entitled to a better standard than this."[2]

Gillard's experience illuminates the obstacles women experience in top executive offices. The United States has yet to see a woman president, and women did not become prime ministers and presidents of other countries in significant numbers until the 1990s. In that decade, 26 women served as executives worldwide as opposed to only seven in the 1980s.[3] Because women are rare in top executive positions, men like Tony Abbott are inclined to think women lack leadership skills and don't belong in these positions. When women do achieve top positions, their actions are thought of as being different, and perhaps inferior, to those of men. In this chapter, we explore how politicians, the media, and the public make these types of assumptions about women in executive positions.

We begin with a discussion of how gender stereotypes of leadership construct our understanding of the executive. We then document the descriptive representation of women in the executive in the United States and around the world. The final part of the chapter discusses whether and how executive institutions provide symbolic and substantive representation.

A few caveats are necessary. First, research about political executives is stymied by the lack of women who have campaigned for or occupied the highest political positions in their countries. With few women to study, it is difficult to evaluate whether women as executives advocate for women in ways that could constitute substantive representation. Second, because few women are in top positions, we also must look to other parts of the executive—such as cabinet positions and in women's policy agencies—to locate women leaders who are representing other women. We also look to women who are governors and mayors.

PATRIARCHY, MILITARY MASCULINITY, AND EXECUTIVE STEREOTYPES

Masculinity and femininity in the Western cultural tradition, though varied over time and place, are associated with opposing, binary gender stereotypes. A **stereotype** is a "cognitive structure that contains the perceiver's knowledge, beliefs, and expectations about human groups," and it allows people to make quick judgments about other people's characteristics and behavior.[4] Media perpetuate these stereotypes through gender framing, or interpretations of gender that are accentuated in media texts (see Chapters 3 and 5 for further discussion of framing).

In reality, gender is not binary nor fixed to one sex, but people tend to assume women and men respectively embody femininity and masculinity. Recall from Chapter 1 that masculinity is associated with toughness, rationality, seriousness, honor, and emotional constraint. Men are thought to be decisive or what political scientists refer to as **agentic**, that is, acting decisively and of their own volition. Femininity, on the other hand, is usually constructed and framed as emotional, soft, gentle, relational, compassionate, coquettish, and sometimes wily or scheming. These gender stereotypes feed into negative assumptions about and evaluations of women as political leaders. But, when and why did these contrasting stereotypes emerge, as they relate to political leaders?

The Enlightenment era (seventeenth and eighteenth centuries) is one source of masculine and feminine stereotypes. Gender stereotypes shaped who Enlightenment theorists, like Rousseau, thought was qualified to be citizens in emerging democracies. As discussed in Chapter 1, men were considered ideal citizens and leaders during the development of liberal democracy at the time of the Enlightenment. On the other hand, women during this era were not considered fit to be citizens.[5] Political revolutions in the United States and France occurred in the midst of the Enlightenment, and they, too, cemented opposing gender identities for women and men. The fact that fledgling democracies emerged from revolutions meant that military leadership became integrally linked to executive authority. Take the example of George Washington, a war general and the first president of the United States. Washington embodied American masculinity during the Revolution by being brave, honorable, and serious.[6,7] Even the way Washington appears in paintings, provokes the conception of a strong man. Roman Hinojosa (2007), a scholar of masculinity, explains,

> Cultural lore holds George Washington as a man of integrity. His admission to cutting down a cherry tree highlights the cultural value of honesty and accepting responsibility no matter the personal costs. As the leader of

American revolutionary forces, he is also the personification of American dedication and tenacity; faced with long odds, he is famed for leading an ill-trained, poorly equipped American Army to victory over what was then the mightiest military force on the planet. . . . Emanuel Leutze's famous painting, Washington Crossing the Delaware, depicts American troop movements before the battle [of Trenton]. More importantly, it captures the essence of Mr. Washington's character; he stands erect on the prow of the boat leaning slightly forward as it nears the shore. While others are huddled against the cold, anxiety on their faces, Washington appears serene as he intensely stares ahead, standing resolute against the strong, cold wind that tugs at his cape. One is left with the sense that he is unafraid of being spotted as he leads his troops into battle, a man who is eager to engage his enemy and does not fear the consequences.[8]

Despite a historical narrative focused on men as heroes, women were actively engaged in revolutions (see Chapter 2); for example, 16-year-old Sybil Ludington road over twice as far as Paul Revere on his midnight ride, on her own in dangerous territory, to raise troops for a battle. Women at this time, however, mostly were associated with the home front, as incipient national-

▶ **Photo 7.1** Emanuel Leutze's painting, *Washington Crossing the Delaware.*

isms emphasized that their reproductive capacity was essential to population growth.[9]

The connection between political leadership and the military also upholds the masculine and feminine binary. The strong masculinity of military men reflects what scholars call **hegemonic masculinity** or what is thought of as the ideal masculinity associated with able-bodiness, "physical size and strength, assertiveness, aggressiveness, and skills in warfare."[10] The aggressiveness of hegemonic masculinity, when associated with the military, is considered honorable because service members are virtuous warriors fighting for liberty, peace, and freedom.[11] By maintaining the security of the homeland, the virtuous warrior protects women who are stereotyped along with children as weak and in need of protection. The above example of George Washington displays how hegemonic masculinity is linked to military action and the U.S. presidency; Washington was strong in his appearance, did not show fear, and succeeded at warfare. In the United States, presidential "responsibilities" are "exceedingly 'masculine,' particularly regarding the president's role as commander in chief."[12,13] A president, as commander in chief and as the foremost foreign policy leader, must demonstrate "strength and an ability to command authority, act quickly, determinedly, and often unilaterally."[14,15]

Women do not fit the masculine expectations of the military and presidential leadership. Hegemonic masculinity is associated with white, heterosexual, cissexual men, and is expressly not associated with femininity.[16, 17] It becomes difficult to see a woman as a potential leader and protector of the country when she herself is thought of as in need of protection; this helps explain why some voters are still reluctant to cast a ballot for a woman presidential candidate, as described in Chapter 5 and later in this chapter. Moreover, though women have participated in militaries throughout history, their contributions have been "unseen," and their femininity belies military toughness (e.g., they have been military wives, camp followers, and laundresses).[18,19] A good example of stigmatized femininity in the military is the reaction to military women in uniform who breastfeed their babies.[20] The idea of a woman in uniform breastfeeding is shocking because military service is understood as masculine and breastfeeding upends "the notion that female soldiers must deny their female bodies" in order to serve.[21] Military women therefore face the lose-lose scenario called a **double bind**, that is, women being punished for acting on feminine stereotypes when masculine standards are expected as normal *and* for acting on masculine stereotypes because they are women who should be feminine (see Chapter 5 for more on how the double bind makes it difficult for women to serve in traditionally masculine roles). A servicewoman may choose to emphasize the masculine characteristics of toughness and downplay feminine characteristics that are stigmatized, but she also might feel obliged to act in traditionally feminine ways because military masculinity situates her as opposite from men.

Women political executives also face double binds. As we discuss later in the chapter, if a woman politician displays emotions, she violates the expectation that political executives should be tough and rational. However, if she is unemotional, she is judged as cold in demeanor. Women, therefore, need to be tough and rational to be leaders in the military or in politics, but they also need to be soft and emotional to maintain their likability as women.

GENDER STEREOTYPES IN LEADERSHIP AND THE PRESIDENCY: PUBLIC SUPPORT AND MEDIA

Given the stereotypes faced by women historically, it is not surprising that until recent decades the public has considered men better candidates for U.S. president than women. As we discussed in Chapter 5, the Gallup poll first asked the American public if it would vote for a woman president in 1937. At that time, approximately one third of the American public said yes.[22] From the late 1950s until the 1970s, about 50% to 55% of Americans answered that they would vote for a woman.[23] In the 1970s, over 70% of Americans were willing to vote for a woman, and, by the 1990s, over 90% of Americans answered the Gallup question in the affirmative. The last time the question was asked in 2015, 92% of Americans stated that they were willing to vote for a woman as president.[24]

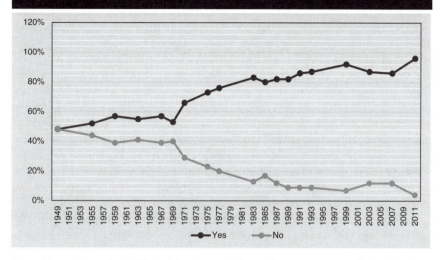

Figure 7.1 Vote for a Woman as President

Source: Roper Center for Public Opinion Research, https://ropercenter.cornell.edu/changing-attitudes-about-a-woman-president/.

With a high level of reported public support for voting for a woman as president, one might question why the United States has yet to elect a woman president. Explanations vary, as will be discussed in other sections of this chapter, but it might be that the public continues to hold gender stereotypes about leadership, or it simply does not prioritize having women as leaders. As described in Chapter 5, a list experiment in 2008 showed that even though respondents do not want to admit stereotypes to pollsters approximately "26 percent of the public is 'angry or upset' about the prospect of a female president."[25] Data from 2018 suggest that parts of the American public remain skeptical about the ability of women to reach high political offices. As discussed in Chapter 3, 59% of women (and 36% of men) think sex-based discrimination is a major obstacle to women in politics, and 69% of women (and 48% of men) believe there are too few women in top political offices. However, Republicans are less concerned than Democrats about women's representation. Only "44 percent of Republican women think there are too few women in high political offices, compared with 24 percent of Republican men. Among Democrats, majorities of men (73 percent) and women (84 percent) say there are too few women in these positions."[26] Therefore, a good share of voters do not prioritize having women in high political offices even as gender stereotypes appear to be waning, and *most* people are supportive of women in higher office.[27]

Women Leaders and Gender Stereotypes

Psychology experiments and analyses of public opinion provide further evidence that the public buys into gender stereotypes related to leadership. When researchers ask subjects in experiments about jobs that are thought of as masculine (for example, doctor, lawyer, soldier, firefighter), the subjects do not prefer women for those jobs.[28] Moreover, in 1992, Alice H. Eagly and her colleagues asked whether women are "evaluated less favorably than men when performing leadership and managerial behaviors."[29] Their findings indicate that, yes, when subjects are presented with a scenario in which a woman is a leader, they judge her in a way that they do not judge men. Subjects prefer men leaders for masculine jobs,[30] and men subjects more favorably rate men leaders.[31] This means women are rated lower than men when they do masculine jobs or demonstrate masculine leadership traits, which are identified as "being independent, masterful, assertive, and instrumentally competent."[32] Subjects do not like women acting like men but instead prefer **gender-role congruency**, or when "leaders behave in a manner that is congruent with gender-role expectations."[33] The leadership traits that are expected out of women are "communal attributes, including being friendly, unselfish, concerned with others, and emotionally expressive."[34]

These expectations would be tricky for a woman leader to embody, and especially a president, because subjects in experiments also believe that women leaders in work contexts are too emotional when making decisions and subsequently rate them negatively.[35] Brescoll (2016) presented subjects with scenarios in which women and men are making decisions and seeking employment. She did not mention the emotional state of the decision-makers; however, "participants viewed the female leader's (identical) decision as fundamentally worse than her male counterpart's decision" because they inferred that the woman was emotional, and, as a result, they "were also less willing to hire her."[36] Why do these findings matter for presidential politics? If women are expected to be emotional but are judged negatively for it, they are presented with a double bind. Also, if women are not expected to be agentic, that is, competent and assertive, and actually are judged negatively when they are, they are likely to be critiqued and rejected.[37] Research by Okimoto and Brescoll (2010) suggest that women politicians can begin to overcome negative judgements associated with being tough by concurrently expressing the stereotyped feminine traits of warmth and sensitivity.[38]

Political science studies from the 1970s, 1980s, and early 1990s[39–44] corroborate these findings. In an experiment evaluating hypothetical candidates for office, Huddy and Terkildsen (1993) ask if masculine personality traits and competence with masculine issues, for example, the military or economy, were thought of as essential for leaders.[45] They found that having feminine traits like compassion does not privilege candidates for legislative and executive positions at any administrative level, but also that feminine traits did not hurt national candidates. Military competence was important for national office, whether legislative or executive. Furthermore, masculine traits were important for all candidates, presidential candidates included.

Public opinion following September 11, 2001, also proves the influence of masculine stereotypes on the U.S. presidency. Jennifer L. Lawless (2004) reports that 28% of respondents in 2002 were "unsure whether they are willing to vote for a woman."[46] Most respondents in her study wanted an elected official who is self-confident (70%) and assertive (63%), and "more than one-quarter of respondents did not believe that men and women in politics are equally likely to be self-confident." She continues,

> About 50 percent think that men and women are not equally assertive and tough.
>
> More than 35 percent of sample respondents assert that men are more competent than women when it comes to punishing those responsible for the September 11th attacks. Forty percent believe that men are better able than women to protect the United States from future attacks. And 30 percent of the individuals in the sample contend that men in politics are superior to women when it comes to bringing about peace in the Middle East.[47]

Furthermore, Lawless's analysis shows that respondents who believe men are more capable leaders regarding terrorism are less likely to want to vote for a woman president.

Stereotypes about women's emotions and traits are substantial as well. Data show that almost a fifth of the American public (19%) agree to some extent that women are not emotionally suited to be president.[48] Similarly, data from a 2008

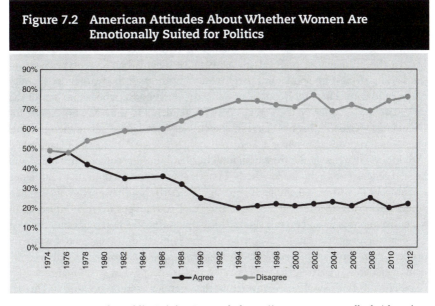

Figure 7.2 American Attitudes About Whether Women Are Emotionally Suited for Politics

Source: Roper Center for Public Opinion Research, https://ropercenter.cornell.edu/changing-attitudes-about-a-woman-president

public opinion survey demonstrate that about one fifth of respondents (21%) think men make better political leaders than women. These same respondents feel "that women (85 percent), not men (5 percent), are the more emotional sex, and by a two-to-one margin they say women (52 percent) rather than men (26 percent) are more manipulative."[49] These data also show that the public rates men better than women on the political leadership trait of decisiveness. On the other hand, the public believes women exceed men on the leadership traits of honesty, intelligence, compassion, creativity, and outgoingness.[50]

Recent political science research shows that the public is becoming less likely to stereotype. Deborah Jordan Brooks (2013), in the book *He Runs, She Runs: Why Gender Stereotypes Do Not Harm Women Candidates*, argues that gender stereotypes exist but do not limit women's performance in elections. Her survey experiments show that women and men face similar expectations for public office, including the presidency, and that the public rates their traits, including emotions, similarly.[51] Even when Brooks presented the respondents with a mock news story about a man or woman candidate crying or demonstrating anger, the ratings were equal. Crying makes candidates—women or men—appear less strong and unable to handle international crises in the eyes of respondents. Women are considered more emotional when they demonstrate anger, but women aren't rated as bad politicians for doing so. Dolan and Lynch (2016), using public opinion data from 2010, argue that overall gender stereotypes are lessening over time, with women and men being judged equally as consensus oriented and women being judged more intelligent than men.[52] In their study, some people see men as more able to handle national security (42%) and the economy (18%), but this male-stereotyped policy expertise does not influence whether voters choose a man or woman candidate.

Why do we find the wavering influence of gender stereotypes? First, it might be that the influence of political parties is more salient than stereotypes, and, in statistical analyses, a respondent's party matters more than the sex/gender identity of the candidate. That is, a Republican wants to vote for a Republican no matter the candidate's sex/gender or the voter's views on gender, and the same holds true for Democrats.[53] Second, Brooks suggests the "leaders-not-ladies" phenomenon. This phenomenon poses that when a woman becomes a leader, and is well established with experience, the public stops assigning her feminine stereotypes of "ladies" and instead judges her as the leader she is. Whether stereotypes continue to influence elections is, therefore, debatable. If voters in the 2010s hold fewer stereotypes than voters in previous decades, it can be argued that stereotypes make a difference in fewer electoral races and do not significantly determine election outcomes for *most* women who are candidates.[54] Nevertheless, the public's misgivings about women's propensity toward emotions or lack of decisiveness could be consequential in presidential elections, in which victories in key states are decided by small margins.

Scholars find much more evidence that gender stereotypes survive in the media. As discussed in Chapter 5, media employ gender frames that construct women's identities and actions. The media tend to discuss women politicians more than men when they report on political issues perceived to be less important (such as education) and culture, while stories about men politicians center on issues perceived to be more important in the political domain (such as economics, foreign policy, or terrorism).[55] Women in politics have been covered less often and more negatively.[56] Instead of discussing a woman candidate's major issues and ideas, the media tend to focus on her appearance, personality, and family.[57] Though women in recent years receive more media coverage than they used to and the press does not always discuss their appearance, media often continue to emphasize women's personal traits over political issues.[58] Women governors, especially, received media attention about their personal lives at the start of their terms.[59] When the media focus on women as physically attractive, as mothers, or as not interested in issues such as terrorism or the economy, they are framed as being too feminine or unprepared to be president.

We focus here on the examples of Sarah Palin, as a vice presidential candidate in 2008; Australian Prime Minister Julia Gillard, discussed in the introduction to the chapter; and Hillary Rodham Clinton, a candidate for U.S. president in both 2008 and 2016. Blatant sexism toward Palin and Clinton appeared in mainstream media in 2008, and even trustworthy media sources, such as *The Washington Post* and *The New York Times*, used sexualized language to discuss Palin as she ran for the vice-presidency. Media also regularly and prominently discussed Palin as a "a 44-year-old mother of five."[60] Sarah Palin and Hillary Clinton were also judged on their fashion choices, and Clinton was pegged as an "Iron Lady." (See Table 7.1 as well as Chapter 5 for a discussion of iron ladies.)

Table 7.1 Sarah Palin and Hillary Clinton Media Frames in 2008

Candidate	Focus	Media Comment	Source (Author/ Commentator)	Date
Palin	Beauty Queen Experience	"Palin entered the Miss Wasilla beauty pageant and won, playing the flute for her talent. She went on to compete for Miss Alaska and was a runner up."	*The Washington Post* (Amy Goldstein and Michael D. Shear)	August 30, 2008
Palin	Clothing	"Palin seems to dress for pretty rather than powerful."	*The Washington Post* (Robin Givhan)	September 28, 2008

(Continued)

(Continued)

Palin	Sexiness	"Men want a sexy woman. Women want to idealize about a sexy woman. . . . Women want to be her; men want to mate with her."	*CNBC* (Donny Deutsch)	September 5, 2008
Palin	Youth	"Palin can seem like the young, trophy running mate."	*ABC* (David Wright)	September 3, 2008
Palin	Mother	"Adding to the brutality of a national campaign, the Palin family also has an infant with special needs. What leads you, the Senator, and the Governor to believe that one won't affect the other in the next couple of months?"	*ABC's Good Morning America* (Bill Weir)	August 30, 2008
Clinton	Sexiness	"There was cleavage on display Wednesday afternoon on C-SPAN2. It belonged to Sen. Hillary Clinton. She was talking on the Senate floor about the burdensome cost of higher education. She was wearing a rose-colored blazer over a black top. The neckline sat low on her chest and had a subtle V-shape."	*The Washington Post* (Robin Givhan)	July 20, 2007

Clinton	Clothing	"By the time this column appears in print, the Post's fashion maven, Robin Gavhen, might well have done a feature on the front-running Democrat's attire, discreetly sidestepping a reference to her frequent wearing of dark pants suits that conceal her bottom-heavy figure."	*The Oklahoman* (Robert Haught)	February 2, 2007
Clinton	Mother	"I always thought of Hillary as the Ma Barker of the Clinton gang in those years. . . . Well, there are a lot of Ma Barkers in northern Ohio just now and across the U.S. With the economy on edge, their lives stressed and their men moping, these women are the ones who've got to suck it up and hold the house together until the troubles fade."	*The Wall Street Journal* (Daniel Henninger)	March 6, 2008
Clinton	Iron Lady	"When she comes on television, I involuntarily cross my legs."	*MSNBC* (Tucker Carlson)	July 16, 2007

Whereas the media focused on Palin's perceived femininity, media fixated on gender-role incongruity in the case of Prime Minister Gillard,[61] or, rather, how she did not conform to feminine expectations. Recall Gillard's misogyny speech; she is known for being assertive and ambitious. The media suggested that women voters would not like these traits because they do not come across as feminine; however, the media also argued that her "ruthlessness" and likeable "Aussie blokey," or masculine, "quality" would help her be a better executive.[62] Gillard thus faced a double bind: She was praised for acting like a man but also critiqued for it. Media discussed her more positively when her ambitiousness could be tied to the feminine traits of cooperation and care.

Gender stereotypes can cut both ways for women candidates; for example, Hillary Rodham Clinton has been politically punished *and* rewarded for displays of emotion. In the 2008 election cycle, Clinton generally projected a powerful and tough demeanor, even to the point of seeming unfeminine or impersonal.[63,64] However, when a photographer, before the New Hampshire primary, asked her to describe the pressures of campaigning, she answered, "It's not easy," and she paused and choked up. Clinton went on to win the primary, and many think her display of emotion advantaged her.[65] However, it presented a double bind because although it made her more likeable and human, it also elicited a sense of incompetence and sharp critiques from pundits.[66]

Hillary Clinton also fought stereotypes during her time as secretary of state (2009–2013). Clinton was secretary of state in 2011 when American forces captured and killed Osama bin Laden, and she was present in the Situation Room at the time, where policy leaders watched the raid and where a famous photo was taken.[67] In the photo Clinton appears to be gasping out of emotion with her hand over her mouth, and, though she claimed she was coughing, the media framed her as acting emotionally. In a content analysis of 201 articles, the press attributed emotion to Clinton more so than the men in the room with her, even though the moment was tense and stressful for all of those involved. What is more, the press believed she showed extreme emotion, to the point of being timid, and that her eyes "tell the entire story." This is curious given that Clinton was one of the strongest proponents of the raid and that she is often charged with showing little emotion or being cold.[68]

The 2016 presidential campaign provides a third example of Clinton's perceived emotionalism and public and media responses to it. It is well-known that Clinton made an attempt to show warmth and emotions in her 2016 campaign. She embraced the label of grandmother, and, in one instance, she released an advertisement in which she comforted a young Latina girl, who says she is scared her parents will be deported.[69] In response to this ad, she was mocked for crying

The White House via Flickr

▶ **Photo 7.2** Situation room photo, taken on May 1, 2011.

"crocodile tears" and was labeled a potential "worrier-in-chief."[70] In the You-Tube video "Hillary Clinton Crying Compilation," posted in May of 2016, Clinton is portrayed as an emotional woman who cannot handle herself. The video is set to dismal music, and it rapidly presents clips of Clinton reacting to political and social issues throughout her career. Viewers are not meant to sympathize with Clinton but instead mock her for overemotionalism and weakness.

Donald Trump received more positive media coverage than Clinton even though many argue he was the more emotional candidate of 2016. Trump as a candidate and as president has used anger in public speeches and on Twitter to convey whatever is on his mind. He does so in order to be a "straight shooter," and his base considers his emotionalism to be appealing.[71,72] Combined "ratings from 75 domestic and international experts in US politics and elections" judged the candidate Trump as lacking emotional stability and being disagreeable.[73] Clinton, oppositely, was rated as emotionally stable, though cold in demeanor. We argue that it is possible for President Trump to succeed while being disagreeable because his anger dovetails with the expectations of hegemonic masculinity. When the presidency is stereotyped as masculine and tough, Trump's anger translates as an admirable trait.

BOX 7.1: DONALD TRUMP "DOING GENDER" BY USING GENDER FRAMES

Politicians, like the media, invoke gender frames to present themselves and their opponents in a gendered light.[74] For instance, Hillary Clinton attempted to soften her image in 2016 by using the "mother frame" to emphasize her caring nature. Another way to say that politicians invoke gender frames is to use the terminology of **"doing gender,"** which means a person conveys and constructs gender in everyday social situations.[75] Donald Trump is a politician, and now president, who uses traditional and social media to "do gender." By drawing upon the mother and seductress frames presented in Chapter 5, we summarize how Trump, as a candidate and president, discusses women, and particularly, his political opponents. We conclude with the candidate Trump's use of the **marginalized masculinity frame**, defined as references to men that call attention to how they do not meet the expectations of hegemonic masculinity.[76]

Trump frames women as attractive and sexy or points out when they are not. By casting women as physically beautiful and feminine (or not), he assigns

(Continued)

(Continued)

women's worth in terms of their appearances. For example, in *Rolling Stone* magazine, he said of Carly Fiorina, his political opponent in the Republican primaries, "Look at that face. Would anybody vote for that?" The implication here is that a lack of physical beauty hinders a woman's political trajectory. He called a political aide in his administration, Omarosa Manigault Newman, a dog, and he said Arianna Huffington, a businesswoman and news columnist, was "unattractive both inside and out." An example of him praising a woman's looks involves the first lady of France. He told Brigitte Macron in 2017, "You know, you're in such good shape," and he then told her husband, President Emmanuel Macron, she is "beautiful." Brigitte Macron is older than her husband; thus, Trump's comment can be interpreted as related to her age. His comments to the Macrons show his prioritization of a women's appearance, and its maintenance into middle-age, but also suggest that a woman's appearance is a matter of consideration for men, for he made his "beautiful" comment to Emmanuel Macron as if it were a compliment for him to "have" a wife that looks good.

The mother frame discussed in Chapter 5 is similar to the **private lives frame**, or a frame that emphasizes women's work in the home and for her family.[77] On several occasions, Trump has suggested women and men's private lives should be distinct or that women's private lives should not transverse the public sphere. For instance, he has said, "I think that putting a wife to work is a very dangerous thing." Also, he believes women should do child rearing: "I like kids. . . . I won't do anything to take care of them. I'll supply funds and she'll take care of the kids." He once told a lawyer of his, when she had to leave the room to pump breastmilk, "You're disgusting, you're disgusting." The implication here is that the private task of breastfeeding does not belong in the public sphere of employment.

Trump does not reserve his sharp comments for women. He also denigrated his opponents who were men during the Republican primaries for their supposed lack of masculinity. Trump made fun of Senator Marco Rubio (R-FL) for his small stature, by calling him by the pet name of Lil' Marco and evaluating his shoe choice: "I don't know what to think of those boots. . . . It helps to be tall. . . . I don't know, they're big heels. They're big heels." Trump also claimed Jeb Bush was "low energy." What did he mean by this? He had previously called Hillary Clinton "low energy," and Trump's surrogates, and some campaign ads, implied to the press that low energy meant "low T," as in low testosterone.[78] In contrast, Trump framed himself as a large man with high testosterone.

DESCRIPTIVE REPRESENTATION
IN PARTS OF THE EXECUTIVE

Because we want to know the extent of women's descriptive representation, that is, where women are located and serving in the executive branch, and how women's descriptive representation in the United States compares to other countries, we start this section with definitions of executive positions.

The top executive post in the United States is the president, whereas a prime minister is what the top political leader in many other countries is called. What's the difference? Presidents are the foremost leaders of presidential systems, and prime ministers govern in parliamentary systems. In **presidential systems** a president is directly elected by the people (though sometimes through an electoral college) for a fixed term of time, whereas in a **parliamentary system** the prime minister is elected from the parliament, that is, the legislature, and is beholden to the legislature, which can remove the prime minister in given circumstances. The job of a president is typically broader and more powerful than that of the prime minister. In the United States, as in other presidential systems, the president is the head of state and head of government at the same time. The **head of state** is an apolitical role, wherein the president acts as a symbolic representative of his or her country. As head of state, a president, for example, gives speeches in times of crisis and meets with foreign dignitaries. The **head of government** is a political role, where a public official serves as a policy leader. As the head of government, the president is not neutral but brokers deals and promotes policy change in line with her or his political party. The president of the United States is also a commander in chief and chief administrator, respectively leading the armed forces and sitting above all cabinet departments and the bureaucracy. A prime minister is only a head of government, the top minister amongst her or his cabinet ministers. In parliamentary systems, a second executive exists as a head of state, and that person might be a monarch or what is called a president, such as in Italy or Germany. Worldwide, both in presidential and parliamentary systems, executives are becoming more influential vis-à-vis their cabinets and legislatures. This shift means executives are the center of power in most countries, and the judicial and legislative institutions that might challenge them are hard pressed to reign in the executive.

In the United States, cabinet positions are situated under the presidency and called departments, but in other countries, they are called ministries. Women and men who lead cabinet departments in the United States are called secretaries, and in other countries, the equivalent position is that of a minister. A cabinet secretary (or minister) arguably is more essential to policymaking than any individual legislator.[79] A minister works directly to develop the policy ideas desired by the executive, whereas a legislator works in cooperation with many other legislators to pass policy. In many countries, unlike the United States, the executive branch proposes legislation rather than the legislature itself, making it so that the legislature mostly works on the executive's and cabinet's agenda. Even in the Unites States, the president through the executive departments, can unilaterally change how policy is carried out. For instance, during 2018, the Secretary of Education, Betsy DeVos, worked to change federal sexual harassment requirements on college campuses to give more rights to the accused and to colleges themselves. Therefore, when women occupy positions in the cabinet, they have significant policy influence and control over resources.

Given patriarchy, women are not expected to hold the most power in any society, and women often succeed in executive positions that are perceived as less powerful, as described in each section below. But recall, institutional context is essential because the authority granted to presidents and prime ministers can vary significantly across countries.

Women in Top Executive Positions: The United States and Comparative Perspective

Because no woman has been president of the United States, or vice president for that matter, there has been no descriptive representation for women in terms of the top executive position in the United States. That is, women have never "stood in" at this level to represent other women. Since the 1960s, however, women from major parties have been candidates in presidential primaries and caucuses (see Table 7.2), yet only Hillary Rodham Clinton has won a major party primary election and ran on the top of a presidential ticket in a general election.

Table 7.2 Women Presidential Candidates From Major Parties

Name	Party	Year
Margaret Chase Smith	Republican	1964
Shirley Anita Chisholm	Democrat	1972
Patsy Takemoto Mink	Democrat	1972
Ellen McCormack	Democrat	1976, 1980
Michele Bachmann	Republican	2012
Elizabeth Hanford Dole	Republican	2000
Carol Moseley Braun	Democrat	2004
Hillary Rodham Clinton	Democrat	2008, 2016
Carly Fiorina	Republican	2016

Source: Data from http://www.cawp.rutgers.edu/facts/levels_of_office/federal_executive.

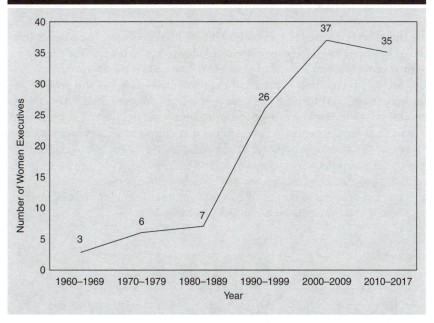

Figure 7.3   Number of Women Executives Worldwide, 1960–2017

Source: Jalalzai, F. (2018). Hillary Clinton's 2016 presidential bid—A gendered and comparative perspective. *Socius: Sociological Research for a Dynamic World, 4,* 1-11. https://doi .org/10.1177/2378023117732441.

Women have run in the general election as vice presidential candidates twice: Geraldine Ferraro in 1984 and Sarah Palin in 2008.

Descriptive representation of women in the top executive positions is more promising worldwide. Farida Jalalzai's (2018) research details trends since the 1960s and explains why some countries, like the United States, have yet to see a woman president or prime minister.

The first woman political executive in the world was Sirimavo Bandaranaike, who was prime minister of Sri Lanka, first in 1960 but also for terms in the 1970s and 1990s. As of January 2017, 114 different women have been either a president or prime minister of a country. There have been more prime ministers than presidents who were women (57% versus 43%), even though more countries have presidential systems with presidents. Women have been the top executive in countries in most world regions. Europe has elected many women to top executive positions, but Latin America and Asia have also had a great deal of women serving as presidents or prime ministers (see Box 7.2 about Latin America).

Why do we find women as top executives in some countries and regions more than in others? Jalalzai posits the following trends regarding women in the highest office in the land.[80] First, women rarely obtain executive positions associated with the greatest amount of political power. As explained above, presidents are more institutionally powerful than prime ministers; thus, women have occupied presidencies to a lesser degree than prime ministerships. Women are more likely to occupy a presidency if it is in a country where power is shared with a prime minister. Furthermore, some women who have been president, like Mary Robinson of Ireland (1990–1997), were not incredibly powerful because the presidency of their country serves as head of state and the position is mostly ceremonial.

Second, the position of president in presidential systems is also problematic for women aspirants because it is popularly elected. Women candidates in these systems must compete twice: in primaries and in a general election. Elections costs a great deal, thereby necessitating resources that women often lack in comparison to men, as described in Chapter 5. Prime ministers, on the other hand, arise from the legislature itself. One exception to these trends, is Latin America, where presidents are popularly elected, do not share power with a prime minister, and thus are both head of state and head of government. In Latin America, many women have served as president in recent decades (see Box 7.2).

BOX 7.2: COMPARATIVE FEATURE

Latin American Women Presidents

Latin American women serving as elected presidents seems unlikely for a number of reasons. First, the presidencies of Latin America tend to be very institutionally powerful. Second, the social and political culture of Latin America is sexist, or, typical of what is called *machismo*. **Machismo** is a word that describes a tough and aggressive masculinity, and political leaders, including many dictators in Latin America's past, have had this trait. Women in Latin America are more likely to be thought of in terms of **marianismo**, or the pure and moral attributes associated with the Virgin Mary. Nevertheless, behind Europe, Latin America and Asia are the world regions with the most women having served as political executives (see Table 7.3).

How is this so? Reasons for women's political success include the social acceptance of women as mothers who lead, the positive impact of gender quotas, and the wave of leftist leadership in recent decades. Women do not fit the expectations of machismo, but they are accepted as political leaders when they have a maternal touch. In 1979, Elsa Chaney labeled this the **supermadre phenomenon**—that a woman politician succeeds because it is believed she can "tend to the needs of her big family in the larger casa of the municipality or even the nation."[81] Women also might be accepted in Latin American politics if they are related to or somehow connected to powerful men in politics,

Table 7.3 Women Presidents in Latin America

Name	Country	Years Served
Isabel "Isabelita" Perón	Argentina	1974–1976
Lidia Gueiler Tejada	Bolivia	1979–1980
Ertha Pascal-Trouillot	Haiti	1990–1991
Violeta Barrios de Chamorro	Nicaragua	1990–1997
Rosaliá Arteaga	Ecuador	1997
Janet Jagan	Guyana	1997–1999
Mireya Elisa Moscoso	Panama	1999–2004
Michelle Bachelet	Chile	2006–2010, 2014–2018
Cristina Fernández de Kirchner	Argentina	2007–2015
Laura Chinchilla	Costa Rica	2010–2014
Dilma Rousseff	Brazil	2011–2016

much like the widow's succession in the United States described in Chapter 6. This is true of the first women presidents in Latin America. Isabel Perón was the first woman president of the region and of Argentina (1974–1976), and she was the widow of the country's demagogic political leader and past president, Juan Perón. Violeta Chamorro became president of Nicaragua in 1990, and she did so by invoking the image of a mother and widow, for she had been married to Pedro Chamorro, a famous activist who had been assassinated. To mimic the Virgin Mary, she wore white clothing and a crucifix. Chamorro represented *marianismo* and maternal leadership in an era when Nicaragua needed stability and peace. More recently, Cristina Fernández de Kirchner governed Argentina (2007–2015) after winning the presidency by assuring the continuity of her husband's policies. Néstor Kirchner preceded Fernández as president (2003–2007), but she had political experience of her own, as an elected representative in a regional legislature and in the national Senate.

Other recent women presidents in the region do not have family ties to politics nor do they embody *marianismo*. Michelle Bachelet of Chile is the daughter of a military general, and she is a mother, but, as a divorcee and atheist, she does not fit the strict mold of Catholic womanhood. She does have previous expertise that qualified her for the presidency. She is a medical

(Continued)

doctor and had been a health minister as well as a defense minister. Dilma Rousseff of Brazil also had substantial political experience before winning the presidency. She was a left-wing resistance fighter during the Brazilian dictatorship of the 1960s. Before becoming president, she was chief of staff to President Luiz Inácio Lula de Silva (2003–2011) and an energy minister (2003–2005). Some have argued that her relationship to the powerful ex-president "Lula" made it possible for her to obtain the presidency, yet her rise to politics is nonetheless notable given that women are very much underrepresented in the Brazilian political system.

Brazil is indeed an outlier in the region, with very weak gender quota laws and only about 11% of women in its lower legislature as of 2018 (see Chapter 6). Many countries in the region have strong quota laws, and women hold more than 35% of legislative seats in Bolivia, Costa Rica, Ecuador, Mexico, and Nicaragua. This is likely another reason why women have been able to ascend to the presidencies of Latin America. Quotas create a pipeline of women politicians who gain expertise and name recognition and are able to run for higher office. It also must be noted that Chile, like Brazil, lacks effective quotas; thus, Bachelet's rise to power cannot be attributed to quotas.

Scholars also have argued that women have succeeded as president in Latin America because they favored the social reform policies that marked an era of leftist government in the region during the 2000s and beyond.[82] This era provided a political opportunity for women, but it has ended, and the region is shifting in a rightward direction. As of late 2018, women presidents—Bachelet, Rousseff, Fernández—are no longer in power, although Bachelet is serving in the United Nations as the High Commissioner on Human Rights. In Brazil, backlash to women's empowerment is evident. The president who came into office in 2019, Jair Bolsonaro, is a right-wing, former military officer who makes disparaging comments about women and minorities, to the point of belittling the seriousness of rape and femicide.

In what ways have women presidents in Latin America made a difference? These women were trailblazers who set an example for the next generation of Latin American leaders. They also favored some policies that influence women's lives. Bachelet addressed women's education, women's healthcare, and abortion, and Rousseff favored policies to help women in poverty. On the other hand, Fernández was critiqued by feminists for her lackluster advocacy of women's rights. Additionally, several of these presidents found themselves in political controversies that are typical of Latin American political systems. Rousseff was impeached in 2016 after numerous scandals. Bachelet's approval ratings, once very high, fell when her son was implicated in illegal real estate deals. Meanwhile, Fernández, accused of money laundering, was being investigated as of 2018.

An explanation for women's success in occupying the position of prime minister is tied to the consensus-orientation of parliamentary systems. Presidential systems are based on conflict, as the executive and legislature are separate institutions expected to check and balance each other's power; whereas the legislature and executive are fused in a parliamentary system, with the same party leading both, thus making policymaking faster and more cooperative. As we know from the earlier discussion, women are stereotyped as cooperative; hence, it is thought that they may fare better in the parliamentary environment as a "collaborative" prime minister rather than as a "conflictual" president. Furthermore, gender quotas are common in parliamentary systems (see Chapter 6), and this creates a pipeline of experienced women candidates who could become a prime minister.[83]

These institutional explanations must be held in balance with the enormous influence of family connections in politics. Women often succeed in countries in which a politician's success is tied to a family political dynasty. A good example of this is Benazir Bhutto who served as prime minister of Pakistan from 1993 to 1996 and 1988 to 1990 and was hoping to become prime minister again in 2008. Bhutto's father, Zulfikar Ali Bhutto, founded a prominent political party and served as both prime minister (1973–1977) and president (1971–1973). Many believed Benazir Bhutto would become prime minister after the 2008 elections, but she was assassinated by a suicide bomber in late 2007. Family connections can supersede cultural and structural variables that impede women candidates. Bhutto, as well as Indira Gandhi from India (prime minister 1966–1977, 1980–1984), come from countries where women do not have the same educational opportunities as men, and patriarchal views persists, yet they demonstrate that elite women from prominent families can leverage their class status to achieve political success. Family connections serve as a primary explanation for women's success in top executive positions in Asia.

Women typically do not reach top executive positions when a country is powerful internationally, and, particularly, when it is a nuclear power. These countries are thought of as global leaders with extreme power, and women "seldom join this even more exclusive club of leaders."[84] On the other hand, post-conflict contexts provide an opportunity for women's election to the executive, because people often surmise that men cause and fight wars, but women are able to mend a country and set it back on track. Rhetoric reinforcing these assumptions was present in the election of Ellen Johnson Sirleaf in Liberia. She served as president from 2006 to 2018, and she represented a change from the warlord leadership that mired Liberia in civil wars from the late 1980s into the 2000s.

Applying these generalities to the United States helps explain why it has failed to elect a woman president. The United States has a presidential system, which requires candidates to compete in primaries and general elections and expects the executive and legislature to check one another's power. The U.S. president does not share power with a prime minister but is instead both head of state and head of government. Further, the United States is a nuclear power and a world leader.

Because the U.S. president is perceived as a powerful executive, a woman might struggle to convince the public she is capable of fighting terrorism, maintaining the country's status as a global power, and being tough enough to navigate a divided government. We see this concern with Hillary Clinton, who was thought to be "tough" in terms of personality but was judged by her challenger Donald Trump as being too weak and beset by health problems to fight terrorism. He once stated that Clinton "lacks the mental and physical stamina to take on ISIS, and all the many adversaries we face—not only in terrorism, but in trade and every other challenge we must confront to turn this country around."[85] Family connections are sometimes present in U.S. politics, with multiple famous political families such as the Bushes, Clintons, and Kennedys; however, the American public often is critical of political hopefuls who rely on family connections. In the case of Hillary Clinton, a family connection to former president Bill Clinton hurt her with many Democratic, blue collar voters who blamed the North American Free Trade Agreement (NAFTA), one of Bill Clinton's significant achievements from the 1990s, for the erosion of high-paying, unionized manufacturing jobs in the Midwest. With these factors in mind, it becomes clearer why women in the United States have been less successful in the executive than women elsewhere in the world.

WOMEN IN CABINETS: THE UNITED STATES AND IN COMPARATIVE PERSPECTIVE

Women are not equally represented in cabinets in the United States and worldwide, and they do not tend to occupy cabinet positions in the **inner cabinet**, or the cabinet positions on which the executive most relies. The inner cabinet in the United States includes the departments of state, treasury, and justice. The inner cabinet is associated with masculinity in that it wields substantial power over male-coded policy issues related to war, terrorism, and finances. Additional departments that have been associated more with men than women are labor, housing and urban development, and commerce. Because women are viewed as caregivers or as mothers who are compassionate, they are often assigned policy areas related to family and social services.

Since the Industrial Revolution, the American workplace has been associated with unions, working men, and waged labor,[86] but the first woman ever to serve in a U.S. cabinet was Frances Perkins, who was appointed by Franklin D. Roosevelt as Secretary of Labor (1933–1945). Few women served in the cabinet from this point until the administration of Jimmy Carter (1977–1981), which had a cabinet of 11% women. Recent presidents in the United States have had 20% to 30% of their cabinet secretaries who are women (see Table 7.4). The highest level of descriptive representation of women in the U.S. cabinet was during the second term of President Bill Clinton, when 9 of 22 cabinet members were women (41%). Obama's first and second terms were similarly high at 30% and 35% women, respectively. Presidents Donald Trump and George W. Bush appointed cabinets with around 20% to 25% women. According to

Maryanne Borrelli (2010), the administrations of Clinton, Bush, and Obama are examples of gender integration in cabinets, whereas all administrations from 1933 until Clinton were cabinets with gender desegregation.[87] **Gender desegregation** is typified by few women in the cabinet who are marginalized and men who are central leaders. With **gender integration,** a cabinet is less masculinized and has a significant proportion of women. The women who serve are thought of as capable leaders and are not only assigned to positions associated with caregiving.[88]

In gender integrated cabinets in the United States, we find women occupying some inner cabinet positions previously associated with men (see Table 7.4). Women have been U.S. Secretary of State three times and Attorney General (i.e., head of the Department of Justice) two times. In the Trump administration (2016–2019), Kirstjen Nielsen served as Secretary of Homeland Security, which oversees terrorism, crime, and immigration issues within U.S. borders. Women have been secretary of labor an additional six times since Frances Perkins. Women have never led the inner cabinet positions of defense, veterans' affairs, or treasury.

Internationally, we find increasing descriptive representation of women in

▸ **Photo 7.3** Cabinet of President Donald J. Trump, March 13, 2017.

Table 7.4 Women Cabinet Officials in the United States, Obama and Trump Administrations

Name	Position	Years Served	Administration	Term
Christina D. Romer	Chair, Council of Economic Advisors	2009–2010	Obama	1st
Hilda Solis	Secretary of Labor	2009–2013	Obama	1st
Susan E. Rice	UN Ambassador	2009–2013	Obama	1st
Lisa P. Jackson	Administrator, Environmental Protection Agency	2009–2013	Obama	1st
Hillary Rodham Clinton	Secretary of State	2009–2013	Obama	1st

(Continued)

Name	Position	Years Served	Administration	Term
Janet Napolitano	Secretary of Homeland Security	2009–2013	Obama	1st
Kathleen Sebelius	Secretary of Health and Human Services	2009–2014	Obama	1st/2nd
Karen G. Mills	Administrator, Small Business Administration	2012–2013	Obama	1st/2nd
Sylvia Burwell	Director, Office of Management and Budget	2013–2014	Obama	2nd
Loretta Lynch	Attorney General	2015–2017	Obama	2nd
Sally Jewell	Secretary of the Interior	2013–2017	Obama	2nd
Penny Pritzker	Secretary of Commerce	2013–2017	Obama	2nd
Sylvia Burwell	Secretary of Health and Human Services	2014–2017	Obama	2nd
Gina McCarthy	Administrator, Environmental Protection Agency	2013–2017	Obama	2nd
Samantha Power	UN Ambassador	2013–2017	Obama	2nd
Maria Contreras-Sweet	Administrator, Small Business Administration	2014–2017	Obama	2nd
Elaine Chao	Secretary of Transportation	2017–	Trump	1st
Betsy DeVos	Secretary of Education	2017–	Trump	1st
Kirstjen Nielsen	Secretary of Homeland Security	2017–2019	Trump	1st
Nikki Haley	UN Ambassador	2017–2018	Trump	1st

Name	Position	Years Served	Administration	Term
Gina Haspel	Director, CIA	2018–	Trump	1st
Linda McMahon	Administrator, Small Business Administration	2017–	Trump	1st

cabinets, especially since the 1990s.[89] In fact, countries such as Chile, Spain, Canada, Italy, and France have had **parity cabinets**, or cabinets with half women and half men as ministers. Parity cabinets are becoming more common,[90] and scholars argue that this is because it is fairly easy to choose women for cabinet posts. Cabinet positions are small in number, and most countries now have women with relevant experience and expertise who could fill those few positions.[91] Furthermore, heads of government are largely free to appoint the number of women they want, which means women entering cabinet posts do not need to campaign or face elections. Most countries with parity cabinets are in advanced democracies, but newer democracies have appointed them as well. For instance, Spain and Chile have only been democracies since the late 1970s and early 1990s, respectively.

Nevertheless, as of 2019, women are on average only 18% of cabinet ministers worldwide. The variables linked to the number of women in cabinets include the masculine nature of some cabinet positions, legislative representation of women, executive type, international norms, and pressure from feminist activists. In previous decades, women tended to lead ministries or departments that were stereotyped as feminine (i.e., family, culture, education, women's affairs, and social services), rather than masculine (i.e., defense, economic, finance, security, and agriculture).[92–94] Even though newer data show that women are being appointed to diverse posts, including ones previously associated with men,[95] it is likely that women are fewer in number because of remaining stereotypes. Second, quantitative research suggests that a greater number of women in a legislature is associated with more women in cabinets.[96] This is true for presidential and parliamentary systems but especially so for parliamentary systems where legislators are often directly tapped to serve as cabinet members. If legislatures have a high proportion of women, a greater pool exists from which to select cabinet members. Third, an international norm of women being descriptively represented is growing. As Prime Minister of Canada, Justin Trudeau (2015-present) famously stated, he appointed a parity cabinet "Because it's 2015." This norm proves to be the most influential in countries whose neighbors have many women in the cabinet and who form alliances via international treaties.[97] Finally, women's groups now expect descriptive representation in cabinets and pressure governments to appoint enough women to accomplish it.[98] Overall, we would expect to find fewer women in cabinets in countries with weak women's movements, fewer women in the legislature, and less incentive to follow international norms.

Research also shows that the women who gain cabinet posts have political resources and backgrounds similar to the men they serve alongside.[99] And, in recent years, women have not been overwhelmingly stereotyped into feminine cabinet posts. Tiffany Barnes and Diana O'Brien (2018) find that 41 countries had women defense ministers by 2012.[100] These authors find that "women are more likely to be ministers of defense in countries with large numbers of women parliamentarians and women chief executives, as well as in those where the essence of defense takes on new meanings—particularly in countries concerned with peacekeeping as a central policy goal and in former military states governed by left-leaning parties."[101] Women are less likely to be ministers of defense "in countries engaged in fatal disputes, governed by military dictators, and in those that invest heavily in military operations while forgoing peacekeeping."[102]

Argentina and the United States demonstrate Barnes and O'Brien's arguments. Argentina was a military state during the late 1970s and early 1980s, but in much of the past decades has been governed by leftists who see security as meaning more than raw military power. Since 1989, women have been ministers over defense, internal security, and foreign affairs (see Table 7.5). As minister of defense in Argentina, Nilda Garré "sought to modernize the military with a focus on human rights, and, part of doing so, included, in her own words, 'giving particular attention to the question of gender.'"[103] The United States has a lesser percentage of women legislators in comparison to other democratic (and some nondemocratic) countries and does not have a gender quota (see Chapter 6). The United States does emphasize raw military power, is present in military operations around the world, and considers terrorism a high priority issue. Thus, the meaning of defense in the United States continues to be firmly masculine.

The United States, on the other hand, has had several women serve as secretaries of state and, arguably, these secretaries pursued women's rights during their mandates. Hillary Clinton practiced what is known as **security feminism**, a soft approach to American foreign policy that promotes women's rights as a mode of counterterrorism and national security (see Box 7.3).[104] Condoleeza Rice also

Table 7.5 Women Ministers of Defense, Internal Security, and Foreign Affairs, Argentina

Name	Cabinet Position	Year(s)
Susana Myrta Ruíz Cerutti	Secretary of External Relations	1989
Nilda Garré	Minister of Defense	2005–2010
Nilda Garré	Minister of Security	2010–2013
María Cecilia Rodríguez	Minister of Security	2013–2015
Susana Malcorra	Minister of Foreign Affairs	2015–2017
Patricia Bullrich	Minister of Security	2015–Present

pursued women's rights while secretary of state (2005–2009). She was instrumental in getting the UN Security Council to recognize rape as a weapon of war,[105] and she launched the One Woman Initiative, which awards grants to Muslim women who are entrepreneurs. Although many recognize concrete ways in which Clinton's security feminism empowers women, she is not without critics. In the estimation of some feminist activists and scholars,[106–109] she is a policy hawk who uses **hard power** (e.g., support of activating troops, use of drones, and covert actions) in a way similar to her many male predecessors. Hawkish choices, because they entail armed violence, could further oppress women (and men).[110] Similarly, Condoleeza Rice was criticized for her service in the Bush Administration. The administration used tough measures to counter terrorism that arguably violated human rights, and critics could not disassociate her from those measures.[111]

BOX 7.3: POLICY FEATURE

Women and National Security Policy

Three women have been secretary of state in the United States (Madeleine K. Albright [1997–2001], Condoleezza Rice [2005-2009], and Hillary Clinton [2009–2013]), and five have been United Nations Ambassador (Jeane Kirkpatrick [1981–1985], Madeleine K. Albright [1997-2001], Susan Rice [2013–2017], Samantha Power [2013-2017], and Nikki Haley [2017–2018]). How can women leaders influence policies related to national security and do so in a way that empowers women? Secretary Clinton is the most recent woman who served as secretary of state in the United States, and she emphasized the political and social empowerment of women and girls as she traveled extensively and interacted with local women's groups around the world. As secretary, she instituted the State Department's Office of Global Women's Issues as well as the position of ambassador-at-large for Global Women's Issues. Scholars and policy practitioners labeled her gendered approach to national security as security feminism or the **Hillary Doctrine**.[112] Clinton believed that "the subjugation of women is a direct threat to the common security of the world and to the national security of the [United States]."[113] As women's rights increase worldwide, she believed world affairs would become more stable, and the United States' foreign interests would be protected. The phrase she coined as first lady in 1995, "women's rights are human rights," rings true in the Hillary Doctrine. The doctrine suggests that human security is intrinsically linked to national security.[114]

How might the Hillary Doctrine work in real life? Or, in other words, what policies could a cabinet secretary like Clinton pursue that would influence the lives of women and national security at the same time? Two examples come from the U.S. National Action Plans on Women, Peace, and Security, which were enacted by the Office of Global Women's Issues. The plan stipulates

(Continued)

(Continued)

initiatives for the health and economic empowerment of women as well as responses to terrorism. For instance, when women participate in agricultural programs, they become empowered and, as a country's economy improves with such programs, its national security increases as well.[115] Regarding terrorism, one could argue that women are essential to preventing terrorism, especially as mothers who influence children and communities but also that they bear the brunt of terrorism's sexual violence. We see policy responses to both of these realities in Secretary Clinton's State Department. In 2014, the department created a public-private network of service providers called the Gender-Based Violence Emergency Response and Protection Initiative. This network "has supported more than 130 women and girls who survived . . . captivity" and sexual assault in Iraq by ISIL (Islamic State of Iraq and the Levant).[116] The State Department also supported counterextremism initiatives that mobilize women to identify and resist terrorist radicalization in places such as Africa, Asia, and the Middle East.[117] Therefore, the State Department under Clinton believed that empowering women could help to reduce terrorism and to increase security.

WOMEN'S POLICY AGENCIES

During the Decade for Women (1975–1985), the United Nations encouraged all countries to establish a national-level women's policy agency to serve as the country's focal point for addressing inequalities between men and women. Women's policy agencies are government bureaucracies that advocate for women in the policy process, and they do so by influencing legislators, administering programs for women, connecting leaders in the women's movement to government officials, and helping to enforce policy suited to women's interests.[118–120] Women's policy agencies research the status of women and issue reports and policy recommendations. Many countries have one bureaucratic body that oversees policies related to women, and they are typically called, for example, a women's institute, ministry of women's affairs, council for equality, or so on.

State feminism is the idea that women's policy agencies can work toward the goals of women's movements by providing representation and producing policy outcomes for them.[121] In other words, state feminism is the idea that government agencies, ministers, and other bureaucrats can be woman friendly.[122] When bureaucrats engage in state feminism, they may be called **femocrats**. For example, in 2018, Soledad Murillo de la Vega and Marlène Schiappa were appointed to be secretaries of equality in, respectively, Spain and France. Secretaries Murillo and Schiappa can be considered femocrats because they seek feminist change in policy, and they represent the issues of interest to women's movements (see Box 7.4).

Although the United States established the world's first women's policy agency, the United States has never had one central bureaucratic institution to oversee all women's affairs. The Women's Bureau was created in 1920 in the Department of Labor, with the charge to investigate the status of working women and comment on bills that would affect women in the workforce. The

Table 7.6 Women's Policy Agencies in the United States Bureaucracy		
Women's Policy Agency	Cabinet Department	Sample Policies
Office of Global Women's Issues	Department of State	• **Accountability Initiative:** Funding for prosecution of gender-based violence in justice systems of other countries • **Afghan Women's Leadership Initiative:** Funding to create safe havens for victims of gender-based violence, to train women in life skills to make them economically competitive in the workplace, and to provide education and job-training for young girls to delay early marriage
Office on Women's Health	Department of Health & Human Services	• **College Sexual Assault Policy and Prevention Initiative:** Funding to states to work with campuses on issues of sexual assault • **Supporting Nursing Moms at Work:** Works to ensure that employees who are breastfeeding have adequate space and time at work to pump breast milk; provides resources for both employees and employers on what current laws dictate and how to have conversations about meeting these needs
Office on Violence Against Women	Department of Justice	• **Training and Services to End Violence Against Women With Disabilities Grant Program:** Funding to groups that work to prevent sexual assault, domestic and dating violence, and stalking of women with disabilities • **Tribal Sexual Assault Services Program:** Works with federally recognized tribes to create greater infrastructure prevention of and justice related to violent crimes against women

United States has agencies like the Women's Bureau in other cabinet departments (Table 7.6). Therefore, the United States' policy landscape is complex as it is a mix of policy agencies in individual cabinet departments. The landscape also includes presidential commissions. A president may establish a special commission to study women's issues and address them by way of policy recommendations. President John F. Kennedy was the first to do so in 1961. His commission was chaired by Eleanor Roosevelt, and it is credited with recommending equal pay legislation, which eventually resulted in the 1963 Equal Pay Act, as described in Chapter 2. The most recent presidential initiative is the White House Council on Women and Girls. President Barack Obama created it by Executive Order in 2009, but it has not been used by the Trump administration. President George W. Bush also did not maintain the commission created by his predecessor, President Bill Clinton. Tina Tchen, who directed the White House Council on Women and Girls under Obama, has argued that the council "served as a signal to career staff [in the federal bureaucracy] that they needed to consider equality gaps."[123] Thus, forgoing a presidential commission or office on women can be seen as a lack of prioritization of women's affairs by a presidential administration.

Women's policy agencies are fairly common worldwide. Most political scientists have studied women's policy agencies in Western Europe,[124,125] but they

BOX 7.4: COMPARATIVE FEATURE

State Feminism in Spain and France

Women's policy agencies at the subnational and national levels were first created in Spain in the 1980s, following the right-wing authoritarian regime of Francisco Franco that ended in the 1970s.[126] The national Women's Institute was established by a socialist, center-left government in 1983, and it was maintained under center-right governments during the 1990s and 2000s. Spain has historically been a land of intense *machista* patriarchy, but norms of equality diffused rapidly following the country's democratization and its incorporation into the European Union.[127] During the past three decades, for example, the Women's Institute has been instrumental in advocating for nonsexist education and job training, as well as responding to violence against women. The women's movement in Spain is fragmented, and though women's policy agencies have engaged women's activists at times, relationships between activists and the state have been strained at other times.[128]

Pedro Sánchez from the Socialist Party was installed as prime minister in Spain in June 2018, and he appointed a cabinet comprised of almost 65% of women ministers. The Women's Institute is situated in the Ministry of the Presidency, which is led by Deputy Prime Minister María del Carmen Calvo Poyato, who is a feminist and who previously led the Socialist Party on matters of equality. The Women's Institute's director is Silvia Buabent Vallejo, who is a self-described feminist. Buabent is trained in political science, is an expert in gender violence, and has been an elected municipal councilor. A sub-Ministry of Equality exists within the Ministry of the Presidency, and it is led by Soledad Murillo, a feminist sociologist and professor who was the Minister for Equality from 2004 to 2008. Murillo is an academic expert on the women's movement in Spain and is well respected in activist circles.

Actions by the Women's Institute and by Ministers Calvo and Murillo substantiate Spain's practice of state feminism. The Business Support Program for Women (PAEM) is a joint initiative between the Women's Institute, the European Social Fund, and the Spanish Chamber of Commerce, and it offers women entrepreneurs access to microcredit so that they can start new businesses. The Women's Institute also has participated in a roundtable about women's career advancement in fields such as construction. Ministers Calvo and Murillo have spoken publicly about the role of women in Spanish universities, and, specifically have argued that women must obtain higher positions of leadership in universities, especially considering that women are now the majority of university students. Another example of the work of femocrats in Spain is Secretary Murrillo's meeting with women from the Federation of Rural Women's Associations. This women's organization conveyed to the minister that rural women lack services and are more vulnerable to gender violence because of their geographic isolation. Murillo also advocates for LGBTQIA+ women; she tweeted, "Today the misogyny is over," when the government announced free fertility treatment for single women and lesbians.

Bureaucratic institutions related to women's employment existed in France from 1919 to 1963, and, in the 1960s, a bureau was created to explicitly address women's rights.[129] Women's policy agencies existed in various forms from that point until 1981 when the socialist president, François Mitterrand, appointed a minister of women's rights, which in 1985 transitioned into a full minister position. The Ministry of Women's Rights has been eliminated or downgraded at various points since that time, by administrations of both the political right and left. In 1990, the Women's Rights and Equality Service was established by executive decree under a political left government. The service produces reports on how women are faring in areas such as employment, leisure, and family. The Women's Rights and Equality Service offers women's organizations funding, but activists have pressured the bureaucracy to be more than a symbolic institution. In 2012, the political left elevated women's rights to the Ministry of Women's Affairs, and, in 2018, this agency was renamed the Ministry of Gender Equality. Through the work of women's policy agencies, France has developed a system of over 100 women's rights centers where citizens can seek information and hear public lectures about women's rights. Women's policy agencies and femocrats also have been credited with advancing the country's parity law and working with police responding to sexual violence.[130]

(Continued)

(Continued)

The centrist government of Emmanuel Macron, installed in May 2018, has an equal number of women and men ministers, and Macron has stated that gender equality is a top priority of his government. He appointed Marlène Schiappa as minister of state for gender equality. She identifies as a feminist, but her trajectory into politics is not through activism in feminist movements. She is a famous blogger who wrote about the balance of work and family for working mothers. She is also famous for editing an anthology called, *Letters to My Uterus*, in which various authors write letters addressing the uterus as it relates to pregnancy, menstruation, menopause, and sex. Although she and Macron have received criticism from feminists, Schiappa believes she is moving France in the direction of feminism. She states that "France is actually the birthplace of philosophical feminism. The problem is, we want to now go from philosophy to action."[131]

Having been moved by the #MeToo movement (called the #BalanceTonPorc or "expose your pig" campaign in French), Schiappa's policy goals have centered on combatting sexual harassment and violence. She established a task force that defined sexual harassment and worked on a sexual harassment law, which was passed in August 2018. The law stipulates fines for street harassment and an age of consent for sex of 15 years. Sex with people younger than 15 is now considered child rape. As for street harassment, the police can issue fines for up to 90 euros to people who "annoy, bother and threaten" women in public. Schiappa also focuses on the pay gap between men and women. French businesses will be required to implement software attached to payroll systems that can monitor pay equality, and Schiappa intends to publicly shame companies that pay women less than men. Schiappa's policy actions appear to empower women, but some argue that she has too few resources to accomplish all her goals. Arguably it is a distraction and an impossibility to police all street harassment if France cannot first stop or respond to egregious cases of gender violence. Furthermore, LGBTQIA+ protesters assert that homophobic attacks are common, and they urge the government to implement educational and cultural programs to address discrimination.

can be found in all world regions. Examples of women's policy agencies at the national level include, for example, the National Commission for Women in India in the Ministry of Women and Child Development and the Ministry of Family, Solidarity, Equality, and Social Development in Morocco. Gender policy in India includes a focus on enhancing education, improving the economy, promoting health (through food security and nutrition), and bolstering women's representation (by increasing the number of women in government). The agency in India also supports home birth professionals in rural regions and women's collective farming. The ministry in Morocco has penalized *taharrush* (sexual harassment in the streets) and has changed policies related to domestic abuse.

What makes women's policy agencies more or less effective for furthering women-friendly policies? Researchers have suggested that agencies are more effective when they work closely with women's movements and have significant resources and administrative powers.[132,133] There are examples of leftist administrations being more attentive to gender policy, yet rightist governments can also maintain and lead women's policy agencies.[134] Thus, keep in mind, "there is no one recipe for success."[135] *The Politics of State Feminism: Innovation in Comparative Research* explains, that neither politics surrounding agencies (i.e., the party in charge), their relationship with women's groups, nor the resources available to them consistently make them influential. Overall women's policy agencies tend to support the women's movement, but their actions are sometimes more symbolic than substantial.[136]

WOMEN IN STATE AND LOCAL INSTITUTIONS

Women also are represented in the executive in subnational institutions. The first women to serve as governors in the United States were spouses of governors who had died. The first woman to become governor in her own right was Ella Grasso (D-CT) in 1974, and a woman first served as lieutenant governor in Vermont from 1955 to 1956 (Consuelo N. Bailey [R]). The first and only women of color became governors in 2011 (Nikki Haley from South Carolina [R] and Susana Martinez [R] from New Mexico). The most women to ever serve as governor at one time is nine, and this has happened twice (2004–2007 and 2019–present). As of 2016, 60% of women governors in all of U.S. history "served all or part of their terms during the first few years of the twenty-first century."[137] The midterm elections of 2018 proved to be a notable year for women governors, considering that 16 women ran for office, the number of women governors in 2019 ties the all-time record of nine, and women of color made substantial strides. Stacey Abrams (D) narrowly lost her race in Georgia, and Paulette Jordan, a Native American woman, was the Democratic nominee for governor in Idaho. Peggy Flanagan, also a Native American woman, campaigned for and won the lieutenant governorship of Minnesota (see Table 7.8).

The paucity of women governors can be linked to several variables. For one, most women who are elected to political office are Democrats, but most governors across the country in recent years are Republicans, because of election cycles (2010 and 2014) favoring Republicans and a greater number of "red states" than "blue states." The Republican Party draws from much smaller pool of women candidates than the Democratic Party, which results in fewer women being elected to governorships.[138,139] The political culture of a state also influences a woman's success in primaries and gubernatorial elections.[140] According to Windett (2011),

> states with a more progressive female sociopolitical subculture have a
> history of treating women as equal to men and have a nontraditionalistic
> view of women in general. States with a traditional female sociopolitical
> subculture do not foster an environment that allows females to run for

political office and pursue careers that will eventually allow them to run for governor. In states with strict gender roles and traditional gender stereotypes, women are not seen as qualified public servants.[141]

Progressive states include, for example, Washington, Vermont, and Colorado, whereas Southern states are traditionalistic. It should also be noted that few women of color are governors because statewide elections do not provide the electoral advantage of majority-minority districts, as discussed in Chapter 6.

One further victory for women in 2018 in the state executive should be noted. In Michigan, voters elected women into three top executive positions: governor (Gretchen Whitmer-D), secretary of state (Jocelyn Benson-D), and attorney general (Dana Nessel-D). According to Senator Debbie Stabenow (D-MI)

> We didn't win because of the novelty of an all-women slate of candidates. We didn't win thanks to some kind of "pink wave." We didn't win because we focused on "women's issues," because every issue is a women's issue. Instead, we won because we had strong, highly qualified candidates who each earned their nomination.[142]

Scholars lack comprehensive data regarding women mayors in the United States, but we do know that as of December 2017, women only made up 22% of the mayors of the largest 100 American cities,[143] and of the 1,362 mayors of U.S. cities with populations over 30,000, 286 were women (21%). As with women in statewide and national elections, there was significant growth in women in local government in the 1990s, but growth has since stabilized.[144] Women of color and white women are represented at the local level in similar proportions, with the former holding both large municipalities as well as smaller ones.[145] One example of a women of color in a prominent local position is Muriel Bowser, who has been mayor of Washington DC since 2015. Bowser explains that she wants to inspire young Black girls to "be anything they want to be," and that, in return, they energize and motivate her.[146]

▸ **Photo 7.4** Peggy Flanagan campaigning at an LGBTQIA+ event for Lieutenant Governor of Minnesota.

Women are more likely to be mayors when they have been appointed by a city council rather than elected by the public. Research suggests that one reason this is so is because local level parties, often led by men, do not recruit many women to run for office.[147] Another reason for fewer women than men as mayors is the difficulty of balancing work and private obligations. Being a local

BOX 7.5: COMPARATIVE FEATURE

Women in Local Politics Balancing Home and Work

Scholarship from different countries and regions show that women in local office are constrained by a triple workload. In personal interviews, women in local government in France spoke to two of the coauthors about what it was like to work as a woman in government.[148] While many were happy with their work, they bemoaned the difficulty in balancing their paid work, their city council work, and their work in the home. The women we talked to explained this as working three "shifts." One interviewee stated, "[a]s with every woman who works outside the home, women who are dedicated to politics suffer, especially the difficulties of reconciling work and family life."[149] In fact, studies show that women in France do more childcare than men.[150,151] Since local political positions are unpaid in France, "this makes it harder for women, especially young women, to engage in politics. Women, unlike men, will have three jobs—family, politics and their paid work."[152] This interviewee explained that women may lead portfolios dealing with children and education rather than "masculine" portfolios of security or economics because the more caring portfolios dovetail closely with women's private responsibilities, which then reduces the triple workload. The respondent also indicated women were first placed into "women's portfolios" (culture, education, Basque language) by men in leadership positions who did not consider them for more masculine portfolios like security.[153]

An example from Mexico substantiates our own findings. Laura Loyola-Hernández interviewed women mayors in Yucatecan indigenous municipalities (2017). The mayors conveyed to Loyola-Hernández that their constituents expected them to keep up "maternal and spousal obligations" while serving as mayor.[154] One of her interviewees explained,

> I am a mom of two girls and one boy. Let me tell you, I do everything, a little bit of this, a little bit of that. I make small gaps in my schedule so I can take my kids to their respective activities. I leave here [city hall] about 3 or 4 o'clock; if I have a chance I have lunch; if not, I don't. I take my kids to their activities then go pick them up. I go back home, come to city hall again then go home at around 10 p.m. There is not a moment to rest.[155]

Therefore, as with women who are local officials in France, women mayors in the Yucatan have many tasks to perform at the same time.

official is often not one's full-time job; thus, serving in local office must be balanced with one's employment and family responsibilities. Women continue to shoulder more responsibility for the home, even in advanced economies and democracies, thus making it more difficult for them to hold local office (see Chapter 4 and Box 7.5).

It is also difficult to find systematic data on women in meso-level and municipal government worldwide, because "internationally agreed standards, definitions and indicators for monitoring" local governments do not exist.[156] **Meso-level governments** (like states, regions, and provinces) as well as municipal government structures vary from one country to the next, making comparisons difficult.[157] Limited data about the municipal level, however, show that women's representation has grown throughout much of the world over the last decade, but that it remains far from parity, with women underrepresented compared to men throughout all regions of the world.[158] When women are present, they tend to be mayors or councilors in smaller municipalities.[159] For example, as of 2017, there were only 26 women mayors among the world's largest 300 cities—which constitutes only 8.7% (see Table 7.7).[160]

Table 7.7	Large Cities in the World With Women Mayors, 2017				
World Rank	City	Country	City Population	Metro Population	Mayor
6	Tokyo	Japan	13,617,000	37,800,000	Yuriko Koike
56	Sydney	Australia	5,005,000	5,005,000	Clover Moore
62	Surat	India	4,467,000	4,591,000	Asmita Shiroya
74	Yokohama	Japan	3,733,000	3,733,000	Fumiko Hayashi
93	Madrid	Spain	3,141,000	6,240,000	Manuela Carmena
107	Rome	Italy	2,877,000	4,353,000	Virgina Raggi
108	Surabaya	Indonesia	2,865,000	6,485,000	Tri Rismaharini
131	Nagpur	India	2,405,000	2,498,000	Nanda Jichkar
142	Paris	France	2,230,000	12,405,000	Anne Hidalgo
144	Managua	Nicaragua	2,206,000	2,561,000	Daisy Torres
150	Bucharest	Romania	2,106,000	2,281,000	Gabriela Firea
151	Havana	Cuba	2,106,000	2,125,000	Marta Hernández Romero

157	Maracaibo	Venezuela	2,002,000	2,451,000	Eveling Trejo de Rosales
159	Perth	Australia	1,980,000	1,980,000	Lisa Scaffidi
175	Warsaw	Poland	1,749,000	3,101,000	Hanna Gronkiewicz-Waltz
183	Montreal	Canada	1,704,000	4,099,000	Valérie Plant
197	Barcelona	Spain	1,605,000	4,740,000	Ada Colau Ballano
240	Prague	Czech Republic	1,280,000	2,156,000	Adrianna Krnacova
242	Sofia	Bulgaria	1,260,000	1,680,000	Yordanka Asenova Fandakova
249	Rosario	Argentina	1,194,000	1,267,000	Mónica Fein
264	Rostov on Don	Russia	1,115,000	1,115,000	Zinaida Neyarokhina
272	Ranchi	India	1,073,000	1,127,000	Asha Lakra
290	Stockholm	Sweden	936,000	2,226,000	Karin Wanngård
297	Durban	South Africa	595,000	3,842,000	Zandile Gumede
299	Cape Town	South Africa	433,000	3,740,000	Patricia de Lille

Women face obstacles when they aspire to become the governing executive in municipalities and meso-level governments. For example, the meso or local level is where national monies flow to fund policy programs. Because these administrative levels manage large budgets, they are attractive positions for politicians to hold. This chapter has argued that women do not always capture the especially attractive and powerful political positions, and, for this reason, subnational positions may be hard for them to obtain. Furthermore, the local level is often a place of intense patronage and masculinism.[161] In Latin America, mayors and governors are central figures who can use their political capital to determine whether other politicians will succeed. Women tend to be locked out of the informal, men's networks where these decisions are made. Obstacles such as these are particularly disappointing given that women's participation in local government has been shown to be "an essential step towards creating gender equal opportunities and gender sensitive policies."[162] Not all women live in national capitals where policies are influenced and made; therefore, if policies are going to reach all women, the local sphere must administer gender sensitive policies and foment equality as well.

A final space where women can be represented is tribal governance. During American colonialism (see Chapter 2), Native women were respected leaders in tribes, but colonists refused to acknowledge women leaders. Given this history, Native women lack equal representation in tribes over time; however, educated Native women increasingly have been encouraged to run for positions as they intend to influence younger generations.[163] They are inspired to

Table 7.8 Prominent Native Women in Executive Positions

Federal, state, and local government

Name	Tribe	Location	Position (years)
Ada E. Deer	Menominee Tribe	U.S. Federal Government	Bureau of Indian Affairs, Department of Justice (1993–1997)
Debora Juarez	Blackfeet Nation	Seattle, Washington	City Councilor (2016–)
Jodi Gillette	Standing Rock Sioux Tribe of North and South Dakota	U.S. Federal Government	Various positions in Obama administration: Special Assistant to the President for Native American Affairs in the White House Domestic Policy Council; Deputy Assistant Secretary to the Assistant-Secretary Indian Affairs in the U.S. Department of the Interior, and Associate Director of Intergovernmental Affairs at the White House (2009–2015)
Denise Juneau	Blackfeet Tribe	Montana	Superintendent of Public Instruction (2009–2017)
Peggy Flanagan	White Earth Band of Ojibwe	Minnesota	Lieutenant Governor (2019–)
Karen Diver	Fond du Lac Band of Lake Superior Chippewa	U.S. Federal Government	Special Assistant to the President on Native American Affairs (2015–2017)

Tribal government	
Name	**Position (years)**
Betty Mae Jumper	Chief of the Seminole Tribe of Florida (1967–1971)
Wilma Mankiller	Chief of the Cherokee Nation (1983–1985)
Cecilia Fire Thunder	President of the Oglala Sioux Tribe, South Dakota (2004–2006)
Karen Diver	Chair of the Fond du Lac Band of Lake Superior Chippewa, Minnesota (2007–2015)
Lynn Valbuena	Chair of San Manuel Band of Mission Indians, Southern California (2014–)

do so out of their family and communal obligations, and have been welcomed in their careers as community leaders[164] (see Table 7.8).

SUBSTANTIVE AND SYMBOLIC REPRESENTATION IN EXECUTIVE INSTITUTIONS

Emerging research suggests that women's presence in the executive branch furthers symbolic and substantive representation. As we discussed in Chapter 6, **symbolic representation** entails citizens attaching meaning to representation. As executive leaders emerge from marginalized groups, citizens may begin to view government more favorably because they see it as fairer and more inclusive. If a woman is a leader, women might sense greater opportunities to participate in **masculine-coded public settings** (i.e., those typically considered the domain of men, as we discussed in Chapter 2, like town hall meetings or the military). A good example of this phenomenon is the leadership of defense minister Carme Chacón, in Spain from 2008 to 2011. Chacón was pregnant while serving as defense minister, and several iconic photos of her walking in front of troops with her pregnancy prominently showing were taken. Political scientists Emanuela Lombardo and Petra Meier (2014) argue that Chacón's "pregnant body," "evokes a shift in symbolic representation, as the typical characteristic that society has attributed to military leaders is being male." Her pregnant body therefore symbolized that the male space of the military was becoming more open to women. It also symbolized a commitment to gender equality from the Spanish parity cabinet in which she served.[165] In other words, when women are leaders in executive institutions, they may increase the profile of gender policies and they "may inspire other women to enter politics."[166]

▶ **Photo 7.5** Carme Chacón, Spain's first female Minister of Defense.

Three recent, quantitative studies suggest the positive influence of women's leadership on symbolic representation. In 2018, Amy C. Alexander and Farida Jalalzai, using data from 40 countries in multiple world regions, found that people in a country with a woman political executive increase their support of women leaders, voting, and interest in politics; and, in fact, women's *and* men's support was positively related to women's leadership.[167] That is, a woman as head of state or government is a symbolic marker that increases citizens' interest in politics and the belief that women are suitable leaders. It is precisely because a head of state or government is incredibly visible to the public, arguably much more so than any individual legislator, that women as top executive leaders are consequential.

In 2016, Catherine Reyes-Housholder and Leslie Schwindt-Bayer found a connection between a woman as president (*presidenta*) and women's political participation in Latin America. These authors estimate that,

> women living under a *presidenta* have almost a 5 percent higher probability of saying how they would vote if the presidential election were this week than women living under a male president. The probability that women will participate in a campaign is 3 percent higher in a country with a *presidenta* than one with a *presidente* (male president). Women in countries with female presidents have a 3.4 percent higher probability of participating in local political meetings than women in countries run by male presidents.[168]

In this study, men's self-reported participation, however, did not increase when a woman was president. As a result, the gap in political participation between men and women began to disappear under women presidents.

Although women as cabinet ministers are not as visible as top political executives, they, too, can provide symbolic representation. Sarah Liu Shan-Jan and Lee Ann Banaszak (2017) make the argument that cabinet ministers become highly visible upon taking their positions.[169] Angela Merkel, they suggest, is an example of visibility and influence. She was not well-known before she became a minister for women and youth in Germany, but her public profile increased as she served. This led her to a place of prominence in her party and influenced her later political success in becoming chancellor, and she also potentially impacted other women by increasing their interest in public service. To research this dynamic, Shan-Jan and Banaszak used survey data from 2010, and they find that women cabinet ministers, like women legislators, can serve as role models whose presence encourages women's political engagement. However, the authors only find that women as cabinet ministers positively and significantly influences political behavior related to voting, party membership, signing petitions, and peaceful demonstrations but not political behavior defined as boycotts and strikes.[170] The authors are not surprised by the latter finding, because, as they explain, confrontational actions pose higher costs and risks, and cabinet ministers are not likely to be role models for these actions.

Additional research complicates the abovementioned findings. In looking at Latin American women as presidents, Jalalzai found that women's symbolic representation was enhanced in Brazil on account of the presidency of Dilma Rousseff, but that was not conclusively the case in Chile with Michelle Bachelet.[171] In Costa Rica (Laura Chinchilla) and Argentina (Cristina Fernández), citizens negatively assessed the presidents' time in office.[172] Dilma Rousseff also provided substantive representation for poor women, as is detailed in Box 7.6. Recall, from Chapter 6, **substantive representation** entails elected officials reflecting the policy preferences, priorities, and interests of those who are represented.

BOX 7.6: POLICY FEATURE

Antipoverty Policies and Substantive Representation by Executives

Women have gained access to education and waged labor in many countries, but many women remain in poverty for various reasons. Women globally are paid less than men by 23%, are twice as likely to be unpaid for care work (i.e., childcare and eldercare), and often work in lower paying "pink-collar" jobs, such as waitressing, teaching, or nursing.[173] Moreover, women in America lose 8 million days of work each year due to gender violence.[174] Gender violence puts women in a cycle of missing work, losing employment, and losing housing. Given these inequalities, policies that address poverty must be formulated with women in mind. Both women and men face poverty worldwide, but single mothers and elderly women (65+) particularly vie with poverty.[175] In the United States, Black and Latina women are more likely than white women to live in poverty.[176]

(Continued)

(Continued)

How have women as presidents advanced policies aimed at poverty reduction? Herein we compare proposals and initiatives for poverty relief in the United States and Brazil. In the United States, this inquiry is limited to what Hillary Clinton proposed in her political platform for the presidency in 2016. In Brazil, we examine the actions of Dilma Rousseff, who was president from 2011 to 2016.

If she had become president, Clinton planned on aiding women in poverty by addressing equal pay and childcare. She advocated improved wages for women by increasing the minimum wage and passing the Paycheck Fairness Act, a bill that has been introduced several times in Congress with the aim to make employers more transparent about wages so that women can spot pay discrimination and address it. To ease the financial burden of childcare, she proposed that no family pay more than 10% of its income on childcare.[177] Affordable healthcare was equally important to Clinton as a solution to poverty. She sought reductions in copays, deductibles, and the price of prescription drugs. To address poverty in older women, she focused on Social Security benefits in two ways: She wanted to credit caregivers for unpaid work by giving them social security benefits, and she wanted to maintain the benefit levels for families after one spouse dies.[178] Despite her electoral platform's inclusion of poverty, critics noted that Clinton emphasized solutions for the middle and working classes more so than those struggling at the very bottom. Clinton did not advocate housing policies to help those who can't afford rent and are in danger of homelessness. Although Clinton often focused on job creation, she had fewer answers for people who have no income and no way to afford basics such as meals or clothing.[179]

President Dilma Rousseff's advocacy for women focused on women's and families' nutrition and housing. This makes sense given that many families in Brazil face inequality and poverty, particularly in the slums called *favelas*. The president before Rousseff established *Bolsa Família* to address poverty, and it offered cash transfers to families to pay for children's school or health needs. Rousseff, continuing the program, specifically promoted it as a policy "made for women."[180] More than 90% of these cash transfers were given to women. In 2012, with the goal to diminish infant and maternal mortality, Rousseff established the *Rede Cegonha* program that increased social assistance to expectant mothers and newborn babies. In 2013, she initiated tax cuts on household staples like beef, butter, coffee, sugar, and oil. She also championed women's property ownership through the *Minha Casa Minha Vida* program (My House, My Life) program. This program entails the construction of affordable housing for the poor, and the houses built become the property of women in cases of separations or divorces.[181]

As with Clinton, Rousseff has critics. In fact, Rousseff was impeached in 2016 for misrepresenting Brazil's budget ahead of her reelection campaign in 2014. Her opponents also likely sought impeachment because of her less than successful management of the country's economy. This intersection, of corruption and declining economics, spells trouble for poverty reduction. Although the aforementioned programs in Brazil are said to have moved 40 million people out of poverty, some people believe they amounted to a vote-getting scheme for Rousseff's party (i.e., cash transfers incentivized voting for her party). Moreover, the ability of Brazil to sustain programs in a poor economic climate is questionable. It is likely that Rousseff's opposition will continue poverty programs, but they might be cut back.[182]

Turning to the bureaucracy and local level of politics is another way to evaluate women in the executive. Researchers find that workers in U.S. federal agencies led by women bureaucrats perceive their agencies to be more high performing than those in agencies led by men.[183] Arguably, this result is due to differences in women's leadership styles, as public administration studies have shown that women are more likely to place higher emphasis on equity, long-term outlook, sense of community, and representation.[184] Similarly, in Yucatan, Mexico, women who are mayors are known to treat constituents in a personal and caring way. In fact, constituents come to the homes of women mayors for help, at all hours of the day, because, as one mayor explained, they are viewed as "more compassionate" and do things in a way that "a man will not understand."[185]

Although large-scale studies about substantive representation and women mayors have not been conducted, some evidence shows that women mayors further policy favorable to women constituents. In the Yucatan, for example, women mayors developed exercise and sports programs for women. This is notable given that women do not typically go out on their own, even to do something healthy like exercising, because doing so can be seen as scandalous.[186] In the United States, cities with women mayors tend to spend more money on social welfare policies. Such spending can be particularly helpful to single mothers who face the repercussions of poverty.[187] In India, when women are leaders of local councils, they spend more money on infrastructure related to the needs of rural women, namely, improvements in water, fuel, and roads.[188]

Despite these findings, more research is needed to conclusively say how women leaders influence substantive representation. Two studies in particular complicate how we see women as leaders in local executive institutions. First, Adrienne R. Smith (2014) studied whether cities with many women as elected officials have policies favorable to women, and she found that when women mayors have significant policy authority they can devote a large percentage of resources to women's issues.[189] This happened in Tulsa, Oklahoma, in 2006, when Kathy Taylor (D) used $635,546 of the city's $2,830,304 in federal block grant disbursements for women-friendly programs. An Omaha mayor at the time, a man, devoted $0 out of $4,779,382 to such programs.[190] However, Smith notes that not all women mayors have the power to make such decisions and that cities are more likely to devote resources to women's issues when they have done so in the past. That is, the institutions women serve in matter as much as their individual intentions to represent women. Second, though women mayors in Brazil are likely to increase the wages of women bureaucrats, some men mayors do the same, and not all women mayors attempt to increase women's presence in bureaucracies.[191] In this way, findings at the local level mirror findings about chief executives—some women executives offer more representation than others. According to Funk, Silva, and Escobar-Lemmon (2017),

> In the same way that some female presidents (like Michelle Bachelet) appointed parity cabinets, and others (most) do not, some female mayors appear to do more to improve the representation of women in particular by raising salaries and thus prestige within the organization, while others do not. At the same time some men (like Justin Trudeau) have also proven at the national level that they will take steps to advance women's representation in high-level positions. The same is also true at the local level. Women mayors are neither unambiguously good nor bad for a more gender balanced bureaucracy. The same is also true for men.[192]

CONCLUSION

Findings in this chapter point to progress in the executive. Women are becoming chief executives in greater number, and women who serve in cabinets have similar qualifications and political capital as men who are cabinet ministers. Furthermore, in recent years, the U.S. public has expressed willingness to vote for a woman as president and has become less likely to stereotype women politicians. Other countries have experienced profound change in that they have elected women as presidents or prime ministers and/or they have parity cabinets and women in inner cabinet positions such as minister of defense. Political opportunities for women's representation also exist at the local level and by way of women's policy agencies.

That said, women leaders often face gendered media coverage about their looks and personal life, and they must balance expectations about their private lives with their public duties. This balancing act, along with judgments about their emotions, reflects the long held patriarchal stereotypes that emerged with the spread of agriculture and were cemented in Western culture during the era of the Enlightenment and democratic revolutions. That is, men are more free to be political leaders who are assertive and dedicated to public life. Women, on the other hand, are still to this day often associated with the domestic sphere, which makes some people wonder whether they have the ability and emotional capacity to lead—especially during foreign policy crises or war. Arguably, we will see more women political leaders as patriarchal notions of gender expectations wane and women are freer to express themselves without the burden of the double bind.

REVIEW QUESTIONS

1. How would you rate women's overall representation in the executive? Consider their presence in top executive positions as well as their potential actions in cabinets, women policy agencies, and local government?

2. Some scholars have argued that women's presence in the cabinet is even more essential to women's substantive interests than their presence in the legislature. Why is this so? Explain what cabinet ministers can do (in the United States and in other countries), and compare them to the actions of legislators. If you wanted to be a public servant one day, do you think you would make a bigger impact as a cabinet minister or legislator, and why?

3. Women's policy agencies can be very active or can largely take symbolic actions. Using the U.S. women's policy agencies discussed in the chapter, make an argument that women's policy agencies make a significant difference in the larger bureaucracy. What evidence points to this conclusion, and what evidence challenges it?

4. Hegemonic masculinity is associated with the military and the U.S. presidency. Define hegemonic masculinity, and think of historical figures or current events that demonstrate either the president or military displaying hegemonic masculinity.

5. What world regions have had many women as the top political executive? Why do some regions or countries excel at electing women to top positions whereas others do not?

AMBITION ACTIVITIES

Speaking Confidently About Politics and Public Policies: We learned in this chapter that women who are candidates for executive positions or serve in them have extensive expertise even if media and the public sometimes presume otherwise. Nevertheless, recall from previous chapters that women often feel as if they are unqualified to speak on certain topics. This was called the "imposter syndrome." To combat this effect, practice speaking authoritatively about a political topic. Hold a press conference about this topic with some of your classmates as an audience. Devise questions in a group, and take turns being the expert. Practice answering questions on topics posed by classmates.

Here are some helpful hints for all public speakers that women should especially consider in order to portray themselves as authoritative and not tentative.[193] Try to avoid the following:

- Using disclaimers such as "I can't say for sure, but I think . . . "

- Hedging your claims with words like "I guess" or "kind of".

- Inserting tag questions, or immediately asking for confirmation of one's statement (e.g., "Representation of women is very important, isn't it?").

- Using intensifiers such as "really," "so," or "very" because they distract from the "directness and strength of an assertion" (e.g., "Maternity leave is a really important policy").

- Apologizing for your speaking style or the words you choose to describe your thoughts.

- Inserting fillers such as "like," "just," "totally," "you know," and "um."

Evaluate how you felt as you stood in front of your peers. In what ways were you confident? If you had nagging thoughts of pessimism, what were they focused on? What strategies did or could have helped you get past negative thoughts about your speaking skills or knowledge?

Practicing Leadership in Foreign Policy Decision-Making: Undertake a simulation of a foreign policy decision. Students should assume different roles as advisors, cabinet members, and the chief executive. Allow the simulation to play out unimpeded. After the simulations ends, discuss whether or how the sex of the participants affected the decisions made. In what ways did the presence of men and women influence who spoke during the simulation or who was listened to and emerged as a leader? How did these identities affect reactions to the different roles? Did issues of gender (in war, economics, etc.) become part of the discussion as the foreign policy was being discussed? In what ways did the decision reflect the gender dimensions of the foreign policy under consideration?

Gauging Gendered Reactions to Leadership: How do you give directions without being bossy? Some scholars suggest that women are penalized for displaying emotions related to dominance such as pride and anger.[194] Thus, women often remark that they must practice a leadership style that is distinct from that of men. That often means that women leaders are expected to smile more and be more caring and cooperative, and they are perceived as cold or demanding when they are not. This chapter also affirmed that the public and media often favor gender-role congruency, or when "leaders behave in a manner that is congruent with gender-role expectations." In small groups, have a woman practice leadership by giving instructions (about how to vote, how to complete an assignment, or any other topic). Have other students in the group check their reactions. Are you having gendered reactions? Did you think the woman was being bossy or a strong leader? Do you or other members of your group expect gender-role congruency when it comes to leadership? Why, or why not?

Recommitting to Amplification: Amplification check-in. How is amplification working for you? Is it now part of your routine or does it require thought? Discuss successes and failures with amplification thus far. Recommit to practicing amplification.

KEY WORDS

REFERENCES

1. Gillard, J. (2012). Transcript of Julia Gillard's speech. *The Sydney Morning Herald*. Retrieved from https://www.smh.com.au/politics/federal/transcript-of-julia-gillards-speech-20121010-27c36.html.

2. Ibid.

3. Jalalzai, F. (2018). A comparative assessment of Hillary Clinton's 2016 presidential race. *Socius: Sociological Research for a Dynamic World, 4*, 1–11.

4. Trolier, D. L., & Hamilton, T. K. (1986). Stereotypes and stereotyping: An overview of the cognitive approach. In J. F. Dovidio & S. L. Gaertner (Eds.), *Prejudice, discrimination, and racism* (pp. 127–163). Orlando, FL: Academic Press.

5. Honeywill, R. (2014). *Masculine madness: The normality of evil in the Western cultural imaginary* (doctoral dissertation). University of Tasmania.

6. Hinojosa, R. (2007). *"Recruiting" the self: The military and the making of masculinities* (doctoral dissertation). University of Florida.

7. Hinojosa, R. (2010). Doing hegemony: Military, men, and constructing a hegemonic masculinity. *The Journal of Men's Studies, 18*(2), 179–194.

8. Hinojosa, R. (2007). *"Recruiting" the self: The military and the making of masculinities.*

9. Howard, J., & Prividera, L. (2006). Gendered nationalism: A critical analysis of militarism, patriarchy, and the ideal soldier. *Texas Speech Communication Journal, 30*(2), 134–145.

10. Zaretti, A. (2005). Lesbian gay bi-sexual transgender (LGBT) personnel: A military challenge. In G. Caforior & M. Nuciari (Eds.), *Handbook of the sociology of the military* (pp. 391–404). New York, NY: Springer.

11. Ibid.

12. Jalalzai, F. (2018). A comparative assessment of Hillary Clinton's 2016 presidential race. *Socius: Sociological Research for a Dynamic World, 4,* 1–11.

13. Duerst-Lahti, G. (2008). Seeing what has always been: Opening study of the presidency. *PS–Political Science & Politics, 41*(4), 733–737.

14. Jalalzai, F. (2018). A comparative assessment of Hillary Clinton's 2016 presidential race. *Socius: Sociological Research for a Dynamic World, 4,* 1–11.

15. Duerst-Lahti, G. (2008). "Seeing what has always been": Opening study of the presidency.

16. Connell, R. W., &. Messerschmidt, J. W. (2005, December). Hegemonic masculinity: Rethinking the concept. *Gender & Society, 19*(6), 829–859.

17. Locke, B. (2013). *The military-masculinity complex: Hegemonic masculinity and the United States Armed Forces, 1940–1963* (doctoral dissertation). University of Nebraska-Lincoln.

18. Cockburn, C. (2001). The gendered dynamics of armed conflict and political violence." In C. Moser & F. Clark (Eds.), *Victims, perpetrators or actors? Gender, armed conflict and political violence.* London, UK: Zed Books.

19. Enloe, C. (2000). *Maneuvers: The international politics of militarizing women's lives.* Oakland: University of California Press.

20. Midberry, J. (2015). Photos of breastfeeding in uniform: Contesting discourses of masculinity, nationalism, and the military. *Feminist Media Studies 17*(6), 972–987.

21. Ibid.

22. Cornell University Roper Center. (2016). *Madame president: Changing attitudes about a woman president.* Retrieved from https://ropercenter.cornell.edu/changing-attitudes-about-a-woman-president.

23. Ferree, M. M. (1974). A woman for president? Changing responses: 1958–1972. *Public Opinion Quarterly, 38*(3), 390-399. Retrieved from https://www.jstor.org/stable/2748167.

24. McCarthy, J. (2015). In U.S., socialist presidential candidates least appealing. *Gallop*. Retrieved from https://news.gallup.com/poll/183713/socialist-presidential-candidates-least-appealing.aspx.

25. Streb, M., Burrell, B., Frederick, B., & Genovese, M. A. (2008). Social desirability effects and support for a female American president. *Public Opinion Quarterly, 72*(1), 76–89.

26. Horowitz, J. M., Igielnik, R., & Parker, K. (2018). 1. Views on the state of gender and leadership and obstacles for women. *Pew Research Center*. Retrieved from http://www.pewsocialtrends.org/2018/09/20/1-views-on-the-state-of-gender-and-leadership-and-obstacles-for-women.

27. Dolan, K. (2014). *When does gender matter?: Women candidates and gender stereotypes in American elections*. New York, NY: Oxford University Press.

28. Davidson, M., & Burke, R. (2016). Women in management worldwide: Progress and prospects—An overview. In J. Burke (Ed.), *Women in management worldwide: Progress and prospects* (pp. 1–18). London, UK: Gower.

29. Eagly, A. H., Karau, S. J., & Makhijani, M. G. (1992). Gender and the evaluation of leaders: A meta-analysis. *Psychological Bulletin, 111*(1), 3–22.

30. Ibid.

31. Eagly, A. H., Karau, S. J., & Makhijani, M. G. (1995). Gender and the effectiveness of leaders: A meta-analysis. *Psychological Bulletin, 117*, 125–145.

32. Eagly, A. H., Karau, S. J., & Makhijani, M. G. (1992). Gender and the evaluation of leaders: A meta-analysis.

33. Ibid.

34. Ibid.

35. Brescoll, V. (2016). Leading with their hearts? How gender stereotypes of emotion lead to biased evaluations of female leaders. *The Leadership Quarterly, 27*(3), 415–428.

36. Ibid.

37. Carroll, S. J. (2009). Reflections on gender and Hillary Clinton's presidential campaign: The good, the bad, and the misogynic. *Politics & Gender, 5*(1), 1–20.

38. Okimoto, T., & Brescoll, V. (2010). The price of power: Power seeking and backlash against female politicians. *Personality and Social Psychology Bulletin, 36*(7), 923–936.

39. Adams, W. (1975). Candidate characteristics, office of election, and voter responses. *Experimental Study of Politics, 4*(1), 76–88.

40. Dolan, K. (1997). Gender differences in support for women candidates: Is there a glass ceiling in American politics? *Women & Politics, 17*(2), 27–41.

41. Huddy, L., & Terkildsen, N. (1993). The consequences of gender stereotypes for women candidates at different levels and types of offices. *Political Research Quarterly, 46*(3), 503–525.

42. Mueller, C. M. (1986). Nurturance and mastery: Competing qualifications for women's access to high public office? In G. Moore & G. Spitze (Eds.), *Women and politics: Activism, attitudes, and office-holding* (pp. 211–232). Greenwich, CT: JAI Press.

43. Rosenwasser, S. M., & Seale, J. (1988). Attitudes toward a hypothetical male or female candidate for president—A research note. *Political Psychology, 9*(4), 591–598.

44. Sigelman, L., Sigelman, C., & Fowler, C. (1987). A bird of a different feather? An experimental investigation of physical attractiveness and the electability of female candidates. *Social Psychology Quarterly, 50*(1), 32–43.

45. Huddy, L., & Terkildsen, N. (1993). The consequences of gender stereotypes for women candidates at different levels and types of offices.

46. Lawless, J. L. (2004). Women, war, and winning elections: Gender stereotyping in the post-September 11th Era. *Political Research Quarterly, 57*(3), 479–490.

47. Ibid.

48. Cornell University Roper Center. (2016). *Madame president: Changing attitudes about a woman president.*

49. Pew Research Center. (2008). Men or women: Who's the better leader?: A paradox in public attitudes. Retrieved from http://www.pewsocialtrends.org/2008/08/25/men-or-women-whos-the-better-leader.

50. Ibid.

51. Brooks, D. J. (2013). *He runs, she runs: Why gender stereotypes do not harm women candidates.* Princeton, NJ: Princeton University Press.

52. Dolan, K., & Lynch, T. (2016). The impact of gender stereotypes on voting for women candidates by level and type of office. *Politics & Gender, 12*(3), 573–594.

53. Ibid.

54. Dolan, K. (2014). *When does gender matter?: Women candidates and gender stereotypes in American elections.*

55. Pantti, M. (2011). Literary review for the project gender, politics and media: Challenging stereotypes, promoting diversity, strengthening equality. *Portraying Politics.* Retrieved from http://www.portrayingpolitics.net/research.php.

56. Heldman, C., Carroll, S. J., & Olson, S. (2005). She brought only a skirt. *Political Communication, 22*, 313–335.

57. Aday, S., & Devitt, J. (2001). Style over substance: Newspaper coverage of Elizabeth Dole's presidential bid. *The Harvard International Journal of Press/ Politics, 6*(2), 52–73.

58. Bystrom, D. (2018). Gender and communication on the campaign trail: Media coverage, advertising, and online outreach." In S. Carroll & R. Fox (Eds.), *Gender and elections: Shaping the future of American politics* (pp. 250–279). Cambridge, MA: Cambridge University Press.

59. Bryant, L. H. (2014). *Gender balanced or gender biased? An examination of news coverage of male and female governors* (doctoral dissertation). State University of New York at Albany, ProQuest Dissertations.

60. Carlin, D., & Winfrey, K. (2009). Have you come a long way, baby? Hillary Clinton, Sarah Palin, and sexism in 2008 campaign coverage. *Communication Studies, 60*(4), 326–343.

61. Hall, L., & Donaghue, N. (2013). "Nice girls don't carry knives": Constructions of ambition in media coverage of Australia's first female prime minister. *British Journal of Social Psychology, 52*(4), 631–647.

62. Ibid.

63. Carlin, D., & Winfrey, K. (2009). Have you come a long way, baby? Hillary Clinton, Sarah Palin, and sexism in 2008 campaign coverage.

64. Carroll, S. J. (2009). Reflections on gender and Hillary Clinton's presidential campaign: The good, the bad, and the misogynic.

65. Shepard, R. (2017). Confronting gender bias, finding a voice: Hillary Clinton and the New Hampshire crying incident. *Argumentation and Advocacy, 46*(1), 64–77.

66. Curnalia, R., & Mermer, D. (2014). The "Ice Queen" melted and it won her the primary: Evidence of gender stereotypes and the double bind in news frames of Hillary Clinton's "emotional moment." *Qualitative Research Reports in Communication, 15*(1), 26–32.

67. Poloni-Staudinger, L., & Ortbals, C. (2014). Gendering Abbottabad: Agency and hegemonic masculinity in an age of global terrorism. *Gender Issues, 31*(1), 34.

68. Ortbals, C., & Poloni-Staudinger, L. (2016). Women policymakers framing their leadership and lives in relation to terrorism: The Basque case. *Journal of Women, Politics, and Policy, 37*(2), 121–144.

69. Corasaniti, N. (2016). Hillary Clinton ad makes an emotional pitch to Hispanics. *The New York Times*. Retrieved from https://www.nytimes.com/2016/02/19/us/politics/hillary-clinton-ad-immigrants.html.

70. Figueroa, M. (2016). Hillary Clinton cries crocodile tears for Latin American immigrants. *Truthdig*. Retrieved from https://www.truthdig.com/articles/hillary-clinton-cries-crocodile-tears-for-latin-american-immigrants.

71. Schneider, C. (2018). Donald Trump's Twitter assault on the English language weakens him and America. *USA Today*. Retrieved from https://www.usatoday.com/story/opinion/2018/05/29/donald-trump-tweets-assault-english-language-undermine-america-column/638888002.

72. Goren, L. J. (2018). Authenticity and emotion: Hillary Rodham Clinton's dual constraints. *Politics & Gender* 14(1): 111–115.

73. Nai, A., and J. Maier. 2018. Perceived personality and campaign style of Hillary Clinton and Donald Trump. *Personality and Individual Differences* 121: 80–83.

74. Ortbals, C., & Poloni-Staudinger, L. (2016). Women policymakers framing their leadership and lives in relation to terrorism: The Basque case.

75. West, C., & Zimmerman, D. H. (1987, June). Doing gender. *Gender & Society*, *1*(2), 125–151.

76. Poloni-Staudinger, L., & Ortbals, C. (2014). Gendering Abbottabad: Agency and hegemonic masculinity in an age of global terrorism.

77. Ortbals, C., & Poloni-Staudinger, L. (2016). Women policymakers framing their leadership and lives in relation to terrorism: The Basque case.

78. Ortbals, C. D., & Poloni-Staudinger, L. (2018). *Gender and political violence: Women changing the politics of terrorism*. Cham, Switzerland: Springer.

79. Shan-Jan, S. L., & Banaszak, L. A. (2017, March). Do government positions held by women matter? A cross-national examination of female ministers' impacts on women's political participation. *Politics & Gender*, *13*(1), 132–162.

80. Jalalzai, F. (2018). A comparative assessment of Hillary Clinton's 2016 presidential race. *Socius: Sociological Research for a Dynamic World*, *4*, 1–11.

81. Chaney, E. (2014). *Supermadre: Women in politics in Latin America*. Austin: University of Texas Press.

82. Reyes-Housholder, C., & Thomas, G. (2018). Latin America's *Presidentas*: Overcoming challenges, forging new pathways. In Schwindt-Bayer, L. (Ed.), *Gender and representation in Latin America* (pp. 19–38). New York, NY: Oxford.

83. Jalalzai, F. (2016). *Women presidents of Latin America: Beyond family ties?* New York, NY: Routledge.

84. Jalalzai, F. (2018). A comparative assessment of Hillary Clinton's 2016 presidential race. *Socius: Sociological Research for a Dynamic World, 4*, 1–11.

85. Politico Staff. (2016). Full text: Donald Trump's speech on fighting terrorism. *Politco*. Retrieved from https://www.politico.com/story/2016/08/donald-trump-terrorism-speech-227025.

86. Krook, M. L., & O'Brien, D. (2012). All the president's men? The appointment of female cabinet ministers worldwide. *Journal of Politics, 74*(3), 840–855.

87. Borrelli, M. (2010). The contemporary presidency: Gender desegregation and gender integration in the president's cabinet, 1933-2010. *Presidential Studies Quarterly, 40*(4), 734–749.

88. Ibid.

89. Suraj, J., Scherpereel, J., & Adams, M. (2014). Gender norms and women's political representation: A global analysis of cabinets, 1979–2009. *Governance, 28*(2), 321–345.

90. Krook, M. L., & O'Brien, D. (2012). All the president's men? The appointment of female cabinet ministers worldwide.

91. Beckwith, K., Franceschet, S., & Annesley, C. (2017). What do women symbolize? Symbolic representation and cabinet appointments. *Politics, Groups, and Identities, 5*(3), 488–493.

92. Escobar-Lemmon, & Taylor-Robinson. (2009). Getting to the top: Career paths of women in Latin American cabinets. *Political Research Quarterly, 62*(4), 685–699.

93. Krook, M. L., & O'Brien, D. (2012). All the president's men? The appointment of female cabinet ministers worldwide.

94. Lovenduski, J. (1986). *Women and European politics*. Brighton, UK: Harvester.

95. Escobar-Lemmon, M, & Taylor-Robinson, M. (2016). *Women in presidential cabinets: Power players or abundant tokens?* New York, NY: Oxford University Press.

96. Stockemer, D. (2017). The proportion of women in legislatures and cabinets: What is the empirical link? *Polity, 49*(3), 434–460.

97. Suraj, J., Scherpereel, J., & Adams, M. (2014). Gender norms and women's political representation: A global analysis of cabinets, 1979–2009.

98. Beckwith, K., Mather, F. L., & Annesley,C. (2016). Evolving norms and the demand for equal female inclusion in governing cabinets. *Scholars Strategy Network*. Retrieved from https://scholars.org/brief/evolving-norms-and-demand-equal-female-inclusion-governing-cabinets.

99. Escobar-Lemmon, M, & Taylor-Robinson, M. (2016). *Women in presidential cabinets: Power players or abundant tokens?*

100. Barnes, T., & O'Brien, D. (2018). Defending the realm: The appointment of female defense ministers worldwide. *American Journal of Political Science, 62*(2), 355–368.

101. Ibid.

102. Ibid.

103. Ortbals, C., & Poloni-Staudinger, L. (2016). Women policymakers framing their leadership and lives in relation to terrorism: The Basque case.

104. Nesiah, V. (2012). Feminism as counterterrorism? *Foreign Policy in Focus*. Retrieved from http://fpif.org/feminism_as_counterterrorism.

105. United Nations. (2008). Security Council demands immediate and complete halt to acts of sexual violence against civilians in conflict zones, unanimously adopting Resolution 1820 (2008). *United Nations: Meetings Coverages and Presse Releases*. Retrieved from https://www.un.org/press/en/2008/sc9364. doc.htm.

106. Nesiah, V. (2012). Feminism as counterterrorism?

107. Geier, K. (2016). Why feminists shouldn't trust Hillary Clinton. *New Republic*. Retrieved from https://newrepublic.com/article/137862/feminists-shouldnt-trust-hillary-clinton.

108. Khalek, R. (2015). Hillary Clinton and the feminism of exclusion. *Fair*. Retrieved from http://fair.org/extra/hillary-clinton-and-the-feminism-of-exclusion.

109. Gentry, C. (2015). Epistemological failures: Everyday terrorism in the West. *Critical Studies on Terrorism, 8*(3), 362–382.

110. Shah, B. (2016, August 20). Can Hillary Clinton change gender roles in politics? *Al Jazeera*. Retrieved from http://www.aljazeera.com/indepth/opinion/2016/08/hillary-clinton-change-gender-roles-politics-160817142422440.html.

111. Dolan, J. (2010). Women as leaders in executive service." In K. O'Connor (Ed.), *Gender and women's leadership: A reference handbook*. Thousand Oaks, CA: SAGE.

112. Ortbals, C., & Poloni-Staudinger, L. (2018). *Gender and political violence: Women changing the politics of terrorism*. New York, NY: Springer.

113. Hudson, V. M., Leidl, P., & Hunt, S. (2015). *The Hillary doctrine: Sex and American foreign policy*. New York, NY: Columbia University Press.

114. Caldwell, D., & Williams, R. E. J. (2016). *Seeking security in an insecure world.* New York, NY: Rowman & Littlefield.

115. The White House. (2016). *United States national action plan on women, peace, and security.* Retrieved from https://www.usaid.gov/sites/default/files/documents/1868/National%20Action%20Plan%20on%20Women%2C%20Peace%2C%20and%20Security.pdf.

116. Ibid.

117. Ibid.

118. Stetson, D. M., & Mazur, A. G. (1995). *Comparative state feminism.* Thousand Oaks, CA: SAGE.

119. Mazur, A. G. (2007). Women's policy agencies, women's movements and a shifting political context: Towards a gendered republic in France? In J. Outshoorn & J. Kantola (Eds.), *Changing state feminism* (pp. 102–123). London, UK: Palgrave Macmillan.

120. Outshooren, J., & Kantola. J. (2007). *Changing state feminism.* New York, NY: Palgrave Macmillan.

121. Mazur, A., & McBride, D. (2007). State feminism since 1980s: From loose notion to operationalized concept. *Politics & Gender, 3*(4), 501–513.

122. Hernes, H. M. (1987). *Welfare state and woman power: Essays in state feminism.* Oslo: Scandinavian University Press.

123. Palmeri, T. (2017). White House Council for Women and Girls goes dark under Trump. *Politico.* Retrieved from https://www.politico.com/story/2017/06/30/donald-trump-white-house-council-for-women-and-girls-239979.

124. Stetson, D. M., & Mazur, A. G. (1995). *Comparative state feminism.*

125. Outshooren, J., & Kantola. J. (2007). *Changing state feminism.*

126. Ortbals, C. D. (2008). Subnational politics in Spain: New avenues for feminist policymaking and activism. *Politics & Gender, 4*(1), 93–119.

127. Bustelo, M. (2016). Three decades of state feminism and gender equality policies in multi-governed Spain. *Sex Roles, 74*(3–4), 107–120.

128. Bustelo, M., & Ortbals, C. (2007). The evolution of Spanish state feminism: A fragmented landscape. In J. Outshoorn and J. Kantola (Eds.), *Changing state feminism* (pp. 201–223). London, UK: Palgrave Macmillian.

129. Mazur, A. (1995). Strong state and symbolic reform in France: le Ministère des Droits de la Femme." In D. M. Stetson & A. G. Mazur (Eds.), *Comparative state feminism* (pp. 76–94). Thousand Oaks, CA: SAGE.

130. Mazur, A. G. (2007). Women's policy agencies, women's movements and a shifting political context: Towards a gendered republic in France?

131. Wulfhorst, E. (2018). France is "Feminist Country" battling to put thought into action, minister says." *Reuters*. Retrieved from https://www.reuters.com/article/us-un-france-women-feminism/france-is-feminist-country-battling-to-put-thought-into-action-minister-says-idUSKCN1GQ0LM.

132. Weldon, S. L. (2002). Beyond bodies: Institutional sources of representation for women in Democratic policymaking. *The Journal of Politics, 64*(4), 1153–1174.

133. Ortbals, C. D. (2008). Subnational politics in Spain: New avenues for feminist policymaking and activism.

134. Ibid.

135. Mazur, A., & McBride, D. (2007). State feminism since 1980s: From loose notion to operationalized concept.

136. Ibid.

137. Carroll, S. J. (2016). Women in state government: Still too few. *Center for American Women and Politics*. Retrieved from http://www.cawp.rutgers.edu/sites/default/files/resources/stilltoofew-carroll.pdf.

138. Sanbonmatsu, K. (2018). Women's election to office in the fifty states: Opportunities and challenges. In S. J. Carroll & R. L. Fox (Eds.), *Gender and elections: Shaping the future of American politics* (pp. 280–302). Cambridge, MA: Cambridge University Press.

139. Windett, J. (2014). Differing paths to the top: Gender, ambition, and running for governor. *Journal of Women, Politics, & Policy, 35*(4), 287–314.

140. Windett, J. H. (2011). State effects and the emergence and success of female gubernatorial candidates. *State Politics & Policy Quarterly, 11*(4), 460–482.

141. Ibid.

142. Stabenow, D. (2018). In Michigan, the best candidates just happened to be women. *The New York Times*. Retrieved from https://www.nytimes.com/2018/11/12/opinion/election-michigan-women-stabenow-whitmer.html.

143. Center for American Women and Politics. (2018). Women mayors among the 100 largest cities. Retrieved from http://www.cawp.rutgers.edu/levels_of_office/women-mayors-us-cities-2018.

144. Osborn, T. (2012). *How women represent women: Political parties, gender and representation in the state legislatures*. New York, NY: Oxford University Press.

145. Holman, M. (2017). Women in local government: What we know and where we go from here. *State and Local Government Review, 49*(4), 285–296.

146. Bowser, M. (2017). Dissatisfied with the number of women of color in office? You can help change that. *Cosmopolitan*. Retrieved from https://www .cosmopolitan.com/politics/a12486319/muriel-bowser-woman-of-color-politics.

147. Crowder-Meyer, M. (2013). Gendered recruitment without trying: How local party recruiters affect women's representation. *Politics & Gender, 9*(4), 390–413.

148. Ortbals, C., & Poloni-Staudinger, L. (2016). Women policymakers framing their leadership and lives in relation to terrorism: The Basque case.

149. Ibid., 137.

150. Garcia-Mainar, I., Molina, J. A., & Victor Montuenga, V. (2011). Gender differences in childcare: Time allocation in five European countries. *Feminist Economics, 17*(1), 119–150.

151. Ortbals, C., & Poloni-Staudinger, L. (2016). Women policymakers framing their leadership and lives in relation to terrorism: The Basque case.

152. Ibid., 136.

153. Ibid.

154. Loyola-Henandez, L. (2018). The porous state: Female mayors performing the state in Yucatecan Maya municipalities. *Political Geography, 62*, 48–57.

155. Ibid.

156. United Nations. (2015). *Power and decision-making*. Retrieved from https:// unstats.un.org/unsd/gender/downloads/WorldsWomen2015_chapter5_t.pdf.

157. Ibid.

158. Ibid.

159. Ibid.

160. City Mayors. (n.d.). Largest cities with women mayors. Retrieved from http:// www.citymayors.com/statistics/largest-cities-women-mayors.html.

161. Vidal C., F. (2017). *Women in Mexican politics: A study of representation in a renewed federal and democratic state*. Lanham, MD: Lexington Books.

162. Shanker, R. (2014). Measurement of women's political participation at the local level: India experience. Retrieved from https://unstats.un.org/unsd/gender/ mexico_nov2014/Session%206%20India%20paper.pdf.

163. Young, M. (2018). Native women move to the front of tribal leadership. *Native Daughters*. Retrieved from http://cojmc.unl.edu/nativedaughters/leaders/native-women-move-to-the-front-of-tribal-leadership.

164. Smithsonian. (2016). Strong women/strong nations 6: Panel 2, tribal governance. *National Museum of the American Indian*. Retrieved from https://www.youtube.com/watch?reload=9&v=L6LAZ4IbyBE.

165. Lombardo, E., & Meier, P. (2014). *The symbolic representation of gender: A discursive approach*. Burlington, VT: Ashgate.

166. Jalalzai, F. (2013). *Shattered, cracked, or firmly intact?: Women and the executive glass ceiling worldwide* (p. 81). Oxford, UK: Oxford University Press.

167. Alexander, A. C., & Jalalzai, F. (2018). Symbolic empowerment and female heads of states and government: A global, multilevel analysis. *Politics, Groups, and Identities*.

168. Reyes-Housholder, C., & Schwindt-Bayer, L. (2016). The impact of presidents on political activity. In J. M. Martin & M. Borrelli (Eds.), *The gendered executive: A comparative analysis of presidents, prime ministers, and chief executives* (pp. 103–122). Philadelphia, PA: Temple University Press.

169. Shan-Jan, S. L., & Banaszak, L. A. (2017, March). Do government positions held by women matter? A cross-national examination of female ministers' impacts on women's political participation.

170. Ibid.

171. Jalalzai, F. (2016). *Women presidents of Latin America: Beyond family ties?*

172. Ibid.

173. Oxfam International. (2018). *Why the majority of the world's poor are women*. Retrieved from https://www.oxfam.org/en/even-it/why-majorty-worlds-poor-are-women.

174. Cawthorne, A. The straight facts on women in poverty. *Center for American Progress*. Retrieved from https://www.americanprogress.org/issues/women/reports/2008/10/08/5103/the-straight-facts-on-women-in-poverty.

175. The United Nations. (2015). The world's women 2015: Poverty. *United Nations Statistics*. Retrieved from https://unstats.un.org/unsd/gender/downloads/Ch8_Poverty_info.pdf.

176. Cawthorne, A. (2008). The straight facts on women in poverty. *Center for American Progress*.

177. Clinton, H. (2018). Issues: Poverty. *Hillary for America*. Retrieved from https://www.hillaryclinton.com/issues/poverty.

178. Clinton, H. (2018). Issues: Social security and Medicare. *Hillary for America*. Retrieved from https://www.hillaryclinton.com/issues/social-security-and-medicare.

179. Appelbaum, B. (2016). The millions of Americans Donald Trump and Hillary Clinton barely mention: The poor. *The New York Times*. Retrieved from https://www.nytimes.com/2016/08/12/us/politics/trump-clinton-poverty.html.

180. Jalalzai, F., & dos Santos, P. G. (2015). The Dilma effect? Women's representation under Dilma Rousseff's presidency. *Politics & Gender, 11*(1), 117–145.

181. Ibid.

182. Kwong, M. (2016). Rousseff impeachment: How Brazil lost its way to economic stability. *CBC News*. Retrieved from https://www.cbc.ca/news/world/brazil-rousseff-impeachment-1.3577394.

183. D'Agostino, M. J. (2015). The difference that women make: Government performance and women-led agencies. *Administration & Society, 47*(5), 532–548.

184. Riccucci, N. M., Hamidullah, M. F., & Pandey, S. K. (2015). Women in city hall: Gender dimensions of managerial values. *The American Review of Public Administration, 45*(3), 247–262.

185. Loyola-Henandez, L. (2018). The porous state: Female mayors performing the state in Yucatecan Maya municipalities (p.52).

186. Ibid.

187. Holman, M. R. (2014). Sex and the city: Female leaders and spending on social welfare. *Journal of Urban Affairs, 36*(4), 701–715.

188. Chattopadhyay, R., & Duflo, E. (2004). Women as policy makers: Evidence from a randomized policy experiment in India. *Econometrica, 72*, 1409–1443.

189. Smith, A. (2014). Cities where women rule: Female political incorporation and the allocation of community development block grant funding. *Politics & Gender, 10*(03), 313–340.

190. Ibid.

191. Funk, K. D., Silva, T., & Escobar-Lemmon, M. (2017). *The leading ladies: How the election of women executives impacts gender diversity and gender equality in subnational bureaucracies*. Paper presented at the Midwest Political Science Association, Chicago, IL. Retrieved from people.tamu.edu/~nsthiago/TheLeadingLadies_MPSA2016.pdf.

192. Ibid., 27.

193. Leaper, C., & Robnett, R D. (2011). Women are more likely than men to use tentative language, aren't they? A meta-analysis testing for gender differences and moderators. *Psychology of Women Quarterly*, *35*(1), 129–142.

194. Brescoll, V. (2016). Leading with their hearts? How gender stereotypes of emotion lead to biased evaluations of female leaders.

CHAPTER EIGHT

WOMEN IN THE JUDICIARY

The advancement of the status of women has long depended on decisions made in the judicial system. When legislatures have been slow to act, women's rights have frequently been moved forward by individuals and groups challenging the status quo in the courts. Historically, women have had to rely on men lawyers and judges to put forward rulings to advance their cause, but increasingly, women have been making inroads into these positions and have been at the forefront of some important decisions. For example, in 2003, the Massachusetts Supreme Court recognized the right of same sex couples to marry in *Goodridge v. Department of Public Health* (2003), making it the first state in the United States to legalize same sex marriage.[1] The decision was written by Chief Justice Margaret Marshall; Marshall was born in South Africa and active in the anti-apartheid movement.[2] She came to the United States to study but was unable to return home due to her activism; while in the United States, she became involved in the second wave of the women's movement. During her legal career, she continued to work for the advancement of human rights for all, and she was the first woman appointed to serve as the Chief Justice of the Massachusetts Supreme Court. The *Goodridge* decision was a close one; just five of the nine justices signed on to the opinion recognizing same sex marriage, so Marshall's role was critical in advancing the rights of same sex couples to marry. Her opinion noted the similarities between bans on interracial marriages and same sex marriages and insisted that "simple principles of decency" require that we extend to same sex couples "full acceptance, tolerance, and respect." While Marshall herself downplays her role in this historic decision, some have noted parallels between the lived experience of Marshall, working to extend rights to all, and her most famous ruling extending the rights associated with marriage to same sex couples. Indeed, this is one of the critical questions about the impact of women in the judiciary—to what extent do the different life experiences of women and the presence of women generally influence the decisions made by the judicial branch?

Prior to the 1900s, women were largely excluded from the legal profession and thus serving in the judicial branch, as becoming a professional attorney is the most common path to becoming a judge. Women sometimes practiced as lawyers in the 1700s and 1800s because a legal education or admission to the bar was not always required to do so. For instance, Mary Magoon opened a law practice in Iowa in the 1860s; while she had not been admitted to the state bar, this was not required to practice law at the county level. Also in Iowa, Arabella Mansfield was permitted to take the bar exam in 1869, despite the fact that state law restricted admission to the field to white men; she passed after studying informally in her brother's law practice, making her the first officially recognized woman lawyer in the United States.[3] A year later, Esther Morris was appointed to be a justice of the peace in Wyoming, making her the first woman in the United States to be appointed to the judiciary.[4] Charlotte Ray became the first African American admitted to the bar in 1872.[5] Around the globe, women began making inroads into the legal profession around the same time frame. In Brazil, Myrthes Gomes de Campos was the first woman to graduate from law school in 1898; in England and New Zealand, the first women graduated from law school in 1888 and 1897, respectively.[6]

These gains were piecemeal. As noted in Chapter 2, the U.S. Supreme Court denied Myra Bradwell the right to a license to practice law under the Equal Protection Clause in 1873; that decision permitted states to deny women access to the bar. Women had to fight for access to the bar on a state-by-state basis, and it wasn't until 1920 that they had the right to do so in every state. The American Bar Association, the most powerful group representing lawyers' interests, prohibited women until 1918; during this time frame, women were "kept from the networks through which lawyers gain contacts, referrals, and power."[7] Even as women gained entry to law school and the bar, they were not accepted into the legal profession upon graduation. When Sandra Day O'Connor, the first woman appointed to the U.S. Supreme Court, graduated from Stanford Law ranked third in her class in 1952, she could not find employment; so, she worked for free for the county attorney of California's San Mateo region to gain experience, after turning down a paid position as a legal secretary.[8] Ruth Bader Ginsburg, a current U.S. Supreme Court justice, was chastised for taking a man's spot at Harvard Law school; after she eventually graduated first in her class from Columbia Law School, she was only able to obtain a clerk position (which is the common path to a high-paying job and career) after one of her professors refused to recommend any other students until Ginsburg was hired. After clerking for two years, Ginsburg was offered jobs at some law firms but at a substantially lower salary than her men counterparts.[9]

The legal field looks different these days as there are now more women in the profession. For example, in 2016, women outnumbered men in law school in the United States for the first time ever. However, there are still many barriers to women's advancement in the profession, and they are not well represented in positions of power. Women are just over 25% of partners in law firms and just under 25% of all Fortune 500 general counsels;[10] The current U.S. Supreme Court is just one third women, and only 36% of federal appellate court judges are women.[11]

While women have been making slow, steady progress in the field of law since the late-1800s, they are still a minority of judges in the United States and around the world. There is evidence to suggest that women act differently from men when they are on the bench; thus, as with the legislative and executive branches, the underrepresentation of women in the judicial branch matters. In this chapter, we examine the advancement of women as public officials in the legal system. Because the most common path to the judicial branch is through the legal profession, we start by examining the advancement of women in law school and as lawyers. Next, we examine women's status as public defenders, prosecutors, and judges. As in Chapter 6, we examine theories about the intersection of sex and the law and then look at the research about the impact of women on the legal system and the decisions and outcomes it produces. We also look at how these decisions and outcomes affect women generally. Finally, we conclude with ways to rework the legal system to increase the representation of women and to improve the status of women.

WOMEN AS LAWYERS AND IN LAW SCHOOL

Generally speaking, the path to an elected or appointed position in the judicial branch starts in law school. Not all judges are lawyers; for instance, in New York, town and village justices who preside over town and village courts are not required to have a law degree, and in Pennsylvania, law degrees are not required to serve in some lower courts. But 28 U.S. states require all judges presiding over misdemeanor cases to have a law degree, and in 14 of the remaining states, a defendant who is sentenced to jail by a judge without a law degree has the right to request a new trial before a judge with a law degree.[12] Thus, it is important to trace the path of women through law school and as lawyers to understand the role and impact of women in the judicial system.

As noted above, the path through law school for early women pioneers in the field of law was not easy. Like Justice Ginsburg, many were resented for taking the place of men; and like Justice O'Connor, many had difficulty finding employment after graduation. It's worth quoting Professor Cynthia Bowman (2009) extensively to describe the experience of Jane M.G. Foster, a Cornell Law School alum for whom one of the law school buildings on the Cornell Law campus is named; what Bowman describes was a typical experience for these women:

> Jane Foster graduated from Cornell Law School in 1918, having served as an editor of the law review and being elected to the Order of the Coif. But no law firm wanted her services. She obtained employment not as a lawyer but as a legal assistant in a New York City firm, and that only with the aid of a faculty member. She worked at the firm from 1918 to 1929, in the postwar era of optimism, the New Woman, and economic

expansion. One after another man made partner while she was there, but advancement was closed to her. After ten years of experience in corporate finance and banking and with strong recommendations from her Cornell sponsors and former employer, she again sought employment as an attorney, only to be rebuffed repeatedly. . . . Discouraged, Jane Foster dropped out of law and put her business and financial skills to work for her own benefit, amassing the fortune that made her benevolence to Cornell Law School possible. In the 1950s, she returned to the Ohio town where she had been born, to care for her aged mother, and remained there until her death, never having practiced law.[13]

There were very few women admitted to law school in the early to mid-1900s; few of those admitted overcame the barriers that were placed in their way. While some law schools admitted more women during World War II to make up for decreasing men's enrollment, enrollment of women declined again when these men returned from the war, such that just 3.3% of all law school students were women in 1947.[14] With the passage of federal civil rights legislation, including Title VII and Title IX, along with court challenges to sex-based discrimination in law school admissions and employment, the number of women enrolling in law school began to grow. From 1947 to 1967, the percentage of women in law school grew from 3.3% to 4.5%; from 1968 to 1988, that number grew from 6.0% to 40.7%. By 2016, women had become the majority of all law school students, a trend that continues into the present.

Women have also made gains into practicing law, but it has not been easy. As Bowman (2009) describes, early women law school graduates were told by employers they were not interested in hiring women; it wasn't until World War II that these firms started hiring women lawyers.[15] Prior to this, a few women were lucky enough to find employment in law, but as men associates were drafted during the war, law firms were forced to hire more women to do their work. Of course, as in other occupations, these women were often hired temporarily, to be replaced by men when they returned from the war. The list of women law school graduates from the 1950s and 1960s who were rejected by major law firms upon graduation includes not only Justices O'Connor and Ginsburg but also U.S. Attorney General Janet Reno, Democratic Vice-Presidential Nominee Geraldine Ferraro, and U.S. Senator Elizabeth Dole (R-NC).[16]

Despite the fact that women now make up a majority of law school students and graduates, sex-based disparities in legal employment persist. Only 35% of lawyers working at the top law firms are women; and just 20% of equity partners, those who hold shares in their firms, are women.[17] The percentage of women who are associates in law firms, the lowest level in these firms, peaked in 2009 at just under 46% of all associates; during the Great Recession, law firms had widespread layoffs, and the employment of women associates only returned to near peak 2009 levels in 2017.[18] This gap in legal employment between the sexes is true not only in the United States but in other countries as well. For instance, the majority of law school graduates in Canada are also women, but just 9.7% of those women lawyers were law firm partners in 2014, compared to 23.5% of men lawyers who were partners.[19] The higher up one looks in law firms, the larger the gap grows. The gap in employment is smallest for associates and largest for equity partners. The National Association of Women Lawyers (NAWL) terms this the 50/15/15 problem—for 15 years, nearly 50% of law school graduates have been women, yet only about 15% of law firm equity partners and corporate chief legal officers are women.[20] The figures are even worse for other groups; only 8% of equity partners are lawyers of color and just 2% are LGBTQIA+.[21] Lawyers with disabilities make up just 0.4% of all equity partners.[22] Across all levels, women of color leave law firms at very high rates; in 2008, 75% of women lawyers of color had left their law firm by their fifth year, likely driven by the fact that nearly half of women lawyers of color report having to make adjustments to fit in to their law firm's culture.[23] Nearly two thirds of women lawyers of color say they have been shut out of networking opportunities, and 44% said they had been passed over for the best work assignments.[24]

The NAWL reported in 2015 that firms have made no appreciable advance in the rate at which they are promoting women to equity partners, and the pay gap persists as women equity partners earn just 78% of men equity partners. This pay gap is also present in other countries; in Canada, one study found a pay gap between men and women lawyers of $5,500 on average emerges by the second year of employment. Yet in the U.K., one prestigious law firm, reporting in compliance with pay gap legislation, found that the hourly rate for women lawyers was 32.8% less than for men lawyers, and bonus pay was 30.4% lower.[25] These gaps emerge despite the fact there is some evidence that women work and bill more hours than men.[26,27]

Upon graduation, many law school graduates pursue clerkship positions at the local, state, or federal level. In these roles, clerks serve as assistants to judges. Clerks do legal research and writing for judges, and these positions help clerks build professional experience and networks that are very valuable to their future careers. Data on the distribution of clerkships is somewhat dated, but what is available is telling. Overall, women received 51% of all clerkships upon graduating law school in 2009, but they were a larger proportion of local clerkships (54.3%) than federal clerkships (45.6%). This is problematic, as federal clerkships are seen as more prestigious pathways to better employment opportunities and to becoming a judge. For instance, the *National Law Journal* published a report on the diversity of Supreme Court clerks, a position they describe as "a golden ticket to career success" and found that since 2005, twice as many men as women served in these roles, and 85% of these clerks have been white.[28]

Thus, women have made significant progress to the point where they are the majority of all law school students; yet, large gaps in employment in the legal field remain, and women are still underrepresented at the highest levels of law employment and in those positions that are most likely to yield a position as a judge.

WOMEN AS PUBLIC LEGAL OFFICIALS

At the front line of the judicial system are the **public defenders** appointed to represent those who cannot afford private legal representation and district attorneys who are responsible for enforcing our laws in court. Public defenders often receive very low pay for very high caseloads; for example, in New Orleans, 60 public defenders manage nearly 20,000 cases per year;[29] the estimated time a New Orleans public defender has to spend on each case in order to manage this workload is just 7 minutes.[30] The median entry level salary for a public defender in 2018 was just $58,300, compared to an entry level salary of $180,000 in a large private law firm.[31] Women public defenders face additional challenges; for instance, in 2017, numerous women public defenders in Cook County, Illinois, filed a sexual harassment lawsuit against the county, arguing county officials had not acted to protect them from inmates who regularly exposed themselves and masturbated in front of the women attorneys during visits to jail and courtroom holding cells.[32]

On the flip side of the coin are those attorneys responsible for enforcing the law and prosecuting those charged with violations. The heads of these offices, commonly called **district attorneys**, are often elected by the voters. Of the over 2,400 elected prosecutors in the United States in 2015, just 16% were women, and only

▶ **Photo 8.1** Guatemalan prosecutor Thelma Aldana.

1% were women of color; in 14 states in the United States, *all* elected prosecutors were white.[33,34] Underneath these lead prosecutors are a vast array of public prosecutors, and like public defenders, women who serve in these roles face unique challenges, particularly for those women who work in countries where women's rights are less advanced and who challenge the status quo. The only woman prosecutor in Kandahar, Afghanistan, Zainab Fayez, focuses on prosecuting crimes against women and "risks her life daily fighting for women's rights."[35] In Guatemala, prosecutor Thelma Aldana, whose investigation into government corruption led to the resignation of President Otto Pérez Molina in 2015, has faced death threats and harassment, leading her to live under protective measures provided by the Inter-American Commission on Human Rights.[36]

Despite the important role both defenders and prosecutors play in our legal system, data about the representation of women in these roles is very hard to come by. For instance, the ABA Commission on Women in the Profession reports employment data for women as private attorneys, corporate attorneys, and as law school educators but provides no statistics on women as lawyers in public roles. There is reason to believe that women are underrepresented in these roles, though; for instance, the first Black woman district attorney in New York took her job in 2016.[37] Given that we know very little about the representation of women in these roles, there is little research about whether this underrepresentation matters, but circumstantial evidence suggests it does. For instance, public prosecutors play a large role in determining when to bring a case forward or to drop charges, whether to offer plea bargains to those accused of a crime, what level of charges to pursue, and how long of a sentence to pursue. The overwhelming majority of felony convictions are the result of plea bargains—nearly 94% at the state level and 97% at the federal level.[38] Research demonstrates there is a racial bias in the extent to which prosecutors exercise discretion in offering plea bargains; white defendants are more likely to have serious charges dropped, and as a result, are less likely to be convicted of a felony than Black defendants.[39] Additionally, men defendants generally receive longer sentences than women defendants, even when the crimes are similar.[40] Research establishes that prosecutorial discretion explains some of this variation,[41] so it may be that having different people serve in these roles would change the outcomes in these cases. As an example, the entire justice system in South Fulton, Georgia, is led by Black women. A photo of these women in their official attire went viral in 2018, serving as an inspiration to many. But these women, who all have years of experience in their roles, also argue that their presence makes a difference substantively, too. They have implemented a pretrial diversion program, given every defendant a public attorney from their first appearance in court, and have created special education programs.[42]

Both prosecutors and public defenders appear regularly in court rooms, as do many private attorneys, and the research suggests that sex influences nearly every part of their experience. While women make up a majority of law school graduates now, one study by the New York Bar found they were just 25% of attorneys appearing in cases across the state, and the more complex the case, the less likely a woman was to appear as lead counsel.[43] As former public defender Lara Bazelon (2018) explains,

> what makes the issue especially vexing are the sources of the bias—judges, senior attorneys, juries, and even the clients themselves. Sexism infects every kind of courtroom encounter, from pretrial motions to closing arguments—a glum ubiquity that makes clear how difficult it will be to eradicate gender bias not just from the practice of law, but from society as a whole.[44]

She recounts stories from a variety of women attorneys, both in public and private roles, who have been scrutinized for their makeup, hair styles, clothing, and display of emotion in the courtroom. In 2016, the American Bar Association (ABA) passed a rule to reduce the use of terms such as "honey" and "sweetheart" in the court room.[45] Bazelon, who is now a law professor, concludes by saying she tells her students "the truth: their body and demeanor will be under relentless scrutiny from every corner of the courtroom."[46] As Rhode (2001) argues, women lawyers face a double standard and double bind, such that they do not receive the same presumption of competence as men attorneys when they appear in court.[47]

As a result of the underrepresentation in other public and private roles in the courts, women are less likely to serve in the other important public positions in the legal system—as a judge, either in the federal or state court system. The U.S. court system has two separate but very distinct legal systems: federal and state/local. Federal criminal courts hear cases related to violations of federal law, while state and local criminal court systems deal with violations of state and local law. There are also federal and state civil courts, which deal with private disputes between two parties; the rules of jurisdiction are more complicated in civil courts in the United States, as compared to criminal courts, but judges preside over these cases, too. All judges in the federal court system are appointed; the president nominates them for the position, then they must be confirmed for this position by the U.S. Senate. At the state level in the United States, the method of judicial selection varies; some states appoint these judges, while others elect them. Whether the method of judicial selection matters for the representation of minorities and women is an issue we will examine later in this chapter.

At the top of the federal court system is the U.S. Supreme Court. Currently, three of the nine Supreme Court justices are women—Ruth Bader Ginsburg, Elena Kagan, and Sonia Sotomayor. All three were appointed by Democratic presidents. Over the course of U.S. history, just four women have served as Supreme Court justices out of 112 people who have ever served in that role; Sandra O'Connor was the first woman to serve and was the only woman Supreme Court justice appointed by a Republican president. Table 8.1 contains information about all four of these women Supreme Court justices.

When asked what sex-based parity on the Supreme Court would look like, Justice Ginsburg has routinely told people that she thinks there will be enough women when there are nine women justices. This may seem like a bit much to some, but as others have pointed out, the Supreme Court was all men for centuries. Below the Supreme Court, there are federal appellate and district/circuit federal courts. As of 2016, 36% of the judges on the appellate courts are women, while 33% of district court judges are women.[48] Very few women of color serve as federal judges; Sotomayor is the only woman of color on the Supreme Court. Just 12 women of color serve on the appellate courts, and just 82 of the approximately 2,750 district court

Table 8.1 Career Paths of Women on the U.S. Supreme Court

Justice	Birthplace (year)	Years on Supreme Court	President who appointed	Law School (Year of degree)	First job out of law school	Career position before appointment to Supreme Court	Judicial leaning
Sandra Day O'Connor	El Paso, Texas (1930)	(1981–2006)	Ronald Reagan	Stanford (1952)	Deputy County Attorney in San Mateo, CA	Arizona State Court of Appeals—Division One	Moderate
Ruth Bader Ginsburg	Brooklyn, New York (1933)	(1993–)	Bill Clinton	Columbia (1959)	Clerk for Southern District of New York under Edmund Palmieri	U.S. Court of Appeals in the District of Columbia	Liberal
Sonia Sotomayor	New York City (1954)	(2009–)	Barack Obama	Yale (1979)	Assistant District Attorney of New York County under Robert Morgenthau	U.S. Court of Appeals for the Second Circuit	Liberal
Elena Kagan	New York City (1960)	(2010–)	Barack Obama	Harvard (1986)	Clerk for U.S. Court of Appeals for the District of Columbia under Judge Abner J. Mikva	Solicitor General	Liberal

Steve Petteway

▶ **Photo 8.2** Women justices of the U.S. Supreme Court: O'Connor, Sotomayor, Ginsburg, and Kagan.

judges are women of color. Across the federal courts then, approximately one third of all judges are women, and most of these women are white.

At the state level, overall numbers are similar; just over 31% of state court judges were women (5,596 out of 18,006) in 2016.[49] This average masks considerable variation across states. At the low end, approximately 17% of all judges were women in Idaho in 2014, while in Oregon, a bit over 50% of all judges were women.[50] Just 8% of all state judges are women of color. Across both the state and federal levels, these numbers represent an increase in the number of women on the bench; in 2010, for example, women were just 22% of all federal judges and 26% of all state judges.[51] Comparatively, there are slightly more women judges in the United States as compared to the global average of 27% in 2012. As at the state level, this global average masks considerable variation across regions. In Central and Eastern Europe and Central Asia, over 40% of judges are women, while in South Asia, they make up less than 10% of judges.[52]

BOX 8.1: COMPARATIVE FEATURE

Women Judges Worldwide

Legal systems vary widely, and two important factors that differ between them are: 1) how judges are selected, and 2) the degree to which judges can interpret the law. In this textbox, we focus on how interpretation varies across countries; later in the chapter, we examine judicial selection. A good starting point for this conversation is the distinction between civil law and common law systems. The United States has a **common law system**—a legal system in which laws develop over time based on the decisions made by judges. Although judges in this system use their own intellect and understandings to shape law, they are expected to uphold **precedent** (i.e., principles engendered by past rulings). In **civil law systems**, the law comes from a comprehensive legal code. Typically, legislatures in these systems pass laws, and they accumulate to comprise a detailed body of law that judges apply during cases. Because the legal code is detailed and comprehensive, judges in civil law systems have less discretion to shape the law and instead play the role of investigators, asking questions and seeking facts about the case so that they can apply the law correctly. The United Kingdom and Commonwealth nations such as Canada, the United States, and Australia have common law systems, whereas most of Europe and Latin America have civil law systems. Africa and Asia have a mix of civil and common law countries typically reflecting colonial influences, and MENA (Middle East and North Africa) countries have legal systems based on religious law as well as civil and common law principles inherited from colonialism.

Women judges' potential to use feminist interpretation is shaped by these differences. As we describe the following U.S. case in greater detail, it is difficult to say with certainty that women judges rule in a way that represents women or in a feminist way. However, scholars tend to believe women judges in common law systems have a greater chance to represent women, because a common law system allows judges to interpret laws, whereas civil law systems are not based on interpretation.[53] For example, the Feminist Judgments Project in the United Kingdom, which is an academic group reimagining judicial outcomes in feminist ways, argues that a feminist judge in the U.K. could rule differently than a nonfeminist about family law and specifically visitation agreements for fathers who are violent. Although many judges insist it is " 'almost always' in children's best interests" for a violent father to visit his children in some way, a feminist judge would recognize the "dangers to mothers and children posed by" domestic violence and rule against the tradition of granting a father's visitation.[54]

Three caveats, however, are in order. First, the traditions of precedent, separation of powers, and a limited judiciary in the common law tradition can stand in the way of feminist interpretations.[55] A woman judge in a common law system might not be a feminist, or she might care about sex-based issues but not want to display difference based on feminism, because doing so is not within the norms of the legal tradition. The following exchange comes from a study about the Australian judiciary:

Facilitator: Do you think there's scope for a feminist approach to judging?

Woman Judge Respondent: Judging is judging. You judge on the criteria that you are supposed to judge [on]. There is a religious approach. I don't think there's room for religion. I don't think there's room for feminism. . . . I think you judge on the criteria you're supposed to judge [on]. Those extraneous things are extraneous things and they shouldn't be brought to bear on a judgment.[56]

(Continued)

(Continued)

Second, though research about women judges in civil law systems is sparse, Jeandidier, Bourreau-Dubois, Ray, and Doriat-Duban (2016) show that women judges in France act differently than their men counterparts when it comes to child support decisions. Two political opportunities exists for women judges in France: 1) women are the majority of French judges since the 2000s and 2) the French civil code does not have detailed guidelines on how to award child support. This means that the judge must make a decision based on the principles of the law and the circumstances of the parents. Jeandidier et al. (2016) find that "women judges set higher child support amounts, on average, than those fixed by men judges . . . [and] the amounts they fix are more often favorable to mothers [i.e., amounts requested by mothers] than they are when it is a male judge who makes the decision."[57] However, in Rwanda, also a civil law country with many women judges (39% women judges as of 2014), Kamatali finds that women and men judges rule similarly in rape and abortion cases, even if there is a perception that women judges are "more patient and understanding."[58]

Third, the influence of civil law and common law principles is muddied in split legal systems, in which secular law coexists with religious laws. Although the interpretation and application of religious law is diverse in Muslim countries (see Box 1.6), feminist interpretations of family law (i.e., marriage, divorce, child custody, etc.), for example, are less established there than in many developed democracies. Whereas family law in the West has been liberalized over the latter half of the twentieth century, women's legal movements in Muslim countries continue to advocate for liberalized interpretations of family law, with different levels of success achieved in each country (see Box 1.6).[59]

While women have achieved parity in law school, women are underrepresented as practicing lawyers, public attorneys, and judges in the United States and around the world. Thus, as in other chapters, an important question to ask is whether women's underrepresentation matters. Given the centrality of laws and our legal system to advancing the status of women in society generally, not just in the legal profession, examining the status of women in our system of laws and as workers in that legal system is critical.

Feminist Jurisprudence

As with Chapters 5 and 6, feminist theory can help us understand why having more women in the judicial branch might alter the way the system operates. But in thinking about the judiciary, it is useful here to take another step back to look at the ways feminist thought, and particularly feminist jurisprudence, has helped change the way we think about the law and our legal system. **Feminist jurisprudence** examines the legal system both theoretically and practically with the interests of women and women's lives at the forefront; importantly, feminist legal theory sees the law and our legal system as fundamental to the oppression of women. Weisberg (1992) argues

> Feminist legal theorists, despite differences in schools of thought, are united in their basic belief that society is patriarchal—shaped by and dominated by men. Feminist jurisprudence, then, provides an analysis and critique of women's position in patriarchal society and examines the nature and extent of women's subordination. It explores the role of law in maintaining and perpetuating the patriarchy. It also examines methods of eliminating the patriarchy.[60]

She goes on to explain the two main focuses of feminist jurisprudence. First, it explores the theoretical interaction between the law and gender. Second, feminist jurisprudence has been critical to raising practical questions about and changing our understanding of a wide variety of issues, including but not limited to pregnancy, divorce, rape, and sexual harassment. The development of feminist jurisprudence follows closely with the development of the Second Wave of the feminist movement overall. For instance, the development of feminist legal theory coincides with the growth of women's studies as a discipline and in other fields in the 1970s and 1980s. A complete review of the breadth and depth of feminist jurisprudence is not possible here, but it is important to look briefly as some of the key theoretical and practical concerns in feminist legal theory.

Theoretically, feminist jurisprudence is focused on uncovering the patriarchal origins of our legal system and questioning whether this is the proper foundation for our legal system. Baer (2011) identifies three fundamental premises of feminist legal theory.[61] First, because conventional legal doctrines have been developed by men, they have a fundamental male bias even when they are "gender-neutral." For instance, equality is a critical component of the Anglo-American legal tradition, yet for centuries, women were denied equal protection under these laws, which largely denies them access to the public sphere.[62] Second, women's lives are so different from men's lives that legal theory developed by men does not match with women's reality. As Wishik (1992) argues, "male-vision legal scholarship is to law what law is to patriarchy: each legitimizes, by masking and by giving an appearance of neutrality to, the maleness of the institution it serves."[63] Third, feminist legal theory must come from women's own experiences and perspectives because they are different to those of men. For example, Wishik (1992) argues that our legal system operates from the assumption that people are naturally dangerous, so our rules and laws are designed to protect us from this danger.[64] But, she continues, this assumes that the aggression typical to patriarchal societies is "human" and so legitimates aggression and dominance facilitated by fear of this aggression. Thus, our legal system is dominated by a stereotypical male focus on fairness, rights, and rules. But Gilligan (1982) argues that women approach ethical problems differently from men with men using an ethics of justice and women using an ethics of care; these two approaches are fundamentally incompatible for Gilligan, such that a legal system built around an ethics of care might look far different from the one we currently have.[65]

Critical to feminist legal theory are questions about equality; what does equality mean and how ought our legal system and laws be organized to best recognize and promote the equality of women? These questions have very practical implications, the second focus of feminist legal theory.

One of the key debates in this area is known as the **sameness/difference** or **equal treatment/special treatment** debate about sex-based equality under the law. Liberal feminist legal scholars, including early works by Ruth Bader Ginsburg (1978), argue for equality with no special status or treatment for women; in other words, they argue for men and women to be treated the same under the law.[66] The law should be sex-neutral, with no differential consideration for women at all. The concern of these sameness feminists is that when differences are enshrined in the law, these recognized differences can and will be used to discriminate against women. Difference feminists, however, point out that women are different; one of the most important of these differences is the fact that they bear children, which puts them at a disadvantage in a system that treats men and women the same. Indeed, early Supreme Court rulings on how pregnant women ought to be treated under the law declined to extend disability or sick leave benefits to pregnant workers. These decisions, for feminist theorists such as Scales (1981), demonstrated the need to develop a legislative and judicial policy that would "account fully, economically as well as legally, for the sex-unique aspects of procreation, namely childbearing and breast feeding," not as a special favor for women but as a way to achieve equality.[67] These feminist legal theorists believe women will only be equal when our legal system recognizes the differences that are relevant to women's lives and gives special treatment to those differences. Thus, the critical questions at the heart of this debate are how to promote the legal equality of women. "Does equality mean that women should wish to be treated exactly the same as men or does it mean that women should wish to be treated differently, because their differences are such that same treatment cannot provide equality?"[68] Other feminists argue that questions about whether our current legal system should treat women the same or differently miss the point. MacKinnon (1987) offers instead **dominance theory** as a critique of this debate; by asking whether women are the same or different, she argues we accept the male as the standard of measure, thereby cementing this standard of dominance into our legal system.[69]

As noted above, the scope of feminist legal theory is vast, and there are a variety of debates within this field of thought, both theoretical and practical. But common to all feminist legal scholars is the recognition of the critical importance of the legal system as a tool for advancing the status of women, whether that path be through modifications to our existing legal system or a complete transformation of this system. Regardless of the approach or school of thought, the women who work and participate in the legal system are seen as critical to this change.

THE IMPACT OF WOMEN IN THE JUDICIAL BRANCH

As with the other branches of the U.S. government and indeed governments around the world, women are underrepresented in the judicial branch, and while women have made significant inroads into the judicial branch, progress has slowed. Yet, there are reasons to believe that diversity matters in the judicial branch, as in other branches of government. Hunter (2015) summarizes six reasons why diversity in the judiciary might matter, and these reasons closely parallel the arguments for increasing women's representation in politics more generally.[70] First, having more women judges increases the democratic legitimacy of the judiciary because it is more representative of society at large. Second, having more women judges signals equality of opportunity for women who aspire to such positions, and third, those women judges can serve as mentors to women seeking similar careers. Fourth, women judges are more likely to have empathy with women litigants, witnesses, and victims of crimes, protecting them from sexist behavior and gender bias. Fifth, women judges will also act as a curb on sexism and gender bias from their men colleagues. Finally, the sixth argument is that women will bring a "gendered sensibility" to decision-making, changing the outcomes of cases either by bringing their life experiences to bear on their decision-making or by applying an ethic of care as opposed to an ethic of justice. It should be noted that in much of the theorizing about women judges, scholars are speaking about cis women and not necessarily femme-identified or trans women.

As noted above, there is little data and research on women as public defenders and prosecutors. Of the research that exists, most examines the behavior of women judges. In particular, many have looked at how women judges affect the decisions courts make. Research on the decision-making of women judges has focused on two key questions: whether men and women judges come to different conclusions, an **individual effect**, and whether serving with women can cause men judges to decide differently, a **panel effect**.[71] In looking at these questions, there are four main theories as to how and why these effects might occur, identified by Boyd, Epstein, and Martin (2010).[72] The first, the **different voice theory**, draws largely on the work of Carol Gilligan (1982), described previously; while Gilligan was a psychologist who studied moral development, her work has been critical to the development of feminist thought and particularly those who study the judiciary.[73] Gilligan was interested in how the moral reasoning of men and women differed. Although she recognized there was a good deal of variation within each sex as to how they approached moral problems, she found that men tended to define morality in a hierarchical framework, with a focus on rules and rights, but women emphasized connections with and responsibilities to others. Thus, when confronted with a problem, men were more inclined to look to the rules for solutions, while women were more likely to pursue solutions that would preserve their relations with others. While her research has been the subject of a great deal of scrutiny and critique, it has also inspired feminist legal scholars to think about how men and women might approach the practice of law differently. From this perspective, women judges bring a feminine perspective to the bench that shapes their decision-making across a wide variety of cases. But because this approach is based on different world views and different approaches to problems, these effects should not carry over to their men counterparts.

The next theory identified by Boyd, Epstein, and Martin draws on the work of Hanna Pitkin, discussed in Chapter 5. According to **representative theory**, women judges serve as representatives of other women and so seek to advance the cause of women generally. As such, differences in decision-making between men and women judges ought to be confined to those directly affecting the lives of women. **Informational theory** shares with representational theory the implication that the effect of sex on decision-making will be confined to those issues that affect women, but the reasons for this are different. In this case, it is argued that women will decide differently because their unique personal and professional experiences with the issues at hand gives them more and better information about the issues, particularly issues of sex discrimination in employment. In these cases, women judges may influence the decisions of their men counterparts, because of the additional information (personal experience) they bring to bear on the case. Supreme Court Justice Sonia Sotomayor's "wise Latina" speech best exemplifies the thinking behind this theory. In a speech in 2001, she said, "I would hope that a wise Latina woman with the richness of her experiences would more often than not reach a better conclusion than a white man who hasn't lived that life." In explaining these comments at her confirmation hearing, Sotomayor has said, "I was trying to inspire (students) to believe their experiences would enrich the legal system."[74]

Finally, some argue there will likely be no differences in the decision-making of women judges due to professional constraints, the **socialization theory**. Both men and women judges have been socialized into the legal profession via the same process, law school, and are constrained by the rules of judicial decision-making. After all, in order to be appointed or elected to the bench, women have to adopt traditional rules of legal reasoning and adapt to the requirements of a men-oriented power structure.[75]

Despite a wide variety of theories positing that women judges may decide differently, the research findings on this have been mixed, at best. Boyd et al. (2010) identify over 30 studies that have examined the decisions of women judges; they estimate that about one third of these studies find either individual or panel effects for women judges, one third find mixed results, and one third find no sex-based differences at all.[76] Their own study of the decision-making of women judges across a wide variety of areas finds differences only in cases involving sex discrimination. They find women judges are more likely to rule in favor of those alleging discrimination (an individual effect) as are their men counterparts when there is a woman judge (a panel effect), supporting the informational theory. In subsequent research, Boyd (2016) also claims that the majority of studies find no impact of sex on judicial decision-making, but she finds that Black and women judges are more likely to rule in favor of those claiming discrimination (race-based and sex-based respectively) than their white and men counterparts.[77] For example, Palmer (2002) found that both Justice O'Connor and Justice Ginsburg were supportive of women's rights in their decisions and wrote more opinions for women's issues cases, but the addition of Justice Ginsburg to the Supreme Court did not lead to an increase in the Court's overall support for women's rights claims; in other words, Palmer found an individual effect but not a panel effect.[78] A few other studies have found differences in some other issues areas, such as search and seizure cases[79] and the death penalty and obscenity.[80] Interestingly, studies have also found that women judges are more likely to sentence women defendants to prison time than their men counterparts.[81–83]

BOX 8.2: POLICY FEATURE

Employment Discrimination— Lilly Ledbetter

While Title VII of the Civil Rights Act of 1964 prohibits employers from discriminating against employees on the basis of sex, race, color, national origin, or religion in any aspect of employment, including hiring, assignments, promotion, training, benefits, pay and more, discrimination in employment is still a problem. For instance, in a recent survey, 4 in 10 working women reported experiencing sex-based employment discrimination; for Black women, that number rose to 53%.[84] Employees who believe they have been discriminated against must file a claim with the Equal Employment Opportunity Commission (EEOC) within 180 days of the discriminatory activity to preserve their rights.

In 1979, Lilly Ledbetter was hired as a shift manager at Goodyear Tire in Alabama; at the time of her hire, she signed a company policy that prohibited employees from discussing their pay. As such, Ms. Ledbetter did not know she was the victim of employment discrimination until she received an anonymous note that disclosed the salary of three men with the same title; those men were paid approximately $500 to $1500 more per month than her. In 1998, she filed a claim with the EEOC and also sued the Goodyear Company. In the initial trial, Ms. Ledbetter was awarded $3.8 million dollars in back pay and damages by a jury, but Goodyear appealed and won when the 11th Circuit Appeals Court ruled that the 180-day time frame from the Civil Rights Act had expired. Ms. Ledbetter appealed that decision to the U.S. Supreme Court. In *Ledbetter v. Goodyear Tire & Rubber*

(Continued)

(Continued)

Co. (2007), the Supreme Court found in favor of Goodyear, ruling that the original discriminatory act had to occur within the 180 day timeframe.[85] In effect, that meant Ms. Ledbetter, or any employee who was the victim of discriminatory practices, needed to have filed a claim the very first time she was paid differently than her men counterparts, a practice she wasn't even aware of at that time.

Justice Ginsberg led the four dissenting judges on this case and read the opinion she wrote from the bench. Reading a dissenting opinion from the bench is rare, and "to read a dissent aloud is an act of theater that justices use to convey their view that the majority is not only mistaken, but profoundly wrong."[86] As part of her dissent, Justice Ginsberg argued that "the Court does not comprehend or is indifferent to the insidious way in which women can be victims of pay discrimination" and called on Congress to remedy this.[87] After Democrats took control of the House and the Senate in the 2008 elections, Congress responded by passing the Lilly Ledbetter Fair Pay Act of 2009; just five Republican Senators voted for the bill, four of whom were women. It was the first piece of substantial legislation signed into law by newly elected President Obama. Under the act, each discriminatory act resets the 180-day window for filing a claim. Thus, each time a victim receives a paycheck, is passed over for a promotion, or is subject to any act of repeated discrimination, they may file a claim. As the only woman judge on the Supreme Court at the time, Justice Ginsburg took the lead in providing a voice for women and others who are the victims of employment discrimination. Ledbetter herself noted that she expected to lose the Supreme Court case, given the Court's sex composition but noted that she "gets chills and goosebumps today [in 2018] just thinking about it . . . knowing how fierce she was."[88]

Joyce N. Boghosian

▶ **Photo 8.3** U.S. President Barack Obama signs the Lilly Ledbetter Fair Pay Act.

Ultimately then, there is not much support for the difference theory, which would expect to find differences between men and women in decision-making across a wide variety of issues. Instead, the existing research tends to support the informational theory, as the most consistent effects of sex are on sex-based discrimination cases. The dearth of consistent findings that women judges act differently may be because the women judges are socialized professionally in the same way men judges are. This socialization process is not just confined to the United States; Hunter (2015) cites interviews with women judges from the U.K., South Asia, and other places where women judges express the need to fit their decisions into the existing framework for legal decisions, regardless of what they themselves personally wanted to decide.[89] They express feeling like an outsider and the need to decide rightly; in other words, they felt pressured to conform to existing norms. The development of feminist legal theory is a relatively new phenomena, with courses in feminist legal theory first being taught in the 1980s, so it may be a while before we see a new crop of women judges who are socialized differently. Also, it may be that as women's representation on the bench grows, they reach a critical mass in the judicial system (see Chapter 5 for a discussion of critical mass theory) that allows them to transform the legal system. Indeed, Collins, Manning, and Carp (2010) find that behavioral differences between men and women judges begin to emerge when there is a critical mass of women on the bench, particularly in criminal justice cases.[90] For Menkel-Meadow (1985), this is the goal of feminist legal education and diversifying the bench.[91] "The growing strength of women's voice in the legal profession may change the adversarial system into a more cooperative, less war-like system of communication between disputants in which solutions are mutually agreed upon rather than dictated by an outsider, won by the victor, and imposed on the loser."[92]

BOX 8.3: COMPARATIVE FEATURE

Women's Representation on International Courts and the Response of Women's Tribunals

The 1997 documentary *Calling the Ghosts: A Story About Rape, War and Women* presents the stories of two women who experienced violence in concentration camps during the Yugoslavian conflicts of the 1990s. In the documentary, one of the women, a judge, who was tortured and raped, proclaims "there will be no justice unless women are part of that justice."[93] Scholars who since have studied the legal proceedings of the International Criminal Tribunal for the former Yugoslavia (ICTY) find that judges' and attorneys' sex mattered to legal outcomes, and particularly in sexual violence cases.[94] In those cases, women judges on judging

(Continued)

(Continued)

panels and women lawyers as prosecutors resulted in longer sentences for perpetrators.[95] Nevertheless, the representation of women in international courts as judges is paltry; thus, scholars question these courts' ability to engender justice. Table 8.2 shows that international courts at most include about one third women judges and, in some instances, less than 10% of judges are women. The International Criminal Court (ICC) and the European Court of Human Rights (ECHR) are outliers; they provide more descriptive representation because they have rules on fair sex-based balance (i.e., when a judging position come open, the selection process for a new judge must include women candidates).

These data are disconcerting for several reasons. First, as Sally Kenney (2002) states, "an all-male bench is no longer legitimate."[96] She was referencing the poor representation of women judges on the European Court of Justice (ECJ), which did not include a woman judge until 1999, the court's 47th year of operation. A woman lawyer in the U.K. at that time, who advocated for greater representation on the ECJ succinctly argued, "if the higher ranks of lawyers and judges did not become more representative of the [European] community, public confidence in the law and justice system would not be maintained."[97] International courts, more so than national courts, suffer from a lack of confidence when they do not include judges with diverse identities. Because international institutions do not carry the sovereignty imbued in the nation-state, international courts lack "strong enforcement mechanisms and guaranteed funding;" thus, when people perceive them as

Table 8.2 Women's Representation on International Courts

Name of Court	Number of Women Out of Total Number	Percentage (year of data)
European Court of Human Rights	15 women (of 47)	31.9% (2019)
European Court of Justice	5 women (of 28)	17.9% (2019)
International Court of Justice	3 women (of 15)	20.0% (2019)
International Criminal Court	6 women (of 18)	33.3% (2019)
International Criminal Tribunal for the Former Yugoslavia	0 women (of 8)	0.0% (2017)
International Criminal Court for Rwanda	2 women (of 10)	20.0% (2015)
Inter-American Court of Human Rights	1 woman (of 7)	14.3% (2019)

Sources: https://www.echr.coe.int/pages/home.aspx?p=court/judges; https://curia.europa .eu/jcms/jcms/Jo2_7026/en; https://www.icc-cpi.int/bios-2; http://www.corteidh.or.cr/ index.php/en/about-us/composicion; http://unictr.irmct.org/en/tribunal/chambers; https:// www.icj-cij.org/en/current-members; http://www.icty.org/en/about/chambers/judges

illegitimate, their rulings will hold less weight and countries might not want to cooperate with them.[98] Without a diverse bench, international courts could become irrelevant. Given that international courts such as the ICC are often tasked with pursuing gender issues, particularly regarding sex- and gender-based crimes during political conflict, these courts' legitimacy and their ongoing development of case law is imperative to women's rights worldwide. Problematically, without a large number of women on international courts, scholars find it difficult to empirically test whether and how women impact court proceedings and rulings. The limited data suggest women judges and lawyers do act differently than men.[99-101] For instance, Judge Navanethem Pillay was the only woman judge in The International Criminal Tribunal for Rwanda (ICTR), and, as a human rights advocate, she is well regarded for pursuing questioning about rape, and the ICTR became the first international body to recognize rape as a form of genocide.[102] Additionally, King, Meernik, and Kelly, as stated above, found women lawyers and judges influenced the ICTY rulings (2017).[103]

In the absence of women's representation on international courts, and given that courts only manage to try a small number of the most egregious perpetrators of gender crimes, activists have pursued **women's tribunals** as an alternative form of justice. Women's tribunals may be defined as "tribunals of opinion" that "create a 'public' space for people to draw attention . . . or make visible gender-based abuses often hidden in the 'private' contexts of the home, family, personal relationships and traditional practices."[104] Put simply, women's civil society groups hold public proceedings in which women tell their stories, and, to them, this is justice in action and a form of political memory. Personal stories often are not welcome in international court proceedings, as cases are geared to determining "whether the perpetrator is guilty. Thus, the survivor will not be able to give a therapeutic retelling of events, as the court is not interested in the complex impact violence has had on her life."[105] Women's tribunals can be held regarding various topics, including the ill effects of poverty, climate change, sexual violence, "forced pregnancy and sterilization, forced marriage and sexual and domestic slavery."[106,107] An example from Guatemala demonstrates how women's tribunals can fill the gap left by state-level and international courts. Guatemala experienced intense political violence from the 1960s to 1990s, which included human rights violations and many sex-based crimes. In 2010, after decades of waiting, women, and particularly indigenous women, gave testimonies of the atrocities against them at a women's tribunal. The tribunal concluded by ruling that "insurgents [had] violated international humanitarian law, and international human rights law. The State of Guatemala was found in violation of its due diligence obligations to investigate, prevent and prosecute crimes, contributing to the creation of a climate of impunity."[108]

THE EFFECT OF THE COURTS ON WOMEN'S LIVES

While the evidence that having more women on the courts only has limited effects, those effects are important to improving the status of women generally. Issues like sexual harassment and sex-based employment discrimination were largely seen as private or nonexistent issues. It was the women's movement that brought these issues out in the open, and the presence of women judges on these courts, who have their own personal experience with these issues, has led to the courts taking these issues seriously. Indeed, the effect of the law and courts on women's lives, broadly speaking, cannot be understated. Thinking back to Chapter 2, at the founding of the United States, women did not have a separate legal existence. From a broad historical scope then, the status of women has advanced tremendously.

However, not all women have enjoyed equally in the advancement of these rights, and there are signs that some of these gains may be under threat. The impact of mass incarceration on women and communities of color is an example of these disparities. The United States is an outlier in its incarceration rates, as the United States imprisons a larger share of the population than any other country. The incarceration rate in the United States is 655 inmates per 100,000 people, which is 7% higher than the next closest country, El Salvador; this is despite the fact that the U.S. incarceration rate fell to its lowest levels in 20 years in 2016.[109] Racial disparities in incarceration rates are well established, but what is less well known is that these disparities extend to women as well. African Americans in the United States are incarcerated at more than five times the rate of white Americans, and the imprisonment rate for African American women is twice that of white women.[110] One in 18 Black women born in 2001 is likely to be incarcerated sometime in her life, compared to one in 45 Latina women and one in 111 white women. These disparities are due to differences in the rates at which Black people are stopped, searched, and arrested by law enforcement officials; harsher outcomes pursued by prosecutors; and judicial biases—not to differences in rates of criminal activity.[111] These racial and gender disparities in judicial outcomes have profound impacts on communities of color, as incarceration has negative links to employment and access to housing and positive links to poverty, poor health, and justice system involvement.[112]

While state bans on same sex marriage were overturned by the United States Supreme Court in *Obergefell v. Hodges (2015)*, the rights of LGBTQIA+ individuals are under attack. Indeed, in October of 2018, news leaked that the Department of Health and Human Services under the Trump administration was seeking to redefine gender as a "biological, immutable condition determined by genitalia at birth."[113] Thus, protection for LGBTQIA+ individuals in the United States is under attack, leaving many unequal before the eyes of the law and courts, as described in Box 8.4.[114]

BOX 8.4: POLICY FEATURE

Equal Protection for LGBTQIA+ Individuals

The Courts have played a considerable role in advancing the status of women generally, and they have also stepped in to protect the rights of LGBTQIA+ individuals, although true legal equality in the United States lags considerably. The courts have, at times, stepped in to protect the rights of LGBTQIA+ persons. Initially, many of these rulings rested on logic put forth in *Price Waterhouse v. Hopkins* (1989).[115] Price Waterhouse had denied Ann Hopkins a promotion because she was not feminine enough; in ruling in favor of Hopkins, the Court argued that discrimination based on stereotypes of how persons of a certain sex ought to look or act is unlawful sex discrimination. Thus, court rulings did not expressly say that discrimination based on gender orientation or identity was prohibited; rather, they ruled that this discrimination was a form of sex discrimination. However, in 2015, the 7th Circuit of the U.S. Court of Appeals ruled that discrimination based on sexual orientation in and of itself is a form of discrimination that violates federal law in *Hively v. Ivy Tech Community College (2017)*.[116] Importantly, the opinion of the 7th Circuit was written by Chief Judge Diane Wood, herself a woman. While this distinction may seem trivial, legally it is not, at is was the first major federal court case in which the courts ruled that sexual orientation is a protected class.[117]

The courts have also moved at times to prevent state and local governments from writing discrimination based on sexual orientation into their laws; importantly, in *Romer v. Evans* (1996), the Supreme Court overturned a Colorado ballot initiative to prevent the state from passing a law to prohibit discrimination against gays and lesbians.[118] Thus, the courts have on many occasions been instrumental in extending equal protection to LGBTQIA+ people. Indeed, the EEOC maintains a list of over 40 federal court cases that support the rights of LGBTQIA+ individuals.[119]

But at other times recently, the courts have issued rulings that failed to protect the rights of LGBTQIA+ people; in 2018, the U.S. Supreme Court ruled in favor of a baker who refused to sell a cake to a same sex couple in *Masterpiece Cakeshop vs. Colorado Civil Rights Commission (2018)*.[120] Also in 2018, the Supreme Court refused to hear a case on a Missouri law that allowed state employees and private business to deny services to LGBTQIA+ people. As such, the federal courts have not always been allies in recognizing that "equal protection under the law" applies to LGBTQIA+ individuals.

Given that the courts have not extended full constitutional protection to LGBTQIA+ people, they must rely on a patchwork of state laws for protection,

(Continued)

which leaves many legally exposed. Additionally, most cases have focused on sexual orientation, meaning TQIA+ individuals are even more vulnerable. In the United States, 50% of the LGBTQIA+ population lives in states that do not prohibit employment discrimination based on sexual orientation or gender identity,[121] despite the fact that 26% of transgender people report having lost a job due to bias.[122] Similarly, 20% of trans individuals report having been evicted or denied housing, yet only 41% of individuals live in states prohibiting housing discrimination based on sexual orientation and gender identity.

Furthermore, as mentioned earlier, many of the advances that have been achieved in recent years are under attack. In 2017, lawmakers across 30 states introduced 129 anti-LGBTQIA+ bills,[123] and in 2018, enough signatures were gathered in Massachusetts to put a question on the ballot that would repeal a law that prohibits discrimination based on gender identity in public places. Voters in Anchorage, Alaska, rejected a similar measure in early 2018, allowing transgender people to use public facilities that correspond to their gender identities. Under President Obama, rules prohibiting transgender individuals from serving in the military were lifted in 2016; however, that rule was reinstated by President Trump via a Twitter announcement, meaning transgender individuals were barred from serving openly in the military. That ban has been challenged in court, and as of July 2018, seven separate federal courts have ruled against the Trump administration, thus preventing the implementation of this policy change.[124]

In January 2019, the Supreme Court lifted several of these injunctions while legal issues play out in federal court. Meanwhile, the Trump administration instead now—while technically still allowing trans service members to continue to serve, but without any real protection against discrimination or retaliation—prevents anyone with gender dysphoria or who has undergone gender transition from enlisting in the military. In short, previously enlisted trans military personnel are subject to the "don't ask, don't tell" policy that was in place for LGB soldiers in the past. Newly enlisted members of the military can only sign up if they agree to serve as and are held to military standards for their assigned sex at birth.[125]

Not only has the extension of rights to women been uneven across different groups of women, the advancement of women's rights generally is threatened. Recently, the United States was ranked among the top 10 most dangerous countries in the world for women, the only Western democracy to be listed among the top 10. The ranking, based on a survey of aid professionals, academics, nongovernmental organization workers, and others, gave that ranking to the United States because of the "risks women face in terms of sexual violence, harassment, sexual coercion, and women's lack of access to justice in cases of rape," all areas of our political system where the courts play an important role.[126] Additionally, the federal courts are becoming more conservative as President Trump's nominees are skeptical about abortion rights and workplace and environmental protections.[127] In President Trump's first six months in office, he nominated 27 lower court judges, which is the most of any modern president; President Obama only appointed 10 judges during the same time frame in his tenure, the second highest number among modern presidents.[128] As of 2018, President Trump has had the opportunity to nominate two justices to the U.S. Supreme Court. It is through these appointments that President Trump will have his most profound and long-lasting impact on U.S. policy, as these positions are lifetime appointments. Scheindlin (2017) argues, "as a group, the nominees are deeply conservative. It is likely they would reverse abortion rights, gay rights, and affirmative action. . . . These rulings could dramatically shape the course of American social and cultural life over the next 30 to 40 years."[129]

INCREASING THE REPRESENTATION OF WOMEN IN THE JUDICIAL BRANCH

Given the centrality of the courts to improving the status of women and the limited but significant impact women jurists have on court outcomes, an important question to ask is, what are the mechanisms that have been shown to increase women's representation in the courts? Scholars have sought to understand whether the way judges are selected affects judicial diversity. Around the world, most judges are appointed to the bench via processes that focus on technical skill and expertise.[130,131] Typically, judges are appointed by public officials or a board and serve for an extended period of time. Indeed, this is how federal judges in the United States secure their positions—they are nominated by the president and confirmed by the U.S. Senate to life appointments. Appointment selection mechanisms emphasize the independence of the judicial branch, isolating judges from worrying about public approval and allowing them the space to make potentially unpopular but technically correct decisions. However, not all judges are selected via appointment. In the United States, 87% of all state court judges face some sort of elections; 39 states elect at least some of their judges.[132] In most countries around the world, judges are appointed, but in Switzerland, the cantons elect judges, and judges on the Japanese Supreme Court sometimes face election. Focusing on the U.S. states, there are a variety of mechanisms for electing judges, but there are three main ways that judges can be elected. First, some states hold nonpartisan judicial elections, where judges stand for election without party labels. Second, other states hold partisan elections, where judges run under party labels, typically Democratic or Republican. Finally, some states use merit selection, where judges are initially appointed by the executive branch but stand for retention elections. In retention elections, judges have no opponents, but voters are given a chance to indicate whether the judge should retain his or her seat. Whereas appointment systems focus on judicial independence from public opinion, judicial elections, regardless of the mechanism, focus on judicial accountability by giving voters a means to hold judges responsible for the decisions they make.

Looking at all types of selection systems, research suggests political incentives, religion, and economic development influence selection. Valdini and Shortell (2016) find that selectors are more likely to choose women as judges when the selectors are "exposed," meaning that the public can hold them accountable for their actions and they have the political incentive to choose based on diversity. For example, the United States is "exposed" in terms of Supreme Court nominations—the public pays attention and the selectors (i.e., the president and confirmation by the Senate) often mention sex as a salient factor in the nomination process.[133] The U.K. provides an alternative example. Until the 2000s, the position of Lord Chancellor chose high level judges in the U.K., and chancellors were insulated from popular opinion and largely didn't seek diverse appointments.[134] Selection since 2006 has been by the Judicial Appointments Commission, comprised of lay members and legal practitioners. Even though the commission aims to create diversity, the U.K. still has one of the lowest representation rates for women judges in Europe.

There is a good deal of debate in the academic literature about which method of judicial selection is more appropriate, depending on whether one holds judicial accountability or judicial independence in higher regard; regardless of which position one takes on this debate, the variation in the method of judicial selection allows us to examine whether this affects the representation of women in the judicial branch.

Given that differences in political ambition are one of the key causes of the lack of representation in other branches of government, as described in Chapter 4, it would seem reasonable to assume that elections might suppress the representation of women in the judiciary if they are less likely to run. But this is not the case; in fact, women attorneys are more likely to express a desire to run for the judicial branch as compared to men attorneys.[135] Frederick and Streb (2008) find that women who run in judicial elections are just as likely, and may even be more likely, to win than their men opponents.[136] Thus, Hurwitz and Lanier (2013) argue that while there are a variety of reasons for picking one method of judicial selection over another, diversity is not one of those arguments, as the method of judicial selection is not linked to either sex or racial diversity on the bench.[137] The similar levels of women's representation in the U.S. states, where most judges are elected, and in the federal judiciary, where judges are appointed, illustrates that selection mechanisms are not strongly linked to the diversity of the judiciary at least in the United States.

Returning to the distinction between civil and common law systems, comparative scholars argue that civil law systems are generally more conducive to representation than common law ones.[138] This is because legal practitioners become judges at a younger age in civil law systems (between 25 and 30 years), and they are chosen based on merit—typically, an academic qualification and performance on exams. On the other hand, in common law systems, judges are selected at a later age based on career achievements and social networks. This is true in the United States; Supreme Court judges in particular are older and have been chosen based on their long legal careers. How does this affect women? Women historically have been left out of the "old boys club" in the legal profession, and even today they lack the networks (e.g., golf outings, grabbing a drink after work, etc.) that men possess. Who you know matters; or as the saying goes in the United States, "a federal judge is a lawyer who knows a senator." Conversely, when women compete on merit in civil law systems, they tend to qualify as judges just as men do.

Of course, it is exceedingly difficult to change the basis of a legal system in a given country, so other factors seem to do a better job of explaining when and where there are more women judges. First, Hurwitz and Lanier (2003) find there are more women on the bench when there are more positions available.[139] Additionally, women are more likely to serve on the bench when there are more women who are eligible to serve.[140] As the number of women law graduates increases, this may point toward increased representation for women on the bench, although the continued barriers to women's advancement to partner status may prevent this from happening. Thus, having more positions to fill and more women qualified to fill these positions increases women's representation in the judiciary.

The biggest factor influencing judicial diversity may be the partisan environment in which the courts reside; Democratic states have more diverse benches than Republican states.[141,142] Importantly, even though most states have some method for electing judges, it is actually common for judges in these states to be appointed initially. Oftentimes, current judges will retire midterm, and most states allow for an appointment to fill a judicial vacancy that occurs midterm. In states with partisan and nonpartisan elections, 45% of all judges in these states were initially appointed to their seats.[143] When this happens, women are more likely to be appointed to these vacancies when there are Democrats in office. This is also true at the federal level in the United States. President Obama and President Clinton appointed the most women judges, 42% and 28% respectively, compared to 21% for President Trump (as of March 2018) and 22% for President George W. Bush.[144]

In the U.S. federal judiciary, presidential staffers develop a list of qualified candidates from which the president makes a selection. Typically, a variety of factors such as ideology, age, ethnicity, and sex are considered. Other countries have different mechanisms for selecting judges, although they consider similar factors. While sex is one of the factors considered, few countries have requirements that these lists contain qualified women—nor do they require the appointment of women to these positions. Sex-based quotas, as described in Chapter 6, are rare in the judiciary, as some argue they violate the principle of merit-based selection for the judiciary, particularly in appointment systems. But there have been informal quotas on many courts for years. For instance, in the United States in the early twentieth century, it was assumed there was a Jewish seat and a Catholic seat on the Supreme Court, such that when a justice of that faith retired, he would be replaced by someone of the same denomination. The U.K. Supreme Court has a de facto geographic quota system, where two judges come from Scotland and one comes from Northern Ireland.[145] Judicial sex-based quotas do exist in some places such as the Belgian Constitutional Court, the International Criminal Court, and the European Court of Human Rights. As a result, over 30% of ICC judges and ECHR judges are women.[146] Thus, quotas are best described at this point in time as a potential way to diversify the judiciary, but they are not in widespread use.

CONCLUSION

The courts have been important in advancing the status of women. Thinking back to the founding era, described in Chapter 2, women in the United States had no legal rights nor personhood. Over the course of the past 200 plus years, women have gained their own independent legal personhood. They have won the right to work, the right to own property, and the right to bodily autonomy. While some of these victories have been secured in the legislative arena, many of them have been secured in the courts. For instance, many U.S. states banned the purchase and use of contraceptives prior to the Supreme Court's *Griswold v. Connecticut* (1965) decision.[147] In this case, the Supreme Court ruled that the state did not have the right to ban contraceptives for married couples, a decision that paved the way for access to birth control for unmarried persons. Now, even though 99% of women between the ages of 15 and 44 who are sexually active have used birth control at some point, Box 8.5 indicates that the courts will continue to influence many women's ability to access contraception.[148]

BOX 8.5: POLICY FEATURE

The Courts and Women's Access to Contraception

Without using any form of contraception, a sexually active, fertile woman with a fertile man as a partner has an 85% chance of becoming pregnant over the course of a single year. Meanwhile, the desired family size in the United States is two children. To achieve this ideal family size, a typical cisgender, sexually active woman will spend 30 years of her life avoiding pregnancy.[149]

Managing fertility provides additional benefits beyond attaining an ideal family size. Avoiding pregnancy at the earliest and latest years of a woman's fertility—as well as spacing pregnancies 18 months apart—are all best practices that not only promote maternal health but that also prevent repeated miscarriages, premature births, and low birth weights. Studies show that women's ability to delay and prevent pregnancy also has a positive impact on family income, which in turn improves family stability and children's long-term well-being. After the 1960s, access to contraception dramatically enhanced women's ability to pursue these outcomes. Contraception use is now a nearly a universal practice. An estimated 60% of people in the United States capable of becoming pregnant currently use contraception, and contraception use among women aged 15 to 44 who have ever had sexual intercourse is nearly universal.[150]

Birth control advocates spent decades fighting U.S. laws that not only made it illegal to purchase or use contraceptive devices but that also prohibited publicly disseminating so-called "obscene" information about how to prevent pregnancy. Birth control advocate Margaret Sanger, for example, was determined to share information about how to avoid pregnancy, as well as contraceptive devices, with women across the country. Sanger purposefully violated federal and state laws—by sending diaphragms through the mail and opening a birth control clinic—so that she could challenge them in court. Planned Parenthood, the legacy of the clinics she helped to found, continued in this tradition.[151] The same tactic of purposefully violating a state law was undertaken by the executive director of the Connecticut Planned Parenthood League. Her conviction as an accessory to a crime for giving a married couple advice about how to prevent pregnancy and prescribing a contraceptive device for the wife's use, resulted in the 1965 Supreme Court decision *Griswold v. Connecticut.*[152]

Frustrated with the limited types of contraceptive devices available in the 1950s (only condoms and diaphragms), Sanger and her financial supporter, Katharine McCormick, commissioned two doctors to invent an effective birth control pill. Envoid, the first birth control pill, was approved by the Food and Drug Administration in 1960. By 1965, nearly 6.5 million U.S. women had a prescription—paving the way for the even wider array of effective contraceptive devices (ranging from intrauterine devices or IUDs to other long-active reversible contraception).[153]

Despite a better array of options, the cost associated with contraception and associated medical care made pregnancy prevention difficult for all women to obtain. Hence, Second Wave feminists focused on making access affordable. Federal funding to expand reproductive health care to low-income women has come from two sources. One is Title X of the 1970 Public Health Services Act, signed into law by Republican President Richard M. Nixon to fund family-planning initiatives, especially those providing services to low-income families. The second is Medicaid, which provides public medical insurance to those living below the federal poverty line. Historically, many low-income women have sought out preventive reproductive health care—including services such as birth control, cervical cancer screening, mammograms, STD treatment/testing, well-woman exams, (and after the procedure

(Continued)

(Continued)

was legalized nationwide in 1973) abortions, from Planned Parenthood clinics (which track their legacy back to Margaret Sanger's Birth Control League). Planned Parenthood accepts Medicaid; it also services 41% of Title X's clients and operates 13% of clinics funded by the program. According to Planned Parenthood's web page, 60% of its patients rely on these two public health programs.[154] Yet, social conservatives oppose funding Planned Parenthood because many of its clinics also provide abortions, even though federal funds are not used to pay for them. In 2017, the Trump administration proposed a rule that would accomplish this end by prohibiting Title X–funded clinics from sharing physical space and financial resources with abortion providers and from clinics referring clients to other abortion providers. At the time this text went to press, those new rules had not been finalized but will likely trigger a legal challenge from Title X–funded clinics when they are published.[155]

The Trump administration has also drafted new Title X guidelines. These prioritize funding for clinics that emphasize natural family planning methods and would not require Title X providers to provide clients access to all forms of medically approved birth control. Similarly, the administration's new rules for funding programs to prevent teen pregnancy prioritized initiatives that promote abstinence or "sexual risk avoidance" over programs that focus on contraception use and safe sex. At the time this text went to press, a federal appellate court was considering whether to uphold a lower court decision upholding these changes.[156,157]

The Affordable Care Act of 2010, also known as ACA or Obamacare, also expanded women's access to birth control by reducing cost barriers. The law, affecting 55 million women's private insurance policies, required companies to cover a list of reproductive health care services (including all 18 FDA-approved contraceptive methods) without charging a copayment.[158] In 2017, the Trump administration released new interim guidelines regarding the ACA's contraception coverage mandate. After reminding health insurance companies that federal subsidies cannot be used to pay for abortion even if policies cover the procedure (a compromise built into the law when it was first drafted), the administration expanded the type of employers (beyond privately held companies offered this exemption in the 2014 Supreme Court case *Burwell v. Hobby Lobby*) who can cite religious and moral objections to providing insurance policies that cover specific types, or even all types, of contraception. Two federal courts issued preliminary injunctions preventing these interim rules from being enforced. Similar final regulations will go into effect in January 2019 and will likely be subject to similar legal challenges.[159]

It seems clear that state and federal courts will continue to hear cases affecting women's access to contraception for the foreseeable future.

As Box 8.6 makes clear, the effects of reliable access to contraception, put in motion by the *Griswold* decision, have been profound:

> In the United States, a high income country, research shows that greater access to contraception had rapid and significant implications for women's economic and social equality. . . . [Women] were able to envision and pursue a less constrained future, one where they could prevent pregnancy, invest in their education, find the right partner, build a career, and perhaps most importantly plan for the lives they wanted.[160]

BOX 8.6: LORETTA LYNN—CHANGING CULTURAL NORMS ABOUT CONTRACEPTION

Widespread contraception use makes it difficult to remember that just one to two generations ago, preventing pregnancy was controversial, and discussion of women's sexuality was taboo. It makes it difficult to recognize how fundamentally different women's lives are now than they were prior to the Second Wave. Both the life and music catalogue of Grammy-winning country music singer-songwriter Loretta Lynn serves as a poignant reminder of the radical transformation these cultural norms and practices underwent.

Born in 1932, Loretta Lynn, née Webb, grew up in a small cabin in an Appalachian coal-mining region of Kentucky. She married while still a young teenager—and without access to contraception, quickly gave birth to four of her six children before turning 20 years old. (Her last two children, twins, were born in 1964 after Lynn had successfully launched her career.)[161]

At her husband's suggestion, Lynn taught herself to play guitar and compose song lyrics. Unlike most other songwriters at the time, she wrote from a woman's perspective and bluntly shared her own lived experiences—which included being a working-class housewife and mother for 15 years before becoming an entertainer. According to Lynn, she was "the first to ever go into Nashville, singin' it like the women lived it."[162]

For example, Lynn's 1971 song *One's On the Way* documented how the cycle of unplanned (and sometimes unwanted) pregnancies and childcare distracted most women from both careers and social reform, by focusing all of their energy on reproductive labor and domestic work. The last verse of the song reads,

(Continued)

(Continued)

> The girls in New York City, they all march for women's lib
>
> And *Better Homes and Garden* shows the modern way to live
>
> And the pill may change the world tomorrow, but meanwhile, today
>
> Here in Topeka, the flies are a buzzin'
>
> The dog is a barkin' and the floor needs a scrubbin'
>
> One needs a spankin' and one needs a huggin'
>
> Lord, one's on the way
>
> (I hope it ain't twins again).[163]

Lynn's early career spanned the 1970s, and she celebrated the way access to contraception affected her own and other women's lives. Her willingness to address intimate issues meant radio stations sometimes refused to play her songs. Yet, in Lynn's own words, "I was writing about things that nobody talked about in public, and I didn't realize that they didn't. I was having babies and staying at home. I was writing about life. That's why I had songs banned."[164]

Juxtaposing repeated pregnancies not only with newfound freedom but also with the ability to enjoy sex, her 1975 hit *The Pill* was one such song. It includes blunt verses such as the following:

> All these years I've stayed at home
>
> While you had all your fun
>
> And every year that's gone by
>
> Another baby's come
>
> There's a gonna be some changes made
>
> Right here on nursery hill
>
> You've set this chicken your last time
>
> 'Cause now I've got the pill.[165]

By the end of the decade, Lynn insisted on a new shared power dynamic with her husband when she released *We've Come a Long Way Baby* in 1979. In the first verse, she questions their past relationship, singing,

> Well, I'm a good ol' girl an' I would like to please every way I can.
>
> I've loved you an' I've always let you have the upper hand.

How come you think you're so smart, an' I'm the weaker sex?

There ain't a man alive can match a woman, trick for trick.[166]

In the refrain, she emphasizes how much things have changed by repeating the lines, "We've come a long way, baby," and "Second class don't turn me on at all." The last verse includes the phrases, "I'm gonna have my say," and "From now on lover-boy, it's fifty-fifty, all the way," before closing with a couplet, below, celebrating women's sexuality:

Up to now I've been an object made for pleasin' you.

Times have changed and I'm demanding satisfaction too.[167]

Lynn acknowledges that she purposefully wrote songs for and about women, claiming, "That's who I'm singing about and singing to during my shows . . . most of my fan club is women, which is how I want it."[168] Lynn's choice—to sing songs about women, for other women—helped to normalize using contraception, limiting family size, and insisting on an egalitarian marriage. Her life and songs vividly illustrate an alternative to the patriarchal status quo, especially for rural, conservative, and working-class women whose experiences and needs were often overlooked by Second Wave activism.

Although the courts and court rulings have been instrumental in advancing the rights of women, there is no guarantee that they will continue to act in this way. Proponents of judicial independence argue that having an independent court system is critical to ensuring courts act to protect and advance rights, even when it may not be popular to do so. But research suggests that the courts, even those with judges who are appointed with lifelong terms, are in fact sensitive to public opinion, which influences their decisions. Barnum (1985) finds that in the 1900s, the U.S. Supreme Court's decisions to protect minority rights followed trends in public opinion that revealed increasing support for these actions, and in the absence of such public approval, the Court was reluctant to act.[169] Even when public opinion supports protecting these rights, the Court may choose to favor other values. For example, a majority of Americans believe that insurance companies ought to provide coverage for contraceptives.[170] Despite this, the U.S. Supreme Court recently ruled in *Burwell v. Hobby Lobby* (2014) in favor of the company Hobby Lobby—which argued it should not be required to provide access to birth control in company insurance plans, as it violated deeply held religious beliefs.[171] Additionally, the Supreme Court refused to hear Planned Parenthood's challenge

▶ **Photo 8.4** Protestors in support of Planned Parenthood.

to an Arkansas state law banning abortion-inducing medication, leading Planned Parenthood to cancel all abortion appointments in the state.[172] As such, it cannot be assumed that the courts will act as the protectors of the rights of women and minorities. Access to contraception, which is central to women's economic and social empowerment, is declining in the United States, as more legislatures introduce obstacles and the courts accept challenges to laws protecting such access. Thus, the political activism of those supporting these rights is critical, not just within government but also through conventional means of political participation and through extrainstitutional participation via social movements and beyond, which we examine in Chapter 9.

REVIEW QUESTIONS

1. How has the experience of women in the legal field changed over time? Describe the barriers to women's advancement in the legal field and judiciary that still exist.

2. What is feminist jurisprudence? Describe the key debates in this field. With which position do you agree? Why?

3. Compare and contrast common and civil law systems. How does the type of legal system in which women serve affect the types of decisions they make?

4. Describe the different theories for how women in the judicial branch might make an impact. For which of these theories is there evidence? In other words, how does the presence of women in the judiciary matter in terms of the decisions that are made?

5. What impact have the decisions of the courts had on the advancement of the rights of women? In what areas are these rights under threat? Do you think the courts will continue to act to advance the rights of women? Why, or why not?

6. Explain the different mechanisms for increasing the representation of women in the judiciary. If you wanted to increase women's representation in this branch of government, what strategies would you recommend? Why?

AMBITION ACTIVITIES

Charting the Paths of Women in the Judicial System: The career path of Ruth Bader Ginsburg has been featured in popular media in recent years—in podcasts (*RBG Beyond Notorious* by CNN), documentaries (*RBG*), and magazine articles (e.g., *The New Yorker*'s "Ruth Bader Ginsburg's Unlikely Path to the Supreme Court"). We know far less about the paths of other women in the justice system—federal women district attorneys, public defenders, and judges. Using Table 8.1 as a starting place, chart the career path of a Supreme Court justice and then compare it to the background of a lesser known woman in the legal field. Where did these women go to law school? What work experiences did they have before becoming attorneys or judges? How were they selected for their positions—through elections or appointments? How might these women's personal, educational, and career backgrounds affect their decision-making? If you are considering a legal career, compare your personal and educational backgrounds to the backgrounds of these women.

Pursuing a Legal Career and Making Social Change: If you are considering a legal career, what is your motivation? Many young people pursue careers, including law, because they want to make a difference in the world around them. Data from the National Society of High School Scholars' 2018 Career Interest Survey show that the majority of high school students are "willing to advocate for social justice issues, with women leading the charge—81 percent compared to 66 percent of men."[173] Reflect on whether you want your legal career to address social justice. After doing so, research law schools, and identify the best law school for you given your motivations; academic and community accomplishments to date; and personal, geographic and financial constraints. What obstacles do you foresee in your future experience in the legal field? Consider work-life balance, sexual harassment, sex and gender bias, and the cost of law school.

Learning to Negotiate: Lawyers practice the art of negotiation. They negotiate as they work with clients and as they draft settlements. Consider how negotiation skills could help you in the area of pay equality. Women lag men in terms of pay, and, with the pay gap persisting, equal pay is not a reality. As we know from this chapter, the gap is even larger for women of color. Knowing how to negotiate a starting salary using vetted techniques might make a difference in your future paycheck and the overall pay gap. Women's lower salary expectations and lower likelihood to negotiate salary increases contribute to the pay gap between men and women.

Linda Babcock and Sara Laschever (2007) in *Women Don't Ask: Negotiation and the Gender Divide* suggest several strategies for negotiation.[174] Watch this video of Linda Babcock discussing her suggested techniques, and practice negotiating a salary for a first job of your choice: https://www.coursera.org/learn/negotiation/lecture/k1WcI/when-women-negotiate.

After watching this video, conduct a mock salary negotiation for a job you might have following college. Keep in mind that when women negotiate for higher salaries and seek to close the pay gap between men and women, they incur more social costs than men who negotiate higher salaries. Other employees often do not want to work with women who ask for higher salaries because they view them as less nice and too demanding. However, women can achieve better outcomes in salary negotiations without experiencing social backlash by providing a legitimate rationale for what they are negotiating, while at the same time communicating their concern for maintaining good organizational relationships. (See also https://progress.heinz.cmu.edu/publications-and-news/publications.)

KEY WORDS

Civil law system 362

Common law system 362

Different voice theory 367

District attorneys 358

Dominance theory 366

Equal treatment/special treatment 366

Feminist jurisprudence 364

Individual effect 367

Informational theory 368

Panel effect 367

Precedent 362

Public defenders 358

Representative theory 368

Sameness/difference 366

Socialization theory 368

Women's tribunals 373

REFERENCES

1. *Goodridge v. Department of Public Health*, 440 Mass. 309 (2003).

2. Totenberg, N. (2013). Former Mass. Chief Justice on life, liberty and gay marriage. *National Public Radio*. Retrieved from https://www.npr.org/2013/06/07/189288605/former-mass-chief-justice-on-life-liberty-and-gay-marriage.

3. Small, L. (1998). *A timeline of women's legal history in the United States*. Retrieved from http://wlh-static.law.stanford.edu/articles/cunnea-timeline.pdf.

4. Buchanan, K. (2015). *Women in history: Lawyers and judges*. Retrieved from https://blogs.loc.gov/law/2015/03/women-in-history-lawyers-and-judges.

5. Martin, S. E., & Jurik, N. J. (2007). *Doing justice, doing gender: Women in legal and criminal justice occupations*, 2nd edition. London, UK: SAGE.

6. Buchanan, K. (2015). *Women in history: Lawyers and judges*.

7. Martin, S. E., & Jurik, N. J. (2007). *Doing justice, doing gender: Women in legal and criminal justice occupations*, 2nd edition.

8. Sandra Day O'Connor. (n.d.). *Oyez*. Retrieved from https://www.oyez.org/justices/sandra_day_oconnor.

9. Ruth Bader Ginsburg. (n.d.).*Oyez*. Retrieved from https://www.oyez.org/justices/ruth_bader_ginsburg.

10. American Bar Association (ABA). (2017). *A current glance at women in the law: January 2017*. Retrieved from https://www.americanbar.org/content/dam/aba/marketing/women/current_glance_statistics_january2017.authcheckdam.pdf.

11. National Women's Law Center (NWLC). (2016). Women in the federal judiciary: Still a long way to go. Retrieved from https://nwlc-ciw49tixgw5lbab.stackpathdns.com/wp-content/uploads/2016/07/JudgesCourtsWomeninFedJud10.13.2016.pdf.

12. Ford, M. (2017). When your judge isn't a lawyer. *The Atlantic*. Retrieved from https://www.theatlantic.com/politics/archive/2017/02/when-your-judge-isnt-a-lawyer/515568/s.

13. Bowman, C. G. (2009). Women in the legal profession from the 1920s to the 1970s: What can we learn from their experience about law and social change? *Maine Law Review, 61*, 1–25.

14. American Bar Association (ABA). (2011). First year and total J.D. enrollment by gender 1947–2011. Retrieved from https://www.americanbar.org/content/dam/aba/administrative/legal_education_and_admissions_to_the_bar/statistics/jd_enrollment_1yr_total_gender.authcheckdam.pdf.

15. Bowman, C. G. (2009). Women in the legal profession from the 1920s to the 1970s: What can we learn from their experience about law and social change?

16. Ibid.

17. Olson, E. (2017). "A bleak picture" for women trying to rise at law firms. *The New York Times*. Retrieved from https://www.nytimes.com/2017/07/24/business/dealbook/women-law-firm-partners.html.

18. National Association for Law Placement (NALP). (2017). *2017 report on diversity in U.S. law firms*. Retrieved from https://www.nalp.org/uploads/2017NALPReportonDiversityinUSLawFirms.pdf.

19. Catalyst. (2017). *Women in the law in Canada and the U.S.* Retrieved from http://www.catalyst.org/knowledge/women-law-canada-and-us.

20. Rikleen, L. S. (2015). Women lawyers continue to lag behind male colleagues. *National Association of Women Lawyers.* Retrieved from https://www.nawl.org/2015nawlsurvey.

21. Ibid.

22. National Association for Law Placement (NALP). (2017). *2017 report on diversity in U.S. law firms.* Retrieved from http://www.catalyst.org/system/files/Women_of_Color_in_U.S._Law_Firms.pdf

24. Bazelon, L. (2018). What it takes to be a lawyer if you're not a man. *The Atlantic.* Retrieved from https://www.theatlantic.com/magazine/archive/2018/09/female-lawyers-sexism-courtroom/565778.

25. Cowling, E C. (2018). Ending the gender pay gap in law. *Law Practice Today.* Retrieved from http://www.lawpracticetoday.org/article/ending-gender-pay-gap-law.

26. Rikleen, L. S. (2015). Women lawyers continue to lag behind male colleagues. *National Association of Women Lawyers.*

27. Wilkins, D. B., Fong, B., & Dinovitzer, R. (2015). The women and men of Harvard Law School: Preliminary results from the HLS Career Study. *Harvard Law School Center on the Legal Profession.* Retrieved from https://clp.law.harvard.edu/assets/HLS-Career-Study-FINAL.pdf.

28. Mauro, T. (2017). Mostly white and male: Diversity still lags among SCOTUS law clerks. *The National Law Journal.* Retrieved from https://www.law.com/nationallawjournal/sites/nationallawjournal/2017/12/11/mostly-white-and-male-diversity-still-lags-among-scotus-law-clerks.

29. Wiltz, T. (2017). Public defenders fight back against budget cuts, growing caseloads." *PEW Stateline.* Retrieved from http://www.pewtrusts.org/en/research-and-analysis/blogs/stateline/2017/11/21/public-defenders-fight-back-against-budget-cuts-growing-caseloads.

30. Lee, J., Levintova, H., & Brownell, B. (2013). Charts: Why you're in deep trouble if you can't afford a lawyer. *Mother Jones.* Retrieved from https://www.motherjones.com/politics/2013/05/public-defenders-gideon-supreme-court-charts.

31. National Association for Law Placement (NALP). (2018). Findings from the NALP/PSJD Public Service Attorney Salary Survey." Retrieved from https://www.nalp.org/0618research.

32. Grimm, A. (2017). Assistant public defenders file lawsuit over masturbating jail inmates. *Chicago Sun Times*. Retrieved from https://chicago.suntimes.com/news/assistant-public-defenders-file-lawsuit-over-masturbating-jail-inmates.

33. Women's Donor Network. (2015). Justice for all? Retrieved from https://wholeads.us/justice.

34. George, T. E., &. Yoon, A. H. (2016). Who sits in judgement on state courts? *The Gavel Gap*. Retrieved from http://gavelgap.org/pdf/gavel-gap-report.pdf.

35. Liutho, M. (2018). The lone female prosecutor in Kandahar risks her life daily fighting for women's rights. Retrieved from https://womenintheworld.com/2018/04/06/the-lone-female-prosecutor-in-kandahar-risks-her-life-daily-fighting-for-womens-rights.

36. Perez, S. D. (2018). Guatemala's crusading prosecutor exits amid praise, threats. *The Standard Examiner*. Retrieved from http://www.standard.net/World/2018/05/07/Guatemala-s-crusading-prosecutor-exits-amid-praise-threats.

37. Kochman, B. (2016). New York's first female district attorney, Darcel Clark, takes office in the Bronx. *New York Daily News*. Retrieved from http://www.nydailynews.com/new-york/bronx/new-york-black-female-district-attorney-takes-office-article-1.2499138.

38. Yoffee, E. (2017). Innocence is irrelevant. *The Atlantic*. Retrieved from https://www.theatlantic.com/magazine/archive/2017/09/innocence-is-irrelevant/534171.

39. Berdejo, C. (2018). Criminalizing race: Racial disparities in plea bargaining. *Boston College Law Review*. Retrieved from https://lawdigitalcommons.bc.edu/bclr/vol59/iss4/2.

40. Mustard, D. (2001). Racial, ethnic, and gender disparities in sentencing. *The Journal of Law and Economics, 44*, 285–314.

41. Kim, B., Spohn, C., & Hedberg, E. C. (2015). Federal sentencing as a complex collaborative process: Judges, prosecutors, judge-prosecutor dyads, and disparity in sentencing." *Criminology* 53: 597–623.

42. Criss, D. (2018). The entire justice system here is run by Black women. It's not a diversity experiment. They do things differently. *CNN*. Retrieved from https://www.cnn.com/2018/06/22/us/south-fulton-georgia-women-leaders-trnd/index.html?no-st=1531160934.

43. New York Bar Association. (2017). *If not now, when? Achieving equality for women attorneys in the courtroom and ADR*. Retrieved from http://www.nysba.org/WomensTaskForceReport.

44. Bazelon, L. (2018). What it takes to be a lawyer if you're not a man.

45. Ibid.

46. Ibid.

47. Rhode, D. L. (2001). The unfinished agenda: Women and the legal profession. *American Bar Association*. Retrieved from http://womenlaw.stanford.edu/pdf/aba .unfinished.agenda.pdf.

48. National Women's Law Center (NWLC). (2016). Women in the federal judiciary: Still a long way to go.

49. National Association of Women Judges (NAWJ). (2016). *2016 state court women judges*. Retrieved from https://www.nawj.org/statistics/2016-us-state-court-women-judges.

50. George, T. E., &. Yoon, A. H. (2016). Who sits in judgement on state courts?

51. Center for Women in Government & Civil Society. (2010). Women in federal and state-level judgeships. Retrieved from https://www.albany.edu/womeningov/ judgeships_report_final_web.pdf.

52. Kalantry, S. (2012). Women in robes. *Americas Quarterly*. Retrieved from http:// www.americasquarterly.org/women-in-robes.

53. Hunter, R. (2015). More than just a different face? Judicial diversity and decision-making. *Current Legal Problems*, *68*, 119–141.

54. Feminist Judgements Project. (2018). *University of Kent*. Retrieved from https:// www.kent.ac.uk/law/fjp/cases/parenting.html#ReL.

55. Hunter, R. (2015). More than just a different face? Judicial diversity and decision-making.

56. Ibid.

57. Jeandidier, B., Bourreau-Dubois, C., Ray, J-C., & Doriat-Duban, M. (2016). Does gender matter in the civil law judiciary? Evidence from French child support court decisions. *BETA, UMR CNRS 7522, Université de Lorraine*. Retrieved from https://ideas.repec.org/p/ulp/sbbeta/2016-55.html.

58. Kamatali, J-M. (2016). Rwanda: Balancing gender quotas and an independent judiciary. In G. Bauer & J. Dawuni (Eds.), *Gender and the judiciary in Africa: From obscurity to parity?* New York, NY: Routledge.

59. Htun, M., & Laurel, W. S. (2011). State power, religion, and women's rights: A comparative analysis of family law. *Indiana Journal of Global Legal Studies 18*(1): Article 7. Retrieved from https://www.repository.law.indiana.edu/ijgls/ vol18/iss1/7.

60. Weisberg, D. K. (1992). Introduction. In D. K. Weisberg (Ed.), *Feminist legal theory: Foundations* (pp. xv–xx). Philadelphia, PA: Temple University Press.

61. Baer, J. (2011). Feminist theory and the law. In R. E. Goodin (Ed.), *The Oxford handbook of political science*. DOI: 10.1093/oxfordhb/9780199604456.013.0016.

62. Taub, N, & Schneider. E. M. (1992). Women's subordination and the role of law. In D. K. Weisberg (Ed.), *Feminist legal theory: Foundations* (pp. 9–21). Philadelphia, PA: Temple University Press.

63. Wishik, H. R. (1992). To question everything: The inquiries of feminist jurisprudence. In D. K. Weisberg (Ed.), *Feminist legal theory: Foundations* (pp. 22–31). Philadelphia, PA: Temple University Press.

64. Ibid., 24–25.

65. Gilligan, C. (1982). *In a different voice: Psychological theory and women's development.* Cambridge, MA: Harvard University Press.

66. Ginsburg, R. B. (1978). Sex equality and the constitution. *Tulane Law Review, 52,* 451–453.

67. Scales, A. C. (1981). Towards a feminist jurisprudence. *Indiana Law Journal, 56,* 375–444.

68. Burchard, M. (n.d). Feminist jurisprudence. *Internet Encyclopedia of Philosophy.* Retrieved from https://www.iep.utm.edu/jurisfem.

69. MacKinnon, C. A. (1987). *Feminism unmodified.* Cambridge, MA: Harvard University Press.

70. Hunter, R. (2015). More than just a different face? Judicial diversity and decision-making.

71. Boyd, C. L., Epstein, L., & Martin, A. D. (2010). Untangling the causal effects of sex on judging. *American Journal of Political Science, 54,* 389–411.

72. Ibid.

73. Gilligan, C. (1982). *In a different voice: Psychological theory and women's development.*

74. CBS. (2009). *Sotomayor explains "Wise Latina" comment.* Retrieved from https://www.cbsnews.com/news/sotomayor-explains-wise-latina-comment.

75. Davis, S. (1992). Do women judges speak in a different voice—Carol Gilligan, feminist legal theory, and the 9th Circuit. *Wisconsin Women's Law Journal, 8,* 143–173.

76. Boyd, C. L., Epstein, L., & Martin, A D. 2010). Untangling the causal effects of sex on judging.

77. Boyd, C. (2016). Representation on the courts? The effects of trial judges' sex and race. *Political Research Quarterly, 69*, 788–799.

78. Palmer, B. (2008). Justice Ruth Bader Ginsburg and the Supreme Court's reaction to its second female member. *Journal of Women, Politics, & Policy, 24*, 1–23.

79. Davis, S., Haire, S., & Songer, D. R. (1993). Voting behavior and gender on the U.S. Court of Appeals. *Judicature*, 77, 129–133.

80. Songer, D. R., & Crews-Meyer, K. A. (2000). Does judge gender matter? Decision making in state supreme courts. *Social Science Quarterly, 81*, 750–762.

81. Collins, P. M., Jr., Manning, K. L., & Carp, R. A. (2010). Gender, critical mass, and judicial decision making in the U.S. Court of Appeals. *Social Science Quarterly, 91*, 397–414.

82. Gruhl, J., Spohn, C., & Welch, S. (1981). Women as policymakers: The case of trial judges. *American Journal of Political Science, 25*, 308–322.

83. Steffensmeier, D., Kramer, J., & Streifel, C. (1993). Gender and imprisonment decisions. *Criminology, 31*, 411–446.

84. Parker, K., & Funk, C. (2017). Gender discrimination comes in many forms for today's working woman. *PEW Research Center.* Retrieved from http://www.pewresearch.org/fact-tank/2017/12/14/gender-discrimination-comes-in-many-forms-for-todays-working-women.

85. *Ledbetter v. Goodyear Tire & Rubber Co.*, 550 U.S. 618 (2007).

86. Greenhouse, L. (2007). In dissent, Ginsburg finds her voice at Supreme Court. *New York Times.* Retrieved from https://www.nytimes.com/2007/05/31/world/americas/31iht-court.4.5946972.html.

87. Zients, S. (2018). Lilly Ledbetter: RBG's dissent in landmark case still gives me "Chills." *CNN.* Retrieved from https://www.cnn.com/2018/08/22/politics/rbg-podcast-lilly-ledbetter-cnntv/index.html.

88. Ibid.

89. Hunter, R. (2015). More than just a different face? Judicial diversity and decision-making.

90. Collins, P. M., Jr., Manning, K. L., & Carp, R. A. (2010). Gender, critical mass, and judicial decision making in the U.S. Court of Appeals.

91. Menkel-Meadow, C. (1985). Portia in a different voice: Speculations on a women's lawyering process. *Berkley Women's Law Journal, 1*, 39–63.

92. Ibid., 54–55.

93. Hoefgen, A. M. (1999). There will be no justice unless women are part of that justice: Rape in Bosnia, the ICTY and "gender sensitive" prosecution. *Wisconsin Women's Law Journal, 14*, 155–79.

94. King, K. L., Meernik, J. D., & Kelly, E. G. (2017). Deborah's voice: The role of women in sexual assault cases at the International Criminal Tribunal for the former Yugoslavia. *Social Science Quarterly, 98*(2), 548–565.

95. Ibid.

96. Kenney, S. J. (2002). Breaking the silence: Gender mainstreaming and the composition of the European Court of Justice. *Feminist Legal* Studies, *10*(3-4), 257–270.

97. Ibid.

98. Grossman, N. (2012). Sex on the bench: Do women judges matter to the legitimacy of international courts? *Chicago Journal of International Law, 12*(2), Article 9.

99. King, K. L., Meernik, J. D., & Kelly, E. G. (2017). Deborah's voice: The role of women in sexual assault cases at the International Criminal Tribunal for the former Yugoslavia.

100. Van Schaack, B. (2008). Engendering genocide: The Akayesu case before the International Criminal Tribunal for Rwanda. *Legal Studies Research Papers Series. Working paper 08-55.* Santa Clara, CA: Santa Clara University School of Law.

101. Waibely, M., & Wu, Y. (2017). *Are arbitrators political? Evidence from international investment arbitration.* Retrieved from http://www-bcf.usc.edu/~yanhuiwu/arbitrator.pdf.

102. Grossman, N. (2012). Sex on the bench: Do women judges matter to the legitimacy of international courts?

103. King, K. L., Meernik, J. D., & Kelly, E. G. (2017). Deborah's voice: The role of women in sexual assault cases at the International Criminal Tribunal for the former Yugoslavia.

104. Feminist Task Force. (2018). *Women's tribunals.* Retrieved from https://feministtaskforce.org/reports/womens-tribunals.

105. Poloni-Staudinger, L., & Ortbals, C. (2012). *Terrorism and violent conflict: Women's agency, leadership, and responses.* New York, NY: Springer.

106. UN Women. (2011). *2001–2012 progress of the world's women: In pursuit of justice.* Retrieved from http://www.unwomen.org/-/media/headquarters/attachments/sections/library/publications/2011/progressoftheworldswomen-2011-en.pdf?la=en&vs=2835.

107. Feminist Task Force. (2018). *Women's tribunals.*

108. De Vido, S. (2017). Women's tribunals to counter impunity and forgetfulness: Why are they relevant for international law? *Deportate, Esuli, Profughe*, (33). Retrieved from https://ssrn.com/abstract=2900879.

109. Gramlich, J. (2018). America's incarceration rate is at a two-decade low. *PEW Research Center*. Retrieved from http://www.pewresearch.org/fact-tank/2018/05/02/americas-incarceration-rate-is-at-a-two-decade-low.

110. NAACP. (2018). Criminal justice fact sheet. Retrieved from https://www.naacp.org/criminal-justice-fact-sheet.

111. Hinton, E., Henderson, L., & Reed, C. (2018). An unjust burden: The disparate treatment of Black Americans in the criminal justice system. *VERA Institute*. Retrieved from https://www.vera.org/publications/for-the-record-unjust-burden.

112. Fruedenberg, N. (2002). Adverse effects of U.S. jail and prison policies on the health and well-being of women of color. *American Journal of Public Health*, *92*, 1895–1899.

113. Green, E. L., Benner, K., & Pear, R. (2018). "Transgender" could be defined out of existence under Trump administration. *New York Times*. Retrieved from https://www.nytimes.com/2018/10/21/us/politics/transgender-trump-administration-sex-definition.html.

114. *Obergefell v. Hodges*, 576 US __ (2015).

115. *Price Waterhouse v. Hopkins*, 490 U.S. 228 (1989).

116. *Hively v. Ivy Tech Community College*, 853 F.3d 339 (2017).

117. National Law Review. (2017). Seventh Circuit rules sexual orientation is protected class: *Kimberly Hively v. Ivy Tech Community College*. Retrieved from https://www.natlawreview.com/article/seventh-circuit-court-rules-sexual-orientation-protected-class-kimberly-hively-v-ivy.

118. *Romer v. Evans*, 517 U.S. 620 (1996).

119. United States Equal Employment Opportunity Commission (EEOC). (n.d.). *Examples of court decisions supporting coverage of LGBT-related discrimination under Title VII*. Retrieved from https://www.eeoc.gov/eeoc/newsroom/wysk/lgbt_examples_decisions.cfm.

120. *Masterpiece Cakeshop vs. Colorado Civil Rights Commission*, 584 US __ (2018).

121. Movement Advancement Project (MAP). (2018). *Non-discrimination laws*. Retrieved from http://www.lgbtmap.org/equality-maps/non_discrimination_laws.

122. National Center for Transgender Equality (NCTE). (n.d.). *Non-discrimination laws*. Retrieved from https://transequality.org/issues/non-discrimination-laws.

123. Human Rights Campaign (HRC). (2017). *State equality index 2017: A review of state legislation affecting the lesbian, gay, bisexual, transgender, and queer community and a look ahead in 2018*. Retrieved from http://www.hrc.org/resources/2017-state-equality-index-view-your-states-scorecard.

124. Lambda Legal. (2018). *Ninth circuit denies another Trump administration effort to implement transgender military ban*. Retrieved from https://www.lambdalegal .org/blog/20180718_karnoski-stay-decision.

125. Jackson, H. and Kube, C. (2019). *Trump's controversial military policy goes into effect*. NBC News, Retrieved from https://www.nbcnews.com/feature/nbc-out/ trump-s-controversial-transgender-military-policy-goes-effect-n993826

126. Foley, A. (2018). U.S. makes list of the top 10 most dangerous countries for women. *The Hill*. Retrieved from http://thehill.com/blogs/blog-briefing-room/ news/394152-us-makes-the-list-of-top-10-most-dangerous-countries-for-women.

127. Berenson, T. (2018). Inside Trump's plan to dramatically reshape U.S. courts. *Time*. Retrieved from http://time.com/5139118/inside-trumps-plan-to-dramatically-reshape-us-courts.

128. Scheindlin, S. A. (2017). Trump's new ream of judges will radically change American society. *The Guardian*. Retrieved from https://www.theguardian.com/ commentisfree/2017/nov/30/donald-trump-legacy-judiciary.

129. Ibid.

130. Liptak, A. (2008). U.S. voting for judges perplexes other nations. *The New York Times*. Retrieved from https://www.nytimes.com/2008/05/25/world/ americas/25iht-judge.4.13194819.html.

131. Valdini, M. E., & Shortell, C. (2016). Women's representation in the highest court: A comparative analysis of the appointment of female justices. *Political Research Quarterly*, *69*(4), 865–876.

132. Liptak, A. (2008). U.S. voting for judges perplexes other nations.

133. Valdini, M. E., & Shortell, C. (2016). Women's representation in the highest court: A comparative analysis of the appointment of female justices.

134. Kenney, S. J. (2013). *Gender and justice: Why women in the judiciary really matter*. New York and London, UK: Routledge.

135. Williams, M. (2008). Ambition, gender, and the judiciary. *Political Research Quarterly*, *61*, 68–78.

136. Frederick, B., and Streb, M. J. (2008). Women running for judge: The impact of sex on candidate success in state intermediate appellate court elections. *Social Science Quarterly*, *89*, 937–854.

137. Hurwitz, M. S., & Lanier, D. L. (2013). Diversity in state and federal appellate courts: Change and continuity across 20 years. *Justice System Journal, 29,* 47–70.

138. Kenney, S. J. (2013). *Gender and justice: Why women in the judiciary really matter.*

139. Hurwitz, M. S., & Lanier, D. L. (2013). Diversity in state and federal appellate courts: Change and continuity across 20 years.

140. Williams, M. (2007). Women's representation on state trial and appellate courts. *Social Science Quarterly, 88,* 1192–1204.

141. Hurtwiz, M. S., & Lanier, D. N. (2003). Explaining judicial diversity: The differential ability of women and minorities to attain seats on state supreme and appellate courts. *State Politics and Policy Quarterly, 3,* 329–352.

142. Reddick, M, Nelson, M. J., & Caufield, R. P. (2009). Racial and gender diversity on state courts: An AJS study. *Judges Journal, 48,* 28–32.

143. Ibid.

144. Gramlich, J. (2018). Trump's appointed judges are a less diverse group than Obama's. *Pew Research Center.* Retrieved from http://www.pewresearch.org/fact-tank/2018/03/20/trumps-appointed-judges-are-a-less-diverse-group-than-obamas.

145. Malleson, K. (2014). The case for gender quotas for appointments to the Supreme Court. Retrieved from http://ukscblog.com/case-gender-quotas-appointments-supreme-court.

146. International Criminal Court (n.d.). Current judges. Retrieved from https://www.icc-cpi.int/bios-2, and European Court of Human Rights (n.d.). Composition of the court. Retrieved from https://www.echr.coe.int/pages/home.aspx?p=court/judges.

147. *Griswold v. Connecticut,* 381 US 479 (1965)

148. Daniels, K., Mosher, W. D., & Jones, Jo. (2013). Contraceptive methods women have ever used: 1982–2010. *National Health Statistics Reports, 62,* 1–15.

149. Guttmacher Institute. (2018). *Contraceptive use in the United States.* Retrieved from https://www.guttmacher.org/fact-sheet/contraceptive-use-united-states.

150. Ibid.

151. Margaret Sanger (1879-1966). (n.d.). *PBS: American Experience.* Retrieved from https://www.pbs.org/wgbh/americanexperience/features/pill-margaret-sanger-1879-1966.

152. *Griswold v. Connecticut*, 381 U.S. 479 (1965)

153. Thompson, L. M., & Murillo, L. M. (2018). The Trump administration's assault on contraception. *The Washington Post*. Retrieved from https://www .washingtonpost.com/news/made-by-history/wp/2018/06/18/the-trump-administrations-assault-on-contraception/?utm_term=.e62f9535407d.

154. Berg, M. (2017). How federal funding works at Planned Parenthood. *Planned Parenthood*. Retrieved from https://www.plannedparenthoodaction.org/blog/how-federal-funding-works-at-planned-parenthood.

155. Marimow, A. (2018). Trump administration approach to funding family planning challenged in court. *The Washington Post*. Retrieved from https://www .washingtonpost.com/local/legal-issues/trump-administrations-approach-to-funding-family-planning-is-back-in-court/2018/12/11/eaeccc68-fd60-11e8-862a-b6a6f3ce8199_story.html?utm_term=.c6920ccbce16.

156. Belluck, P. (2018). Trump administration pushes abstinence in teen pregnancy programs. *The New York Times*. Retrieved from https://www.nytimes .com/2018/04/23/health/trump-teen-pregnancy-abstinence.html.

157. Alonso-Zaldlvar, R., & Crary, D. (2018). How the Trump administration is remaking federal policy on women's reproductive health. *PBS*. Retrieved from https://www.pbs.org/newshour/politics/how-the-trump-administration-is-remaking-federal-policy-on-womens-reproductive-health.

158. Pear, R. (2018). Trump proposes a new way around birth control mandate: Religious exemptions and Title X. *The New York Times*. Retrieved from https:// www.nytimes.com/2018/11/17/us/politics/trump-birth-control.html.

159. Goldstein, A. (2018). Trump administrations issues rules letting some employers deny contraceptive coverage. *The Washington Post*. Retrieved from https://www.washingtonpost.com/national/health-science/trump-administration-issues-rules-letting-some-employers-deny-contraceptive-coverage/2018/11/07/9402173a-e2d7-11e8-8f5f-a55347f48762_story. html?utm_term=.d9e5f6ce9480.

160. Silverman, R., Birdsall, N., & Glassman, A. (2016). Can access to contraception deliver for women's economic empowerment? What we know—and what we must learn. *Center for Global Development*. Retrieved from https://www.cgdev .org/publication/can-access-contraception-deliver-women%E2%80%99s-economic-empowerment-what-we-know.

161. Biography. (n.d.). *Loretta Lynn biography*. Retrieved from https://www.biography .com/people/loretta-lynn-9389831.

162. Loretta Lynn. (n.d). *Loretta Lynn*. Retrieved from https://www.lorettalynn.com/bio.

163. Lynn, L. One's On the Way. Decca DL 75334, 1972, vinyl.

164. Loretta Lynn. (n.d.). *Loretta Lynn*.

165. Lynn, L. (1975). The pill (Single). *MCA Records*, MCA-40358, vinyl.

166. Lynn, L. (1979). We've come a long way, baby. *MCA Records MCA-3073*, vinyl.

167. Ibid.

168. Loretta Lynn. (n.d.). *Loretta Lynn*.

169. Barnum, D. (1985). The Supreme Court and public opinion: Judicial decision-making in the post-new deal period. *The Journal of Politics*, 47, 652–666.

170. Pew Research Center. (2016). Most say birth control should be covered by employers, regardless of religious objections. Retrieved from http://www.pewforum.org/2016/09/28/1-most-say-birth-control-should-be-covered-by-employers-regardless-of-religious-objections.

171. *Burwell v. Hobby Lobby Stores*, 573 U.S. (2014)

172. Kasana, M. (2018). The Supreme Court's Arkansas abortion law decision is already having a devastating effect on women. *Bustle*. Retrieved from https://www.bustle.com/p/the-supreme-courts-arkansas-abortion-law-decision-is-already-having-a-devastating-effect-on-women-9262390.

173. National Society of High School Scholars. (2018). New survey of Gen Z high achievers shows vast majority plan to vote in the next presidential election. Retrieved from https://www.nshss.org/press-room/nshss-press/new-survey-of-gen-z-high-achievers-shows-vast-majority-plan-to-vote-in-the-next-presidential-election.

174. Babcock, L., & Laschever, S. (2007). *Women don't ask: Negotiation and the gender divide*. Princeton, NJ: Princeton University Press.

CHAPTER NINE

WOMEN IN SOCIAL MOVEMENTS

On January 21, 2017, the day after Donald Trump's inauguration, the largest single day protest in U.S. history took place—the Women's March (Box 9.1). The march in Washington, DC, is estimated to have been as big as 1 million people. Up to 5 million people are thought to have participated throughout the United States and up to 7 million worldwide. Why did people march? Upset with what was seen as sexist and degrading policies and rhetoric toward women by Donald Trump as a candidate, organizers stated that the march was intended to show that "women's rights are human rights." The march grew into a movement, with organizers putting out "10 Actions for 100 Days" for the first 100 days of the Trump Administration.

BOX 9.1: WOMEN'S MARCH

What began as nothing more than a series of posts on Facebook calling for action after the announcement of Donald Trump as president-elect, became the largest, single day, cross-country demonstration in United States history. The **Women's March on Washington** took place on January 21, 2017, to protest the inauguration of Donald Trump. Though the march on Washington was the focus of the day, demonstrations took place throughout the country and even internationally.

Teresa Shook is widely credited with originating the idea of the Women's March after she created an event page on Facebook proposing a women's march on Washington shortly after Donald Trump won the presidency.[1] Initially, her page gained little attention, having only 40 RSVPs. Then, literally overnight, that number grew to 10,000. In other locations around the Unites States, people had similar ideas. Fashion designer Bob Bland (also known as Mari Lynn Foulger), the current

(Continued)

(Continued)

co-president of Women's March, had proposed a million-pussy march on Washington. Eventually, all of these events were consolidated into one, the Women's March. The first march became synonymous with the pink pussy hats in response to Donald Trump's on-tape statement that he grabbed women "by the pussy."

Several New York-based activists were later recruited to chair the national march, while Teresa Shook focused on organizing one in her home state of Hawaii. These activists were Tamika Mallory, Carmen Perez, and Linda Sarsour.[2] Since the first Women's March on January 21, 2017, the organization has created a youth branch called Youth Empower. They have established chapters abroad in places like Lagos, Jakarta, Oslo, Melbourne, Buenos Aires, and Taipei. Most notably, they held the second annual Women's March on January 20, 2018 and the third on January 19, 2019.

According to the Women's March official website, "Women's March is a women-led movement providing intersectional education on a diverse range of issues and creating entry points for new grassroots activities and organizations."[3] Their goals are consistent for each chapter no matter location, with a slim degree of variation between chapters in the United States and chapters around the world. In addition to promoting intersectional education, the other main goal of the movement is to dismantle oppressive systems. In the United States, Women's March calls for justice in cases of police brutality, ending racial profiling, and targeting communities of color. They advocate for reproductive freedom, including access to safe, legal, and affordable abortion. They acknowledge the challenges faced by the LGBTQIA+ community, disabled, workers, and immigrants; and they assert that gender norms and expectations should be abolished; disabled individuals should have the right to full access and enjoyment of citizenship both here and abroad; all workers deserve equal pay, the right to organize, and a living wage; and that immigration is a human right, no one is illegal, and immigrants and refugees have rights regardless of status. Women's March also advocates for environmental justice and demands a new, all-inclusive Equal Rights Amendment to the U.S. Constitution.

Globally, Women's March goals are defined by the **H.E.R.S. framework**. The "H" in H.E.R.S. stands for health. This is a call for universal healthcare services, protection of the environment, and the right of all people to have access to clean water and air. "E" stands for economic security. The framework asserts that jobs need to provide a living wage and humane work conditions and call for the dismantling of all barriers that "obstruct women's full participation in local, national, and global economic systems."[4] "R" stands for representation. Women must have

fair representation at all levels of government and work; minority, disabled, elder, and indigenous representation is essential. And "S" stands for safety. The safety portion of the H.E.R.S. framework insists on ending violence against women, police brutality, and sex trafficking. It calls for the dismantling of gender and racial inequities within the criminal

▶ **Photo 9.1** Scenes from the first Women's March.

justice system. Finally, the framework indicates that it is our moral obligation to always advocate for refugees and asylum seekers.

The second Women's March took place in 2018 to commemorate the work of the year, to continue to press for the rights of women, and to protest what was seen as infringement on women's and other marginalized group's rights by the Trump Administration. Additionally, the second Women's March corresponded with the #MeToo movement (Box 9.2), which was a major focus of the action. The third women's march took place January 19, 2019, under the theme of #Women's Wave (a play on the idea of a blue wave of Democratic victory in the 2018 midterm elections). Organizers stated, "We are outraged. We are organized. They forgot that 5 million women lit the world on fire two years ago. On January 19, 2019, we're going to remind them when we flood the streets of Washington, DC, and with sister marches in cities across the globe. . . . The #WomensWave is coming, and we're sweeping the world forward with us."[5]

Criticisms of the Women's March are often rooted in patriarchy (other criticisms rooted in intersectionality are discussed in more detail later in the chapter). Critics said the women's march accomplished nothing; true heroes were women who stayed home to work or take care of kids instead of wasting time marching. Activists were accused of being a farce and essentially accomplishing nothing by marching. In short, critiques focused on belittling women or making their actions invisible.[6]

This chapter will begin with an overview of women's groups and some key definitions. We will next turn to how ideology, resources, and institutions shape women's movements actions. The chapter then explores how women's movements frame themselves, paying particular attention to the frame of motherhood. Throughout the chapter, we also make note of how women's movements provide forms of representation for women. We end our discussion with an exploration of the challenges women and feminist groups face and the likelihood of an intersectional movement in the post-Trump era.

BOX 9.2: COMPARATIVE FEATURE

#MeToo in South Korea and India

The #MeToo movement began to garner mainstream attention in 2017 when actress Alyssa Milano used the hashtag on social media as a way to urge women to speak up about sexual harassment and assault. Tarana Burke had first used the phrase "Me Too" in 2006 to speak to her own experience as a sexual assault survivor, and she encouraged high school students to do the same at Me Too workshops. At the workshops, which she first held well over a decade ago, girls could safely ask for help if they had endured harassment by writing "Me Too" on a piece of paper, rather than raising their hands and "outing" themselves as survivors.[7] Along with celebrities, Burke ushered in a new way of creating safe spaces for women and camaraderie between women. The hashtag #MeToo, though originally a response to the actions of Hollywood mogul Harvey Weinstein, soon began to expose other perpetrators in media, politics, and women's everyday lives; it even spread into the field of political science, sociology and other academic disciplines.

The #MeToo movement spread to many countries. According to CNN, the five countries that had the most tweets and posts about #MeToo were the United States, France, India, Canada, and United Kingdom.[8] The movement also has cropped up in China, a country known for its social media censorship. Chinese activists claim #MeToo, which first started on university campuses in early 2018, has been censored because it threatens "government officials and powerful business executives [who] are often protected from allegations of wrongdoing."[9] As in the United States, movements in other countries often began with actresses sharing their stories on social media. For example, Karla Souza, a Mexican actress, spoke out about how a director made sexual advances on her. In the two countries we discuss next, South Korea and India, the movement began in light of sexual harassment in the entertainment industry and also encompassed stories of sexual harassment in politics. In India, the movement garnered a critique that we also find in the United States, specifically that #MeToo lacked diversity and didn't elevate the voices of all women who might need to share their stories.

South Korea: A young Korean woman celebrity was found dead in 2009, and many controversial investigations led to the conclusion that she had committed suicide due to sexual abuse and harassment. This incident started a conversation about sexual harassment in South Korea, but it was not until the movement of #MeToo that people began calling for an end to sexual harassment in the entertainment industry. In January 2018, #MeToo began in South Korea when a woman prosecutor announced on national television that a senior level officer at the Ministry of Justice had groped her in 2010. Because of the social media response to this announcement, the prosecutor's case was investigated, and many actresses and celebrities then posted online about their experiences with sexual harassment and abuses by high profile men directors and actors. The #MeToo movement further spread to politics when Kim Ji-Eun, a secretary of Ahn Hee-Jung, a major politician, claimed on national television that the politician had groped and touched her inappropriately. He also was accused of raping another woman. This accusation came as a shock as Ahn Hee-Jung was considered a potential presidential candidate. He eventually stepped down as the governor of South Chungcheong Province in February 2018. In addition, in March 2018, young students came out with sexual allegations against their professor, the actor Jo Min-Ki. The allegations were proven to be true, but Jo Min-Ki committed suicide before he could be prosecuted.

Support for the movement has been widespread, and the #MeToo movement also includes the hashtag of #WithYou, which allows supporters to show solidarity with women on social media. The widespread acceptability of the movement is also evidenced by the many media outlets that have engaged the topic of sexual harassment. Korean dramas have incorporated talks about discrimination and sexual harassment in the workplace, and Webtoons, a comic strip, has brought up harassment in the workplace and in everyday settings such as the classrooms or social gatherings.

India: The Indian #MeToo movement began with Bollywood actress Usha Jadhav, who publicly addressed the sexual assaults happening in the Indian entertainment industry in a BBC Documentary on April 28, 2018. She cited instances in which she was instructed to sleep with directors or producers to help secure a role in a film. Politicians in India also have been called out for their sexual misconduct. Kuldeep Singh Sengar, an elected member of the Uttar Pradesh state legislative assembly, allegedly raped a girl. He denied the accusations, but an investigation showed the police tried to intimidate the girl by saying that Sengar would kill her family members if she proceeded with the case. Sengar was arrested in the spring of 2018. A leader in the Congress Party and parliamentary member, Renuka Chowdhury, spoke about sexual harassment in Indian Parliament. She explained that "casting couch," a term used in Bollywood to explain how actresses are cast in exchange for a sexual favors, is not only happening in Bollywood but it is also prevalent in politics. Other politicians disagreed, but she said the culture of parliament represents

(Continued)

the essence of the casting couch in that men politicians make derogatory remarks against women politicians. Young women also face sexual assault and have become a part of the #MeToo movement. One of the most controversial cases in India's recent past involved a 23-year-old medical school student who was gang raped in 2012 and died from her injuries. This incident sparked a conversation about sexual assault, violence against women, and feminism, particularly among Indian youth. Statistics show that rape occurs every 20 minutes in the country;[10] thus, #MeToo could be considered a logical extension of Indian feminism as well as an outlet for many women in the country who have experienced sexual assault As described in Chapter 2, the feminist movement has deep roots and is active on a variety of issues in India.

On the other hand, some argue that the movement cannot connect all women in India because only a quarter of the population have access to the Internet, and many are more concerned about basic needs rather than activity on social media.[11] Priya Varadarajan, who works for an NGO, explains how the #MeToo is a class-based phenomenon:

> The #MeToo campaign has resonated with the educated middle-class women who are employed, who dare to speak, and who are fighting for their space and are active on social media. . . . But very few women belong to this class. When you move out of the cities, you see women for whom survival is the most basic question and for whom #MeToo will make no difference.[12]

> Devi Sharma, a woman who lives in rural India, is a good example of a woman who is excluded from the movement. She states, "I work in the fields and get a lower daily wage than a man. I want that to change."[13] She knows nothing about #MeToo or urban women's activism but considers herself a feminist. Thus, similar to critiques in the United States that #MeToo privileges "white, affluent, and educated women,"[14] some Indian observers view #MeToo as exclusionary to rural and nonaffluent women.

In Iceland, the #MeToo movement has expanded to the #karlmennskan movement, which translates as #masculinity. The point of the movement is for men to take responsibility for inequality between men and women and to speak out about the ways in which toxic masculinity has been damaging for them.[15] **Toxic masculinity** refers to the idea that men and boys are cast into very narrow, very masculine gender roles that do not allow for the expression of emotion and the expectations that men and boys act in alpha male type ways. We refer elsewhere in the book to hegemonic masculinity, which is a similar concept.

The Women's March and #MeToo movements are unique in terms of their size and worldwide scale. That said, the fact that women and their allies would band together in protest is not particularly unique. Citizens in all democracies have interests and try to influence the political system. A country's political culture and institutions shape the form and function of this influence. For example, in France protest is a common tactic for women's groups because it is an accepted (often privileged) form of political participation, a legacy of the French Revolution. Additionally, ideology of groups and the resources available to them also influence how social groups, women's groups included, act.[16] (See Box 9.4 for an additional example.)

▸ **Photo 9.2** #MeToo on a sign from a protest.

Two important vehicles through which interests are conveyed in democracies are political parties and interest groups. **Intermediary institutions**, like parties and interest groups, make citizens' political behavior easier to achieve and understand by providing key information and political cues to voters, transmitting political values to guide political leaders, organizing the avenues of political behavior, and providing access to elected officials. In this way, intermediary institutions enable political representation. Parties and interest groups differ greatly in many regards, but they share the above-mentioned functions, as well as two crucial democratic functions: they articulate and aggregate the public's opinions to political leaders.[17]

INTEREST GROUPS, SOCIAL MOVEMENTS, AND SOCIAL MOVEMENT ORGANIZATIONS

In advanced industrial democracies, interest groups, sometimes called social movements in comparative politics, are powerful and important interest articulation and mobilization vehicles. An **interest group** is defined as an organization of people with similar policy goals who enter the political process to try to achieve those aims. For example, those who passionately champion breastfeeding may join La Leche League or First Right. Those passionate about reproductive rights may join the National Organization of Women (NOW) or the National Abortion and Reproductive Rights Action League (or NARAL Pro-Choice America). In short, interest groups bring together people who share common purpose and interest to act jointly and in a coordinated fashion. Interest groups and social movements differ from political parties in that they do not run their own slate of candidates for election. This chapter later shows, though, how the line between interest group and political party can be blurred.

Observers of American politics often strictly refer to interest groups, but *social movement* is a term usually used more broadly by comparativists and sociologists. Kriesi et al. (1995) defines a **social movement** as "an organized, sustained, self-conscious challenge to existing authorities on behalf of constituencies whose goals are not taken into account by these authorities."[18] Sidney Tarrow (1994), a prominent American social movement scholar, defines social movements as "collective challenges [to elites, authorities, other groups, or cultural codes] by people with common purposes and solidarity in sustained interactions with elites, opponents and authorities."[19] Women's movements fit these definitions in that their interests historically, and currently, have not been taken into account. Thus, they challenge political elites and cultural codes as they work toward policy change, and in some cases, the dismantling of patriarchal structures of power and privilege.

The conceptual differences between social movements and interest groups are blurry, with some scholars arguing that there is no difference at all.[20] Other scholars argue that social movements are political outsiders, and interest groups are political insiders.[21] This means that social movements act through noninstitutional means (outside political institutions), while interest groups work institutionally. Poloni-Staudinger and Wolf (2019) explain that many groups start off acting through non-institutional avenues, and over time, adopt more institutional actions that they use alongside other tactics.[22] For example, the Women's March started as a protest, but over time, it began to engage in lobbying activities and campaign contributions, actions it uses alongside more protest-type activities. That said, a group like Code Pink, a feminist, women-led grassroots protest group that formed to protest the Iraq War in 2002 and today advocates to "end U.S. wars and militarism, support peace and human rights initiatives, and redirect our tax dollars into healthcare, education, green jobs and other life-affirming programs," has continued to engage in extra-institutional action throughout its more than 15 year history.[23] In fact, CodePink states that they act "with an emphasis on joy and humor, our tactics include satire, street theatre, creative visuals, civil resistance, and directly challenging powerful decision-makers in government and corporations. And of course, wearing pink!"[24]

Yahya Ahmed/Kurdish Service (VOA)

▶ **Photo 9.3** Code Pink protestors.

Other scholars refer to the term **social movement organization (SMO)** to mean essentially the same thing as an interest group, defining SMO as "a complex, or formal, organization which identifies its goals with the preferences of a social movement."[25] In short, a social movement like the women's movement can be comprised of many different interest groups or social movement organizations.

Poloni-Staudinger and Wolf (2019) conclude that any real distinction between SMOs and interest groups has largely evaporated in advanced industrial democracies.[26] Most groups engage in similar types of activity (from protest and unconventional activities to lobbying and conventional activities) and have been incorporated, either formally or informally, into the policy-making process. Thus, in this chapter, the terms "social movement organization" and "interest group" will be used interchangeably when discussing women's groups.

It is important to distinguish between "women in movements" and "women's movements." **Women's movements** are groups with central goals pertaining to "women's gendered experiences, women's issues, and women's leadership and decision making."[27] **"Women in movements"** refers to activism by women in movements not primarily focussed on women's issues and experiences. Black Lives Matter provides a good example of women in movements. While we see in Box 9.7 that women founded this movement, and these women express gendered discourses, they are not in a "women's movement" because gender issues do not guide the groups' actions, and men may lead the groups.[28]

The definition of a women's movement may be applied to feminist, antifeminist, and nonfeminist movements.[29] Whereas **feminist women's movements** challenge "political, social and other power arrangements of domination and subordination on the basis of gender,"[30] **antifeminist women's movements** "protect women's socially ascribed gender roles" in the private sphere.[31] **Nonfeminist women's movements**, unlike antifeminists, accept women's entry into the public sphere, yet they do not actively seek changes in gender relations. In fact, nonfeminist groups reproduce gender relations as they often uphold feminine, wifely, and maternal ideals.[32] Nonfeminists, however, can respond to issues important to women and families like education and childcare.

How Do Women's Movements Act?

The claims of women activists typically do not make front-page news; rather, they are marginalized. Thus, women often use social movement activity to influence authorities and the general public. At a broad level, we can characterize action among women's movements as **institutional** (working though institutions in the form of lobbying, sitting on commissions, advising on policy) or **extra-institutional** (working outside institutions mainly through engagement in protest). Thus, women's groups like other SMOs engage in all types of activities, including protests and demonstrations, lobbying, and serving in consultative roles with policymakers. Arguably, they are essential to substantive representation because policymaking is dynamic and forged through the work of many actors, and women in legislative and executive institutions must interact with movements if they are to be a voice of "dispossessed subgroups of women." That is, women's movements can open policy discussion to the voices of many more women.[33] By and large, however, women's groups work disproportionally on service. That is, service related to education, health, or other women's issues, such as sponsoring voter education drives, self breast exams, or law clinics. Additionally, the type of activity available to women is constrained when they do not live in a democracy. For example, in Saudi Arabia, the political opportunity structure (see discussion of opportunity structures in later sections) is closed to women's collective action, yet as Box 9.3 shows, even in authoritarian systems, women have found ways to organize and address the interests of some women.

BOX 9.3: COMPARATIVE FEATURE

Women's Activism in Saudi Arabia

Political participation for women (and men) is constrained in Saudi Arabia, a monarchy that practices **Wahhabism**—an austere, fundamentalist form of Islam that restricts alcohol and tobacco use, maintains a strict separation of the sexes, and requires modest dress for women and men. Women and families eat in designated places in restaurants, for example, while men eat in men's-only sections. *Sharia* law is the law of the country, and a religious police (*mutaween*) monitors social interactions and has reprimanded women for their dress or even their nail polish color. As of 2016, "the government declared that the *mutaween* could no longer stop, pursue, or arrest people and ought to be 'gentle and kind' in their conduct;"[34] however, judges can sanction offenders as they see fit for sexual relations or nonconforming gender identities because *sharia* law pertaining to personal status is uncodified (see Chapter 1). This also means that injustices like sexual assault and marital rape are not "on the books."[35] Women can vote for and be elected to municipal councils as of 2015, but these positions are not incredibly influential, and national-level officials remain appointed by the king.

Given that Saudi Arabia is not democratic, it comes as no surprise that social movement organizations, including women's groups, are disallowed. Furthermore, dissent against the government is illegal and can be met with imprisonment. The women's movement in Saudi Arabia by and large consists of individual activists who primarily use social media to criticize current policies and push for social and political change. Some women use social media anonymously, while others, like Loujain al-Hathloul, dare to use their own identities (names *and* faces) as an additional form of protest. Traditional media in the country is state-controlled, and public forms of entertainment, such as movie theaters, have largely been prohibited; thus, social media provides

Saudis, and especially young people, a space for recreation. This space serves as dialogue about political and social change. The two campaigns reviewed below, the right to drive and the guardianship movements, occupy this space.

Until 2018, Saudi Arabia was the only country in the world to ban women drivers. Arguments against women driving included that it would lead to promiscuous behavior by women traveling alone, and, as a result, would diminish the Saudi family. In fact, "one cleric claimed—with no evidence—that driving harmed women's ovaries."[36] Women's activists are partially to thank for the ban being lifted in 2018. The #Women2Drive movement on Twitter hastened change, and its roots lie in a 1990 protest in which 47 women drove vehicles around Riyadh, the Saudi capital. Many of the women in this protest were treated harshly by the regime. They lost their jobs, and feminist activism waned as a result of their treatment. The right to drive campaign continued, when in 2007, 1,100 Saudis signed a petition to then King Abdullah to strike down the driving ban.[37] In 2011, a Facebook group called "Women to Drive" launched a Twitter campaign with the hashtag #Women2Drive. Tweets from the movement over the years (2011–2017) include the following:

Manal al-Sharif https://twitter.com/manal_alsharif Verified account **@manal_alsharif**

Today, the last country on earth to allow women to drive

#Women2Drive#Daring2Drive we did it

Another major tactic of the movement was to video record women drivers and post videos to YouTube. Loujain al-Hathloul, 25 years old at the time, filmed herself attempting to drive from the United Arab Emirates into Saudi Arabia in 2014. She was imprisoned for 10 weeks for her actions, which were labeled an act of subversion. Protest alone did not convince the kingdom to permit driving for women. An economic incentive existed for Crown Prince Moham-med bin Salman, who—prior to becoming infamous for his likely involvement in coordinating the assassination of Saudi ex-pat and *Washington Post* reporter Jamal Khashoggi—had garnered an international reputation as a reformer who wanted to change the country socially and economically through his "Vision 2030" plan. A key component of the plan is to increase "women's workforce participation to 30 percent from 22 percent."[38] With the driving ban lifted, women can more easily work, and the Saudi economy can grow. Whereas rich women had mobility even during the ban due to private drivers who worked regularly for their families, many other women had to pay for taxis, thereby decreasing their incentive and ability to work outside the home.

(Continued)

(Continued)

Obstacles to women's independence and mobility persist, however. Backlash to women driving and a counter hashtag campaign roughly translating to "you won't drive, you won't drive" have cropped up. Some women fear that men with this sentiment might come across women driving, and then chase down and harass them. What is more, the government has furthered backlash. In 2017, it told activists not to speak to the foreign press about driving campaigns and, during summer 2018, it imprisoned leading feminists, including Loujain al-Hathloul, on charges of subversion and conspiring with hostile forces abroad. In fact, Saudi officials are prosecuting human rights activists who have been accused of inciting activism against the government. Israa al-Ghomgham may be the first woman activist put to death in Saudi Arabia. She is accused of inciting demonstrations in the eastern part of the country. Human Rights Watch and supporters argue the activists were engaging in peaceful protest to push for rights for the Shiite minority. As of 2019, al-Ghomgham's trial was ongoing with the government originally seeking the death penalty by beheading.[39] Reports in early 2019 suggest that the government may be reversing calls for beheading based on international pressure. Reports in late 2018 suggested that the state was physically and sexually torturing women who are activists, with some having been flogged and electrocuted to the point of being unable to walk.

Finally, women face the constraints of the country's guardianship system. Under the Saudi interpretation of *sharia* law, "a woman remains a legal dependent, no matter her age, education level or marital status. She needs a man as a guardian—a father, uncle, husband, brother or son—to consent to a variety of basic needs" such as traveling outside the country.[40] Although a royal decree specified in 2017 that women did not need their guardian's permission to go to university, take a job, or have surgery, most employers want a guardian's permission for a woman to work, and women cannot open bank accounts or consent to marry on their own. For this reason, feminists since 2016 stepped up activism against guardianship. Almost 15,000 women signed an online petition against guardianship in 2016, and after the government announced the end of the driving ban, activists can now focus on guardianship. As one woman tweeted: "#Women2Drive done #IamMyOwnGuardian in progress" (12:34 PM-Sep 26, 2017).

What Explains Differences in Women's Groups' Activities

Early social movement work suggested that groups take action based on the idea of **relative deprivation.** That is, they are less concerned about what they don't have but rather about what they do or don't have in relation to others in society. In short, relative deprivation theory asserts that groups are motivated to action when they perceive their position in society to be relatively depressed compared to others, rather on objective measures. On the other hand, previous work by Poloni-Staudinger and Ortbals (2011) out of Europe suggests that how women's groups act is influenced by the resources available to them, their ideology, and the political opportunity structures with which they are confronted. **Resource mobilization** approaches to understanding group action focus on the degree to which groups have the resources—money, personnel, time, volunteers—to achieve their goals. **Ideological** examinations of group activity suggest that groups with different ideologies, such as feminist versus not, will engage in different types of action. For example, protest and satire may appeal to members of Code Pink, but it may be less palatable to Daughters of the American Revolution, a lineage-based membership service organization for women who are directly descended from a person involved in the United States' efforts toward independence. **Political opportunity structure** explanations explore how different institutional arrangements constrain or promote different types of group activity. Opportunity structures can be defined as "filters between the mobilization of groups and their choice of strategies and actions."[41]

Much research examining social movement activity, including women's movements, does so from the political opportunity perspective,[42] though the approach is critiqued for being overly deterministic.[43] Women and politics literature discusses whether opportunity structures are consistently closed to women or whether there can be instances where the opportunity structure is hospitable to women's group activity. We've highlighted elsewhere in this book how most feminists believe that the state is built upon patriarchal principles, or as Beckwith (2005) suggests, "systematic gendered arrangements of [masculinist] power and privilege."[44] This structure can help to explain why even in progressive groups, women can be treated as outsiders, an impediment to women's movements we discuss at the end of this chapter.[45] That said, research shows that political parties on the left can serve as opportunities for women's activism when they become important allies for women's groups;[46] although as we have seen in Chapters 6 and 7, leftist governance does not guarantee feminist policymaking.

Social groups act differently when faced with open (those hospitable to them) and closed (those inhospitable to them) opportunity structures. When confronted with closed structures, groups are more likely to engage in domestic protest or act in larger coalitions. Alternatively, when faced with open structures, groups lobby and seek consultation with state officials.[47] While there is confusion in the literature around opportunity structures because the term was overused to describe many aspects of politics, one specifically defined opportunity structure—elite allies—was found to impact activity choices by women's groups.[48] For instance, when the left is in charge, women's movements are more likely to lobby and less likely to engage in protest. There is one important caveat: Women's movements are less likely to be invited into consultation with the government than other social groups, no matter the party in power.[49] This means women's movements are not equally present at the proverbial table to hasten political change and produce greater substantive representation.

Research shows that in countries with a variable party structure (most democracies), parties of the left often balance the desires of a varied constituency. When the left is under pressure from the working-class vote, it may ignore groups like women's and feminist groups, advocating instead for their traditional working-class base.[50] During such times, social movement organizations tend to choose confrontational tactics. While this finding holds among many types of social movements, it is different for women's movements. Women's movements tend to protest significantly less than other social groups.[51] Furthermore, groups are likely to expect the most and be the most critical of governments led by parties who are allies. According to the **expectation-punishment axiom**, social movements are more critical of political parties with which one would expect them to have the greatest affinity.[52] Thus, even when political opportunities are open, women's movements issue critical statements of their leftist allies. This criticism is more likely to come from groups that identify as feminist, that is, they challenge structures of patriarchy, than from groups that identify as women's groups without a feminist agenda. This criticism tends to stay at the level of rhetoric, however, since women's movements are less likely to engage in protest.[53] There are, of course, some exceptions to this rule. Some of the major advances of the women's movement in the First and Second Wave were accompanied with protest. Resistance to Donald Trump, discussed elsewhere in this book and chapter, also appears to be ushering in a new wave of women's movement protest. It is perhaps precisely because they are less likely to protest that women have a strong impact when they do (see discussion of the Madres movement in Box 9.6).

Authoritarian systems, like that seen in Saudi Arabia, provide few opportunities for women's groups' actions. While we know that allies in government can potentially make the path for women's groups smoother, in democracies, the type of interest group arrangement—whether it is (neo)corporatist or pluralist—influences the nature and type of women's movements' actions and organizations as well. **Neo corporatist interest group** arrangements are defined as those where there is tight policy making between government, labor interests, and business interests. These three large interests are in constant negotiation to influence, in particular, fiscal policy. As modern democracies have evolved to take on more issues, like women's issues, neo corporatism has evolved to consider these issue areas as well. The Nordic countries are considered typical neo corporatist states, but the arrangement exists in Germany and Austria as well.[54] **Pluralist interest group** arrangements are characterized by large numbers of interest groups competing for policy influence. For example, in the reproductive policy area, prolife and prochoice groups compete to influence public policy related to abortion and reproductive policy. The United States has the most pluralist interest group arrangement in the world.

Women's Groups in the United States and Germany

Earlier sections of this chapter addressed the difference between feminist, non-feminist, and antifeminist women's groups. All advanced industrial societies have these groups. In the United States, however, compared to a country like Germany, the concentration of such groups is different.

The first thing you notice when you look at a listing of women's groups in the United States and Germany is the stark difference in the sheer number of groups in each country. In Germany, a more neo-corporatist state, there are relatively few groups. Groups work in "federations." In fact, in Germany, there are fewer than a dozen nationally active women's groups. The group Deutscher Frauenring is a good example. This federated group has about 60 local branches, but it operates as a single organization. Because of its federated structure, it focuses on activities from protesting sexism in society to a capital campaign to invest in job training for women in West Africa. Groups moderate their message in neo-corporatist countries as well. While few groups in Germany could be strictly classified as feminist, there are also few antifeminist groups. Most would be considered nonfeminist because of the wide range of issues upon which they focus. While there are groups with federated structures in the United States, there are many, many more groups in the United States than in Germany. While in Germany, you would have one group that took on both sexism and fair trade/work empowerment issues of women in Africa; in the United States, these issues would be addressed by many different groups. This is because the United States has a pluralist interest group arrangement. This means that the United States has a much broader differentiation between groups. Many groups would fall in to the feminist and antifeminist camps. In Chapter 2, we mentioned antifeminist groups, such as the Concerned Women for America, that worked to block the Equal Rights Amendment; this group is still active and lobbying the Trump administration, and at the same time, we observe active feminist groups protesting against Trump. Nevertheless, most women's groups would be considered nonfeminist in all advanced democracies, including the United States.

The type of interest group arrangement influences how groups act in the two different countries as well. In Germany, given its neocorporatist structure, research has shown that protest makes up less than 1% of activity among women's groups. That said, according to research by Poloni-Staudinger and Ortbals (2014),[55] women's groups are less likely to engage in consultation with the government over policies in Germany (a characteristic of a neo-corporatist state) than social groups in other sectors, indicating that women's groups continue to be less likely to be invited to the proverbial policy-making table. In the United States, women's groups are also not often seen consulting with government; yet, given

(Continued)

the sheer number of groups, some often engage in protest as an activity choice, and others choose more conventional activities such as lobbying. In all countries, however, research points to the idea that women's groups are most likely to engage in "service" work, such as educational campaigns or social gatherings.[56]

Organizing Women's Issues Outside of Social Movement Organizations

With a few exceptions, women's movements, feminist movements, and groups pushing women's issues usually coalesce through social movement organizations rather than through political parties. This does not mean that parties do not discuss sexism and women's issues, but in most countries, this is *one* aspect of a political party's wider platform, not the sole or defining aspect of a party's platform. There are a few notable exceptions to this rule. In some countries, we see women's political parties. When asked why a party was needed, one U.K. Women's Equality representative told the authors, "we will know we have been successful when a separate women's equality party is no longer needed." Box 9.5 lists women's political parties around the world and provides a brief introduction to each party. In the United States, we only see a women's party at the state level in New York. Given our electoral system (majoritarian, single member districts), small niche parties, like feminist parties, are unlikely to compete for power in any real way. Thus, in the United States, women's interests are more likely to be articulated through groups.

BOX 9.5: COMPARATIVE FEATURE

When Women Organize in Parties in Addition to Movements

Table 9.1   Current Women's Political Parties Around the World (as of 2018)

Party	Country	Year Created
Feminist Initiative	Sweden and Norway	2005
Women's Equality Party	United Kingdom	2015
GABRIELA Women's Party	Philippines	2000
United Women Front	India	2007
U'Bizchutan	Israel	2015
Women's Equality Party	United States (New York State)	2014

Feminist Initiative: Feminist Initiative was founded in 2005 by the former leader of the Left Party and one of Sweden's most well-known political feminists, Gudrun Schyman,[57] and operates with the following slogan: "We are the open hand mobilizing the growing social movements seeking equality, accessibility and social justice. We are bringing a new dimension into politics." Initially, the party was nothing more than a small pressure group led by Schyman who had recently abandoned her previous party. They made their presence known at a press conference on April 4, 2005, at which point its founding members stated that it was not yet a political party. However, the group began to gain quite a bit of attention. As a result, they launched a website, announced the creation of both local and regional chapters, and on September 9, 2005, it was decided that the group would officially be a political party, allowing them to run in the general parliamentary election of 2006.

Despite a considerable amount of media attention, in the 2006 election, Feminist Initiative only received 0.68% of the vote. As a result, the party was not admitted into the Riksdag (parliament) because 4% of the vote is necessary for entry. In 2010, the party experienced an even greater blow when it was revealed that they had lost support, garnering only 0.4% of the vote. Then in the 2014 European Parliament Election, the party made an astonishing come back, receiving 5.3% of the vote and earning them a seat as a Member of the European Parliament (MEP). Since 2014, the party has continued to grow and has even expanded to Norway. Feminist Initiative calls for open borders, protection of democracy, and a peaceful Europe that is accessible for all. They also demand freedom from violence and sexual exploitation; prioritization of gender equality; rights to sexuality, identity, and reproductive health; and early childhood care.[58]

Women's Equality Party (UK): The Women's Equality Party (WEP) of the United Kingdom was cofounded by Catherine Mayer and Sandi Toksvig in March 2015.[59] After its founding, the party moved quite quickly to gain legitimacy and prepare for elections the following year, announcing that Sophie Walker would be their new leader. The party participated in its first major election in May 2016, backing candidates in Lothian, Glasgow, South Wales Central, and London. In total, across all four areas, the party received 352,322 votes. In London, in particular, where leader of the party Sophie Walker was running for mayor, the party garnered 251,775 of those votes. Walker and the party viewed this as a major success and a step in the right direction, acknowledging the fact that she did not win but still received 5.2% of the vote in London. The party has yet to replicate the success that they had in 2016. In the 2017 General Election, the party-backed candidates in seven different areas all garnered less than 2% of the vote. Part of the fizzling of the party has to do with its hostility toward "outsiders" and its stance on sex workers. The WEP is accused of being insular and hostile to critique or dialogue. In reference to

(Continued)

(Continued)

the former, the authors attempted an in-person interview with the party, and a wrought iron gate was slammed in their faces. Further attempts at e-mail correspondence were eventually thoroughly answered, indicating this is not a widespread stance among party operatives. Its stance toward sex workers has proven problematic as it has come out strongly against prostitution, angering many who believe the decision to participate in sex work is a woman's choice.

The goals of the Women's Equality Party are similar to those of other women's political parties around the world; however, they diverge from the norm in seeking equal media treatment and equal parenting and caregiving. The party asserts that "equality for women requires real cultural change, and the media has to be at the centre of that."[60] The media must change to make it clear to youth that equality is indeed normal. When asked via an e-mail interview why they chose a political party over an interest group, a WEP representative replied,

> Women make up half the population but are still treated as a special interest group by political parties. Having seen how effective UKIP [United Kingdom Independence Party] was in the U.K. as a single issue political party that achieved its aims (a referendum on membership of the European Union and then exiting the EU) having only ever elected one MP, we saw an opportunity to pressure the other political parties by threatening their vote share. We also saw some highly effective individual women MPs who don't have backing of their parties. By providing external pressure, we aim to give those women a better chance of being heard in their own parties.

They believe that if shared parenting and caregiving can be achieved, the pay gap will be reduced, women could take on more decision-making roles, enable men to take part in the childcare process, and give children the benefit of having time with each parent. Their other objectives include equal representation, equal pay and opportunity, equal education, equality in healthcare and medical research, and an end to violence against women.

GABRIELA Women's Party: The GABRIELA Women's party (Philippines) was first founded in April, 1984. GABRIELA stands for General Assembly Binding Women for Reforms, Integrity, Equality, Leadership, and Action. Initially, the party began as a feminist organization and began to be seen as a leader of third world feminism.

In 2003, the organization launched GABRIELA Women's Party so that it could run in elections. In their first election in 2004 they received 3.65% of the vote and gained one seat. This percentage increased slightly to 3.89% in 2007 for which they were awarded two seats. Since 2007, they have continued to win seats in the legislature, despite a decrease in support in 2013. In the most recent election in 2016, the party once again won two seats after receiving 4.22% of the vote, the most successful year the party has had to date.[61] The GABRIELA Women's Party continues to grow and gain support for their progressive platform that focuses on human rights, poverty, globalization, antimilitarism, violence, rape culture, health, censorship, and sex trafficking.

United Women Front: The United Women Front is a political party in India that was founded in 2007 by Suman Krishan Kant, the wife of the former vice-president, Krishan Kant.[62] She created United Women Front to provide a political party for women. Historically, women in India have not had strong voices in government, and United Women Front aims to make women's voices heard. The party focuses on women's illiteracy, early marriage, and the safety of women.[63]

U'Bizchutan: U'Bizchutan in Israel was founded by Ruth Colian in 2015 after the party she had previously been associated with, Shas, refused to let her run in a state election because she was a woman. Colian is a member of the Haredi Jewish community, a conservative Jewish sect. Colian petitioned the Israeli High Court to make sex-based discrimination in political parties illegal, but the court refused, so Colian created her own party.[64,65] The party focuses on overall progress on women's issues, especially in education, employment, and health. U'Bizchutan faced many obstacles while campaigning in 2015.[66] Colian and members of the party faced harassment and threats by individuals who believed women did not belong in politics. Newspapers initially refused to give them ad space, causing them to be dependent on social media to get the word out about their campaign while they took the newspapers to court. Ultimately, the party failed to pass the electoral threshold to win a seat in parliament after only receiving 1,802 votes. Since this loss, the party has had no major political activity.[67]

Women's Equality Party (New York): The Women's Equality Party of New York state was founded by Andrew Cuomo in 2014.[68] The party is named after the Women's Equality Act, a bill that Cuomo was attempting to push through the New York State Legislature at the time. Since its inception, many have criticized the party and Cuomo, because Cuomo is not a woman and seems to have only created the party so that he could get elected. While Cuomo is a Democrat, New York electoral rules allow for ballot fusion, which allows two or more parties to list the same candidate on the ballot. As such, the party was granted ballot access as a political party for the next four years after it gained over 50,000 votes for the Cuomo-Hochul ticket during the 2014 New York gubernatorial election. Since the 2014 election, there was a change in leadership. In 2018, Susan Zimet became chair of the party after Rachel Gold was chair in 2016.[69] The party backed Cuomo for reelection again in 2018, despite the fact that once again, he was challenged by a woman.

Using Motherhood as an Organizing Tool

We saw in Box 9.5 that some women's groups choose to organize as a party rather than an interest group because of the message they think it sends about how they want to frame policy debates. **Frames,** as discussed in Chapters 5 and 7, present "little tacit theories about what exists, what happens, and what matters."[70] According to Entman (2004), "a frame operates to select and highlight some features of reality and obscure others in a way that tells a consistent story about problems, their causes, moral implications, and remedies."[71] In Chapter 7, we discussed how frames can be constructed by the media but also by politicians such as President Trump. Social groups, such as women's movements, use frames as well. A common frame associated with women is one of motherhood, or maternal politics.

Maternal politics (or the politics that focus on mothers and children) and women's group organizations have a long history. Women focused on shaping maternal and child welfare policy in the early twentieth century, and through their work, claimed new roles for themselves.[72] In doing so, they transformed motherhood from primarily a *private* responsibility into *public* policy. This policy area became a way for women reformers, individually and through organizations, to enter the political realm, a way to challenge existing power arrangements and the state writ large, and a way to expand notions of the welfare state. Even before the advent of the Nineteenth Amendment in the United States, and before women in most countries had full suffrage, women working in the area of maternal politics "envisioned a state which not only had the qualities of mothering we associate with welfare, but in which women played active roles as electors, policy makers, bureaucrats, and workers, within and outside the home."[73] Women activists in the late 1800s addressed poverty, homelessness, the needs of widows, and the dangers of industrial work.[74]

Motherhood historically and today is a powerful frame to use for groups when organizing because it is a "safe" space in which women can operate. Why is it a safe space? Motherhood is an identity assigned to women that does not disrupt the status quo or socially ascribed gender roles. In fact, it is one of the most socially acceptable identities for women.[75] Therefore, when women operate *as mothers* they are often able to make headway and work in spaces not always open to other social movements or activists, allowing them to fly below the radar.[76] The Madres de Plaza de Mayo are a potent example of using motherhood as an organizing tool (Box 9.6).

Further, motherhood is acceptable politically because it is key to nationalism.[77] (See Chapter 10 for examples of the way rising authoritarian leaders frame women and motherhood.) In Chapter 7, we explained that nationalism positions men as heroes, leaders, and protectors whereas it groups women with children and considers both in need of men's help. Women bear and raise each generation of a nation; thus, they are a revered representation of entire publics.[78] That said, historically motherhood as an organizing tool operated on two levels. "It extolled the virtues of domesticity while simultaneously legitimating women's public relationships to politics and the state, to community, workplace, and marketplace."[79] While materialist politics evokes traditional images of womanliness, it also has the potential to implicitly challenge the boundaries between public and private, women and men, and state and civil society.[80] Nevertheless, there can be a danger in using motherhood as a "shield" in social movement organizations. Women can become confined to activism only on "motherhood issues," and backlash against women or groups that deviate outside the space of motherhood can often be met with harsher consequences as they are seen as not occupying their acceptable "space."[81] Additionally, not all women are mothers, and not all who identify as women were born with a uterus. Essentializing women on their ability to bear children, then, can be problematical and exclusionary. (See Chapter 10 to review tensions between individual and fetal rights that emerge, in the form of personhood legislation, when women are essentialized as mothers.)

BOX 9.6: COMPARATIVE FEATURE

Madres de Plaza de Mayo

In Argentina, in the late 1960s and early 1970s, radical leftists launched terrorist attacks against symbols of capitalism, including bankers, whom they kidnapped or assassinated. Right wing extremists formed militias and enacted terror in response. When Argentinian President Juan Perón died in 1974, the ideological terror escalated, creating a cycle of violence between the police and terrorists, which prompted the military to take over the government in a coup. A *junta* of three military commanders ruled the country between 1976 and 1983. The military waged the Dirty War during this time, committing atrocities to root out leftist extremists and anyone tangentially associated with them.

Between 9,000 and 30,000 people "were disappeared" and killed during the Dirty War. Victims were typically young people from the working class. Prisoners were tortured by electrocution and sexual abuse, and people were killed in heinous ways—including death flights over the Atlantic, where prisoners were drugged and dropped alive to drown in the ocean. The disappeared, known as the *desaparecidos*, mostly were not heard from again, leaving families with no information of their deaths or ability to bury their remains. More men than women were disappeared during the Dirty War; however, some women prisoners who gave birth in jail were later killed, and military families adopted their children.

(Continued)

(Continued)

Women largely were not represented in politics and economics at this point in Argentine history. Many women were housewives, and the country's culture reflected *machismo* and *marianismo*. Recall from previous chapters that *machismo* is exaggerated masculinity and indicates male dominance in society and politics (similar to **hegemonic masculinity** and our discussion about Latin American presidents in Chapter 7), whereas *marianismo* reflects the adoration of the religious mother Mary and conveys the expectation that women's life pursuits are sacrifice and motherhood. The **Madres de (or Mothers of the) Plaza de Mayo** reflect these expectations, as their reason for mobilization was to find their disappeared sons and daughters. The women became activists as they sought information about the disappeared from authorities, and they turned to one another as they began to recognize their common plight. The Madres began meeting in churches and eventually moved their protest to the Plaza de Mayo in Buenos Aires in 1977, gathering in a large circle in the plaza located in front of the Argentine Presidential Palace, Casa Rosada.[82] The mothers were mostly from the working class, were middle aged, and had minimal education. One mother explained,

> Each of us Mothers is born again in the circle. . . . One Mother leaves her apron in the kitchen, another her sewing machine, yet another her typewriter. We have to be present at three-thirty in the afternoon. . . . Not one Mother fails. . . . What mysterious hand convokes us? The puzzle of our children's fate, which didn't stop us from going on . . . the son's photograph on the night table; every Thursday it would point the way—Today is the circle, Mom: "to the Plaza!"[83]

While protesting, the mothers wore white scarves embroidered with the names of their children. Their maternal politics struck a cord and hastened democracies like the Netherlands, Norway, and the United States to put pressure on the Argentine government; however, even as mothers, the women were harassed by police officers and sometimes arrested. One of their founders, Azucena Villaflor de De Vincenti, was disappeared in 1977. The mothers empowered themselves through camaraderie.[84] One mother stated,

> My first time in the circle I was very scared . . . and deeply moved. . . . Once we were in the Plaza, the fact of being arm in arm, or of walking together compelled us to return . . . we could talk [to each other] about our concerns without any problem, without fear, and the person by our side listened very, attentively.[85]

The women protested by walking peacefully around the Plaza de Mayo, every Thursday, and their protests continue to this day because many mothers still want information about their family members' whereabouts.

By demanding information about their children from Argentine officials, thus garnering international attention, the mothers helped to facilitate the transition back to democracy in Argentina (in 1983). They won the 1999 Prize for Peace Education from the United Nations. Moreover, they have inspired many women's activists worldwide, as their repertoire of maternal politics and peaceful demonstrations translates into other contexts in which women also confront state terrorism or warfare that endanger their families. The Madres splintered in 1986, and some of the mothers since have become controversial. One group of mothers, Madres de Plaza de Mayo Línea-Fundadora, desired information about the remains of relatives, and these Madres approved of exhumations by the then-democratic government. Other mothers within the Asociación Madres de Plaza de Mayo refuse exhumation and closure, insisting that their loved ones deserve justice, not burial, as dead persons.

▶ **Photo 9.4** Madres with Argentine President Néstor Kirchner.

Why do women themselves incorporate maternal politics into their activism? Ortbals and Poloni-Staudinger (2018) discuss three main reasons. First, women use maternal politics because their maternal identity ties to their everyday experiences and those of their children. For example, Latina janitors in Los Angeles in the 1990s operating around labor politics participated in protests to better their children's lives. Labor benefits were connected to motherhood because, "women take the children to the doctor, and they see how much it costs. And that's why we are fighting for health insurance."[86] Similarly, the Million Mom March, a movement for gun control, framed their movement not in terms of gun control but in terms of motherhood, because of the special harm guns could cause their children.

Second, framing activism, particularly protest, as an extension of motherhood is strategic.[87] As seen in the Madres case earlier, motherhood is a safe identity to activate, particularly when advocated against an authoritarian or repressive regime. This is because motherhood implies care for one's children, which is not overtly suspect in the eyes of authoritarian regimes.[88] As Koven and Michel (1993) explain, women were able to organize under the guise of motherhood in advanced democracies even before (sometimes long before) they had the right to vote. Motherhood (and grandmotherhood) is also a strategic way to garner public sympathy for social groups' activities.[89]

Finally, other political actors (the state, other NGOs) mobilize politically inactive women through compelling maternal discourses.[90] In this way, motherhood is used as a way to convince other women to politically support a cause. Ortbals and Poloni-Staudinger (2018) use the 1980s in Nicaragua as an example. The Sandinistas of the ruling, leftist regime organized mothers' groups and used pressure from mothers to conscript young men into the regime's revolutionary cause.[91] Thus, rather than women organizing themselves from the grassroots, sometimes social groups or governments may mobilize women by way of maternal identity. Moms Demand Action in the United States organizes women around issues of gun control through a maternal discourse of protecting children in much the same way. Black Lives Matter, discussed in Box 9.7, was started by three radical Black organizers, all women. These women "created a Black-centered political will and movement building project called #BlackLivesMatter" in response to the acquittal of Trayvon Martin's murderer, George Zimmerman. The early movement drew upon discourses of motherhood and parenthood, especially as connected to the murder of a child, Trayvon Martin.

BOX 9.7: POLICY FEATURE

Black Lives Matter, Maternal Politics, and the Policy of Policing

The Black Lives Matter hashtag was created in 2013 by three Black women organizers, Alicia Garza, Patrisse Cullors, and Opal Tometi. They created #BlackLivesMatter as a way to build movements and create a political will centered around blackness. From 2013 to 2014, the hashtag began to grow and develop into an organizational tool for groups and individuals who wanted to amplify and combat any and all forms of anti-black discrimination that occurred across the nation. #BlackLivesMatter provided a platform for people to broadcast incidents that they had either directly experienced or that they had witnessed. The hashtag became essential in projecting the conversation about the policy area of policing, particularly militarization of the police and state-sanctioned violence. It also amplified the murders of Tamir Rice, Walter Scott, Sandra Bland, and countless others whose stories were either being omitted from mainstream media or had been picked up and distorted, demonizing these individuals and attempting to justify their murders. It has been many years since the hashtag's inception, and it is still used as a tool to make the public aware of deadly police brutality.[92]

In 2014, an unarmed teenager named Mike Brown was murdered in Ferguson by Officer Darren Wilson. His death prompted weeks of protest from communities in both Ferguson and St. Louis—with much of the rhetoric focused on the loss of Black children—and was often led by mothers. Darnell L. Moore and cocreator Patrisse Cullors organized a national ride, the Black Life Matters "Freedom Ride" to Ferguson, to stand in solidarity with the protestors. Over 600 people participated. Activists experienced police brutality during these protests and saw their protests slandered by the media. Eventually, 18 activists decided they would establish Black Lives Matter chapters to organize and actively combat policies that promoted racism and violence within their own communities. The creators of #BlackLivesMatter credit the events that took place in Ferguson, and especially the brave people who stood up to protest, as the reason why they were able to create the Black Lives Matter Global Network.[93] They believe that without those who fought back in Ferguson, they would not have been able to make the transition from a simple hashtag to a global, well-respected organization. The goal of Black Lives Matter is to create a network of Black empowerment and support the development of new Black leaders, while also standing against inequality and the destruction of Black lives and communities.

In their Herstory, Black Lives Matter acknowledges that historically, Black liberation movements have been led by and created more space and opportunities for cisgender, heterosexual, Black men, leaving those who did not fit that mold—especially women, queer, and transgender people—on the sidelines. Because of this, since their inception, they have vowed to be inclusive and place special emphasis on providing a platform for female, queer, and transgender individuals interested in leading. "To maximize our movement muscle, and to be intentional about not replicating harmful practices that excluded so many movements for liberation, we made a commitment to placing those at the margins closer to the center."[94] They have also asserted that #BlackLivesMatter was created in support of all Black lives; that includes Black women, Black queer people, Black transgender people, Black disabled people, and all those who deal with discrimination not only because of their blackness but also because of another minority status.

In the era of the Trump presidency, Black Lives Matter has held on to their inclusive principles and their goal of combatting state-sanctioned violence; however, they have had to change their tactics. Though protesting is still a widely used method by chapters throughout the nation, there

(Continued)

(Continued)

has been a general shift from protest to policy. In an interview, Alicia Garza stated that much of the work concerning policy is done at the local level by individual chapters. For example, African Americans and Latinx experience greater criminal justice consequences for possession of marijuana.[95] In Atlanta, activists put pressure on the city council to make the possession of small quantities of marijuana punishable by a $75 fine instead of an arrest. This could limit the amount of physical interaction between an individual and the police.

Beyond the local level, several prominent activists, including DeRay Mckesson, have created a website called Campaign ZERO. Mckesson is an activist from Baltimore who rose to fame after live-tweeting the events taking place in Ferguson. He is now known to many as one of the leading faces of Black Lives Matter. Mckesson, along with Johnetta Elzie and Brittany Packnett (who also emerged from Ferguson), and Samuel Sinyangwe developed Campaign ZERO to end police brutality in America "by limiting police interventions, improving community interactions, and ensuring accountability."[96] The website makes it clear that the key to ending police violence is change in policy. The "Solutions" section outlines 10 points to help bring an end to police brutality, and under each point, there is a list of necessary policy reforms. In addition to the reforms, there are examples of a state act, state or city law, and/or organization policy that they believe should be a national standard. For example, "Limit Use of Force" calls for the establishment of standards and reporting when officers use deadly force. Clause A states, "authorize deadly force only when there is imminent threat to an officer's life or the life of another person" and then lists the International Deadly Force Standard and Tennessee Deadly Force Law as examples. Campaign ZERO outlines what the movement is fighting, describes how they plan

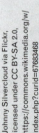

▶ **Photo 9.5** Black Lives Matter protestors.

to fight it, publishes reports on police departments, and even provides a tool to track the progress of federal, state, and local legislation that deals with police violence.[97] Although protest has been the main tactic used by the Black Lives Matter movement and has helped advance their cause, it is clear that now, and in the future, policy reform will be an important focus at all levels of government.

The use of motherhood as a mobilizing identity has ebbed and flowed in the United States. In the early 1900s, women won the right to vote and secured many social benefits (as highlighted in earlier sections and chapters) based in part by framing their activism as actual or potential mothers, claiming special status and invoking moral authority because they were mothers.[98] Stavrianos (2015) reveals that by the 1960s, the use of motherhood as an organizing frame had declined in the United States.[99] Instead, women, particularly those who identified as feminists, actively moved away from this frame in favor of arguing for policy based on equal rights.[100] The use of motherhood as an organizing tool was mainly seen in countermovements, those that we would describe as antifeminist, particularly among conservative women's groups opposing abortion rights.[101] In the latter half of the 2000s, it appears that the motherhood frame is reemerging, particularly with regard to gun regulation, with increased calls for political change couched in the frame of motherhood.[102]

The discussion of motherhood and maternal politics as an organizing tool should be taken with a caveat. While motherhood is a powerful organizing space that may be used with great benefit for the advancement of women's issues, it also has dangers of **essentialism**, the belief that groups with given identities are born with certain characteristics. In the case of gender, essentialism incorrectly assumes men and women have a fixed essence that is fundamentally distinct from one another and that women can be defined by their ability to bear children. Maternalism as an organizing tool invokes the idea that women have biological and perhaps psychological differences from men.[103] This can be dangerous and pigeonhole women to work on "women's issues" or essentializes women according to biological creation. We can sometimes see this in the discussion of women and peace movements (see Box 9.8 for examples) as women are thought to be somehow more peaceful than men. This caution according to some may be overstated. Goss and Heaney (2010) argue that maternal frames can be flexible and used in a playful way to emphasize equality and reclaim feminine stereotypes.[104] In short, motherhood can be a way to motivate political action of all types of women but should be looked at critically. Elsewhere in this chapter and book we discuss how women can engage other frames, for example a critical or intersectional feminist frame, in undertaking their activities.

BOX 9.8: COMPARATIVE FEATURE

Women and Peace Activism—Liberia and Korea

The late Judy El-Bushra, an international development expert, asked in 2007 "are men inherently territorial and aggressive, and women naturally nurturing and peaceable?"[105] In doing so, she was drawing attention to the commonly held

(Continued)

(Continued)

belief that women as mothers or as caregivers are more peaceful and thus are especially capable of pursuing peace in local, national, and international politics. Men, on the other hand, are traditionally viewed as armed perpetrators in political conflicts and are likely to violate women—physically, sexually, and economically—during war. El-Bushra called these assumptions the **"womenandpeace"** view. This view reflects essentialism. It is empirically incorrect to consider women peaceful (and men violent). Women are combatants in war and terrorism, and many women support the actions of men combatants. El Bushra points out another pitfall of the "womenandpeace" view. She explains that assuming all women are inherently peaceful, and thus the same in terms of fighting for peace, ignores the specifics of women's local activism for peace.[106] The "womenandpeace" view, therefore, denies women agency as unique political actors who can contribute to violence or peace.

Although we must call attention to the cultural specificities of women's peace movements in order to fully capture women's political agency, scholars do see commonalities present in women's peace movements. First, following political conflicts, mainstream actors in peace negotiations tend to ignore women's movements.[107] Thus, women's interests are not always brought to the proverbial table. Second, as a result, women's movements typically use informal mechanisms to pursue peace.[108] For instance, they provide communities with basic necessities like food and medical services, and they often initiate community reconciliation and healing processes.[109] Third, though women's peace movements have local goals, pertaining to the specific conflicts in their region, they often receive assistance from international sources, which brings them into a transnational community of women activists.[110] Lastly, movements have the ability to provide "bridges across political divides" in order to find solutions to local conflicts.[111] For example, as El-Bushra explains, in Somalia, "women have much weaker clan allegiances than men since they have close links both with their own, natal clan and with that of their husbands."[112] During Somalia's political transition in the early 2000s, women thought of themselves as a "sixth clan" when they fought for reserved seats for women in the Transitional Federal Government. In the following paragraphs, we briefly examine these commonalities, as well as case specificities, in Liberia and South Korea. We particularly focus on the movements' forms of mobilization and how various actors responded to these mobilizations.

Liberia: Liberia's 14 years of extremely violent civil wars, fought between rival warlords, ended in 2003, with fatalities reaching 200,000. Women's movements mobilized in numerous ways to hasten the end of the conflict. In 2002, Crystal Roh Gawding, Leymah Gbowee, and Comfort Freeman established the Women of Liberia Mass Action for Peace (WIPNET). WIPNET held protests against the leader of one side of the civil war, President Charles Taylor. At a fish market near the president's residence, the women wore white as a symbol of peace and sang and danced for peace. During the early 2000s, Christian and Muslim women held prayer meetings together in an effort to foment peace. The women also used "a brilliant media strategy" to mobilize men for peace;[113] specifically, they called for a sex strike, asking women to withhold sex from men until the end of the conflict. The strike, though more of a wake-up call than a literal strike, made men acutely aware of women's resolve and brought them to the side of peace. In 2003, women marched through the country's capital and presented Taylor a position paper demanding peace, after which, he agreed to peace talks. When peace talks did occur in Ghana, women made a human wall to force delegates to come to an agreement; and, when security guards attempted to remove them, Gbowee threatened to strip her clothes, thus using "the threat of her own naked body—an act considered a curse in her country" as a way to ensure peace.[114] In order to get the peace candidate (Ellen Johnson Sirleaf) elected to the presidency in 2006, Gbowee mobilized women to vote, and

> some women hid their sons' voter ID cards to prevent them from vot-ing for Sirleaf's opponent; others tricked the young men into exchang-ing their cards for beer; still others managed market stalls while their women owners went to register to vote and watched babies so that mothers could vote on Election Day.[115]

In 2011, Leymah Gbowee, a social worker, won the Nobel Peace Prize. Finally, in 2011, women's groups established peace huts, with assistance from the United Nations and the Swedish government; the huts parallel the Palaver Huts, which are a traditional institution of men that serve as community centers and pursue truth and reconciliation. Peace huts provide job training, education about rights, and strategies to overcome situations of sex-based violence, such as working with the local police to apprehend perpetrators. By resolving conflicts in com-munities and responding to domestic violence, the huts allow women to become local leaders and to take control of their lives and safety.[116] In 2014, the huts treated patients during the deadly Ebola crisis in Western Africa, with some of the women activists dying from the disease in the process of caring for others.

Korea: The Korean peninsula has been in a state of war for much of the past 200 years; however, women have come together to fight for peace in various eras.[117] For example, in 1992, Women in Patriot Missiles created a Joint Committee for the Reduction of the Defense Budget to advocate for the transfer of funds from the military budget to the social budget, which deals with gender violence and promoting peace between North and South Korea. Furthermore, in 2000, Women Making Peace—a nonprofit organization for peace—organized an Inter-Korean forum that discussed how women can be involved in the peace-making and unification process, in response to the 2000

(Continued)

(Continued)

Inter-Korean Summit. In 2015, women from all over the world came together to walk through the Demilitarized Zone (DMZ) in Korea. About 30 women from the organization Women Cross DMZ joined other international organizations and walked across the DMZ from North Korea to South Korea as a way to show their commitment to peace. Women Cross DMZ argued the walk was a symbolic movement to end war and to reunite the two Koreas. However, the walk did not receive much media attention, and conservative South Korean nongovernmental organizations, who help North Korean defectors, opposed the walk because the protesters walking came across as sympathetic to North Korea. More recent peace talks in 2018 also have not given voice to women's movements. Because patriarchy is still dominant in South Korea (as well as North Korea), women are easily dismissed from official peacemaking. On April 27, 2018, Chairman Kim Jong-Un from North Korea and President Moon Jae-In from South Korea met for the first time. This was a historic moment as it was the first time the chairman of North Korea embraced a South Korean president and mentioned the idea of denuclearization. However, women's groups have criticized the talks for not including them. Women organizations mainly mobilize by creating nonprofit and nongovernmental organizations. Their main method is peaceful protests in front of the American Embassy or in front of Gwang-Hwa Moon Plaza, one of the busiest and well-known spots in South Korea. Women organizations explain that they are calling for denuclearization and the creation of a specific road map for a peace treaty between the two Koreas. Women's peace groups in South Korea face other obstacles. Although they may want to bridge across political divides, they largely cannot collaborate with North Korean women for peace.[118] Because North Korea is an oppressive regime, North Korean women lack autonomy, and South Korean women can only network with North Korean women who are permitted to contact them or attend conferences; and these women are often from the North Korean government itself. Additionally, conversations with North Korean women result in disagreements about reunification, nuclear weapons, arms reduction, and the role of women in the peacemaking process.

CHALLENGES FOR WOMEN'S AND FEMINIST MOVEMENTS

While women's movements have been successful with organizing under the frame of motherhood, definite challenges exist for women's organizing. These challenges can be broadly grouped around societal expectations about women's roles in the public sphere—which can also make getting a seat at the table difficult—and challenges related to forging a shared identity.

There are historical and societal expectations of women as the "silent sex." This means that women are not supposed to act in the public sphere. When they do act, for example by participating in social movements, there tends to be societal sanctions for this action. Scholars have long expressed concern that minorities and women, as well as those with a lower socioeconomic status, can be excluded from participation in deliberative settings, like social movements, and that their contributions may not be given equal consideration (we see this as well with the Women's March). Even when organized in groups, women can be marginalized, with women's groups less likely to be heard in the halls of government. In fact, marginalized groups, like women and particularly women of color, may be more likely to engage in protest politics because they are shut out from other forms of political expression (even though we know protest is rarer for women's groups than other social movement organizations).[119]

Marginalized groups gain their seat at the table and their right to be heard when they have gained enough power that they can no longer be ignored. Thus, people who lack power or sufficient resources may first gain access to decision-making by being argumentative and purposefully disruptive. Such disruptions, especially by those previously expected to be subordinate and deferential (i.e., women who are supposed to be the silent sex), are often perceived as rude and inappropriate.[120] Even when marginalized groups have access to decision-making, there is no guarantee they will be able to participate effectively. Lynn Sanders (1997) argues,

> some Americans are apparently less likely than others to be listened to; even when their arguments are stated according to conventions of reason, they are more likely to be disregarded. Although deliberators will always choose to disregard some arguments, when this disregard is systematically associated with the arguments made by those we know already to be systematically disadvantaged, we should at least reevaluate our assumptions. (p. 349)[121]

Aside from voting, women participate in all forms of political activity—especially discursive political activity found in social movements—at far lower rates than men (as discussed in Chapters 4 and 5). Given that women are socialized to avoid disagreement within their social networks and are subject to social sanction if they are perceived to be self-promoting or ambitious, it is not surprising that scholars have labeled women "the silent sex" after observing their limited participation in traditional deliberative forums.[122] This silence reinforces societal expectations of women as quiet and agreeable.

More recent scholarship is beginning to identify features of deliberative spaces that facilitate women's participation. For example, in the United States, women's influence wanes when discussions are framed as traditional political discussions, because American politics is still largely perceived as a competitive, "hypermasculine" zero-sum game with clear winners and losers. Women are much more likely to participate when politics is reframed as way to help solve public issues that affect their communities. We saw this in women's use of the motherhood frame to situate their actions. The composition of participants also matters. Being in a numerical minority not only reduces women's status and authority but also results in reliance on more competitive and assertive communication styles; this further reduces the likelihood that women will contribute and be heard. Indeed, women are more likely to engage in politics around local concerns, but as Hardy-Fanta (1995) argues, the definition of political participation and leadership has a deep bias in favor of men, such that only public and formally organized participation is counted as such. Because women, and particularly Black and Latina women, are more active on community issues, their activism is seen as community activism or "disorderly" but not political thus underestimating the degree to which these women engage in political participation, as we described in Chapter 3.[123]

When women make up at least half of the room, on the other hand, the communication styles they have been socialized to adopt—which focus on listening, facilitating, and collaborating—begin to influence the way all group members interact. This shift makes it easier for women to participate without being perceived as too aggressive or interrupting too frequently—perceptions that erode their likability and their ability to influence others. Finally, decision rules affect women's participation, with majority rule suppressing women's influence and voice, particularly if they are a numerical minority. On the other hand, decision rules that emphasize unanimous agreement empower women's voices.[124] Many of these same features may impact racial and ethnic minorities and possibly also have intersectional effects.[125]

Some have heralded a new era in women's participation in the Trump era. In fact, the majority of resistance groups that emerged in the face of the Trump presidency are run by women. These numbers may give women the critical mass necessary to change the norms of interaction and to influence policy debates. The Women's March that opened this chapter is an example of one of these groups. After the first Women's March, however, there were criticisms from many that the march was "white-washed;" that is, it focused on the experiences and needs of white women and ignored issues of importance to women of color and trans women. The march was also criticized for centering cisgender, heteronormative, able-bodied white women in its execution, a complaint we have seen at various waves of the women's movement. In Chapter 2, we discussed how the forging of a shared identity has been difficult for each wave of the women's movement.

The critiques surrounding the Women's March serve to illustrate where many of the problems lie. Some have argued that the Women's March was just another display of white privilege.[126] How, in the words of a *Washington Post* editorial, "did Madonna get away with talk of 'blowing up the White House' in a speech on the Mall when those with darker skin fear saying such things even in private company?"[127] People of color, both men and women, pointed to the fact that the overwhelming number of people at the marches in DC and in major metropolitan areas were white women; and as white women, they could hold space on public streets—and even shut down streets—because they were allowed to do so in a way that never happens for people of color. Critics contrasted pictures of white women in pussy hats posing with police with pictures of Black and brown people at Black Lives Matter protests being barreled down by police. In fact, white women's "chumminess" with police at the rally was a focus of concern as it showed a lack of allyship with communities of color who are not met with the same sort of camaraderie from police when they choose to peacefully organize.

Organizers of the March were quick to point out that the intention was to be inclusive of all people, noting three of its leaders were women of color and stating "the Women's March on Washington was a women-led grass-roots movement that served to bring people of all genders and backgrounds together to take a stand on social justice and human rights issues ranging from race, ethnicity, gender, sexual orientation, religion, immigration, and health care."[128] People of color have acknowledged this while also suggesting that white women ought to understand and acknowledge the privilege they are given due to their skin color.

The March was originally organized by white women who called it the Million Women March. This name showed a lack of sensitivity to women of color, as Black women organized a march of the same name in Philadelphia in 1997 on the heels of the Million Man March in Washington, DC, which was a protest by Black men to draw attention to urban issues and Black solidarity. While organizers attempted to appoint a more diverse committee, criticisms persisted that the voices of women of color were not listened to during the planning. Critics also expressed concerns that some attendees of the Women's March participated as activists for the first time and ignored communities who have been doing the work on the front lines of social justice movements for years, usually under more dangerous conditions. In short,

> Black women, queer folks, disabled people, et al. existing at the intersection of multiple marginalized identities have been setting up the framework for this kind of activism for a very long time, only to be discredited, silenced, excluded, and betrayed in the execution of this large-scale event. White women who had never been to a protest before were showing up to this one, performing resistance, and taking all the credit, while forgetting to listen to and take their cues from the people who have already been on the front lines, making this possible for them.[129]

As we highlighted in Chapters 1 and 2, trans women also criticized the March, in particular the pink pussy hats. They argued there was not room in the movement for those who were not born with a vagina (aka pussy). Criticisms harkened back to a feminist slogan from the Second Wave of "no uterus, no opinion" in discussions of women's reproductive health. As Mosthof (2017) explains,

Cis women reclaiming their vulvas as a political act in protest of their bodies being the sites of violence is powerful. There is absolutely room to stand up for all these ideas in an intersectionally feminist movement. But when we center these narratives as the be-all-end-all of woman-hood and what we're fighting for, we cut ourselves off from meaningfully including marginalized bodies and identities.[130]

This brings back a point made earlier. Equating womanhood with the ability to have children can be problematic, and this is particularly problematic for trans women.

BOX 9.9: POLICY FEATURE

Trans Women's Activism and Gay Rights Policy

Concerns from trans women that the women's movement excludes them are not unique to post-Trump politics nor entirely to the women's movement. Trans women were responsible for much of the activism around gay rights in the 1960s, only to be pushed out of the movement as it gained traction and became dominated by gay white men. In fact, much of the criticism leveled at heteronormative cis women for not including trans women in activism has also been leveled at the cis gay community.

Marsha P. Johnson (1945–1992) was an African American transgender woman who was an advocate for LGBTQIA+ rights and particularly for trans people of color. She helped to spearhead the Stonewall uprising in 1969 with Sylvia Rivera. Johnson and Rivera were fixtures in the **gay liberation movement**, a movement that advocated for a change in government policy around gay rights. Johnson and Rivera also pushed to align gay rights with other social justice movements; however, they were not always met with warmth from fellow activists. At a gay pride event in New York City in 1973, Rivera was booed off the stage for calling out the white, middle-class complacency of the LGBTQIA+ movement, a movement Johnson and Rivera suggested had left behind the trans community. Ms. Johnson, together with Ms. Rivera, argued that the policies surrounding the trans community needed special attention. To that end, they established the Street Transvestite (now Transgender) Action Revolutionaries (STAR). This group is committed to helping transgender youth in New York City and bringing pressure to bear on policies related to homelessness and the transgender community while advocating for "free gender expression, an end to prison injustice and homelessness, and the creation of an inclusive community that rejected binding definitions of gender and sexual identity."[131]

Marsha P. Johnson was murdered on July 6, 1992. Her life has been the focus of numerous movies, documentaries, and essays, and was also invoked at the 2017 Women's March. Raquel Willis, National Organizer for the Trans Law Center, accused march organizers of silencing trans voices when she invoked the names of Johnson and Rivera, in a moment and with discourse reminiscent of Rivera's 1973 experience.

Raquel Willis ✓
@RaquelWillis_   Follow ⌄

Still silencing trans women.

Cutting my mic off mid-speech after I just discussed Sylvia and Marsha... I see you & so does everyone else.

11:58 AM - 21 Jan 2017

2,656 Retweets **4,162** Likes

♡ 72   ⟲ 2.7K   ♡ 4.2K

▶ **Photo 9.6** Raquel Willis's tweet about the inclusion of trans women in the Women's March.

Raquel Willis via Twitter

CONCLUSION: INTERSECTIONAL RESISTANCE IN THE POST-TRUMP ERA

Given the criticisms of the Women's March, what chances are there for intersectional resistance in the post-Trump era? Already hinted at in this chapter, we see that the resistance that has formed in opposition to the Trump presidency has mainly been organized and directed by women. While not perfect, initial indications are that this movement is intersectional in nature. In the words of one feminist blogger, the Trump presidency has "undeniably served to usher in a new wave of feminist activism, starkly different from any of the previous three." (Some are referring to this as the Fourth Wave of the women's movement, see Chapter 2.)[132] The second Women's March, for example, took lessons from the first, didn't focus on the pussy hat as the key symbol of the movement, and in some places, like Phoenix, Arizona, was led by Native women to draw attention to the disproportionate violence faced by this group. And while the third march was marred by accusations that some national organizers exhibited anti-Semitic language, local marches extended efforts to include a myriad of voices in continuing attempts at intersectionality.

The book *Nasty Women* addresses the question of feminism and resistance in Trump's America. The book, comprised of individual essays, tackles this idea of intersectionality from several perspectives. Most authors echo sentiments by Alicia Garza, who states, "We can build a movement in the millions, across our differences. We will need to guild a movement across divides of class, race, gender, age, documentation, religion and disability . . . we can tell people a hundred times over that because they haven't been here before they have no right to be here now. But I promise the only place that will get us is nowhere."[133]

The nascent intersectionality of the movement is perhaps best illustrated by the work of Aditi Juneja. Juneja, who created what is known as the Resistance Manual, an open-source online platform where the public can contribute information about state and local elections, proposed legislation, executive actions, rallies, resources, and events. Juneja states, "For us, the creation of the *Resistance Manual* was an exercise of intersectionality. The goal was to try to demonstrate how all of these seemingly different issue areas are related and are important."[134] According to Juneja, the content on the page is representative of the issues facing America. While contributors are apt to be highly educated, on other metrics, the work includes multiple perspectives. One goal of the *Resistance Manual* is to ensure that multiple viewpoints and voices are included in discussions. While open source, individuals are self-selecting to contribute with multiple voices in an intersectional fashion.

Thus, while it is too early to know if we are seeing a Fourth Wave of a women's movement and intersectional resistance in the era of Trump, we are seeing attempts by social movement organizations in some cases to move toward more of an intersectional approach to movement activism. The growth in activity in the Trump era is probably due in large part to the fact that the opportunity structure is perceived as closed by many feminist groups and women's groups. Thus, women's movements are protesting in larger numbers than we have seen with previous U.S. movements. There is some indication that maternal framing is used by these movements. That said, early analysis indicates that the anti-Trump movements go beyond thinking of women based on anatomy or their ability to bear children, taking on a wider array of issues of importance to women and feminists. Additionally, movements in the era of Trump are providing an important way for both the substantive and descriptive representation of women outside of traditional modes of representation discussed in earlier chapters.

REVIEW QUESTIONS

1. What was significant about the Women's March? Why was it controversial? How do criticisms of the Women's March fit with the "TERF"-based criticisms discussed elsewhere in the book?

2. What is maternal framing? How do groups use the maternal frame to influence politics? Give some examples of groups that have used this frame. How can it be powerful? How can it be essentializing?

3. What are social movements? What are women's movements, feminist movements, nonfeminist movements, antifeminist movements, and "women in movements"? Give an example of each.

4. How do women's movements act? How does the opportunity structure influence how groups act? What explains differences in women's group activities?

5. Describe challenges for women's movements and feminist activism overall and in the Trump administration. How do you think the movements will develop? Where are the tensions? Where are their opportunities for collaboration?

AMBITION ACTIVITIES

Evaluating Campus Advocacy: Think of a pressing issue on your university's campus that is tied to broader political issues or current events. For example, are there debates on campus about courses that address political and social diversity or about statues that celebrate the lives of historical figures who were exclusionary in their actions? In order to evaluate the nature of advocacy on your campus, answer the following questions about the issue.

1. Why is this topic relevant at this point in time and in your university context? Who are the main voices speaking up about the issue? Are these voices representative of various constituencies and perspectives? Why, or why not?

2. Has a group formed around the issue to call for or against change? What sort of rules does the group employ for decision-making? If possible, attend a meeting of the group, and report on who speaks and who listens at the meeting. How would you evaluate the group in terms of representation of men and women, cis and trans individuals, and attention to gender issues?

3. How did the group (or individuals speaking about the issue) frame concerns about the issue at hand? Does the frame appeal to you as an individual, and what would it take to get you to become involved with this group on a regular basis?

Researching and Experiencing Local Activism: Conduct online research about your local National Organization of Women, Women's March, Black Lives Matter group, or another group of your choice. According to the definitions provided in this chapter, would you characterize the group as a women's, feminist, nonfeminist, or antifeminist group? How does the group frame its activities? What major policy issues does the group focus on? Would you say the group takes an intersectional approach to policy? Why, or why not?

After your initial research, consider attending a meeting of the group. Did you feel comfortable attending the meeting or speaking up in the group? Why, or why not? What would it take to get you to become involved with this group on a regular basis?

Planning Activism and Framing It: Think of a political issue of interest to you (and your classmates). Attempt to conduct activism that could address this issue. The following are two ideas for activism:

1. Organize an event by way of social media, for example, through a Facebook page or event. What photos and phrases would you use to draw people's attention to the issue? How do your choices influence how the issue is framed? Do you consider your actions a type of "slactivism" (actions taken via the Internet or social media but requiring little investment of time) or an effective strategy to influence others? To what extent will your efforts change the issue?

2. Design a protest sign that you believe best frames the issue. What are clever ways to get your points across on the sign? Consider using the sign in an actual protest or hanging it up on campus to gauge its impact. How easy was it to design a persuasive sign, and what type of resources did it require?

Checking in About Amplification: We learned in this chapter that women do not always make it to the proverbial table of policy discussions. Some movements receive more attention from political elites than others, and some voices are elevated within movements more than others. Given these realities, discuss how amplification as a strategy could matter in social movements. Who in social movements (leaders in groups, politicians engaging with groups, individual group members, etc.) should use this strategy and for what reasons? Recommit to practicing amplification.

KEY WORDS

Antifeminist women's movements 409

Essentialism 427

Expectation-punishment axiom 414

Extra-institutional 409

Feminist women's movements 409

Frames 420

Gay liberation movement 434

Hegemonic masculinity 422

H.E.R.S. framework 402

Ideological 413

Institutional 409

Interest group 407

Intermediary institutions 407

Machismo 422

Madres de Plaza de Mayo 422

Marianismo 422

Maternal politics 420

Neo corporatist interest group 414

Non-feminist women's movements 409

Pluralist interest group 414

Political opportunity structure 413

Relative deprivation 412

Resource mobilization 413

Social movement 408

Social movement organization (SMO) 409

Toxic masculinity 406

Women's March on Washington 401

REFERENCES

1. Stein, P. (2017). The woman who started the Women's March with a Facebook post reflects: "It was mind-boggling." *The Washington Post*. Retrieved from https://www.washingtonpost.com/news/local/wp/2017/01/31/the-woman-who-started-the-womens-march-with-a-facebook-post-reflects-it-was-mind-boggling/?utm_term=.502af21725a0.

2. Agrawal, N. (2017). How the Women's March came into being. *Los Angeles Times*. Retrieved from http://www.latimes.com/nation/la-na-pol-womens-march-live-how-the-women-s-march-came-into-1484865755-htmlstory.html.

3. Home. (n.d.). *Women's March*. Retrieved September 07, 2018 from https://www.womensmarch.com.

4. Ibid.

5. https://www.womensmarch.com/2019/.

6. See, for example, the thread at https://www.reddit.com/r/unpopularopinion/comments/6x4ctt/the_womens_march_didnt_accomplish_anything or https://reason.com/archives/2017/01/12/the-pointless-upcoming-womens-march-agai.

7. Brockes, E. (2018). Me Too founder Tarana Burke: "You have to use your privilege to serve other people." Tarana Burke at her office in Brooklyn, New York. *The Guardian*. Retrieved from https://www.theguardian.com/world/2018/jan/15/me-too-founder-tarana-burke-women-sexual-assault.

8. Ox, K., & Diehm, J. (2017). #MeToo's global moment: The anatomy of a viral campaign. *CNN*. Retrieved from https://www.cnn.com/2017/11/09/world/metoo-hashtag-global-movement/index.html?no-st=1532639338.

9. Ngo, M. (2018). #MeToo is growing in China—Despite government efforts to stop it. The government has censored hundreds of social media posts supporting the #MeToo campaign. *Vox*. Retrieved from https://www.vox.com/world/2018/7/27/17621420/china-me-too-chinese-women-social-censor-sexual-assault.

10. Feingold, S. (2013). One rape every 20 minutes in country. *Times of India*. Retrieved from https://timesofindia.indiatimes.com/city/delhi/One-rape-every-20-minutes-in-country/articleshow/22040599.cms.

11. Urian, A. (2018). The #MeToo movement marks the rise of a new era in Indian feminism. *Quartz India*. Retrieved from https://qz.com/1195569/the-metoo-movement-marks-the-rise-of-a-new-era-in-indian-feminism.

12. Dhillon, A. (2018). India's #MeToo moment is still about the struggle to survive. *Sydney Morning Herald*. Retrieved from https://www.smh.com.au/world/asia/india-s-metoo-moment-is-still-about-the-struggle-to-survive-20180330-p4z750.html.

13. Ibid.

14. White, G. B. 2017. The glaring blind spot of the 'Me Too' movement: Lena Dunham's defense of a *Girls* writer accused of sexual assault highlights how frequently allegations from women of color are dismissed. *The Atlantic*. Retrieved from https://www.theatlantic.com/entertainment/archive/2017/11/the-glaring-blind-spot-of-the-me-too-movement/546458.

15. Fontaine, P. (2018). Icelandic men launch campaign against toxic masculinity. *Grapevine News*. Retrieved from https://grapevine.is/news/2018/03/14/icelandic-men-launch-campaign-against-toxic-masculinity.

16. Poloni-Staudinger, L., & Ortbals, C. (2014). The domestic determinants of transnational activity: An examination of women's groups in the United Kingdom, France and Germany. *International Studies Quarterly, 58*(1), 68–78.

17. Almond, G., & Coleman, J. (1960). *The politics of the developing areas.* Princeton, NJ: Princeton University Press.

18. Kriesi, H., Koopmans, R., Duyvendak, J. W., & Guigni, M. (1995). *New social movements in Western Europe.* Minneapolis: University of Minneapolis Press.

19. Tarrow, S. (1994). *Power in movement: Collective action, social movements and politics.* New York, NY: Cambridge University Press.

20. Burstein, P. (1999). Social movements and public policy. In M. Giugni, D. McAdam, & C. Tilly (Eds.), *How social movements matter*. Minneapolis: University of Minnesota Press; Burstein claims that there is "no theoretical justification for distinguishing between social movement organizations and interest groups."

21. Snow, D., Soule, S., & Kriesi, H. (Eds). (2004). *The Blackwell companion to social movements*, 7–8. Malden: Blackwell. In this view, social movements are much less formal, but both are "different kinds of collectivities."

22. Poloni-Staudinger, L., & Wolf, M. (2019). *American difference: A guide to American politics in comparative perspective.* Washington, DC: CQ Press.

23. Issues and campaigns. (n.d.). *Code Pink*. Retrieved September 21, 2018 from https://www.codepink.org.

24. Ibid.

25. McCarthy, J., & Zald, M. (1977). Resource mobilization and social movements: A partial theory. *American Journal of Sociology, 82*(6), 1212–1241; see pages 1217–1218.

26. Poloni-Staudinger, L., & Wolf, M. (2019). *American difference: A guide to American politics in comparative perspective;* See also Meyer, D., & Tarrow, S. (Eds.). (1998). *The social movement society.* Lanham, MD: Rowman and Littlefield.

27. Beckwith, K. (1996). Lancashire women against pit closures: Women's standing in a men's movement. *Signs, 21,*1038.

28. Beckwith, K. (2000). Beyond compare? Women's movements in comparative perspective. *European Journal of Political Research, 37,* 431–468.

29. Ibid.

30. Ibid., 437.

31. Alvarez, S. E. (2000). Translating the global: Effects of transnational organizing on Latin American feminist discourses and practices. *Meridians: A Journal of Feminisms, Race and Transnationalism, 1,* 29–67.

32. Ortbals, C. D. (2008). Subnational politics in Spain: New avenues for feminist policymaking and activism. *Politics and Gender, 4,* 93–119.

33. Dovi, S. (2002). Preferable descriptive representatives: Will just any woman, Black, or Latino do? *The American Political Science Review, 96*(4), 729–743.

34. Saudi Arabia's religious police: Advice for the vice squad. (2016). *The Economist.* Retrieved from https://www.economist.com/middle-east-and-africa/2016/10/20/advice-for-the-vice-squad.

35. Human Rights Watch. (2018). Saudi Arabia—Events of 2017. Retrieved from https://www.hrw.org/world-report/2018/country-chapters/saudi-arabia.

36. Jamjoom, M. (2013). Saudi cleric warns driving could damage women's ovaries. *CNN.* Retrieved from https://www.cnn.com/2013/09/29/world/meast/saudi-arabia-women-driving-cleric/index.html.

37. Yuce, S. T., Agarwal, N., Wigand, R. T., Lim, M., &. Robinson, R. S. (2013). *Blogging, bridging, and brokering: Analyzing interconnected networks in online collective actions.* PACIS 2013 Proceedings. 225. Retrieved from http://aisel.aisnet.org/pacis2013/225.

38. Al Omran, A. (2017). Saudi Arabia edges more women into work. *Financial Times.* Retrieved from https://www.ft.com/content/c55d6cf4-8cd3-11e7-9084-d0c17942ba93.

39. Taylor, A. (2018). Saudi Arabia seeking first death penalty for female activist, rights groups say. *The Washington Post.* Retrieved from https://www.washingtonpost.com/world/2018/08/22/saudi-arabia-seeking-first-death-penalty-female-activist-rights-groups-say/?noredirect=on&utm_term=.9205e20e5403.

40. Coker, M. (2018). How guardianship laws still control Saudi women: The right to drive is only one small step toward full legal equality. *New York Times*. Retrieved from https://www.nytimes.com/2018/06/22/world/middleeast/saudi-women-guardianship.html.

41. Kitschelt, H. (1986). Political opportunity structures and political protest: Anti-nuclear movements in four democracies. *British Journal of Political Science*, *16*(1), pp. 57–85.

42. Kriesi, H., Koopmans, R., Duyvendak, J. W., & Guigni, M. (1995). New social movements in Western Europe; Tarrow, Sidney. (1998). *Power in movement: social movements and contentious Politics*. Cambridge: Cambridge University Press.

43. Meyer, D. (2004). Protest and political opportunities. *Annual Review of Sociology*, *30*, 125–145.

44. Beckwith, K. (2005). The comparative politics of women's movements. *Perspectives on Politics*, *3*(3), 583–596.

45. Poloni-Staudinger, L., & Ortbals, C. (2014). The domestic determinants of transnational activity: An examination of women's groups in the United Kingdom, France and Germany.

46. See for example Banaszak, L., Beckwith, K., & Rucht, D. (2003). *Women's movements facing the reconfigured state*. Cambridge, MA: Cambridge University Press; Ortbals, C. D. (2008). Subnational politics in Spain: New avenues for feminist policymaking and activism.

47. Poloni-Staudinger, L., & Ortbals, C. (2014). The domestic determinants of transnational activity: An examination of women's groups in the United Kingdom, France and Germany.

48. Ibid.

49. Ibid.

50. Kriesi, H., Koopmans, R., Duyvendak, J. W., & Guigni, M. (1995). *New social movements in Western Europe*.

51. Poloni-Staudinger, L., & Ortbals, C. (2014). The domestic determinants of transnational activity: An examination of women's groups in the United Kingdom, France and Germany.

52. Poloni-Staudinger, L. (2005). *How to act and where to act: The dynamic determinants of environmental social movement activity in the United Kingdom, France and Germany*. (Doctoral dissertation, Indiana University.)

53. Poloni-Staudinger, L., & Ortbals, C. (2014). The domestic determinants of transnational activity: An examination of women's groups in the United Kingdom, France and Germany.

54. Poloni-Staudinger, L., & Wolf, M. (2019). *American difference: A guide to American politics in comparative perspective.*

55. Poloni-Staudinger, L., & Ortbals, C. (2014). The domestic determinants of transnational activity: An examination of women's groups in the United Kingdom, France and Germany.

56. Ibid.

57. English Feministiskt Initiativ. (n.d.). *Feministiskt Initiativ*. Retrieved from https://feministisktinitiativ.se/sprak/english.

58. Feminist Initiative (Sweden). (n.d.). *Wikipedia*. Retrieved from https://en.wikipedia.org/wiki/Feminist_Initiative_(Sweden).

59. The story so far. (n.d.). *Women's Equality*. Retrieved from http://www.womensequality.org.uk/our_history.

60. Ibid.

61. Gabriela Women's Party. (n.d.). *Wikipedia*. Retrieved from https://en.wikipedia.org/wiki/Gabriela_Women's_Party.

62. Thorpe, J. R. (2018). 6 feminist political parties you should know. *Bustle*. Retrieved from https://www.bustle.com/articles/81055-6-feminist-political-parties-around-the-world-you-should-know-about.

63. United Women Front. (2018). *Wikipedia*. Retrieved from https://en.wikipedia.org/wiki/United_Women_Front.

64. Thorpe, J. R. (2018). 6 feminist political parties you should know.

65. U'Bizchutan. (n.d.). *Wikipedia*. Retrieved from https://en.wikipedia.org/wiki/U'Bizchutan.

66. Chabin, M. (2015). Israel's ultra-orthodox Haredi women form political party. *USA Today*. Retrieved from https://www.usatoday.com/story/news/world/2015/02/28/israel-jerusalem-haredi-jewish-women-political-party/23892059.

67. U'Bizchutan. (n.d.). *Wikipedia*.

68. Stand up for Women's equality—Sign the pledge. (n.d.). *Women's Equality Party*. Retrieved from http://womensequalityparty.org.

69. Women's Equality Party (New York). (n.d.). *Wikipedia*. Retrieved from https://en.wikipedia.org/wiki/Women's_Equality_Party_(New_York).

70. Gitlin, T. (1980). *The whole world is watching: Mass media in the making and unmaking of the new left.* Berkeley: University of California Press.

71. Entman, R. M. 2004. Reporting environmental policy debate: The real media biases. *Harvard International Journal of Press/Politics, 1*(3), 77–78.

72. Koven, S., & Michel, S. (Eds.). (1993). *Mothers of a new world: Maternalist politics and the origins of welfare states.* New York, NY: Routledge Press.

73. Ibid.

74. Ibid.

75. Sjoberg, L., & Gentry, C. (2007). *Mothers, monsters, whores: Women's violence in global politics.* London, UK: Zed Books.

76. Stavrianos, C. (2014). *The political uses of motherhood in America.* New York, NY: Routledge Press.

77. Ortbals, C., & Poloni-Staudinger, L. (2018). *Gender and political violence: Women changing the politics of terrorism.* New York, NY: Springer Press.

78. McClintock, A. (1993). Family feuds: Gender, nationalism and the family. *Feminist Review, 44*, 61–80.

79. Koven, S., & Michel, S. (Eds.). (1993). *Mothers of a new world: Maternalist politics and the origins of welfare states.*

80. Ibid.

81. Stavrianos, C. (2014). *The political uses of motherhood in America.*

82. Bouvard, M. G. (1994). *Revolutionizing motherhood: The mothers of the Plaza de Mayo.* Lanham, MD: SR Books.

83. Ibid.

84. Bosco, F. (2006). The madres de Plaza de Mayo and three decades of human rights' activism: Embeddedness, emotions, and social movements. *Annals of the Association of American Geographers, 96*(2), 342–365.

85. Mellibovsky, M. (1997). *Circle of love over death: Testimonies of the mothers of the Plaza de Mayo* (Trans. by Proser, M., and Proser, M.). Willimantic, CT: Curbstone Press.

86. Cranford, C. (2007). Constructing union motherhood: Gender and social reproduction in the Los Angeles "Justice for Janitors" movement. *Qualitative Sociology, 30*, 361–381.

87. Ortbals, C., & Poloni-Staudinger, L. (2018). *Gender and political violence: Women changing the politics of terrorism.*

88. Ibid.

89. Ibid.

90. Ibid.

91. Ibid.

92. About. (n.d.). *Black Lives Matter*. Retrieved September 17, 2018, from https://blacklivesmatter.com/about.

93. Ibid.

94. Ibid.

95. Ross, J., & Lowery, W. (2017). Turning away from street protests, Black Lives Matter tries a new tactic in the age of Trump. *The Washington Post*. Retrieved from https://www.washingtonpost.com/national/in-trumps-america-black-lives-matter-shifts-from-protests-to-policy/2017/05/04/a2acf37a-28fe-11e7-b605-33413c691853_story.html?utm_term=.c3c8907c6985.

96. Solutions. (n.d.). *Campaign Zero*. Retrieved from https://www.joincampaignzero.org/solutions/#solutionsoverview.

97. Ibid.

98. Stavrianos, C. (2014). *The political uses of motherhood in America*.

99. Ibid.; see also Goss, K. (2013). *The paradox of gender equality: How American women's groups gained and lost their public voices*. Ann Arbor: University of Michigan Press.

100. Stavrianos, C. (2014). *The political uses of motherhood in America*.

101. Ibid.

102. Ibid.

103. Ibid.

104. Goss, K., & Heany, M. (2010). Organizing women as women: Hybridity and grassroots collective action in the 21st century. *Perspectives on Politics*, *8*(1), 27–52.

105. El-Bushra, J. (2007). Feminism, gender, and women's peace activism. *Development and Change*, *38*(1), 131–147.

106. Mazurana, D., & McKay, S. (1999). *Women and peace-building*. Montreal: International Centre for Human Rights and Democratic Development.

107. El-Bushra, J. (2007). Feminism, gender, and women's peace activism; Tripp, A. M. (2017). Women's organizations and peace initiatives. In F. N. Aolain, N. R. Cahn, D. Francesca, & N. Valii (Eds.), *The Oxford handbook of gender and conflict* (pp. 430–441). New York, NY: Oxford University Press.

108. Tripp, A. M. (2017). Women's organizations and peace initiatives.

109. Ibid.

110. Ibid.

111. El-Bushra, J. (2007). Feminism, gender, and women's peace activism.

112. Ibid.

113. Torres, L. (2018). Fearless women: Leymah Gbowee—Nobel Peace Center—Medium. *Medium*. Retrieved from https://medium.com/nobel-peace-center/fearless-women-leymah-gbowee-59e66e1108f.

114. Schulte, E. (2011). How Nobel Peace Prize winner Leymah Gbowee unified Liberian women. *Fast Company*. Retrieved from https://www.fastcompany.com/1786780/how-nobel-peace-prize-winner-leymah-gbowee-unified.

115. Lawson, E. (2017). How women bring about peace and change in Liberia. *The Conversation*. Retrieved from https://theconversation.com/how-women-bring-about-peace-and-change-in-liberia-86670.

116. Douglas, S. (2014). This hut is working for me. *International Feminist Journal of Politics, 16*(1), 148–155.

117. Cockburn, C. (2012). *Antimilitarism: Political and gender dynamics of peace movements*. New York, NY: Palgrave Macmillan.

118. Ibid.

119. Benhabib, S. (1996). *Democracy and difference: Contesting the boundaries of the political*. Princeton, NJ: Princeton University Press.

120. Strachan, J. C., & Wolf, M. R. (2012). Calls for civility: An invitation to deliberate or a means of political control? In M. P. Fiorina & D. M. Shea (Eds.), *Can we talk? The Rise of rude, nasty and stubborn politics*. New York, NY: Pearson Longman.

121. Sanders, L. (1997). Against deliberation. *Political Theory, 25,* 3:347–376.

122. Karpowitz, C., & Mendelberg, T. (2014). *The silent sex: Gender, deliberation, and institutions.* Princeton, NJ: Princeton University Press.

123. Hardy-Fanta, C. (1995). Latina women and political leadership: Implications for Latino community empowerment. *New England Journal of Public Policy, 11,* 221–235.

124. Ibid.

125. Strachan, J. C. (2017). Deliberative pedagogy's feminist potential: Teaching our students to cultivate a more inclusive public sphere. In T. J. Schaffer, N. V. Longo, & M. S Thomas (Eds.), *Deliberative pedagogy, Teaching and learning for democratic engagement*. East Lansing: Michigan State University Press.

126. Ramanathan, L. (2017). Was the Women's March just another display of white privilege? Some think so. *The Washington Post*. Retrieved from https://www.washingtonpost.com/lifestyle/style/was-the-womens-march-just-another-display-of-white-privilege-some-think-so/2017/01/24/00bbdcca-e1a0-11e6-a547-5fb9411d332c_story.html?noredirect=on&utm_term=.7a2a5895972c.

127. Ibid.

128. Ibid.

129. Mosthof, M. (2017). If you're not talking about the criticism surrounding the Women's March then you're part of the problem. *Bustle*. Retrieved from https://www.bustle.com/p/if-youre-not-talking-about-the-criticism-surrounding-the-womens-march-then-youre-part-of-the-problem-33491.

130. Ibid.

131. Chan, S. (2018). Overlooked—Marsha P. Johnson, a transgender pioneer and activist. *The New York Times*. Retrieved from https://www.nytimes.com/interactive/2018/obituaries/overlooked-marsha-p-johnson.html.

132. Global Gender Justice. (2017). *Post-Trump feminism: A new age for the feminist agenda*. Retrieved from https://globalgenderjustice.wordpress.com/2017/11/05/post-trump-feminism-a-new-age-for-the-feminist-agenda.

133. Garza, A. (2017). How to Build a Movement. In S. Mukhopadhyay & K. Harding (Eds.), *Nasty women: Feminism, resistance and revolution in Trump's America* (pp. 225–230). New York, NY: Picador Press.

134. Aberra, N. (2017). Inside the Resistance Manual, a guide to Trump-era policies—And how to protest them. *Vox*. Retrieved from https://www.vox.com/conversations/2017/3/7/14834692/resistance-manual-aditi-juneja.

CHAPTER TEN

CONCLUSION

S logans on t-shirts often make jokes about social dynamics in real life. Take for example the t-shirt that reads *A Woman's Place Is in the House and in the Senate*. This shirt advocates for women in public office but is phrased in a way that pokes fun at the older, commonplace saying that a woman's place is in the home. Another t-shirt that helps summarize the major points of this book is one with the slogan *My Favorite Season Is the Fall of Patriarchy*. The t-shirt design accompanying this slogan captures the season of autumn, with colorful leaves falling from the trees. The slogan is catchy, but has the patriarchy fallen yet? If it started to fall, has backlash against sexual equality propped it back up again? More recently, women have been seen sporting t-shirts with a harsher edge, bluntly proclaiming, *I've Heard Enough from Old White Men*—implying that some women believe the patriarchal legacy we inherited from the Neolithic Era still exists, and that they find it frustrating. These t-shirt slogans are problematized here to initiate a final assessment of patriarchy's remaining influence in politics today. Has the patriarchy described in Chapter 1 subsided in recent decades, making it possible for women to control their own lives, and for women politicians to wield influence alongside men? Or are women still oppressed within their households and excluded from the public sphere? How much progress have women made in the United States? Across the globe? Moreover, what can average people do to make sure women no longer have subordinate status, are free from oppression and violence, and are encouraged to fully and freely participate in public life? These questions are addressed in this concluding chapter in five steps: 1. Admit that patriarchy exists; 2. Listen to women's complaints and take their anger seriously; 3. Understand the roots of women's anger; 4. Monitor progress and backlash to establish priorities; and 5. Decide what to do and act.

THE FIRST STEP: ADMIT THAT PATRIARCHY EXISTS

Many will always find it easier to think of patriarchy as an ancient system of masculine dominance—one that existed alongside slavery, premodern agriculture, and monarchies (or other authoritarian governance structures).

Similarly, many Americans will find it easier to identify patriarchal legacies in other countries before they see it in their own. One reason for denying that patriarchy still exists is because men and women live such intertwined lives, often needing each other in "profound" ways, in roles as romantic/sexual partners, family members, parents, children, friends, and/or colleagues.[1] Sociologist Allan G. Johnson (2014) argues that both men and women are often reluctant to acknowledge how much patriarchy affects their lives, noting, "Who wants to know how dependent we are on patriarchy as a system, how deeply our thoughts, feelings and behavior are embedded in it?"[2]

However, reading this book should have made clear that patriarchy was deeply embedded not only in the archaic city states that produced the fear–control cycle and warrior culture shaping so many civilizations as they evolved but even in modern democracies where leaders were overtly masculine, and citizens were exclusively men. Indeed, the authors have argued throughout this book that patriarchy remains front page news in the United States and in other countries—in both developed and developing ones. The first step in making a difference, therefore, is simply acknowledging that varying versions of patriarchy still exist.[3]

THE SECOND STEP: LISTEN TO WOMEN'S COMPLAINTS AND TAKE THEIR ANGER SERIOUSLY

Despite the difficulty of recognizing and grappling with inequality when it is threaded through our everyday lives, the last t-shirt described above indicates that some women have overcome the human inclination to help reify a world socially constructed to deny them agency over their own lives. As noted in Chapters 2 and 9, organized groups dedicated to women's activism have become a permanent part of civic infrastructure, and gender studies programs have been institutionalized in the academy. (See Box 10.5, however, for insight into how quickly these seemingly permanent realties can be undone by those with hierarchical, authoritarian impulses.) These groups work continuously to raise women's awareness of inequality and to bolster women's group consciousness in countries like the United States.

Hence, the second step to overcoming patriarchy is to listen to women's complaints and to take their anger seriously. Yet, after 7,000 years of subordinate status, people became accustomed to treating women as "childish creatures who had little of consequence to say." As a result, "any views expressed by women on important matters [including who they should marry or whether they were raped] could be treated with little regard or simply ignored."[4] In the past, as now, political commentary dismissed women's political activism and anger. The following cartoons, for example, depict scenes objectifying and patronizing suffragettes to make light of their concerns.

Learning to listen can be hard. Traditional gender role socialization encourages people to patronize women who complain, attributing their concerns to fluctuating hormones, uncontrolled emotions, or child-like irrationality. "When the stories originate from women of so many ages and racial, class, and ethnic backgrounds, and when they echo across cultures and so much of history, they call on men [along with everyone else] to have enough respect and humility to be silent for a while and listen."[5] Learning to listen will require not only hearing women who complain quietly and politely but also women who are angry. When men—even men with other marginalized identities such as class, race, or sexual orientation—experience injustice, their anger is often perceived as righteous indignation. Ambivalent sexism's double bind means women are rarely afforded this reaction.[6] Even when they are angry over the type of serious issues detailed throughout this text, furious women are subject to social sanctions—ranging from being told that they cannot take a joke or that they are overreacting, to being labeled frigid, a bitch, or even unhinged. Women's anger is unacceptable because it "threatens the entire patriarchal order," by placing "women and their concerns at center stage in a male-centered world."[7] Moreover, many men's intrinsic identities—how they are socialized to think of themselves—are still so intertwined with patriarchy's idealized masculine gender roles that criticisms of patriarchy are sometimes incorrectly heard as a criticism of all men. The #NotAllMen trend provides ample evidence of this reaction. Why, men might ask, should they "question, much less give up, what they have and risk other men's disapproval, anger, and rejection, not to mention feeling disempowered, diminished and 'softened' to a position of equality with women," especially when intersectional identities mean that they may not feel "terribly good about their own lives in the first place?"[8] The inclination to compartmentalize and minimize women's concerns, along with the impulse to pacify their anger without working for change, must be overcome. As feminist author Rebecca Traister (2018) outlines in *Good and Mad, The Revolutionary Power of Women's Anger*, "female fury" has inspired every instance of successful women's organizing in the United States, from suffragette marches on the White House up through the Women's March and the #MeToo movement.[9]

Cobb x Shinn Series 895 T.P. & Co.

Cobb x Shinn Series 895 T.P. & Co.

Brian L. Bossier Collection

▸ **Photos 10.1–10.3** Anti-suffragette postcards circulated in the early 1900s.

Anger fed women's willingness to undergo hardship just to gain publicity for their cause—as when Susan B. Anthony purposefully voted in a presidential election before women were enfranchised, creating the opportunity to give an inspired speech in court when she refused to pay the fine, or when Alice Paul staged protests knowing they would result in marchers' arrests so that she could wage hunger strikes. Anger fed birth control and abortion activists, who purposefully committed acts of civil disobedience with every intention of being arrested, just so they would have legal standing to challenge and overturn restrictive laws as unconstitutional in court. As these and numerous anecdotes relayed throughout previous chapters make clear, women must be heard because their anger, their righteous indignation at unjust treatment, "is an important engine for social change."[10]

THE THIRD STEP: UNDERSTAND THE ROOTS OF WOMEN'S ANGER

The aftermath of the 2016 presidential election provides an important opportunity to understand women's anger. Although U.S. women's post-2016 activism spiked, some political observers have overlooked the overtly political nature of their efforts. Much in the same way that John Adams patronized Abigail Adams after her appeal that he "remember the ladies," some downplayed the seriousness of women's concerns, predicting that their political engagement would amount to nothing more than a temporary distraction. Others overlooked women's legitimate policy concerns, framing women's activism as an angry but largely emotional and personal reaction to Trump's overt sexism on the campaign trail. The pussy hats women knitted to wear to his protest indicate many women *were* angry at Trump's audio-taped comments, aired during the campaign season, that because he was a reality show TV star he could "grab [women] by the pussy," that he could "do anything." Yet, the scale and intensity of women's response hints at a root cause far beyond personal offense at a rude comment.

As discussed in Chapter 9, activism in reaction to Donald Trump's presidency has been unprecedented. Protests organized by women were followed by a groundswell of grassroots organizing activism—signing petitions, contacting elected officials, mobilizing the "the resistance"—and running for office. For the first time, the gap between the two parties widened because women, especially the youngest generation of women voters, shifted their allegiances, away from Republicans to identify as Democrats. (Recall from Chapter 3 that in the past, this gap was driven primarily by men shifting away from the Democratic Party.)[11] The pattern continued as pollsters gauged registered voters' intentions in the 2018 midterms. Between June 2018 and September 2018, for example, men registered voters slightly shifted away from Democrats, initially being split at 45% voting Democratic and 44% Republican, to preferring Republicans by a six-point margin of 50% to 44%. Across the same time period, women's preference for Democratic candidates widened from an eight-point margin in June—51% Democratic and 43% Republican—to a 24-point lead of 58% to 34%.[12] At least one exit poll showed women of all education levels—and not just college educated, urban, and minority women—moved toward Democrats in the 2018 midterm elections.[13]

However, Democratic women, even more so than Democratic men, had the most intense, visceral reaction to Trump. Lawless's and Fox's 2017 survey of potential candidates, for example, found that more Democratic women described being appalled (at 70%) and angry (at 55%) by Trump's win, compared to Democratic men (of whom 60% reported being appalled, and 45% reported being angry.) Similarly, 73% of Democratic women agreed that seeing Donald Trump on the news made them sick to their stomach, a reaction reported by only 61% of Democratic men. Even more so than Democratic men, Democratic women (at 47% compared to 33%) became more attentive to then national news after 2016 and more likely to take political action (at 40% compared to 34%).[14]

These reactions were not merely personal but rooted in Democratic women's distinct policy concerns. Democratic women and men were equally motivated by Trump's willingness to cut environmental regulations (at 57% to 55%). Democratic women, however, were far more upset by the possibility that Obamacare would be repealed (at 57% to 49%) and that Planned Parenthood would be defunded (at 57% to 45%). "The gap [on environmental policy] closes, therefore, not because women were less motivated, but rather, because men are more driven by environmental concerns than they are by health care or reproductive rights."[15]

Why would Democratic women be incensed and motivated to undertake political action when Obamacare and Planned Parenthood were threatened? Both policies provide access to reproductive health care—which has been essential to women's progress over the past half century. Consider that the lynch pin of U.S. women's movement toward equality since the Second Wave has been 1) the ability to control reproduction, 2) combined with access to higher education and professions, and 3) the anticipation of fair treatment in these settings. Democratic women likely have such a visceral response to Donald Trump because he represents not only a direct threat to their bodily autonomy (e.g., access to reproductive health care and physical safety in the public sphere) but is also a tangible symbol of patriarchal equilibrium, demonstrating to women that their decades-long investment in earning educational and professional credentials has not resulted in fair treatment or a level playing field at work.

Early feminist activist Susan B. Anthony, as explained in her essay *The Homes of Single Women*, thought that women would gain equal status in the United States first by gaining access to education and professions, and then by avoiding the "obligations" (i.e., domestic duties, mandatory sexual services, uncontrolled pregnancies, and childcare) typically accompanying traditional marriages by avoiding the institution altogether until relationships between the sexes were fundamentally transformed. Political cartoons from early 1900s suggest some feared women would not only follow Susan B. Anthony's advice about foregoing the institution of marriage but would become lesbians and abandon men altogether. Currently, as Box 10.1 indicates, women living in countries with more restrictive versions of patriarchy and limited access to reproductive health care are more apt to follow Anthony's advice about women-only spaces.

▶ **Photos 10.4 and 10.5** Anti-suffragette postcards circulated in the early 1900s.

BOX 10.1: COMPARATIVE FEATURE

Women's-Only Communities as an Alternative Solution

One longstanding women-only community, Umoja, is a village founded in 1990 by Samburu women in northern Kenya. The Samburu, an ethnic group closely related to the Maasai tribe, are patriarchal nomadic pastoralists. Men elders make important decisions for each village, and cultural practices give women little control over their own lives. Members of the tribe wear ornately beaded jewelry, and young girls receive their first necklaces from their fathers in a ceremony known as "beading." At the same time, they enter into temporary marriages with older "warrior" men—and despite having no access to contraception, are forbidden to become pregnant. Girls who do are forced to have abortions performed by other women in their villages. The women who founded Umoja over 25 years ago were raped by British soldiers and Gurkhas (Nepalese soldiers who fight with the British

▶ **Photo 10.6** A woman and her children stand in front of their home in the village of Umoja in 2008.

army) stationed nearby and beaten by their husbands or rejected by their communities as a result. One resident described this reaction, noting that once a woman is raped, she is considered unclean. Another recalled, "After what the British did to me, I would never be able to marry."[16] Over the years, the village matriarch, Rebecca Lolosoli, has welcomed women and girls escaping child marriage, female genital mutilation, domestic violence, and sexual assault—all of which are cultural norms among the Samburu. In 2015, the village housed 47 women, who made their money largely by selling beaded jewelry to tourists, and their 200 children.[17] As suggested by the number of children, some Umoja women seek sexual relationships with men who live nearby, in part, because they still want to have children. Few, however, want husbands, claiming, "Outside, women are being ruled by men so they can't get any change"; "The women in Umoja have freedom"; and "I don't want to ever leave this supportive community of women."[18]

Women have sought similar refuge in the violent nation of El Salvador. Approximately 10% of Salvadorans are gang-affiliated, making it the most dangerous country around the globe, except for those currently at war. Men-dominated gangs are territorial, and women and girls often become part of the territorial resources they control. For example, women often fear being in public places and try to make themselves appear as unattractive as possible, because those chosen as "girlfriends" by gang members cannot refuse. Although the gang leader or *palabrero* will choose one woman who has sex exclusively with him, other women and girls are expected to be sexually available to an entire gang. Gang members admit that their standard practice is to kill any who refuse, which helps to explain why a woman is murdered in El Salvador every 19 hours. Meanwhile, the suicide rate among teenage girls is high, as their alternatives are often to have nonconsensual sex on demand or to be violently raped and murdered. While these femicides should be treated as hate crimes, investigations are often dropped when authorities realize they are gang-related.[19] According to one Salvadoran woman living in hiding to avoid retaliation for trying, unsuccessfully, to flee to the United States: "We live in a deeply patriarchal system, we're taught to say yes to men, [to] accept violence and that men are superior. If you are a man you must prove you are strong, aggressive, [and] capable of violence."[20]

In a mountainous region of the country near the city of Tonacatepeque, widowed women and single mothers who lost their homes (either to civil war in the 1980s or to an earthquake in 2001) avoided poverty and violence in gang-infested areas by banding together to found Romero Community. The Community, recently granted land rights, has 450 residents, of whom 90% are women. All of the community's leaders are women who have tackled illiteracy rates by helping residents learn to read and write, have founded a school for their children to attend, and have taught others to earn an income from organic farming.[21] The women have no plans to leave, because as the community's president, Carmen Acevedo, explains, "Outside the Romero Community, being a woman is a liability. But inside, it is something to be celebrated. . . . We're our own bosses here. . . . We don't suffer for being women and we can move forward."[22]

Anthony, however, could not have predicted U.S. women's widespread access to reproductive health care, which allowed women to control family size and, thus, succeed in education and professions without entirely abandoning the institution of marriage but working to reform it from within instead. Success in altering marriage and family life does not mean there is not room for improvement. Remnants of patriarchal attitudes still affect domestic relations in the United States, as evidenced by rates of domestic violence. Nearly 1 in 4 adult women and approximately 1 in 4 adult men will experience intimate partner physical violence in their lifetime. Women, at one in seven compared to 1 in 25 men, are more likely to sustain injuries from these incidents.[23] They are also more likely to be murdered. More than two thirds of intimate partner homicides involve a man perpetrator and a woman victim, in comparison to the one fifth of incidents in which women kill men. Moreover, nearly 45% of women homicide victims are killed by an intimate partner, compared to only 5% of men homicide victims.[24]

Even so, women have arguably been more successful at fundamentally transforming the institution of marriage and the nature of domestic partnerships than they have the workplace or politics.[25] As Box 10.2 notes, however, progress in the domestic sphere may be a more important feminist accomplishment than many realize.

BOX 10.2: SUSAN M. OKIN, EGALITARIAN FAMILIES AS THE BUILDING BLOCKS OF EGALITARIAN POLITICS

Failure to make even more progress toward equality in the workplace and in politics may be discouraging. Consider the possibility, however, that Americans' success in transforming the institution of marriage and promoting more egalitarian family structures may be a prerequisite to achieving those goals. In her classic work *Gender, Justice, & the Family*, theorist Susan M. Okin (1987) criticized previous political philosophers for applying theories of justice to men's relationship with the governing structure, while refusing to extend the same analyses to families and the domestic sphere.[26] She argued Western culture's gender system was the equivalent of a caste system, granting privileges, duties, and opportunities based on demographic traits assigned at birth. This caste system damaged the cherished democratic value of equality of opportunity, as disparities in the way women and girls were treated within the family limited the opportunities available to them for their entire lives. Moreover, Okin concluded that family dynamics based on justice, equality, and reciprocity were the only way that children would ever learn to truly be just. One of the first things children notice is sex-based differences in their own home. Hence, relationships within the home become children's first political order, affecting the type they find acceptable and expect to see replicated in the public sphere. Egalitarian homes normalize women's political leadership. Yet, when children observe their mothers' and sisters' subordination within the family, women's political power feels unnatural and is hard to accept. Just as patriarchal states grew out of men's subordination over women within the household, egalitarian relationships within the household could well be patriarchy's undoing. Okin's arguments help to clarify the meaning of the women's rights slogan of the Second Wave, which was "The Personal Is Political." In short, what happens within the confines of the domestic sphere affects our ability to establish a just, egalitarian society. Around the globe, women typically have more representation in government in nations where family life is more egalitarian. Moreover, in countries characterized by domestic inequality, authoritarians are more apt to be elected immediately after a prominent feminist leader, because powerful women are perceived as an unnatural threat to men's authority.[27] Thus, promoting women's equality in the home may be one of the most important things societies can do to promote democracy at home and abroad.

Meanwhile, U.S. workplace and political institutions still prefer ideal workers who can fully dedicate themselves to their work and public service and who have no conflicting domestic responsibilities. As Box 10.3 underscores, this expectation means women still face considerable obstacles in the workplace. Meanwhile, as noted in Chapter 6, political institutions like Congress and state legislatures often lack even basic physical infrastructure (like adequate bathrooms and lactation rooms) let alone policies (like maternity leave and sexual harassment protocols) that accommodate women's different lived experiences. Hence, cisgender women transformed marriage and controlled their fertility in order to achieve success in workplace and political institutions that were purposefully designed to exclude them and were never fully transformed to include them. Access to contraception and reproductive health care, however, reinforced **choice feminism**, or the notion that each cisgender woman can make a choice. She can choose to have more children and to prioritize family life, or she can choose to control her fertility to pursue professional and career success. After the successes of the Second Wave, many women earnestly believed that if they chose the latter, they would be treated fairly and achieve success comparable to similarly credentialed men, even if they had to work harder for it. Hence, women, especially Democratic women, are angry because they believe the Trump administration will undermine their bodily autonomy (in terms of access to reproductive health care), and they perceive Trump himself as a vivid reminder that patriarchy continues to undermine both their bodily autonomy (in terms of physical safety) and their credentials in the workplace.

BOX 10.3: POLICY FEATURE

The Motherhood Penalty and Pregnancy Discrimination in the United States

In 2018, investigative journalists at the *New York Times* reviewed court documents and public records and interviewed women, their lawyers, and government officials. Their findings support social science research indicating that U.S. women often face pregnancy discrimination and a steep motherhood penalty. The journalists conclude, "Many of the country's largest and most prestigious companies still systematically sideline pregnant women. They pass them over for promotions and raises. They fire them when they complain."[28] Unlike new fathers, who are perceived as more committed employees, pregnant women and mothers are perceived as less committed to their jobs and less capable of performing at work. Research using otherwise identical résumés, for example, reveals employers prefer fathers over all other types of employees but are much less likely to contact mothers for an interview. Further, employers more closely scrutinize mothers' job performance and are less understanding when they are tardy.[29] In lab experiments, again relying on identical résumés, participants offered mothers $11,000 less, on average, than childless women and $13,000 less than fathers.[30] Controlling for employees' experience, education, marital status, and hours worked (which takes women who purposefully reduce their hours after child birth into account), a 2014 study found that men receive a 6% "fatherhood bump" in wages after having a child, while women experience a 4% "motherhood penalty" for each child.[31]

These biases mean that women with white collar jobs are often demoted, as well as discouraged from taking prestigious assignments, left out of meetings with high-end clients, and given smaller bonuses. Yet, such biases, combined with few protections against pregnancy discrimination, often result in more serious consequences for women with physical, blue collar jobs—where requests for alternative duties or more frequent breaks to accommodate at-risk pregnancies are often ignored.[32] Efforts to prevent pregnancy discrimination were a reaction to the 1976 Supreme Court decision in *General Electric Company v. Gilbert*, which determined that the company was not required to give expectant mothers paid time off, even though it did so for other disabled workers.[33] The result was the 1978 federal Pregnancy Discrimination Act, which requires employers to accommodate pregnant women—but only if they were already doing so for other people "similar in their ability or inability to work." Yet, employers still often refused pregnant women, arguing that they were not injured on the job and did not deserve accommodations. This position was rejected by the Court when it decided *Young v. United Parcel Service* in 2015.[34] Based on her doctor's recommendation, Peggy Young asked UPS for an alternative assignment—in particular one that would not require delivering packages—so that she would not have to lift heavy boxes during her pregnancy. UPS refused, despite honoring such requests for other workers, including not only those injured on the job but also those who lost driver's licenses for driving drunk. After losing two federal court cases, Young appealed to the Supreme Court. During oral arguments, Justice Ruth Bader Ginsburg asked the company's lawyer to cite "a single instance of anyone who needed a lifting dispensation who didn't get it except for pregnant people."[35] He could not, and the Court ruled 6-3 in Young's favor.

The decision hinged on UPS's treatment of other employees. Hence, under federal law, companies that do not adjust duties for any employees are under no obligation to adjust duties for pregnant women, even when their obstetricians document the need for alternative duties, and such tasks are available. And many do not. Hence the *New York Times* investigation revealed numerous instances when denied requests resulted in miscarriages and premature labor, and in one instance, a stillbirth.[36]

In 23 states, legislatures have passed policies with stronger workplace protections for pregnant women than the federal law provides. They were spearheaded by Republicans in Utah, Delaware, Colorado, and New York and by an antiabortion Democrat in Nebraska. Meanwhile, new legislation supported by antiabortion groups such as Americans United for Life has been proposed in every congressional session since 2012. Modeled after the American With Disabilities Act, it would simply require employers to make accommodations for people whose health depends on it.[37]

Meanwhile, the U.S. Equal Employment Opportunity Commission (EEOC) received 3,184 pregnancy discrimination complaints in 2017, twice as many as in 1992 when the agency began keeping electronic records, and tens of thousands of women have taken legal action against their employers, who represent a wide array of American companies and organizations including, somewhat ironically, Planned Parenthood.[38,39]

Undermining Women's Bodily Autonomy

Some women's intense, negative reaction to Donald Trump is a rejection of policies that undermine women's bodily autonomy by limiting access to all forms of reproductive health care and that have the potential to stymie gains in equality achieved since the Second Wave. Policy text boxes in Chapters 3 and 8 explained how the Trump administration, by appointing socially conservatives judges and attempting to change rules and regulations related to Title X funding and the Affordable Care Act's contraception mandate, is methodically "remaking government policy on reproductive health—moving to limit access to birth control and abortion and bolstering abstinence-only sex education."[40] Many Democratic women, who were motivated to defend organizations like Planned Parenthood, are inclined to agree with Rep. Diana DeGette (D-CO), who responded to these changes, noting, "It's across the spectrum of women's health services. . . . They're [i.e., Trump administration officials] proposing abstinence only sex education—which study after study has shown doesn't work—restrictions to family planning, and more and more restrictions to abortion."[41]

Beyond reproductive freedom, however, Trump's pussy-grabbing comments during the 2016 campaign reminded women that patriarchy threatens their bodily autonomy by continuing to frame unchaperoned women outside the domestic sphere and the protection of a man guardian as sexually available—as **Publica** (or a public woman associated with prostitution and illicit behavior) rather than **Publius** (or a public man associated with civic virtue and patriotism).[42]

When so many voters, including so many other women, were willing to cast ballots for Donald Trump even after hearing him boast about his irrepressible impulse to kiss and grope beautiful women without their consent, many worried that fewer women would be willing to complain about workplace harassment and assault. Instead, women got angry, triggering not only the #MeToo movement in the United States but an array of sister-movements overseas (as described in Chapter 9). It is impossible to predict whether women would have been angry enough to risk sharing stories about powerful men committing sexual harassment and assault if Hillary Clinton had won. It is possible that a Clinton victory in 2016 would have made women more complacent about sex-based equality, or, as described in Box 10.5, would have resulted in backlash against a highly visible, powerful woman. Yet, some women were angrier about Donald Trump's win than they were about Hillary Clinton's loss. Linda Sarsour, a cofounder of the Women's March, conveyed this sentiment when she noted, "People were so aghast and felt betrayed that so many of our fellow Americans voted for a misogynist, accused sexual predator."[43]

Women were angry because, as the stories that emerged from the #MeToo movement revealed, sexual harassment and assault in the workplace were far more widespread, across all types of workplaces in the United States, than many people realized. As they shared their lived experiences, women explained why they coped with these harrowing experiences individually, rarely sharing stories (for fear of being belittled or blamed) and often choosing not to file formal complaints with workplace human resource departments (for fear of retaliation).

As novelist Jennifer Weiner (2018), who authored a *New York Times* editorial titled "The Patriarchy Will Always Have Its Revenge" explained,

> By 21, like most women, I'd had experience with the way the world makes excuses for young men (and old ones), and instead trains its scrutiny on the women who dare to complain. What's your problem? Was it really such a big deal? C'mon, it wasn't like he raped you. Better to tell yourself that the boss who groped you at the office party was just an old goat and the teenage boy who grabbed you at the pool party was just high-spirited and that all the ones in between were just . . . men.[44]

Sharing these stories provided women with the group consciousness and rising expectations that serve as precursors to collective action. First, women recognized themselves in stories like Weiner's and realized they were all being treated unfairly because of their shared identity as women. Second, judging the perpetrators in others' stories resulted in rising expectations, helping women realize that they all deserved better. Anger about powerful men and their ability to avoid punishment for sexual harassment and assault was reignited by controversy surrounding the confirmation of Supreme Court Justice Brett Kavanaugh in October 2018 (discussed in Chapter 8). During the confirmation hearings, novelist Jennifer Weiner published the editorial noted earlier, dedicating her column to voicing anger, engendered by an expectation, shared by her peers, that if they worked diligently to excel in the workplace they would be rewarded in an egalitarian society that honored their hard work. Weiner experienced sexism as a young, working woman but believed she and her women colleagues would work hard to achieve higher status positions where "men like that" would have "no sway" over them.[45] (Note the unintended expression of privilege implied in Weiner's narrative. She and her friends anticipated moving up into positions of authority, where they could avoid sexual harassment, in a way that not all women can.) Conveying a deep sense of betrayal, she wrote, "Except guess what? The joke's on us. There's no such place."[46] Weiner's column resonated with women across the country, who see patriarchy restricting their ability to function in the public sphere by continuing to normalize behavior that threatens their bodily autonomy.

Undermining Women's Credentials

Hillary Clinton's loss though, particularly to Donald Trump, also cultivated group consciousness, and anger, especially among working women who recognized a familiar pattern in the way her credentials were overlooked and dismissed. Even those who disagreed with Clinton's policy positions could recognize that she made all the sacrifices that Second Wave women who chose to pursue an education and a career were expected to make. She delayed marriage and family until after law school and limited her family's size. She prioritized her husband's career, setting aside her own opportunities to move to Arkansas. She waited to pursue her own political ambition, running for a U.S. Senate seat only after her daughter was an adult. Despite Clinton's late start, Barack Obama could reasonably argue at the 2016 Democratic National Convention—with the touch of hyperbole expected in a nominating speech—that, "There has never been a man or a woman, not me, not Bill, nobody more qualified to serve as president of the United States."[47] By the time she ran for president, Clinton had survived two competitive Democratic primaries and two general elections to serve as the junior U.S. senator from New York for eight years. In addition, serving as Secretary of State provided her with significant foreign policy experience, while overseeing her husband's push for health care reform as First Lady provided significant domestic policy experience. One political reporter summarized her list of qualifications with the understatement, "So yes, she's pretty qualified."[48] Meanwhile, in terms of political experience as an elected, appointed, or military official, Donald Trump was one of the least qualified and most controversial presidential candidates in U.S. history. In an editorial explaining why Hillary Clinton's loss to Donald Trump made Democratic women so angry, one *New York Times* columnist explained that white men's "death grip on power in America" is precisely the kind of "identity politics" conservatives claim to "abhor." She argued that "conservative identity politics" (i.e., their blinkered preference for white men) meant that highly qualified women were regularly overlooked and discredited. "Meanwhile, as a reminder of the bar for male competence, Donald Trump is the president."[49]

Another columnist expressed solidarity with Clinton, noting, "Her career brings to light the truth . . . that the harder [women] strive, the higher we climb, we all become that woman."[50]

Journalists report that when Hillary Clinton's campaign manager, Robby Mook, delivered the news that she was going to lose, she was not surprised and immediately responded, "I knew this would happen to me. . . . They were never going to let me win."[51] Clinton never elaborated on who "they" were. But many women across the country nodded in agreement with one interpretation that "they" "were the patriarchy that could never let an ambitious former first lady finally shatter 'that highest, hardest, glass ceiling.'"[52] In 2018, they similarly nodded along with former First Lady Michelle Obama when she reacted to a prominent women executive's self-help book advising women to stop being passive and more aggressively "Lean In"[53] to achieve professional advancement, saying, "It's not always enough to lean in, because that [expletive] doesn't work."[54]

These sentiments may have resonated with women at this particular historical moment not only out of empathy for Hillary Clinton but because their own credentials, as well as the higher education institutions where they are earning those credentials, are under duress. Since the 1950s, whenever women have become associated with a particular job or profession, the result has been diminished prestige and lower compensation.[55] More recently, however, women are not only succeeding in particular professions but in college and graduate/professional school overall (see Chapter 4). Education scholar Nancy S. Niemi (2017), author of *Degrees of Difference*, points out that every time American girls and women have come close to surpassing American boys' and men's educational achievements, the result has been public angst over the fate of boys. Women's academic success was tolerated as long as women still accepted remnants of patriarchy's gendered caste system. For example, even though women graduated from high school at twice the rate of men in the 1890s, their success was acceptable because access to political and economic power was still sex-based. Similarly, even though women outperformed men on college campuses during the 1950s and 1960s, most complied with what Mary Bunting, then president of Radcliffe College (the women's liberal arts college that functioned as a counterpart to Harvard College) labeled a "Climate of Unexpectation." "They could go to college, but with the silent understanding that they would marry and stay home with children thereafter."[56]

The more academia becomes associated with women, and the more women use their credentials to achieve positions of authority, Niemi argues, the more likely men, particularly white men, are to seek status and credentials elsewhere—such as traditional men-dominated workplaces and men-dominated professions—to "regain their cultural and economic advantage."[57] She notes that women and minorities will continue to need college degrees, because they yield professional opportunities and higher pay than members of these demographic groups can achieve without them—but not the same pay or influential positions available to similarly and less credentialed white men. As Carole Pateman (1988) made clear in *The Sexual Contract*, traditional patriarchal authority is associated with men, as men agreed to be ruled by one another, in exchange for all men ruling over women.[58] Hence, patriarchal equilibrium (a concept first defined in Chapter 1) requires that institutions where women gain access and begin to wield power in large numbers or in prominent positions must be scrutinized, found wanting, and discredited or dismantled. (See Box 10.5 for examples of the way efforts to sustain patriarchal equilibrium in reaction to women political leaders have played out in recent authoritarian regimes, and Box 10.6 for what such efforts might look like in America.) Niemi concludes,

> American women fought hard to be included in the privileges of higher education; without it, millions of women and their country would be diminished in countless ways. But in America, the idea that women's attainment of formal higher-education credentials created gender equity is simply untrue.[59]

Hence, Hillary Clinton's loss made so many women angry because it provided a prominent, tangible example confirming their suspicion that patriarchy continues to find ways to undermine their credentials and deny them leadership positions.

BOX 10.4: COMPARATIVE FEATURE

Patriarchal Equilibrium and the Resurgence of Authoritarian Regimes

Several authoritarian leaders have won elections around the world in the past decade. All have followed a similar winning campaign strategy by portraying a return to patriarchal, strong-man leadership, unconstrained by democratic institutions and rule of law, as the only way to overcome a national crisis. In the Philippines, President Rodrigo Duterte equated an epidemic of illegal drugs with a national disaster, while newly elected Brazilian President Jair Bolsonaro focused on his predecessor's inability to address widespread crime and a foundering economy. Meanwhile, authoritarianism in Hungary, associated with Prime Minister Viktor Orbán, and in Poland, associated with the far-right Law and Justice Party, has focused on loss of national and cultural identity, in the face of rising immigration in the former and deference to Russia and the European Union in the latter. All, under the guise of a need for strict "law and order" to reimpose stability, have already undertaken or have threatened actions that undermine liberal democracy. Bolsonaro, for example, has promised to return Brazil to its "glorious past" when it was ruled by a military dictator, while Duterte, similarly glamorizing his nation's autocratic history, has overseen state-sponsored killing of thousands of alleged drug dealers without the benefit of a trial. Orbán undermined freedom of the press and of academia by threatening journalists and firing university administrators, while Poland's Law and Justice Party eroded judicial autonomy by stripping power from the nation's Supreme Court.

Their actions indicate that they all want to revert to the original social contract's justification of legitimate political authority—where a ruler became "the Patriarch" of an entire nation based on his strength and on his ability to seize power through force, while other men deferred in exchange for their ability to rule over women[60,61] For those still grounded in a patriarchal worldview, "women's empowerment ruptures this order."[62] Despite the various types of "crises" used to justify their power-grabs, all of the new autocrats have one thing in common—they use women's power in public life to delegitimize the preceding democratic regime and call for resubordination of women under their own rule. Moreover, these authoritarians' "efforts to denigrate and subordinate women cemented—for their supporters—the belief that the nation, having been turned upside down [by empowering women in a democracy], was being turned right-side up."[63]

Appeals to supporters often include attempts to publicly humiliate and attack powerful women. While still a legislator, for example, Bolsonaro voted to impeach Brazil's first woman president, who had been tortured by Brazil's military rulers in the early 1970s. Bolsonaro publicly dedicated his vote to an infamous torturer. After a prominent woman senator demanded an investigation into Duterte's drug war, he publicly vowed that he would "make her cry."[64] He had her detained on drug-trafficking charges, leaking evidence intended to prove that she was (in his words) "screwing her driver" like she was "screwing the nation."[65] Other crass appeals include crowds at Bolsonaro rallies chanting about feeding dogfood to feminists, and Duterte announcing that soldiers carrying out military actions on Midnanao Island in 2017 could rape up to three women without fearing consequences. In 2018, Duterete also encouraged soldiers to shoot women rebels in the vagina to make them "useless."[66] In less violent appeals that still underscore the link between fertility and women's value, far-right conservatives in Poland have aired advertisements encouraging Poles to "breed like rabbits."[67] Meanwhile, Orbán suggested providing Hungarian women a debt-free education—but only after they fulfill their duty to reproduce by bearing at least three children.[68] In an interview with Redden (2018), Kevin Moss, the Jean Thomson Fulton Professor of Modern Languages and Literature at Middlebury College, posited that opposition to feminists, which extends to attacks on equality for LGBTQIA+, occur because "authoritarian regimes require for somebody to have more power than somebody else; once you overthrow the idea that the patriarchy is something natural, for [authoritarians] that is the destruction of a . . . building block of [their] culture."[69]

Everywhere authoritarian far-right politicians have come to power, universities' gender studies programs have also come under attack—with programs denigrated in the media, gender scholars harassed and blacklisted, and university classrooms/events censored.[70] This turn of events is not surprising, given that gender studies is a subgenre of critical theory, which emerged to ensure that the humanities and social science remained committed to extending the normative, egalitarian values of the Enlightenment to all types of people (see Chapter 1). Some of the most egregious examples of the backlash against gender studies have taken place, again not surprisingly, in Hungary and Brazil. In Brazil, the National Congress is currently considering a bill (first introduced in 2014) that would ban teachers from using the word *gender* in the classroom, in order to "privilege family values in [students'] school education related to moral, sexual, and religious education."[71] If passed, the law would effectively prohibit teaching topics related to gender in Brazilian schools and universities. Marlene de Fáveri, professor of history at Brazil's State University of Santa Caterina described the bill as a political tool designed to discredit the field of gender studies. "It takes a great deal of effort to deny the world-renowned research efforts and the vast body of knowledge regarding women, gender as a category of social analysis and gendered violence, as well as the hard and numerous battles women had to fight throughout history to be legally recognized," she said in Redden (2018).[72]

Judith Butler, a prominent U.S. gender scholar who traveled to Brazil to participate in an academic conference in 2017, was met at the airport by protesters

(Continued)

(Continued)

who burned her in effigy. She described Bolsonaro supporters' authoritarian, patriarchal worldview to Redden (2018), noting, "They want boys to be boys and girls to be girls, and for there to be no complexity in questions such as these."[73]

Hungary, meanwhile, withdrew accreditation from gender studies programs in 2018, after releasing a statement that gender studies "has no business [being taught] in universities" because it is "an ideology not a science."[74] A deputy to Prime Minister Orbán went on to claim that the decision was guided by the need to prepare students for the Hungarian workplace, noting, "No one wants to employ a gender-ologist."[75] A professor of gender studies at the Central European University—which was forced out of Hungary and moved its main campus to Vienna—linked the decision to the country's rising authoritarianism, explaining, "Every undemocratic government wants to control knowledge production and sexuality, which explains why gender studies becomes a target in the first place."[76] The actions of the latest wave of authoritarian leaders demonstrate the lengths those motivated by the fear-control cycle at the heart of patriarchal worldview will go to reestablish, reify, and police binary gender roles—demanding that men be "warriors," while women and others serve a subordinate role as resources—when given the chance.

BOX 10.5: POLICY FEATURE

Was the Michigan Legislature's Lame Duck Session an Example of Patriarchal Equilibrium?

Efforts to sustain patriarchal equilibrium may cause Americans to devalue not only higher education but also democratic practices, particularly when elections empower prominent feminists. In the 2018 midterms, voters in the state of Michigan overwhelmingly voted to support women candidates up and down the slate, in particular, Governor Gretchen Whitmer (D-MI), a former state legislator and county prosecutor; Attorney General Dana Nessel (D-MI), the first openly gay official elected to a statewide office in Michigan; and Secretary of State Jocelyn Benson (D-MI), the first Democrat elected to the position in 20 years. These three women violated patriarchal norms not only by stepping into the most powerful statewide executive positions of authority—or the apex of political power that women have found elusive— but also by having well-established feminist credentials.

Benson enthusiastically endorsed ballot initiatives that would eliminate gerrymandered district lines and would increase many Michigan voters' access to the polls. Meanwhile, both Nessel and Whitmer were well known for their commitment to progressive and feminist issues. As the state Senate's minority leader, Whitmer had vehemently opposed a bill banning insurance companies from covering abortion procedures unless women proactively purchased an additional "abortion rider," noting that most women, who rarely anticipate needing an abortion, would be left without coverage. She garnered national attention for describing her own rape as an example on the floor of the Michigan Senate,[77] as well as for defending two fellow women legislators who were censured for using so-called "vulgar" terms (such as vagina and vasectomy) while aggressively criticizing the bill during debate, as described in Chapter 6.[78] Nessel also had a national reputation after dedicating much of her legal career to helping same-sex couples challenge Michigan's same-sex marriage ban, and in 2012, helping to overturn a state law preventing same-sex couples from adopting children.[79] During the 2018 campaign, she produced an online ad reminiscent of a Samantha Bee skit that went viral. In it, she leveraged concerns raised by the #MeToo movement, telling voters,

> If the last few weeks has taught us anything, it's that we need more women in positions of power, not less. So when you're choosing Michigan's next attorney general, ask yourself this: Who can you trust most not to show you their penis in a professional setting? Is it the candidate who doesn't have a penis? I'd say so.[80]

She continued, "I want to tell you what you can expect me not to do. I will not sexually harass my staff, and I won't tolerate it in your workplace either. I won't walk around in a half-open bathrobe, and I'll continue to take all sex crimes seriously, just like I did as a prosecutor." The ad concludes with her claiming, "Yes, I'm a woman. That's not a liability. That's an asset."[81]

Michigan voters embraced these candidates, with some claiming that they purposefully supported women candidates. One millennial woman voter, interviewed by a local journalist, claimed she felt a sense of urgency to vote for Democrats—and for women. "I actually voted for 17 women. It felt really, really good."[82]

Yet, Republican legislators' first move in the **lame duck legislative session**—which occurs after gubernatorial and state legislative races have been decided but before new public officials have been sworn in—was to introduce bills gutting the ballot initiative reforms and restricting power traditionally associated with statewide positions, with hopes that the outgoing Republican incumbent governor would sign them into law on his way out the door. One bill removes the incoming secretary of state's power to oversee campaign finance issues, handing it to a newly created bipartisan committee. Another grants the state legislature, which Republicans will still control, standing in court cases affecting the state. Such standing will allow the

(Continued)

legislature to intervene if Nessel (a Democrat) refuses to defend laws enacted by the Republican legislature in court and limits her ability to advocate for Democratic Governor Whitmer's interests in court.

The bills—criticized in the national press for undermining a legitimate democracy's respect for electoral outcomes[83] and by state press as "bombshell legislation" intended to "curb Ms. Benson's powers and circumvent Ms. Nessel"—mimic laws enacted two years ago in North Carolina and in 2018 in Wisconsin after Democrats were elected governor there. Republicans describe the bills as good government reform, claiming that they need to strengthen their authority to preserve GOP initiatives such as voter ID and to prevent more litigation challenging Donald Trump's policies.[84]

Yet, the effort to undermine women leaders resulted in pushback. The first line in a *Detroit Free Press* editorial, titled "Michigan Voters Elected Women. The GOP Is Trying to Limit Their Power," read, "Because of course they are."[85] The columnist went on to reject Republican claims that they would have tried to enact the legislation regardless of election outcomes, as well as any effort to claim that the sex and sexual orientation of Michigan's newly elected statewide executives did not trigger their "unprecedented power grab." She noted that the incoming executives are women, "and it's both impossible *and* insulting to suggest that *minor* detail just doesn't signify."[86] She concludes with a warning, pointing out that women's electoral success "is a lesson that women—and those who would seek to hobble them—should remember."[87] If the two major parties continue to be polarized, not only over feminist issues such as access to contraception and abortion or sexual harassment and discrimination in the workplace but also over the number of women who serve as elected officials in each, it is worth asking, are efforts to undermine power traditionally associated with elected positions merely polarized partisan politics, or are they efforts to achieve patriarchal equilibrium at the expense of rule of law and democracy?

THE FOURTH STEP: MONITOR PROGRESS AND BACKLASH TO ESTABLISH PRIORITIES

As these accounts make clear, promoting women's equality is an ongoing process. It is important to continue to monitor progress toward equality and to adjust priorities for individual and collective activism for the movement toward egalitarianism to continue to advance. Such efforts are important for several reasons. The first is that anytime women make substantial progress in improving their status in a given society, their success is often met with backlash that results in patriarchal equilibrium. For women, two steps forward toward progress are often followed by at least one step (and hopefully not two or more steps) back—which results in maintenance of some version of an unjust status quo. Progress requires ongoing vigilance against backlash. Second, on a more optimistic note, progress toward equality should be monitored because transforming hierarchical institutions often creates new and unanticipated opportunities to uproot additional forms of oppression. Opportunities can emerge because small, subtle shifts made at one point have accrued into substantial changes years later—a transformation described as butterfly politics in Chapter 1. Previous efforts may have resulted in access to new resources or radically different cultural norms years later. People

"In the Year 2001," The Standard, 27 April 1895

▶ **Photo 10.7** Anti-suffrage cartoon from 1895 depicting transposed gender roles.

once denied access to education and professions may now have resources and status that can be used to achieve goals that were once completely out-of-reach. Radically new ways of thinking may also reveal new egalitarian goals that can only now be conceived and labeled. Monitoring progress ensures that new resources will not be underutilized and that new goals will not go unrecognized.

For example, an 1895 cartoon, Photo 10.7, representing what a society wedding would look like in 2001 if women got the vote, illustrates how new goals and agendas emerge over time. The caption of the cartoon read,

> In The Year 2001: A brilliant society wedding took place last night at Grace Church, the contracting parties being Miss Helen Strongmind, the well-known young stock broker of Wall Street, and Mr. Percy Lightweight, the beautiful and fascinating brunette whose come-out ball was such a society event of the early season. The bridesmen were the most beautiful that have been seen at any wedding this year. They were Clarence Tulip, Chauncey Maybud, and Willie Highfly, all of whom were chums of the groom at Madame Devere's Seminary for Young Men. The bridegroom was attired in a handsome close-fitting silk dress, which showed to advantage the lines of his svelte form, and he held in his hands a magnificent bunch of lilies. The officiating minister was the Rev. Mary Walker.

At the time, imagining a world where people rejected binary gender roles was intended to ridicule the suffrage movement. Now, eliminating binary gender roles has been embraced by feminists and LGBTQIA+ activists alike.

Finally, it is essential to monitor progress because intersectionality guarantees that different types of women with different lived experiences, backgrounds, and values will notice and voice concerns about different aspects of inequality. While it is important to listen and to be allies for one another, those most affected by particular types of inequality will not only be most motivated to pursue reform, they will be the most articulate and persuasive advocates for changes that can dramatically improve their own lives. Hence all women—and not just prominent feminist scholars or well-known feminist activists —should pay attention and help to establish priorities for future activism, thus keeping efforts to promote egalitarianism relevant and vital. Accommodating diverse perspectives and agendas might appear to make efforts to promote equality fragmented. It is important to keep in mind that dismantling any form of oppression should be welcome, because all such efforts ultimately help to undermine the need for control over others that feeds patriarchy.

Despite patriarchy's ongoing influence on their lives, women have made progress both in the United States and in other countries. Hence, the following paragraphs chart the balance of progress, lack of change, and retrenchment detailed throughout previous chapters of this book, with hopes that these insights will provide readers with the overview they need to begin monitoring women's progress and developing their own priorities. Evidence of progress implies that women are closer to influencing decisions that affect their lives than in decades past, but many examples prove that even as change occurs, patriarchal dominance has survived and reemerged in new forms.

One huge step toward women's ability to lead in local, state, national, and world politics is women's growing independence in recent generations. As discussed in Chapter 4, in the United States, women now delay marriage and have fewer children, which allows them to more fully participate in the workforce and in public affairs. Women's lived experiences are dramatically different from earlier historical periods when marriage and the law of coverture guaranteed men's control over women's bodies and when women were expected to bear children and prioritize work within the home. Progress in marriage relations has occurred not only in the United States but in many other countries, including those with socially conservative cultures and legal systems. For example, a Moroccan law from 2004 disallowed underage marriage for women and stated that women no longer owed obedience to their husbands.

Women's ability to enter professions previously associated with men, including pursuing legal careers, provides women one significant pathway to politics. Recall that some believed that Ruth Bader Ginsburg, a current U.S. Supreme Court justice, had taken a man's spot at Harvard Law School when she first arrived on campus. Now it is common for women to attend law school, and, as noted in

Chapter 8, women outnumbered men in law school in the United States as of 2016. With more women "on deck" in legal careers, as well as other professions, more women will have job experiences and networks (providing the resources, engagement, and invitations described in Chapters 4 and 5) necessary to reach powerful political positions—whether as justices on the Supreme Court, as state legislators and members of Congress, or, perhaps, as president of the United States. Although women have reached the apex of power in a small handful of countries, and some would argue that enough qualified U.S. women already exist for more of these posts to be filled by them, an even greater number of highly qualified women in rising generations will increase the pool of likely candidates who can be recruited into politics. Their presence increases the likelihood that women will continue to wield more political influence in the future.

Not only are women's experiences in the home and in the professions changing, but the attitudes of women (and men) are beginning to point in the direction of equality. Chapter 3, about public opinion, revealed that more than half of the citizens in all countries around the globe, with the exception of Burkina Faso, embrace equality in principle. The Middle East and Africa have far fewer people who report the importance of gender equality, but in Europe 86% say gender equality is important, as do 91% of people in United States. Although women are more likely than men to support gender equality, a number as high as 80% to 90% of all citizens indicates that many men are on board with equality, too. Changing attitudes are also reflected in the gender stereotypes voters hold about women candidates, as discussed in Chapter 5. For example, public opinion as early as 2008 suggested voters think women have the leadership traits needed for public office. In fact, a Pew Survey that year showed that people believe women are more honest, intelligent, ambitious, compassionate, outgoing, and creative (albeit less decisive) than men as political leaders. Research shows such a decline in sex-based stereotyping that some scholars believe they rarely make a difference in determining the outcomes of electoral races.[88]

Women's descriptive representation is far from perfect worldwide or in the United States, but it is another example of progress in recent decades, as discussed in Chapter 6. At the turn of this century, 17% of Congress members were women. By 2019, that number had jumped to nearly 25%. An increase of women in public office occurred at the state level as well; women are over 28% of state legislators as of 2019—and for the first time, women have hit parity in a U.S. legislature, as women legislators comprised 50% of Nevada's state legislature after the 2018 midterm elections. This uptick is a significant change, especially given that a plateau for women's representation occurred after the 1980s. Meanwhile, although President Trump has appointed fewer women to his cabinet than did President Obama, the percentage of women serving in the U.S. cabinet has generally hovered around 25% since the early 1990s. Three decades of women in significant executive positions should not be overlooked, even though women are more than 50% of the population and deserve an even greater voice in political institutions.

Furthermore, the greater number of women of color in politics in recent years should be noted. More women of color and LGBTQIA+ women were candidates in 2018 than in any past election, and, as of 2019, 43 women of color are representatives in the House—a record number that includes Black women, Latinas, Asian/Pacific Islanders, Native Americans, and one Middle Eastern/North African woman. In local politics, women of color are even better represented, at a level comparable to white women.

Many studies show that when women are elected to politics, they create change. They fashion policy with an eye toward women, inspire other women to care about politics, and pay attention to women constituents. Although research shows women judges often choose a neutral stance instead of a decisively feminist one, women in legislative and executive positions often promote policies that address women's issues such as health care, sexual discrimination, and poverty. Women legislators are more likely to think representing women is a part of their job responsibility, and they speak more frequently about women's issues. Moreover, women's policy agencies in the executive can represent feminist interests when they consult with women's movements. These examples mean that women can change politics through institutions as well as through mobilization via social movements. Women legislators serve as surrogate representatives, thereby inspiring women even outside of their own constituencies, and when women are in top executive posts and in cabinets, symbolic representation generates positive feelings about politics and higher levels of political participation overall.

Even given the changes for women mentioned in the preceding paragraphs, more changes are needed, and women are angry about changes that have not yet transpired. Recall the anger Jennifer Weiner expressed in her op-ed about patriarchy, described earlier in this chapter. She is mad, and many women join her in this anger. What are they mad about? They are mad that sexism continues to affect their lives, and many worry that it will persist, continuing to affect future generations. They are also mad that prominent leaders in the country speak disparagingly about women, and that many men politicians care very little about women's representation or the policy issues experienced most closely by women. They are also angered by men who make or administer laws regarding their bodies and do so with very little or no input from women. This anger has been directed into action, particularly after the 2016 election. Women are running for office at higher levels and are willing to work extrainstitutionally when they cannot change politics from within institutions of power. Women's activism in the era of the Trump presidency provided the organizing skills they needed to trigger the "blue wave" and the women's wave in the 2018 midterm elections. A feeling prevails in some circles that women have laid the groundwork for even more fundamental change in which both sexes have access to political power. In a recent news interview, prominent historian Doris Kearns Goodwin, for example, speculated that Hillary Clinton may have joined a "select club of losing presidential candidates whose defeats lead to larger cultural movements"[89] by encouraging disappointed supporters to organize and run for office. Goodwin sees parallels between Clinton's loss, and the Republicans' loss in 1964, which led to Ronald Reagan's ability to revitalize conservatism in the 1980s, noting that something similar could happen for women. "It's hard to see when you're in the middle of it," she said. "But it feels like something's happening, a fervor, an excitement, an optimism."[90]

It is irresponsible, however, to close this book with such sanguine predictions. Women are still targets for sex-based violence and femicide worldwide, and traditional gender roles have uncanny staying power. Even in the midst of #MeToo, women's stories of harassment and abuse are doubted, and abusive men go unchecked. The fact that #MeToo was an international phenomenon shows that sexual abuse is a worldwide phenomenon affecting many women. In fact, Chapter 1 relays the World Health Organization statistic that 1 in 3 women will experience physical or sexual violence during her lifetime. Although women are no longer the property of men, as they once were, violence against women remains a crucial concern and will remain one as long as a significant number of men embrace patriarchal values that justify using violence to establish emotional and physical control over women.

Another disturbing reality counters women's ability to give voice to women's concerns within political institutions. Simply put, women's voices are often ignored or judged harshly. It is not a stretch to say that legislative institutions are still hostile to women; women legislators have to work longer and harder than their men counterparts to enact policy. Men continue to interrupt and speak over and silence women even in these formal deliberative settings, and states invest fewer resources to implement legislation sponsored by women. Women in politics at times are also subjected to violence that comes in the form of rape, economic threats, and even assassination. Without a doubt, violence against women politicians aims to silence women's voices in politics. Furthermore, women's voices often are ignored when women participate in social movements. Women's groups are less likely than other social groups to be invited to the proverbial table of policy negotiations with government leaders. And, when women assertively speak up and use more eye-raising or strident tactics to draw attention to desired change, they are faced with critiques centered on social constructions of appropriate feminine behavior. Yet, if women have behaved "improperly," ambivalent sexism justifies labeling them as pushy and overzealous and justifies dismissing them and their concerns as "unnatural." Additionally, the fear of being subjected to such social sanction leads some women to avoid speaking up in deliberative contexts. In an ironic cycle, women are dismissed when they speak but also fail to speak because they fear being dismissed. Unfortunately, it is still difficult to listen to and respond to women's voices, denying them the respect and consideration they deserve.

While ongoing social sanction experienced by women in the public sphere contradicts the attitudinal changes in the direction of equality documented above, attitudes often do not change in a consistently progressive direction. As discussed in Chapter 3, some young people in the United States hold traditional views of women or are ambivalent about men's and women's expected roles, and many millennial men revert to traditional views once they move into adulthood, especially after becoming fathers. This trend emerged in the 1990s, when scholars claimed the United States was experiencing a "stalled gender revolution."[91] In this book, Chapter 4 questions how women can continue to advance in public life if they are expected to and continue to perform more of the domestic chores required to sustain their homes and families. Despite progress on this front, advances have come at a glacially slow pace. As late as 2016, more people in the United States reported support for equality in the workplace than equality at home.[92]

Connected to these "stalled" gender attitudes is a U.S. policy context that does little to support work-life balance. On the one hand, women continue to be essentialized as mothers in politics; however, the political system in the United States has done very little to help them balance motherhood with careers or political engagement. Although women can often gain a political advantage by framing their political interests in terms of motherhood, there are dangers to associating women's concerns with an ability to bear children (see Box 10.6 that addresses fetal personhood legislation in order to address such concerns). This view not only distracts from women's political agency on issues unrelated to children but also delegitimizes the policy agendas of women who are not mothers.

BOX 10.6: POLICY FEATURE

Personhood Legislation and Women's Rights

The tension between women as mothers and women as autonomous individuals with other interests is perhaps made most stark by personhood legislation, which seeks to establish that a fetus is a person due all individual constitutional and legal rights from the point of conception. While moderate policymakers may be interested in balancing women's rights with fetal rights, the most extreme activists, who fully embrace fetal personhood, are sometimes willing to prioritize fetal rights even over a woman's life. In 1984, for example, conservative activist Paul Weyrich, the founding president of the Heritage Foundation, explained his position: "I believe that if you have to choose between new life and existing life, you should choose new life. The person who has had an opportunity to live at least has been given that gift by God and should make way for new life on earth."[93]

The push for fetal personhood first emerged as a reaction to the Supreme Court's decision in *Roe v. Wade* (1973). During oral arguments, justices asked Roe's lawyer what would happen if a fetus was deemed a person under the Constitution. She replied, "I would have a very difficult case."[94] While drafting the majority opinion, Justice Harry Blackmun noted that the Supreme Court found no basis for granting a fetus this status, and wrote, "If this suggestion of personhood is established, [Roe's] case, of course, collapses, for the fetus' [sic] right to life would then be guaranteed specifically by the [14th] Amendment."

A week later, a Maryland member of Congress proposed a Human Life Amendment—the first of more than 330 versions proposed or introduced over the next four decades. While unsuccessful, either at promoting a constitutional personhood amendment or federal legislation to accomplish the same ends (such as the 2013 Life at Conception Act sponsored by Senator Rand Paul, R-KY), advocates of fetal personhood were more successful at embedding this legal concept into state feticide laws. These laws, often enacted after a highly publicized tragic incident results in a lost pregnancy and public outcry, typically recognize an act that negligently or purposefully causes the loss of a pregnancy as manslaughter or murder. While initially targeting perpetrators who harm pregnant women, the laws often purposefully include language that establishes fetal personhood rights and that later allows states to charge women whose behavior is believed to have harmed their own fetuses with a crime. In 2004, Congress passed the Unborn Victims of Violence Act, the first federal law making it a crime to harm or kill a fetus during an act of violence against the mother. By 2018, 29 states had laws defining ending any state of pregnancy from the point of fertilization as murder, except in the case of a legal abortion. Meanwhile, nine states recognized feticide only after a fetus is viable and could survive outside of the womb.[95,96]

Women's rights advocates, including the staff of the nonprofit National Advocates for Pregnant Women, worry that these laws allow states to prioritize the interests of a fetus at the expense of a mother's autonomy. Indeed, such laws have been used to charge women across the United States with a variety of crimes, including murder, manslaughter, neglect, criminal recklessness, and chemical endangerment. Behaviors that triggered these charges include taking legal and illegal drugs, attempting suicide, failing to wear a seatbelt, delivering a baby at home, refusing a doctor's recommendation to have a Caesarean section (or C-section), and behaving in other ways police and prosecutors perceived as dangerous during pregnancy.[97] For example, a New York woman was convicted of manslaughter because she failed to wear her seat belt and caused a car accident. As a result, her infant daughter was born one month early via a C-section and died five days later. The manslaughter conviction was overturned three years later on appeal.[98] Meanwhile, a New Jersey woman's healthy newborn was placed in foster care because she was accused of child endangerment after refusing to have the C-section recommended by her doctor.[99]

The concept of fetal personhood has also affected pregnant women's ability to make end-of-life decisions in 31 states, even if they have a living will and do not want to be placed on life support. Twelve states prohibit doctors

(Continued)

(Continued)

from removing women from life support even in the earliest stages of pregnancy, while 19 do so after a fetus is viable. These laws garnered nationwide attention in 2014, when the family of a brain-dead Texas woman, Marlise Munoz who was 14 weeks pregnant, fought to honor her wishes by having her removed from life support. Hospital officials refused because Texas updated its definition of a human being to include an "unborn child at every stage of gestation" in 2013, and they did not want to be charged with homicide for causing the death of a fetus. After a two-month delay, during which time Munoz's fetus was deemed unviable, a judge approved her removal from life support. Legislation titled Marlise's Law, granting pregnant women more control over such decisions, is expected to be considered by the Texas State Legislature in 2019.[100]

Pregnant women across the country have also been arrested for using illegal drugs, and in more than half of those cases, they risk losing custody if they or their newborns test positive for controlled substances. Tennessee enacted legislation to specifically criminalize pregnant women's use of controlled substances in 2014.[101] In most other states, law enforcement and prosecutors apply existing laws to pregnant mothers with hopes that juries and appeals courts will agree with their interpretation and uphold convictions. In Alabama, for example, the state's highest court upheld convictions of chemical endangerment against addicted pregnant women, even though the law was initially intended to protect children from being exposed to fumes and chemicals in illegal in-home meth labs.[102,103] In 2018, however, Pennsylvania's Supreme Court determined that women who use illegal drugs while pregnant cannot be convicted of child abuse, because the state law refers specifically to children and does not use the terms *unborn children* or *fetuses*.[104]

Infertile women who have used in vitro fertilization (IVF) to have children are leery of personhood legislation. Most IVF procedures involve fertilizing multiple eggs, even though most will never result in viable pregnancies. Hence, the procedure would likely be illegal if fetal personhood were fully established.[105]

Finally, women's rights advocates further question what other types of behavior could be deemed negligent if fetal personhood were fully embraced. They ask, "What if a judge rules, or a police officer believes, she [a pregnant woman] is risking the life of a fetus by, say, climbing a mountain, or riding a roller coaster, or undertaking a humanitarian mission in a war zone? Who will decide whether a pregnant woman diagnosed with cancer may undergo chemotherapy?"[106] People with different lived experiences, religious faiths, and value systems will likely continue to answer these questions differently, but the concept of fetal rights and personhood legislation intended to establish those rights helps to highlight that essentializing women as mothers overlooks inherent tensions between women as mothers and women as autonomous individuals.

Finally, this text notes the disappointing fact that women have failed to reach the pinnacle of power—or the highest political executive positions—in most countries of the world, including the United States. As Chapter 7 notes, women are historically absent from not only top executive positions but also from any institutional position associated with great power. Women struggle to occupy these positions. They are more likely to be prime ministers than presidents, for example, because most presidencies are imbued with greater power; women are also less likely to be mayors of large cities or to be appointed to the "inner cabinet" that works most closely with the president.

So, where does the United States stand comparatively in terms of progress and lack of progress? The United States is similar to other countries in terms of women's activism; it is neither the foremost beacon of equality nor a place where society and politics is entirely stacked against women. Like their counterparts in the rest of the world, women in the United States face discrimination and have sufficient reasons to participate in the #MeToo movement. When it comes to representation, the United States is in the middle of the pack. In addition, the United States does not have gender quotas or a majoritarian electoral system that would produce parity or anything close to it. Unlike other countries, the United States has not had a woman president, nor has any president chosen to appoint a parity cabinet. On the other hand, women in the United States do not face jail time—or worse, physical punishment from the state—as a means of suppressing their collective action, social movements, and political participation. Yet, such consequences are regularly meted out in other countries like Saudi Arabia. Finally, women's movements in the United States have historically been plagued by a lack of inclusivity—typically excluding agendas prioritized by working-class women, lesbians, trans women, women of color, women with disabilities, and so on—as have women's movements across the globe. Intersectional feminism deserves more attention everywhere.

THE FIFTH STEP: DECIDE WHAT TO DO AND ACT

At the same time, awareness of the need to make progress for all women is growing, as evidenced by another t-shirt that has become popular over the past two years. It reads *The Future Is Intersectional.* This sentiment is another way of restating the reminder at the end of Chapter 1, that the title of the book, which asks the question *Why Don't Women Rule the World?*, is a play on words. Women have been denied positions of authority as "rulers" in most civilizations around the world. Yet, feminists do not simply want women to displace men as rulers in the hierarchical governing structures that spread across the globe 7,000 years ago. Rather, they want to replace hierarchy, along with the oppression and subordination that inevitably accompany it, with egalitarianism. They reject the notion that anyone should have inherent authority to rule over others. In order to do so, they must uproot the caste systems based on demographic traits—sex, orientation, class, race, and ethnicity—that have provided patriarchy with sustaining resources for thousands of years.

For those who focus on all the substantial obstacles that must be overcome, the task of creating a more just, egalitarian world can feel overwhelming. But this last t-shirt slogan is an important reminder that the future can indeed be intersectional and egalitarian, if people remember that they are the ones who collectively construct the social world around them, through their compliance with cultural norms that constrain their behavior and through their participation in the institutions that socialize and govern them. Hence if enough people collectively take steps to make our world intersectional and egalitarian—by altering cultural norms and transforming institutions—a sea change in the way the world is organized will inevitably happen. Allan G. Johnson (2014) expresses this same conviction when he argues,

> The transformation of patriarchy has been unfolding ever since it emerged 7,000 years ago, and it is still going on. We cannot know what will replace it, but we can be confident that patriarchy will go, that it is going at every moment. It is only a matter of how quickly, by what means, at what cost, and toward what alternatives, and whether each of us will do our part to make it happen sooner rather than later and with less rather than more destruction and suffering in the process.[107]

As women continue to make progress, backlash is inevitable. Yet, when backlash occurs after periods of substantial progress, women and their allies can use newfound access to resources and altered cultural norms to resist. In Brazil, for example, women who became politically engaged in order to oppose far-right President Bolsonaro's election (see Box 10.4) immediately shifted their attention to limiting his administration's influence after he won. A social media campaign encouraged women to change their social media profiles to a simple black square with the word *luto*, which conveys two meanings in Portuguese. One meaning is "mourning," while the other is "I fight." As Ludmilla Teixeira, the 36-year-old advertising professional who founded the 3.8 million member Facebook group Women Against Bolsonaro simply put it, "We will fight back." One columnist for a prominent Brazilian newspaper explained that efforts to promote women's rights as universal human rights "will influence Brazil far beyond these elections."[108] Activists have been subject to backlash from Bolsonaro supporters. Images of their women's march activists were photoshopped and altered to create the impression that they were violent, vulgar, and sacrilegious, while some prominent spokeswomen and celebrity supporters received death threats.

Although the technology has changed, the nature of misogynist attacks on women in the public sphere has not. Caricatures of suffragettes, shown in Photos 10.9, 10.10, and 10.11, also depicted feminist activists as unattractive, dim-witted, promiscuous, angry, and violent.

Despite the pushback, Brazilian women activists plan to use the skills they gained launching social media sites and coordinating large-scale street protests during the election to coordinate an array of activities intended to undermine the Bolsonaro administration's legislative agenda. As Teixeira relayed in a recent newspaper interview, "Women realized they are stronger together. . . . Bolsonaro won, but he won't govern without resistance."[109]

▸ **Photos 10.8–10.11** Anti-suffragette postcards circulated in the early 1900s.

Similarly, American women and their allies can rely on resources (including access to education, careers, economic independence, and altered cultural norms) that were unavailable to previous generations as they develop their own contemporary priorities and agendas for undermining patriarchy's legacy in America and across the globe. The array of tactics and strategies for doing so are also myriad. More specifically, these include speaking up when outcomes are unfair and avoiding unthinkingly performing traditional gender roles in personal and professional relationships out of habit or fear of social sanction. Purposefully making alternative everyday and life choices is also important, as simply choosing not to participate in oppressive practices sets an example and normalizes egalitarian alternatives, creating a well-trod path for succeeding generations to follow. This suggestion can be extended to openly supporting others who step off the path of least resistance by refusing to police binary gender roles.[110] Additional steps extend to extrainstitutional civic and political action—which includes coordinated collective action intended to influence the political system. Examples range from participating in phone-banking and letter-writing campaigns, get-out-the-vote drives, product boycotts and "buycotts," rallies, disruptive politics, protests, and social movement activism. As this text makes clear, U.S. women have achieved enough progress in the past several decades that they can and should successfully seek appointed and elected offices. By doing so, they can reform institutions from within and can address issues that affect their lives by developing, interpreting, and implementing policies as legislative, judicial, and executive officials. Despite the strong likelihood that such efforts will still result in social sanction in their personal lives and in more organized backlash in their public lives, the authors hope that women reading this text will prepare for this potential and will use the full array of tactics and strategies now available to them. In particular, they hope that many women readers will throw their hats in the proverbial ring and decide to run for elected office—not so that women can take their turn at ruling the world and oppressing others but so that they can speed the ongoing transition from patriarchy's hierarchical order to a more just and egalitarian world.

REVIEW QUESTIONS

1. Is it still easier to recognize patriarchy in other countries and cultures than in your own? Why, or why not?

2. Do you agree that it is difficult to hear women when they are angry? What steps can you undertake to be a better listener?

3. Would U.S. women have been more likely to embrace women's only communities like those in Kenya or El Salvador if they had not gained access to contraception? Would they be even more likely to delay or avoid marriage, as Susan B. Anthony predicted in her essay *On the Homes of Single Women*?

4. Susan M. Okin argues that just families are the cornerstone of a just society. Explain why, as well as whether you agree or disagree with her position.

5. Describe how remaining issues such as the motherhood penalty and pregnancy discrimination affect women's experiences in the workplace.

6. Explain the three reasons why women, especially Democratic women, were angry after the 2016 presidential election. Do any of these reasons resonate with you? Why. or why not? If not, what issues affecting women's equality would you prioritize?

7. How does patriarchal equilibrium benefit those seeking to reestablish authoritarian leadership in formerly autocratic countries? How does it look different in democratic regimes?

8. Explain three reasons why it is important to continue to monitor women's progress toward equality, as well as any backlash against their success. What priorities do you think contemporary activists should address? Can you recognize and label any new issues that have emerged as a result of past successes?

9. How should knowing about the social construction of reality help to motivate those who want to continue to reform patriarchy and promote a more egalitarian society?

10. The conclusion outlines a number of steps that can be taken in efforts to make a difference. Which of these strategies and tactics do you think are most effective? Why?

AMBITION ACTIVITY

Dismantling Systems of Oppression by Building Alliances and Taking Action: The very first ambition activity in Chapter 1 asked you to make a list of all the things you actually could imagine doing to reduce the influence of a given system of oppression. Consider how these actions help to overcome patriarchy, the subordination of women, and other kinds of oppression. Review the prompts for completing this exercise.

1. **By yourself or with a group, update your list**: Review your list, making any changes required to reflect your current commitment to activism and the types of issues you currently prioritize.

2. **Discuss: Has your list evolved throughout the semester?** If so, how has it changed? If not, why has it remained the same? Did you add run for office to your list? Why, or why not?

KEY WORDS

Choice feminism 457

Lame duck legislative session 467

Publica 460

Publius 460

REFERENCES

1. Johnson, A. G. (2014). *The gender knot: Unraveling our patriarchal legacy*, 3rd ed. Philadelphia, PA: Temple University Press.

2. Ibid.

3. Ibid.

4. Kann, M. (1999). *The gendering of American politics: Founding mothers, founding fathers, and political patriarchy*. Westport, CT: Praeger.

5. Johnson, A. G. (2014). *The gender knot: Unraveling our patriarchal legacy*, 3rd ed.

6. Traister, R. (2018). *Good and mad, the revolutionary power of women's anger*. New York, NY: Simon and Schuster.

7. Johnson, A. G. (2014). *The gender knot: Unraveling our patriarchal legacy*, 3rd ed.

8. Ibid.

9. Traister, R. (2018). *Good and mad, the revolutionary power of women's anger.*

10. Johnson, A. G. (2014). *The gender knot: Unraveling our patriarchal legacy*, 3rd ed.

11. Pew Research Center. (2018). Wide gender gap, growing educational divide in voters' party identification. Retrieved from http://www.people-press .org/2018/03/20/1-trends-in-party-affiliation-among-demographic-groups.

12. Saad, L. (2018). Both parties' voters are keyed up for midterm elections. *Gallup*. Retrieved from https://news.gallup.com/poll/243173/parties-voters-keyed-midterm-elections.aspx.

13. Greenberg, S. (2018). Trump is beginning to lose his grip. *The New York Times*. Retrieved from https://www.nytimes.com/2018/11/17/opinion/sunday/trump-is-beginning-to-lose-his-grip.html?module=inline.

14. Lawless, J. L., & Fox, R. L. (2017). *The Trump effect*. Washington, DC: American University. Retrieved from https://www.american.edu/spa/wpi/upload/The-Trump-Effect.pdf.

15. Ibid.

16. Bindel, J. (2015). The village where men are banned. *The Guardian*. Retrieved from https://www.theguardian.com/global-development/2015/aug/16/village-where-men-are-banned-womens-rights-kenya.

17. Ibid.

18. Ibid.

19. Townsend, M. (2018). Women deported by Trump face deadly welcome from street gangs in El Salvador. *The Guardian*. Retrieved from https://www .theguardian.com/global-development/2018/jan/13/el-salvador-women-deported-by-trump-face-deadly-welcome-street-gangs.

20. Ibid.

21. Bolanos, C. (2016). The Salvadoran community where women take the lead. *News Deeply*. Retrieved from https://www.newsdeeply.com/womenandgirls/ articles/2016/12/06/salvadoran-community-women-take-lead.

22. Ibid.

23. Black, M. C., Basile, K. C., Breiding, M. J., Smith, S. G., Walters, M. L., Merrick, M. J., Chen, J., & Stevens, M. (2011). *The National Intimate Partner and Sexual Violence Survey: 2010 summary report*. National Center for Injury Prevention and Control: Division of Violence Prevention. Retrieved from http://www.cdc.gov/ violenceprevention/pdf/nisvs_report2010-a.pdf.

24. Fox, J. A., & Fridel, E. E. (2017). Gender differences in patterns and trends in U.S. homicide, 1976–2015. *Violence and Gender 4*(2).

25. Coontz, S., & Henderson, P. (1986). *Women's work, men's property: The origins of gender and class*. Thetford, Norfolk: Thetford Press.

26. Okin, S. M. (1987). *Gender, justice, and the family*. Princeton, NJ: Princeton University Press.

27. Beinart, P. (2018). The new authoritarians are waging war on women. *The Atlantic*. Retrieved from https://www.theatlantic.com/magazine/archive/2019/01/authoritarian-sexism-trump-duterte/576382/.

28. Miller, C. C. (2014). The motherhood penalty vs. the fatherhood bonus. *The New York Times*. Retrieved from https://www.nytimes.com/2014/09/07/upshot/a-child-helps-your-career-if-youre-a-man.html.

29. Correll, S., Benard, S., & Paik, I. (2007). Getting a job: Is there a motherhood penalty? *American Journal of Sociology, 112*(5), 1297–1338. Retrieved from https://www.jstor.org/stable/pdf/10.1086/511799.pdf?refreqid=excelsior:8de432a6895fa02cd5ebce297ceb3faa

30. Ibid.

31. Budig, M. (2014). The fatherhood bonus and the motherhood penalty: Parenthood and the gender gap in pay. *Third Way*. Retrieved from https://www.thirdway.org/report/the-fatherhood-bonus-and-the-motherhood-penalty-parenthood-and-the-gender-gap-in-pay.

32. Miller, C. C. (2014). The motherhood penalty vs. the fatherhood bonus.

33. *General Electric Company v. Gilbert*, 429 U.S. 125 (1976)

34. *Young v. United Parcel Service*, 575 U.S. ___ (2015)

35. Silver-Greenberg, J., & Kitroeff, N. (2018). Miscarrying at work: The physical toll of pregnancy discrimination. *The New York Times*. Retrieved from https://www.nytimes.com/interactive/2018/10/21/business/pregnancy-discrimination-miscarriages.html.

36. Ibid.

37. Ibid.

38. Ibid.

39. Kitroeff, N., & Silver-Greenberg. J. (2018). Planned Parenthood is accused of mistreating pregnant employees. *The New York Times*. Retrieved from https://www.nytimes.com/2018/12/20/business/planned-parenthood-pregnant-employee-discrimination-women.html.

40. Alonso-Zaldlvar, R., & Crary, D. (2018). How the Trump administration is remaking federal policy on women's reproductive health. *PBS*. Retrieved from https://www.pbs.org/newshour/politics/how-the-trump-administration-is-remaking-federal-policy-on-womens-reproductive-health.

41. Ibid.

42. Kann, M. E. (1999). *The gendering of American politics: Founding mothers, founding fathers, and political patriarchy*.

43. Chozick, A. (2018). Hillary Clinton ignited a feminist movement by losing. *The New York Times*. Retrieved from https://www.nytimes.com/2018/01/13/sunday-review/hillary-clinton-feminist-movement.html.

44. Weiner, J. (2018). The patriarchy will always have its revenge. *The New York Times*. Retrieved from https://www.nytimes.com/2018/09/22/opinion/sunday/brett-kavanaugh-anger-women-metoo.html.

45. Ibid.

46. Ibid.

47. Nelson, L. (2016). Is Hillary Clinton really the most qualified candidate ever? An investigation. *Vox*. Retrieved from https://www.vox.com/2016/8/1/12316646/hillary-clinton-qualified.

48. Ibid.

49. West, L. (2017). Brave enough to be angry. *The New York Times*. Retrieved from https://www.nytimes.com/2017/11/08/opinion/anger-women-weinstein-assault.html.

50. Chozick, A. (2018). Hillary Clinton ignited a feminist movement by losing.

51. Chozick, A. (2018). They were never going to let me be president. *The New York Times*. Retrieved from https://www.nytimes.com/2018/04/20/sunday-review/hillary-clinton-chasing-hillary.html.

52. Ibid.

53. Sandberg, S. (2013). *Lean in: Women, work, and the will to lead*. New York, NY: Alfred A. Knopf.

54. Weaver, H. (2018). Michelle Obama got especially comfortable during her book-tour stop in Brooklyn. *Vanity Fair*. Retrieved from https://www.vanityfair.com/style/2018/12/michelle-obama-book-tour-at-barclays-center.

55. Levanon, A., England, P., & Allison, P. (2009). Occupational feminization and pay. Assessing casual dynamics using 1950–2000 U.S. Census data. *Social Forces, 88*(2), 865–891. Retrieved from https://academic.oup.com/sf/article-abstract/88/2/865/2235342.

56. Niemi, N. (2018). Why does the public distrust higher ed? Too many women. *The Chronicle of Higher Education*. Retrieved from https://www.chronicle.com/article/Why-Does-the-Public-Distrust/243114.

57. Ibid.

58. Pateman, C. (1988). *The sexual contract.* Stanford, CT: Stanford University Press.

59. Niemi, N. (2018). Why does the public distrust higher ed? Too many women. *The Chronicle of Higher Education.*

60. Pateman, C. (1988). *The sexual contract.*

61. Filmer, R. (1685). *Patriarcha, or, the natural power of kings.* London, UK: Printed for R. Chiswel, W. Hensman, M. Gilliflower, and G. Wells.

62. Beinart, P. (2018). The new authoritarians are waging war on women.

63. Ibid.

64. Ibid.

65. Ibid.

66. Ibid.

67. Ibid.

68. Ibid.

69. Redden, E. (2018). Global attack on gender studies. *Inside Higher Ed*. Retrieved from https://www.insidehighered.com/news/2018/12/05/gender-studies-scholars-say-field-coming-under-attack-many-countries-around-globe.

70. Kuhar, R., & Paternotte, D. (2017). *Anti-gender campaigns in Europe: Mobilizing against equality.* Lanham, MD: Rowman and Littlefield International.

71. Redden, E. (2018). Global attack on gender studies.

72. Ibid.

73. Ibid.

74. Ibid.

75. Ibid.

76. Ibid.

77. Oosting, J. (2013). Whitmer blasts "rape insurance" bill: "It's one of the most misogynistic proposals I have ever seen." *MLive*. Retrieved from https://www.mlive.com/politics/index.ssf/2013/12/whitmer_blasts_rape_insurance.html.

78. Murray, D. (2012). Michigan Rep. Lisa Lyons calls Sen. Gretchen Whitmer "a liar" and Rep. Lisa Brown's actions "disgraceful" in growing melee. *MLive*. Retrieved from https://www.mlive.com/politics/index.ssf/2012/06/michigan_rep_lisa_lyons_calls.html.

79. Gray, K. (2018). Nessel's quest for AG's office began on steps of U.S. Supreme Court. *Detroit Free Press*. Retrieved from https://www.freep.com/story/news/politics/2018/10/19/dana-nessels-michigan-attorney-general/1678321002.

80. Singer, J. (2017). "I Won't Show You My Penis"—Jewish candidate's campaign ad goes viral. *Forward*. Retrieved from https://forward.com/schmooze/388734/i-wont-show-you-my-penis-jewish-candidates-campaign-ad-goes-viral.

81. Ibid.

82. Ibid.

83. Dionne, E. J., Jr. (2018). Are Republicans abandoning democracy? *The Washington Post*. Retrieved from https://www.washingtonpost.com/opinions/are-republicans-abandoning-democracy/2018/12/09/8ad0b278-fa62-11e8-8c9a-860ce2a8148f_story.html?utm_term=.07128bdafe9a.

84. Kaffer, N. (2018). Michigan voters elected women. The GOP is trying to limit their power. *Detroit Free Press*. Retrieved from https://www.freep.com/story/opinion/columnists/nancy-kaffer/2018/11/30/michigan-women-gop-election/2161043002.

85. Ibid.

86. Ibid.; emphasis in original.

87. Ibid.

88. Dolan, K. (2014). Gender stereotypes, candidate evaluations, and voting for women candidates: What really matters? *Political Research Quarterly, 67*(1), 96–107.

89. Chozick, A. (2018). Hillary Clinton ignited a feminist movement by losing.

90. Ibid.

91. Scarborough, W., Sin, R., & Risman, B. (2018). Attitudes and the stalled gender revolution: Egalitarianism, traditionalism, and ambivalence from 1977 through 2016. *Gender and Sociology*.

92. Ibid.

93. Editorial Board. (2018). Can a corpse give birth? The *New York Times*. Retrieved from https://www.nytimes.com/interactive/2018/12/28/opinion/pregnancy-exclusion-law.html.

94. Roe v. Wade 1971 Oral Argument. (1971). *C-Span*. Retrieved from https://www.c-span.org/video/?59719-1/roe-v-wade-1971-oral-argument.

95. Martin, N. (2014). This Alabama judge has figured out how to dismantle *Roe v. Wade*: His writings fuel the biggest threat to abortion rights in a generation. *Pro Publica*. Retrieved from https://www.propublica.org/article/this-alabama-judge-has-figured-out-how-to-dismantle-roe-v-wade.

96. Editorial Board. (2018). The feticide playbook, explained. *The New York Times*. Retrieved from https://www.nytimes.com/interactive/2018/12/28/opinion/abortion-murder-charge.html.

97. Editorial Board. (2018). The future of personhood nation. *The New York Times*. Retrieved from https://www.nytimes.com/interactive/2018/12/28/opinion/abortion-law-pro-life.html.

98. Ibid.

99. Editorial Board. (2018). Can a corpse give birth?

100. Ibid.

101. The personhood movement: Where it came from and where it stands today. (n.d.). *Pro Publica*. Retrieved from https://www.propublica.org/article/the-personhood-movement-timeline.

102. *Ex Parte Kimbrough*, 1110219 (2013).

103. *Ex Parte Ankrom*, 1110176 (2013).

104. Pa. court rules pregnant women's illegal drug use isn't child abuse. (2018). *CBS Pittsburgh*. Retrieved from https://pittsburgh.cbslocal.com/2018/12/29/pregnant-women-illegal-drug-use-child-abuse.

105. Editorial Board. (2018). The future of personhood nation.

106. Ibid.

107. Johnson, A. G. (2014). *The gender knot: Unraveling our patriarchal legacy, 3rd ed.*

108. Carranca, A. (2018). The women-led opposition to Brazil's far-right leader. *The Atlantic*. Retrieved from https://www.theatlantic.com/international/archive/2018/11/brazil-women-bolsonaro-haddad-election/574792.

109. Ibid.

110. Johnson, A. G. (2014). *The gender knot: Unraveling our patriarchal legacy, 3rd ed.*

APPENDICES

APPENDIX 1: CONDUCTING INTERVIEWS

Students are often surprised by what it takes to conduct an interview for a research project. Not only do you have to set up the time and place of the interview, but you have to prepare questions and anticipate follow-up questions to use when the interviewee doesn't answer your initial ones as you expected. Because about 90% of all social science investigations rely on interview data, students in social science fields need to know how to conduct one.[1] By doing an interview for an ambition activity you might discover interesting gender dynamics at play in politics, and you'll also develop interview skills that could assist you in other educational or employment endeavors.

Roulston, deMarrais, and Lewis (2003) trained graduate students to do social science interviews, and they found that students were surprised by the process of interviewing.[2] Here are some of the things that surprise students in interviews and some helpful suggestions for how to conduct one.

What might surprise you?

- **Actions and emotions of the interviewee:** Sometimes the interviewees' actions will distract you as you interview them. They might take an outside phone call as you sit there, loudly eat a snack, or act impatient. It also might be the case that they show emotions, which requires a careful response from you. For instance, when discussing gender, race, and class identities, interviewees might talk about experiences of discrimination, and, these experiences might convey deep emotions.

- **Your own feelings, expectations, and identity:** You might be nervous to interview someone in a position of power relative to you, or you might not know how to respond to references about race or gender, if you are not of the same race or gender as the interviewee. Or, you might share an identity with the interviewees and expect them to feel the same way as you about certain issues. You might be surprised or even disappointed if the interviewee is less interested in the advocacy issues you care most about.

- **How many things you need to pay attention to while still being a good listener**: It's obvious that you need to listen to the interviewee's verbal responses and write them down, but there are more things going on in an interview that require your attention. You should pay attention to the time, as you probably only made the appointment for 30 minutes to an hour. It's easy to lose track of time, veer away from the prepared questions, and never get back to some of them! You should also pay attention to facial expressions and body movements; these convey meaning as well as tell you the amount of time the interviewee wants to dedicate to the interview. While you are listening, you will also be trying to build rapport with the interviewee by physically demonstrating your interest in what is being said. You need to maintain eye contact and perhaps nod to show understanding.

- **How often you'll want to talk—but don't!**: Roulston et al. (2003) suggest students aim for "an 80/20 or 90/10 ratio in their interviews (that is, 80% to 90% respondent/10% to 20% researcher talk)."[3] You'll be tempted to constantly clarify what you are saying, and, if nervous, you might repeat yourself. Try not to! You might be frustrated when the conversation gets off track, and you'll want to overpolice it, but you need to allow the interviewees to answer questions as they see fit.

Here are some recommendations:

- **Clearly state your purpose and intentions:** If you tell the interviewees why you are conducting the interview, how you will be using the information from it, how many questions you will ask, and that you will be taking notes, they won't need clarifications about these matters throughout the interview, which means you can talk less.

- **Prepare a few, simple and open-ended questions and brainstorm follow-up questions:** Interviewees don't have time for 50 questions! But, they will make time for a few questions and typically will allow you to insert follow-up questions. Type about 3 questions to share with the interviewee beforehand, and brainstorm questions you might want to say as follow-ups. Phrase open-ended questions; never, ask yes-or-no questions because once an interviewee answers "yes" or "no," the conversation tends to stop abruptly. Open-ended questions "ask respondents to respond to a question in their own terms," and typically use phrases such as "to what extent," "why do you believe/not believe," and "what do you think about."[4]

- **Use active listening skills:** Don't interrupt the interviewee, and maintain eye contact. Eliminate distractions by turning off your cell phone. Get enough sleep to prepare yourself to "be on."

- **Practice self-reflection before and after:** Beforehand, ask how your identity or the identity of the interviewee might elicit emotions or distractions that could hinder or facilitate the interview. Take notes about the interview immediately afterward. Jot down what you didn't have time to write during the interview. Recall the interviewee's facial expressions, moments of laughter or seriousness, or your own emotions. All of these will help you analyze the significance of your interview data.

APPENDIX 2: COMPARISON

How do we compare in political science? Researchers often say they want to compare "apples to apples" and not "apples to oranges." This means that they want to compare cases (countries, political parties, politicians, etc.) that are somewhat similar rather than entirely different.

Why? If we compare two instances that are very different it is difficult to understand all the differences at once, which ones are most significant, and why they might be significant. On the other hand, if we compare two "apples" that are relatively similar we can more easily understand the fewer differences between them and examine those differences more closely. In this way, we can isolate the most theoretically interesting differences, which in the case of our ambition activities might be, for example, the gender, race, age, or political party of a member of Congress (MOC) and how that influences a MOC's personal or career trajectory. Also, by comparing similar cases, we can rule out the significance of factors that are the same between cases (e.g., if we compare two Republican women, and their experiences are different, we cannot attribute the differences to simply being a Republican). The basic point here is to know who or what you are comparing in political science and why.

1. Briggs, C. (1986). *Learning how to ask: A sociolinguistic appraisal of the role of the interview in social science research*. Cambridge, UK: Cambridge University Press.

2. Roulston, K., deMarrais, K., & Lewis, J. B. (2003). Learning to interview in the social sciences. *Qualitative Inquiry, 9*(4), 643–668.

3. Ibid, 651.

4. Harvard University Program on Survey Research. (2007). Tip sheet on question wording. Retrieved from https://psr.iq.harvard.edu/files/psr/files/PSRQuestionnaireTipSheet_0.pdf.

INDEX

women's credentials, 461–463
women's voice, 450–452
Chao, Elaine, 316t
Cherokee Indian Removal Act, 54
Child care responsibilities:
    delayed childbirth, 166–167
    labor force participation, 64
    political ambition impact, 164–167
Chile:
    cabinet positions, 317
    executive representation, 311–312, 333
China:
    cultural backlash, 176–177
    political candidacy, 209
Chinchilla, Laura, 311t, 333
Chisholm, Shirley, 308t
Choice feminism, 457–458
Chowdhury, Renuka, 405
Christianity, 95
Cisgender women, 1–2
City council representation, 248–249
Civil law system, 362–364, 378–379
Civil Rights Act (1964), 62
Clinton, Bill, 314, 322
Clinton, Hillary:
    double bind, 220–221
    executive representation, 301, 302–303t,
        304–305, 308t
    family politics, 314
    framing stereotypes, 208, 301, 302–303t,
        304–305
    Hillary Doctrine, 319–320
    law school attendance, 153
    linked-fate ideology, 96
    media coverage, 208, 210, 225
    nascent political ambition, 156
    political qualifications, 461–462
    polling data (2016), 91
    Secretary of State, 304, 315t, 319–320
    security feminism, 318, 319
Closed list system, 268, 269, 270–272t
Code Pink, 408
Colian, Ruth, 419
Collins, Susan, 123, 246, 259, 261
Collum, Kristin, 218
Colombia, political ambition, 147t
Colonial era, 50, 52–53
Colorado:
    executive representation, 325
    legislative representation, 252–253
    LGBTQIA+ community, 375
    voting rights, 58

Commentaries on the Laws of England
    (Blackstone), 52–53
Common law (England), 50, 53
Common law system (judiciary), 362–364,
    378–379
Communal female ideology, 167, 169, 170
Communist Party, 59
Comparativists, 146–147
Complementarian society, 6–7
Concept of Representation, The (Pitkin), 253–256
Concerned Women for America, 73
Congo, hunter-gatherers tribes, 7
Congressional Black Caucus, 197
Connecticut, legislative
    representation, 272
Consciousness-raising
    groups, 65–66, 96
Contraception:
    cultural norms, 383–385
    judicial policy, 380–382
Contreras-Sweet, Maria, 316t
Coontz, Stephanie, 3
Costa Rica:
    executive representation, 311t, 333
    political ambition, 148t
    violence against women politicians
        (VAWP), 163
Coverture ideology, 52–53
Creation of Patriarchy, The (Lerner), 8
Crenshaw, Kimberlé, 13, 14–16
Critical mass theory, 266–267
Critical race theory, 24
Critical theory, 23–24
Crowley, Joe, 267–268
C-suite phenomenon, 155
Cuba, legislative representation,
    246, 273–274
Culberson, John, 202–203
Cullman, Susan, 123
Cullors, Patrisse, 78, 424
Cult of true womanhood, 53
Cultural backlash:
    for change strategies, 473–477
    judicial representation, 376–377
    legislative representation, 263–267
    to political ambition, 175–177
    See also Change strategies; Patriarchal
        history; Patriarchal systems;
        Traditional family values
Cultural feminism, 30
Cuomo, Andrew, 419
Curbelo, Carlos, 202

state court judges, 360, 362
study guide, 386–388
Switzerland, 377
United States, 353–357, 358, 359–362,
    369–370, 376–377, 378, 379
U.S. Supreme Court, 354, 360, 361*t*
women of color, 357, 360, 362
women's rights impact, 374–377, 380–382
women's safety, 376
women's tribunals, 373
Wyoming, 354
Yugoslavia, 371–372
Judicial rulings:
Baehr v. Lewin (1993), 3
Burwell v. Hobby Lobby (2014), 382, 385
General Electric Company v. Gilbert (1976),
    458–459
Goodridge v. Department of Public Health
    (2003), 3, 353
Griswold v. Connecticut (1965), 380
Hively v. Ivy Tech Community
    College (2017), 375
Ledbetter v. Goodyear Tire & Rubber Co.
    (2007), 369–370
Masterpiece Cakeshop vs. Colorado Civil Rights
    Commission (2018), 375
Minor v. Happersett (1875), 57
Obergefell v. Hodges (2015), 374
Pittsburgh Press v. Pittsburgh Commission on
    Human Relations (1973), 67
Planned Parenthood of Southeastern
    Pennsylvania v. Casey (1992), 117
Price Waterhouse v. Hopkins (1989), 375
Roe v. Wade (1973), 69, 116–117,
    474–475
Romer v. Evans (1996), 375
R. v. Morgentaler (1988), 115
U.S. v. Morrison (2000), 160
Young v. United Parcel Service
    (2015), 459
Jumper, Betty Mae, 331*t*
Juneau, Denise, 330*t*
Juneja, Aditi, 436

Kagan, Elena, 360, 361*t*
Kant, Suman Krishan, 419
Kanyi, Ann, 161
Katz, Jackson, 40
Kavanaugh, Brett, 98, 117, 461
Kazakhstan, *sharia* law, 26
Kennedy, John F., 61–62, 322
Kentucky, abortion rights, 117

Kenya:
    violence against women politicians
        (VAWP), 161
    women-only communities, 454–455
Khashoggi, Jamal, 411
Kirchner, Néstor, 311
Kirkpatrick, Jeane, 319
Koike, Yuriko, 328*t*
Kosciusklo-Morizet, Nathalie, 162
Krnacova, Adrianna, 329*t*

Labor force participation:
    child care responsibilities, 64
    family leave, 64
    glass ceiling, 74
    global context, 9–12
    invisible labor of women, 164–165
    occupational segregation, 63–64, 67
    patriarchal history, 9–12
    pay gap, 62, 63–64
    Rosie the Riveter, 59, 60, 176
    sex discrimination, 61–62, 67, 369–370
    sex-segregated help-wanted ads, 63
    slave labor, 8–9, 13
    Spain, 10
    Switzerland, 10
    Syria, 10
    World War II, 59–60, 175–176
    Yemen, 10
Ladies Home Journal, 67
LaHaye, Beverly, 73
Lakra, Asha, 329*t*
Lame duck legislative session, 467–468
Landon, Alfred, 91
Laschever, Sara, 388
Latin American women:
    double jeopardy, 120
    incarceration rates, 374
    party identification, 123–124
    pay gap, 63, 120
    political candidacy, 199
    political participation, 119
    presidential election (2016), 124
Lauer, Matt, 78
Lavender menace, 73
Lawless, Jennifer L., 155
Law school graduates,
    353–354, 355–357
Lawyers, 353–354, 356–360
Lazarus, Jeffrey, 214
League of Women Voters, 59
Ledbetter, Lilly, 369–370

lesbian feminism, 72–73
political ambition, 166
political candidacy, 197–198
queer feminism, 72–73
queer theorists, 73
same-sex marriage, 2–4, 353
social movements, 434–435
state feminism, 323, 324
Trans-Exclusionary Radical Feminism
    (TERF), 31–33, 75–76
Trump, Donald, 374, 376
violence against women, 160
Liberal feminism:
    characteristics of, 24–25
    in political ambition, 172–175
    in political history, 62–63, 65, 67
Liberal representation, 255
Liberia:
    executive representation, 313
    iron maiden frame, 209
    social movements, 428–429
Life at Conception Act (2013), 475
Lille, Patricia de, 329*t*
Lilly Ledbetter Fair
    Pay Act (2009), 370
Linked fate, 94, 95–96
Local representation:
    executive positions, 325–331
    legislative positions, 248–251
Locke, John, 19
Logan Adella Hunt, 58
Lolosoli, Rebecca, 455
Ludington, Sybil, 295
Lula de Silva, Luiz Inácio, 312
Lynch, Loretta, 316*t*
Lynn, Loretta, 383–385

Machismo, 274, 310, 422
MacKinnon, Catharine, 70
Macron, Brigitte, 306
Macron, Emmanuel, 306, 324
Madres de Plaza de Mayo
    (Argentina), 421–423
Magoon, Mary, 354
Maine:
    legislative representation, 245–246
    same-sex marriage, 3
Malcorra, Susana, 318*t*
Male privilege, 14
Mallory, Tamika, 402
Malta, legislative representation, 247
Mankiller, Wilma, 331*t*

Mansbridge, Jane, 68–69
Mansfield, Arabella, 354
Manyala, Elizabeth, 161
Marginalized masculinity frame, 305
Marianismo, 310–311, 422
Marriage:
    delayed marriage, 166–167
    patriarchal history, 3–4
    See also Same-sex marriage
Marriage, a History (Coontz), 3
Marshall, Margaret, 353
Marshner, Connie, 73
Martin, Trayvon, 424
Martinez, Susana, 325
Marx, Karl, 96
Maryland, same-sex marriage, 3
Masculine-coded public settings, 146, 331
Masculine ethos of politics,
    167–169, 220–227
Massachusetts:
    industrial labor activism, 54
    LGBTQIA+ community, 376
    pay equity, 64
    political candidacy, 197
    same-sex marriage, 3, 353
Mass media:
    candidate coverage, 205–211
    executive representation, 300–305
    public opinion impact, 93–94, 106–107
*Masterpiece Cakeshop vs. Colorado Civil Rights
    Commission* (2018), 375
Maternal politics, 420–430
Matricentries, 4–6
Matristic societies, 4–6
May, Catherine Dean, 70
Mayer, Catherine, 417
Mayor positions, 326, 327, 328, 328–329*t*
McCain, John, 245–246
McCarthy, Gina, 316*t*
McCormick, Katharine, 381
McGath, Amy, 223–224
Mckesson, DeRay, 426
McKinney, Louise, 246
McMahon, Linda, 317*t*
McSally, Martha, 223
Media. *See* Mass media
Medicaid, 381–382
Meir, Golda, 209
Menstruation, 32–33
Mentors in Violence Prevention, 40
Merkel, Angela, 208, 209, 332–333
Meso-level government, 328

forced sterilization, 70
Fourth Wave of feminism, 77–78
glass ceiling, 74
Industrial Revolution, 53
labor force participation, 59–60,
    61–62, 63–64
lesbian feminism, 72–73
LGBTQIA+ community, 72–73
liberal feminism, 62–63, 65, 67
occupational segregation, 63–64, 67
pay gap, 62, 63–64
policy feature, 63–64
pornography, 70
queer feminism, 72–73
queer theorists, 73
radical feminism, 65–66
relative deprivation theory, 63
Second Wave of feminism, 59–69
sex-positive feminism, 72–73
social class, 61
social justice feminism, 65
study guide, 79–82
temperance movement, 54
Third Wave of feminism, 70–78
traditional family values, 73
Trans-Exclusionary Radical Feminism
    (TERF), 75–76
transnational feminism, 71
voting rights, 54–59
womanist feminism, 71
World War II, 59–60
Political interest, 118
Political opportunity structure, 413–414
Political participation, 118–119, 150–151
Political party identification:
    anti-Trump reaction, 452–453
    public opinion impact, 121–124
    race-based, 123–124
    for social movements, 416–419
Political qualifications, 171–172, 461–462
Political socialization, 93, 168
Political training (Pakistan), 226–227
Politics of Presence, The (Phillips),
    255–256
Polling organization, 90–92
Polling sample, 91–92
Pollsters, 91
Pornography, 70
Postcolonial criticism, 24
Postcolonial feminism, 28–29
Power, Samantha, 316*t*, 319
Precedent, 362–364

Predispositions, 92, 94–95
Pregnancy discrimination, 458–459
Pregnancy Discrimination Act (1978), 459
Prehistory, 7
Presidential Commission
    on the Status of Women (1961), 61–63
Presidential system, 307
Pressley, Ayanna, 197,
    227–228, 267–268
Price Waterhouse v. Hopkins (1989), 375
Prikzker, Penny, 316*t*
Primary socialization, 21
Private lives frame, 306
Proportional representation, 268,
    269–273, 275–276
Prosecutors, 358–360
Publica frame, 460
Public defenders, 358–360
Public opinion:
    abortion rights, 109–117
    African Americans, 108–109
    agenda setting, 93
    aggregate statistical voting approach, 121
    ambivalent sexism, 97–98
    asymmetry, 106
    benevolent sexism, 97–98
    comparative feature, 99–105
    defined, 90
    disadvantaged perspective, 119
    double jeopardy, 120
    election priorities (2012/2016), 108*t*
    enfranchisement, 121
    equity policy, 92
    on executive representation, 296–300
    fair wage, 120
    formation influences, 92–105
    formation theories, 92
    framing stereotypes, 93
    Gallup Organization, 90–91
    gender, 89
    gender equality, 99–105
    gender gap, 89, 99–105, 106–120
    gender issues, 92
    gender predisposition, 94
    gender socialization perspective, 119
    hegemonic masculinity, 98
    hostile sexism, 97–98
    identity-protective cognition, 94
    interdependence, 94, 95–96
    intersectionality, 90, 95, 120
    linked fate, 94, 95–96
    mass media, 93–94, 106–107